Making Cities Livable

Wege zur menschlichen Stadt

Suzanne H. Crowhurst Lennard
Sven von Ungern-Sternberg
Henry L. Lennard
Editors

A Gondolier Press Book
Making Cities Livable Conferences

Library of Congress Catalogue Card Number: 97-72973
ISBN: 0-935824-07-3 (hardcover); 0-937824-08-1 (paperbound)

Printed in the U.S.

A Gondolier Press Book
Published by the International Making Cities Livable Conferences
P.O.Box 7586, Carmel, California 93921, U.S.A.

CONTENTS / INHALT

Public Realm
Öffentlichkeit

Children in the City
Kinder in der Stadt

Community Participation
Bürgerbeteiligung

PART THREE - New Urban Neighborhoods: Work in Progress
DRITTER TEIL - Neue Stadtteile für urbanes Leben: zum derzeitigen Sachstand

Principles
Grundsätze

New Urban Neighborhoods: Case Studies
Neue Stadtteile für urbanes Leben: Beispiele

Chapter/ Kapitel		Page/ Seite

PART FOUR - Recommendations
VIERTER TEIL - Empfehlungen

Introduction

Suzanne H. Crowhurst Lennard
Henry L. Lennard

The purpose of Making Cities Livable is to provide city officials, planners, architects, and urban designers with a state-of-the-art handbook on the nature of livable cities, and approporiate strategies for combatting urban sprawl.

Making Cities Livable brings together the most advanced concepts and ground breaking projects for new urban neighborhoods. The essays were selected from over one hundred presentations at the 17th International Making Cities Livable Conference in Freiburg, Germany, September 5-9, 1995.

At this conference speakers were drawn from around the world to address the special theme of "New Urban Neighborhoods", a topic of particular relevance to the City of Freiburg, which hosted the Conference: Freiburg, which has been a leader in ecological transportation planning, is currently developing two new urban neighborhoods, one on a greenfield site, "Rieselfeld", at the city's periphery, the other on the "Vauban" site (formerly a French military barracks).

Making Cities Livable is unique in that it is based on a foundation of ten years of dialogue among professionals and city officials from around the world, who have gathered together twice a year at the International Making Cities Livable Conferences, to broaden their understanding of the city as an organism, and how urban policies affect inhabitants' quality of life.

For some time the major problems facing cities have been urban sprawl, the concurrent destruction of the landscape, and the unifunctional mass housing areas on the periphery. This issue transcends national borders. Partial solutions are attempted in many parts of the world: the IMCL Conferences provide a forum for exchanging lessons learned from around the world, and examining potential model

solutions. A multidisciplinary approach is the only way to understand the complexity of the issues, and also to analyze the advantages and disadvantages of proposed solutions.

The problems that have been created by urban sprawl are multifaceted: sprawl is devastating from an ecological perspective, creating air pollution, damaging nature, wasting energy, and draining the aquifer. Sprawl is also devastating from a social and psychological viewpoint: it estranges different sectors of the population, fosters distrust, and inhibits the development of community spirit. Suburban sprawl creates an unfavorable environment for children and young people, and for the elderly.

The dialogue that has taken place among participants at the IMCL Conferences over the last ten years has established certain fundamental principles:

1. A systemic conception of the city as a social organism is as important as the vision of the city as an ecological entity.

2. The city is not only an economic engine; its function, as Lewis Mumford proposed, must also be the socialization and optimal development of its citizens.

3. The livable city must provide the opportunity for all, and especially for young people, to develop their social skills, sense of autonomy and identity.

4. Every decision and policy regarding the physical environment of the city, its periphery and suburbs (whether or not to provide public transportation, neglect of the city center, construction of gated housing compounds, proliferation of shopping malls, separation of functions, etc.) has significant social consequences for citizens' sense of well-being, as well as ecological consequences.

5. The city must not increase distrust, but rather, must bring people together and offer a favorable environment for understanding and resolving social and cultural differences.

6. To be healthy, the city as a whole must have a functioning "heart" that draws all citizens together, that helps to develop a sense of their shared identity.

7. For the city to be healthy from a social as well as ecological point of view, every neighborhood needs to function as a microcosm of the whole, each with its own center that helps to develop a sense of neighborhood community.

8. To understand how to create a neighborhood that is socially "healthy" and ecologically "sustainable", we must learn from examples of traditional city centers and small towns that have proved over time to be successful.

The Freiburg Conference on Making Cities Livable addressed the issue of what makes a city center work, and the importance of the city center for the operations of the whole metropolitan region. At the same time, this conference presented the first comprehensive focus on "New Urban Neighborhoods", and what makes them work, both by themselves, and as part of the whole city.

In reviewing the presentations included in Making Cities Livable, it is interesting to observe the similarities between the characteristics of a good city, and the characteristics of a good urban neighborhood. To design successful new urban neighborhoods, one must first understand the nature of the city.

Speakers and panelists agreed that this is a lesson that has not yet been learned, as we can see from the design of too many peripheral urban settlements that ignore the wisdom of the traditional city; but this lesson must be learned if our cities are to survive.

Since there were more than 110 presentations, and 45 exhibits in Freiburg, it is not feasible to include all of the contributions. Some presentations had to be abridged so that they could be included. But there is enough of a selection on each of the major issues for city officials, architects, planners, and all others concerned with the human habitat to find inspiration, and to obtain useful suggestions.

Part One presents an overview vision of the livable city. Civic leaders, scholars, and practitioners associated with the Making Cities Livable movement present their definition of the livable city, and the interrelationships among the diverse elements necessary to achieve quality of everyday life for the citizens. Part One also presents background information about the Freiburg Conference on New Urban Neighborhoods.

In Part Two each of the elements necessary to achieve a livable city (or a livable neighborhood) are examined in turn by experts in their field. These elements include the importance of social life in public places, the design of public space, appropriate urban architecture, mixed use, ecological principles, balanced transportation system, community participation in planning, and children in the city.

Part Three deals with the practical application of new "city making" criteria in relation to specific large scale planning projects. Guidelines for the design of new urban neighborhoods and the reuse of military and industrial areas are followed by specific planning projects. These projects are at the forefront of current efforts to design new urban neighborhoods on greenfield sites, to turn former military and industrial areas into new urban neighborhoods, to restructure dysfuntional urban areas such as mass housing, and to reclaim waterfront areas.

Part Four, prepared at the conclusion of the Freiburg Conference by IMCL Board members and conference participants, is a concise statement of recommendations for the design of new urban neighborhoods, a primary theme of the Freiburg Conference.

Einleitung

Sven von Ungern-Sternberg

Dieses Buch soll denjenigen, die sich hauptberuflich oder ehrenamtlich mit der Gestaltung und Entwicklung der Lebenswirklichkeit in unseren Städten beschäftigen, einen Einblick in den Stand der internationalen Diskussion verschaffen, die im Sinne von Making Cities Livable auf eine Verbesserung der Verhältnisse in unseren Städten zielt.

Making Cities Livable bringt seit 10 Jahren aufgrund der Initiative von Frau Dr. Suzanne H. Crowhurst Lennard und Herrn Professor Dr. Henry Lennard sehr unterschiedliche Menschen zusammen. Es sind Praktiker und Wissenschaftler, Regional- und Kommunalpolitiker, Landes- und Stadtplaner, Architekten, Soziologen, Vertreter der Wirtschaft, Kulturschaffende und Sozialarbeiter aus vielen Ländern und allen Kontinenten. So unterschiedlich ihr Tätigkeitsfeld auch sein mag: Sie alle sind besorgt um die Zukunft unserer Kommunen und engagieren sich für eine menschlichere Stadt.

Der Austausch von Erfahrungen und Erkenntnissen, aber auch von Leitbildern und Visionen führt zu Tagungen, die einen ganz besonderen und einzigartigen Charakter haben. Sie finden abwechselnd in Nordamerika und Europa statt, zuletzt im April 1997 in Sante Fe. Die Freiburger Tagung im Herbst 1995 hatte den Schwerpunkt in den gerade für Deutschland so wichtigen aktuellen Fragen der Planung neuer Stadtteile und der Konzepte von Konversionsflächen. Die zahlreichen Beiträge zu diesem Thema bilden die Substanz des vorliegenden Buches. Es sind Themen, die weit über den aktuellen Bezug einer Tagung für das vorliegende Jahrzehnt und darüber hinaus von entscheidender Bedeutung für die Kommunalpolitik sein werden.

Die Entwicklung des "urban sprawl", die Zersiedlung des Umfeldes unserer Städte und insbesondere die eintönige Monostruktur reiner Wohngebiete mit großem Flächenverbrauch hat bereits jetzt schlimme Auswirkungen. Zum einen sind die Umweltschäden unübersehbar. Wertvolle Flächen werden geopfert. Wunderschöne (Erholungs-) Landschaften werden zerstört. Ein unverhältnismäßiger Anstieg des Straßenverkehrs mit Umweltschäden, mit zusätzlichem Energieverbrauch und stark versiegelten Flächen sind die negativen ökologischen Folgen. Deshalb sind bereits aus Umweltgesichtspunkten heraus regionale und kommunale Strategien gegen die Zersiedlung unseres Raumes zugunsten urbaner neuer Stadtteile mit hoher Dichte notwendig. Eine rechtlich verbindliche Regionalplanung wird hierzu in allen Ländern unverzichtbar sein.

Eine angemessene hohe Dichte neuer Stadtteile ist aber auch eine kommunale Schlüsselentscheidung zugunsten einer höheren Wohnqualität. Denn in reinen Wohngebieten mit hohem Flächenverbrauch ist es faktisch unmöglich, die notwendigen Infrastrukturen zu schaffen. Dies gilt für kulturelle und soziale Einrichtungen wie Kindergarten, Schulen sowie Stätten der Begegnung unterschiedlichster Art. Dies gilt ebenso für Infrastrukturen des öffentlichen Nahverkehrs wie für Angebote des täglichen Einkaufs. Und dies gilt für die Gestaltung des öffentlichen Raumes, der mit Leben und insoweit mit Dichte gefüllt sein muß. Einrichtungen, die die Monostruktur reiner Wohngebiete aufbrechen und Mischnutzungen, die eine "Urbanität" beibehalten, setzen eine ausreichende Dichte voraus. Sie ermöglichen dann Qualitäten des menschlichen Miteinander und brechen die Isolierung auf, die flächenfressende reine Wohngebiete im städtischen Umfeld haben. Deswegen ist eine der Grundpositionen von Making Cities Livable, ein menschliches Antlitz unserer Städte in urbanen Wohnformen zu erreichen.

Aus den Diskussionen der IMCL-Konferenzen der letzten 10 Jahren sind folgende Grundsätze entstanden:

1. Eine grundsätzliche Sicht der Stadt als ein "sozialer" Organismus ist genau so wichtig wie die Vision der Stadt im Sinne eines "ökologischen Wesens".

2. *Die Stadt ist nicht nur eine "ökonomische Maschine". Sie muß auch, wie Lewis Mumford vorgetragen hat, der Sozialisierung, dem "menschlichen Miteinander" und einer möglichst guten Entwicklung ihrer Bürger dienen.*

3. *Eine lebenswerte Stadt muß diese Entwicklungsmöglichkeiten für alle Mitbürgerinnen und Mitbürger entfalten. Dies gilt insbesondere für Jugend, um ihre sozialen Fertigkeiten, ihre Selbständigkeit und Identität zu fördern.*

4. *Jede politische Entscheidung, die die äußere Entwicklung der Stadt, ihres Umfeldes und ihrer Vororte betrifft, hat auch erkennbar bedeutende soziale Folgen für das Wohlbefinden der Bürger sowie ökologische Konsequenzen.*

5. *Eine Stadt darf nicht Mißtrauen und Angst fördern, sondern sie muß die Menschen näher zusammenbringen und eine günstige Voraussetzung für gegenseitiges Verständnis und die Lösung sozialer und kultureller Konflikte schaffen. Sie muß das Gegenteil einer städtebaulichen "Apartheid"-Politik sein, die trennend wirkt und polarisiert.*

6. *Eine Stadt muß als "Herz" dienen, das alle Bürger miteinander verbindet und das hilft, gemeinsame Identität zu entwickeln.*

7. *Damit eine Stadt sozial und ökologisch "gesund" und "dauerhaft" ist, muß jedes Wohnquartier und jeder Stadtteil so gestaltet sein wie die Stadt insgesamt. Jeder Stadtteil muß einen eigenen Mittelpunkt haben, der den Gemeinschaftsgeist fördert.*

8. *Um zu verstehen, daß auch neue Stadtteile sozial "gesund" und "dauerhaft" sind, müssen wir Beispiele von historischen Stadtkernen und kleineren Städten zum Vorbild nehmen, die sich über Jahrhunderte bewährt haben.*

Gerade im Rahmen der Freiburger Konferenz Making Cities Livable wurde festgestellt, daß es auffällige Ähnlichkeiten zwischen den allgemein gültigen Maßstäben einer lebenswerten Stadt insgesamt und den Kriterien für einzelne gute Stadtteile gibt. Um einen "guten" und "dauerhaften" Stadtteil

überhaupt entwickeln zu können, muß man die Natur, die Grundidee einer Stadt und ihren "sozialen Organismus" verstehen. Die gemeinsame Erkenntnis dieser und anderer Tagungen war, daß diese Einsichten vielfach noch nicht vorhanden sind. Die Wirklichkeit der insbesondere in den letzten Jahrzehnten entstandenen neuen Stadtteile und Vororte zeigt dies zu deutlich. Die geschichtlich entstandenen Städte bieten deutliches Anschauungsmaterial und weise planerische Erkenntnisse. Sollen unsere Städte künftig überleben, so müssen wir daraus lernen.

Aus der Vielzahl der Präsentationen (110 Referate, 45 Ausstellungen) der Freiburger Tagung konnte naturgemäß nur ausgewählt werden. Manches mußte auf den Zweck des Buches hin zugeschnitten, verändert und gekürzt werden. Es bleibt aber genügend aus dieser Auswahl, um die entscheidenden Positionen des Vorgetragenen aufzuzeigen und um ausreichend Inspiration und nützliche Vorschläge vorzufinden.

Der erste Teil enthält generelle Leitbilder und Visionen einer lebenswerten Stadt. Kommunalpolitiker, Wissenschaftler und Praktiker, die mit Making Cities Livable verbunden sind, bringen ihre Definition von einer lebenswerten Stadt. Die Zusammenhänge zwischen den verschiedenen notwendigen Kriterien für die Lebensqualität für den Alltag des Bürgers werden aufgezeigt. Der erste Teil informiert zugleich über den Hintergrund der Freiburger Konferenz.

Im zweiten Teil werden einzelne der notwendigen Elemente der lebenswerten Stadt untersucht und zwar durch verschiedene Fachleute auf ihren Spezialgebieten. Diese Elemente beziehen die Bedeutung des sozialen Kontaktes im öffentlichen Raum ein sowie die Gestaltqualität des öffentlichen Raumes. Sie umfassen die Qualität städtischer Architektur, gemischte Nutzungskonzeptionen, ökologische Grundsätze, ausbalancierte Verkehrskonzepte, Bürgerbeteiligungen und Ansätze, unsere Städte kinderfreundlicher zu gestalten.

Der dritte Teil beschäftigt sich mit der praktischen Umsetzung, nach welchen Gesichtspunkten neue Stadtteile geplant und verwirklicht werden. Leitlinien für die Gestaltung neuer Stadtteile und die Umwandlung von Konversionsflächen werden aufgezeigt. Im Anschluß daran werden spezielle Planungsprojekte besprochen.

Der vierte Teil enthält Empfehlungen, die auf der Freiburger Konferenz von Mitgliedern des Vorstandes von Making Cities Livable und ausgewählten Konferenzteilnehmern vorbereitet worden sind und sich auf das vorherrschende Thema der Freiburger Konferenz beziehen: Planungsansätze und Entwicklungsmodelle für neue Stadtteile.

Möge das Buch, das im Zuge der Bearbeitung einen immer größeren Umfang angenommen hat, allen Praktikern und Wissenschaftlern bei der Beschäftigung mit neuen Konzepten nicht nur ein sachdienlicher Überblick über den aktuellen Diskussionsstand zu diesem Themenbereich sein, sondern auch konkrete Hilfe in dem gemeinsamen Bemühen, die Lebenswirklichkeit unserer Städte entscheidend zu verbessern. Werden die Sünden der Vergangenheit bei der Konzeption neuer Stadtteile fortgesetzt oder noch verschärft, so wird das "menschliche Antlitz" in unseren Städten verkümmern, werden die Beziehungen der Menschen zueinander entscheidend geschwächt und dauerhaft Gemeinschaftsgeist und Bürgersinn verschwinden. Deshalb sind für die Autoren die Grundgedanken von Making Cities Livable auch eine Kernfrage des Überlebens unserer Städte schlechthin.

PART ONE
The Livable City

ERSTER TEIL
Die Lebenswerte Stadt

Historisches Kaufhaus, Münsterplatz, Freiburg
Site of the 17th IMCL Conference, September 5-9, 1995

Kaisersaal, Historisches Kaufhaus

Fotostudio Frank Iwan

Chapter One

Welcome

Suzanne H. Crowhurst Lennard

I want to thank the City of Freiburg first, for having invited us to come to this beautiful city. We have known it and loved it for many years, and we were very pleased to have been invited.

I want to thank Oberbürgermeister Dr. Rolf Böhme especially, and for being so hospitable as to have provided the Rathaus for the very extensive Exhibit Program of the Conference. I'd like to thank also Erster Bürgermeister Dr. Sven von Ungern-Sternberg who has worked so very closely with us, for his extraordinary effort as the conference grew to the unanticipated size and complexity that it is today.

This is indeed an even richer program than we have ever brought together before. There is a panoply of stars in this room today; each of you very well known and outstanding in your own field, and here brought together perhaps for the very first time with people from so many different areas. I would like to thank all of you who have come – many from so far away – and taken time out from your busy schedules; and in particular to mention a very few names: Mayor Dietmar Hahlweg from Erlangen; Mayor Bob Cools from Antwerp; Mayor Christa Meier from Regensburg; Mayor Antonio Casellati from Venice; Hans Stimman, Senatsbaudirektor from Berlin; and Klaus Humpert from Freiburg itself.

Just a few words about the conference itself: the concept of the IMCL Conferences was from the very beginning, rather a unique idea. We began in 1985, and it was the result of having traveled to many European and North American cities looking for the people who were responsible for having made improvements in their city, in whatever field they were in, whether it was appropriate human scale architecture, whether it was the creation of pedestrian areas or traffic calming, whether it was the creation of farmers' markets or festivals, or whether it was a program for the involvement of the community in planning projects – in all of these different areas we were looking for the best people, and we wanted to create a forum for them to come together, because we discovered that most of them did not know each other, even when they were in the same country.

We held our first International Making Cities Livable Conference in Venice in 1985, and since then we have held IMCL Conferences in Siena, also in Italy, and in Charleston and San Francisco in North America.

The Conferences are interdisciplinary as well as international, and they are for people who can see the larger picture, who are generalists, who can transcend their own professional boundaries and see the connection between their own work and the work of other professionals; but also, more importantly, who can see how their decisions in their particular field, impact the everyday lives of the citizens. And we are especially always concerned with the impact these city-making decisions have on children, as well as older people; because our philosophy is based on the belief that cities must be livable for children and older people if it is to be livable for everyone.

You will hear more about the actual conference themes as the day goes on. I just wish you all a most enjoyable personal, as well as professional, experience at the conference. I hope you will get a lot out of meeting some of the amazing people who are gathered together here; enjoy each other's presence, enjoy the themes of the conference, and I wish you all "Buon lavoro", as Edoardo Salzano said on behalf of the City of Venice, when he greeted our first IMCL Conference in 1985.

Suzanne H. Crowhurst Lennard, Ph.D. (Arch.) is Director of the International Making Cities Livable Council, Carmel, California, and Co-Chair, Program Committee for the 17th IMCL Conference.

Sven von Ungern-Sternberg

We are very, very happy that so many outstanding speakers and so many interesting and interested participants join our conference. This, I think, is a guarantee of the quality of our conference, a guarantee of its success. We appreciate that our proposal to focus the main issue of our conference on new urban neighborhoods and conversion issues has met with such a good response!

In 1993, I had the privilege to attend the International Making Cities Livable Conference in Charleston and was honored to receive on behalf of the City of Freiburg, the Award of "Making Cities Livable". And frankly speaking, I was at once overwhelmed, not only by the hospitality of the City of Charleston itself, but by the specific character of this unique sort of conference, by its international flair, and by the composition of the participants with completely different professional backgrounds, being active in the administrative branch, being politicians, being in university life, or in business, being town planners, or architects, or engaged in cultural or social affairs. They all have one thing in common – they are engaged in the future of our cities, the quality of life of our towns. And I very soon wished – this is the

thing for our City of Freiburg; I wished we could have the opportunity to have such a conference in Freiburg.

We are asked by the press and other people about the practical results of this kind of conference. The mere fact that there is a platform, that such a variety of people from different countries and with different professional backgrounds have the opportunity to meet each other, to get into contact, to talk about the future of the cities, to exchange experiences, to get new ideas – or to get a fair warning, as far as mistakes are concerned – is very important by itself.

It is very difficult to measure those things, but I can only tell you from the point of view of the City of Freiburg, I am convinced that to move our city forwards, as far as its quality of life is concerned, we will benefit a great deal from your experiences and ideas!

We do hope that you enjoy your stay in the City of Freiburg, but more than this, enjoy the topics and issues of this conference and take back many ideas for your professional work and for improving the quality of our lives in cities and towns.

And therefore, I thank you for coming and welcome you to our city. We are looking forward to very exciting and fascinating days.

Sven von Ungern-Sternberg is Erster Bürgermeister (Deputy Mayor) for the City of Freiburg, and Co-Chair, Program Committee for the 17th IMCL Conference.

Chapter Two

The Future of the City

Bob Cools

Fotostudio Frank Iwan

It is more opportune than ever that we think about the future of the CITY and consider the city of the FUTURE. For the world is beginning to look increasingly like a string of "urbanising areas". The old city centres are entombed there somewhere, stripped of their substance, fossilised or converted into a business centre and/or recreational area. Sometimes it is very difficult to say where a city begins and ends. So we can speak of "une ville ruban" - "a ribbon town". In Flanders, where I come from, 40% of the territory is given over to housing.

Is this, I wonder, the ideal living pattern for the future? Neither city nor country, but somewhere in between, where the scenery is tower blocks and off-the-peg glass constructions, a mono-office culture, a few shopping silos, the occasional vague vestige of the past, all located alongside barren asphalt; on the outskirts, public housing and, in the greener beyond, the homes of the new breed of "city dwellers". They are increasingly turning the green areas around the cities into zones where the "fermier" lives next to the new "fermetier". This is how Richard Sennett puts it in his very recent book, "Flesh and Stone. The body and the city in Western civilisation":

"This is first of all so because of the physical experience which made the new geography possible, the experience of speed. People travel today at speeds our forebears could not at all conceive. The technologies of motion - from automobiles to continuous, poured concrete highways - made it possible for human settlements to extend beyond tight-packed centres out into peripheral space."

And yet surely we are not heading for complete disurbanisation and sliding into a sort of "rurbanisation"? The danger there is that we lose the essential characteristics of the city, the cradle of civilisation. These nebulous areas are displaying fewer and fewer of the characteristics of a city and, indeed, are increasingly becoming the very negation of it. The so typically human - or should I say physical - contact with the city is also disappearing. "The traveler, like the television viewer", and we might also add, "the computer screen watcher", experiences the world in narcotic terms; the body moves passively, desensitized in space, to destinations set in a fragmented or discontinuous urban geography. And to quote Sennett again: "The geography of the modern city, like modern technology, brings to the fore deep-seated problems in Western civilisation in imagining spaces for the human body which might make human bodies aware of one another."

So we make a plea "In the Name of the City" for their preservation, renewal and revival.

I. The city as the basis of our civilisation

The city must remain, but at the same time try to exert a greater influence on the surrounding urban areas, yet without reducing them to characterless urbanisations. The reason being that, as Le Corbusier wrote back in the thirties: "the city is only a part of a socioeconomic and political whole which constitutes the region".

And that is exactly where a great deal has gone wrong because the administrative unit has always been at variance with the environmental and morphological unit. So instead of environmental planning this causes disorder and also weakens the financial basis of the cities. Moreover, it accounts for the imbalance among the citizen and the non-citizen! So we need to look at the city as a whole, on its natural foundations one might say, at the metropolitan region, metropolitan district or urban community, call it what you will.

This encompasses a European view. For cities are an important aspect of European civilization. After all, they bear the European identity and should in practice propagate its spirit. So in fact what it all comes down to is rehabilitating urban Europe. It is vital that the city continues to perform its original function, adapts to the technological evolution and safeguards and builds on its urbanity. So our European vision is that we in Europe must try to shape a number of large, strong and vigorous metropolitan districts, which are the motor of economic events. Not metropolitan districts which compete, but metropolitan districts which complement one another. This will create an opportunity to protect the large open zones and scenic areas from development, so that we can give our continent a clear ecological profile.

For many the city is a dream world, an ideal, for others a place of doom but, whichever way you look at it, it is and will continue to be the cradle of our civilisation. You can best compare it to people themselves: a long, tenacious life which should have masculine as well as feminine traits. But yes, cities, like people, can show symptoms of an often virulent disease. These diseases may remain repressed for a long time but then suddenly manifest themselves. Often by then it is too late. Hence the need to prevent urban society from degenerating into an incurable state. Hence the need for a "long-term care programme". But usually curative intervention is urgently needed and in many cases an "instant action plan" is also desirable. The problem, however, lies in convincing the whole community that the cities need preferential treatment and this does not happen very often! Or it happens abruptly, in fits and starts or by means of shortsighted, prestige projects.

It is, after all, a fact that these new, large-scale projects never have more than a temporary value in a city's development. Every ten years a new urban development fashion seems to come along ... and no one wants to hear that he fell victim to some fad. Hence the need for a global view of the city. Moreover, there can be no urban renewal without an economic base. It is also a mistake to limit city renewal to the treatment of social symptoms. We must not of course forget that cities were created by people, for people. This means that the most important aspect of the city is man himself, but also the interaction between man, city, urban development and culture. This is what I like to call "urbanity", by which I mean that higher form of society with a philosophy all of its own. It is this typical metropolitan lifestyle which makes a "concentration area" a city in the real sense of the word. That is why so many inhabitants feel so very much at one with that city and why they react so forcefully when they believe that their city risks losing its identity through some technical or cultural intervention.

Living in a large city means living within view of the world. And so it is in Antwerp, my city, but a metropolis to the extent that as a large port it is in touch with the whole world. If Antwerp was to turn inwards upon itself, adopt an egocentric attitude, then it would not be a metropolis. Urbanity can burgeon in a cosmopolitan climate of openness, not in a tribal atmosphere. The city dweller is someone who is conscious that he is part of a higher form of cohabitation and he is constantly looking to improve it. And if this is accompanied by an intoxicating play of light and shadow over the roofs, towers, facades, streets and squares, patined by the glories of the past, then the pictorial effect is so intense that it can inspire great things. Through the ages such cities have become centres of culture. Even Socrates said it: "the fields and the trees do not teach me, but the people in the city do." It is in urban spaces that the sense of public life is strongest, it is here that people can associate freely, that the social traffic is intense and varied, the street the extension of the sitting room. "It is the relation between person and place that makes the identity" (K. Lynch). No doubt romanticism plays a role here, and why not?

Unfortunately the postwar, poorly-understood functionalist movement dealt our cities a hard blow. Uniformity and lack of identity threaten to nip public life in the bud and to turn the European network of cities into a "ruban betonne" (concrete ribbon). "In the Name of the City", we must try to avert this calamity, because the cities are the very basis of our civilisation.

Wrath, resentment and discord about the city can be heard almost everywhere. The national authorities show very little real interest in the city. Any interest there might be is all too often, as Peter Hall says, triggered by financial revenue and profit and not by all those fine things I have just described. And yet it is curious that those new spaces that "we" have created nip that uniformity, that tastelessness, all public life in the bud, so that a gap threatens to appear between life and city with the result that people shun that city and even abandon it. Rather fatalistically they see it as the result of the welfare state and general motorisation. It is that mentality which upsets those conscientious city administrators as well as many true city dwellers.

II. Threatening or threatened city?

a) Threatening city

So for many people today there is also a threatening side to cities. They are, they believe, dangerous, unhealthy and unsavoury places to live, but they nevertheless descend upon them every day to pluck a little of their prosperity. And of course if the environment in which people spend their working days is on a large scale, unpleasant and depressing, then people will be inclined to leave the place as quickly as possible, jump into their cars and escape to the green belt. And the result is this quasi office mono-culture. Every exodus leaves unoccupied dwellings and neglect in its wake and this causes further exoduses and in that way of course the basis of the urban fabric is undermined, the city is no longer safe, it attracts vandalism and criminality and it becomes a meeting place for junkies, tourists, adventure seekers, fringe groups, you name it. And the city acquires a reputation for being threatening. Those who have abandoned the city complain about it, they forget that they themselves are in part responsible for that problem and are merely weakening its basis by their desertion. It is true that cities have a tenacious life, but they can decay and die. Therefore we must protect them from the squanderers and the speculators, otherwise they become threatened places. Cities must be a long-term investment, not a short-term object of gain.

b) Threatened city

First and foremost the city is threatened from the outside, that is to say that the city is under constant pressure from its outskirts, and particularly from the incessant carving up of the green peripheral areas. The trend is perhaps stronger in some countries than in others but it is certainly a Belgian specialty! Dividing land into lots is one of the main depopulation processes. Any attempt at urban renewal is futile if the spatial tension between city and suburban areas cannot be reduced. So long as the municipalities located around the cities are allowed to implement an independent planning policy, then urban renewal will never make headway. The low burden of taxation in these peripheral areas also plays the cities false.

This negative development can only be stemmed by a forceful planning policy implemented at metropolitan district level. Otherwise the upshot of all this is that the only people who stay behind in the city are the underprivileged who are not in a position to maintain the city's financial basis.

But of course the city is also threatened from within. The older parts of the city and the 19th-century areas are most at risk. I will summarise the problems: squalid, seedy conditions, abandoned and decaying buildings, often impoverished residents, a feeling of alienation and, finally, traffic nuisance. The nature and intensity of these conditions do of course vary from place to place, but usually the cause of one evil is to be found in another.

In certain areas of the city industrial activity, transport companies or night-time entertainment can also make cohabitation difficult. All this of course goes hand in hand with a feeling - if not of danger - then of unease. Often the very substance of the city is damaged because the population is either too old or too young. This is the case in many neighbour-hoods and districts in our European cities.

The city can also be threatened from within when the splitting up of the city into areas or districts is taken to extremes. When this happens, the city becomes less of a city and there is no longer a clear-cut urban administration. There is then a great danger that certain parts - the problem areas - will be cut off from other parts thereby erasing the urbanity or urban solidarity.

It is not the city which is threatening but the city which is threatened. So we must fight for its preservation. An urban renaissance is an absolute must, even if we have to take account of the perverse effects of well-intentioned, local social campaigns. But what is essential is that we have a good understanding of the city and its working.

III. The city: a subtle balancing act

We experience the city as an ongoing interaction between rational and irrational elements, often contradictory, fanciful and sometimes pleasant, like life itself. So we must treat the city like a living organism which is precariously balanced between growth and death, between health and the onset of disease. The larger the body, the greater the demands on the heart.

The urban phenomenon then, like life, is founded on a subtle balancing act. If we want a city to function properly as a society, then that balance must not be upset, as is sometimes the case today. Let us examine the equilibrium of a few of these components.

a) Living and working in the city

Perfection in urban development terms is living and working in the same area, insofar, of course, as the latter does not interfere with the former. A walking distance of 20 to 25 minutes between the two is ideal. That is the situation urban development planning should do everything in its power to achieve. Unfortunately, the living-working situation in the city is often unbalanced. This causes traffic nuisance and is one of the problems I referred to above. In terms of the metropolitan district, of course, the picture is broader. Hence the need once again to emphasise a regional approach to the urban phenomenon. There is a tendency these days for employment to abandon the urban area and to shift more towards the outskirts. This then is another form of imbalance which can shake the very foundations of the city. At the moment the situation in the city of Antwerp - with its 465,000 inhabitants and 247,000 employed - is fairly healthy, but if the trend continues for the jobs and the people to move out of the city then those foundations are really going to be in trouble. Once more it must be emphasised that a balance in this regard can only be achieved by dialogue between city and region. Jobs must not be allowed to disperse over a whole region, as the population has done. Urban integration is necessary. We fought long and hard for people to be able to live right in the heart of our city. It would be dreadful if the jobs were now to move away.

b) On cities and their inhabitants

This brings us on to what is, or should be, regarded as the most important characteristic of a city: the number of inhabitants. That is a simple statistic which is regularly available and which can be used on almost every level. In many cases you can look at the number of inhabitants from a historical viewpoint and in that way draw what are sometimes clear-cut

conclusions. Peter Hall, whom I referred to above, thinks that the metropolitan areas will continue to grow in ever-wider circles. So we should consider the problem of the city and its inhabitants at European level, perhaps tomorrow at world level, given the great migratory movements. Because all things considered, European demography is, with one or two exceptions, very weak and the migration from the "south" to the north will persist. Fifty-five percent of the central parts of urban concentrated Europe is suffering a loss. If one makes an abstraction of the tendency in Spain, Portugal and a number of less concentrated parts of France and Italy, then that loss comes to almost 90%. A falling-off of the urban population is irrevocably explained by the tendency for families to have fewer children. So in Europe we have the parallel situation of a weak demography and an exodus from the cities. And this phenomenon causes an imbalance between inhabitant and city.

Then we find a number of unbalanced situations within the urban population itself which have a great influence on the urban pattern. Of the approximately 4,000 hours per year which people used to work, today we do no more than 1,600. So free time is far more important than working time. This means that cities will increasingly become the stamping ground of young adults in search of leisure activities. An interesting fact to the extent that they will succeed in making a contribution to the urban basis and the city administrators will succeed in offering them a livable city which meets their requirements. Typical of the cities, too, is the number of one-person families, both young and old. This sort of information about the population, then, is relevant to the urban development pattern and more specifically to the range of living accommodation which may or may not be available. An effort must also be made to enable young families to acquire or build a home of their own.

c) On city dwellers and city residents

A balanced age structure and inhabitants who also make a direct contribution to the urban basis or mainstay constitute the backbone around which a healthy urban fabric can be spun. If a city's own demography is weak, then the migratory movements are important factual information for that city. For example, a city needs to know where the newcomers come from and where those who are leaving are going to. Until the twenties it was mainly contributions from the surrounding municipalities which assured the continued growth of the cities. Things are of course different today. The main additions to the population come from abroad. The same trend is found almost all over Europe. You might of course put it down to the draw which a city exercises and therefore to its metropolitan characteristics.

However, coming to live in the city is a commitment! Many who have done it felt ill at ease in the early years. They were drawn to the city because of the job opportunities. But you do not automatically become a city dweller just by going and living in a city. So there is on the one hand the draw of the city but as a corollary it must have the ability to integrate, to assimilate the inhabitants. An important instrument here is of course education.

The resentment I alluded to earlier is of course largely rooted in the unbalanced situations I am going on to describe. Coming as they do from distant parts, which had little to do with urbanity, many of our immigrants are suddenly plunged into an urban environment for which they were not in the least prepared. And their large families arouse a feeling of alienation in the native population. It is in fact a cultural confrontation.

In "la défaite de la pensée" the French philosopher Alain Finkielkraut wrote: "the spirit of modern times in Europe easily accepts the existence of national or religious minorities, provided that, after the example of the nation, they are made up of free and equal individuals". So, if we want to correct the imbalance which has emerged in these areas, we must facilitate the urbanisation process of these newcomers. In many of these areas urban renewal should be seen not so much as a building process, but more as a process that promotes communal living.

And this brings us on to one of the delicate aspects of the findings of the city today. Newcomers from around the city, from other provinces and from abroad have moulded the cities, they have often kept the cities going and they have given them a new and bigger dimension; this has also often created internal areas of tension. So it is all a question of how and to what extent.

When all is said and done, it is basically a question of the balance that we must try to achieve between the draw of the city and its capacity to integrate. In integrating newcomers, the cities must try to find a dynamic for their future expression.

d) The liberalism-urbanism dilemma

I have already referred to cities which have fallen prey to commercial interests and prestige projects. Everything that can be done in a city is, in fact, determined by real estate. There is often a discrepancy between the owner and the city council's or higher government's views on urban development. Even if occasionally they move in the same direction, again the general urban interest is sacrificed to this private interest, often with catastrophic consequences. Indeed, this explains why many European cities soon began to grow skywards.

The owner-tenant ratio is another important factor in striving to achieve a balance. Throwing tenants out when a property is sold is a very disturbing and antisocial act and one the legislator should often be made to answer for. What we need to avoid is the speculative purchase, which is frequently the cause of neglect and decay.

Project development has often resulted in people being forced out of their homes and this creates very unbalanced environmental situations. So we need to look for a different framework in which public-private cooperation can create bonds of solidarity. Cooperation between the municipality and the business community does not have to be restricted to economic projects, however important they may be in terms of employment; it is now quite clear that a lively sociocultural climate is also important for business activity. New forms of cooperation between the business community, residents and the city administration can be a good way of steering the "liberalism-urbanism" dilemma in the right direction.

e) Lack of balance between pedestrians and other traffic in the city

The cheapest form of transport is transport which does not exist! This is the ideal we must strive for, like the idealised picture referred to earlier of working close to home. We are not concerned here with trying to stifle traffic and transport. It is again a question of how and how not, where and where not.

A first useful step would be to make a drastic distinction between pedestrians and motorised traffic on the blocked arterial roads. Secondly, trucks must be given their own lanes. Thirdly, we need to consider transit roads for long-distance traffic. These would be quite separate from the ordinary roads which are designed only for local traffic.

The consistent application of these principles should create a better balance, in favour of public transport. It was this which led me to adopt a consistent philosophy of pedestrian zones in our city in the seventies. More than 200,000 m2 in the centre of Antwerp have been made into pedestrian areas so that 20% of the historic inner city is now traffic free. This policy has been carried out consistently and it is one which I expect my successors to continue. In so doing we cannot allow ourselves to be misled or diverted by private interests of whatever sort. It is a fact that wherever this policy was implemented, immediate signs of a revival sprang up. Of course there must be parking in the vicinity of such areas and it must be possible to reach them by means of a reliable public transport system.

f) Balance between development of the surrounding area and open spaces

It should be enough in environmental planning to indicate what must remain undeveloped. Alas, every environmental planner begins by indicating what should be developed. So in postwar Europe this prerequisite for balance was greatly violated. Consequently, the balance between develop-ment areas and open spaces is again one which needs to be considered mainly at regional level and not so much within the urban agglomeration itself. This is certainly not to say that the agglomeration must be purely ribbon development.

The city is by definition of stone, but parks, wooded walks and greenery are also an essential part of it. In building and renovation work we must try to ensure that not only new traffic-free areas are created, but also new open spaces. The 19th-century areas are a logical choice. We need to consider whether less suitable, poorly located 19th-century develop-ment should not make way for green areas, particularly on the outskirts on the approach to the city. The issue of new development versus open spaces is a key factor in environmental planning. It also means, in looking to the future, an attempt to incorporate nature into the cityscape. In this respect, the garden city concept can have a bearing on the future.

g) Preservation, renovation or renewal

Here we come to one of the essential factors in connection with the preservation of the European city. If the prestige, concrete-and-glass urban development continues, monotony and uniformity will become the characteristics of a sort of universal urban landscape. It is true that the European city is typified by a number of similarities, and yet each city has acquired its own "look", atmosphere and style, has an identity, its own heritage. So in preserving historical buildings and monuments and the appearance of the city, we must allow ourselves to be guided first and foremost by the characteristics of this individual being, the city. It is a well-known fact that from the 11th century on, we Flemings made a considerable contribution to shaping a certain style of European urban civilisation. So it is also our duty to give that past a future.

It is my belief that there also has to be a balance between the structure, the design of the city and the city's architectural heritage, which gives it its identity, and the possibility of adapting to the evolution of time and changed living conditions.

So we try to achieve an urban development model, which is able to reconcile both renewal and preservation. After all, it is important that the city continues to be a living organism, not a mausoleum. A healthy urban fabric may change from day to day, some parts will age and may disappear, so renewal must be given a chance. We must therefore avoid dogmatically advocating new development over and above renovation. These are spurious problems, for

old and new have always existed side by side. But, in the case of new development, the architect must take account of the existing environment, of what we call the harmony of the place. And here we part company with the so-called modernistic avant-garde, for it has a tendency to spin totally new fabric and to leave just a few monuments as scars from bygone days. Their postwar adaptation, "the poorly-understood functionalism", is the proof that those sort of urban constructions spell the end of a city in the long term. Take, for instance, La Defense in Paris.

So new development in a city must be able to be seen as an attempt to complement the personality of that city. On this subject, William Morris was, I believe, right when he said: "We must keep what we know to be still useful or believe to be beautiful". A city without historical architecture would be a city without a memory. In our city I wanted to make sure that the essential part of our architectural heritage was protected by Royal Decree. But later buildings, including 20th-century buildings, have their place on the list of protected buildings, too. It is essential that in the case of new buildings and renovation work an on-going dialogue can be stimulated between old and new so that the adaptation to the evolution of time can be a smooth one.

Our ideal is a conciliatory urban development model between preserving what is valuable from the past and contemporary architectural values. Today's good architecture should be able to become tomorrow's monument.

Bob Cools, former Lord Mayor of Antwerp, is currently the President of the Municipal Centre for Health Care and Social Welfare, Antwerp, Belgium.

Chapter Three

The City as a Family

Dietmar Hahlweg

Fotostudio Frank Iwan

I would like to mention five points which are not new for you, or for me, but I hope it is worthwhile to keep them always in mind in our work, and in our discussion in the next days.

I start with the point, multi-functional planning of our cities' variety. Nothing new, but we know that the segregation of functions in cities over the last decades produced a lot of the problems we have today. For myself, the livable city is, as the Mayor said, a city where I can have my house or apartment, where I can work, where my children can go to school, where we have recreation and culture.

The second point: a livable city for me is a city where I can have a healthy life and where I have the chance for easy mobility – by foot, by bicycle, by public transportation, and even by car when there is no other choice. The healthy city means that I can rest at least during the night: that I can breathe the air and I am not afraid that I will be harmed by breathing this air. And the healthy city, also, is where I have the chance, when I leave my apartment, to go to a green area, of whatever size, within a five or ten minutes' distance. That sounds very idealistic, but I think as a goal this is very important.

Third point: the livable city is a city for all people. That means that the livable city should be attractive, worthwhile, safe for our children, for our older people, not only for the people who earn money there and then go and live outside in the suburbs and in the surrounding communities.

For the children and the elderly people it is especially important to have easy access to areas with green, where they have a place to play and meet each other, and talk with each other. The livable city is a city for <u>all</u>.

Fourth point: A livable city, of whatever size, must try to act as a great family. A great family cannot live together every day, every hour of each day. This would be very complicated. But a family lives together if they have the possibility to meet from time to time in public places, in events of the city which happen every year at a certain time, when everybody in the city feels they are invited.

In Erlangen we have the "Bergkirchweih" – it is a wonderful thing to have such a Fest, and most of our cities, the bigger and smaller cities have festivals like this. At this kind of festival, especially in the southern part of Germany, the kinds of things happen where older people talk to a young man from whom they had a feeling that he is a problem. Such conversation cannot be organized, it just happens if the situation is there.

But you need no only the event, you need the places where this can happen. So this is very important for the topic, the design of public places.

Fifth point: The livable city should be the tolerant city. The livable city should be the city which brings solidarity to the people who need the help of other people; and the livable city should be a shelter for people who are in danger or are afraid. This also has to do with open spaces: it is important that every citizen should not look aside if something bad happens to other citizens, but really be engaged. I think it is important in our cities to create an atmosphere where every citizen knows that he has a certain obligation to help in the case where it is needed.

Last word: with the livable city, I am convinced that wherever people are living around the globe, whether in a mega-city, a city with 150,000 inhabitants, or the village with one hundred inhabitants, that all people try to have a worthwhile life and to overcome problems. So every community is a livable community. But our task, as planners, as politicians, is to give them the chance that their daily life is easier, and not to do things by planning and urban decisions that make their life more complicated.

Dr. Dietmar Hahlweg is the former Lord Mayor of Erlangen, Germany and member of the IMCL Board.

Chapter Four

Principles for the Livable City

Henry L. Lennard

Fotostudio Frank Iwan

The following principles are suggested as basic to the livable city:

One, in the livable city, all can see and hear each other! It is the opposite of the dead city, where people are segregated and isolated. In a livable city the noise you hear is of people talking, not of cars! Children have not vanished from the face of the earth, but are part of the daily life of the city.

Two, in a good city dialogue is important. Hannah Arendt said the world is not <u>human</u>, because it is made up of human beings, but only because it has become the subject of discourse. And for Lewis Mumford, the best definition of the city was "a place designed to offer the widest facilities for significant conversation."

This dialogue, which can take many forms, makes possible the bringing together of different views and perspectives. The most revealing symbol of city failure is the absence of dialogue, "not necessarily a silence, but the sound of a chorus or mass uttering the same words in cowed and complacent conformity".

The reality of the public realm relies on the simultaneous presence of innumerable perspectives and aspects in which the common world presents itself.

Three, in a good city, the public realm offers many activities, celebrations, festivals that bring all of its inhabitants together, events that bring opportunities for its citizens to be together, not in the specialized roles and functions that they usually occupy, but as full human beings!

Four, a good city is <u>not</u> dominated by fear, <u>not</u> by a conception of fellow human beings as evil and subhuman. Inhabitants do not panic at insignificant disturbances or troublesome behavior, especially on the part of its young people. Fear of the vital city, with the occasional tension and friction among its different groups, has dominated planning policies in too many cities.

Five, a good city offers the public realm as a place of social learning and socialization that is indispensable for children and young people. All of the inhabitants of the community serve as models and teachers.

As Jane Jacobs observed, "In real life, only from the ordinary adults of the city sidewalks do children learn - it they learn it at all - the first fundamentals of successful city life: people must take a modicum of public responsibility for each other even if they have no ties to each other. This is a lesson nobody learns by being told. It is learned from the experience of having other people without ties of kinship or close friendship or formal responsibility to you take a modicum of public responsibility for you."

"It is folly to build cities in a way that wastes this normal, casual manpower for child rearing and either leaves this essential job undone - with terrible consequences - or makes it necessary to hire substitutes. The myth that playgrounds and hired guards or supervisors are innately wholesome for children and that city streets filled with ordinary people, are innately evil for children, boils down to a deep contempt for ordinary people..."

Children are not taught to become full members of a community by professionals or experts or by technology, but by participating in the life of the city, by being with diverse people, young and old, similar and different from themselves. They can only learn the human competencies, social skills and functional values through contact with their fellow city inhabitants. They learn about caring, responsibility and trust by observing examples of such behavior. Such learning does not occur in cyberspace, in the virtual city, but only by human example.

Six, cities must meet many functions - economic, social and cultural. In so doing, however, there has been a trend for the modern city to over-specialize in one or two functions; other functions are being sacrificied. For example, in order to move working adults efficiently, traffic planners thought they needed wide traffic arteries that are impassable and dangerous for children. In order to accommodate parked cars, public urban spaces are sacrificed which could be utilized for the co-presence of all the city's inhabitants. The emphasis on maximizing business efficiency led to the creation of city centers or suburbs devoted totally to economic activities (office or industrial parks).

A good city does not favor one function at the expense of other functions. It does not sacrifice one population group for the sake of other groups. That would be as ludicrous as if a physician were to favor one organ, or organ system, the heart or cardiovascular system, at the expense of another organ, such as the kidney or liver.

But this is what has been done in many of our cities. There has been an amputation of some population groups, especially children and young people, to favor commercial functions by segregating and excluding children and youth from vast areas of the city.

For the city as a whole to be healthy, every citizen group - children, the elderly, working males, the handicapped, disabled, etc. - must have a sense of being part of the whole, and indeed have their particular needs served, so that they in turn can help maintain the life of the city in the future.

Seven, in a good city, all inhabitants confirm and value each other. This is not possible if the only definition of self esteem and one's value as a person is tied to economic success. Each human being must be valued for their uniqueness and contribution to their fellow citizens, even if their talents are not marketable.

Eight, in a good city, aesthetic considerations, beauty, and meaning of the physical environment must have high priority. The physical and social environment are two aspects of the same reality. Just as it was a mistake to maintain the body-mind dichotomy, so it is a mistake to think that city inhabitants can have a good civic and social life in an ugly, brutal, and physically inhospitable city.

Finally, in a good city, the wisdom and knowledge of all inhabitants are appreciated and used. People are not intimidated by experts, whether architects or planners, but show a sense of caution and distrust of those who make decisions about their lives.

Make no mistake, every decision about the city's physical reality has social consequences! Consider the ill-conceived zoning practices and their consequences, the failure of public housing projects, the subsidization of the move to the suburbs, destructive transportation policies and architectural ideologies that celebrate and emphasize architecture as an esoteric art, rather than a social art! The result is an urban physical environment that is inhospitable and meaningless for many city dwellers!

Henry L. Lennard, Ph.D. is Chairman of the Advisory Board of the IMCL Council.

Chapter Five

Seven Aims for the Livable City

Edoardo Salzano

Fotostudio Frank Iwan

First of all, Where are We From, Where Do We Go?

No society, no culture, no civilization can live without the consciousness of its history. The roots of our life, and of our capacity to be active and responsible members of mankind, are in our history: they are in the history of our civilization, of our country, of our city and our family. Without our roots we become as sterile as uprooted trees.

And no society, no culture, no civilization can progress unless it cares for its posterity: for men and women, for coming generations, for the civilizations that will appear in our universe after us, and will live, utilize and enjoy it as we will have left it.

The Livable City: A Link Between the Past and the Future

Therefore I think that we must consider, first of all, the livable city as a link between the past and the future: the livable city respects the imprint of history (our roots), and respects those who are not born yet (our posterity).

A livable city is a city that preserves the signs (the sites, the buildings, the layouts) of history. It preserves the historical centers and the castles, the cathedrals and the palaces of the lords and of the city powers, surely. But it also preserves and restores the common houses lived in by common people (what we call "edilizia minore" or "edilizia di base"), which can testify to a rich and wise culture of living and building, and the traces of the historic design of the city, the narrow streets and the neighborhoods square, the traditional relationship between the house and private open space, and private space and community space and public space, and indoors and outdoors.

A livable city is also a city that fights against any waste of the natural resources and that we must leave intact for the humankind, that is, for our posterity. In the livable city all the care of planners and designers, all the care of technicians and administrators - and first of all the care of citizens - is applied to use the minimum resources of earth and water and energy: resources that, as now we know, are limited. Therefore a livable city it also a "sustainable city": a city that satisfies the needs of the present inhabitants without reducing the capacity of the future generation to satisfy their needs.

Social Elements and Physical Elements

History tells us that in a city social and physical elements are strictly tied together. As the home is the expression and the instrument of family life, in the same way, the city is the expression of social life, and the tool for well being and progress of the community.

It is not possible to separate, in the city, social elements and physical elements: it is only possible to distinguish them.

In the livable city both social and physical elements must collaborate for the well being and the progress of the community, and of the individual persons as members of the community.

The Seven Aims for the Livable City

1. A livable city has no boundaries: it is open to the whole world, and it has no ghettos nor segregated areas.

The city was born, in the history of our civilization, as the site where people became free and equal. The city has been transformed as the site where social and economic differences, as well as ethnic and religious ones, created barriers and confined and constituted sharply defined ghettos. In the livable city policies for public services and those for house rent must collaborate with town planning in order to abolish the constraint of boundaries and the disease of segregation.

2. A livable city is marked by the complexity of its functions and by the richness of the interpersonal exchanges it fosters.

The city is traditionally the site of exchanges and of the larger scores of opportunities. The historical centers (where they have not been reduced in tourist Disneylands) tell us how livable is the city where the different functions live together: inhabiting, working, shopping, meeting, recreation, health care. With the rigid application of functional zoning modern town planning menaces to destroy the complexity of the city, and to implement more and more traffic.

3. A livable city is a city where the town planners are able to manage the complexity and the dynamics so that it does not degenerate into congestion and anxiety.

If they are not carefully managed, complexity of functions and dynamics of life can transform the richness of exchanges into chaos. Congestion of traffic and anxiety in individual lives are more and more characteristics of urban life, especially in the bigger cities. Only a wise policy of town planning can enable the public administrators to manage urban development to increase the livability of the city.

4. A livable city has a good relationship with its site and with the environment.

The city is part of the balance between nature and history, between the action and culture of man, and the forces and rhythms of nature. The design of the city (in new developments as well as in restoration of the ancient settlements) must demonstrate respect and place value on the characteristics of sites and care for the environment.

5. A livable city is the home of the community.

In its golden ages the identity of the city is strictly tied to the dominant interests of the whole community over the interests of groups and individuals. A livable city is not merely an agglomeration of houses: in its organization, as well as in its stones and spaces it must show its reality as home of a community.

6. A livable city is a city where common spaces are the centers of social life and the foci of the entire community.

A livable city must be built up, or restored, as a continuous network - from the central areas to the more distant settlements -- where pedestrian paths and bicycle-paths bind together all the sites of social quality and of the community life.

7. And finally, a livable city is not built for the appearance and the glory of architects and city administrators, but for the well-being of the citizens.

Town design and town planning are not the result of the imagination and the work of one person (a genius or a hero), but the result of a dialectic and the produce of group work, where the different competences and the different responsibilities (those of the technicians, the administrators, the politicians) systematically collaborate. Only in that way can the city really be, as in its golden ages, the home of the community.

Edoardo Salzano is Dean of the School of Urban Planning at the University of Venice, Italy, and Member of the IMCL Board.

Chapter Six

The Nature of Livability

Antonio Casellati

Fotostudio Frank Iwan

It's late, and what can I add about the concept of livability, about livable cities, after so many interesting speeches. For me, it's more difficult because I'm not professionally involved in the problems. I'm not an architect. And, of course, I'm not even a professional politician, even when I was Burgermeister in Venice. And, I'm an amateur! But to put attention on it, I didn't say I am ONLY an amateur. Because amateur comes from amo, amore in Italian, lieben, love. And love for our cities, love for livability of our cities unifies us all in the problem, in this question which is so interesting and so important for the future of our lives because it's important for the future of our cities.

As it is so late, I don't make examples, but I ask you to allow me to remind you that in the Lennard's book, Livable Cities Observed, there is a wonderful chapter written by our friends Mr. and Mrs. Lennard about Venice. And this chapter, which is wonderful, passionate, and affectionate, precisely describes the quality of life in my town, my city of Venice.

It describes the ideal urban spaces, the life in the narrow streets. The life of children and their place in the numerous squares, we call them campi. Not squares, because we have only one square, the San Marco Square. Campi are irregular squares where the most part of our social life takes place. It is important to conserve such a quality of life as you find in Venice.

The Lennards wrote that Venice has changed not so much. It comes not only from history but also from the concerns of the population, from the will of the population. In Venice, it was difficult to defend its quality of life. It was difficult to conserve the city as it was. But through the centuries, we can say it has remained almost intact. So, it is necessary to have a strong will, a will to defend it now and always, because the livability of a city must be fought for step by step, year after year.

But when I think about Freiburg, and how it has been restored after the damage of the war, and how it is now, and about a decision of restoring it and rebuilding the old city as it was, I think it has been a more difficult decision and it has needed a very, very strong will. I visited this nice, beautiful city long ago in 1950, when it was so damaged from the war, around the wonderful Münster which was preserved almost intact. And the old city of Freiburg in our times, see how it grew up again, and now it has been rebuilt. And I now enjoy to be here, and to see how she is, with rebuilt old houses, with the streets all pedestrianized around the Münster Platz. This is a city where we all can say there is a livable city, an example of livability.

Coming here today, crossing the Münster Platz, hearing the voices of the women who are buying fruits, vegetables, the children, the fountains, the water coming from the fountains, the distant sound of the dogs of the Münster, seeing a crowded square, I experienced an example of life and of livability. But not only when the square is crowded, also in the evening. Yesterday when I saw a lonesome woman crossing the square, I felt that this human being was not only a human being, she was a person because the dimension, the human dimension of the Münster, of the Platz, of the whole city allows that every human being feels himself a person. I don't presume I can give a different definition of livability. I think livability means only one thing: livability means that we experience ourselves as real persons in the city.

Antonio Casellati, former Lord Mayor, City of Venice, Italy.

Chapter Seven

The Mission of the IMCL Conferences

Dietmar Hahlweg

The Advisory Board comprises almost thirty people from the United States and several European countries. The people who are engaged in the Advisory Board are doing this not only because of their commitment to "livable cities", but also because they are fascinated by the two people who are the soul and the motor of this project and impressed by the passion and energy with which they are advancing the work of "Making Cities Livable".

The Board is also very pleased that we changed the emphasis in the Freiburg program from the downtown areas to new city developments or new urban areas. We think that the downtown area is very important in every city, but the majority of the citizens do not live in the downtown area; they live in other parts of the city, and here the results of what we have planned and realized after the 2nd World War, after 1945, is not very good, and not sufficient.

There is in Germany now a new trend to develop new urban areas – not only settlements for people to live, but really new urban parts of the city. To improve existing urban areas as well as planning good new urban areas is an important task of this conference!

The last point I would like to mention is the "genius loci", Freiburg. From the beginning, the City of Freiburg played an important role in the work of Making Cities Livable. Competent people from Freiburg came to Venice, came to Charleston, came to San Francisco and the participants at these conferences were always very much impressed by the quality of life in this city – as far as it was possible to describe this in words, or to show this in slides.

I think we are all very grateful that we now are able to have this conference in this wonderful city, which is a pilot city for "making cities livable". I think what makes Freiburg so important for this conference is that we have this wonderful downtown area, and many fine areas of the city surrounding the downtown area.

But Freiburg does not only preserve what has grown from the history, as Lord Mayor Böhme described; Freiburg is also open for new developments. They started their work ten years ago – which was very early in the Federal Republic. At that time only a few cities were even thinking about creating a new part of the city. The Advisory Board is very thankful to Lord Mayor Böhme, to Mayor Ungern-Sternberg, and to the City Council that they were ready to support this conference. I am certain that as a result of this conference, Freiburg will become even more popular than it already is in Germay, in Europe, and in the United States!

Dr. Dietmar Hahlweg is former Lord Mayor, City of Erlangen, Germany, and Member of the IMCL Board.

Edoardo Salzano

I think it is very good to be part of an International Making Cities Livable Conference. First of all, I would say it is a pleasure. And I say this because we live in a world that is becoming more and more hard and anxious. I think we all have a need to have sometimes the opportunity to be together in an enjoyable way, in a good city, with interesting people, under the wise and loving leadership of Suzanne and Henry Lennard.

It is certainly also a pleasure to spend some time in one of the beautiful cities of the world selected by the IMCL Council once or twice a year. Every time I was at an International Making Cities Livable Conference in Venice or in Carmel or in San Francisco or Charleston, I had the pleasure to get to know or to appreciate the town or city, or to see with new eyes a city where there is a good balance between history and natu_, between culture and society on one hand and its natural environment.

These few days I am here I learned much about this wonderful Freiburg im Breisgau, so near to Venice; and like Venice, it has its feet in water.

It is surely a pleasure to participate in an IMCL Conference. But it is not only a pleasure. It is also a very interesting and useful opportunity to enrich ourselves – our professional and cultural knowledge; an opportunity to hear and learn something new and useful, hearing, observing and discussing experiences with persons working in many cities, and _for_ the cities and the citizens; by persons that work using the tools of town planning or town design or town management, but first of all with the tool, the very indispensable tool of the _love_ for their city, and therefore of the comprehension of its dynamics, its crises, its struggles and its hopes. And this is a main characteristic of these conferences – to bring together persons that work in different countries, in different tasks, coming from different backgrounds and experiences, having often different ideas about society and the world, but persons having all the same purpose and the same aim, to make our cities more livable.

Edoardo Salzano is Dean of the School of Planning, University of Venice, and Member of the IMCL Board.

Gianni Longo

I would like to start by making a simple observation, that is, how international this conference has become. It was always called International Making Cities Livable Conference, but I think here in Freiburg we have reached something like 29 different nations who are represented here from every continent. I think that's both a challenge and a responsibility. I think that we should think very carefully about the complexity of the issues that we are talking about, and how different some of the themes that are central to this conference are for each of us.

It's simple just to talk about suburban developments in the United States. It's very different to talk about new urban neighborhoods here in Germany or in Europe. The rules of the game are different. The players are different. And the images evoked by those words are different. And I think we should look at the exhibits, because they're very clear about that. We should make a real effort to listen because there's so much richness and experience that is represented here by so many of us.

There are two characteristics of this conference. One - this is the most holistic conference you will ever participate in. And two - this is a thoroughly inter-disciplinary conference. What do we mean by holistic? Holistic, essentially, is the profound belief that urban problems can not be solved in a vacuum. The belief that urban problems just don't go away if we suppress whatever symptoms they present to us. This has been the approach of the past and we know it fails. When crime came to the cities, we went to the suburbs. And when crime came to the suburbs we began to build gates and then we put lights and then we put guards and then dogs and televisions. So that our office parks began to look like fortresses and our residential areas really look like prisons. Did we solve the problem? Of course we did not solve the problem.

Because by not focusing on the issues holistically, we essentially destroyed the basic underpinning of what creates livable cities. A sense of honor of place, the dignity of the public realm. The idea of citizenship. And the idea of tolerance in our communities. So this theme of place, citizenship, and community are really the cornerstone, or some of the cornerstones, of this conference.

The inter-disciplinary aspect is clearly almost self-explanatory. Just this morning we heard so many points of view. There were architects, and planners, and elected officials, and people that deal with the administration of cities. I think that really the solution of problems in our cities is not just a question of good design or bad design, good economics or bad economics. It really takes the expertise of all of us.

There are essentially three themes that will be discussed at the conference. The first one is the theme of fairness and justice. I think that the new urban neighborhoods must be built in ways that provide for inclusiveness, diversity and social justice. They should allow for citizens regardless of age or economic status, and offer the opportunity to become active and engaged members of the community. They must provide the tools to strengthen citizenship among their residents. They must also provide jobs and the opportunities that bring prosperity and equity to residents.

The second theme is the theme of good design. You'll be surprised how interested and focused citizens are about the designs that we submit to them. Good design is critical to the success of a new urban neighborhood. Now I understand that there are limits to what good design can achieve, but let me tell you, there's almost no limit to the damage that bad design can do to our communities.

And the third theme is the theme of comprehensiveness. That, to me is really that as we develop new communities and new urban neighborhoods, we need to do so in a context that stretches from the existing urban core to the immediate countryside, to the wildest of wilderness that surrounds our cities. We must recognize that the urban neighborhood is more than a neighborhood. It is first and foremost part of a community. That a community is more than can be defined by the boundaries of a city. It is part of a region. And a new urban neighborhood is more than just a step toward the future. It is also part of the past. And a subtext of this principle is the special responsibility that we have to make a relationship between the man-made environments and the public and the natural environment. We need to fit it in, and we need to protect the special features. We need to be kind to it.

I hope that all these ideas and thoughts will challenge us. The structure of this conference is complex. It reflects the inter-disciplinary character of the problems addressed and it will reflect the holistic aspect of the solutions. And I hope that as the city of Freiburg is inspiring us with its beauty, the conference will inspire us to create better places in our communities.

Gianni Longo is President of Urban Initiatives, New York, and Member of the IMCL Board.

Chapter Eight

A Message from the Prince of Wales

John Thompson

Fotostudio Frank Iwan

I bring with me a message of goodwill to the conference from His Royal Highness the Prince of Wales, who sadly cannot be with us today, although he would love to be here. He would be most impressed with the work of this conference, and would appreciate the way in which Freiburg has restored the center of the historic city. There are some wonderful lessons here.

He would have loved to have joined in the debate that is going to take place in the next few days, particularly as he speaks more German than I do. He continues to enjoy his copy of <u>Livable Cities Observed</u>.

I am reminded that his particular campaign is twinned with yours, because you started in 1985, which is when His Royal Highness, very innocently, made the remark at a gathering of the Royal Institute of British Architects at Hampton Court Palace to the effect that the proposed extension to the National Gallery on Trafalgar Square was like a carbuncle on the face of an old friend. And he was fairly inundated with mail from around the country, much to his amazement. And subsequently,

since you have been so active yourselves and running these marvelous conferences, he has also been very hard at work.

In this period he has been running summer schools in civil architecture in England, France and Italy (and next year we hope to bring the summer school to Germany, possibly to Berlin and Potsdam) and at the same time as running a school for students we shall actually have a cities workshop on the very pressing problem of mass housing (Grosssiedlungen) which are represented in the Conference Exhibition. With a hundred million people living in such housing east of the River Elbe, it is one of the most pressing social and making cities livable problems the world faces.

It seems to me that there are two things that perhaps we could do to bring closer these two campaigns. At the Institute we run a research publication project called "Tools for Community Design" and it does seem to me that the lessons you are distilling out from all of your conferences could form the basis for joint cooperation and publications.

And last but not least, why not bring the IMCL Conference to the United Kingdom, because then His Royal Highness will be able to attend!

Thank you very much.

John Thompson, RIBA, John Thompson and Partners, London, UK.

Chapter Nine

The Freiburg Conference Themes

Rolf Böhme

This conference is dealing with many aspects of the "livable city" topic:

- new city neighborhoods and urban life

- conversion of military facilities to residential and commercial ones for civilian use in Germany - an important topic in Germany after reunification and the withdrawal of Allied and Soviet troops

- road planning and public transportation, living in a city without a car

- citizen participation in shaping new city neighborhoods

- the city for children and youth

- ecologically-sound city development and

- social issues of urban development

All these issues are important, but there is a general question underlying all these aspects: what kind of person are we basing our urban planning and development on? We have dealt a great deal with this question concerning the "philosophy" of current urban policy during the planning and construction of our new city neighborhood, "Rieselfeld". Prior to this, there was a long debate about whether we should build new city neighborhoods at all or whether maintaining our natural basis of life in accordance with sound ecological principals prohibits additional "asphalting" of our landscape. The Green party members in our city council are still opposed to construction in the Rieselfeld area for this reason. The decision made at that time was not based on ecology versus economy, but rather ecology versus the social issue of finding a solution for the many thousands of people who are looking for housing.

The majority in the city council voted in favor of the social aspect, to construct new housing and consequently create a new city neighborhood.

At that time, the participation models for the citizens were important in constructing the new city neighborhood. We devoted a lot of time discussing these basic issues and deciding them democratically. This was the only way to overcome the basic opposition to constructing a new city neighborhood at all.

These participation issues are also very important today. A city is composed not only of streets, squares, schools, kindergartens, public transportation and the like, but also requires a mental infrastructure of its citizens. Democratic endorsement and the process of public planning with the participation of citizens and the media are not only essential characteristics of a livable city, but also its brains.

Our cities act according to the principles of freedom and self-government of its citizens. A policy of "making cities livable" cannot be achieved without a positive mental infrastructure of the citizens involved.

Consequently it is not only a question of achieving the correct result, but also a question of the process involved in making decisions and having them accepted.

I especially wanted to mention this point, because it is the most difficult one in my experience. There are architects for architecture, specialists for all issues, but the political management and the public debate in the media with an affirmative vote on the final decision is a difficult but important matter for a livable city, that is based on the principles of freedom and self-government.

I would like to mention an additional matter: public transportation. Most cities in Europe are suffering from automobile traffic today. Our policy in Freiburg has clearly made public transportation its priority for quite some time. The dense infrastructure in our city center with its services and shopping facilities is only possible with a good public transportation system. The public spaces are too small for a great amount of automobile traffic, and the same applies to the parking spaces. There are "No Parking" signs everywhere. But there are so few parking spaces and the demand is so great, that we should post signs saying "Don't even think about parking". However, priority given to local public transportation is always controversial. There is a conflict every time

automobile traffic is reduced on an important street.

This issue is especially important when constructing a traffic system in so-called threshold countries, that are aiming at the level of industrialization and prosperity enjoyed by Western countries.

Problems of urban development are going to be created when the mega-cities in China or other Far Eastern countries achieve the same degree of motorization as is normal in America or Europe. I believe that the globalization of the economy and lifestyles make it imperative for us to include this international aspect of the "Making Cities Livable" topic, too.

The makeup of this conference is suitable for dealing with these issues - over 30% of the over 350 participants are from other European countries and abroad, and the interesting mixture of professions provides starting points for discussion and dialogue, for getting to know the problems and solutions in other cities and countries.

The great chances of this event as well as the exhibition, which is taking place in our city hall at the same time, are the result of its wide range of topics extending beyond urban planning, to include urban culture and psychological and social aspects. Precisely these aspects of inter-disciplinary planning are becoming decisively important given the current economic situation of almost all cities at home and abroad.

I want to thank you for coming and I am confident the conference will produce good results.

Dr. Rolf Böhme is the Lord Mayor of Freiburg im Breisgau, Germany.

PART TWO

Essential Elements

ZWEITER TEIL
Wichtige Grundüberlegungen

Public Space

Öffentlicher Raum

Piazza Umberto I, Capri

Suzanne H. Crowhurst Lennard

Chapter Ten

Designing for Urban Life

Edoardo Salzano

Can a good design of the city help the well-being of people? Sincerely, I'm not sure. But I'm absolutely sure that a bad design, or a bad layout, or the absence of any design and layout are a formidable help for the disease of people.

In general terms, we can say that the modern city is built up as a lot of houses linked by a lot of roads covered by a lot of cars. It is built as a continuous conglomerate of concrete and asphalt: on the back of houses and roads lies some open space - free for the children and garbage, often for the two of them together.

I'm convinced that we must fight this way of building and living in the city. I'm convinced that the livable city must be built, or restored and up-graded, as a continuous network - from central areas till the more distant settlements - where pedestrian paths and bicycle-paths link together all the sites of social, physical and environmental quality.

The sites of social quality, that means the spaces and the buildings that people use not as individuals, but as members of a community: churches and schools, community buildings and sports grounds, theaters and museums, libraries and markets, hospitals and cemeteries, parks and public gardens, clubs and - finally - open spaces dedicated to meetings and to being together, to converse and to discuss.

The sites of physical and environmental quality, that means all the spaces, and buildings, and monuments where nature and history have imprinted the sign of beauty or rarity or

memory: riversides and woods, historical centers and castles, panoramic views and archeological zones, geological and natural monuments and cultural resources.

In other words, the design of the city must show the city as it was in history, and as it must be again: not merely an aggregate of individual homes, but the home of the community.

Therefore the aim is to organize an ideal network to tie together the "spaces for livability": but to achieve this we must preview, plan, designed and realize such spaces, and they must have an adequate quality. Then we must ask ourselves: what does it mean "to have an adequate quality"? In other words, what do we need from spaces for livability?

Not only do we need settled, canonized and standardized functions (such as schools and hospitals, playgrounds and gardens and so on), but we need a special competency of the public spaces: we need the capability to be designed and planned as spaces where it is easy, enjoyable, comfortable to stay together, and chat, and converse, and play together. And we need spaces not suitable to only one kind of person: to the elderly or to younger people, to handicapped or to women, but spaces in which persons of different generations and different social status are together, each learning from the others.

In Venice we have such spaces: their name is "campi". The terrific book of Suzanne H. Crowhurst Lennard and Henry L. Lennard,

Livable Cities Observed, is a lovely guide for people who know Venice, and an amazing reporting for people who yet don't know this wonderful city (only for those very young then, I suppose!). But let me now open a brief parenthesis, and dedicate some words to the city where I have been living for many years.

Venice is a wonderful city for several reasons. In general terms the design of Venice testifies to a perfect balance between the action of man and the forces of nature: between the needs of society, culture and the work of man on one side, and the rules and rhythms of nature on the other side. The layout of the city, of its streets and squares (the "calli" and the "campi"), shows you still today, with all evidence, how the wise Venetians of the past were able to use the natural factors (without forcing or violating them), to synthesize them with the needs of social life and with the thought and work of man, to design the shape of the city.

And the design of the open spaces of Venice shows us how the care for human needs and the primacy granted to community values, both joined with a high and consolidated "culture of building" (and "culture of living") could create spaces where it is a pleasure to meditate and to chat, to meet friends and to make a new acquaintance, to stay and to play, to walk and to buy, to look at people who pass and to exhibit yourself.

But Venice has one more trump: something more to teach to the other cities of the world. Egon Grund explains it in a very good way: Venice has no cars. In Venice all the heavy and the fast traffic goes in waterstreets (the canals), with specialized boats: water-buses (vaporetti and traghetti) for the public service; water-trucks (mototopi, peate, burci) for the wares; watercars (gondole, sandoli, tope and sampierotte) for the private transportation; watertaxis (lance) for those that are in a hurry (and for the rich ones).

In Venice we have the perfect separation of the different kinds of traffic. Since the birth of the city, they have realized, in a natural way, one of the basic principles of modern town planning. In Venice the streets - as all open spaces - are free for people: you can walk chatting or with your nose at the clouds or looking at the nice girls or reading the newspaper, without being anxious for cars or motorcycles. Very little kids and old people too can walk, without any fear of being klaxoned or run over.

I am convinced that a livable city is a city where more space than today is reserved to pedestrians, and much less to cars. I am convinced that the traffic is now destroying not only the cities, but the idea of the city. The city was invented and produced by men for being together, for exchanging wares, goods, information, work. We can say that the city is the "site of exchanges". Nowadays the city, especially big cities (I'm thinking Rome, Naples, Milan, Florence, as well as Cairo, Madrid, Athens), but also-many medium-size cities, became the sites where traffic not only prevents you to promenade, not only menaces your health with pollution, but also obliges you to reach your work or your friends wasting a great deal of time and fuel in the big carrousels of congestion.

There was once in the USA an association whose name was: "More streets for people". I don't know if it is still alive. But I think that in every country and in every city groups of citizens should organize to fight for that aim. In the interest not only of people today, but also for the generations of the future.

Edoardo Salzano is Dean of the School of Urban Planning at the University of Venice, Italy, and Member of the IMCL Board.

Chapter Eleven (a)

Designing the Heart of a New Urban Neighborhood

Suzanne H. Crowhurst Lennard

The single most important element in the creation of a new urban neighborhood may be the design of a central public place.

Consider some of the social goals of a new urban neighborhood:

- a neighborhood in which people feel recognized and known to others;

- where all persons play a valued role;

- where children grow up within a familiar, yet varied social environment, and can learn a broad repertoire of social competence from observation and contact with different kinds of people;

- a neighborhood with a sense of its own identity, but where a sense of membership in a larger community exists;

- where persons of different backgrounds are not segregated from one another; and where cultural and social differences are accepted and celebrated.

Each of these social goals has implications for the design of public urban spaces.

Good public places facilitate the co-presence of a variety of people, old and young, little children and the handicapped, those well-to-do and those less well off.

Good public places offer many opportunities for informal and unplanned meetings of friends, neighbors, workmates and acquaintances. These social contacts confirm to each that they are known, and valued by others.

Meetings in public promote significant conversation. The exchange of information about each other's lives, and about mutual friends, cements the social bonds among community members.

Extended conversations unfold in a good urban space, or the conversation may move to the more comfortable setting of a cafe.

When people are happy in a good urban space they show pleasure in each other's company, they show affection for one another, and they share a common feeling of delight in watching street performers and musicians.

Frequent use of a public space can be achieved in a number of ways:

- the space can be located at the crossing point of routes through the neighborhood, or adjacent to a major public transportation point;

- the space can be designed to accommodate a weekly activity that is necessary, and appealing to everyone, such as a farmers' market;

- the space can be enclosed with buildings that contain shops serving everyday needs, such as a grocery, bakery, pharmacy, etc.. If inhabitants of a new neighborhood are to spend enough time in each other's presence that they begin to recognize and talk with one another, they need a neighborhood space that is hospitable for all, and comfortable for longer stays.

In good urban spaces children can take part in the life of the city; they meet other children, and observe how different people relate. This way, they learn the social skills of talking, negotiating differences, and taking pleasure in social relationships. Little children are taught how to talk with adults, adults pay attention to children, and treat them with respect, and little children learn to talk to adult strangers as an equal.

Children learn to interact through watching others, and through practice. The more opportunity they have to watch all kinds of people in a variety of relationships the more versatile they become in social interaction.

This varied social life takes place in public spaces, not in the more limited realm of home or school; and in major, centrally located public places, not in smaller courtyards or neighborhood corners.

Therefore, if it is important in a new urban neighborhood to develop children's social competence, a central public space that facilitates social interaction among all residents is extremely important.

Good urban spaces make possible all kinds of pleasurable festive events in which everyone can participate. At some festivals this means that everyone joins in to create an object of great beauty, such as the carpets of flower petals made at Corpus Domini in the little town of Cannara. At other festivals people practice for months to perfect a skill, or to perform wonderful feats, as at Siena's Palio and neighborhood processions.

At many festivals neighbors eat and drink together, at a meal prepared by the community, and served on the neighborhood's main public space. If it is considered important for the community to acknowledge that everyone can play a valued role in society, then public social events, and community festivals will be organized at which everyone can be seen to play an important role.

When all inhabitants of a neighborhood use a common central place on a regular basis, and for special festive occasions, the shared experiences begin to create a neighborhood's sense of its own unique identity. A new neighborhood, therefore, needs a centrally located public space large enough to accommodate a variety of social activities -- a farmers' market, neighborhood festivals, outdoor cafes and restaurants, as well as all inhabitants.

In Venice each district, or sestieri, has its own centrally located public space (or campo) that evolved to accommodate social life in public. Each of these campi serves as the central gathering place for a population of between ten and fifteen thousand inhabitants. In the district of Dorsoduro, for example, the main campo, Campo Santa Margherita is 150 meters long, and up to 35 meters wide. Additional smaller campi and courtyards abound.

Rather than relying on police, or video monitoring devices a neighborhood works best, and is safest, if it is designed to promote informal social monitoring by the whole society.

As Jane Jacobs showed, this is best achieved if the public space is surrounded by traditional shop/houses. The dwellings above provide "eyes on the street", and a permanent population with jurisdiction over the space; at street level small shopkeepers, waiters and vendors can provide immediate control or assistance, and these commercial enterprises generate increased presence of people.

Informal social monitoring of children by all adults, not only teachers and parents, helps to socialize children and make them more aware of other people's needs. For this to occur, children's play must be accommodated within public spaces used by all members of the community, not in playgrounds. Adults shopping, or on business errands, must pass close by.

Different people in the public realm, and different occasions, need different physical settings. Some may prefer a sunny cafe sheltered from the wind; others a cool shady cafe with a breeze. Some people are drawn to a dramatic location center stage; others prefer a more secluded location.

While it is difficult, if not impossible, to accommodate such a wide range of activities and preferences within a geometrically designed square, it is possible to design a piazza -- possibly of irregular shape -- around the activities that one wants to accommodate.

This is the process by which the Venetian campi and the most successful urban spaces came into existence; and this method can be simulated today to design new neighborhood urban spaces. It is a method which I myself use in teaching architecture and urban design.

In general, urban spaces work best when they are roughly square shaped or rounded, but not symmetrical. Symmetrical spaces are more formal, and suggest the power of the city planner, but may not be so suitable for the

informal, multifunctional character of social life.

In general, streets are not so hospitable. They encourage movement, not sojourn. Those streets that are more successful are visually closed, for example by a tower gate; or slightly curved, so that one cannot see far down the street, and the space may be divided into smaller areas by outdoor cafes and planters.

If one wants young people and adults to pay attention to other human beings co-present with them in a public space, then one will design a space that is visually enclosed, so that a person's attention does not wander into the distance.

The space will be traffic-free, so that attention need not be directed to the danger of moving vehicles, noise and fumes, and people can really see, and hear each other.

The sense of having arrived at a destination is enhanced by a "threshold experience". Moving from a narrow, dark passage into a bright, open plaza awakens the pedestrian from their private inner reverie and dramatically announces that they are now entering the public social realm.

Trees and flowering plants encourage people to linger in public, and water always provides a gathering point. Erlangen, of course, has been internationally recognized as a leader in efforts to restore nature in the urban environment. In the design of new urban neighborhoods, nature must be incorporated to play its important social, as well as ecological role.

If one wants to encourage people to linger in the public space, then seating is essential. Not everyone needs, or would choose the same kind of seating. The most successful public spaces offer a combination of informal seating - ledges, walls or steps, that allow for more spontaneity -as well as formal seating, chairs and benches.

If it is considered important for strangers to see and acknowledge one another, for acquaintances and friends to talk with one another, then seating in public must be placed to allow eye contact, and to facilitate conversation. For example, traditional straight benches must be grouped facing towards each other.

A great deal of subtle social contact takes place in public, even between strangers. An arrangement of benches in a circle permits this eye contact. A few European cities have designed benches curved or angled inwards. At Sterntor in Bonn, three semicircular benches above the stream are very popular, especially for small groups of friends.

The spatial organization of a plaza, defining places for people to gather, areas to move through, locations for conversations, is suggested by the placement of focal points, trees and planters, by paving design and differences in level. Stone bollards locate people in space and define locations that one may, temporarily, make one's own.

Paving designs identify certain areas as a space to move through, other areas as a place to pause, or to change direction. There is no city in the world that has perfected paving design to the extent that Freiburg has.

People are naturally gregarious and like to gather where others are present, but they need anchors, or focal points around which they can cluster.

Public art can function as a focus of social life in public, if it is hospitable and friendly to people. Peter Lehmann's pigherd and pigs is an important focal point in Bremen; it provides seating and opportunities for children's play.

Of all the sculptors working in the public realm, no one contributes more to public life than Bonifatius Stirnberg. His works are a powerful magnet for old and young, and they create a topic of conversation among strangers - a process that Holly Whyte calls "triangulation".

To build public social life and community spirit in a new urban neighborhood cannot be done piecemeal. Many factors must be coordinated so that all the necessary elements fall into place -- the design of a neighborhood "heart", together with revival of "shop/houses", appropriate architecture, pedestrian networks to work, school and shops, traffic control, public transportation, social events such as farmers' markets and community festivals.

But it is the central urban place, the "heart" of the community that is the axis around which all other elements must revolve.

In designing a new urban neighborhood, before any street arrangement is considered, or the location of any building is determined, the first task should be to define the public social life that will characterize the spirit of the community; to identify social events and occasions that will support public social life; and to design urban spaces to accommodate these social events.

Suzanne H. Crowhurst Lennard Ph.D. (Arch.) is Director of the International Making Cities Livable Council, Carmel, California, and Co-Chair, Program Committee for the 17th IMCL Conference.

Die Gestaltung eines Herzens für einen neuen Stadtteil

Suzanne H. Crowhurst Lennard

Die Einrichtung eines zentralen, öffentlichen Platzes ist vielleicht das wichtigste Element in der Gestaltung eines neuen Stadtteils. Denken wir nach, über die zentralen sozialen Ziele eines neuen Stadtteils:

- In so einem Stadtteil sollen alle Menschen fühlen, daß sie erkannt, sind;

- Hier spielen alle Menschen eine Rolle, die von andern eingeschätzt wird;

- In so einem Stadtteil wachsen Kinder auf in einer bekannten und mannigfalten sozialen Umgebung. Sie lernen sozialen Kompetenz von der Beobachtung, Kontakt, und Umgang mit verschiedenen Menschen;

- So ein neuer Stadtteil soll seine eigene Identität entwickeln, aber auch das Gefühl, daß man auch ein Mitglied einer größeren Gemeinschaft ist;

- Hier sollen Menschen mit verschiedenen Lebensumständen nicht von einander segregiert sein, aber auch akzeptiert und sogar gefeiert sind.

Jedes einzelnes dieser sozialen Ziele hat bestimmte Konsequenzen für die Gestaltung öffentlicher Räume. Öffentliche Räume bieten viele Möglichkeiten für informale und ungeplante Begegnungen zwischen Freunden, Nachbarn, Kollegen und Bekannten. Diese sozialen Kontakte bestätigen den Menschen, daß sie bekannt und geschätzt sind.

Begegnungen in der Öffentlichkeit fördern ein bedeutsames Gespräch. Der Informationsaustausch über ihr Leben und über gemeinsame Freunde befestigt soziale Beziehungen.

- Die Menschen zeigen Freude miteinander zu sein.

- In guten öffentlichen Räumen nehmen Kinder in dem Leben der Stadt teil. Sie begegnen anderen Kindern und beobachten wie Menschen mit-einander umgehen. Auf diese Art lernen sie soziale Fähigkeiten miteinander zu sprechen, miteinander zu verhandeln, und, daß man sich auf dem Umgang mit anderen Menschen freuen kann.

- Kinder lernen miteinander umzugehen, durchdem sie andere beobachten, und durch Übung. Umsomehr Möglichkeiten sie haben, allerlei Menschen zu beobachten, in einer Vielfalt von Beziehungen, desto mehr begabt werden sie, im Leben der Stadtteil teil zu nehmen.

- Diese Vielfalt soziales Lebens spielt sich im öffentlichen Raum ab, und nicht in dem mehr begrenzten Bereich der Wohnung oder der Schule. Es ereignet sich in zentralen, großen öffentlichen Räumen, und nicht in den kleinen Innenhöfen.

Wenn es wichtig ist, in einem neuen Stadtteil die soziale Kompetenz der Kinder zu entwickeln, dann ist ein zentraler öffentlicher

Platz der soziales Leben unter allen Einwohnern fördert, sehr wichtig.

Allerlei angenehme spezielle Ereignisse spielen sich im öffentlichen Raum ab -- Ereignisse in denen alle teilnehmen können. Wenn es wichtig ist, für die Gemeinschaft zu erkennen, daß Jeder eine wichtige Rolle hat, dann werden soziale Ereignisse und Gemeinschaftsfeste so im zentralen öffentlichen Raum organisiert, daß alle sehen können, daß Jeder eine wichtige Rolle spielt.

Wenn alle Einwohner eines neuen Stadtteils einen gemeinsamen zentralen Raum auf regelmäßige Basis benutzen, und für spezielle Ereignisse und Veranlassungen, dann werden diese gemeinsamen Erfahrungen eine einzigartige Identität prägen. Ein neuer Stadtteil darum, braucht einen zentralen öffentlichen Raum, groß genug für eine Vielfalt von sozialen Aktivitäten -- einen Bauernmarkt, Feste, und so weiter.

Jeder Stadtteil in Venedig hat seinen eigenen zentralen öffentlichen Platz (oder Campo), der sich entwickelt hat, um öffentliches Leben zu fassen. Jedes Campo ist der zentrale Sammlungspunkt für eine Bevölkerungszahl von 10-15,000.

Häufiger Gebrauch des öffentlichen Raums von allen, die im Stadtteil leben, kann auf verschiedene Weisen erreicht werden.

- Der Raum kann auf einer Kreuzung von verschiedenen Wegen liegen, oder angrenzend zu öffentlichem Verkehr.

- Der Raum kann so gestaltet sein, daß er sich eignet für eine wöchentliche Aktivität die notwendig ist, und allen gefällt, wie, zum Beispiel, ein Bauernmarkt.

- Der Raum kann mit Gebäuden umgeben sein, die die täglichen Bedürfnisse erfüllen, wie eine Bäckerei, Lebensmittelgeschäft, Apotheke, und so weiter.

Die Menschen brauchen einen Nachbarschaftsraum der freundlich und komfortabel ist, für ein längeres Verweilen. Es ist besser, und sicherer, wenn der Stadtteil so gestaltet ist, daß alle Leute die dort wohnen, selbst alles überwachen können. Wie Jane Jacobs uns gezeigt hat, ist es bestens, wenn der öffentliche Raum mit traditionellen gemischte-nutzung-Häusern ungeben ist. Die Wohnungen über den Geschäften sorgen für "Augen auf die Straße". die Geschäfte im Erdgeschoß versichern, daß Leute auf der Straße sind.

Informales Überwachen von Kindern von allen Erwachsenen, helfen Kinder mit anderen Kindern besser umzugehen, und gleichzeitig werden sie mehr bewußt von den Bedürfnissen von anderen Menschen. Damit dieses geschieht, müssen Kinder sich in öffentlichen Plätzen aufhalten, die von der gesamten Gemeinschaft benutzt werden. Erwachsene wärend des Einkaufs, oder während sie geschäftliche Angelegenheiten erledigen, müssen den Kindern vorbei kommen.

Verschiedene Menschen im öffentlichen Raum und während verschiedener Ereignisse, brauchen unterschiedliche Räumlichkeiten. Da es sehr schwierig ist, sogar fast unmöglich so eine Vielfalt von Aktivitäten und Veranstaltungen beschränkt auf eine quadratisch geformte Fläche, unterzubringen, ist es möglich, ein "Piazza" zu entwerfen, möglicherweise in einer unregelmäßigen Form, um die Aktivitäten unterzubringen.

Durch diesen Prozeß entstanden die Venezianische "Campi", aber auch viele andere Plätze; und diesen Prozeß kann man auch heute noch zunutze machen, um öffentliche Plätze in neuen Stadtteilen zu entwerfen. Dies ist eine Methode die ich selber verwendete, als ich Architektur und Stadtgestaltung unter-richte.

Öffentliche Räume sind am besten, wenn sie entweder eine quadratische oder runde Form annehmen, allerdings nicht symmetrisch. Symmetrische Flächen wirken etwas formal, und deuten auf die Macht der Stadtplaner hin. Aus diesem Grunde, sind sie nicht für den vielseitigen Charakter des sozialen Gefüges geeignet. Um Gemeinschaftsleben zu fördern, sollten die Formen der öffentlichen Räume aus dem Charakter der Gesellschaft entstehen, und sie gleichzeitig einbeziehen.

Im allgemeinen, wirken Straßen nicht so sehr einladend. Sie fordern dazu auf, in Bewegung zu bleiben, nicht zu verweilen. Die Straßen die erfolgreicher sind, wirken visuell geschlossen. Wenn man beabsichtigt, daß junge Leute und Erwachsene auf andere Menschen im öffentlichen Raum aufmerksam werden, dann wird man einen geschlossenen Platz entwerfen, in dem die visuelle Aufmerksamfähigkeit nicht in der Ferne verloren geht. Ein solcher Platz soll Verkehrsfrei sein, daß Menschen sich wirklich sehen und hören können.

Den Eindruck zu erwecken, daß man an einem Ziel angekommen ist, wird durch ein "Schwellen Ereignis" verstärkt.

Bäume und Blumen fördern Menschen auf sich in der Öffentlichkeit aufzuhalten. Wasser hat die Eigenschaft, als ein Versammlungsort zu wirken. Es ist sehr wichtig, daß in der Gestaltung von neuen Stadtteilen, Natur so eingebaut ist, daß sie eine soziale, wie auch eine ökologische Rolle spielt.

Daher sind Sitzgelegenheiten eine fundamentale Bedingung. Nicht jederman benötigt oder würde die selbe Sitzgelegenheit wählen.

Ein großer Anteil vom sozialen Kontakt findet in öffentlichen Räumen statt, sogar zwischen Fremden. Hierbei ist es wichtig, daß Fremde sich gegenseitig sehen können. Aus diesem Grunde müssen öffentliche Sitzgelegenheiten so plaziert werden, daß sie Blick-kontakt und Unterhaltungen fördern. Traditionelle gerade Bänke müssen so aufgestellt sein, daß sie sich gegenüber stehen.

Der Rahmen in welchem ein öffentlicher Raum gestaltet ist, kann das Zusammenbringen von Menschen unterstützen, und es möglich machen, daß unterschiedliche Aktivitäten am gleichen Ort stattfinden.

Diese räumliche Anordnung, die Definition wo Menschen sich treffen können und miteinander sprechen können, wird durch Bäume und Kunstwerke, Pflaster, Höhenunterschiede, usw. unterstützt.

Um öffentliches Leben und Gemeinschaftssinn zu erwecken, müssen viele Elemente zusammenkommen: die Gestaltung des Herzens der Nachbarschaft, mit der Wiederentdeckung gemischter Nutzung Shop/House; umgebungsangemessenen Architektur, Fußgänger-verbindungen zu der Arbeit, Schule oder Einkaufen; Öffentlicher Verkehr, und soziale Ereignisse wie Gemeindefeste und Bauernmärkte.

Aber der zentrale urbane Platz ist das Herz der Gemeinschaft, mit dem alle andere Elemente verbunden sein müssen.

Prof. Dr. Suzanne H. Crowhurst Lennard Ph.D.(Arch.) ist Direktorin der International Making Cities Livable Council, Carmel, Californien, und Vorsitzende des Programm-Komitees der 17. IMCL Konferenz.

Chapter Twelve (a)

Historical Marketplaces and New Urban Neighborhoods

Klaus Andrä

Introduction

An interesting starting point for a talk on the subject of contemporary urban planning might be to pose the question: what can one learn from historical marketplaces in the outlining of new urban neighborhoods?

Over the years, my studies of historic town cores, as well as my conversations and correspondences, illustrate that, despite the many differences between Europe and the United States, there are many similar answers to similar questions regarding urban life and town culture. This is also so when speaking of public town squares. In town squares, the essence of urbanity can be found. Such squares provide a kind of gauge by which to judge both the existence of urban culture as well as the social and economic standard of the urban society. Town squares both reflect and manifest the soul of the town to visitors who happen by. And, we can find beautiful souls in even simple conditions or a kind of hopelessness and soullessness in town-building structures erected with much pomp and glamour.

Appropriateness is demanded. The determinate of this appropriateness is man, with his wishes, capabilities and potential. Man's standards are then used as guidelines by which the shape and texture of the square is determined in order to insure a maximum of options as provided by its spatial architectonic form. And these two aspects of shape and texture must also harmonize in the same way that an individual's personality and clothing also go together. Perhaps we should ask historic town squares themselves for the message which they portray.

Calculated Changes for Successful Marketplaces

At first glance, any attempt to pull useful new ideas from medieval town squares and apply them to the planning of new urban neighborhoods seems rather hopeless. The immense richness in optic wonderment and atmosphere of old charm, along with the dignity achieved through centuries of existence, makes such structures unique. But this seeming disconnection can be changed after a more in-depth look.

One might at first be surprised by the purposefulness and rationality with which town-founders centuries ago weighed various possibilities and created prerequisites by which to develop new centers for urban prosperity and culture, sometimes even several of such centers in one town. It is remarkable how energetically they strove to create significant design ideas, and combined these with a sound business sense.

Location was very important for the success of a new urban square. It was, and continues to be, advantageous to place the square not only in the middle of the "settlement," but in an area where regional traffic streams come together.

When an additional marketplace was necessary in the German town of Halle at the beginning of the 12th century, the town founder chose a distinctive topographical point, directly on the edge of a high embankment. The towers were also a kind of symbol of prosperity, promising travelers a wealth of business opportunities. The various regional trade routes were then systematically joined at the new square. The topographical placement of the square allowed the towers to be seen from great distance and they became an orientation point and marker for travelers. These trade route junctions brought tremendous economic profits to the town lords as they received a part of all trading sales.

Simple Geometry and Simple Designing of the Squares

This structure is similar in other towns. The squares are located at points of traffic confluence and of topographical distinction: on top of a hill or embankment or in the bend of a river. Where the land is flat, the square is located in the center of the settlement. The form of the square is usually very simple: quadratic, rectangular or in the shape of a trapezium. In time, the boundaries of the square became more and more defined as a result of an ever decreasing area within the town walls upon which to build. Town hall and church were the most important buildings in the square and, up to the last century, the square area was often left unpaved. As the most essential public drinking water source, the well also served as a favorite meeting place (as we know from many old folk songs). Time also had its effect on these wells, as they were transformed by the community into objects of art and thus became self-representative. In everyday life, the square became a familiar center for the common exchange of community gossip and information, for meeting and for the discussion of daily religious and communal activities. Everyday the square was frequented only by the inhabitants.

A High Degree of Urban Quality in a Very Small Area

The importance and power of an urban center result not only from its ability to provide for the daily needs of the people living in the settlement itself. The wider the regional function and appeal, the more vital and successful the new center. It is astonishing to realize what a highly developed degree of urban quality could grow out of a very small area. The famous town of Wittenberg, for example, only covered an area of 33 hectares when the great religious reformer Martin Luther lived there in the 16th century - but what an urban quality! And the marketplace, as was also the case in many town squares, was no more than 5000 square meters. And also in this case, we find the square to have a simple geometrical design.

Attaining Urban Quality Through Regional Institutions

If communities today are seriously interested in creating new, powerful urban centers in contemporary housing areas, then they should forcefully develop a kind of program that also includes some elements which are important not only for the settlement, but for the entire city and region as well. And, such programs must be carried out with fervor. Naturally, real success is also contingent upon an effective traffic system. An immense advantage for a new housing area would also be the inclusion of several educational institutions. Students and youngsters have always given public squares an appealing flair. A high degree of shopping appeal must also be present such as to attract not only consumers, but also small facilities and services which are essential to providing an urban, yet comfortable atmosphere: shops and boutiques, cafes and nice restaurants, book shops, galleries, fitness and beauty centers.

Of course no historical marketplace is without its impressive architectural features. Today these features need not be presented by buildings such as the church and city hall. Sky scrapers filled with many anonymous offices and institutions would, however, not do the job. In Wernigerode, for example, the beauty and fascination is conveyed through the smallish form of an old dance or wedding hall. I think it could be a fascinating project for students to design this type of building as an attraction of part of the housing area's center with such features as banquet rooms, indoor gardens, manicured surroundings, and interesting technical artwork or touches, an example of which might be the admirable artistic clocks of the Renaissance-epoch of the 15th/16th century. This example from Görlitz is like many others, an imposing masterwork connecting art and the technical along with a solid dollop of fun for observers. And this picture of a town hall front entrance illustrates how a single architectural detail like a house door can have a powerful emotional effect. In this case the effect is supported essentially by the green on the walls.

Functions and Building Structures in Transition

Historical places communicate another important concept: a vital town square can not prosper without somehow having elements intertwining it with the surrounding urban and regional structures. Such a reality can rarely be achieved immediately, but rather depends on time for the area to mature and develop on its own, perhaps over the span of a generation. It needs a chance to change in both function and construction and mold itself to the needs of those living in and using the area. Form and content should be able to transform as life in the town itself transforms - over a period of years. But in no case should this change lead to the use of transitory/provisional types of architecture in town squares. This "throw-away architecture" would be especially disastrous in urban squares because the development of an individual urban identity would be seriously interrupted. History has shown us that many of the most greatly prized buildings are those which have won individuality and cultural values through respectful and confident modernization and the addition of new elements by later generations.

The unity of architectural styles is appealing and thus in some ways serves to suggest that we of today should also design our buildings in such a manner as to make them worthy of being preserved and one day becoming the monuments of tomorrow.

Festivals in Urban Communities

Reports and pictures convey a huge variety of information dealing with public activities in medieval town squares. Rambunctious festivals with miracle healers, musicians and clowns were frequently held in connection with the traditional markets or fairs. Showmen brought and showed their exotic animals: calves with two heads or other anatomic abnormalities. Religious proceedings ranging from Easter games and homages to feudal lords were organized with fireworks, flags and expensive decorations. There were also duels and riding tournaments - in Dresden, feudal lords even shot wild bears, sows and stags in the marketplace. Thanksgiving processions were a common sight. And of course all ate and drank in a festive and opulent manner.

The connection between commerce and culture was both tightly knit and successful. The tradition of festivities and activity in old town marketplaces is continued on today with musical, dance, sport and cultural events often being held there. In older times as also today, there are many highlights to urban life, where the doldrums of everyday are momentarily broken and people far and wide come to take part and/or observe the festivities.

Because of the fact that individual initiative tends to grow slowly in newly settled areas (then and now), cultural as well as business successes depend at first rather heavily on a high quality of professional management. Also important is the support of a coming together of people of all ages and social groups based on mutual values such as tolerance and acceptance. Understanding between and among different societal and ethnic communities can be promoted in such a way.

A Few Infamous Traditions

There are a few infamous traditions belonging to the history of old marketplaces: they were a showplace for executions, burnings or the denouncement of suspected "evil" doers. Until the beginning of the last century, public denouncements as a sign of warning and means of education were a usual occurrence at the town square. Nowadays, verdicts against law breakers are not given or punishments carried out in public squares, but rather are portrayed on television or through newspapers. A contemporary responsibility carried out in public areas has now become the ensuring of security and order to visitors. Should there be a police station in every square? Can we place our confidence in the courage of the individual citizen to act with braveness and in selflessness and aid others in conflict? More unorthodox solutions to such issues, perhaps eliminating the need to resort to the use of police stations, can be obtained from historical market traditions. One such example is the so-called master of the market.

His responsibility was to punish the petty thieves and, for example, the female shoppers who stuck their hair pins into the butter to test its quality and taste. The master of the market's other duties included ensuring that merchants correctly measured and weighed their goods and that the start and end of the trading day was punctual. Today one can imagine a new kind of market master whose job it would be to act as a combination policeman, social worker and manager. His apartment would be located directly on the square and he would be able to observe all activities from above. He would be able to command the respect of the young people, as well as be able to call a taxi for an elderly woman. A further important criteria for the master of the market would be his ability to organize an array of programs in the square, such as cultural and sporting events and provide advice and his services in a number of areas. But perhaps such a master of the market is already in existence here and we can turn to him and learn from his experiences.

Living at the Market

In earlier times, buildings at the marketplace were used for a combination of living and shopping. Shops and offices were situated on the ground floor in front of which one often found large arcades to provide protection from the elements for the shopkeepers' wares and customers. Above these shops one could find apartments on some of the floors. Attics were often used as storage space. To live on the marketplace was considered a high status - giving those with such fortune a higher social standing in the community. Thus, individuals such as merchants, heads of trade agencies, pharmacists, nobility and other prominent persons resided there together often along with their large families, domestic servants and live stock, such as horses, pigs and poultry. All this resulted in the existence of a lively flair and aroma. In today's society, town prominents prefer living in the greener suburbs, generally at quite a distance from the city's core. I find this to be quite a pity as the good urban atmosphere of a square is rather contingent upon the residence of members of several social groups including individuals such as the mayor, merchants, scientists, artists, and men and women of the press and business community.

Earlier such individuals were attracted to urban communities as a result of the many apparent privileges and benefits such as the receipt of building materials free of charge. The connection between the social status of the residents and the quality of the area is significant: in Paris, for example, a very dilapidated area became revitalized as a result of a government minister taking up his residency there.

Conclusion

In Europe we find that it goes without saying that many of our historic squares, right down to the pavement, are protected as monuments and valued as famous objects of art at the regional, national and/or even world-wide level - attracting tourists from around the globe, including the United States. But, we have difficulties imagining that any modern urban square, which is designed and created nowadays, could one day be considered a historical tourist attraction and as such appear in tour books or be considered a highlight and definite must for every visitor to the city. Are we too timid? Is there not an abundance of intelligent and daring town fathers, creative planners, and young and talented architects with gusto whose sole concern is not fame and fortune? Are there not people connected with their home town as well as sponsors who may be interested and capable of creating a livable town square with love and patience, a little utopia or small but modern Garden of Eden?

I think that despite the many problems, there are good chances for such endeavors - creating a great deal of fun for not only those in the surrounding areas, but for those from far away as well. And I wish you much vigor, luck and success in making use of your opportunities.

Dr. Klaus Andrä is an architect and author in Berlin, Germany.

Kapitel Zwölf (b)

Was ist von historischen Marktplätzen für neue urbane Kristallisationskerne zu lernen?

Klaus Andrä

Durch die sehr freundliche Einladung von Suzanne und Henry Lennard bin ich zum ersten mal in Freiburg. Obwohl die Erwartungen durch viele Berichte aus Presse und von Freunden sehr hoch waren, bin ich von dem Stadtkern stark beeindruckt. Ich fand auch nicht eine Museums-atmosphäre, auch keine Zonen oder Szenen bedrohlicher Kriminalität. Ich fand eine menschlich angenehme Atmosphäre auf Straßen und

Der Marktplatz in Leipzig, um 1800. Radierung von Christian Gottfried Geißler.

Plätzen, besonders durch die vielen Studenten und anderen jungen Leuten. Beeindruckend der menschliche Maßstab in der Stadt-Architektur und die selten so gelungene Verbindung zwischen tatsächlich alten, rekonstruierten und modern entworfenen Bauten. Ablesbar ist der Wandel des Stadtbildes über die Jahre und sogar täglich, wie man sehen und hören kann.

Freiburg scheint mir eine Stadt, deren einzigartig liebenswerter Charakter auch für die Zukunft, nicht zuletzt dank des stetigen Engagements seiner "Stadtherren", Fachleute und Bürger, erhalten blieb.

Meine Anregungen für neue urbane Kristallisationskerne wie z.B. das Rieselfeld stützen sich auf Studien von ost-deutschen Marktplätzen. Man hätte für das meiste - wie ich inzwischen weiß - Beispiele aus Freiburg nutzen können. Bei der gebotenen Selektion von Beispielen habe ich bewußt Provozierendes bevorzugt. Nicht Persönlichkeiten oder gar Kollegen, sondern neues Denken soll provoziert werden:

1. Überraschend, mit welcher Zielstrebigkeit und Rationalität Stadtherren zurückliegender Jahrhunderte Chancen kalkulierten und Voraussetzungen schufen, um neue Kristallisationskerne städtischer Prosperität und Kultur zu entwickeln, nicht selten mehrere in einer Stadt. Für bemerkenswerte historische Leistungen ist charakteristisch, daß mit Entschiedenheit große Gestaltideen gesucht und mit gesundem Geschäftssinn verknüpft waren.

2. Die Lokalisierung ist für den Erfolg bereits wichtig: Auf topographisch markanten Stellen (höchste Erhebung, Geländebruch, Flußbiegung) und mit konsequenter Bündelung der Handelwege an diesem Punkt begann es. Heute würde dem eine planvolle Entwicklung einer hohen Erschließungsqualität entsprechen.

3. Entwicklungen wurden seit altersher durch verschiedene Privilegien (heute: Förderungen, Begünstigungen, Bonus-Systeme) unterstützt. Marktprivilegien - die eine Art Standortbezogenes und termingebundenes Handelsmonopol schufen, waren besonders wirksam. Privilegien stimulierten wesentlich Heraus-

bildung und Stärkung zentraler Orte und regionaler Hierarchien, die kulturell und ökonomisch ihren Sinn haben.

4. Bedeutung und Potenz eines Siedlungskerns ergaben sich nicht allein, nicht einmal vorrangig aus den Versorgungsaufgaben der unmittelbar Anwohnenden. Je stärker die überörtliche Funktion, desto vitaler, erfolgreicher das neue Zentrum. Urbanität nährt sich - so scheint es - wesentlich von Bedeutungsüberschuß, aus übergreifendem Wirkungsfeld.

5. Was wäre an Urbanität auf den 78 ha des Rieselfeldes zu leisten? Alte Städte hatten in ihrer Blüte oft geringere Flächen. Rostock und Wismar je 74 ha, das berühmte Wittenberg zu Luthers Zeiten nur 33 ha - und welche Urbanität!

6. Will die Kommune ernsthaft ein neues urbanes Zentrum, muß sie mit aller Energie ein Programm mit Elementen von gesamtstädtischem, besser noch von regionalem Rang disponieren und durchsetzen. Natürlich ist das nur mit einem entsprechenden Erschließungssystem chancenreich.

7. Anregungen für übergreifende Funktionen braucht man für Freiburg nicht lange suchen. Naheliegend wäre eine Interpretation von Bereichen der Universität. Studenten gaben und geben zu allen Zeiten öffentlichen Plätzen ihr jugendlich unbekümmertes Flair. Auch stadt-übergreifende Institute (etwa einige der 70 berichteten Institute auf dem Gebiet der Ökologie und des Umweltschutzes mit z.T. europäischem Rang) würden ein urbanes Zentrum aufwerten.

8. Selbstverständlich müssen qualifizierte Verkaufsmagneten da sein. Im Gefolge derartiger "Lokomotiven" entwickeln sich die erwünschten kleineren Elemente: Shops und Boutiquen, Cafes und Weinstuben, Buchhandlungen, Galerien ...

9. Besonders gilt es über markante Architekturzeichen und eine Dominante nachzudenken. (Wenn auch heute Geld für Planung und Realisierung fehlt, könnten durch Studentenarbeiten Anregungen gesammelt werden. Es müssen nicht wie früher Kirche und Rathaus sein, mit dem ein Stadtteil Zeichen setzt und Ausstrahlung gewinnt. Auch ein Bürositz wäre kein Gewinn. Eine Anregung könnte z.B. der historische Bautyp des Tanz- oder Hochzeitshauses geben. Eine höchst reizvolle Aufgabe für kreative Architekturstudenten (mit Wintergärten, Festräumen, aber auch mit Wasser- und Glockenspielen, technischen Raffinessen unserer Zeit, wie etwa den noch heute viel bewunderten Kunstuhren der Renaissance als Synthese aus Kunst, Technik und Spaß). Würde ganz im Sinne der Förderung neuer Urbanität noch ein Standesamt hinzugefügt, wäre eine Stätte lebensvoller kulturverbindender Geselligkeit geschaffen. Angehörige verschiedener Bevölkerungs- und Volksgruppen könnten ihre Lebensart zeigen. These: Im Interesse einer Profilierung neuer Kerne und der Verkehrsentflechtung sollte Hierarchienabschwächung (also z.B. Delegierung von Einrichtungen des Hauptzentrums in das Nebenzentrum) nicht ausgeschlossen werden.

10. Ein vitaler Stadtplatz - diese Erfahrung vermitteln die historischen Marktplätze - kann nicht ohne enge Verflechtung mit dem gesamten Stadt- und Siedlungsgefüge gedeihen. Er läßt sich auch nicht in einem Wurf realisieren. Es braucht Zeit (u.U. über Generationen) zur Reife, dabei auch Möglichkeiten zur Veränderung in Bebauung und Funktion. Aus diesem Sachverhalt soll aber nicht Verschleiß- und Wegwerfarchitektur gefolgert werden. Im Gegenteil: wie viele herausragende Bauwerke haben (auch in Freiburg) durch selbstbewußtes Um- und Weiterbauen nachfolgender Generationen an Individualität und Kulturwert gewonnen. Wir sollten auch unseren neuen Kernen Zeiten zur Reife und zur Wandlung einräumen.

Wichtig: Für Künftiges sollte auch Raum bleiben, der z.B. eine Zwischennutzung als Grünbereich haben könnte.

11. Vielfältiges städtisches Leben auf öffentlichen Plätzen ist zu allen Zeiten auch bewußt inszeniert worden (Prozessionen, Huldigungszeremonien, Oster- und Fastnachtsspiele ...)

Bemerkenswert: Die Verbindung zwischen Kultur und Kommerz war zu allen Zeiten sehr eng und erfolgreich. Anzuregen wäre durch ein sozial-kulturell engagiertes, aber ebenso organisatorisch professionelles Management auch die neuen urbanen Kerne zu stärken. Man sollte gute Traditionen der Altstadt übertragen auf die neuen Gebiete ohne die Ansätze der "Kiez-Kultur" zu negieren.

12. Die unrühmliche Tradition historischer Plätze als Orte von Hinrichtungen, Verbrennungen oder Anprangerung von vermeintlichen oder tatsächlichen Übeltätern sollte angesichts zunehmender Sorge um die Sicherheit in unseren Städten Anregung sein, unorthodoxe Lösungen zu suchen, die eine Polizeistation überflüssig machen, sich aber auch nicht allein auf die Notrufsäule oder das couragierte Eingreifen von Bürgern in Konfliktsituationen verlassen.

Vorschlag: Die Funktion des Marktmeisters neu bestimmen, und ihn direkt am neuen Markt (u.U. in einer Dienstwohnung und mit anderen Privilegien wie Zeitungs- und Eisverkauf o.ä.) ausstatten.

13. Wohnen am Markt war früher Statussymbol. Rats- und Handelsherren, Apotheker, Hofbeamte u.a. Honoratioren residierten dort. Heutzutage wohnt Stadtprominenz lieber im Grünen, zumeist fernab der Zentren. So wichtig und richtig es ist, nach einer Balance der Wohnformen und Sozialstrukturen zu streben: Zur Aufwertung eines urbanen Kerns, also z.B. im Rieselfeld gehört, daß dort auch Stadtprominenz wohnt, z.B. ein Bürgermeister, Wissenschaftler, Künstler, Männer und Frauen der Wirtschaft. In Paris bekam ein baulich stark heruntergekommenes Ensemble einen starken Aufschwung, als dort ein Minister einzog.
P.S. ein Wettbewerb über eine Zeitung, um für das Rieselfeld einen guten Namen zu finden, wäre an der Zeit und könnte auch auf seine Weise indentitätsstiftend wirken.

Ein Letztes: Wir finden es selbstverständlich und voll berechtigt, daß unsere historischen Plätze oft als Gesamtanlage bis hin zu den alten Pflasterungen als Denkmale von regionalem, nationalem oder europäischem Rang geschützt und geschätzt werden. Nur schwer vorstellbar ist uns, daß ein in unseren Tagen geschaffenes Ensemble in die Reise- und Kunstführer als Attraktion und Highlight eingeht. Sind wir nicht etwas zu kleinmütig? Im Vertrauen auf Klugheit, Ausdauer und Courage der Freiburger Stadtväter, auf Kreativität seiner Planer und Esprit der Architekten greife ich etwas vor und zitiere abschließend aus einem Reiseführer des Jahres 2025:

Dort heißt es u.a. Freiburg i.Br.: Ein moderner Garten Eden (vormals Rieselfeld). Dafür großer UNESCO-Preis "Lebenswerte und tolerante Stadt". Urbaner Kristallisationskern mit multifunktionaler Agora, weltweit wirkende Lehr- und Forschungsstätten besonders auf dem Gebiet der Ökologie und Toleranzforschung, mehrere Kulturfestivals von internationalem Rang, Ensemble mit Hochzeitshaus, vorbildliche Verknüpfung von Natur (Wasser), Kunst, Technik. Eindruckvolle Architektur der Jahrtausendwende, in Flair und Charme der weltberühmten Altstadt ebenbürtig.

Klaus Andrä ist freier Architekt in Berlin, Deutschland.

Chapter Thirteen (a)

Squares in Berlin

Hans Stimmann

Fotostudio Frank Iwan

Last Sunday the world's biggest electronic entertainment fair ended, the 40th International Broadcast Exhibition. The organizers of this fair expected decisive signals for "new departures in the information society". Grandpa's television, telecommunication and computer technology are growing close. A vast number of television programs, video movies, and most of all new forms of home computer consumption: teleshopping and telebanking, are at the consumers' disposal.

Because of this, the traditional city is tending towards a substitution by a virtual city with a **network** without centers, without outskirts, without streets and squares. In this way, information and virtual communication become possible at each point. Berlin, of all cities, where since a few years the continuity of the European City has become the basis for city planning and architecture policy, gives the impetus to the often predicted end of the traditional city.

According to a common hypothesis, the more or less totally **interlinked** citizens, and the therefore useless conditions of the real life city realm, make redundant the type of European city with streets and squares **that are lined**

with trees, and an architecture with façades towards the public realm. "The place of residence, the house, the street, the square, the city, the country - who still needs those anyway, those outdated things, when life goes on without them in **interlinked knots**?" wonders Oswald Matthias Ungers in a skeptical reaction to those current tendencies.

While politics and planning have been preoccupied for years to contain the foreseeable consequences for the public places by building shopping malls and isolated shopping centers, the large telecommunication enterprises are "reinventing shopping again", says the commercial for teleshopping of the company Deutsche Telekom with partner Otto-Versand. Multimedia, online-services, interactive television, shopping malls in the city, shopping and entertainment centers in the outskirts on one hand, and meeting places for communication near airports on the other hand, render the traditional city pointless. The citizen turns into a consumer, who only meets his isolated neighbor for a couple of hours in the controlled and air-conditioned artificial world of shopping centers and soon in virtual cities.

You do not have to be an enemy of technology to recognize the tremendous negative effects on social, cultural and therefore also on political life of the unbridled realization of these tendencies.

With our reconstruction and new building plans for traditional streets, squares and houses, we deliberately emphasize to resist the economic trend toward commercialized and virtualized city life. The measures of urban planning in the new suburbs and the downtown area are against the power of virtualization by electronic media as well as against the sliding loss of meaning and appearance of the **downtown** public areas due to the formation of almost identical shopping malls.

To avoid misunderstandings: the problem does not lie within the mediocre architecture of such shopping centers, but in the effect on the principle of the city. The traditional city is based on the cooperation of private houses and streets and squares, where the "public realm can unfold itself, the public realm being something social and political, that results from individual and collective actions, but actions that refer to each other and are related to each other" (H. Häuserman). In concrete terms: it has to be possible to use streets and squares without feeling obliged to behave in a certain way (namely **angepaßt**) and even to buy something.

The Berlin program for the development of traditional public streets and squares has more than one main focus. It is about the public places in the suburbs, in the **building concentrations,** in the redevelopment areas and finally in the historical city center.

In the suburbs on the outskirts of Berlin the rediscovery of public city places is the starting point of the designs. The main elements are streets, squares and parks **lined with trees** as a basic framework for identity and order. The situation is different in the **building concentrations** of Marzahn, Hohenschön-hausen and Hellersdorf. Following their earlier design logic, in spite of a building pattern with wide, open spaces and large low-built constructions, it is not inviting because of the indifference. The Senate has set up a program to solve this deficiency. The new city center Hellersdorf represents a good example. Hellerdorf receives a spatial and a functional center, shaped after traditional city centers.

From the outskirts back to the center. To the special qualities also of downtown Berlin, belonged until the devastation the clearly visible evolution from the city centers of the middle ages, over the expansion of the suburbs in the baroque period, to the Hobrecht city expansion of the second half of the 19th century. Each transition was marked by dominant squares: Spittelmarkt and Alexanderplatz immediately next to the old part of the town and then on the border of the baroque city, the three famous gate squares, Pariser Platz, Leipziger Platz and Belle-Alliance-Platz (Mehringplatz at present).

This document of the history of the city Berlin has been unrecognizably disturbed by the war destruction, the construction of the wall and most of all by the city planning after the war.

Within the framework of the "critical reconstruction", an attempt is made to regain the city qualities of those places that are so important for the understanding and for the function of the city as a place where real people meet.

Dr. Ing. Hans Stimmann is Senatsbaudirektor (Planning Commissioner) for the City of Berlin, Germany.

Berliner Plätze

Hans Stimmann

Am vergangenen Sonntag endete die größte Messe der Welt für Unterhaltungselektronik, die 40. Internationale Funkausstellung. Von dieser Messe erwarteten die Veranstalter entscheidende "Signale zum Aufbruch in die Informations-gesellschaft". Die vernetzten Branchen der Telekommunikation sind elektrisiert oder zeitgeistiger digitalisiert. Opas Fernsehen, Telekommunikation und Computertechnik wachsen zusammen. Eine unübersehbare Anzahl von Fernseh-programmen, Videofilme und vor allem die neuen Formen des Konsums am Heimcomputer: Teleshopping und Telebanking bieten sich den Verbrauchern an.

Die traditionelle Stadt wird damit tendenziell durch eine virtuelle Stadt mit einem Netz ohne Zentren, ohne Peripherie, ohne Straßen und Plätze ersetzt. Information und virtuelle Kommunikation wird so an jedem Punkt möglich. Ausgerechnet von Berlin aus, dem Ort, an dem seit einigen Jahren die Kontinuität der europäischen Stadt zur Grundlage der Städtebau- und Architekturpolitik gemacht wurde, gehen so Anstöße zum schon öfter prognostizierten Ende der traditionellen Stadt aus.

Die mehr oder weniger totale Vernetzung aller Bewohner und die - so eine gängige These - damit verbundene Ablösung von den Bedingungen der realen Stadträume macht den Typus der europäischen Stadt mit baumbestandenen Straßen, Plätzen und einer Architektur, die sich mit ihren Fassaden auf die öffentlichen Räume bezieht, tendenziell überflüssig. "Der Wohnort, das Haus, die Straße, der Platz, die Stadt, das Land - wer braucht sie noch, die veralteten Dinge, wenn das Leben sich ohne dies in vernetzten Knoten abspielt?", fragt Oswald Matthias Ungers in einer skeptischen Reaktion auf diese aktuellen Tendenzen.

Während Politik und Planung seit Jahren damit beschäftigt sind, die absehbaren Folgen für die öffentlichen Räume durch den Bau von Shoppingmalls und isolierter Einkaufszentren in Grenzen zu halten, sind also die Großunternehmen der Telekommunikation dabei, "das Einkaufen noch einmal neu zu erfinden", so die Werbung der Deutschen Telekom für das Teleshopping mit dem Partner Otto-Versand. Multimedia, Online-Dienste, interaktives Fernsehen, Shoppingmalls in der City, Einkaufs- und Freizeitzentren an der Peripherie auf der einen und Treffpunkte der Kommunikation in der Umgebung der Flughäfen auf der anderen Seite machen die traditionelle Stadt scheinbar überflüssig.

Der Stadtbewohner mutiert zum Konsumenten, der sich nur noch stundenweise in der kontrollierten und klimatisierten Kunstwelt der Einkaufszentren und dennächst in virtuellen Städten mit seinen isoliert wohnenden Nachbarn trifft.

Man muß kein Technikfeind sein, um zu erkennen, daß die ungehemmte Konkretisierung dieser Tendenzen für das soziale, kulturelle und damit auch für das politische Leben unabsehbare negative Folgen hat.

Mit unseren Planungen zur Rekonstruktion bzw. zum Neubau traditioneller Straßen, Plätze und Häuser wird ganz bewußt ein Akzent gesetzt, sich dem ökonomischen Trend zur Kommerzialisierung und Virtualisierung des Lebens in der Stadt entgegenzustellen. Die städtebaulichen Maßnahmen in den neuen Vororten und im Zentrum richten sich gegen die Macht der Virtualisierung durch die elektronischen Medien sowie gegen den schleichenden Gesichts- und Bedeutungsverlust der innerstädtischen öffentlichen Räume durch die Anordnung von nahezu identischen Shopping malls.

Um Mißverständnissen vorzubeugen: das Problem liegt nicht in der durchweg mittelmäßigen Architektur solcher Shopping-Center, sondern in der Wirkung auf das Prinzip Stadt. Die traditionelle Stadt basiert auf dem Miteinander privater Häuser und Straßen und Plätzen, in denen sich "Öffentlichkeit herstellen kann - Öffentlichkeit als etwas Soziales und Politisches, das sich aus individuellen und kollektiven, aber aufeinander bezogenem Handeln ergibt" (H. Häußermann). Konkret: Die Benutzung von Straßen und Plätzen muß möglich sein, ohne sich verpflichtet zu fühlen, sich in einer bestimmten Art und Weise zu verhalten (nämlich angepaßt) und gar etwas zu kaufen.

Das Berliner Programm zur Weiterentwicklung traditioneller öffentlicher Straßen und Plätze hat mehrere Schwerpunkte. Es geht um die öffentlichen Räume in den Vorstädten, in den Großsiedlungen, in den Sanierungsgebieten und schließlich in der historischen Innenstadt.

In den Vorstädten an der Berliner Peripherie ist die Wiederentdeckung des öffentlichen städtischen Raumes Ausgangspunkt der Entwürfe. Hauptelemente sind baumbestandene Straßen, Plätze und Parkanlagen als Grundgerüst für Identität und Ordnung. Anders gelagert stellt sich die Situation in den Berliner Großsiedlungen von Marzahn, Hohenschönhausen und Hellersdorf dar. Ihrer früheren Entwurfslogik folgend gibt es hier zwar weite, offene Stadträume zwischen den Großfiguren des Plattenbaus, die jedoch wegen ihrer Indifferenz wenig zum Aufenthalt einladen. Der Senat hat auch hier ein Programm zur Beseitigung dieses Defizits aufgelegt. Exemplarischer geschieht dies im neuen Stadtzentrum Hellersdorf. Hellersdorf erhält einen räumlichen und funktionalen Mittelpunkt, der sich in seiner Gestaltung an traditionellen Stadtzentren orientiert.

Von der Peripherie zurück ins Zentrum. Zu den besonderen Qualitäten auch der Berliner Innenstadt gehörte bis zur Zerstörung die klar ablesbare Entwicklung von den mittelalterlichen Kernstädten über die barocken Erweiterungen der Vorstädte hin zu der Hobrecht'schen Stadterweiterung aus der zweiten Hälfte des 19. Jahrhunderts. Die jeweiligen Übergangsbereiche waren immer markiert durch dominante Plätze: dem Spittelmarkt und dem Alexanderplatz in unmittelbarer Nähe der Altstadt und dann am Rande der barocken Stadt die drei berühmten Torplätze, Pariser Platz, Leipziger Platz und Belle-Alliance-Platz (heute Mehringplatz).

Dieses Dokument Berliner Stadtgeschichte ist durch die Kriegszerstörung, Mauerbau und vor allen Dingen Nachkriegsplanung bis zur Unkenntlichkeit zerstört worden. Im Rahmen der "Kritischen Rekonstruktion" wird versucht, die stadträumlichen Qualitäten dieser für das Verständnis und für die Funktion der Stadt als Ort der Begegnung realer Menschen so wichtigen Orte wiederzugewinnen.

Dr. Hans Stimmann ist Senatsbaudirektor, Stadt Berlin, Deutschland.

Chapter Fourteen

Climatic Factors and Public Space

Norman Pressman

Introduction

The climate in which we live has a tendency to determine our outlooks and life ways. It can sharply influence particular environments -- and their effects -- for every type of civilization. Even from the slightest variations in climate, one can witness different kinds of social systems and cultural attributes which are frequently reflected in architectural styles, building traditions, and the design of open spaces.

Climate has often been called upon to explain personality, especially in extreme settings -both hot and cold. It is even believed, by many, to shape national characteristics and to define a common identity. Drastic shifts in weather systems can affect human behaviour to more than simply a limited extent where dramatic seasonal variation exists. Climate has also served as a modifying or determining force in architectural and urban design. People living in harsh regions have often ignored the need to accept climatic demands in formulating policy and design guidelines, and few designers have embodied the practice of "thinking seasonally". Hence, the typical form and structure of open spaces, located in less than ideal settings, have generally not been shaped according to climatological dictates and, not infrequently, this has resulted in impoverished design and user-unfriendly attributes, particularly in public urban space.

Designing Public-Urban Spaces

Climatic factors should be taken into account if safe, healthy, and comfortable public spaces are to result in a given environment. Particular emphasis should be attached to ensuring compatibility between local and microclimatic factors -- the air quality, noise, shade, temperature, humidity, wind, rain, and snow -- and the design and location of the spaces and equipment included therein.

Recreation areas and all kinds of public spaces should be sufficiently well sheltered from cold winds (in northern regions). Warm spots -- for winter areas -- and areas which are cool (during summer) should be set aside within the same project. They should not be sited in polluted places and should not be the recipients of pollution from traffic or industrial sources.

Care should be taken so that they are not positioned on low-lying areas which collect cold air. They should be in locations which benefit from direct solar radiation for the greater part of the day and provision should be made for shady spots by employing vegetation or built forms which cast shadows during the warmer part of the year. Provision should be made for play areas to receive as much solar radiation as possible between the hours of 9 a.m. and 5 p.m. during the spring and autumn equinoxes, in northern regions. Shadows which can be cast by tall buildings -- and wind turbulence around these buildings -- should be considered during the initial site planning stages.

Provision should be made for surrounding sources of pollution with protective vegetation covered areas to prevent impurities in the air from spreading to recreational zones of intensive public use. Plans being made for an area should retain enough of the area's own woods (should these exist? to ensure that the major part of any air impurities is dealt with satisfactorily. Alternatively, newly treed areas can be planted for absorption purposes, and to serve as a dust "sponge". Finally, attempts to mitigate surrounding noise sources should be made by using natural or artificial noise attenuating barriers. Often, an abundance of bushes or trees will be sufficient.

The benefits of planting extensive areas go well beyond the efforts to control noise or poor air -- or even to modify wind speeds. Dense planting enhances the aesthetic quality and provides a good natural habit for flora and fauna. However, its use may be limited due to lack of available land as well as by the fact that dense and non-transparent plantings in open spaces are often undesirable due to security and safety considerations. When weather or pollution protection, by using trees or hedgerows (or even fences and walls) occurs, there should be a balance between the use of porous and non-porous material or planting (for protection) for improved visual permeability and resulting public safety.

Recreational routes which provide access to play areas and public spaces -- including paths for biking, walking, and tracks for jogging, skiing and hiking -- should be carefully sited, safe, and preferably illuminated when dark. This is critical at high latitudes during the winter periods when daylight hours are extremely brief. They should be within easy reach, particularly for children, and should

form a network throughout the municipality or the local neighbourhoods.

Attempts should be made to develop local climate and micro-climate models. With their help, it would be possible to obtain qualitative data about the area's climatic characteristics. Attention should be paid to the development of synoptic climatic data when the models are being created. The manner in which the climatic parameters are combined is crucial in order that planners and designers have access to the data in a usable, practical form.

It is essential to analyze the air and noise quality in order to discover the most healthy and favourable sites for recreational and public space activities. Analysis also aims at dividing the area, to be developed, between different forms of ground use so that, for instance, green belts may improve the air quality and so that the protective zones around noisy sectors are sufficiently encompassing.

The results of an inventory of the air and noise quality can be employed to elaborate the technological, planning, and legislative measures used for improving air quality. These measures should be incorporated when both general and detailed plans are made for recreational areas. Playgrounds, for example, should not be sited on areas where the air quality does not meet the norms in use for ensuring sufficiently good air in residential areas or where the noise level does not adhere to acceptable standards. Neither should they be sited in areas where contaminated soil exists. Qualitative and quantitative analysis of wind conditions aims at siting recreation (and housing) areas so that the impact of industrial plants releasing impurities into the air is reduced or entirely eliminated.

A further objective, in site analysis, is the resistance against uncomfortable wind conditions and velocity. This can be achieved through positioning protective structures which deflect and minimize cold winds -- and snow drifts. Tree stands and shelterbelts (in northern regions) working against such forces should be planted in appropriate locations.

Regulations and norms should be drafted (if these do not exist) for the design of children's day care centres, playgrounds, buildings, plazas, and recreation and sports facilities locations. Furthermore, active and passive outdoor spaces should be arranged, oriented, and sheltered so that they provide warmer zones during winter and cooler ones during summer. Ancillary measures can include the provision of landscaping elements with plant material situated so as to modify extremes of air temperature in publicly accessible outdoor spaces. Such material can be located so as to absorb the sun's rays (when necessary), to prevent paved surfaces from acting as a heat sink, and to reduce or redirect wind flows thus creating more comfortable conditions.

Encouraging Walking and Cycling

Achieving suitable micro-climatic conditions will undoubtedly enhance the environmental quality of life. Therefore, performance standards which protect pedestrians and cyclists from increased wind speeds induced by design and positioning of buildings must be formulated. These should be combined with measures to guarantee daylighting requirements, proper air circulation and sunlight access -- through regulating built form, using front and rear sky exposure planes -- especially in areas of intense public use.

The environments benefiting from climate-protection strategies and improved micro-climatic conditions should be those which connect important nodes of activity such as shops and public transport stops, public squares and cycle-parking zones, major institu-tional buildings and high-use functions (e.g. railway or bus stations). If these strategies also contribute toward energy conservation and environmental protection, they will have made a powerful impact in improving urban quality. Both physical design and social organization have to work together to support daily life, and urban architecture has an important role to play.

In deciding the levels of priority for weather-protection, the needs of various user groups must be carefully specified. User characteristics vis-a-vis trips (origins and destinations) will determine the movement network, its specific locations and the detailing of the sheltering elements, within the overall framework of the town or district. The extent of protection will have to be seen as a function of both need and cost.

In areas of significant pedestrian and cycle activity, consideration should be given to the requirement for weather protection devices such as canopies, awnings, arcades and colon-nades. Urban design concept plans should indicate major pedestrian links between origins and destinations suggesting where climatically sheltered zones might be realized.

Climate protection also increases the power of economic attraction when a regional centre competes with others for business and shoppers. A project for total climate protection (by glazing-over the entire major pedestrian shopping street and adjacent car-free zone) in the town of Vlissingen, The Netherlands (which experiences abundant wind and rain), completed in 1992, has met with immense success by increasing the regional shopping radius by an additional 10 kilometers.

Guidelines for Successful Walking and Cycling Networks

If walking and cycling -- the soft/slow modes -- could be encouraged (by further restricting car movements and through improvement of collective transport modes) and continuous paths and networks for pedestrians implemented where people live, work and play, then the public and semi-public spaces of the city's fabric which are woven into these paths could be appropriated for a wider range of uses.

Clearly, new attitudes -- especially in North America -- will be required if funding, participatory measures, legislative means and marketing are to evolve with the intent of making serious changes to our behaviour with respect to how we move around. The micro, meso, and macro scales will have to be tackled simultaneously. Solutions developed for an urban region will significantly affect strategies targeted at specific, localized parts of the city. If quality in urban life is demanded, then walking and cycling must ultimately be viewed as part of the overall plan, and as a constituent element of the broader civic space.

Recent trends indicate a strong concern for climatic protection, among all the other social, economic and political goals operative in urban centres. Combined with functional considerations -- which provide the 'raison d'etre' of central zones -- aesthetic qualities, climatic comfort and programmed events (such as parades, carnivals, musicians, street performers, etc.) are becoming more important in sustaining the urban tempo and rhythm we have come to expect of downtowns. In addition to total, or even partial, protection from the elements the following principles should be followed in developing areas for walking, cycling, standing and sitting:

- provide shelter from the wind.

- create an urban form which avoids increased windspeeds.

- designate sunny and sheltered open spaces for non-motorized activities.
- save existing vegetation (for wind protection) or provide windbreaks.

- make provision for comfortable walking (design effective rainwater run-off areas, provide selected snow deposit areas and respective drainage for melting, eliminate or modify curb-cut details for ease of movement, etc.)

- include ramps (as well as stairs) where changes in elevation occur. Heat them in cold, winter season.

- design for ease and simplicity of access.

- extend the outdoor comfort zone, especially in the marginal seasons, providing "transition areas" mediating between indoor and outdoor spaces and activities.

- furnish the public spaces with comfortable, visually pleasing, and well located "urban furniture".

- serve the pedestrian zones and networks with highly visible and accessible collective transport.

- provide overhead protection at critical urban locations.

Some complementary guidelines should likely be followed if intensive use is to be anticipated in the pedestrian and cycle zones:

- concentrate on the whole area not just the downtown.

- balance the traffic system with the pedestrian system and cycle-path network.

- ensure accessibility to motorists in locations where they are welcome.

- design public spaces for users of all ages and physical needs.

- plan for the rainy day, noise and other disturbances.

- animate space with light and graphics.

- zone for a mix of uses such as retail and housing.

- educate motorists to pedestrians' and cyclists' needs.

- support the growth of public transport systems.

- keep the streets alive with cultural and recreational activities.

The recent wave of underground passages and above-grade skyways linking private "atrium-style" developments and enclosed shopping malls (often connected to railways' terminals and subway systems) has created a pseudo-public environment of substantial size. While offering weather-protection, these projects guarantee social filtering and careful "selection" of patron users. Commercial objectives are first and foremost on the "development agenda". Hence, increasingly, the traditional role of the city centre -- to provide goods, services and amenities to the entire urban population -- no longer can be said to prevail, as the newer projects generate incremental privatization, resulting in traditional users being displaced elsewhere to find locations which meet their needs. This dilemma must be offset by opening up more genuinely public space -- parks, streets, lanes, green-areas, squares -- to counteract the erosion of the public domain.

Public space has become one of the most critically studied areas falling within the scope of urban design, architecture, and planning for human well-being. The configuration of this public space, its appropriation, its meaning and content, its connection to the natural elements and the symbolic interpretations given to "genius loci" (sense and spirit of 'place') have strong implications for affecting and shaping the quality of urban life. Participation in public events, the relationship among the various urban functions, the siting of "solid" objects within the spatial "void" of the city -- all contain opportunities for attracting or repelling human life; for making people proud of being citizens of certain towns or alternatively, for causing depression, and even debilitating illness. So-called healthy places must exhibit a powerful combination of factors enhancing sociability in well-designed public space so as to promote connectedness between people when this is desirable; to offer a range of choices between the extremes of solitude, on the one hand, and togetherness, on the other.

Social enjoyment (in the spaces of which the city is composed), visual pleasure, climatic comfort, security, strong identity, contact with nature, and sensory stimulation should be viewed as goals to which the physical organization of the city must aspire. "Genius loci" will occur when ordinary space is elevated, in the minds and hearts of urban dwellers, to a sense of place, with very special attributes, universally recognized and appreciated.

Attractive and well-managed streets and open spaces -- and the activities both planned and spontaneous which occur in them -- form the essence of urban life. They should be genuinely public in nature as a counterthrust to the gradual disappearance of public life resulting from large "atrium-style" pseudo-public environments and shopping malls downtown and in the suburbs. Once out of either the car or public transportation, everyone eventually becomes a pedestrian. Therefore, it is essential to direct greater attention to the achievement of a milieu in which the slow-mode is dominant.

The most critical goal is to extend the outdoor season (in colder regions) encouraging people to remain outdoors at times when they might normally withdraw and spend more time indoors. Climatic modification of the environment is required if human animation is to thrive in our urban centres during the colder periods. Even if outdoor social space and the activities which it harbours suffer a reduction during the cold part of the year, social activity can still be supported and maintained.

If improved bioclimatic conditions are to be incorporated within public urban space - including movement systems -- then the following issues will have to be accorded high priority:

a) Careful decisions must be taken regarding the types and location of vegetation and planting for modifying climatic conditions.

b) Multiple use of public space over varying times of the day (or night), week or even year, will ensure greater activity and animation adding to the perceived importance of the space as well as to user safety and satisfaction.

c) Degree of shelter, especially at public transport stops and high-intensity cycle use areas, will achieve greater comfort for all users.

d) Alternative microclimates should optimally be possible in the same space (some areas in shade, others exposed to sun -- with varying degrees of protection from wind).

e) Comfort criteria should be established for all seasons, where possible (especially if considerable seasonal variation occurs).

f) The attempt to minimize both travel time and distance for cycle users and pedestrians constitutes the most important principle if reduction of motor car traffic is desired. The concepts of short-cutting and climatic protection can serve either as determining or modifying factors vis-a-vis movement patterns within the urban fabric.

Flexible utilization of the public realm, in different seasons, will ensure more improved livability for users regardless of their needs or trip destinations. Adopting a climate sensitive approach (in less than ideal climatic regions) is clearly the best strategy (when combined with appropriate, user-responsive, ergonomic design) for obtaining a sustained lifestyle well into the 21st century.

Managing of a large scale 'climatic environment' where the sub-components are town and region, involves accommodation to the rhythm of annual seasons. This begins to determine the character of the urban design and structure of the land-use. The criterion for a livable town is its potential to respond to weather agents during different seasons of the year.

Norman Pressman is Professor at the School of Urban and Regional Planning at the University of Waterloo, Waterloo, Ontario, Canada.

Circular 5/94 Planning out Crime

The Department of the Environment issued this circular to all local planning authorities in 1994. It appeared at the time that the title was wildly optimistic, but the circular did acknowledge that good planning alone cannot solve the problem of crime.

This Circular suggests:

- For development plans

  - Aim to create attractive, well managed environments as opposed to desolate, sterile and featureless surroundings.

  - Aim for a wide and varied range of land-uses to create a lively and well-used environment- in residential, commercial and leisure developments.

  - Establish principles for design of commercial and residential areas which will reassure the public about more secure surroundings.

  - Avoid overlarge single use developments which are sparsely populated at night.

  - Positively encourage provision of leisure and social facilities for the young.

  - Introduce positive policies for Town and city center revitalization, including restrictions on out of town shopping; flats over shops; passive surveillance and the night economy of centers.

- For development control

  - Need to consider crime at outset of design process.

  - Increase residential control over accesses ,for example by having main living areas facing onto access roads.

  - Consultation with Police Liasion officer, not just on big applications.

  - Develop small scale housing areas with good access to amenities.

  - Aim to provide a sense of ownership

  - Encourage landscaping which avoids hidden areas.

  - Importance of sporting leisure and recreational facilities to reduce criminality.

  - Care that traffic segregation does not lead to isolation, and use lighting effectively in such areas as sub-ways.

- For general consideration

  - Consider environmental aspects of security shutters.

  - Imaginative use of Bollards, railings and other street furniture to deter crimes such as "Ram-raiding"

  - Increased use of closed circuit television (CCTV)cameras to deter and help to detect crime. Changes to the planning control system proposed to take such cameras out of planning control, except in the case of Listed Buildings.

What is being achieved?

There are 36 Metropolitan Districts, 32 London Boroughs and over 300 Non Metropolitan authorities in England currently producing development plans. A recent survey of local authorities (Farr 1994) indicates a wide variety of responses.

- Plan policies increasingly tackle the problems- Crime prevention at Gloucester, Intrusion and Safety at Kingston on Thames, Design policies at Bromley, Community safety at Ipswich, Public safety at Doncaster, and Roller shutters at Blackpool.

- Oldham near Manchester has extensive policies covering back entries to house, underpasses, defensible space in public housing, street lighting, and communal entrances to residential tower blocks.

- Southwark, in London, has similar policies relating to dark corners, lighting and mixed land uses when considering new developments and refurbishments.

- City centers, their revitalization and safety occupy significant parts of every plan, - supported by recent Government sponsored research.

- There is, however, less evidence of fewer single use areas in many plans. Where large scale expansion is envisaged, numerous authorities still plan for single use estates whether for commercial/industrial /warehousing uses (often close to major motor way junctions,) or residential or retail expansions.

- Where constraint policies, such as Green Belt, aim for more reuse of land within cities there is evidence of infill sites and conversions bringing residential activity into new areas.

In the control of development, another series of initiatives have been taken

- Probably the most common is the production of specific guidance to developers and the public on design and crime prevention. This is intended to expand the policies of the development plans, and is called supplementary guidance. This has been produced by authorities in the north, (eg.Newcastle, Manchester. Doncaster), in the midlands (eg Birmingham, Corby and Northampton) and many of the London boroughs.

- A series of authorities have published more specific advice- Women and the planned environment from Manchester and Southampton, Shop front security from Derby, Householder safety from Kingston on Thames, Car parking safety from Ipswich, and on CCTV from the Corporation of London.

In their enabling and implementation role, local authorities have

- Introduced Close circuit Television in many areas, especially city centers, but also in retail and residential environments. Newcastle City are currently installing cameras into the West End, a residential and shopping area with numerous problems, after a similar scheme in the city center reduced assaults by 19% and criminal damage by 47%.

- Government funding has been gained for numerous Safer routeway schemes such as one in Wigan, Lancashire, and Kingston on Thames.

- Dramatic growth in neighborhood watch schemes from 1,000 in 1985 to over 100,000 by mid l990s.

- Increased activities to enliven city centers. Leeds city council has promoted itself as a 24 hour city with a five point plan:

  - Renewal of city center shopping

  - An Events strategy for cultural and economic revival
  - Public services must not end at 5.30pm

  - Mixed uses of offices, retail, entertainment and housing must be fostered.

  - Concept of city center managers must be developed.

Some Reservations

In an ever changing society it can be dangerous and ultimately unhelpful to be too dogmatic in our approach to solving social problems by physical means. There is a problem of displacing crime from one area to another rather than reducing overall crime.

There are aspects of design guidance against crime which can conflict with personal choice. With the expansion of low rise housing developments in the social housing sector, and continuing suburbanization of private housing, domestic privacy has become more important. This is often reflected in fast growing conifer hedges and wattle-fencing as domestic boundaries, enclosing patio-doors, barbecues and sun traps. Such individual developments may conflict with a general requirement to reduce hidden vulnerable areas. Similarly, the development of "fortress mentality" in some large expensive housing areas with electronic gates etc. being a new feature in the UK will not foster social cohesion. Likewise, a shopping center of unfriendly steel shutters may encourage vandalism and graffiti whilst discouraging theft.

The extended use of CCTV is viewed by many liberals as an invasion of privacy, and in certain areas, lighting intended to be protective can be intrusive in the environment.

Many areas of our towns and cities will not see significant changes in their built fabric in the coming years. Much of our disposition of land uses will remain as they are. Only by management activities can the operation of these areas be made more safe.

Some of our finest urban environments are found in the older parts of towns, from Edinburgh's wyndes, to York's mediaeval street pattern and Exeter's alleyways. In warmer European climates such development of narrow dark streets is vital for shade, and they are major tourist attractions. Narrow streets and surprise corners cannot be totally condemned as potential crime spots. Nor can parks and public spaces be cast aside. There are fundamental gains to our living cities from the segregation of vehicular traffic from pedestrians. There is a careful balance to be struck in this exercise, and it is important that the overall quality of life in our towns and cities is not forgotten in the desire to reduce and eliminate crime.

There is also the thought that if we eliminate today's crimes they will merely be replaced by those of tomorrow. And we may have done it at the high cost of destroying many valuable features.

Derek Senior J.P., B.A., M.C.D., MRTPI, School of the Environment, Leeds Metropolitan University, Leeds, England, U.K.

Kapitel Sechzehn

Strategien zur Förderung stadträumlicher Gemeinschaft

Klaus Brendle

1.0. Architektur und Alltag

Was verblieb in den Städten - von dem, was historisch einmal war? Es sind nicht nur alte Häuser, repräsentative Monumente oder romantische Straßenbilder. Diese architektonischen und stadträumlichen Gegebenheiten sind gleichermaßen gebaute Erzählungen, steingewordene Ereignisse, überlieferte Beziehungen. Es sind versteckte Lebensweisen, die sich ihren Raum schufen, ihn immer wiederumbauten und den neuen Nutzungsanforderungen anpaßten. In Rostock werden die Schiffsladungen nicht mehr vom Hafen zu den Lagerhäusern und Marktplätzen befordert. In Schwerin sind die umliegenden Seen längst nicht mehr Schutz gegen Angriffe. Die mecklenburgische Kleinstadt Lübz liegt nicht mehr im Schutze der Wasserburg, und der Müller arbeitet dort nicht mehr in der alten Wassermühle. Der historische Gebrauch der Stadt als Ursprung für die öffentlichen Räume ist längst überlagert: der sozialistische Aufbau implantierte in Rostock eine monumentale "Magistrale"; der Schweriner See wurde Freizeitoase; der Lübzer Burgturm ist werbewirksames Brauerei-Symbol und Stadtmuseum. Neue Anforderungen richten sich auf die alten Stadträume: Passagen durchschneiden die Altstadtblöcke; der Cityring trennt die Altstadt von See und Schloß; die kleinen Läden im Zentrum kämpfen gegen den Supermarkt am Rande der Stadt. Vergangenes, Gegenwärtiges und Zukünftiges stehen als Stadt-Teile hart gegeneinander. Es droht Verlust und Zerstörung überlieferter Baugeschichte ebenso

wie leere, historisierende "Fassadenästhetik". Außen und Innen fallen auseinander, das Stadt-Bild spaltet sich ab vom Stadt-Gebrauch; Inszenierung oder blanke Banalität verdrängen Identität und heimatliche "Stadtgefühle".

Die planerischen Arbeiten meines Büros suchen mit einem breiten inhaltlichen Ansatz die Grundlage für den städtebaulichen und architektonischen Entwurf am jeweiligen Ort. Hierzu dient ein offenes, inhaltlich anpassbares Analyse- und Planungsschema, welches sozialräumliche wie bauliche Fragestellungen gleichermaßen umfaßt. Beide sind untrennbar miteinander verknüpft und bedingen einander. Aus arbeitstechnischen und methodischen Gründen werden diese Fragestellungen zwar aufgeteilt, bleiben jedoch über eine feste, bipolare Heuristik inhaltlich verknüpft. Hierdurch gibt es konzeptionell theoretische Möglichkeiten, geeignete architektur-psychologische Konzepte und Methoden (wie Behavior Setting-Konzept, kognitive Karten, Stadt-Image) - je nach Bedarf und Möglichkeit - miteinzusetzen und ähnliche theoretische Vorgehens- bzw. Denkweisen aus anderer Disziplinen (wie pattern language, typologische Verfahren, sozialer Raum, Oral History) zu benutzen.

2.0. Architektur und Stadtbild

" Stadtbild - Was ist Das?"

Die Stadt setzt sich zusammen aus erlebten Alltagsbildern - täglich immer wieder neu oder in den altbekannten Bahnen: der Weg zum Bäcker - zur Arbeit, der Spielplatz und die Bank an der Ecke. Die vielen einzelnen Aktivitäten überlagern sich zu Bewegungen und Verkehrsströmen, zu persönlichen Vorstellungen und allgemeinen Vorstellungsbildern der Stadt. In Rostock zum Beispiel der Hafen mit Warnew-Ufer und Schiffen, die Kröpeliner Straße zum Einkaufen oder die August-Bebel-Straße mit tagtäglichem Stau. Dieser Gebrauch der Stadt ereignet sich in den Straßen, Plätzen und Häusern; er ist dadurch verbunden mit bestimmten Bildern von dieser Stadt. Der Schaugiebel steht für die alte bürgerliche Hansestadt, kleine traufständige Gebäude für die beschauliche Östliche Altstadt und die Weite der Warnow für die landschaftliche Einbettung der Stadt und die Verkehrsflächen für Großstadt-Attraktivität und -Ärgernisse.

Darüber hinaus muß die Persönlichkeit selbst - von Stadt und Stadtbetrachter erkannt werden im skizzierenden Dialog von Sehen und Gesehen-werden. Nun kann verglichen werden: die landschaftliche Lage, die Orientierung der Straßen und Plätze, die Prägnanz der Merkzeichen, die Typen der Häuser, der kleine Brunnen - das Wesentliche, Besondere der einen Situation gegen die Alltäglichkeit der anderen. Maßstäbe bilden sich heraus, ein Überblick entsteht Bewertungen werden bewußt. Die Situation ist erfaßt, der Stadt-Charakter begriffen. Was zählt, ist der wahrhaftige Eindruck um die Einmaligkeit von Stadtsituation und Stadtleben, wie er sich im Stadtbild dokumentiert.

"Stadtbild - wie ist es aufgebaut?"

Das Stadtbild wird erlebt und untersucht auf verschiedenen Maßstabsebenen; beispielsweise in Rostock:

Ausstattung: bauliche und schmückende Details an Gebäuden und im Straßenraum (z.B. gotischer Treppengiebel, Brunnen auf dem Universitätsplatz).

Gebäude: Häuser, bauliche Anlagen (z.B. Fünf-Giebel-Haus, Universitäts- und Barocksaalgebäude) und Ensembles (z.B. Heilig-Kreuzkloster).

Freiraum: Gesamtheit aus Gebäude und Natur- bzw. sozialem Raum (z.B. Eselföterstraße, Universitätsplatz).

Baüzone: städtebauliche Quartiere und Bereiche (z.B. östliche Kröpeliner Straße, Neuer Markt, Katthagen) mit ähnlicher Gebrauchs- und Baustruktur.

Stadtgebiet: Gesamt-Stadtstruktur mit bereichsbildenden Teilgebieten (z.B. Östliche Altstadt, Rosengarten) und übergreifenden Gliederungs- und Beziehungselementen (z.B. Blick zur Warnow).

"Stadtbild - woraus besteht es?"

Jedes Stadtbild bewahrt in sich drei Zeithorizonte: die Stadt-Baugeschichte durch Anwesenheit des Vergangenen, das Stadt-Geschehen als Einsicht in das Gegenwärtige und die Stadt-Tendenzen als Vorwegnahme des Zukünftigen. Das Stadt-Bild setzt sich als Summe des Sichtbaren einer Stadt zusammen aus einer Vielzahl von Komponenten,

Einheiten und Elementen. Schwerpunkt städtebaulicher Planung ist naturgemäß die materiell-räumliche Erscheinung der Stadt. Das Stadt-Bild besteht in diesem Planungs- und Konzeptionsmodell aus drei Komponenten mit jeweils drei Elementfamilien: das Stadt-Raumgefüge beinhaltet die Gesamtform aus Baukörpern ("Figur"), Topografie ("Schichtung") und Anordnung ("Grundriß"). Die Stadt-Raumvorstellung (siehe hierzu auch 3.0.) erfaßt die wahrgenommene Erscheinung durch Raumeindruck ("Wirkung"), Raumabfolge ("Gliederung") und Raumorientierung ("Beziehung"). Die Stadt-Bauweise beschreibt die typischen Vegetations- und Baustrukturen, nämlich ihren Formaufbau ("Komposition"), ihr Traggerüst ("Konstruktion") und die stofflichen Eigenschaften ("Materialität").

"Stadtbild - wie wird es untersucht und geplant?"

Um die Gestaltung des Stadtbildes zu sichern und zu verbessern und den Erfordernissen des Denkmalschutzes Rechnung zu tragen müssen die stadträumlichen und architektonischen Situationen untersucht und stadtgestalterische Leitbilder formuliert werden. Die Gebäude, Ensembles, Freiräume und Bauzonen werden entsprechend ihrer funktionalen und architektonischen Erscheinung in Typologien aufeinanderbezogen, um den Erhalt und die Erneuerung der Innenstadt unter den gegenwärtigen Entwicklungsbedingungen und -zwängen im Zusammenhang zu betrachten. Dies geschieht in vier Schritten: die vorhandene (und geplante) Bebauung wird in der Stadtbild-Untersuchung als Bestand aufgenommen, die Denkmalpflege- und Entwicklungsziele erkundet und anschließend einer qualitativen Stadtbild-Bewertung unterworfen. Der Stadtbild-Entwurf zeigt die vorgeschlagene Weiterentwicklung und Bewahrung auf allen Maßstabsebenen, damit sich ohne Beeinträchtigung der historisch, funktionalen und ästhetisch bedeutsamen Stadtgestalt die neuen Gebäude und Freiräume eingliedern

können. Hierzu dienen die planerischen Maßnahmen der Stadtbild-Regulierung, die sich in präzisen Regeln (z.B. Stadtbild-Satzung und -Empfehlungen) zur Gestaltung der Neubauten sowie bestehender Häuser niederschlagen. Die Resultate der Stadtbild-Planung ergeben generelle Leitlinien und differenzierte Gestaltungsempfehlungen für das Untersuchungsgebiet, und damit Kriterien für die Beurteilung von Einzelvorhaben.

3.0. Architektur und Milieu

"Stadtbild - wie wird es genutzt?"

Im Rahmen derartigen Arbeitens wird - neben den genannten städtebaulichen Aufgaben - immer wieder auch Augenmerk gelegt auf architektur-psychologische Aspekte. Das Erleben der Stadt als alltäglich genutzter Raum wird erfaßt durch die Kartierung der Lage der wichtigsten Stadtfunktionen, z.B. nach eigener Analyse, aber u.a. auch nach BauNVO. Aus diesen in der Stadtplanung üblichen Kategorien wird jedoch die erlebnisprägende Seite herausgeschält, weil diese den Charakter eines Gebietes bestimmbar macht. Städtebauliche Nutzung heißt auch Benutzung bzw. "Stadt-Gebrauch" und beschreibt Orte von Handlungen und Menschen (z.B.: Behavior Setting Konzept), deren Ausübung und Ausstrahlung bestimmte Erlebnisqualitäten erzeugt, gewisse Regelhaftigkeit besitzt und Alltagssituationen für den aufmerksamen Bearbeiter sichtbar macht und erfaßt.

Der Stadt-Gebrauch schlüsselt sich auf in diesem Planungs- und Konzeptionsmodell ebenfalls in drei Komponenten mit jeweils drei Elementfamilien: das Raum-Personal differenziert die Besetzung des Untersuchungsgebietes nach vorhandenen Gruppierungen ("Personengruppen"), sozial-ökonomischen ("Sozialstatus") und aktivitäts-bezogenen ("Verhaltensgruppe") Gesichts-punkten. Die Raum-

67

Bedeutung gliedert sich von funktionaler Affordanz ("Eignung") über Informations-aspekte ("Semantik") bis hin zu individual bzw. sozialpsychologischer Bezogenheit ("ldentität"). Die Raum-Funktion wird aufgeteilt je nach Perspektive als vereinfachte Zuschreibung ("Nutzung"), Handlungs- und Verhaltensweisen ("Aktivitäten") und Bezügen zwischen Menschen bzw. zu Artefakten ("Interaktion").

"Stadtbild - wie wird es erlebt?"

Eine weitere Zugangsweise zur Stadt arbeitet bewußt mit ausschnitt-bildender Perspektivität. Was wird wahrgenommen, welche Räume und Nutzungen sind präsent, welche stehen im Alltag im Vordergrund. Hierdurch ergeben sich bildartige Verdichtungen und gefühlsbezogene Bewertungen in der Vorstellung von einer Stadt ebenso wie "blinde Flächen" und Strukturlosigkeit für andere Teile der Stadt. Diese Gliederung der Stadt in wahrgenommene und weniger gewichtige Räume wird über simulierende Verfahren, Analyse örtlicher literarischer Beschreibungen (z.B. Uwe Johnson) oder auch in Gesprächen mit Bewohnern ermittelt. Qualitative, charakter-isierende Beschreibungen werden erstellt und mittels Karten dargestellt (z.B. "Stadt-Gefühle", "Nutzer-Raumerlebnis"). Ziel ist, charakter-istische Züge herausarbeiten, die das Stadterlebnis hin auf "begriffliche Formeln und Bilder" bringt und präziser ergreifen läßt.

"Stadtbild - wie wird es beschrieben und Bewertet?"

Stadtgestaltung als sozialräumliches Modell greift "hinter" das Stadtbild, sucht den Alltag, beobachtet die Aktivitäten im Raum, simuliert Handlungsströme, erfragt Verhaltensweisen und die Haltungen der Menschen zu ihrer Stadt. Gebrauch und Bild werden begrifflich erfaßt in Typologiereihen aus vorgefundenen örtlichen Situationen. Das modellhafte Zusammenspiel der Themen "Stadt-Gebrauch" und "Stadt-Bild" ermöglicht eine umfassende Bestandsuntersuchung, weil das umfangreiche Analysematerial systematisch zugänglich und verknüpfbar ist. Sozial- und Architektur-räumliches wird gleichermaßen erfaßt und der Wandel durch die Zeiten sichtbar. Die so erarbeitete "Stadt-Charakteristik" kristallisiert als Ergebnis-Zusammenfassung die vorhand-enen "Stadt-Qualitäten" heraus. Die Bewertung des Bestandes ist die Grundlage des nunmehr formulierbaren Stadt-Leitbildes. Kontrovers können Stadtgestalt-Entwicklungsmodelle diskutiert werden, die den Stadtraum als das Gemeinschaftliche der Stadt mehr oder weniger anstreben durch Verwebung, Verknüpfung und Gebrauchssituationen. Jede Maßstabsebene erhält ihre speziellen Entwicklungs- und Bewahrungsziele.

"Stadtbild - wie wird es entworfen?"

Nicht das "schöne Stadtbild" ist das Entwurfsziel, sondern Raum für neue und alte Aneignungsmöglichkeiten. Der Weg zum Verständnis der Stadt über den Gebrauch ergibt ein Stadtbild, welches fußt auf Tradition, Nutzung, Anforderung, Interessen: kurz - auf der erfaßbaren Wirklichkeit.

Die gemeinschaftsfördernden Entwicklungs-faktoren und die architektonischen Absichten und Ziele werden räumlich-sozial betrachtet und damit verknüpfbar. Auf allen Maßstabs-ebenen liegen abgeleitete Entwurfsvorschläge vor: für die Gesamtstadtstruktur, die Bauzonen, die Freiraumtypologie, die Haustypologie und die wesentlichen Ausstattungsdetails an Gebäuden und im Freiraum. Zur Umsetzung werden Regeln und Empfehlungen in Gestaltungsplänen und Regulierungs- maß-nahmen zusammengefaßt und stadtbezogene Organisationsmodelle vorgeschlagen. Jeder Ort erhält die angemessene Umsetzungsstrategie.

4.0 Architektur und Freiraum-Gestaltung

"Stadtbild - wie wird es aufgefunden?"

Im Rahmen innerstädtischer Freiraum-Planung sind solche mehr strukturellen, stadtplanerischen und gesamt-städtischen Erkenntnisse örtlich-materiell präzise und den Alltagshandlungen näher. Das Ringen mit den Bürgern und Ämtern um die Gestaltung örtlicher Situationen ergibt "kürzere, direkte Antworten", weil Planung hier Umsetzen in Nützlichkeit, Material und sichtbare Form erfordert. Hierbei efiahrt der Architekt bei den Gesprächen nur über den Umweg von Interpretationen, welche Poesie, Potentiale und Eigenarten ein Ort beherbergt, da die Betroffenen meist nur blanke Nutzungsinteressen formulieren und diese ihnen und anderen den Weg versperren, um solch "erbauliche Erlebnisaspekte" sich selbst bewußt zu machen. Jedoch erfährt der Planer damit die geforderten Zwänge, um örtlich-angemessene Lösungen zu entwerfen. Die weiteren Gebrauchsmöglichkeiten werden (zum Teil von anderen, z.B. Kindern) erst hinterher nach Fertigstellung wahrgenommen und gelebt.

"Stadtbild - wie wird es gebaut?"

Nach der beschriebenen Planungsmethodik wird derzeit die kleine Altstadt von Lübz in Mecklenburg im Zuge einer vollständigen Freiraum-Neugestaltung umgebaut. Neben der räumlichen Präzisierung einer früheren Wasserburg in Beziehung zur Altstadt auf der Flußinsel, ist die räumlich-soziale Gesamt-Struktur Schwerpunkt. In dieser Stadt Lübz werden örtlich verschüttete, aber vorhandene, zum Teil historische Gegebenheiten genutzt, das landschaftsräumliche Erleben (der Flußquerung) mit einer eindeutigen Hierarchie

kommunikativer Orte zu verbinden. Der erste öffentliche Treffpunkt "An der Pumpe" ist in Gebrauch und erfahrt im Durcheinander von anfänglicher Ablehnung und deutlichem Identitätswunsch nunmehr beobachtbare Aneignungsaktivitäten. Die Ausstrahlung dieses ersten Begegnungsortes ist zur Zeit sichtbarer Initialort für die kleinstädtische Entwicklung und geplante Gesamt-Erlebniskonzeption, auch im Kampf gegen die neue Konkurenz randstädtischer Einkaufszentren. Beim kürzlich fertiggestellten "Altstadt-Markt" ist dieser Aneignungsprozeß in seiner Anfangsphase.

5.0. Architektur und raumliche Gemeinschaft

"Stadtbild - als sozial-raumliche Erscheinung?"

Die verhaltensorientierte Perspektive für die Erforschung von Mensch Umwelt-Phänomenen begann (abgesehen von der ethnologischen Betrachtung fremder Völker) erst in den 50er Jahren als R.G. Barker die Verhaltensmuster in einer amerikanischen Kleinstadt beobachtete und beschrieb. Bis dahin hatte die Psychologie die materielle Umwelt nahezu ausgeblendet. Im Zuge wachsender Umweltprobleme in den USA arbeiteten sich daraufhin Sozialwissenschaftler und interessierte Architekten in die städtebaulichen und architektonischen Felder ein, um Zusammenhänge von Raum und Verhalten zu erkennen. Hierbei entstanden eine Reihe von Erklärungsmodellen und theoretischen Konzeptionen, die bestimmte Verhaltensweisen und Stadtprobleme isolieren und plausibel erläutern. Ergänzend sei auch hingewiesen auf einen anspruchsvollen und umfassenden Ansatz: die "Pattern Language". Sie definiert raumbezogene Verhaltenseinheiten und -ketten vom architektonischen Detail bis zu städtebaulichen Räumen und will über Entwurfsregeln eine bessere Umweltgestaltung erreichen. Trotz des Fehlens einer umfassenden Umwelttheorie liegen eine Fülle von Einzeluntersuchungen vor, die Architekten und Stadtplanern helfen ihre Arbeit bewußter einzuordnen, ihre Möglichkeiten abzuschätzen und verantwortlicher auszuüben. Beim heutigen Stand der Forschung und Praxis liegt die Aufgabe von Architekten und Sozialwissenschaftlern darin, ein Umweltproblem von den verschiedensten Blickwinkeln her anzugehen und - angemessen an Aufwand und Ziel - passende Vorgehensweise (d.h. pragmatisch bis forschungsorientiert) zu entwickeln. Dies erfordert interdisziplinäre Verständigungs- und Arbeitsmöglichkeiten. In diesem Sinn sind die folgenden Arbeitsstrategien als Aktions-forschungs- und Planungsansatz zu werten.

"Stadtbild - als Strategie des Ortes"

"Architektur-psychologische Strategie" meint erstens: ein Ort, eine Stadtstruktur, einen städtebaulichen Raum in der Bestandsuntersuchung zu beschreiben, seine Stadtbaugeschichte, Defizite, Mängel, seine "Unsichtbarkeiten" und Wirkungen freizulegen, um die Kräfte herauszuschälen, die seine Besonderheit, Alltäglichkeiten und Verknüpfung mit der Umgebung ausmachen. Solche Orte benötigen in der anschließenden Gestaltungs-Konzeption nur "Hilfestellungen", die im städtebaulichen und freiraumgestalterischen Entwurf angelegt sein müssen. Eine markierende Beiläufigkeit, ein Kreis im Pflaster (Lübz) oder die Verknüpfung vorhandener Stadtraum-Systeme mit der konzeptionellen Leitplanung eines Ufersaums (Schwerin) oder die bewußte Überlagerung verschieden-epochaler Raumarten in ein vernähtes Fragment-System (Rostock) genügen, um der Situation neues Leben, abgewandelte Ziele einzuhauchen, damit architektonische Lösungen vorzubereiten, die sich in die örtliche Überlieferung einpassen.

"Stadtbild - als Strategie der Vermittlung"

Im zweiten Sinne sind "architekturpsychologische Strategien" die Schritte und die Art der Vermittlung an Ämter, Interessengruppen, Politiker-, Bürger/innen und die sonstige Öffentlichkeit, ebenso an die bauausführenden Fachleute und Firmen. Mit längerfristigen taktischen Überlegungen, durch die Planungsmethodik und bei der Überzeugungsarbeit muß der Planer immer wieder auf die Einhaltung der einmal aufgefundenen Entwurfsidee (Leitbild) bei der Realisierung hinarbeiten. Jedes Detail, jede technische Lösung muß wie Metallspäne mittels eines Magneten immer wieder ausgerichtet und gepolt werden. Die gestaltende Leitlinie ist den Beteiligten oft nicht bewußt, der gedankliche Bezug bei jeweils vorliegenden Entscheidungen zu fern und die Mühsal konsequenter Durchsetzung zu schwierig. Naheliegender Pragmatismus, fehlende Zusammenschau, fachliche Unsensibilität kann aufgedeckt und durch positiv leitende Motive ersetzt und kommunikativ angeleitet werden.

Hierfür ist ständige Teilhabe und Information von größter Wichtigkeit, um Interessen vor Ort aufzuspüren, persönliche Vorlieben zu erkennen, einzupassen und sie zu verstehen. Auch ist eine gewisse Härte vonnöten, wenn Bequemlichkeit oder blanker Eigennutz die Leitidee zu verwässern drohen (z.B. weil unebene Pflasterung "umsatz-mindernd" sei). Strategie meint hier, immer am Ball zu bleiben - Präsenz vor Ort (unbezahlbar im doppelten Sinne) - aber auch immer wieder Rückversicherung und Überprüfung am formulierten Leitbild. Dies hilft klare Entscheidungen zu treffen bzw. ebenso, einen gewissen Grad an Abweichung und Änderung immer wieder aufzunehmen und gegebenenfalls zuzulassen.

"Stadtbild - durch Kooperation und Organisation"

Beide Strategien bedingen einander; ist die aufgefundene örtliche Idee zu einer vorhandenen Situation nicht stark genug herausgearbeitet und wenig überzeugend beim Auftraggeber verankert, bleibt die selbstbildende Eindruckskraft des Ortes ungenutzt. Einsicht erzeugt der Ort selbst, indem er im Einklang mit dem gestalterischen Konzept sich als Argument selbst miteinbringt. Erst dann greift die "zweite Strategie", die vom Planer nur mittels Präsenz geleistet werden kann: immer wieder den Bezug herzustellen, zukünftige Handlungsmöglichkeiten an der Situation aufzuzeigen und kurzfristige Eigeninteressen zurückzuweisen. Den Ort konsequent stark machen, damit er eine gewisse "Selbständigkeit und Offenheit" bewirkt und ausstrahlt. Ein Verständnis aller, die Kooperation und Organisation der Beteiligten sowie die persönliche Glaubwürdigkeit erleichtern dem Architekten als "Anwalt der räumlichen Situation" die Erstellung von städtebaulichen Qualitäten. Diese sollen Anreiz und Möglichkeit binden, damit Neues und Altes sich dort ereignen kann.Wenn diese Förderung konsequent gelingt, schließt sich der Kreis zur vorherigen Analyse: das ehedem aufgefundene, vorhandene Raumerlebnis bekommt eine andere, weiterentwickelte oder gar neue Verhaltenssweise an seine Seite gestellt. Die "Stadt-Geschichte" geht weiter, die eigene planerische Aneignung - baulich umgesetzt - eröffnet und fördert neue Alltagslebensweisen für die Stadtbewohner.

"Stadtbild - als Ausdruck raumlicher Gemeinschaft"

Der Begriff "Gemeinschaft" ist nicht emotional, oder gar politisch gemeint, sondern beinhaltet im Vergleich mit dem Wort „Gesellschaft" gewisse örtliche Bezüge und Beziehungen. Er erfaßt zugleich die Eingrenzung auf eine bestimmte Einheit von Menschen, die im strukturellen und lokalen Sinne miteinander verbunden sind. Der "Gemeinschaftsraum Stadt"beschreibt Möglichkeiten des Kontakts und von Lebensweisen; sei es unverbunden und zufällig im Straßenverkehr oder im direkten, gemeinsamen Erleben einer Festveranstaltung. Die stadträumliche Gemeinschaft birgt "Gelegenheiten" (Jürgen Friedrichs) - örtlich wie funktional; meint die privaten Gebäude ebenso wie den Öffentlichen Raum; weist auf Verhaltensmöglichkeiten wie auf heimatliche Kulturverbundenheit. Der Stadtraum kann schlicht verfügbar sein oder gar deutlich zusammenführen, die Gemeinschaft still geordnet oder bewußt einig erlebt werden.

Die Summe aus Gebrauch und Raum ist Grundlage der stadträumlichen Gemeinschaft im Sinne von Gelegenheiten. Spielräume werden sozial angeregt und materiell gebaut: nun kann die Lebendigkeit des Alltags greifen; einiges wird genutzt wie geplant, vieles anderes entfaltet sich in den neuen Gegebenheiten: "A door is a place and an occasion". Die "ästhetische Wahrhaftigkeit" der Stadtgestalt entsteht aus der Wirklichkeit des Alltags und ist erst damit als urbanes Stadtbild zu evaluieren.

Dipl. Ing. Klaus Brendle ist Architekt in Lübeck, Deutschland.

71

Chapter Seventeen

Public Art, Public Space and City Regeneration

Marion Roberts and Bill Erickson

Britain, whilst lagging behind the rest of Western Europe in terms of its spending on cultural policies, nevertheless can boast two fine examples of the use of public art in the redefinition of the image of an area. It will be argued, though, the use of public art in this manner does not offer an easy solution or panacea to the problems of place-making. Such ventures have to be undertaken with a great deal of forethought and care and can as easily be disastrous as they are successful. Furthermore, the problems of public perception evoked by certain interventions in each of these examples suggests that in the arena of the public realm in British cities, public art needs a strong connection to the particularity of site and place and to bend to the logic of the process of regeneration.

Before moving to a discussion of these case studies the difficulties facing public providers will be considered in more detail. A problem resides in defining the image of the revitalized neighborhood or district. Greene, discussing public art in 1989, noted that there did not exist an appropriate language with which to discuss public art works; "rather understanding of these projects is limited by a language developed in relation to individual works of art in the studio. " Dunlop's recent thesis which studied public art on transport systems takes this argument further in the contention that public art should not be equated to gallery art because, in order to succeed, it requires an interaction with both its site and its audience. In other words, the urban square is not an open air gallery.

The social meanings which may be attached to the production of public space are elusive in this postmodern era. Whilst the honest civic intentions which lie behind providing truly accessible public space in the defensive spaces of the polarized city seems quaintly Modernist, if not pre-Modern, in another interpretation these spaces can be seen as cultural products, objects of mass-consumption. In this sense, the new spaces of urban regeneration are in competition with the privatized space of the shopping mall and the theme park, fragments of a city in which the past is endlessly recycled to be absorbed into the present.

The competition with the mall and the heritage park is real, indeed the driving force behind these developments. At ground level then, the sensory perception which the visitor experiences in walking through these new spaces should be comparable to that experienced in other spaces of consumption. The challenge to the public artist and the urban designer, is considerable: design and art armed with the limited resources from public/private funding has to compete with the full weight of commercial enterprise.

The two case studies discussed below illustrate the limitations and potential of public art programs to meet these challenges.

Birmingham

The provision of public art in Birmingham's city centre is closely related to the City Council's initiative in changing the city's image. Birmingham is England's second city and is a regional centre for the West Midlands. The city centre was laid out in the 1960's employing the urban devices of Modernism: concrete underpasses, an inner ring road and "a dominance of engineering structure". By the middle of the 1980's, it was felt that a new approach needed to be taken to re-thinking the city centre, providing it with a more attractive image and a user-friendly environment.

Following a re-casting of the city centre strategy, a consultation exercise and the adoption of two consultants' reports, a network of high quality squares and pedestrian links was put into place. Two major civic spaces, Centenary Square and Victoria Square, were created. The concept for Centenary Square had been developed prior to the city centre strategy. The Square was thus the opening up of a new rectangular public space framed by distinguished nineteenth century civic buildings, the Convention Centre and some less distinguished modern constructions. The tone of the Square was set by the nineteenth century Hall of Memory set in its eastern portion.

Centenary Square incorporated three major new pieces of sculpture, artist designed tiling and street furniture and a neon sculpture on the canopy of the Convention Centre. Two of the sculptures were in traditional materials, bronze and stone, but the third was in fiberglass. The Square received critical acclaim in the national and professional press and was hailed as a breakthrough in British cultural policy.

However the fiberglass sculpture raised something of a furor in the local press and media.

The sculpture, which had been commissioned from a Birmingham born artist called Raymond Mason, was entitled Forward and depicted "the onward march of the people of Birmingham". Key figures and anonymous people waved goodbye to Birmingham's past and looked towards the future. A Policy Studies Institute report records that the majority of the people whom they interviewed or who wrote letters to the local papers disliked the statue. Criticisms were made of its size ("awful"), shape ("wrong") and the material ("a slab of rancid butter"). Further ridiculing comparisons were made to its resemblance to socialist realist art ("Red Square, Birmingham").

Despite this setback, the City Council continued its use of public art through the pedestrian linkages to its next major public place, Victoria Square. This Square was a former traffic island. It is enclosed by some fine neoclassical building which enjoy historic monument status. Mindful of the problems caused by the Raymond Mason sculpture, the City briefed the chosen artists for the Square, Dhruva Mistry, Bettina Fermet and the Carving Workshop, to achieve a high quality urban landscape using traditional materials. A consultation exercise was carried out and the small number of objections seemed mainly to be motivated by racist objections to the employment of an Indian artist.

Further problems arose when the TSB Bank, who had bought one of the most beautiful of the historic buildings fronting the Square, decided to hold a competition for a sculpture to be placed outside it. The winner of the competition was the artist, Anthony Gormley, who proposed a 9m high Iron Man, constructed from 20mm thick sheets of steel, buried up to his calves and tilted at an angle. As one commentator tactfully pointed out, it ". . . simply cannot be ignored". The City Council headed off potential criticism with advance publicity which made it clear that the £75,000 statue had been donated by the TSB. Letters were received asking "why this horror was being put up in the beautiful new square" and a local paper, the Birmingham Evening Mall ran a campaign to get it removed. The sculpture remained following the opening of the Square in 1993 and in the year which followed the Council received approximately 20 letters of support for the Square, although invidious comparisons were made with Mason sculpture in Centenary Square. Interestingly, despite the popularity of Victoria Square, a further proposal to site a non-traditional sculpture in New Street which leads up to Victoria Square raised an outcry and an alternative site was chosen elsewhere.

Birmingham City Centre was successful in its strategy towards its city centre. The new pattern of spaces changed the image of the city and, combined with other strategic measures, attracted £2 billion of inward investment and thousands of jobs to the city. Nevertheless, the problems raised by certain of the art works suggest that the public's place bound judgments may be more astute than is generally supposed; this will be explored further in relation to Swansea.

Swansea

Swansea is Wales' second city and in British terms, is relatively small, a regional centre serving a population of approximately half a million. The town occupies a marvelous site, on an inlet framed by hills. Swansea, in common with many other waterfront cities, suffered an absolute decline in its port activities throughout this century. By 1969 its commercial shipping activities in the South Dock had finally closed and its activity as a resort town was declining.

The Maritime Quarter was an ambitious project to regenerate the South Dock area which

rejected a monolithic monumental approach in favor of a network of spaces and walks, based on the docks themselves. In a public/private partnership, the City Council and YJ Lovells Holding created a new area comprising housing, hotels, shops, a theatre, a museum and many renovated and renewed buildings. Swansea's Maritime Quarter was very successful; it received several awards, including the Europa Nostra Award. Its success did not only derive from its peaceful squares and cobbled walkways and its rapid increase in property prices in the housing boom of the late 1980's but also from the ambitious public art program which ran through the entire development.

The artworks draw on maritime, literary and astronomical themes and are related to Swansea's tradition of local arts and crafts. The works vary from simple figurative sculptures, such as the statue of Captain Cat - a character from one of local poet Dylan Thomas's poems, to more enigmatic sequences, such as the Spolasco series - a series of 26 bathstone panels celebrating the life of an idiosyncratic nineteenth century Swansea doctor, to the more abstract free-standing sculptures of the Tower of the Winds and the Lighthouse Tower. In the period from 1983 over seventy panels, monuments sculptures and features were installed, 80% of which were made by local artists.

The works, as has been described above, relate closely to the site. They may be read as enhancing the unique particularity of the site, providing articulation and resonance to a post modern development with an otherwise familiar style of architecture. There were some difficulties in relating to the audience, however. Hourahane points out that there was no community involvement between the artists and the resident population because at the time that the Maritime Quarter was built, the docks were derelict. The re-population of the area by outsiders opened up the possibilities for a re-interpretation of meaning in the Quarter and the public art program supported that re-identification. Her conclusion was that the art program succeeds because there is a balance between the more easily understood pieces and the intricate and the poetic.

At the time of its completion the Maritime Quarter was hailed as a commercial and civic success, "it is now the most sought-after area of Swansea to visit and in which to live". It is interesting that the program of public art ran into extreme difficulties when it was extended to the town centre. The progenitor of the public art program wished to give the centre of Swansea a specific identity. In many British cities, not only are the same multiples trading in each High Street, but local authorities use the same design for street furniture - generally a 'heritage' design. To avoid this duplication specialist designs for street furniture, paving and decorative poetry were commissioned. Each of these endeavors drew on Celtic motifs and the poems were written in Swansea dialect. The street furniture was unusual in design, although constructed in metal its color coding in green, mauve or orange gave it the appearance of being made from plastic.

The introduction of the street refurbishment in conjunction with partial pedestrianisation aroused the wrath of the local press and the Civic Society, whose President declared it to be "ghastly". Particular exception was taken to a proposed artwork which through the construction of a fragment of an arch, evoked Swansea's Roman heritage. It was argued that the connection was tenuous, and even worse, the ironic comment in local Swansea dialect appended to the arch, was making fun out of local people. The Celtic references were also obscure in a city where only 14% were Welsh speaking. Although comments recorded in the media by local people were mixed sufficient damage was done by the local press to prevent the extension of the public art program. The City's public art program had been demoted from its former position of prominence to more low key interventions.

Analysis

This paper has illustrated some of the potential and limitations for public art programs used in conjunction with schemes for urban regeneration. The potential is illustrated by the commercial success and recognition given to both Swansea's Maritime Quarter and Birmingham's Civic Centre.

The limitations are spelt out in the controversies which occurred over specific art works in Birmingham and in Swansea's artist designed city centre street furniture. The difficulties may, of course be interpreted in a number of ways. Firstly, on a pragmatic level, the story may be told as the malicious influence of the local press in Britain, which is owned by a relatively small number of proprietors and which likes to raise controversy. Or, it can be recast as the use of art works in accusations of wasteful public expenditure between opposing political parties anxious to make capital out of errors of judgment.

As discussed earlier in this paper, the difficulties may also be considered as symbolic. The common denominator between Mason's heroic sculpture, Gormley's Man and Swansea's street furniture and fragmented arch is that as objects, they did not respond to the dominant interpretations of the spaces in which they were placed.

Urban design theorists such as Gordon Cullen have argued for over three decades that exterior urban spaces should be designed, constructed and used as outdoor rooms. Jameson has argued that the public are well-used to reading cultural products in terms of genres. Conventionally genres are defined in terms of films. Reading these spaces as examples of genres, it can be seen that the contested art works fell outside of the terms of reference of the places themselves. We would argue that where the urban context provides a strong example of a genre, it then becomes difficult for the art works to set themselves at variance to it, without appearing simply odd, or misplaced. A piece of uncompromisingly modernist art is out of place in a "pastiche" Renaissance piazza, or a conventional civic space, as are unusually conceived, brightly colored street furniture in an everyday shopping street. Public responses would suggest that the urban space is read as a whole and not considered as a form of outdoor gallery.

In conclusion, these cases studies have illustrated that, given the right circumstances, public art may be a powerful aid to urban regeneration in its articulation and identification of the uniqueness of place. The effectiveness of the artworks is constrained by the context to which they relate: where a new "genre" is being formed in conjunction with the art works, then the art can play a strong role in the construction of new meanings for that area. Where, however, the urban context is set, then the art installations need to take a more responsive and reflexive contribution to that urban space. To be effective, change needs to be "artful" indeed!

Dr. Marion Roberts, B.Sc. (Hons), Dipl .Arch., School of Urban Development & Planning, Faculty of the Environment, University of Westminster, London, UK.

Bill Erickson, B.Arch., MA, MSc, School of Urban Development and Planning, Faculty of the Environment, University of Westminster, London, UK.

Site Specific Public Art

Crafts Fountain, Euskirchen. Detail of weaver.

The sculptures and fountains by Bonifatius Stirnberg, one of Germany's foremost sculptors specializing in public art, are participatory, and site specific. Stirnberg's works are located in the best public spaces, market places or outside city hall in more than 50 cities in Germany.

These works portray the city's traditional crafts and trades, locally renowned figures, myths and legends. They are designed to appeal to people of all ages and offer opportunities for children's play.

Public Realm

Öffentlichkeit

Suzanne H. Crowhurst Lennard

Chapter Eighteen

The Public Realm and the Good City

Henry L. Lennard

Throughout most of the history of cities, public places have made a significant contribution to the personal, social and economic life of the city's inhabitants.

Much of the city's life took place in squares and streets. Indeed, cities were designed around the market square and the cathedral square. Life on the street was made possible because the shops, services, and facilities needed for everyday life were located on these streets, and because residential accommodations overlooked, or were adjacent to the places and streets.

There was a period in the development of European cities when streets were taken over by the car, and became inhospitable for people. During the last three decades, however, there has been a remarkable change in this trend. Hundreds of cities and towns in Europe have developed extensive pedestrian areas, have freed many public squares from cars, and have begun to provide a mix of uses which makes possible the overlap of the private and public realms. The shop-house, the building with apartments above and shops and services below, has been a major building block of most European cities. Currently, the importance of this arrangement is again being realized, and attempts to diminish this arrangement are being resisted.

Cities and towns differ in the heterogeneity of the population using public places. In some cities there may be an absence of children, or of elderly people, or of strangers. Cities and towns also differ in the intensity and com-plexity of public life: in the form it takes, the functions it serves.

At its best, the public realm is an important element in maintaining social stability.

The essence of the good city is found in its urban public spaces and its differentiated public life. The public realm is essential for the enactment of vital social processes. These processes are connected to the very issues that currently concern many cities in Europe and North America, and are the subject of much public concern and debate: violence, crime, incivility, inter-group conflict, drug use, lack of self-esteem, and diminished social competence.

Public places and the public realm are important social learning, teaching and social equilibrating factors. Indeed, socialization, social learning, and humanization occurs most significantly through life in public.

The public realm is indispensable for the following social processes that are essential for life in a city, in a town, indeed in any community:

- Knowing others and being known by others.

- Showing attention and interest, and being shown attention and interest.

- Being confirmed as fellow human beings.

- Discussing and reconciling different points of view and perspectives.

- Observing and learning (especially for the young) how people relate, comfort, support and take responsibility for each other.

- Negotiating one's place within the public domain (Where do adults talk? Where do children play? From where do the elders monitor?)

- Being in a place that has meaning, either historic association or present significance.

Cities as Living Systems

By thinking about cities as living systems analogous to biological organisms we achieve a greater understanding of factors responsible for instability, and of the ensemble of social patterns needed to promote stability.

The utility of such an analogy has been proposed both by the great scholar of cities, Lewis Mumford, and by the preeminent physiologist, Walter Cannon, in his book, *The Wisdom of the Body*.

In thinking of cities in this way we can apply knowledge from the study of biological organisms as systems. Of prime relevance is the concept of homeostasis (stability) and of the mechanisms that promote homeostasis. This principle of homeostasis has to do with the acceptable range of variation that may occur among the elements constituting a system, so that the system will maintain its stability and identity.

When there is too much variability in organismic processes, when, for example, the sugar supply of the body runs low, or body temperature varies too greatly because of internal factors (disease) or external factors (extreme cold), mechanisms come into play to restore stability.

Many of the organism's systems and functions are brought into play when the stability of any one of the important physiological systems of the body is threatened. As Cannon explains, there are additional safety and monitoring mechanisms built into the functioning human organism that offer protection against loss of stability, and promote homeostasis.

While the elements of the human body, the different organs and organ systems have been delineated, and most of their relationships are well documented and understood, the situation is less clear for systems as complex and large as cities.

Also, while there is consensus on the factors that threaten the human organism (bacteria, trauma, temperature variations, toxic substances, extreme physical or emotional stress, etc.), there is less consensus on the causes of instability for the social organism of the city.

Factors Disrupting Stability

Yet, there has been a good deal of discussion of the factors disrupting the stability and functioning of the city systems. These include rapid technological change, economic policies, priorities and ensuing economic dislocations. But there can also be no doubt that architectural and planning ideologies have had serious destabilizing effects. The destruction of the urban tissue, of the continuous physical fabric of the city through architectural ideologies, especially, the idea of the "modern", has led to the creation of fragmented and chaotic cities with individual buildings often separate, unrelated in character and disconnected in space.

By now, there is agreement that past zoning policies restricting mixed use, and segregation of poor and vulnerable persons in public housing, were errors, if not outright disasters. Traffic planning policies and the creation of highways dissecting many cities were equally destabilizing.

What has, so far, not received the attention it deserves, is the disrupting impact of prevailing myths and values about the nature of society and other human beings.

Leon Eisenberg wrote "The planets will move as they always have, whether we adopt a geocentric or heliocentric view of the heavens... but the behavior of man is *not* independent of the theories of human behavior men adopt."

The conception people hold of other human beings as dangerous or untrustworthy has great destabilizing force. They become a self-fulfilling prophecy by leading people to avoid each other, which leads to further segregation of persons and groups!

To the extent that the media promote and amplify these images of persons, they are also a destabilizing force.

Instability is manifested in lack of complementarity in behavior and expectations. Social process is only possible if a measure of complementarity exists.

Communicational and physical barriers also indicate lack of stability. Physical and communicational barriers are, of course, connected; they are two aspects of the same phenomenon, each mirroring the other. Lack of mutual confirmation and caring reflect system strain.

Homeostatic Mechanisms

Fortunately, through an analysis of many cities that have worked well over the centuries, and cities that are still doing fairly well in maintaining stability, and serve as a good environment for their human inhabitants, we can learn about structures, processes, values, and patterns that promote stability.

What then are some of the mechanisms and arrangements that promote stability?

Significant Conversation:

According to Lewis Mumford, "Perhaps the best definition of the city in its higher aspects is to say that it is a place designed to offer the widest facilities for significant conversation.

Indeed, as the social philosopher Hannah Arendt explains, it is only by speaking about the world to one another that "we humanize what is going on in the world and in ourselves." "For the world is not humane just because it is made by human beings, and it does not become humane just because the human voice sounds in it, but only when it has become the object of discourse. However much we are affected by the things of the world, however deeply they may stir and stimulate us, they become human for us only when we can discuss them with our fellows."

"The dialogue is one of the ultimate expressions of life in the city; if provision for dialogue and drama, in all their ramifications, is one of the essential offices of the city, then one key to urban development should be plain – it lies in the widening of the circle of those capable of participating in it... in a sense the dramatic dialogue is both the fullest symbol and the final justification of the city's life."

"For the same reason, the most revealing symbol of the city's failure, of its very non-existence as a social personality, is the absence of dialogue – not necessarily a silence, but equally the loud sound of a chorus uttering the same words in cowed if complacent conformity." (Lewis Mumford)

Models of Social Life:

Behavior is learned through observation and participation. The public realm provides a great many examples and models on how persons relate with family and friends, with young and old, with those of different social backgrounds, those of different temperament; and with the physically and mentally well or disabled.

It is especially important for children to be exposed to a diversity of people, to observe a range of models of how people relate, and to learn from the skills and flexibility from those they observe.

It is not realized, to paraphrase Jane Jacobs, how many people are required to provide suitable models for the socialization of children. Social skills of talking, initiating and maintaining contact, negotiating differences, taking pleasure in social relationships, cannot be acquired *only* from one's family, especially from families who are already deficient in their verbal and social repertoire.

Social learning is very important if people, different in generation, social and ethnic background, and interest are to live together with some measure of cooperation and harmony.

Major social problems are directly linked to the impoverishment of the public realm: to the absence of good models of relationships and to the lack of practice and skills in human discourse.

One reason for the use of physical violence as a preferred mode for settling differences may be a lack of knowledge about, and competence in utilizing other ways of making one's position known, and achieving the desired ends. Drug users frequently attribute involvement with addictive drugs such as heroin, to an inability to talk and relate to their peers, or to strangers.

Interestingly, of central importance in therapeutic communities are group meetings where members learn the skills of self expression, conversation and dialogue.

Multiple Perspectives:

"The reality of the public realm relies on the simultaneous presence of innumerable perspectives and aspects in which the common world presents itself. Being seen and being heard by others derive their significance from the fact that everybody sees and hears from a different position. This is the meaning of public life, compared to which even the richest and most satisfying family life can offer only the prolongation or multiplication of one's own position with its attending aspects and perspectives." (Arendt)

Exposure to multiple perspectives expands one's own point of reference and tends to exercise a civilizing influence on the relations among persons.

A healthy human organism can deal with destabilizing forces by generating an ensemble of operations that restore equilibrium.

Neighborhood dinners on the main street of each of Siena's 17 districts increase a sense of community well being.

Suzanne H. Crowhurst Lennard

Where should we look for these health promoting mechanisms in cities? In answering this question we are helped by observing, and learning about cities that have *worked*; cities that are not obsessed with coping with pathology, but rather with promoting well being!

Most cities that have this ability to deal with destabilizing factors, that promote a sense of well being among their inhabitants, and where there is tangible evidence of well being among their children and young people, indeed, among a wide range of inhabitants, have some of the following characteristics: A physical fabric that is not chaotic and fragmented; a range of public places and streets that stimulate an active social life and serve as focal points for dialogue, and conversation; a range of commu

nity events, whether public markets, town meetings, festivals, celebrations, or even community kitchens.

All of the places and events are inclusive, not exclusive, permitting and involving the widest possible participation of young and old, rich and poor, native and stranger.

It is only where this, a viable public realm exists, that misconceptions of others can be corrected, that paranoia diminishes, and that a sense of trust can be revived.

Henry L. Lennard is Chairman of the Advisory Board of the IMCL Council.

Kapitel Neunzehn

Panische Angst vor der vitalen Stadt

Andreas Feldtkeller

Ich gebe zu, daß das Thema meines Referats etwas verwunderlich ist. Angst vor der vitalen Stadt, die wir alle doch sehnlich wiederhaben wollen? Aber in Ernst: Bleiben nicht viele unserer guten Ideen zur lebenswerten Stadt Träume, weil uns eine geradezu panische Angst vor den Zumutungen der vitalen Stadt daran hindert, sie wirklich zu wollen?

1. In seinen "Aussichten auf den Bürgerkrieg" hat Hans-Magnus Enzensberger dafür plädiert, der heute täglich drohenden Revolte - dem molekularen Bürgerkrieg zuerst vor der eigenen Haustür entgegenzutreten. Wie das zu machen ist, läßt er offen. Enzensberger sagt aber, daß Sisyphos keineswegs ein existentieller Held sei, sondern "etwas viel Wichtigeres, nämlich eine Figur des Alltags". Nach dem klassischen Verständnis von der Stadt war es selbstverständlich, daß vor der Haustür das Stadtviertel liegt und daß der beste Schutz gegen Revolten der zivile Umgang im Quartier ist. Heute neigen allerdings viele Menschen (etwa angesichts der Ereignisse in Hannover vor einigen Wochen) dazu, sich lieber für eine bessere Überwachung der Grundstücke, für mehr privat kontrollierte Einkaufszonen, für die Entfernung "unerwünschter Personen" aus den Fußgängerzonen und für einen besseren Durchgriff der Polizei stark zu machen.

2. Ich denke, es gibt wirklich eine Angst bei Planern, bei Architekten, auch bei Politikern, - überhaupt in der Gesellschaft-, vor Veränderungen, die die so wunderbar in gut sortierte Inseln aufgeteilte Stadt mit ihren Bequemlichkeiten (und deren Absicherungen durch Gesetze, Verwaltungsvorschriften, höchstrichterliche Urteile und architektonische Qualitätsmaßstäbe) durcheinanderbringen könnten. Städtisches Chaos, unvorhersehbare Veränderungen, die Planung des Unplanbaren, davon möchten wir lieber nichts wissen. Kennzeichnend ist etwa die panische Angst in der Bevölkerung vor jeder Andeutung von "Verdichtung". Wer weiß, was da auf einen zukommt an Dichte, an Mischung, an Fremden, an unordentlichen Jugendlichen, an Kriminalität, an zusätzlichem Verkehr, überhaupt an Unvorhersehbarem. Wir sind uns alle einig, wir brauchen "mehr Stadt" und mehr Städtisches - die Spielregeln sollten aber die gewohnten bleiben; das Abstandgrün darf nicht weggeplant werden.

3. Natürlich waren Stadtplanung und Architektur an der Zerlegung der Stadt, an dem Auseinandernehmen der für die Gesellschaft so wichtigen räumlichen Zusammenhänge ganz unmittelbar beteiligt. Die "gegliederte und aufgelockerte" Stadt ist tendentiell eine Stadt der subtilen Ausgrenzungen, der Zäsuren und der Zäune. Ihr Konzept ist erstaunlich zählebig und das schon etwas mit der Angst vor der vitalen Stadt zu tun. Aber die Revolten - die mehr oder weniger molekulare Revolten - in den sich auflösenden Städten veranlassen neuerdings doch den einen oder anderen Bürgermeister, zu fragen, ob das so bleiben kann:

• 1989 entschließt sich der neugewählte Stadtrat für Stadtentwicklung der Stadt Lyon nach heftigen Unruhen in den trostlosen Vierteln der Vorstädte zu einer Politik der

Rückgewinnung von öffentlichen Raumen als Ort des sozialen Lebens.

• Und der neue Bürgermeister von Bogota in Kolumbien stellt angesichts massiver Gewalt in seiner Stadt fest, daß "die Menschen desinteressiert und indifferent auf Aggressionen reagieren" und "daß die soziale Kontrolle nicht mehr funktioniere"; es bestehe "ein Mangel an öffentlichem Raum". Er veröffentlicht einen 6-Punkte-Plan zur Starkung der Bürgerkultur und zur Schaffung öffentlicher Räume. Unter anderem ermuntert er die Bewohner seiner Stadt, sich mit der Verteilung von roten und weißen Kärtchen auf der Straße gegenseitig zu bescheinigen, ob sie mit dem Verhalten des anderen einverstanden sind oder nicht.

4. Die Stadt ohne öffentlichen Raum ist eine Stadt, bei der das passive Hinsehen, oder eigentlich noch besser das Wegschauen, die Gleichgültigkeit gegenüber dem gesellschaftlichen Alltagsgeschehen, das Zuschauen und Nicht-Partei-Ergreifen zum Gestaltungstenor erhoben ist. Das geht bis ins Detail, wenn etwa die Gebäude sich nicht mehr mit ihren Fenstern auf die Straße orientieren, sondern ins private Grün, auf die "schöne Aussicht" oder ein metropolitanes Stadtpanorama. Es hängt also durchaus auch mit dem Zustand des Städtischen (und nicht allein mit der Verführung durch die Medien) zusammen, wenn wir die Welt immer mehr wie ein widerstandsloses Bild auf dem Monitor sehen. Vor dem Resultat hat kürzlich Jan Ross in einem Artikel in der FAZ mit der Überschrift "Europas Selbstverachtung" gewarnt: "Genau Bescheid zu wissen und nicht einzugreifen, an diesem Widerspruch zerbricht die moralische Integrität. Die Aufmerksamkeit des Zuschauers schärft das moralische Bewußtsein, bietet ihm aber zugleich keinen anderen Gegenstand als das moralische Versagen. Selbstverachtung ist die Konsequenz."

5. Zurück zur konkreten Stadtplanung: Die anwesenden Architekten und Planer werden sagen: wieso, wir sind ja längst auf dem Weg zu neuen städtischen Strukturen, die gegliederte und aufgelockerte Stadt ist doch Vergangenheit.

Ich bin mir da nicht so sicher. Mein Eindruck ist, daß fast überall doch das alte Konzept, nur versehen mit einem neuen Design, wieder angeboten wird. Diese ganzen wunderbaren Modelle: der "ökologische Städtebau", die "Gartenstadt der Zukunft", das "integrierte Wohnmodell", das "Leben ohne Auto", die "Architektur der Stadt" und die "neuen Plätze", die "Stadt am Wasser", die "High-Tech-Architektur" und nicht zuletzt die "Großprojekte" (die urbanen Riesen), bei denen "die Stadt" den technologischen Wandel im Verkehrswesen finanzieren soll - das sind zwar alles Konzepte, bei denen "Mehr Stadt" als Devise ganz vornean steht, bei denen es aber im Ernst nicht unbedingt um die vitale Stadt geht. Sind diese Konzepte geeignet, die Verinselung der Agglomerationen aufzubrechen? Orientieren sie sich an den alltäglichen Bedürfnissen ganz normaler, durchschnittlicher Stadtbewohner, der jungen und älteren, der alteingesessenen gerade erst zugewanderten? Sind sie flexibel angelegt, um auf vehementen gesellschaftlichen Wandel reagieren zu können? Ich sage es bewußt zugespitzt: Ich glaube eher, da wird so getan, als könne per Ökologie oder Design oder durch die Beschwörung der Metropolen aus der Siedlung ein Stück vitale Stadt werden, ohne daß an den Grundfesten der modernen Planungsdoktrinen gerüttelt wird.

6. Richtig ist: der moderne Städtebau hat der breiten Bevölkerung endlich das gebracht, was lange Jahrhunderte Privileg weniger Einzelner war: räumliche Abschottung vor den Belästigungen und Widrigkeiten des normalen Alltags. Nach Regeln der funktionalen Organisation haben sich die Menschen für alle ihre Bedürfnisse besondere, sorgfältig voneinander geschiedene Nachbarschaftsinseln geschaffen, und die moderne Technik hat ihnen mit Auto, Bus und Bahn, Telefon, Radio, Fernsehen und Fax versprochen, daß sie

jederzeit individuell und bequem zwischen diesen Inseln hin- und herspazieren können. Damit sind die wesentlichen Ansprüche, die der Mensch an die Stadt richtet, nämlich Arbeit und Wohnen, Austausch und Geschütztsein, zunächst einmal erfüllt und zwar in einer gesunden Umgebung, abseits von rauchenden Schloten und den zugebauten Hinterhöfen der kompakten Stadt.

7. Inzwischen befinden wir uns allerdings in einer anderen Situation, und zwar in zweierlei Hinsicht: Einmal haben sich die gesellschaftlichen, die wirtschaftlichen und vor allem die technischen Gegebenheiten des Stadtlebens gründlich geändert (und sie werden sich noch weiter ändern) und daneben hat sich das Modell der funktional gegliederten, der verinselten Stadtstruktur gegenüber dem Stadtmodell der Vielfalt und der Kompaktheit so brutal durchgesetzt, daß die vitale Stadt komplett zu verschwinden droht. Abgeschottete Inseln gab es ja schon immer in der Stadt. Aber sie waren eben ein größenmäßig untergeordneter Bestandteil im Stadtgefüge, das ansonsten überall vielfältig und gemischt strukturiert war und dadurch fast an jeder Stelle öffentlichen Raum hervorbringen konnte. Die jetzt entstehende Situation hat also eine besondere Brisanz: die funktionale Anti-Stadt frißt die vitale Stadt auf. Es ist nämlich keineswegs so - wie immer noch viele glauben -, daß innerhalb einer funktional strukturierten Peripherie noch ein vitaler Stadtkern weiterbestehen bleibt. Die Zentren werden doch fast überall von der erlebnis- und konsumhungrigen Peripherie als Freizeit- und Erlebnis-Park zweckentfremdet und damit ebenfalls zu einer Insel mit Spezialeffekt umfunktioniert. Nicht nur in der Peripherie verschwindet die Stadt, sondern auch in der Zone, die so gerne als "das Herz der Stadt" bezeichnet wird. Dort ist zwar noch ein Rest an Vitalität übrig, aber die Bewohner der Stadtkerne haben sich längst von der Straße ihrer Quartieren zurückgezogen. Damit besteht auch hier die hier ehemals so lebendige urbane Nachbarschaft (eine Nachbarschaft unter Fremden, die sich kennen) nicht länger.

8. Man kann den geschilderten Veränderungsprozeß folgendermaßen zusammenfassen: War die Stadt jahrhundertelang ein Mittel, unterschiedliche Interessen an einem gemeinsamen Ort, also räumlich zusammenzubringen, Ausgleich und Austausch zu besorgen, Synergien zu erzeugen - so ist heute auf einmal geradezu das Gegenteil der Fall. Jetzt geht es darum, die unterschiedlichen Interessen möglichst sorgfältig zu trennen und auf diese Weise von gegenseitigen Beeinträchtigungen freizuhalten.

Deshalb werden auch die beiden elementären Aufgaben der Stadt - der Austausch und das Geschütztsein - ganz anders als früher aufgefaßt und gelöst: Die funktionale Stadt rationalisiert diese Aufgaben und löst sie mit technischen Hilfsmitteln, die einfach gegen Bezahlung angeschafft werden können: Waren, Dienste und Informationen werden weniger Ausgetauscht" als durch Werbung angeboten und "abgeholt".

Schutz wird eine Angelegenheit von rechtlichen Ansprüchen, von räumlicher Trennung und Abschirmung, von technischen Sicherheitsmaßnahmen (bis hin zur gerichtlichen Verfolgung der Ansprüche und zum Einsatz von Wachpersonal und Videokameras). Der Markt, der öffentliche Raum, die Straße als Ort des Austauschs, als Ort des zivilen, zwischenmenschlichen Umgangs, der Parteinahme und des Geschütztseins durch Zivilcourage stirbt aus.

Wichtig ist: die beiden Modelle der vitalen Stadt mit dem öffentlichen Raum und der funktionalen Stadt mit der instrumentellen Aufrüstung lassen sich nicht in der Form eines Kompromisses vereinigen. Entweder ist die Straße ein Ort des zivilen Umgangs im Alltag - oder sie ist es eben nicht. Genau das ist auch der Grund, warum die Bestrebungen zur "Belebung" der funktionalen Stadt oder zu ihrer "Vitalisierung" durch ein städtisches Design kaum etwas anderes hervorbringen können als eine Simulation, eine simulierte Stadt. Etwas,

was den Bürgermeistern in Lyon und Bogota mit Sicherheit nicht genügen wird.

9. Öffentlicher Raum ist nicht zu haben ohne Gewerbe und Wohnen an seinem Rand, und zwar müssen diese Nutzungen in großer Mannigfaltigkeit präsent sein. Sich aufhalten im öffentlichen Raum gehört weder zum Arbeiten, noch zum Wohnen, noch zum Erholen, noch zum Verkehr, sondern ist ein Verbindungsglied zwischen diesen "Funktionen". Der Passant im öffentlichen Raum ist - selbst als Flaneur immer dabei, ein Ziel anzusteuern, sei es ein Cafe, ein Schaufenster oder eine Sitzbank. Früher war es selbstverständlich, daß in städtischen Vierteln überall Betriebe (ordentliche und weniger ordentliche) vorhanden waren. Die Stadt war zum übewiegenden Teil ein großes Mischgebiet. Heute ist es gerade umgekehrt. Heute ist die Stadt eine große Siedlung, in der Nutzungsmischungen überall verboten sind, wo sie nicht bereits von altersher bestanden haben. Betriebe, die in traditionellen Stadtvierteln noch vorhanden sind und dort Stadtleben produzieren, sind heute in Wohngebieten nur zum geringsten Teil überhaupt noch erlaubt.

10. Die Arbeit als Beschafferin von Arbeitsplätzen, Ausbildungsstellen, Dienstleistungen, Waren und Material, als Ziel von Passanten, als Ziel von neugierigen Jugendlichen ist aus der Stadt ausgewandert. Und sie wird weiter verdrängt durch die Centrifizierung der alten Vorstädte. Wir haben eine geradezu verrückte Situation. Immer mehr Haushalte suchen Wohnraum in stadtnahen, möglichst urbanen Lagen und verdrängen in diesen Lagen die KMUs, und gleichzeitig geht die Stadtentwicklung davon aus, daß sie den Menschen wegen der damit verbundenen Belästigungen die Präsenz einer Vielfalt von (ordentlichen und weniger ordentlichen) Unternehmen nicht zumuten darf. Sie plant deshalb immer noch segmentierende Gewerbeflächen in die freie Landschaft hinaus (für alle möglichen Zwecke, Bürokomplexe, Fertigungs- und Forschungsbetriebe, Universitäten, Fach-

märkte, was weiß ich. Hier zeigt sich die Angst vor der vitalen Stadt ganz deutlich. Dieses systematische Ignorieren des qualifizierten Mischgebiets als Instrument zur Lenkung der städtischen Entwicklung behindert ganz direkt die Entstehung neuer KMUs in den Städten. Dabei ist es doch so, daß die Arbeitskraft, die während der industriellen Hochphase aus dem Handwerk und den Diensten abgezogen wurde, jetzt, wo die Industrie sie in die Arbeitslosigkeit entläßt, nur dann eine Chance hat, wenn sie wieder dorthin zurückwandert, wo sie früher ihre Existenz hatte, in den Manufakturen und Dienstleistungen der Stadtviertel. Was wir als allererstes brauchen, ist eine wirkliche Neuentdeckung des MISCHGEBIETS. Nur das kann auch den öffentlichen Raum und das Stadtquartier wieder beleben.

11. Die "Individualisierung in modernen Gesellschaften" (um einen aktuellen Buchtitel zu zitieren) beinhaltet nicht nur den Rückzug in die private Nische, sondern zugleich einen Aufbruch in entsicherte Zustände. Das Stadtquartier verliert dabei die traditionellen Bindungen an Wohngenossenschaften, Traditionsvereine, örtliche Sportclubs und Kirchengemeinden. Aber dennoch bleiben die meisten Menschen - große und kleine - auf die zwischenmenschlichen Kontakte in einem städtischen Kommunikationsraum zwingend angewiesen. Meine These ist nun, wie bereits gesagt, daß die Stadt ihre Kommunikationsfunktion im Quartier nur noch über die Präsenz einer Mannigfaltigkeit an Arbeitsplätzen aufrechterhalten kann.

In diesem Zusammenhang muß man bedenken: Die Geschichte ist nicht am Ende. Demnächst werden immer mehr Menschen ihren Bedarf an Kommunikation und Unterhaltung in den Netzen des Global Village decken. Wird also die Multimedia Welt die funktionale Stadt verdrängen, so wie die funktionale Stadt die vitale Stadt bereits heute fast ganz verdrängt hat? Oder lösen gar teleworking, teleshopping, telebanking und telelearning die Verkehrsprobleme der funktionalen Stadt in Nichts auf? Oder führt das Spazierengehen in der virtuellen Welt zu einer Neuentdeckung des Kommunikationsraums im eigenen Stadt-quartier? Ziehen sich die Menschen vollends in ihre vier Wände zurück (das wäre letztlich die perfekte Aufrüstung der Städte) oder kommen sie zurück, um für ein Stadtquartier und seine Lebensqualität Partei zu ergreifen; das sind alles Fragen, die die Stadt und die Stadtplanung ganz akut betreffen, ohne daß sie heute schon beantwortet werden können.

12. Wir brauchen wieder öffentliche Räume, sagen die Bürgermeister großer Städte, in denen die Jugend gegen die Monotonie der Vorstädte mit unverhohlener Gewalt protestiert. Ich sage, das Weiterschaffen dieser öffentlichen Räume ist nicht so sehr eine Frage der künstlerischen Gestaltung als der Nutzungsmischung in dem Quartier, zu dem diese Räume gehören. Meine These ist, daß die Städte nicht immer noch mehr neue Wohngebiete brauchen (auch nicht, wenn sie mit ein paar Büros garniert werden), sondern sich endlich ganz intensiv um die Erhaltung und Neugründung von qualifizierten Mischgebieten mit einem kompakten städtischen Charakter kümmern müssen

13. Neue Mischgebiete werden die funktionale Stadt nicht total umkrempeln. Das ist auch gar nicht nötig. Ich stelle mir eine Stadt vor wie ein Schachbrett, bei dem die schwarzen Felder Mischgebiete und die weißen Felder Bereiche mit Monostrukturen sind. Auf einem solchen Schachbrett wäre von jedem Punkt der Stadt aus ein städtischer Kern mit öffentlichen Räumen und einer attraktiven gewerblichen Infrastruktur leicht zu Fuß für die ganze Stadtbevölkerung erreichbar.

Die vitale Stadt ist eine Stadt, in der nicht Ruhe und unbegrenzte Mobilität für die Qualität maßgebend sind, sondern städtischer Umtrieb, Entwicklungsfähigkeit, konsequente Nutzung der vorhandenen Ressourcen. Ein wichtiges Merkmal für die Vitalität eines Stadtviertel ist,

daß in ihm Kinder und Jugendliche auf der Straße sein können und dort ihren eigenen Lärm machen dürfen, ohne daß irgendwo panische Angst aufkommt.

Andreas Feldtkeller ist Leiter des Stadtsanierungsamts, Stadt Tübingen.

88

Kapitel Zwanzig (a)

Ist Urbanität planbar?

Gertrudis Peters

Die Feststellung Bazon Brocks "Urbanität ist nicht eine Qualität der Städte, sondern ihrer Bewohner" löste während einer Podiumsdiskussion der Architektenkammer Berlin unter Architekten und Stadtplanern heftige Diskussionen aus. Die provokante Aussage stellte Urbanität als Leitbild städtebaulicher Planungen scheinbar in Frage. Sollte sich die Stadtplanung vor dem Hintergrund einer zunehmend unberechenbar gewordenen Zukunft von ihrem sozialen Anspruch auf Gestaltung einer lebenswerten Umwelt lösen und die Stadtstruktur dem freien Spiel der Marktkräfte überlassen? Blieb das Bauen auf formal-ästhetische Regelwerke reduziert? Diese oder ähnliche Fragen schaffen eine produktive Unruhe, die uns veranlaßt, dem Begriff der Urbanität nachzuspüren.

Urbanität - eine Definition

Urbanität bedeutet eine kulturelle Qualität, die aus der ethnischen, sozialen und politischen Heterogenität der Bevölkerung, aus den daraus resultierenden Spannungen und den unterschiedlichen Lebensformen zugleich ein Klima produktiver Unruhe und gelassener Toleranz entstehen läßt.

Urbanität äußert sich im demokratischen Dialog einer städtischen Öffentlichkeit. Sie wird zur politischen Wirklichkeit, wenn es gelingt, aus dem Stadtbewohner, einem Konsumenten städtischer Dienstleistungen, einen Stadtbürger zu machen. Urbanität bedeutet daher mehr als Fassadenästhetik, Inszenierung der Alltagswelt und grobmaschige Funktionsmischung. Sie zielt auf Identifikation der Menschen mit der Stadt als eine Voraussetzung für ein demokratisches Bewußtsein, das über das Eigeninteresse hinaus sich dem Allgemeinwohl verpflichtet weiß und normative Werthierarchien gegen die Macht des Faktischen setzt.

Urbanität zwischen Planung und Wirklichkeit

Urbanität tauchte als Leitbild städtebaulicher Planung das erste Mal zu Beginn der 60er Jahre auf. Das Leitbild reagierte auf die allmählich sich abzeichnenden Folgen des Städtebaus der Moderne, der die Stadtgebiete in einzelne Funktionen unterteilte, sich gegen eine bauliche Fassung des Straßenraumes aussprach und stattdessen für die plastische Gliederung des Raumes durch freistehende Baukörper plädierte. Verdichtung und Verflechtung, so schien es, könne dem Mangel an städtischem Leben vor allen Dingen in den Wohnsiedlungen ein Ende bereiten. Doch trotz baulicher und sozialer Verdichtung erhöhte sich die Zahl der Kontakte nicht, ein Gemeinschaftsgefühl blieb aus. Die autogerechte Stadt leistete einer Verödung der Innenstädte weiteren Vorschub. Ihre Tertiärisierung und die damit verbundenen Verdrängungsmechanismen und Entmischungsvorgänge setzten sich fort.

Die Ölkrise Anfang der 70er Jahre verwies auf die Grenzen uneingeschränkten Wachstums. Ein dadurch gewandeltes Umweltbewußtsein führte bei den Planern nicht nur zu neuen Methoden des ökologischen und energiesparenden Bauens, sondern äußerte sich auch in einem neuen Stadtverständnis: Das Leitbild der Urbanität führte zu einer Rückbesinnung auf die Stadt als Lebensraum. Der Stadtteil sollte durch Wohnumfeldmaßnahmen revitalisiert werden. Der Block wurde als städtebauliches Element teuer gemischter Wohn- und Arbeitsformen rehabilitiert. Durch eine restriktive Verkehrspolitik sollte in den Innenstädten die Aufenthaltsqualität des öffentlichen Raumes zurückgewonnen werden. Es wurde versucht, der gesichtslosen City durch die Rekonstruktion historischer Bauten Identität zu verleihen.

Die 80er Jahre zeigten die zweite Seite dieser Medaille. Die großstädtische Öffentlichkeit drohte durch Verkiezung und Dezentralisierung zu zerfallen. Der Wunsch nach Überschaubarkeit und Kleinteiligkeit entlarvte sich als Feind des Urbanen. Die Auseinandersetzung mit der Geschichte des Ortes äußerte sich häufig in einer Geschichtsinszenierung. Den Planern schien jeglicher Glaube zu fehlen, aus sich heraus eine tragfähige, im Sinne von identitätsstiftende Lösung zu schaffen.

Die Freizeit- und Könsumgesellschaft forderte ihren städtebaulichen Tribut. Die Stadtplaner und allen voran die Kommunalpolitiker versuchten, diesen Erlebnishunger zu stillen. Museumsmeilen verkörperten Kultur als Imagefaktor. Eine zunehmende Ästhetisierung der Geschäftswelten schaffte das notwendige urbane Ambiente im Kampf um werbewirksame Standortfaktoren. Wo Randgruppen das Bild störten, wurden sie ausgelagert. Die Stadt wurde clean, aber fein, bei genauerer Betrachtung eine Perversion an Urbanität. Die Politik schien sich auf die Bedürfnisse einer ausgewählten Gruppe, der Yuppie-Kultur, zu konzentrieren. Ihre Vertreter galten als zukunftträchtiges Kapital der Stadt, als Innovationstrager der Gesellschaft.

Cybercity, City of Bits, Mikropolis bezeichnen einige, teils apokalyptische Vorstellungen. Gelingt es der Stadtplanung der 90er Jahre eine Vision der Stadt des 21.Jahrhunderts zu entwerfen? Verdichtung und Nähe wird durch steigende Mobilität und wachsende Möglichkeiten der Telekommunikation immer weniger räumlich definiert. Faceto-face Kommunikation wird ersetzt durch ein Zusammentreffen im virtuellen Raum. Urbanität - synthetisch erzeugbar?

Unabhängig davon, wie weit die neuen Medien in den einzelnen Lebensbereichen schon Anwendung finden, wir werden, so meine ich, uns weiter von dem Leitbild der Urbanität entfernen. Bei genauerer Betrachtung zeigte die Planungspraxis, dass die "Ordnungsversuche" der Stadtplanung sich auf dem Weg zur Urbanität eher als hinderlich erwiesen, sie teilweise sogar ins Gegenteil verkehrten. Die Ursachen dafür liegen weniger in der Diskrepanz zwischen einer gesellschaftlichen Dynamik und den Realisierungszeiträumen der Planung, sondern vielmehr in einem falschen Stadtverständnis aller Beteiligten und einem daraus resultierenden Mißverständis von Urbanität.

Fünf Thesen auf dem Weg zur Utopie

Der Planer kann dem Wesen der Stadt nur gerecht werden, wenn er Vielfalt und Chaos als wesentliche Strukturelemente akzeptiert. Die Erkenntnis aus der vergangenen Planungspraxis sollte nicht zu einer Kapitulation vor der komplexen städtischen Wirklichkeit, sondern eher zu einer realistischen Einschätzung des Machbaren führen. Seine Planung muß Spielräume eröffnen, die Wahlfreiheit des Städters erhalten und die Wandlungsfähigkeit der Stadt ermöglichen. Das bedeutet:

1. Urbanität braucht Pluralität der Lebensformen

Die Auflösung der traditionellen Familienstruktur und verändertes Rollenverhalten kennzeichnen heute den sozialen Wandel. Es herrscht scheinbar Stillschweigen darüber, welche Konsequenzen er baulich haben soll. Die Stadt kann nur dann ein Ort unterschiedlicher Lebensstile bleiben, wenn sie sich weiterhin als Experimentierfeld neuer Formen des Zusammenlebens versteht und ihnen geeigneten Raum gibt. Eine vorausschauende Wohnungsbaupolitik wird daher ihr Augenmerk im Neubau auf alternative Haustypen richten, deren Raumprogramm weniger funktional-hierarchisch gegliedert ist, sondern durch Variabilität differenzierte Beziehungsformen und Gruppengrößen ermöglicht.

Ungenutzte Flächen und Gebäude ohne direkten Verwertungsdruck bieten vielfach Nischen für das soziale Experiment. Sie stellen ein großes Potential für die Stadtstruktur dar, da sie Unterpriviligierten und Nonkonformisten Lebensraum und Entfaltungsmöglichkeiten bieten und so ein Neben- und Miteinander unterschiedlicher sozialer Situationen erlauben.

Die Forderung nach Pluralität der Lebensformen schließt neben den Bedürfnissen unterschiedlicher Sozial- und Altersstrukturen ebenso ein, den Lebensgewohnheiten anderer Kulturkreise Rechnung zu tragen. Eine neue Offenheit und Interessiertheit ist gefragt - eine Offenheit und Interessiertheit, die Integration nicht mit Assimilation verwechselt.

2. Urbanität braucht neue Formen der Mischung

Dieter Hoffmann-Axthelm schreibt in einem Beitrag der Stadtbauwelt zum Thema "Städte ohne Arbeit": "Eine Stadt, die den Bezug zur Produktion aufgibt und sich auf bloßes Umschichten und Verwalten verlegt, gibt sich ökonomisch, sozial und kulturell selbst auf."

Verschlankung und Flexibilisierung der Produktion, funktionale Differenzierung und Spezialisierung der Unternehmen bezeichnen nur schlagwortig massive Umstrukturierungsvorgänge des industriellen Sektors. Neue qualitative und quantitative Flächenansprüche entstanden sowohl auf der Seite der Endprodukthersteller als auch bei den Zulieferern. Begünstigt durch den Ausbau der Transport- und Kommunikationsnetze sowie dem preiswerten Baulandangebot des Umlandes, besteht derzeit die Gefahr, daß immer mehr neue Produktionscluster im suburbanen Raum entstehen und in den Städten sich häufig nur noch die Steuerungszentralen befinden. Zurückbleiben Industriebranchen im städtischen Kontext, deren "Revitalisierungs" konzepte sich einseitig an Wohnen und Dienstleistungen als profitträchtigste Nutzungen orientieren und somit den noch vorhandenen Bestand an Klein- und Mittelbetrieben immer mehr verdrängen.

Der Stadtplanung allein wird es nicht gelingen, dieser Tendenz entgegenzuwirken. Es ist jedoch ihre Aufgabe, die strukturellen Schwächen aufzuzeigen, die sich für die Stadt aufgrund der einseitigen Standortpolitik ergeben. In Zusammenarbeit mit Politikern und Investoren müssen erneut Trägermodelle diskutiert werden, die einen veränderten Umgang mit Bodenpreisen erlauben und eine differenziertere Nutzungsquotierung garantieren.

Die Forderung nach Re-Integration der produktiven Arbeit in das Stadtgefüge ist verknüpft mit der Forderung nach einer kleinräumigen Zuordnung von Wohnen und Arbeiten. Der Block und die Parzelle haben sich in der Vergangenheit als ein Ordnungsgerüst erwiesen, das auf vielfältige Weise Nutzungsmischungen ermöglichte. Gesellschaftlicher und wirtschaftlicher Wandel fand aufgrund der Veränderbarkeit der Parzelle seinen Ausdruck, ohne daß der städtischen Kontext verloren ging. Felix Zwoch schreibt ergänzend dazu: "...der Block ist die einfachste Form, die Dualität von kollektiver Ordnung und individueller Vielfalt im Stadtraum zu organisieren."

Block und Parzelle bieten meiner Meinung nach auch heute noch aktuelle Ansatzpunkte, um einer städtischen Nutzungsvielfalt Raum zu geben und veränderten Flächenansprüchen zu genügen. Die Berliner Stadtplanungspraxis zeigt derzeit leider auch, wie schnell die Potentiale eines solchen Ordnungsgerüstes sich ins Gegenteil verkehren können, wenn sie in ihrer strukturellen Eigenart verkannt und zum Regelwerk erklärt werden.

3. Urbanität braucht den unverwechselbaren Ort

"Die Welt ist überdeckt von einem einzigen Trude, daß nicht anfängt und nicht aufhört, nur Am Flughafen seinen Namen wechselt." - so Italo Calvino in seinem Roman "Die unsichtbaren Städte".

Trude ist leider nicht nur ein kühnes Phantasiegebilde des Autors, sondern wird immer mehr zum Spiegelbild städtischer Realität. Die derzeitige Stadtentwicklung in den neuen Bundesländern scheint mir dazu ein warnendes Beispiel zu sein. Der Reisende in Calvinos Roman fragt sich letzendlich: "Warum überhaupt nach Trude kommen? ...Und wollte schon wieder abreisen." Identifikation der Bewohner mit ihrer Stadt setzt einerseits Unterscheidbarkeit voraus, andererseits Symbole und Zeichen, die emotional besetzbar sind. Urbanität braucht daher den unverwechselbaren Ort als

materiellen und immateriellen Ausdruck einer einmaligen Mischung von Vielfalt und Ambivalenz städtischer Lebensformen.

Planung muß das Spezifische des städtischen Kontextes analysieren, um entscheiden zu können, welche Qualitäten erhalten, verstärkt oder neu entwickelt werden sollten. Die Kenntnis historischer Bezüge und die Auseinandersetzung mit dem Vorhandenen bieten die Chance, einen über das Programm hinausgehenden Entwurfsansatz zu finden. Spuren geschichtlicher Entwicklungsprozesse sind hilfreich bei der Suche nach Identität eines Ortes. Sie sollten jedoch nicht zu nostalgischer Übernahme von Strukturelementen verleiten, sondern Interpretationshilfen liefern. Colin Rowe und Fred Koetter fordern in ihrem Buch "Collage City" eine "Zweideutigkeit der Lösung". Das bedeutet, die eigentliche Herausforderung der Planung liegt darin, ortsbezogene, kontextuelle Lösungen zu entwickeln, ohne auf eine zeitgemäße Architektursprache zu verzichten. Der unverwechselbare Ort, die Identifikation der Bewohner mit der Stadt setzt meiner Meinung nach eine "Tradition" der Gegenwart als unverzichtbares Zeitzeichen voraus.

4. Urbanität braucht Sensibilität ihrer Akteure

Die Nutzungsqualität der Stadt und ihr gebautes Bild sind das Ergebnis des Zusammmenspiels zahlreicher gesellschaftlicher Kräfte. Der Architekt und Stadtplaner kann den Rahmen gestalten, in dem sich unterschiedliche Lebensmodelle entwickeln können. Hierbei stößt er jedoch oft an die Grenzen des Politisch-Durchsetzbaren, WirtschaftlichTragfähigen und Planungsrechtlich-Erlaubten.

Urbanität als Leitbild braucht daher ein urbanes Bewußtsein der Entscheidungsträger, das sich u.a. einer sozialgerechten, offenen Planung verpflichtet fühlt. Es setzt den demokratischen Dialog voraus, fordert eine kritische Distanz zu vorhandenen Planungsinstrumenten und den Mut aller Beteiligten, unkonventionelle Lösungen umzusetzen.

Ein so verstandenes urbanes Engagement, das einer Polarisierung und damit verbundenen verschärften Ausgrenzung einzelner Kulturen und Lebensformen entgegenwirkt, muß immer wieder neu eingefordert werden, auch von den beteiligten Bürgern. Regulativ für das Gelingen von Urbanität ist daher die politische, kulturelle und soziale Verantwortung jedes einzelnen und die darin zum Ausdruck kommenden allgemein verbindlichen Werte und Konventionen.

5. Urbanität braucht Zeit

Die Aneignung des Stadtraumes durch die Bewohner wird zeigen, ob aus arrangierter Heterogenität Urbanität wachsen kann.

Urbanität braucht Zeit. Der Erfolg neuer Stadterweiterungsgebiete wird meiner Meinung nach im wesentlichen davon abhängen, wie fehlerfreundlich und damit umbaubar sich die Planung erweist.

Berlinische Urbanitiät

Ich möchte Ihnen am Beispiel von Karow-Nord, dem derzeit größten Wohnungsbauprojekt der BRD, eine Interpretation des Leitbildes Urbanität aus der Berliner Planungspraxis vorstellen. Größenordnung und Realisierungszeiträume dieses Projektes legen den Verdacht nahe, die Stadtentwicklung hat die Schwelle vom organischen Stadtwachstum und qualitativen Stadtumbau zur schlüsselfertigen Stadtproduktion überschritten. Hat Urbanität unter diesen Vorzeichen überhaupt eine Chance?

Gertrudis Peters ist Architektin in Berlin.

Chapter Twenty (b)

Can Urbanity be Planned?

Gertrudis Peters

Bazon Brock's comment that "urbanity is not a quality of cities, but rather of their inhabitants," caused heated debate among architects and urban planners at a panel discussion of the Chamber of Architects in Berlin. The provocative statement seemed to cast doubt on whether urbanity can be an ideal of urban design. Should urban planning relinquish its social responsibility to design an environment worth living in at a time in which the future is becoming increasingly unpredictable? Should it leave urban structure to the free play of market forces? Can design be reduced to formal aesthetic principles? These questions or similar ones create a productive uncertainty that leads us to investigate the concept of urbanity.

Urbanity - a Definition

Urbanity signifies a cultural quality that allows a climate of productive restlessness and at the same time complaisant tolerance to arise from the ethnic, social and political heterogeneity of the population and from the resultant tensions and diverse lifestyles.

Urbanity finds expression in the democratic dialogue of an urban public. It becomes political reality when it succeeds in making the city dweller, the consumer of urban services, a citizen of the city.

Urbanity therefore means more than the aesthetics of facades, the dramatization of the mundane or the crude amalgamation of functions. Its goal is the identification of individuals with the city as a pre-condition for a democratic consciousness that perceives beyond it own interests a responsibility to communal well-being and counterposes normative hierarchies of value against the power of immutable matters of facts.

Urbanity Between Planning and Reality

Urbanity became an ideal of urban planning for the first time in the early nineteen-sixties. The ideal was a reaction to the gradual appearance of consequences of the modern style of urban design. which subdivided neighborhoods according to individual functions, which spoke out against an architectural framework for streets and demanded instead the plastic division of space through free-standing buildings. It was thought that increasing population density and circulation would suffice to eliminate the deficit of urban life, above all in the residential neighborhoods. But in spite of the heightened social and architectural density, the number of contacts

did not increase; a feeling of community was absent. The city designed to accommodate automobiles contributed to the decay of city centers. The rapid growth of the services industry and the consequent mechanisms of displacement and the homogenizing of areas continued.

The effects of the oil crisis in the early seventies indicated the limitations of unrestricted growth. The transformed environmental consciousness that resulted led planners to new methods of ecological and energy saving construction and expressed itself in a new understanding of the city: The ideal of urbanity caused a return to the theme of the city as a space for living. The neighborhood was to be revitalized by taking into account the residential environment. The block as a unit of urban design was rehabilitated as an element of new, mixed ways of living and working. Public spaces were to win back their attractiveness for those who use them through restrictive policies governing traffic in the city centers. The attempt was made to lend the faceless city identity by reconstructing historical edifices.

The eighties revealed the other side of the coin. The confrontation with the history of specific sites frequently expressed itself in a staging of history. Planners seemed to lack all faith in being able, by themselves, to find workable solutions that helped articulate the identities of places.

The society of leisure and consumption demanded its architectural tribute. The urban planners and above all the local politicians tried to satisfy this appetite for adventure. Stretches of museums embodied culture as a matter of image. The expanding role of aesthetics in business environments created the necessary urban ambiance in the contest for marketable features of sites. Fringe groups were displaced whenever they disturbed the picture. The city became clean but fine, on closer examination a perversion of urbanity. Politics seemed concentrated on the needs of a select group, the yuppies. Their representatives were considered the capital of the city, the innovators of society.

Cybercity, City of Bits and Micropolis are a few of the partly apocalyptic conceptions of the future. Will the urban planning of the nineties succeed in sketching a vision of the city of the 21 st century? Because of increasing mobility and the growing capabilities of telecommunication, density and proximity are less and less often defined spatially. Gatherings in virtual space are taking the place of face-to-face communication. Can urbanity be created synthetically?

Regardless of the extent to which the new media are already being applied in individual areas of experience, we will, in my opinion, move farther away from the ideal of urbanity. On close examination, one sees that the practice of urban planning proved that its "attempts to create order" were obstacles on the road to urbanity and sometimes even had the opposite effect. The causes of this lie less in the discrepancy between social dynamics and the deadlines for realization of planning than in the participants' faulty understanding of the city and the resultant misunderstanding of urbanity.

Five Theses on the Road to Urbanity

The planners can do justice to the essence of the city only when they accept variety and chaos as essential structural elements. The experiences of planning practice should not lead to a capitulation before complex urban realities, but rather to a realistic appraisal of what can be accomplished. The planning of the latter must allow for contingencies, it should preserve the urban resident's freedom of choice and enable the city to be mutable. That means:

1. Urbanity Requires a Plurality of Life-Styles

Today's social transformation is characterized by the dissolution of the traditional family structure and a shift in roles. Not a word is spoken today of the consequences this should have for construction. The city can remain a place of diverse life-styles only if it can continue to be considered a place of experiment for new ways of living and can allow these the appropriate space. Circumspect policies of apartment construction will therefore devote attention to alternative types of housing when considering new buildings. The spatial programs of those types will permit differentiated forms of relationships and group-sizes through variability, rather than being functionally-hierarchically divided.

Unused lots and buildings that are not in immediate jeopardy of being exploited often offer niches for the social experiment. They represent a large potential for the structure of the city, because they offer the underprivileged and the non-conformists living space and opportunities for self-realization and thus allow diverse social situations to co-exist in proximity of each other.

Just as the demand for a plurality of life-styles includes the needs of diverse age groups and social classes, it requires that the living habits of other cultural groups be taken into account. A new openness and a new interest are needed--openness and interest that do not confuse integration with assimilation.

2. Urbanity Requires New Forms of Mixture

In an article for the "Stadtbauwelt" on the subject of "cities without work", Dieter Hoffmann-Axthelm writes: "A city that neglects its relation to production and is content to act as distributor and administrator neglects itself economically, socially and culturally."

Slimming down production and making it more flexible, functional differentiation and the specialization of the company--these concepts suggest massive processes of restructuring in the industrial sector. The producer of the end-product as well as the providers of raw material have caused demands for land to arise that are qualitatively and quantitatively new. In part because of the expansion of transportation and communications networks, there is a danger that more and more clusters of production facilities will arise in the suburbs and that mostly only the administrative centers will remain in the city. Industries would then be left fallow in the city; the plans for their rejuvenation, which focus on housing and services as the most profitable sectors of the economy, would exert more and more pressure on the stock of small and mid-sized companies.

Urban design will not-succeed in neutralizing this tendency by itself. It is, however, obliged to call attention to the structural weaknesses that result for a city because of one-sided policies that induce businesses to locate operations there. Discussions including politicians and investors must be renewed, so that financing methods allowing different ways of meeting real-estate prices and differentiated quotas of land use can be guaranteed.

The demand for a re-integration of productive labor into the structure of the city is connected to the demand for smaller distances between places of work and residences. The block and the parcel of land have in the past proven themselves to be structural elements that permit mixtures of uses in many ways. Social and economic change found expression through the mutability of the parcel of land without the urban context having been lost. On

this subject Felix Zwoch writes, "...the block is the simplest form that organizes the duality of collective order and individual variety in the urban area."

In my opinion, the block and the parcel of land still offer points of departure for the problems of making room for a variety of land uses and satisfying changed demands for land. Unfortunately, the urban design in Berlin also demonstrates how quickly the potential of such a structural framework can reverse the effects intended when its structural particularity is not recognized and it is propounded as a set of rules.

3. Urbanity Requires the Inimitable Place

In his novel, "The Invisible Cities", Italo Calvino wrote, "The world is covered by a single Trude that neither begins nor ends but only changes its name at the airport."

Trude is unfortunately not only a bold product of the author's imagination; more and more often it reflects urban reality. The contemporary development of cities in the new German states seems to me to be an ominous example of that. The traveler in Calvino's novel finally asked, "Why go to Trude at all? . . And already wanted to depart again." The identification of residents with their city presupposes on the one hand the ability to distinguish the city from others, and on the other hand symbols and signs that can have emotional content. Urbanity therefore requires the inimitable place as a material and non-material expression of a unique mixture of the diversity and multi-valuedness of urban forms of living.

Planning must analyze what is peculiar to the urban context in order to decide which qualities should be kept, strengthened or developed anew. The knowledge of historical relationships and the confrontation with the given offer the opportunity of finding an approach extending beyond the programmatic. Traces of historical processes of development are helpful in the search for the identity of a place. They should not, however, result in adoption of structural elements for reasons of nostalgia, but rather deliver interpretive assistance. In their book, "Collage City", Colin Rowe and Fred Koetter demand an "ambiguity of the solution". That means that the actual challenge of planning is to develop place-specific, contextual solutions without dispensing with a modern architectural language. The inimical place, the identification of residents with the city presupposes, in my opinion, a "tradition" of the present as an indispensable sign of times.

4. Urbanity Requires Sensibility on the Part of its Protagonists

The quality of land use in the city and its architectural reflection are the result of the interaction of numerous social forces. The architect, as urban designer, is able to shape the framework in which diverse models of life can develop. In this attempt, however, he often reaches the limit of what is practicable politically, economically viable and legally permitted.

Urbanity as an ideal therefore requires on the part of the decision makers an urbane consciousness that feels an allegiance to, among other things, a socially just, open planning. That consciousness presupposes a democratic dialogue, and it demands a critical distance to traditional methods of planning and the courage of all participants to follow through with unconventional solutions.

Active partisanship on behalf of this sort of urbanity, which opposes a polarization and exacerbated marginalization of individual cultures and forms of living, must be insisted upon again and again by the residents concerned as well as others. What governs the successful emergence of urbanity is therefore the political, cultural and social responsibility of each individual and the values and conventions that find expression through it and are generally binding.

5. Urbanity Requires Time

The appropriation of the urban environment by the residents will show whether or not urbanity can grow from pre-arranged heterogeneity. Urbanity requires time. The success of new areas of urban expansion will depend essentially, in my opinion, on the degree to which planning is able to respond to mistakes and so remain capable of revision.

Urbanity in Berlin

Using the example of Karow-Nord, currently the largest apartment construction project in the Federal Republic of Germany, I would like to present an interpretation of the ideal of urbanity from the planning practice of Berlin. The scale of the project and the deadlines set for its realization lead one to suspect that the urban development has crossed over a threshold from organic urban growth and qualitative urban restructuring to urban prefabrication. With omens such as these, does urbanity have any chance at all?

Gertrudis Peters is an architect in Berlin, Germany.

zation points where paths cross: "micro-worlds" around which city life is focused.

This network is held together by city design structures, by the social and cultural life, by networks of small enterprises, the economics of the city, by active network of communications and activity spaces. These are the criteria for the quality and daily practicality of cities and of planning. The problem is not the electronic media but the lack or the imperceptible disappearance of such communication zones, of such a public city culture. The multimedia initiative of the City of Tubingen attempts to bring together city structures with new as well as traditional media. Planning, politics and administration have to take care of the distri-bution of resources and access rights, of the creation of large structure, and the essential regulations; urban communication zones and micro-worlds come into concrete existence only as a consequence of planning processes and strategies which are aimed at facilitating communication and responsibility among citizens. The integration of the various commu-nication spheres, traditional as well as new ones -- mixed use and the integration of the various forms of the private and the public spheres are the essential tasks ahead for contemporary and future city planning.

Gabriele Steffen is Erste Bürgermeisterin for the City of Tübingen, Germany.

Kapitel Einundzwanzig (b)

Virtuelle Realität oder konkrete Stadt?

Gabriele Steffen

Die Zukunft der Stadt - die virtuelle Stadt?

Auf dieser Tagung diskutieren wir Modelle für eine künftige Stadt. Aber vielleicht gehört in Zukunft die Stadt schon der Vergangenheit an? Einige Belege für solche Prognosen: Wenn die Entwicklung der Wissenschaft, der Technik und der Wirtschaft nicht mehr von uns verlangen, persönlich am selben Ort anwesend zu sein, um zusammen zu arbeiten, ist das Zeitalter der europäischen Städte endgültig vorbei - so Jean-Louis Arnaud. Wo elektron-ische Medien die optische Ordnung des Gedruckten und seine Denkstrukturen (u.a. Straßen, Geraden, Hierarchien, Kategorien) ablösen, ist auch das Ende der Rolle des Städters oder Bürgers gekommen - so Lewis Lapham. Und Florian Rötzer: "Virtuelle Städte mit allen Funktionen, die auf Distanz ausgeführt werden können, werden die realen Städte mehr und mehr überlagern und vermutlich zu einer stärkeren Adaption an Formen der Tele-Existenz fiihren".

Was haben wir solchen Prognosen eigentlich entgegenzusetzen? Wachsende Kriminalitäts-furcht wird mit dem Einsatz privater Sicherheitsdienste beantwortet. Auf die **wahrgenommene Jugendgewalt reagiert die verschreckte Öffentlichkeit mit dem** Ruf nach mehr Finanzmitteln und pädagogischen Experten. Stadtkultur erschöpft sich vielerorts im Bereitstellen von *events* für den "urbanen Freizeitmenschen". Für den weiter expandierenden Autoverkehr werden fast ausschließlich technische Lösungen gesucht, Verkehrsberuhigung für Straßen, die von Menschen längst entvölkert sind, oder Telematik zur intelligenten Steuerung des Verkehrs durch eine immer weiter auseinanderdriftende Stadtlandschaft. Im Zuge von Haushaltskonsolidierung und Verwaltungsmodernisierung - den Themen, die die Städte derzeit am meisten beschäftigen - wird die Stadt zunehmend als "Konzern" oder als "Dienstleistungsunternehmen" begriffen; die Bürgerinnen und Bürger werden zur Kundschaft, die optimal bedient werden soll.

Diesen Beispielen ist eines gemeinsam: Das eigentlich Städtische wird aufgegeben. Die Lösungsversuche reduzieren die Stadt auf jeweils eine einzige Funktion, anstatt sie als komplexes, vielschichtiges Gefüge zu begreifen. Wo urbane Qualitäten abgeschrieben sind, bieten Multimedia, virtuelle Realitäten und Cybercity perfektere Lösungen: Virtuelle communities, Reisen, Märkte, Museen, Bibliotheken und Unternehmen, die piazza virtuale, ja auch virtuelle Polizei und virtuelle Banküberfälle lassen die konkrete Stadt wie ein historisches Relikt erscheinen, vielleicht noch - wie heute viele öffentliche Verkehrsmittel - als Restkategorie für Alte, Arme und andere, die nicht ans Mediennetz angeschlossen sind. Telecommuting und Haus-Tele-Dienst für Ältere lösen auch das Problem der Pendler oder der Alten-betreuung. Bernd Streich hat es kürzlich in der Bauwelt sehr zurückhaltend formuliert: "Ein wenig drängt sich der Eindruck auf, als wenn diejenigen, die sich um die räumlichen und ästhetischen Konsequenzen kümmern müßten - Architekten und Stadtplaner -, in einer kontemplativen, ja etwas ängstlich anmutenden Erstarrung verharren". Und noch weniger haben sie diese Konsequenzen ins öffentliche Bewußtsein gebracht: Wie anders ist es zu erklären, daß im Multimedia-Bericht der Landesregierung Baden-Württemberg auf über 170 Seiten das Thema "Stadt" überhaupt nicht vorkommt?

Die Wirkung und Verbreitung von Innovationen hängt von einer Vielzahl von Einzelentscheidungen ab und vom gesellschaftlichen Bedarf, auf den sie reagieren. Abstinenz, blinde Euphorie angesichts der neuen technischen Möglichkeiten (und Kritik allenfalls an der Widerständigkeit der Menschen, die sich nicht schnell genug darauf einlassen) oder kulturpessimistisch-arrogante Ablehnung einer Technologie, von der man nichts versteht, lassen sie aber zu einer scheinbar natur- oder schicksalhaften Entwicklung werden. Eine Erfindung wie das Auto wurde zur stadtzerstörerischen Innovation erst durch die ungehemmte private Nutzung, ermöglicht und vorangetrieben durch zahlreiche Weichenstellungen in Politik, Recht, Wissenschaft, Verwaltung und Planung - und durch die Städte, die ihr die Straßen, früher dem tatsächlichen Gemeingebrauch vorbehalten, kostenlos überlassen und dazu eine aufwendige Infrastruktur und Verwaltung aufgebaut haben. Die Kosten wurden dabei (auch von allen mir bekannten Stadtkämmerern) ebenso ausgeblendet wie die soziale, kulturelle und fast religiöse Bedeutung dieses - bekanntlich begrenzt tauglichen - Verkehrsmittels.

Was macht denn die Qualität und die Faszination der virtuellen Stadt aus? Das Internet, eigentlich zu anderen Zwecken geschaffen, dient heute vor allem dem Austausch, der direkten Information. Der Zugang ist freiwillig, billig, kennt keine Klassen- und Rassenschranken, keine Grenzen, Urheberrechte und zentralen Entscheidungsinstanzen, keinen Unterschied zwischen Profis und Amateuren, zwischen Machern und stummem Publikum. Es ist selbstregulierend, kreativ, mit einem gehörigen Anteil an Anarchie, bringt Privatheit und Öffentlichkeit zusammen, ermöglicht immer neue Erfahrungen - in miteinander geteilten Räumen, Ideen-, Handlungs-, Erlebnis-, Spielräumen, einem Patchwork aus sich überlagernden, vernetzten Inseln. Die virtuelle Gemeinschaft mit Mailinglists, Newsgroups, ChatChannels bietet Anonymität und

Vertrautheit, Begegnungen mit Fremden und Bekannten, gegenseitige Hilfe und Teilhabe, passive, aktive wie "beiläufige", auch für Kinder oder Alte. Man kann "dabeisein", man muß nur losspazieren: Es gibt Klatsch, Nachrichten, Liebe, Schauspiel, Forschung, Kuriositäten, Botschaften, Erlebnisse für Augen und Ohren, Gegenstände und Dienstleistungen, die der virtuelle Markt feilbietet, Arbeit, Leben, Gemeinschaft. Kurz: das, was urbane Stadträume bisher geboten haben. "Urbane Lebensweisen werden nicht abgebrochen, sondern im Datennetz fortgesetzt", so Florian Rötzer. Die Metaphorik ist der realen gebauten Welt entlehnt: die digitale Welt hat Daten-autobahnen, Home-Verzeichnisse, Fenster, Briefkästen, Zimmer, Bühnen für Handlungen mit multiplen Akteuren, Host und Server; so wird sie bewohnbar gemacht, ermöglicht es, sich in ihr häuslich einzurichten. Eine Ergänzung der Stadt, eine Fortsetzung der Stadt mit anderen Mitteln, ein Gegenentwurf zur Stadt - oder ein Gegenentwurf zu den Städten, wie wir sie heute vorfinden?

Die konkrete Stadt: Urbane Situationen und urbane Quartiere

Zur Sicherung der Umwelt, der Lebensbedingungen von Tieren und Pflanzen existiert mittlerweile ein ausdifferenziertes Instrumentarium. Für die Lebens- und Arbeitsumwelt von Menschen, die soziale und kulturelle Seite des Städtebaus gibt es weder eine eingeführte Begrifflichkeit, eine anerkannte Professionalität und Lobby noch ein dem "ökologischen" Stadtumbau vergleichbares griffiges Konzept. Ginge es nur um die Bewahrung eingezäunter Reservate, könnte man analog zum "Biotop" den Begriff "Soziotop" verwenden. Besser ist es, von urbanen Situationen und von urbanen Quartieren als gemeinsamen Kommunikations- und Handlungsräumen für Stadtmenschen zu sprechen. Ich möchte 10 Merkmale nennen, die diese von anderen Situationen oder Siedlungsformen - etwa Wohnsiedlungen oder Gewerbegebiete unterscheiden.

1. Der lebendige Straßenraum, in dem eine Vielfalt von Menschen zu unterschiedlichen Zeiten aus unterschiedlichen Gründen anwesend und zu Fuß unterwegs ist und zu dem alle, unabhängig von Alter, Herkunft oder Beruf, freien Zugang haben. Nur die Anwesenheit von Menschen zieht andere an. Auch das Gefühl von Sicherheit hängt davon ab, daß viele Menschen auf der Straße sind.

2. Komplexe face-to-face-Interaktion im Medium der Stadt. Die Menschen begegnen sich auf der städtischen Bühne leibhaftig und in einem Netzwerk komplexer, direkter Beziehungen, die - im Gegensatz zu den unausweichlichen, verbindlichen, engen und manchmal beengenden privaten Bindungen in Familie, Nachbarschaft oder auch pädagogischen Einrichtungen - vielfältig, unverbindlich und auch flüchtig sind, aber ganz bestimmten Spielregeln folgen.

3. Vielfalt, Komplexität und Überlagerung der Aktivitäten und Funktionen. Arbeiten und Muße, Austausch, Versorgung, Teilhabe am öffentlichen Leben und der Stadtkultur überlagern und durchdringen sich gegenseitig und sind auch baulich miteinander verbunden durch mehr-dimensionale Orte und Räume, die unterschiedliche Bedeutungsschichten haben: das Schwimmbad wird morgens zur Altenbegegnungsstätte, der kleine Supermarkt zum Jugendtreff.

4. Wirklichkeit des Stadtlebens: Die ungefilterten, konkreten sinnlichen Eindrücke der Stadt, wechselnd je nach Jahres- oder Tageszeit und Wetter, sind - im Gegensatz zu medial vermittelten oder in Form von *events* simulierten - wirklich und haben Ernstfallcharakter, weil in der Stadt Menschen wirklich leben und arbeiten - wirtschaftende Menschen mit Verantwortung und Beziehung zum Quartier und nicht nur "urbane Freizeitmenschen".

5. Integrationsfähigkeit und Wahlfreiheit: Urbane Situationen und Quartiere sind zumindest prinzipiell offen für Nicht-Zugehörige und Fremde, können Unterschiede verkraften, basieren aber auf Freiwilligkeit der Beziehungen. Sie erlauben Nähe und Distanz.

6. Konfliktfähigkeit: Konflikte, Ungeplantes, Schrilles, Chaotisches, "Anstößiges" gehört zur Stadt. Sie ist robust und kann auch Störungen aushalten - vom brüllenden Baby bis zum Lärm des Handwerkers.

7. Öffentliche Gebäude und Einrichtungen haben nicht nur eine einzige, sondern auch eine soziale und kulturelle Funktion. Sie stehen für die Stadt als gemeinsam, im Austausch mit anderen organisierte, vergesellschaftete Lebensform und für die "öffentliche Ordnung", die Gesamtheit der Regeln für das Verhalten der einzelnen in der Öffentlichkeit. Die öffentlichkeit ist auch in symbolischer Form - z.B. durch Haltestellen, Wegweiser, Telefonzellen - oder durch öffentliche Personen - Polizistinnen wie Müllmänner, Marktmeister und Briefträgerinnen - präsent.

8. Bürgerschaftliche Verantwortung: Solche öffentlichen Personen sind zugleich informelle "Ortswächter", die das Quartier im Auge haben, ebenso wie der Kioskbesitzer oder die alte Frau am Fenster. Soziale Kontrolle ist - im Gegensatz etwa zu Neighbourhood-Watch-Programmen - ein Nebenprodukt anderer Aktivitäten. Bürgerschaftliche Verantwortung meint aber noch mehr: sich für ein in der Umgebung spielendes Kind verantwortlich fühlen, auch wenn es nicht das eigene ist; Anzeichen von Gewalt oder Vereinsamung frühzeitig wahrnehmen; sich als Bürgerin und Bürger für das Gemeinwesen engagieren; Zivilcourage.

9. Autarkie und Interdependenz - Zentren und Netze: Urbane Situationen und Quartiere können sich weitgehend selbst regulieren. Sie sind aber nicht selbstgenügsam, sondern sind in ein dichtes und vielfältiges Netz von Austauschbeziehungen eingebunden. Sie sind polyzentrisch.

10. Geschichtlichkeit und Veränderbarkeit: Menschen interagieren nicht nur im Raum, sondern auch mit dem Raum. Urbane Quartiere bestehen nicht aus "Architektur für Architekten", sondern sind ein Gemeinschaftswerk. Sie bieten die Möglichkeit, sich das eigene Haus und die eigene Umgebung symbolisch oder tatsächlich aneignen zu können; dazu gehört auch die Möglichkeit, auf Entwicklungen Einfluß zu nehmen. Sie können sich - anders als die Monostrukturen etwa von Einfamilienhaus-Wohnsiedlungen, Supermärkten oder Bürobauten - wechselnden Anforderungen anpassen. Geschichte ist, oft im ganz wörtlichen Sinne, ablesbar, als Übereinandergeschichtet-Sein, als Spuren der Auseinandersetzung mit der Stadt.

Mikrowelten: Kommunikationsräume für Stadtmenschen

Die vorgeblich rationale Planungsphilosophie der getrennten Funktionen beruht auf dem Lebensentwurf einer Minderheit, dem des aushäusig berufstätigen, alleinverdienenden Familienvaters. Der Lebensalltag etwa berufstätiger Singles oder Alleinerziehender, von Hausfrauen, Kindern, jobbenden Jugendlichen, Rentnern, Arbeitsuchenden oder Wohnungslosen ließ sich noch nie in diese Funktionen aufteilen. Erst recht gilt dies für den komplexen Alltag voller Koppelungsaktivitäten in einer künftigen Medienwelt, in der sich die Grenzen zwischen Arbeitsplatz und Zuhause, Arbeit und Spiel, Unterhaltung und Bildung weiter auflösen werden. Viele der heute interessanten Existenzgründungen finden sich nicht in anachronistischen Bürobauten, sondern sind klein dimensioniert, brauchen an Fläche zunächst kaum mehr als das Studentenzimmer oder den Keller mit Platz für Rechner und Fax, später vielleicht ein Gemeinschaftsbüro; sie sind auf Kommunikationsräume und auf die richtige Mischung aus Bildungseinrichtungen, Dienstleistern, öffentlichem Leben, Kultur und Verwaltung angewiesen. Qualifizierte Telearbeitsplätze führen zu neuen Anforderungen an das soziale und kulturelle Lebensumfeld. Ein steigender Anteil der Arbeit wird sich - wenn es auf das Elend der Arbeitsgesellschaft überhaupt eine Antwort gibt - in neuen Formen abspielen: Eigenarbeit, Arbeit im dritten Sektor, Arbeit für die Stadt. Postmoderne Lebensentwürfe gleichen einem Patchwork unterschiedlicher Identitäten, die einen Ort des Aushandelns brauchen. Funktionen wie "Wohnen" und "Freizeit" greifen da nicht mehr.

Die künftige Stadt ist nicht als "Stadt der Insellösungen" zu konzipieren, die jeder einzelnen Funktion und Nutzung einen getrennten Bereich oder eine spezielle Einrichtung zuweist, sondern als Gefüge oder Netz miteinander verbundener, sich überlagernder alltäglicher Kommunikationsräume für die unterschiedlichen Stadtmenschen. Dies ist in erster Linie der öffentliche Raum im eigentlichen Sinne. Ferner Räume mit einem unterschiedlichen Grad an Öffentlichkeit: öffentliche Einrichtungen, die trotz ihrer eindeutigen Zweckbestimmung mehrere Funktionen erfüllen, nach bestimmten Regeln - Satzung, Hausrecht - öffentlich zugänglich sind: Rathaus wie Polizeiposten, Stadtteilschulen und Büchereien, Feuerwehrhaus und öffentliche Bedürfnisanstalt; private Nutzungen für die Öffentlichkeit, das, was man zum Alltag braucht: Bank, Post, Kioske, Läden (vom türkischen Gemüseladen bis zum Copy- oder Computer-shop, in dem Alte ebenso Rat und Hilfe finden wie ganz junge Computerfreaks), Werkstätten, Reparaturbetriebe, Kino, Wasch-salon, Imbiß, vielfältige Dienstleister (vom Fahrkartenverkauf bis zum Elektronik-Recycling), die lebens-notwendigen "Third places" zwischen Wohnen und Arbeit, von denen Ray Oldenburg spricht - Café und Kneipe, Frisör und bürgerschaftlichen Treff; private, aber ins Quartier eingebundene Arbeitsstätten und Wohnungen, die miteinander durch ein Netzwerk von Beziehungen verbunden sind; ambulante Dienstleister, die ins Haus kommen von Einkaufsservice und mobiler Fußpflege bis zum Computer- oder Fahrrad-notdienst. Dazu gehören schließlich Knoten oder Kristallisationspunkte, "beiläufige" Gelegenheiten - wo man anhalten kann oder wo sich Wege kreuzen: Abzweigungen und Treppen, Bänke und öffentliche Uhren, Haltestellen und

Telefonzellen, Aushänge, Auslagen, Schaufenster, Spielmöglichkeiten, Punkte des Gedenkens und vieles andere.

Es geht, zusammengefaßt, um Mikrowelten, um die sich städtisches Leben zentriert. Die Dichte, Vielfalt, Robustheit und Vitalität dieses Netzes von Kommunikations- und Handlungsräumen, von Mikrowelten macht die Qualität und Alltagstauglichkeit von Städten und Planungen aus. Es ist wesentlich dafür, daß Zusammenhang, Austausch und Zivilcourage in der Bürgergemeinde überhaupt entstehen können. Zusammengehalten wird dieses Netz durch das soziale und kulturelle Leben, durch Netzwerke aus kleinen Unternehmen, Beziehungen zwischen Dienstleistern und ihren Kundinnen und Kunden, durch das Handeln aktiver Bürgerinnen und Bürger für das Quartier und im politischen Raum, durch gemeinsame Regeln, durch eine öffentliche Verwaltung, insgesamt durch die städtische Öffentlichkeit. Verankert ist es in städtebaulichen Strukturen, die für Dichte, Vielfalt und Vitalität sorgen.

Prüfsteine für die Brauchbarkeit einer Stadt können ganz banal sein: Wo findet man Schutz vor einem plötzlichen Regenschauer oder einem Verfolger, wo kann man ein menschliches Bedürfnis erledigen? Was sieht man, wenn man eine Stunde lang aus dem Fenster schaut? (mehr als auf dem Bildschirm?). Sie können aber auch sehr Wesentliches ansprechen: Wo treffen Kinder und Alte aufeinander? Kann man als Bürgerin oder Bürger die Stadt aktiv mitgestalten (mehr als in der virtuellen community?) - oder wird man nur als lästiger Bittsteller begriffen oder als Kundschaft, die es zu bedienen gilt?

Nicht die elektronischen Medien selbst sind das Problem, sondern das unmerkliche Verschwinden dieser Kommunikationsräume, die Zersplitterung des Öffentlichen im "Konzern Stadt", der Verlust der städtischen Öffentlichkeit. Die Erfindung des bewegten

Bildes hat nicht nur zum Rückzug an den heimischen Fernseher geführt, sondern auch - und zwar zuerst - das Kino geschaffen, einen Kristallisationspunkt der Stadtkultur; und die Innovation der maschinenbetriebenen Verkehrsmittel hat nicht nur das Auto als privaten Rückzugsraum, sondern vorher öffentliche Orte wie Bus und Bahn, Haltestellen und Bahnhöfe entstehen lassen. Es kommt darauf an, ob es gelingt, öffentliche statt nur privater Nutzungen zu etablieren und neue Verbindungen zwischen Medien und Stadtstruktur zu schaffen. Maarten Hajer hat von "Orten des Konsenses" gesprochen, die sich in gemeinsamen Regeln und Praktiken manifestieren, im kollektiven Bewußtsein konstruiert werden und die Idee des Bürgerseins in den Mittelpunkt rücken: Dazu gehörten gemeinsame soziale Räume ebenso wie Zeitschriften, "die einer ständigen Debatte über die Stadt Raum geben, lokale Fernsehprogramme oder ein Nachrichtennetz im Cyberspace, das sich mit besonderen Elementen städtischen Lebens befaßt".

Mit der Initiative "Multimediastadt Tübingen?" versuche ich in unserer Stadt, Stadtisches mit neuen wie traditionellen Medien zu verbinden. Ein ständig wachsender Gesprächskreis hat die Vielfalt der bereits vorhandenen Aktivitäten, der spin offs und anderer innovativer Existenzgründungen, der Formen von Telearbeit deutlich gemacht; oft sind sie getragen von besonders engagierten, an Städtischem interessierten Menschen. Ein Stadtporträt des Stadtarchivars regt internationalen Austausch an, an Projekten wie Standortinformationsdienst oder Citynetz arbeiten Akteure aus Wirtschaft, Kultur und Sozialem, am Projekt "Medien und Stadtstruktur" Stadt und Universität. Das Projekt Internet-Café soll einen öffentlichen Ort schaffen und die Teilhabe für viele ermöglichen. Neue Qualifizierungsmöglichkeiten werden konzipiert. In eigener Initiative hat die Lokalzeitung, das "Schwäbische Tagblatt", einen interaktiven Tübinger Sommerkrimi - auch über das Internet - gestartet, der zu einer ungewöhnlich lebhaften Beteiligung und Kreativität geführt hat; die Diskussion über Multimedia bekommt zunehmend Raum. - Vor allem aber versucht die Stadt Tübingen, nicht nur eine lebendige Stadt zu bleiben, sondern durch die Entwicklung des ehemaligen französischen Garnisonsgeländes einen auch in Zukunft brauchbaren neuen Stadtteil zu schaffen.

Aufgabe des Städtischen ist es, auch in Zukunft für Austausch, zivile Handlungsmöglichkeiten und Geschütztsein zu sorgen in einer Stadt der sich überlagernden Kommunikationsräume, einer konkreten Stadt vitaler Mikrowelten. Was so harmonisch klingt, wird noch zu Konflikten führen: Es geht um die Neuverteilung der Welt, um Wegerechte, Zugangsmöglichkeiten und Berechtigungen (für wen und zu welchem Preis?), um Grundversorgung und Grundrechte, um öffentliches und privates Interesse, um Geld und um die Verteilung von Ressourcen - und um die Rolle der Städte. Es geht um Parteinahme für die Stadt und um Absage an das Stadtmodell der Insellösungen wie an weitere Mono- und Mega-strukturen, die die urbanen Kerne ausbeuten und letztlich zu Reservaten machen. Und es geht um neue Planungsprozesse und Strategien, die auf die *Ermöglichung* von Austausch, dichter Kommunikation und ziviler Verantwortung ausgerichtet sind. Die Verknüpfung der unterschiedlichen Kommunikationsräume auf engem Raum - traditionelle wie neue, virtuelle wie konkrete -, der Nutzungen von Privatem und Öffentlichem ist die wesentliche Aufgabe gegenwärtiger und künftiger Stadtplanung. Die Kunst wird sein, die Vitalität und Existenzberechtigung dieser unterschiedlichen Kommunikationsräume zu erhalten und immer neu zu beweisen.

Gabriele Steffen ist Erste Burgermeister in der Stadt Tübingen.

Children in the City

Kinder in der Stadt

Chapter Twenty-Two

Children and Their Needs

Arno Gruen

We want livable cities for our children. How do we achieve this when we are unclear as to the meaning of livable? Wherever we look we see the increasing brutalization of children: the violence, the drug consumption, the unemployment, the loss of compassion. Overall we have to deal with the diminishment of dignity, of the innermost identity, of humanity itself.

In her talk at the 8th International "Making Cities Livable Conference" in Siena, Suzanne Crowhurst Lennard mourned the loss of the "communal eye". She correctly diagnosed that it is the loss of shared experience, through which we lose the fundamentals of our humanity, our capacity for compassion. The construction and new organization of our cities can make an important contribution to the reversal of this development. It is vital to provide a compassionate existence, the key to being human.

The core of our common task is complex. "More livable" does not only mean building cities which suit humanity, but also promote humanity through the capacity to respond to this environment. This creates an interaction between the buildings we create and people's internal reactions to these which are mirrored in their actions. We would fail to fulfill our duty without the realization that man is more than a reactionary machine. Rather man's internal forces are realized in actions and states. Therefore, in order to create more livable cities we must recognize the needs of our children and build cities which fulfill their needs. However, our perception of what a child and person are comprised of, act as an obstacle. Our

perceptions have been created in order to serve the ideologies of the those in power and the organization itself, not the people. Let us examine the development of a child from birth:

The disposition of a child's own self already begins to develop during gestation in its mother's womb. The inner realm of expectations, determined by diffuse as well as precise perceptions and rhythms, exist in the context of the embryo and child as their preparedness to react to the world. From the very beginning of its life, this preparedness is modulated through the ability of every organism to react to gentle stimulus. For the most part we fail to recognize this reaction, since the huge popularity and scientific prominence which are given to the threatening aspects of evolution has clouded the true meaning of gentle stimuli for the phylogenese leading to cooperation. This is how the current consciousness came to be, wherein survival is understood to be the result of strengths and strong stimuli.

Therefore, we understand the development of our children as determined through learning reality in the form of confrontation and a clear realization of danger. Thus the retreat from danger being the decisive quality of every ontology. We also determine this in how we build. In reality, however, the possibilities for retreat do not dominate the development of a life form, rather the possibility to react to gentle stimuli does. That which further confuses this occurrence in our culture is the identification with authority demanded by society. This leads to a reversal of the current state of stimulation. We are beginning to turn toward the

Chapter Twenty-Three

The Good City for Children

Henry L. Lennard

Ignoring Children

There is a growing concern that children are being ignored in the design of cities; that city officials, planners, architects and developers do not consider children when they make decisions that have far-reaching consequences for their lives. Yet, all decisions about the physical and social character of cities affect the lives of children, whether in the design of urban places, transportation policies, or the aesthetic qualities of their urban environment. Children are the citizens of tomorrow. One day, the future of the world's cities will be their responsibility.

Psychoanalysts have described how the behavior and attitudes of significant persons are internalized by the child. Neglectful or uncaring parents diminish the growing child's self esteem. But just as inattention or brutality in the child's psycho-social environment affects development unfavorably, so can the monotony, indifference and placelessness of the physical environment leave a lasting impact on children's mental, social and emotional development. As Rene Dubos warned, "Young people raised in a featureless environment are likely to suffer from a kind of deprivation that will cripple them intellectually and emotionally."

The urban environment of too many cities and towns represents a form of sensory deprivation for children, with little to engage their curiosity, fantasy or affection.

Children need environments that address them, that challenge them, that provide people, events and objects to attract their attention, to observe and think about. Buildings with intricate facades, or with historic references, do just that. Streets and squares with fountains and accessible public art also invite participation and attention. Attractive shop and street signs can arouse an interest in reading in the preschool child.

Events such as street entertainment, festivals and markets also are a source of perpetual interest and fascination to children and young people.

The City as a Playground

There are essential experiences that cities must provide for children. Children need a variety of places, preferably connected to each other, where they feel at home; places to explore alone or with each other. They need to be able to move about their city by foot or by public transportation when a little older. Cities with a network of pedestrian places and streets are, of course, ideal. There are hundreds of European cities where this has become possible for children, at least in the center of their cities. Unfortunately, the mobility of children is restricted in most North American cities.

At its best, the city as a whole, and all of its resources, should be available to children. In some cities easy access is limited to parks and zoos. Such settings, while important, may often become a means of segregating children. Playgrounds, too, are of limited usefulness as social learning settings. Rudofsky challenges widely accepted planning policies when he states that playgrounds, with their provision for "planned play are a diabolical invention for retarding the child's development." While unrestrained traffic endangers children's play on the street we agree that sandboxes, concrete bunkers and metal cages are not a substitute for playing on the street where children can be part of the everyday life of the city. Ideally, the whole city should be usable as a playground.

Important also for children are activities and events in the city that draw their attention, and engage their interest and fantasy, such as impromptu entertainers, clowns, mimes, puppet shows and musical performances. At these occasions, children are joined with their families, familiar and unknown persons, in a common experience. Where children experience pleasure, others enjoy seeing children experience pleasure as well!

The Public Realm as Teacher

It is essential for children to observe the range of human beings who make up their city, young and old, poor and well to do, of diverse social background and origin; to observe people engaged in different activities, at work and at play and in casual or intense conversation.

Children learn about human relationships by observing how friends relate; how adults talk to visitors or strangers; how they express tenderness or show pleasure in each other's company.

Children must learn to show interest and attention to others. The learn to do this by observing adults showing interest in each other, and in them. They must learn to look, and not to "look away".

Children need to experience themselves as part of the social life of their city, being recognized, and respected. Children need good models to develop their own skills and competency in relating to the fellow inhabitants of their city.

It must be made possible for children to gain access to all areas of their cities. Only if children encounter and get to know their fellow citizens, will they be socialized into their community as full-fledged members. Children growing up today are very unskilled in human relationships because so much of what needs to be learned cannot be learned only within the family or school context.

The opportunity to be in public shapes the development of useful attitudes and emotions. Children who have observed others take responsibility for each other learn to experience positive emotions towards their fellow human beings. As Jane Jacobs puts it: "People must take a modicum of public responsibility for each other even if they have no ties to each other…"

Such functional social behavior cannot be learned from using computer technology and participation in the Internet. To act caringly and responsibly, children and young people need to experience <u>models</u> of such behavior; they must witness <u>adults acting</u> in caring and responsible ways in a variety of settings and towards all kinds of fellow human beings.

To the philosopher, Martin Buber, the wish of every person for confirmation is the basis of social life. For Buber, humanity only exists where this capacity unfolds. Children and youth in the public realm need to be valued and affirmed by others, and not experienced as

113

a nuisance or threat. Social functions and roles where children and youth receive affirmation and respect from adults must be rediscovered and reinforced. Young people still perform such valued functions in traditional community events and festivals in a number of cities and towns. The public realm is indeed a wonderful teacher about the human world!

Meaning in the Urban Environment

It is also important for children to live in a physical environment that makes sense.

During the past few decades, researchers have noted the "meaningless" quality of communication among families with a mentally ill member. Behavior is often unrelated and lacks continuity. One family member introduces an idea or subject, only to find it wholly disregarded by the others. The conversation of family members exhibits a fragmented quality that has been described as a "word salad". Children raised in such communicational environments become confused and experience a sense of meaninglessness.

Living in the urban environment of many cities and towns might well be compared to growing up in a dysfunctional family. Developers and architects construct buildings often irrespective of the character of surrounding buildings or the tradition of the city or town in which they are placed. The dialogue among buildings, that in traditional cityscapes echoed one another in scale, choice of materials and in building elements, is now characterized by fragmentation and discontinuity. Buildings and the spaces created between them rarely represent an "ensemble"; that is, they do not relate to each other in such a way as to make a meaningful whole.

However, some architects celebrate the creation of "urban shock". "The fragmentation and dislocation produced by the scaleless juxtaposition of highways, shopping centers, high rise buildings and small houses is seen as a positive sign of the vitality of urban culture.

While all city inhabitants are exposed to the organization and appearance of cities and towns the effect on children is more profound! Children must visualize their city in order to negotiate its streets and places. Their internalized portrait of the city has become one of disconnected and fragmented shapes. The city has taken on the character of a schizophrenic environment! It is difficult to develop a sense of meaning in a human or physical landscape that does not make any sense.

Traffic planners rank high among those who have unwittingly contributed to the confusing and fragmented appearance of cities. Traffic arteries divide different areas and neighborhoods of many cities and towns and limit mobility and access to children.

The child's freedom to explore, to satisfy curiosity about the urban world, is largely determined by the extent to which the streets and public spaces are safe for children to explore alone and with friends. Inhospitable streets dominated by traffic, and difficult to negotiate, deny children access to the common world.

Function of Public Places for Children

Perception and reality form a vicious cycle. Because the public realm is perceived as dangerous, it is avoided by many of the cities' inhabitants, and subsequently is abandoned. This conception of the public realm too often forms the basis for the work of planners, architects, developers – and city officials.

Suzanne H. Crowhurst Lennard

Negative images held by city inhabitants about each other <u>cannot</u> be maintained where there is a great deal of contact among inhabitants;

where there are lively public places; where the public domain offers many opportunities for a flourishing social life; where children share urban public spaces with adults; where people are known, or at least are familiar to each other!

The greater the sense of community, the more events where all city-dwellers participate, the more difficult it becomes to maintain paranoia about one's fellow citizens!

In North America and on the periphery of too many Western European cities, too little attention is paid to maintaining or creating public places. In older American cities, many have been destroyed or neglected. What is often promoted as a benefit to the public is a poor substitute for genuine public places. As a result, very few good things happen in the public realm to change the perception. The streets and plazas characteristic of most North American cities do not generate the favorable experiences that city dwellers in other countries take for granted.

It would be difficult to frighten the Sienese or Venetians into abandoning the pleasures of their numerous public community events that involve all segments of the population. Nor would the inhabitants of Munich or Freiburg forgo the delight of their daily visits to farmer's markets and contacts with friends, strangers, and vendors on these market errands; nor would the inhabitants of Antwerp be dissuaded to flock afternoons and evenings to their public streets and squares to enjoy coffee, a meal and the sociability of their fellow citizens.

In those and the centers of many Western European cities, children still enjoy much greater freedom and autonomy. They are not always watched or warned against strangers, though they are often unobtrusively monitored by familiar adults.
But being present with their fellow citizens at such occasions reinforces a sense of belonging and trust. Consequently, the public world is not perceived as dangerous for children.

The Good City for Children

To assure children's affection, interest and participation in their cities and towns, the "ideal" city for children would require some of the following:

- Social and physical arrangements that promote trust and a sense of justice, such as public places where the presence of known adults guarantees protection and safety for children, and where the design of the public place enhances contact among persons of different ages and social backgrounds.

- The opportunity to observe people of diverse backgrounds, adults and children engaged in a variety of work activities and social relationships.

- Presence of adults who take responsibility not only for their own children but for other children as well.

- A network of safe, traffic reduced or traffic-free places and streets, that allow children to explore their neighborhoods and cities.

- A legible and meaningful urban environment that can easily be traversed by foot or public transportation.

- Accepted and valued roles for children and youth in community events and rituals.

- Living and work settings located close together so that children and parents may have access to each other during the day.

- An urban environment that exemplifies the best features of public social life: paying attention, showing interest, civil negotiation of differences of opinion and outlook.

- Exposure to public events that generate surprise and delight, including street entertainment.

- Occasions and celebrations that reinforce a sense of history and interest in the community and its traditions.

- Visually interesting characteristics of the built environment (e.g., varied textures, colors, materials, shapes and forms, including public art) that arouse interest.

- Contact with nature in all its forms – water, earth, trees and plants, animals, birds and insects – so that children can understand and learn to love nature.

Henry L. Lennard is Chairman of the Advisory Board of the IMCL Council.

Chapter Twenty-Four

How to Provide Good Cities for Children and Youth

Peter Novak

Academic people usually start with definitions. They would primarily ask, what does the concept "good city" mean, and soon they would be involved in discussing the platonian relationship of "good" and "beautiful", e. g. of aesthetic and moral values. But is that really the starting point of our efforts? I don't think so. We could and should learn so much from philosophy, sociology, also from theology and from other sciences, but keep in mind special and real situations of good or not so good cities for children and youth.

Therefore, proceeding from special and real issues we will ask: Who can, right now, improve what, so that this urban environment will be improved, where these children and young people are now not living well? Inevitably, solutions of problems of the good city for children are dependent upon:

(1) engaged persons having sensible and close contact to the real problems;

(2) city administrators and planners up to the position of mayors who are willing and able to collaborate seriously with representatives of relevant neighborhoods;

(3) the willingness of the members of special neighborhoods to collaborate with each other, with more or less professional helpers, and with people of the administration, this way

taking actively part in decisions concerning their own affairs.

I am arguing for the idea of the city as a living organism involving the interdependence of every structure and function of this living being, like housing, working, industry, traffic, taxes, public realm, including ads, cultural life, etc.

But in order to change actual conditions, where actual things are going wrong, you have to take into account the special perspectives people have of their own situation. And these views are not holistic ones. Admitted, a good physician is treating a patient as a whole person, but very often he should not renounce the advice and collaboration of a specialist. I myself have no problem to confess, that I am a wholist, but this does not prevent me from appreciating the necessary competence of specialists. The members of each neighborhood are specialists concerning their own affairs.

Regarding different neighborhoods of a city as something like a micro world, the special structure of the population of each, its economic situation, its facilities of education, health and culture, public squares etc. represent different and special physical as well as social environments for favorable and unfavorable socialization of children, of youth, and of adults.

As one may see, the approach to the good city for children, I prefer, is something like a piecemeal technology; this term goes back to the philosopher Sir Karl Popper. This piecemeal technology implies, e.g. children's early rehearsal of participation in decision making regarding their special affairs. The city where I am living has introduced a parliament of children. The advantage is, that the young children between 8 and 14 learn that e.g. the city hall is also their house, where they will be heard by the city administration and by the mayor, where they can take part in decision making regarding their own problems. The disadvantage is, that children of the middle classes are more likely to take advantage of this opportunity.

Of more importance, perhaps, are neighborhood related projects, e.g. with the aim of health promotion of children and youth, essentially including their active participation in the project work. Health is here understood in a broader sense. These projects in my country are supported by regional working groups of health promotion and funded by the state government. When also research is emphasized, those projects are sometimes funded within the framework of integrative public health research, funded by the federal government nationwide with more than 50 million Deutschmark for 3 years.

According to the piecemeal technology approach, these projects are working on micro system levels, and I want to give you an example to make concrete their advantages, but also their limitations.

In a city of 30.000 inhabitants in southern Germany, a team of 2 female social workers had identified one neighborhood as quite unfavorable for socialization of children and youth. By means of talks and interviews with the people of this neighborhood and by means of participant observation they found that:

1. A good many of the children and young people were living in cramped housing conditions where no space for privacy was available.

2. The family situation was characterized by a high percentage of single mothers with 2-3 children, and during day time for two-thirds of the children and young people no adult contact person was available all day.

3. Regarding school education and vocational training many of the children and young people had negative experiences and were feeling like drop-outs or were really drop-outs.

4. Small scale criminality and drug abuse of young people was already a problem. Policemen and their cars were frequent but unwelcome visitors.

After these situational analyses and with the mutual interest within the neighborhood the two ladies designed an intervention project which is now funded and has been started.

First of all they organized within the neighborhood a round table concerning the topic "playgrounds in our neighborhood as fields of experience and learning".

Interested people of the neighborhood were invited to participate, above all young people. Children of the neighborhood were showing slides, demonstrating what is already available and what is lacking, e.g., motor car free areas, playgrounds independent of weather, footpaths between house and playgrounds, a cafe as an attractive meeting point for youth, opportunities and facilities for creative organization of leisure time activities.

The next step was to identify young target groups interested and willing to cooperate within sub-projects, like the so-called playground project and the girls/boys project, the last one including group work on "health and our body". Further sub-projects are aimed at.
I want to suggest that:

(1) in order to promote the idea "good city for children and youth" we need many realistic micro system or piecemeal technology approaches and

(2) that these piecemeal technology approaches are in themselves not only of high complexity but have as well holistic aspects that require efforts at integration.

Moving from the micro system level of neighborhoods of a city to the macro system level of a municipal council or a local administration, we cannot deny that what is going on in the neighborhood of a city is, on the one hand to be assessed as an autonomous process, but on the other hand needs to be related to what is happening in the city as a whole. Too often this task of integration will be misunderstood as a process of setting priorities.

And there is another problem: Not only the immediate physical and social environment has an impact on the socialization of children and young people, but also general ideological interpretations of the situations where they perceive themselves. I only want to mention the xenophobia and persecution of foreigners among young Germans, specifically in the new countries of East Germany. These young people are confronted with the poverty and decay of their cities and with mass unemployment they had never experienced before. And at the same time they are urged to adapt to a very important component of western society, that is to competition which implies aggressiveness and even brutality.

Moreover, they are faced with mass immigration from Eastern, African, and Asian countries to which they have never been accustomed.

I think here as well, the piecemeal technology I argued for is needed, but it must also be complemented by social and political intervention on a broader scale.

Peter Novak is Head of the Department of Medical Sociology at the University of Ulm, Germany.

Chapter Twenty-Five

Visions and Beyond

Gianni Longo

When I started fifteen years ago, the field of civic consensus building was in its infancy. The few communities in the United States that had mobilized themselves to conduct visions, Chattanooga and Kingsport in Tennessee, San Antonio in Texas, Scottsdale in Arizona, had done so at the initiative of residents. They were motivated by the apparent inability of local governments to make decisions in step with the community's aspirations, and by the desire to take charge of decisions affecting their future. Today, visions have become an accepted methodology to build consensus and are widely used by planning and transportation agencies. They have also become an integral component of comprehensive and long-range plans adopted by municipalities, counties and regions.

The proliferation of vision programs (initiated by citizens, government or business) has led to inappropriate methodologies, disappointing results, and confusion about the program's goals. Many of the visions I have observed are either top-down, involving a small group of civic leaders, or bottom-up, more like a traditional grass-roots effort. They fail to achieve the balanced participation that lends a broad and lasting base of support to this kind of program. Well-planned visions, on the other hand, have attained exciting and far reaching results that stretch our present understanding of what communities can achieve.

I will take the opportunity of this presentation to clear up this subject. Using examples drawn from the experience of *Vision 2000* in Chattanooga (the first vision I designed in 1984) and

from the many other communities I have worked with, I will define what a vision is and review some general principles that seem to contribute to their success. I will also look at what results we can expect from a well-conceived and well-implemented consensus building process.

Let me start with a simple definition. A vision is a community strategic planning process. It is designed to bring together residents and leaders of a community to discuss common issues and to develop shared goals for the future. These goals can guide a community to develop programs in areas such as economic and community development, transportation, education, culture, the natural and man-made environments, recreation, race relations and human needs. In addition to establishing goals, a vision should also make concrete suggestions on how to achieve them.

A vision can be implemented in a neighborhood, in a city, or in a region. In fact, it can be applied to any complex organizational structure. When implemented in conjunction with a comprehensive plan, its goals define the technical elements of that plan. In a regional process, they illustrate the policies and strategies that the region's local governments need to implement.

Typically, most visions start with an idea gathering phase that consists of large and small facilitated meetings attended by hundreds of residents. The ideas (thousands of them) gathered this way are first organized into categories. They are then distilled into progressively more specific products like vision statements, goals, development scenarios, and funding and implementation strategies. The entire journey from random ideas to a coherent vision is conducted through meetings open to the public.

This common thread runs through most visions. The final program of a vision, however, differs from city to city and should consider local political, environmental and social characteristics. Other variables typically include: the design of the meetings, the duration of the process, who is invited to participate, the involvement (or lack of involvement) of governmental entities, and the budget. Whenever possible, I like to involve local residents and leaders in the design of a program to tailor it to the specific needs of a community.

There are three major challenges that make the design of a vision process a complex task. The first and largest challenge is in the general decline in civic involvement that seems to plague most communities. A successful vision requires participation of hundreds of residents. To get them there, we must reach beyond their frustration, apathy and general disenchantment. Many residents have been involved in past participation efforts and disappointed by them; many do not believe they can make a difference; many do not trust that the ideas they have will be treated fairly; many have become disenfranchised and have no history of civic involvement; and many believe that things are just right the way they are.

Next to the decline in citizenship is the skepticism and sometimes hostility of urban professionals, special interest groups and decision makers. Their involvement is also critical to the success of a vision. Yet, they regard civic involvement as a time consuming and costly

annoyance, or worse, an intrusion in their areas or expertise to be avoided at all costs.

A third challenge is in the scope and duration of the solutions we seek. A vision is about the future and often it looks at a far horizon of 30 and even 50 years. The mind of the participants has to be moved creatively from the constraints of the present to the possibilities of the future, with an understanding that a vision defines a path over time and not a hypothetical end-state.

Finally we must face the fact that urban problems are complex and require complex solutions. A vision challenges the notion that "experts know better" and assumes that those who live in a community are in fact experts. To tap that knowledge and understanding in ways that lead to concrete results, however, we need to create a safe meeting environment, a place and a format where experts and residents can listen and talk to each other.

To meet those challenges, I apply five general principles that give coherence and integrity to the design of a vision. First, **a vision must be inclusive and reflect the diversity of a community or region.** No stone should be left unturned in involving all members of a community, including those groups that exist at the edges of the civic dialogue or tend to be isolated and disenfranchised. No opportunity must be overlooked to provide the place and the format for positive, creative dialogue. This inclusiveness is what lends lasting legitimacy and power to a vision by establishing ownership of the results, support for the implementation, and consistency in decision making over time.

A vision must deal with all issues facing a community (for example, economic development, job creation, the environment, recreation, education, social life, etc.), and should be an intuitive and informed process. It should link issues across specialized professional and institutional boundaries. It should provide a complex, all inclusive and far reaching view of the future.

A vision must be community driven. Even when it is done at the request of a governmental agency, it should be led by a steering committee that can lend legitimacy and visibility to the process. The steering committee must reflect the economic, social and racial make-up of the community, including business and institutional leaders, elected officials, representatives of special interests, community groups, and residents.

All phases of a vision must be carefully designed and facilitated to lead participants toward more concrete and specific decisions and to achieve a right balance of creative visioning and reality, of intuition and information. The design of the vision must include: marketing, to create general awareness of the program's goals; outreach, to ensure broad participation; logistics, to attend to the specific needs of the meetings; and formats, to ensure that the meetings are safe, structured, accessible, consistent, and fun.

A vision must lead seamlessly into implementation. The participation and involvement of the community leadership and the excitement and good will of residents must be harnessed for the implementation of projects and programs. Without a commitment to implementation, a vision is incomplete and will not result in positive change.

A vision implemented following these five general principles is an effective tool for establishing decision making by consensus in cities. It is a key to get things done and to build better communities. It will save time, money and community dissent by gaining support for projects and initiatives before they even start. It will create a positive investment climate as developers like the stability, continuity and commitment to implementation expressed by the vision. Finally, it will provide an incentive to elected officials to make tough decisions with an understanding that consensus is there to support those decisions.

How successful can a vision really be? It can be very successful. Visions have a demonstrated economic impact on the cities that have implemented them. Consider for example *Vision 2000* in Chattanooga, that I designed and implemented with Chattanooga Venture, a citizens' group. *Vision 2000* has been the catalyst for the transformation of that Southern town into one of the country's most progressive communities. In a period of ten years, 223 projects resulting from the vision have generated $793 million in investments and created a total of 1,500 new permanent jobs and 7,000 temporary construction jobs. Of those $793 million, the public sector spent one dollar for each three invested by the private sector.

But Chattanooga is not alone, and the applications of the vision methodology are many. The following is a brief review of cities and regions I have worked with. In Dublin, one of Ohio's fastest growing municipalities, the vision has given elected officials and planners the foundations on which to build on solid grounds the city's comprehensive plan. In Collier County, Florida, a vision is developing a framework for regional decision making on contested issues such as growth, environmental protection, and the quality of life of those who already live there. In the Washington, D.C. area, *Getting There*, possibly the country's most ambitious regional vision program, has brought into a structured dialogue some of the country's most entrenched special interest groups. A promising common ground is emerging from that dialogue that will affect the region's long-range transportation plans.

The traditional mixed use shop/house, Venice

Suzanne H. Crowhurst Lennard

Nutzungsmischung: ein Baustein der "kompakten Stadt"

Klaus Brake

Vor 30/40 Jahren gab es eine sehr engagierte und kritische Auseinandersetzung mit unseren Städten und den Lebensbedingungen dort. Ihre Stimme erhoben z.B. Jane Jacobs (Tod und Leben amerikanischer Städte), Alexander Mitscherlich (Die Unwirtlichkeit unserer Städte) oder auch Jobst Siedler (Die gemordete Stadt).

Was prangerten sie an?

Eine Entwicklung unserer Städte, womit das Leben darin immer stärker geprägt wurde durch eine Desintegration der sozialen und räumlichen Zusammenhänge von Stadt (-Leben); im Einzelnen war vor allem gemeint räumliche Trennung von Arbeit/Wohnen/ Freizeit; "erzwungene Mobilität"; Segretation; Monotonie; unstabile Nachbarschaften; soziale Kälte; Desinteresse; unkommunikative öffentliche Räume; Gefahren; Verschwendung und Armut etc..

Wofür plädierten sie?

Für eine Stadt, die (auch) von ihrer Flächennutzungs- und Baustruktur her ein in vieler Hinsicht vor allem kommunikatives Leben darin ermöglicht; im Einzelnen hieß das besonders: reich an Kontakten, Anregungen, Auseinandersetzungen; Strukturen von (wie H. P. Bahrdt es damals formuliert hatte:) "...Öffentlichkeit + Privatheit"; verschwenderisch mit räumlicher Nähe von Unterschiedlichem - aber sparsam mit Zeit- und Materialverbrauch; "Urbanität" i.w.; etc..,

Jahrzehntelang ist nichts davon (bzw. dafür) **ingang** gekommen. **Jetzt, in diesen Jahren, mehren sich die Stimmen derer, die in diesem Sinne einen Orientierungswechsel der Stadtentwicklung fordern** - sehr energisch, sehr fundiert (und durchaus auch "offiziell" bereits, etwa in der bundesdeutschen Städtebaupolitik)

In dieser Bewegung treffen sich vor allem zwei Linien der Kritik, der Forderungen, der Visionen:

- da wären zum einen (nach wie vor) die "Urbanisten", und zwar mit vielen immer noch (bzw. um so mehr) zutreffenden Argumenten - und bestärkt noch durch die aktuellen Probleme im Umgang mit allem Fremden (ob das unsere neue "Armut im Reichtum" betrifft oder Immigranten): es geht um die (sozial/kulturell) integrierte Stadt!

- und da wären zum anderen (und eher neuerdings); die "Ökologen" ihre Argumente für eine Bau- und Stadtpolitik, mit der dem Verlust (und der Verschwendung) von natürlichen Komponenten unseres Lebens Einhalt geboten wird, werden inzwischen noch bestärkt durch die nicht mehr zu ignorierenden Probleme globaler Ressourcen - und Umweltzerstörung: hier geht es um die - in jeder Dimension - "nachhaltige Stadt"!

Wie diese - integrierte nachhaltige - Stadt aussehen würde (bzw. lebbar wäre), das wissen wir noch nicht so ganz genau. Wir haben aber Vorstellungen davon, welche Elemente von Stadtstruktur wohl hilfreich sein könnten, einer solchen Stadt näher zu kommen. In der Diskussion sind vor allem:

- qualifizierte Dichte der Bebauung (statt Zersiedlung)

- Polyzentralität (und Vernetzung) (statt monozentrischer und hierarchischer städtischer Siedlungsstrukturen)

- örtlich/regionale Kreisläufe von Ressourcen und Stofftransporten (statt eindimensional und räumlich weit ausgreifender Kooperationsstrukturen wie das Beispiel des Johghurtbechers zeigt, der im Zuge seiner Produktion halb Europa durchreist, oder das selektive Einkaufen).

- räumliche Nähe wichtiger Komponenten des alltäglichen Lebens (statt "erzwungener Mobilität")

- kleinräumige Nutzungsmischung (statt funktionaler räumlicher Arbeitsteilung/ Spezialisierung/Trennung).

Manche dieser Elemente werden bereits im Zusammenhang diskutiert, und zwar im Leitbild der "kompakten Stadt" der Stadt der kurzen Wege (so z.B. das Motto einer Studie der deutschen Bundesregierung, bzw. ein Ziel-Begriff der laufenden Münchner Stadtentwicklungsplanung).

Als ein strategisch besonders wichtiger "Baustein" einer (nachhaltig integrierten, d.h.) **lebenswerten Stadt erscheint mir dabei die** "Nutzungsmischung"; sie ist auch unmittelbar verknüpft mit einigen der anderen Elemente veränderter Stadtentwicklung.

Was braucht diese städtebauliche Konzeption ganz konkret? Auch vorbehaltlich aller noch notwendigen Klärungen/Forschung geht es ganz elementar um eine kleinräumige Mischung, d.h. der Nutzungen/Aktivitäten: Wohnen/ Arbeiten/Freizeit/Versorgen jeweils untereinander auf der Ebene Quartier, Block oder Parzelle.

Das bedeutet im Klartext aber eine ziemlich radikale Abkehr von der uns gewohnten Strukturierung und Zonierung von Stadt, nämlich von einer Funktions-Entmischung, wie sie sich in den vergangenen 50-100 Jahren hat durchsetzen können, und zwar im Zuge von vor allem zwei Entwicklungen:

- das eine ist der Wirtschafts- und Sozialstrukturwandel, wie ihn hochentwickelte industrielle Marktwirtschaften - insbesondere nach 1900 - vollzogen haben, und wobei ein betriebliches Prinzip der funktionalen Arbeitsteilung (und Spezialisierung) optimiert und - zur Wahrnehmung "komparativer Standortvorteile" - auch auf die Lokalisierung von Aktivitäten Übertragen worden ist - und damit auch auf die Flächennutzung. Ob im Verhalten von Unternehmen oder auch von privaten Haushalten bzw. von Städten, es gilt das gleiche Motto: hier (d.h. in der (großen) Stadt) hochwertig Arbeiten und Leben, aber die Mülldeponie hinterm Stadtrand, die Naherholung im weiteren Umland, den Absatz im Hinterland und die Niedriglohnarbeit in der Peripherie (vom ländlichen Gebiet in Deutschland bis nach Ost-/Südeuropa oder noch weiter weg).

- die andere Entwicklung manifestiert sich in einer Stadt-Planungs-Philosophie, die ihre Begründung in der "Charta von Athen" findet, und die diese räumliche

Funktionsentmischung begünstigt, indem sie die Flächennutzungstrennung propagiert. Damit wird städtebaulich eigentlich nur das nachvollzogen, was die sozialökonomischen Verhältnisse des "fordistischen" Zeitalters erforderten. Wenngleich auch die "Charta von Athen" in der Traditionslinie der Kritik steht an den Umweltbelastungen der Lebensverhältnisse in den frühindustriellen Städten!

Nutzungsmischung als Baustein einer lebenswerten (integrierten/nachhaltigen) Stadt hat es also mit nicht unerheblichen Rahmenbedingungen bzw. Hypotheken zu tun. Was läßt sich nun darüber sagen, wie dieser Baustein handhabbar gemacht werden könnte?

Ganz unstrittig ist, daß wir dafür förderliche städtebauliche Instrumente und Verfahren brauchen. Das soll hier nicht weiter vertieft werden; daran wird gearbeitet, und zwar in dem Maße, wie klarer wird, wie die Konstellationen einer Veränderung gelagert sind sozioökonomische bzw. stadtstrukturelle Situationen); und Dafür kommen Anregungen ebenso von Veranstaltungen wie dieser wie auch aus einem großen Modellvorhaben etwa der Bundesregierung ("Nutzungsmischung im Städtebau"/Experimenteller Wohnungs- und Städtebau).

Klar muß aber noch etwas anderes werden (und darum geht es mir hier und heute vor allem): obwohl "Nutzungsmischung im Städtebau" in Deutschland schon offiziöses Planungsleitbild ist - verwirklicht werden kann es letztlich nur mit sozialen, ökonomischen und politischen Verbündeten, d.h. in der Ausein-andersetzung mit deren Existenz- und Entwicklungs-Bedingungen. Denn immerhin hat es ja bislang ausreichend hinhaltende Widerstände gegeben gegen eine so andere Art städtischer Nutzungsstrukturierung; so daß

wir uns ganz ernsthaft fragen müssen: warum sollte das nun - und denn doch so plötzlich wohl umstandslos verlaufen?

Was ich daher ins Blickfeld rücken möchte, ist weniger die instrumentelle Dimension von Nutzungsmischung sondern die strategische, die mir in gewisser Weise noch wichtiger erscheint. Denn tendenziell ist jegliches (sozial)politische Leitbild dem Scheitern geweiht - zumal bei einem derartigen Orientierungswechsel -, wenn es nicht auch "aufgesattelt" werden kann auf förderliche Strömungen im jeweiligen Sachgebiet. **Für die Entwicklung städtischer Flächennutzungsstrukturen wäre es also hilfreich, wenn die Strategie der Nutzungsmischung eine Entsprechung fände bei den Erwartungen, die flächennutzende Akteure haben an die Bedingungen von Mikrostandorten bzw. an die Qualitäten des Umfeldes von Standorten. Und dabei sind flächennutzende Akteure der gewerblichen Wirtschaft von besonderer Relevanz,**

- ist für sie doch die Inanspruchnahme von Standortqualitäten enger mit kritischen Aspekten ihrer Aktivität Verknüpft (konkretere betriebliche ökonomische Rationalität als etwa bei Wohnnutzungen oder öffentlichen Einrichtungen);

- ist deren Wahrnehmung von Standortwahlkriterien doch besonders "durchschlagend", und zwar ebenso in vorhandenen Siedlungsstrukturen hinein wie gegenüber den Instanzen ihrer Steuerung (Flächennutzungskonkurrenzen); und

- gelten derartige Nutzungen doch z.T. als besonders empfindlich gegenüber räumlicher Nähe (Emissionen/Erweiterungen).

Im Hinblick auf Umsetzungs-Chancen und -Bedingungen eines neuen Stadtentwicklungs-Konzeptes wie dem der Nutzungsmischung ist es daher wichtig, zu identifizieren, inwieweit der aktuelle (Wirtschafts-)Strukturwandel bei diesen Akteuren Bedarfe an mischgenutzten Siedlungseinheiten erkennen läßt, an die dann anzuknüpfen wäre ("aufsatteln"). Speziell diesen Ausblick (und den entsprechenden thematischen "Ausflug") schlage ich vor, weil es mit Nutzungsmischung ja um Zukunft geht. Im übrigen soll mit dem Aufspüren von förderlichen Potentialen keineswegs ausgeblendet oder gering geachtet wurden, inwieweit es weiterhin auch Tendenzen betrieblicher Konzentration und großformatiger Flächenbeanspruchung gibt, die einer kleinräumigen Nutzungsmischung im Wege stehen. Auch deren Kenntnis verhilft zu mehr Realismus im Umgang mit einem solchen Leitbild.

Zu den Merkmalen flächennutzender Akteure der gewerblichen Wirtschaft (im Spannungsfeld von produzierendem Gewerbe und produktionsorientierten Dienstleistungen), die in diesem Kontext interessieren, würden insbesondere zählen: inwieweit gibt es eine Tendenz zu kleinteiligen Strukturen (betrieblich bzw. Flächenbedarf)/intensivierter Kooperationen (am Standort)/räumlicher Nähe zu anderen Nutzern/zu geringeren Peripherieflächen bzw. erhöhten Dichte-Möglichkeiten bzw. zu weniger gegenseitigem Stör-Potential?

Wie verhält sich dazu also der aktuelle Wirtschafts- (und Sozial-)Strukturwandel? Wesentliche seiner Elemente sind in diesem Zusammenhang:

- flexibilisierte Produktionsmethoden für differenziertere Produkt- und Marktstrategien (anstelle einer "economy of scales")

- deregulierte Arbeitsverhältnisse nach Status, Arbeitszeit und -ort (freie Mitarbeiter, außertarifliche Entgeltmuster, Teilzeit, Heimarbeit etc.)

- (vertikal) dezentralisierte Organisationsstrukturen bei gleichzeitiger Externalisierung von Funktionen und deren Einbettung jeweils in Netzwerke

- ein heterogener Status von Kooperanten unter Aspekten ihrer ökonomischen Potenz, des technologischen Niveaus etc.

Die aktuelle Phase wirtschaftlichen Strukturwandels stellt insgesamt eine Ablösung dar betont regulierter Mechanismen durch eher flexibilisierte. Oder: die "fordistische" Art standardisierter Massenproduktion wird ergänzt/überlagert durch eine differenzierte Art qualifizierter Gütererstellung.

Dieser Strukturwandel hat ein paar charakteristische Begleiterscheinungen, die nicht unerheblich sind für unsere Thematik; in vier Bereichen erscheinen sie mir bemerkenswert:

1. Tertiärisierung:

flexibilisiertes Agieren bei der Leistungserbringung erhöht Bedeutung und Bedarf vor- und nachgelagerter (Produkt-, Markt-, Prozeßorientierter) Dienste; das begründet die besondere Dynamik der produktionsorientierten Dienstleistungen für die Tertiärisierung; sie verläuft gleichermaßen innerhalb des produzierenden Gewerbes (mit entsprechend abnehmendem Anteil fertigender Tätigkeiten) als auch außerhalb, und zwar z.T. als Folge von Externalisierung. Damit verbunden sind Tendenzen zu: mehr auf dem Markt auftretenden Unternehmen/Betrieben in Größen, die durchschnittlich eher auch wieder kleiner sind (als ansonsten typisch)/zu mehr unmittelbaren Kooperationen zwischen Betrieben bzw. Unternehmen/mehr standortsuchenden Akteuren und zu mehr Tätigkeiten, die Büroflächen benötigen.

2. Heterogenisierung:

derartige "Auflockerungen" (insb. von Kooperation) korrespondieren verstärkt mit eher situationsbedingten (statt prinzipiellen) Mustern von Umgang/Organisation, und zwar ebenso für Arbeitsprozesse (Gruppen/"flache" Hierarchien u.ä.) und Unternehmensbeziehungen (strategische Allianzen/Konsortien/ Netzwerke etc., wie auch für soziale Beziehungen (entformalisierte berufliche Positionen/"Lebensstile"/veränderte Haushaltstypen etc.). Das erhöht zugleich die Bedürfnisse intensiverer Identifizierung mit dem institutionellen, personalen wie auch örtlichen - Umfeld (kollektive Individualisierung / "corporate identity" / Quartier / Region, etc.).

3. Komplexe Spezialisierung:

mit der Flexibilisierung wird die Massenproduktion standardisierter Großserien Überführt in diejenige variantenreicher Teilserien, bzw. die tiefgestaffelte Arbeitsteilung und extrem vereinfachende Spezialisierung weicht einer disponibleren Struktur: "Systematische Rationalisierung" eher im Arbeitsprozeß und komplexe Spezialisierung - auch darüber hinaus - bedingen sich.

4. Standörtliche Segmentierung:

Veränderte Muster der Arbeitsteilung innerhalb eines Unternehmens und unter seinen Standorten tendieren demnach zu komplexeren Einheiten und entsprechenden (Makro- wie auch Mikro-)Standorten:

"Das Modell der einfachen Standortspaltung dürfte auch in Deutschland zugunsten dezentraler "schlanker" verkleinerter Unternehmenseinheiten mit direktem Industrie-Dienstleistungsverbund abgedankt haben. Insbesonders in der technikintensiven

Produktentwicklung und Pilotfertigung ist eine enge Verzahnung von Marktbeobachtung, Ingenieurwissen, produktionstechnischem know how und Software von Vorteil, ein Modell, das zu räumlich engster Verzahnung von Fertigungs- und Dienstleistungsarbeitsplätzen, z.T. innerhalb eines Gebäudekomplexes tendiert". (v. Einem/BMBau)

Auch über einzelne Unternehmen hinaus ist räumliche Nähe zumindest bei denjenigen Kooperanten (Zulieferern/Dienstleistungen) notwendig, mit denen permanent hoher Abstimmungs- und Handlungsbedarf besteht (hohe personengebundene Kommunikationsintensität: Fühlungsvorteile bzw. face-to-face Kommunikation nehmen potentiell noch zu).

Der aktuelle Wirtschafts- (und Sozial-Strukturwandel scheint also - generalisierend gesagt - heterogene institutionelle, soziale und auch räumliche Aktivitätsstrukturen zu begünstigen.

Im Hinblick auf das produzierende Gewerbe (das uns als flächennutzender Akteur im Hinblick auf Nutzungsmischung interessiert) bedeutet das: außer daß Emissionsgrade nachlassen (d.h. geringere Störanfälligkeit zur Nachbarschaft) und Büroarbeit und entsprechender Flächenbedarf zunehmen, kann aufkommendes Interesse an räumlicher Nähe daher vermutet werden zwischen überlokal orientiertem Gewerbe ("Industrie") und lokalem (z.T. handwerklichem) Gewerbe bzw. unternehmensorientierten Diensleistungen bzw. lokalen Versorgungs-Dienstleistungen (Technik/Einzelhandel/Gastronomie).

Im Hinblick auf produktionsorientierte Dienstleistungen (als flächennutzende Akteure) kann "plausibles" (d.h. funktional erklärliches) Interesse an räumlicher Nähe - als einer wichtigen Voraussetzung für mischgenutzte Gebiete vermutet werden zwischen

- strategischen unternehmensberatenden Dienstleistungen und anderen Dienstleistungen bzw. lokaler Versorgung bzw. Wohnen;

- betriebs-organisatorischen Dienstleistungen und handwerklichem produzierenden Gewerbe bzw. Verkehr/Handel/Lagerei;

- allgemeinen unternehmensbezogenen Dienstleistungen und anderen Dienstleistungen.

Was nun (kleinräumig) mischgenutzte Gebiete in (groß-)städtischen Siedlungsstrukturen angelangt, so lassen sich in der Zusammenschau von produzierendem Gewerbe, produktionsorientierten Dienstleistungen und Wohnen eine Reihe "plausibler" Typen von Nutzungsmischung herleiten, die zudem mit spezifischen Mikrostandorten- korrespondieren, wie sie (groß-)städtischen Siedlungsstrukturen vorkommen.

Soweit mein Ausflug in die Plausibilität. Und so gut also die Aussichten auf Möglichkeiten, das neuartige Konzept der Nutzungsmischung "aufsatteln" zu können auf Tendenzen des aktuellen Sozial- und Wirtschaftsstrukturwandels.

Drei Fragen mindestens stellen sich nun noch im Rahmen eines derart strategisch gemeinten Beitrages.

Zunächst, in wieweit sich denn - wenigstens in Ansätzen - entsprechend veränderte Raumnutzungsmuster auch schon beobachten lassen? Immerhin wirkt der aktuelle Wirtschafts-strukturwandel ja bereits längere Zeit. Als neuartig möchte ich dabei vier Erscheinungen hervorheben:

1. die "Re-Urbanisierung",

d.h. die ökonomische, soziale und architektonische Aufwertung innerstädtischer Bereiche als Standorte von (tendenziell tertiärisierter) Arbeit, von Wohnen und entsprechender Versorgung i.w.S.. Dabei bilden sich Gebiete heraus, die in sich recht vielfältig sind, zugleich - was Art und Klientel ihrer Inanspruchnahme anbelangt - geschlossen wirken und von daher gern als "homogen in ihrer Heterogenität" bezeichnet werden.

2. die Akzentuierung großstädtischer Peripherie

in Form einer auch kleinräumigeren Verschränkung von Gewerbe- bzw. Wohn-Suburbanisierung.

3. eine "Renaissance" von Mittelstädten,

die im Zuge einer Art von "dezentraler Konzentration" eine Aufwertung erfahren, indem sie Orte sind, an denen ein angehobenes Mindestniveau urbaner Qualitäten realisiert werden kann, wie das offenbar als Standortvoraussetzung zunehmend wichtiger wird ("komplexe Spezialisierung").

4. die Herausbildung multifunktional strukturierter - hauptsächlich: gewerblich geprägter - Mikrostandorte kann beobachtet werden

- indem vormals "homogene" Gewerbe- und Industriegebiete in zunehmend heterogene Mikrostandorte zerfallen mit einer Mischstruktur aus verschiedenen Wirtschaftszweigen, Tätigkeiten, Unternehmens- oder Betriebstypen und -großen; und unterschiedliche Funktionen und Tätigkeiten werden im Rahmen eines Unternehmens so gar auf dem eigenen Gelände auch wieder miteinander vermischt. Bzw.

- indem es in neueren Gewerbegebieten zu gemischter Belebung (kommt) nämlich: Unternehmen mit kleinem und mit großem Flächenbedarf, Handwerk, Handel, Dienstleistungen, Hotel etc.; die Zusammensetzung ist durchaus nicht beliebig: die Verbindungen sind in diesem Fall jedoch weniger in der direkten Kooperation der Betriebe zu sehen als in der Bildung eines gemeinsam genutzten Umfeldes.

Was wir durchgehend an solchen Beispielen beobachten können, ist eine relativ hohe Bewertung wiederum (groß-)städtischer Standorte, verbunden mit einer Flächennutzung, die in ihrer Spezialisierung sehr viel weniger standardisiert und gegliedert ist als die uns gewohnte - zumal: städtische - Siedlungs-struktur. Dem entspricht denn auch ein Raum von "Stadt", der sehr viel geringer zentralisiert gedacht wird, was die räumliche Arbeitsteilung der wesentlichen seiner Aktivitäten angelangt. Auffallend ist - insbesondere in städtischen Bereichen - die enge räumliche Verflechtung eines funktionalen Zusammenhangs ver-schiedener Tätigkeiten. Diese neuartige Tendenz faktischer Flächennutzung erscheint ein wenig bereits wie ein Abschied auch von standardisierter funktionaler Zonierung bei der räumlichen Strukturierung von Stadt (und von ihren Grundsätzen etwa in der "Charta von Athen").

Eine weitere Frage orientiert sich ausdrücklich nicht an dem Strukturwandel, den unsere Sozioökonomie ohnehin derzeit vollzieht, sondern richtet sich darauf, inwieweit ein an sich noch ganz anders gelagerter Strukturwandel womöglich (auch) förderliche Aspekte hervorbrächte für die integrierte Stadt und die Nutzungsmischung. Dabei denke ich an die - in allen Dimensionen, und d.h. auch der räumlichen - nachhaltige Entwicklung. In unserem Kontext wäre sie ersteinmal nur als

diejenige "nachhaltigen Wirtschaftens" zu thematisieren. Wie vielgestalig die Diskussion darüber auch ist; es gibt ein paar zentrale Merkmale, die sich mit unserem Thema verknüpfen lassen. Soweit zwar eine eigene Entwicklung möglich sein soll, jedoch - so die Lösung - "nicht auf Kosten anderer" (hier: Gegenden/Regionen etc.), so erklärt das (auch, um Problemverlagerungen einzuschränken) den Ansatz der- möglichst: regionalen "Kreisläufe", d.h. der eher kleinräumigen Kooperation bei der Organisation von Wirtschaftätigkeiten. Und das hieße, ein solcher Strukturwandel ließe erst recht Anknüpfungspunkte für Nutzungsmischung erwarten.

Und die dritte - abschließende - Frage wäre diese: ist mit solchen ermunternden Beispielen alles klar schon zum "Aufsatteln" - und damit also auch bereits für die Verwirklichung von Nutzungsmischung: quasi als "Selbstläufer"? Keineswegs. Ein schwieriges Unterfangen bleibt es allemal, ein Konzept zu verwirklichen, das einen derartig gravierenden Orientierungswechsel darstellt. Nur kann mit solchen Hinweisen vielleicht auch deutlich werden, wo anzusetzen sich lohnt (und wo nicht). Das könnte hilfreich sein - und motivierend: immerhin geht es um eine Konzeption für eine lebenswerte nachhaltige Stadt!

Prof. Dr. Klaus Brake, Forschungsinstitut Region und Umwelt, Carl von Ossietzky Universität, Oldenburg, Deutschland.

Chapter Twenty-Eight

The Shop/House
Building Block of a Healthy City

Suzanne H. Crowhurst Lennard

Throughout much of the world the primary building block of the healthy city is the "shop/house" with shop, workshop or restaurant at street level, and residential dwelling above. The close proximity of living, working, socializing, of the private and the public realms, are what makes the public realm so hospitable, and the private dwelling so convenient. This arrangement makes a city that is not only socially healthy, but also ecologically sound, eliminating unnecessary travel.

The street facade is the medium that makes possible a public life on the street, and connects the private world to the public world. Interaction between the private and public worlds is facilitated by a variety of different kinds of openings- windows, bay windows, shutters that open fully or halfway, French windows, and balconies. It is essential that these apertures may be opened, so that interaction is possible between inside and outside. Window boxes, curtains and blinds provide additional messages to the public realm about the persons living in surrounding buildings, thus making the street feel safer and more personal.

The street level deserves special handling, since it is here that the greatest degree of interactions takes place between those inside and those outside. The commercial shop fronts and their entrances need to be emphasized as different from the residential accommodation above.

Even if the building is large, the street level section of the facade should be broken into narrower shop frontages, and entrances should be accentuated. In this way the street facade presents an almost continuous succession of shop windows. The more carefully detailed the windows are, the more prestigious the merchandise often appears to be.

Every society has developed its own unique shop/ house design, with its own variations in window and door openings, materials and colours. The typical Parisian shop/house presents tall French windows with narrow wrought iron balconies wide enough for window boxes in a limestone, cream or white painted facade. Mansard roofs often contain windows for additional living quarters.

Many cities now require new buildings to reinterpret their traditional shop/house form in a modern idiom. In Paris facing Place des Innocents near the Les Halles development is a new building that retains the shops and restaurants at street level, the tall windows with iron balconies, the limestone facade, and the mansard roofs typical of the Parisian shop/house.

In Freiburg, Germany the tradition of the shop/ house has been continued in the Konviktstrasse in a post-modern style. The shops at street level are entered from the corner. A diagonal corridor leads to an inner courtyard containing more small shops. Above the shops are private dwellings, each with good visibility to the street, and generous balconies and roof gardens.

Tubingen, Germany recognized the importance of the shop/house and revived an ancient German law that requires upper level accommodations to be used for residential purposes. The gentrification process that in so many cities leads to increased rents and the transformation of apartments into professional offices was thus prevented, and almost every building within the old city now contains residential accommodations. The city maintains affordability by providing loans or grants for renovation and restitution of residential facilities in exchange for being able to place a ceiling on rents.

In Oxford, England the shabby Gloucester Green bus terminal has been splendidly rebuilt with attractive shop/houses enclosing a square. Imaginative detailing, such as the variegated brick designs and whimsical turrets are reminiscent of Oxford's best Victorian architecture. Balconies, bay windows and gently bowed facades overlook a lively square with outdoor cafes and restaurants, used once a week for the market.

In the U.S. and Canada, too, this essential building block has always existed in those parts of our cities that are generally considered to be most livable. New York's Greenwich Village continues to be one of the most desirable neighbourhoods because of its intense mix of residential with shops, cafes and restaurants. The streets are lively and belong to the regular clientele, shopkeepers and local residents.

Complex overlay zoning policies have permitted the retention of the shop/house in San Francisco. A number of older neighbourhoods are centered around a main street where some residential accommodation has survived above the shops. One of the most desirable new neighbourhoods is now considered to be Sacramento Street, where new commercial services are now permitted in what was once a purely residential district, and where new

mixed use buildings, designed along the lines of the traditional San Francisco shop/houses, are being built to meet the demands for a more lively, community oriented urban lifestyle.

Victoria, British Columbia has a wealth of handsome shop/houses that continue to enliven and give character to its old city center. Indeed, much of Victoria's appeal lies in these colourful buildings that create Victoria's dense urban character and active street life.

Suzanne H. Crowhurst Lennard Ph.D. (Arch.) is Director of the International Making Cities Livable Council, Carmel, California, and Co-Chair, Program Committee for the 17th IMCL Conference.

Chapter Twenty-Nine

Village in the City

Donald MacDonald

Results of a real estate corporation study demonstrate that high-density housing of the type found in urban areas is considerably less expensive from both an economic and environmental point of view than the traditional sprawl characterized by block after block of single-family homes lined up in the conventional grid pattern.

The purpose of the study was "to help the mayor, the city manager, the planning board, and other concerned local officials" answer such questions as whether the added tax base provided by residential growth would offset the costs to the community and what were the effects of development on air and water pollution, wildlife, open space, energy and water consumption, and the lives of the new residents and their neighbors.

To every question the answer was that high density is better. For example:

- Costs for roads and utilities are about 55 percent lower. Therefore, local governments save money to the extent that they bear financial responsibility for the installation of infrastructure. Operating and maintenance costs are also lower. In addition, there is less need for public transportation.

- Only about half as much land is required. So the potential for preserving open space, with the trees still standing and the grass still growing, is much higher.

- Air pollution from heating and automobiles is about half, with most of the reduction coming from the fact that residents do not have to drive as far.

- Energy consumption is less because of the reduced use of autos and public transportation. Moreover, single-family homes tend to use more heating and air conditioning than an equal number of apartments or townhouses.

- Pollution from storm water and sediment is less, because the total paved area is smaller.

- Fewer traffic accidents occur.

However, the usual type of high-density development -- multi-unit buildings lined up contiguously – are not acceptable alternatives to sprawl. First of all, they are precisely what people flee. Locked inside their apartments, residents have very little, if any, sense of belonging to a community. Often they do not even know their next-door neighbors. Because the streets outside the buildings are impersonal, belonging to no one in particular, they invite crime. As a matter of fact, the Real Estate Research Corporation study did say that a disadvantage of high-density development is a higher crime rate. Nor is the traditional apartment building satisfactory from the environment point of view. People still jump in their cars to go shopping.

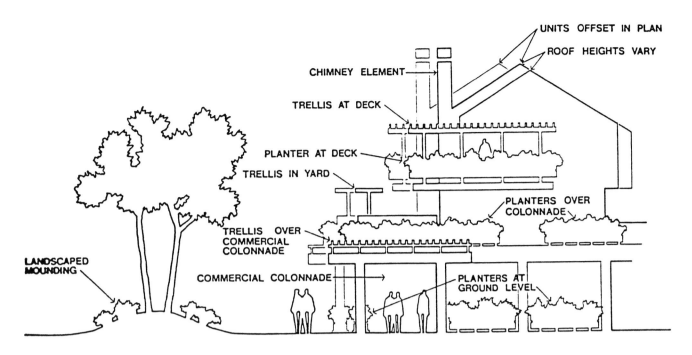

UNITS OFFSET IN PLAN

ROOF HEIGHTS VARY

CHIMNEY ELEMENT

TRELLIS AT DECK

PLANTER AT DECK

TRELLIS IN YARD

PLANTERS OVER COLONNADE

TRELLIS OVER COMMERCIAL COLONNADE

LANDSCAPED MOUNDING

COMMERCIAL COLONNADE

PLANTERS AT GROUND LEVEL

Suburban mixed-use complex, Mountain View, California.

It is the last objection, the use of cars to go shopping, that is the key to a very attractive and practical solution to all the disadvantages. By combining multi-unit housing with commercial development – that is, mixed use – a village-like environment can be created that inspires a sense of community, discourages crime, and in general offers residents and their neighbors the convenience of nearby shopping.

Moreover, the approach lends itself to the efficient use of both urban and suburban infill sites, undeveloped transitional areas between residential and commercial zones, and even built-up commercial land.

The concept of mixed residential and commercial use is by no means new, of course. In many countries, including parts of the United States, the house with a shop on the first floor and living quarters on top of it or in the back used to be the norm for a small family-owned business and in some places still is. Virtually every city in America has designated streets lined with stores on the ground level of apart-

ment buildings. A recent trend is to combine office space and apartments in the same building, usually a high-rise.

But the idea of village-like mixed use is different. Essentially, it is a self-contained community of stores and perhaps a restaurant or two on the street level and individual residential units, each with its own entrance from the outside, on a plaza above the stores. The two levels are quite separate, neither one intruding upon the other, yet they are interdependent in that the residents have food and other shops virtually at their doorsteps and the stores are assured customers from the tenants of the upper level, as well as drawing on the surrounding neighborhood.

On the residential level, groups of three to five units are clustered around courtyards or, where this is impractical, each group is set on its own pedestrian walkway, like houses in an English mews. The level is accessed from the street and ground-level or underground parking spaces by a number of stairways and elevators strategically placed so that tenants can reach their homes more or less directly. There is no central entrance. In addition to the charm and convenience of the grouping of units, the arrangement is crucial to security. The groups or clusters of groups are miniature neighborhoods, and the residents look out for each other. A stranger in the lane or courtyard is observed. Windows in the units are deliberately positioned to facilitate surveillance.

Oscar Newman emphasizes the importance of "subdividing the residential environment into zones toward which adjacent residents easily adopt proprietary attitudes."

Various details of the design enhance the feeling of a village. Pitched roofs evoke the traditional American image of a home —the square box topped with a triangle, which is among the first things kids draw, often adding a chimney with smoke streaming out. Planters in front of the units simulate yards. Whenever possible, units are positioned so that the kitchens receive sunlight in the morning.

One of the great advantages of mixed use is that some built-up commercial and light research and development industrial sites can be utilized. While vacant flat horizontal space is environmentally precious, there is plenty of vertical space available above existing stores and business and industrial parks. They can hook onto an existing infrastructure – instead of chewing up more agricultural land as new towns do. With some renovation of existing structures, housing can be built on top. For people who work in the stores, offices and plants, it is an ideal solution to the expense and stress of the daily commute. For their employers it is a way to reduce absenteeism, especially if a child-care center is included.

The ever-growing population of metropolitan areas can be accommodated without destroying more open space or adding to the thickening layer of smog. Although mixed use certainly is not the entire solution, it is a practical and cost-effective contribution to mitigating the problems. All that is required is imaginative planning and a willingness of the building industry, regulatory agencies and affected neighborhoods to work together to prevent the inevitable catastrophe that would result from continued suburban sprawl.

Donald MacDonald, FAIA, is an architect based in San Francisco.

City Identity

Städtische Identität

A modern interpretation of the traditional Hanseatic-style architecture in Antwerp's new neighborhood, at the heart of the city.

Suzanne H. Crowhurst Lennard

Chapter Thirty

City Identity in New Urban Neighborhoods

Suzanne H. Crowhurst Lennard

Urban Identity

In order to fit into the urban context, a new urban neighborhood must be designed to respect the architectural identity of its host city, through the development of design guidelines that reflect existing patterns, or permit variations in a contemporary idiom.

Every livable city has its own unique character that is expressed in its architecture and arrangement of streets and open places. It is not inappropriate to propose the metaphor that the livable city, like every living thing, has a genetic code, or DNA structure.

The DNA of a city is expressed in those architectural and spatial characteristics best loved by the city's inhabitants, that contribute most to its sense of identity. These may consist of certain building materials and colors, a typical arrangement of scale and architectural forms, building lot size, roof lines, scale of public and semi-public spaces.

As there used to be a consensus about a community's values, so was there also a consensus about what building materials, architectural and spatial forms represented the unique character and structure of one's city.

Each person in the community recognized and understood this unique character, and worked within its constraints, although there was still considerable variation possible, in choice of colors and materials, detailing, degree of elegance, as well as in the architectural expression of the city's varied functions.

This consensus, which the playwright Peter Schaffer calls the "communal eye", has been lost in many places, but there are still many citizens who are intuitively able to recognize their city's unique character, and can identify appropriate or inappropriate development. There are architects who design context specific buildings exemplifying the best of their city's heritage. And mechanisms exist to reinforce a city's special qualities.

Some developers and architects argue that many cities have lost their identity, and the citizens have forgotten the unique character of their city, and that, therefore, they are not obliged to consider the city's identity in their proposals for new urban neighborhoods. The results of this view can be seen in almost every city in the world.

In many North American and some European cities, architects and developers have been allowed to build individual structures and large developments that have no relationship either to the surrounding buildings, or to the city's character and tradition. Buildings compete for attention but do not pay attention to each other. The dialogue among buildings is too often characterized by fragmentation and discontinuity, and the collage of buildings and public spaces creates a profound sense of anomie and dissociation.

We internalize the built environment. But we are gradually eroding our urban sense of identity. A true sense of identity can only be maintained through a dialogue between the community and architects, through community participation programs, and the development of design guidelines sensitive to each city's specific historic heritage.

Through public discourse we need to develop again this "communal eye", this vision of the characteristics of the buildings and places that are valued, that give a sense of place, identity and meaning to the city. And to facilitate this, of course, we need to create public spaces, streets and squares that are hospitable to social contact, connection and civic dialogue.

The architecture of the city embodies the city's memory and shared memories create a community's sense of identity. When a building is destroyed then the memories that each individual had in connection with that building can no longer be passed on to others.

If too much of the architectural heritage is destroyed, the city's communal memory of its unique identity is violated, the importance of the common good is invalidated, and a sense of social disintegration is created. This makes the city susceptible to the development of social problems.

But even a city badly damaged architecturally can recover if the citizens understand its genetic code, and define developmental goals based on this code.

Recognizing the City's Identity

For an organism, the DNA contains instructions on such characteristics as color of eyes, or hair; for a city on such characteristics as building materials, building colors, roof shapes, and size of windows.

These transmitted characteristics vary in small ways, within a limited range, from individual to individual, and from generation to generation, without harm to the individual or to the society. Indeed, these variations are essential to our sense of identity as individuals.

The physical characteristics of the city and its neighborhoods should vary within a limited range. These small and subtle variations give meaning and identity to the street or the neighborhood.

The city with perhaps Europe's most intact genetic structure is Venice. The Venetians have maintained their city's human scale and integrated social structure virtually unchanged since the fifteenth century.

Characteristic of Venice are the white marble base and trim, pinkish-red brick, cream, ochre and brick toned stucco and red tile roofs. From the city's founding in the ninth century until today hardly a single building transgresses this acceptable range of building materials. The fabric of the city is densely packed, to a maximum of six stories in some places. The mix of uses, with shops and workshops below and apartments above, interwoven with courtyards, alleyways, campi and canals, is continuous throughout the city.

Most characteristic are the myriad "campi", the public spaces in every neighborhood, that form the heart of each community, every one unique and irregularly shaped, varying in character from neighborhood to neighborhood, yet similar in their essential function as centers of community life.

Only one new neighborhood (on the Giudecca), which was constructed not according to Venice's genetic structure but on the basis of modern planning principles of isolated apartment blocks, is associated with some of the social problems rampant in most twentieth century cities.

Within its medieval walls, Siena, too, is intact, with a tightly knit physical fabric that supports intense social urban life.

Siena's identity is most distinct in the color of its brickwork, the brownish-red "burnt Siena". In 1309 the ruling council specified the use of brick not only for private but also for many public buildings. The city's heart, the Piazza il Campo, which serves to bind the whole community together, is also paved in brick.

On Siena's outskirts is a new neighborhood that follows modern planning principles and was constructed in pristine white concrete. It is not considered by the Sienese a good place to live and does not contribute favorably to the intense sense of neighborhood community characteristic of the old city. The architect himself, Giancarlo di Carlo, had the grace to admit the development was not a success.

Among European cities, Bologna's architectural identity is clearly recognized in its arcaded streets, in the red earth colors of its brick buildings and tile roofs, and the dark green wood shutters. This pattern repeats itself, with minor variations, throughout the city. The colors vary slightly from building to building; the ubiquitous arcades, too, each have their own character, but provide continuity through the city, connecting building to building, and street to street.

The old city of Lyon in France has a similar palette of rich earth tones. But here the windows and basic construction are in sandstone, the arcades are private, facing onto inner courtyards and are stacked one on another; the streets are not arcaded, and the windows have no wooden shutters.

In Bressanone, a small town in Northern Italy, the city's identity is expressed in its oriel windows and architectural details that are highlighted with white borders. The palette of building colors range from moss green to putty, through pale ochres and sand colors, to gray and cream, but they are all subtle pastel earth tones that blend harmoniously.

Some cities in the U.S. have a clear architectural identity. The antebellum city of Charleston, South Carolina is recognizable for its characteristic pastel wood frame "single houses" with columned terraces along the southern side, narrow alleyways leading to private gardens, quiet tree lined streets, weathered brick walls and uneven bluestone sidewalks.

Those cities that recognize their unique character can develop clear design guidelines for new urban neighborhoods, specifying what building materials, palette of colors, architectural proportions and detailing will be acceptable.

The almost total lack of any guidelines in the economic "enterprise zones" of London's Docklands encouraged its overbuilding and lack of a coherent urban fabric. Clear design guidelines formulated for such North American cities as Santa Barbara, California, Santa Fe, New Mexico, and Nantucket, Massachusetts protect the special character of those towns.

Failure to Maintain the City's Identity

In cities and towns with a well defined architectural identity the intrusiveness of alien architectural forms can seem overpowering.

In Basel, the majority of the old city is of modest scale, with unpretentious architecture that provides a hospitable, human scale setting for urban life. But the living tissue of the city has been invaded by inappropriate buildings such as an office block - the headquarters of the Bank for International Settlements - reminiscent of a nuclear power plant cooling tower.

Inappropriate structures are not always identifiable simply by their size. Sometimes the overall height may be appropriate, but the materials, or the size and proportions of windows and doors may be entirely hostile to the building's context.

On a characteristic street in Amsterdam, where the high gabled, narrow fronted brick houses echo and reinforce the street's identity, the architect Soetjers has been permitted to contravene the building regulations and to create his own personal statement -- a corrugated aluminum sided building with tiny square windows and inappropriate proportions.

The historic fabric of Ulm, Germany consists of three and four story buildings, with gables fronting to the street, and two or three additional floors within the roof frame. A large number of medieval half timbered houses still exist, particularly in the Fischerviertel (the fishermen's district beside the Danube).

Local architects schooled in the careful restoration of the Fischerviertel and other historic sectors have shown a sensitivity to the unique character of Ulm's best architecture, and have designed new infill buildings to reflect this character in scale, form, color and detail. Their efforts were appreciated by the great majority of Ulm's citizens.

Meanwhile, in order to promote Ulm as a world city, the city administration hired Richard Meier to design a major building on the cathedral square.

The appropriateness of Meier's design for this historically extremely significant site was hotly debated in the Ulm press and among its citizens.

Meier's "Cultural Center" is designed without reference or regard to its cultural context. It is a white abstract sculpture, designed to sit in an imaginary white field. Its vast scale and lack of detailing make it appear overblown in relation to its architectural context -- the handsome sixteenth century brick warehouse, the "Neubau", the painted facades of the nearby gothic town hall, and the modest scale of the postwar shop/houses ringing the cathedral square.

In Bonn the construction of a completely scaleless department store on the main cathedral square outraged many people. It completely disregards the DNA of the city, it used materials and colors alien to the setting, there were no windows, and the typical Bonn roof line was abandoned in favor of a flat roof. The building completely lacked any reference to human scale at street level!

More successful was the recent reconstruction of a competing department store on the opposite side of the cathedral square, which continues the light color stone facade of adjacent buildings, the rows of windows, and the typical Bonn roofline.

New buildings, developments and places that do not conform to the basic patterns of a city's architectural tradition are sometimes characterized as deformities. It is this idea that Prince Charles expressed in his famous "carbuncle speech" about London:

What, then, are we doing to our capital city now? What have we done to it since the bombing during the war? What are we shortly going to do to one of its most famous areas -- Trafalgar Square? Instead of designing an extension to the elegant facade of the National Gallery which complements it and continues the concept of columns and domes, it looks as if we may be presented with a kind of vast municipal fire station, complete with the sort of tower that contains the siren . . .

What is proposed is like a monstrous carbuncle on the face of a much-loved and elegant friend.

New Urban Neighborhoods that Reflect the City's Identity

In many European cities we begin to see extensive new developments that reflect the best architectural traditions while encouraging individuality and current needs.

In Annecy, a town renowned for its arcaded streets, earth and ochre-toned walls, and intricate pitched roofs with small dormer windows is a new development built around two plazas that contains low income housing, a supermarket, hotel, four screen cinema, and underground parking while still retaining the traditional architectural elements.

A most exceptional development in Bruges is the "Silver Pand". This is a series of interconnecting inner courtyards and alleys onto which face a mixture of renovated old buildings, and new buildings in the traditional styles, blending harmoniously and hardly identifiable as modern. At ground floor are a variety of shops, restaurants, outdoor cafes, but what makes this development particularly outstanding is that the upper floors are city owned low income housing.

In Antwerp, too, the traditional elements of the Hanseatic city architecture -- three and four story buildings with steeply pitched roofs, the gable fronting to the street and decorated in the style appropriate to the period -- have been successfully reinterpreted in the recent extensive reconstruction of a large neighborhood in the center of the city.

Older buildings, of brick with stone detailing, and textural brick patterns, particularly in the gables, are reflected in adjacent new buildings, and in the detailing, where concrete is used in a decorative-structural manner instead of stone, and where brick designs give subtle texture to the wall surface.

The harmonious blending of old and new has been skillfully accomplished. The monotony that generally characterizes such extensive projects has been avoided here by careful variations in design, brick color and detailing from one building to the next. The palette of brick colors harmonize well, but help to differentiate each building. The individuality of each building is emphasized by a change in the building facade line, and variations in roof and eaves lines.

Montpellier in Southern France has a tightly woven mixed use fabric, on a medieval street plan, and buildings that date from the classical golden age of the seventeenth and eighteenth centuries. The traditional shop/house forms the basic building block of the city, there are many small squares that function as market

149

places in the morning and are then transformed in the afternoon into cafes and restaurants. Many fine town houses are to be found opening to inner courtyards.

In a new controversial mixed-use neighborhood called "Antigone", by the Spanish architect, Ricardo Bofill, Bofill has attempted to recreate the spirit of the seventeenth and eighteenth century style architecture, with continuous mixed use terrace buildings designed around a series of public spaces.

The central axis of plazas and avenues is free from traffic, and paved with stone and crushed limestone. The avenue is lined with trees; arcades and terraces offer pleasant outdoor cafes and restaurants.

The enclosing buildings with their manneristic version of classical style detailing, are arranged in crescents and terraces no more than six stories high. Apartments and offices are placed above stores, services and restaurants.

In these aspects, Antigone seems to be an attractive effort to recreate the eighteenth century urban fabric.

While highly photogenic, the development fails in the eyes of some of its residents and business people, who claim that the beauty is superficial -- visible on the exterior but not evident in the interior planning -- and that the quality of everyday life is unsatisfactory in comparison to the old city. They find it difficult to think of themselves as members of a community.

The architectural plan consists of a series of plazas and boulevards on a symmetrical axis that culminate in a dramatic vista. The scale is suitable for stately processions, but not conducive to the development of a sense of community.

The development lacks the intricacy, complexity and asymmetry typical of the old city and the intimate scale of the old inner courtyards and town houses.

Most unfortunate is that the development is cut off from the rest of the city. While only a few minutes walk from the Place de la Comedie, Antigone is rendered almost inaccessible by the barrier of "Polygon", a disastrous commercial and administrative development from the '60s. While it does not function as an independent neighborhood, its weak connection to the body of the old city makes it difficult for it to function as a part of the historic center.

Louvain La Neuve in Belgium is another interesting effort to create a new university town based on ecological planning principles, and with an urban character. Cars are kept at the periphery; parking, buses and trains are beneath the development, which spans a small valley between three hills.

The whole development is based on a winding, pedestrian street that, for most of its length, is mixed use, on the shop/house principle, with shops, cafes and restaurants at street level, and apartments above.

Along this spine are a variety of public squares, from the Place Rabelais at the very center, to Place de l'Université, and further along, the Place des Wallons – all surrounded by shop/houses.

At one end, the development is anchored by the Place des Science, at the heart of the Science faculty complex, and at the other end, by Grand Place, beside the theological college. Branching off this spine are many pedestrian streets and alleys that lead to other specialized areas of housing, or the clusters of buildings that accommodate the faculties of philosophy, political, economic and social sciences.

As a design for a campus Louvain la Neuve, because of its mixed use spine containing grocery stores, bookstores, pharmacies, supermarkets, photo stores, print shops, restaurants and bars, all with apartments above, is a vast improvement on most new university campus designs. It has an urban quality, and seems very lively during the week, during the university term.

But the very fact that it is still only a university campus means that it becomes deserted at weekends when many students go to their parents, or over vacations when the only people left are the married foreign students.

Despite its interesting physical design, with much attention to the importance of public spaces, it cannot function as a real community because it consists only of students and faculty – no older people, few children, and the full range of professions, occupations, etc. is lacking.

The Structure of a Healthy City and a Healthy Neighborhood

Similarities between the workings of a living organism and the functions of a city have been suggested by many urban analysts, and it is worth exploring this metaphor.

An understanding of the characteristics of a healthy living organism, and how that organism maintains its healthy state also provides a

better understanding of the characteristics of a healthy city, and how each neighborhood can maintain itself in good health.

The role of the DNA in assuring correct form and direction of growth of the organism may also shed some light on the essential characteristics of a healthy and well-functioning neighborhood.

In a healthy body every cell functions not as an independent unit but as part of an integrated ensemble.

In a healthy city, too, the built fabric must be continuous. Buildings similar in height, form and appearance are connected to one another along streets and around urban spaces. The healthy city has an identifiable boundary; there are no wounds in the urban tissue, and no undifferentiated sprawling developments.

As the Nobel prize winner Konrad Lorenz observes,

> "If you look at a cancer under the microscope, a cross section with cells of healthy tissue, it looks exactly like an aerial view of a city in which the old sections are surrounded by new, irregularly built regions or else by those that are monotonously geometrical -- both are possible, after all. The parallels between the formation of malignant tumors and cities in a state of cultural decay are very wide ranging."

The Wisdom of the City

A healthy organism is one that is self regulating, where all the cells coordinate their function smoothly with all other cells, where there is a continuous flow of information back and forth, each cell "reporting" its condition, and receiving appropriate response from the other cells of the body.

Similarly, a healthy city is one in which finely tuned mechanisms exist for recognizing the needs of every individual, and group, and for responding appropriately to those needs. In other words, a city in which a sense of community is very well developed, where individuals monitor the well being of their neighbors and acquaintances, and where individuals take responsibility for each other.

The development of a sense of community in the city requires a constant flow of information. Information concerning the private world of individuals must become public knowledge, and events in the public realm must be reflected on in private. This process requires, also, a physical structure that supports information flow across the public/private barrier. This structure is found in the traditional shop/house.

The variety of activities at street level -- shops, businesses, workshops, coffeehouses, theaters, and restaurants -- generate social life and form the basis for social interaction. The private dwellings above provide for communication with the public realm through the building's apertures -- windows, balconies, doors, shutters and blinds. When residential use is withdrawn to high rise buildings, or is oriented away from the street, it can no longer contribute to the essential dialogue between the public and private realms.

The communal wisdom needed to maintain a city's special identity is dependent on a continuous communication between all members of the community. There must be frequent exchange of information, involving all, and keeping all members up-to-date on the current "health" and well being of others in the community. And the behavior, actions and attitudes of all must, in part, be visible and common knowledge. This implies an active and viable public realm, and appropriate and accessible urban spaces where the social life of the community can be enacted.

For a new neighborhood to be healthy, it must establish appropriate relationships between the different elements -- dwellings, schools, shops, offices, etc.. No single element can be overdeveloped at the expense of any other element, and no single population group such as working adults with cars can be given priority at the expense of other groups such as children.

Vast areas of suburban sprawl and single function zones unnaturally separate neighborhood functions and make impromptu social contact and a sense of community impossible. For new urban neighborhoods to be healthy they must have high density urban nuclei that provide all the necessary functions within walking distance.

As early as 1960 Lewis Mumford was calling for "tightening the loose and scattered pattern of the suburb, turning it from a purely residential dormitory into a balanced community . . . with a more varied population and with sufficient local industry and business to support it."

Suzanne H. Crowhurst Lennard Ph.D. (Arch.) is Director of the International Making Cities Livable Council, Carmel, California, and Co-Chair, Program Committee for the 17th IMCL Conference.

Kapitel Dreißig

Über den Umgang
mit der Nachbarschaft

Peter Breitling

Die isolierte Darstellung progressiver Architekturschöpfung in der Fachpresse war nur folgerichtig, denn Nachbarschaft, Umraum und Übergang von Alt zu Neu waren für die klassische Moderne keine Themen. diese klassische Moderne war vom "Objektdenken" beherrscht und hatte den Blick für den Zusammenhang verloren.

Wenn nun innerhalb von wenigen Jahren mehr Bücher und Artikel über Neues Bauen in alter Umgebung, Häuser in Baulücken, Neu neben Alt und den Genius loci erschienen sind als in Jahrzehnten durchaus intensiver Architekturdiskussion, so muß die Zeit etwas Neues meinen, um mit Hans Scharoun zu sprechen; oder die Umstände, unter denen wir arbeiten, haben sich geändert - wahrscheinlich aber beides.

So oft es auch schon gesagt sein mag - man muß, wenn von Übergängen die Rede ist, wiederholen, daß "Zusammenhang" in der Entstehungszeit der Moderne von vielen als etwas Belastendes empfunden wurde.

Das Hinwegspringen über die Möglichkeiten des Gegebenen, auf das Le Corbusier so stolz war, das Abstreifen von Fesseln und das Lockern beklemmender Bindungen war die Herausforderung für alle Nachdenklichen. Es galt, die belastenden Zusammenhänge zu zerschlagen und Neues an die Stelle des Zerschlagenen zu setzen. Man kann in einer solchen Aufbruchstimmung wohl keine differenzierten, abgewogenen Urteile und Forderungen erwarten. Wenn man mit Bert Brecht glaubte, das schlechte Neue sei besser als das gute Alte, gab es keinen Anlaß zur respektvollen Auseinandersetzung mit alter Nachbarschaft.

Wir leben und bauen heute unter völlig veränderten - umgekehrten - Verhältnissen. In Zahlen: 1875 waren im ganz großen Durchschnitt, wenn man von den damals schon in rasanter Entwicklung begriffenen Metropolen absieht, ungefähr 90% der Bausubstanz, die einen Europäer umgab, älter als 100 Jahre und nur 10% waren jünger. Die offene Bauweise spielte überhaupt noch keine nennenswerte Rolle und beschränkte sich auf Monumentalbauten, Fabriken und die Wohnbauten einer kleinen priviliegierten Minderheit.

1975 hatte sich das Verhältnis umgekehrt. Was älter ist als 100 Jahre, macht heute höchstens noch 10% der Substanz aus. Uber 90% des Gebauten, das uns umgibt, ist jünger, und es gibt Städte, in denen weit mehr als die Hälfte der Bausubstanz aus der letzten Generation stammt.

Die geschlossene Bauweise wurde aufgegeben und alles Verbindende auf triviale Normen reduziert. Zu zerschlagen gibt es in einer solchen Umwelt, die eher aus einem Trümmerhaufen aus ganz oder teilweise zerstörten Ensembles, Systemen und

Übereinküften besteht, nichts mehr. Auch der Störung der selten gewordenen Geschlossenheit fehlt in der Anhäufung des Häßlichen und Gestörten die Faszination der Pioniertat und des neuen Anfangs.

Daß unter diesen Bedingungen viel über den Genius loci, über Einfügung, über den Respekt vor vorhandener Qualität und Übergänge von Alt zu Neu nachgedacht wird, ist fast selbstverständlich. Festzustellen, daß dieses Nachdenken bisher nicht viel vermocht hat, ist aber sicher keine unzulässige Über-Vereinfachung.

Wie in jeder Stadt gibt es auch in meiner Wahlheimat Graz viele Beispiele für den Versuch, sich in einen vorhandenen Kontext einzufügen, aus den verschiedensten Epochen und mit unterschiedlichem Erfolg.

Was in den vielen Veröffentlichungen zum Thema des Übergangs von Neu zu Alt gesagt wird, läßt sich auf eine einfache Formel bringen: Das Vorhandene - namentlich das in seinem Zusammenhang noch weitgehend unversehrte Alte - verdient unsere Aufmerksamkeit und unseren Respekt.

Wie sich dieser Respekt manifestiert, ist mit gutem Grund bis heute umstritten geblieben. Daß beim Bauen Neu neben Alt, sowohl vom Bauhern als auch vom Architekten, besonders viel Rücksicht und Meisterschaft verlangt wird, ist klar. Ebenso klar wie die Tatsache, daß Denkmalpflege im strengen Sinne uns hier nicht weiterhilft, es sei denn, man teilt die Meinung Donald Insalls, Demkmalpflege sei keine Wissenschaft, sondern eine Kunst. Dann nämlich gibt es keinen Unterschied mehr zwischen Denkmalpflege und gutem verantwortungsvollem Umgang mit dem Vorhandenen.

Aber was heißt guter Umgang mit dem Vorhandenen? Wer glaubt, das Falsche berechnen und das Richtige verordnen zu können, geht fehl; und dennoch wird es immer klarer, daß man für ortsbewußtes Bauen ohne Regeln wohl nicht auskommen wird.

Für die Architekten des 19. Jahrhunderts galt es noch für ausgemacht, daß es notwendig sei, "der äußeren Erscheinung des Bauwerks Kunstformen zu verleihen, für welche im Stil ein Kanon geschaffen ist". Die Beschäftigung mit Kompositionsgesetzen und der optischen Wirkung von Größen, Formen und Proportionen nahm in der zeitgenössischen Fachliteratur breiten Raum ein . Zu diesen Verhältnissen - zu Stil und verbindlichem Kanon - führt kein Weg zurück. Aber Aufmerksamkeit für das Wesen und die Gesetzmäßigkeiten des Vorhandenen steht uns in einer aus den Fugen gehenden Welt mehr an als je zuvor. Und daß sich das Verhältnis zu diesen Gesetzmäßigkeiten allmählich verbessert, ist unverkennbar.

Adolf Freiherr von Knigges seit 1788 unendliche Male wieder aufgelegtes Buch "Uber den Umgang mit Menschen" erlebt sicher nicht zufällig heute wieder eine Renaissance, und dem geschärften Bewußtsein für Respekt und Auf merksamkeit würde ein Buch "Uber den Umgang mit dem Ort und der vorhandenen Nachbarbebauung" ganz gut entsprechen. In seiner Abhandlung über "Die verdammten Satzungen" hatte Paulhans Peters ganz deutlich gesagt, worauf es ankommt: "Ähnlichkeiten herzustellen, nicht zu verbalisieren oder herbeizureden. Ähnlichkeiten, die wieder das Gemeinsame erkennen lassen, das Ortstypische, das Regionalistische, auch das Vertraute, was das Gegenteil von üblicher Innovation ist". Doch wie könnte ein solcher Knigge des baulichen Respekts zustande kommen und wie müßte er aussehen? Sicher ist, daß er ohne eine bis ins Detail gehende Beschäftigung mit den

Gestaltgesetzen des Vorhandenen nicht möglich wäre.

An Zeugnissen für eine soche intensive Beschäftigung fehlt es zwar nicht, aber sie haben bisher mehr Unbehagen als freudige Zustimmung erregt. Das dürfte neben den meist fehlgeschlagenen Versuchen, das Erkannte in rechtliche Bindungen umzusetzen, mit der Scheu vor der cartesianischen Zergliederung zusammenhängen, der Theodor Fischer Ausdruck gegeben hat, als er sagte, solche Versuche, die Qualität zu ergründen, "zerkrümeln und vernichten, was als Ganzheit vor dem Empiriker steht".

Wie auch immer: Daß der Genius loci oder die Charakteristika alter Bebauung nicht mit einigen wenigen Merkmalen beschrieben werden können, liegt auf der Hand. Michael Trieb benutzte zur Beschreibung der Gestalt von Alt-Leonberg sechs Kategorien: Gebäudebreite, Traufhöhe, Dachform, Dachneigung, Gebäudeflucht und Fassadengliederung und wies darüberhinaus auf die Bedeutung des Materials hin . Hinter diesen Gesamtmerkmalen liegen zahllose Einzelkennzeichen und Gruppen von Charakteristika in mehreren Schichten übereinander, von der Korngröße der Gesamtbauwerke über ihre Großgliederung und den Maßstab bis zu Material, Farbe und Detailrepertoire. Und selbst innerhalb der Einzelmerkmale gibt es Differenzierungen zwischen rauh und glatt, stark und schwach, einfach und differenziert. Allein die Fassadengliederung der Gebäude aus der vorindustriellen Zeit hat mindestens fünf Ebenen

- Die Baukörperdimensionen und die Grundaufteilung in Sockel, Korpus und Haube sowie in Geschosse, die Höhe der Stockwerke, ihre Differenzierungen und Zusammenfassung in Gestalt von "Ordnungen".

- Die Grobgliederung in Elemente erster Ordnung, Erker, Risalite, Kordongesimse und anderes, zu der man auch die Achsenbildung und Symmetrie zählen könnte.

- Das Verhältnis von Wand zu Loch.

- Die Architekturglieder zweiter Ordnung, wie Fensterüberdachungen und Umrahmungen, Gesimse, Friese und Bänder zwischen den Gliedern erster Ordnung, und

- die Architekturglieder dritter Ordnung, zu denen neben Profilierungen und Teilungen auch der Dekor gehört.

Es ist sicher, daß die Übernahme eines Charakteristikums der alten Bebauung noch keine Einfügung ergibt, so oft wir das auch in Begründungen finden mögen.

Mit der Argumentation beispielsweise, daß die Abmessungen der Felder einer Rasterfassade den Proportionen der Fensteröffnungen in der umgebenden Bebauung entsprächen, kann man die Einfügung des Neuen in der Regel nur herbeireden, aber nicht wirklich erreichen.

Auch die Übernahme der Traufhöhe von Nachbargebäuden wird oft mit Einfügung gleichgesetzt, obwohl mit ihr allein noch kein Respekt vor dem Genius loci bezeugt wird. Ähnliches gilt für die Verwendung des in der Umgebung vorherrschenden Materials als einziger Anpassungsmaßnahme.

Eine Virtuosität in der Einfügung zu erreichen, die von jedermann als selbstverständlich empfunden wird, ist unendlich schwer. Der Grat zwischen der zu getreuen Anlehnung, die zur Imitation führt und zur Fessel werden kann, und der Betonung des

"Zeitgenössischen" mit untauglichen Mitteln ist sehr schmal.

Selbst bei den seit Jahrzenten als Vorbilder anerkannten Meisterbauten in alter Umgebung gibt es in dieser Beziehung Probleme. Wäre die Rathauserweiterung in Göteborg anbiedernd geworden, wenn Gunnar Asplund die Fenster seines Anbaus nicht an die Seite der Fassadenfelder hätte verrutschen lassen?

Haben sich die Auflagen, die Adolf Loos bei seinem Haus am Michaelerplatz zähneknirschend in Kauf nehmen mußte, zum Nachteil seines Bauwerks ausgewirkt? Wäre es schlechter, wenn es noch einige gliedernde Elemente mehr aufwiese?

Daß Anklänge an Vorhandenes selbst in großer Zahl nicht zu einer selbstverständlichen Einfügung führen, wenn sie nur als ironische Zitate auftauchen, versteht sich eigentlich von selbst. Immer wieder werden uns aber Entwürfe dieser Art als vorbildlich präsentiert. In der Dokumentation "Construire en quartier ancien" ist der Geschäftshausneubau in der Avenue Matignon in Paris von Vittorio Mazzuconi unter "Integration" eingeordnet.

Beim Blick auf Neubauten in historischer Umgebung, die von vielen als gut eingefügt empfunden werden, finden wir stets Übereinstimmung mit einer ganzen Reihe von Merkmalen der umgebenden Bebauung. Bei der Lückenbebauung in Brooklyn Heights aus dem Jahre 1986 wurden nicht nur die Traufhöhe, die Gesimsbildung, der betonte Eingang, das Material und die klassische Aufteilung von Wand und Loch mit hochrechteckigen Fensterelementen übernommen, sonden auch der Grundhabitus der umgebenden Gebäude mit dem axial-symmetrischen Fassadenaufbau. Die Abweichung in den Geschoßhöhen fällt überhaupt nicht auf, weil die nach oben abnehmende Höhe der Geschosse und der Fenster das klassische Prinzip der geschoßweise wechselnden Ordnung in eine der Aufgabe entsprechende neue Form übersetzt; ein Entwurf, dessen Meisterschaft sich nicht in auftrumpfender Originalität äußert, sondern sich erst beim genauen Hinschauen in ihrer raffinierten Sublimierung der Beschränkungen zeigt.

Beim Internationalen Lutherischen Studentenzentrum in London wurden als Mittel der Einfügung die Übernahme des Materials und die Vertikalbetonung durch Erker benutzt. Ohne diesen Kunstgriff wäre eine Störung des zwar bescheidenen, aber harmonischen Straßenbildes durch die zahlreichen eng aneinanderliegenden Fenster und den starken Unterschied in der Geschoßhöhe unvermeidlich gewesen. Auch die Ausbildung eines abgesenkten Basements und die geschickte Eingliederung in die gestaffelte Trauflinie durch zurückgesetzte Gelenkbauteile schafft zusätzliche Anknüpfungen an den Bestand. Wichtigste Quelle des Eindrucks einer zwanglosen Einfügung ist jedoch die bescheidene, unverkrampfte Grundhaltung des Gebäudes, die sich sehr gut mit dem Habitus der umgebenden Nutzbauten verträgt.

Je "loyaler" sich der Architekt der Nachbarbebauung gegenüber verhält und je selbstverständlicher er gestaltet, desto weniger tritt meist seine persönliche Leistung hervor. Viele Beispiele guter Übergänge bleiben wegen ihrer Harmlosigkeit anonym, wie etwa das Geschäfts- und Bürohaus in der Karlstraße in Augsburg, für dessen Einfügung ausnahmslos "klassische" Mittel verwendet wurden. Das steile, ziegelgedeckte Dach und das "Ohrwaschel" helfen, den Höhenunterschied zwischen dem siebengeschossigen und dem dreigeschossigen Nachbarhaus zu überwinden; der knappe Dachvorsprung vermittelt zwischen dem starken Traufgesims des Altbaus auf der linken und dem gesimslosen Abschluß des Nachkriegsbaus auf der rechten

Seite; mit dem Erker wird ein gewohntes Gliederungselement der Augsburger Altstadt wiederholt, die Fenster zeigen in Größe und Format deutliche Anklänge an die alte Fensterlandschaft. Die dichtere Reihung der Öffnung und die sehr gestreckten Formate der Fenster in den beiden Obergeschossen lassen trotz der reichen Gliederung durch Kämpfer und Sprossen keinerlei Putzigkeit aufkommen.

Auch hier zeigt sich wieder, daß auch die Verwendung vieler überlieferter Elemente nicht zur Imitation oder Anbiederung führen muß. Andererseits erzeugen manche Abwandlungen des Überlieferten trotz ihrer scheinbaren Geringfügigkeit unbefriedigende Brüche. Der aus einer flachen Betondecke herausgezogene Erker ohne Andeutung eines stützenden Elements widerspricht unseren Seh- und Empfindungsgewohnheiten des Lastens und Tragens und wirkt in einem sonst konsequent aus überlieferten Prinzipien entwiekelten Hausgesicht inkonsequent. Am Augsburger Beispiel wird deutlieh, wie sehmal der Grat zwischen dem positiv harmlosen oder Bescheidenen und dem ärgerlich Belanglosen oder Trivialen ist, und man wird sich beim einzelnen Beispiel darüber immer wieder streiten. "Lieber langweilig als schlecht" ist eben kein allgemein anerkannter Grundsatz.

Man darf es wohl als allgemein akzeptiert ansehen, daß Selbstverständlichkeit im Weiterbauen und Einfügen weder bei der Alltagsarchitektur der "grauen Mäuse" noch bei den Werken prominenter zeitgenössischer Architekten die Regel ist. Manche Fälle könnte man ohne Übertreibung als tragisch bezeichnen. So begann die Auseinandersetzung um den Neubau an Stelle des alten Haas-Hauses am Stephansplatz in Wien mit einem Entwurf Hans Holleins, der zwar vielen Wienern nicht gefiel, in seiner städtebaulichen Eingliederung aber sehr ortsbezogen war und große Vorteile gegenüber der alten Randbebauung hatte. Trotz der technischen Schwierigkeiten mit dem U-Bahn-Tunnel war

es gelungen, durch den Baukörper eine Erinnerung an die frühere Zäsur zwischen Stock am Eisenplatz und Stephansplatz zu erzeugen.

In seiner Formensprache war schon dieser erste Entwurf recht kompromißlos und ohne große Anklänge an Vorhandenes in der Umgebung, aber auch nicht bewußt verletzend. Der neue Entwurf, der jetzt zur Auführung gelangt, ist dagegen ein eher "hochmütiges" Projekt, ein neues Denkmal, das zwar sehr viel Aufmerksamkeit erregt und viele Besucher anlocken wird, aber von den Anhaltspunkten des Ortes außer der Gebäudehöhe fast nichts übernommen hat.

Die Schwierigkeiten, die ein selbstverständliches Weiterbauen behindern, beruhen auf einem vielleicht sehr ehrenwerten, in jedem Fall aber liebevoll gepflegten Mißverständnis.

Immer wieder lesen wir, daß es in historischer Umgebung besonders wichtig sei, gut zu bauen. Qualifizierende Begriffe für diese Gute gibt es aber nicht. Man zieht sich auf die pure Geschichtlichkeit zurück, die zu nichts verpflichtet und verweist darauf, daß sich die Architekten vergangener Epochen mit vorhandener Substanz und Nachbarbebauung nicht auseinandergesetzt hätten und daß wir dieser Rücksichtslosigkeit unsere größten Baudenkmäler verdankten.

Daß diese Behauptung eine völlig unzulässige "fürchterliche Simplifikation" ist, kann man mit zahllosen Zeugnissen belegen.

Ein solches ist zum Beispiel das Ensemble des Grazer Landhauses. Der Komplex, den wir heute als eine harmonische Einheit empfinden, entstand schrittweise von etwa 1500 bis 1890 nach Plänen von mindestens 15 bis 20 teils italienischen, teils österreichischen Baumeistern und Architekten. Deutsche Frührenaissance, Hochrenaissance lombardischer Prägung, Früh- und Spätbarock, Rokoko, Biedermeier und Historismus habe die Architektur des Landhausensembles geprägt, ohne daß es zu "Brüchen" oder Gegensätzlichkeiten gekommen wäre, die wir als solche empfinden.

Theodor Fischer, einer der es wissen mußte, hat von sich gesagt, daß er zu jenen gehöre, "die nicht nur mit der gepriesenen künstlerischen Freiheit oder besser gesagt, Willkür, bauen, sondern die sich ein Gesetz gemacht haben, das ihnen Halt und rechte Freiheit gibt."

So sehr die Nachbarschaft manchmal selbst eine Stütze braucht, so viel an Halt und rechter Freiheit kann sie -- geachtet und richtig verstanden -auch geben.

Dr. Ing. Peter Breitling ist Architekt und Universitäts Professor emeritus, Institut für Städtebau, Graz, Österreich.

Chapter Thirty-Two

Identity, Urban Design in the City State

Ernie Scoffham

Introduction

'We are witnessing in Europe the emergence of a new generation of cities. No, more than that: we are seeing the emergence of a new urban culture. With the relative decline of the nation-state Europe is becoming increasingly defined by its cities. It is becoming, as it was until the seventeenth century, not a national but a city civilisation. And the reappearance of the city-state has ushered in once again a very old and civilising European phenomenon – inter-city rivalry and competition'. (Rogers: 1992)

Events in Eastern Europe today are symptomatic of the quest for ethnic identity, cultural expression and independence from autocratic rule that have been welling up for some time. In the mood of democracy after the end of the second world war, a phenomenon denied to the East, independence from imperial rule began the multi-ethnic transformation of today's city society. Today, these ethnic groups seek expression of their own culture, in another climate, in another place.

Freed from autocratic control the political boundaries of Europe have begun to shift; away from lines drawn by victorious allies, to lines which reflect an older order, more ethnic, and apparently more natural, in its delineation. In the process, territorial rights are upset and blood is spilled, for in the intervening years enforced migrations of population, and political dealings, have blurred those earlier boundaries. Words which have not been used

in a lifetime begin to reappear, as if from a map of Europe at the time of the Hapsburgs. Fresh migrations emerge: either to homelands previously barred by political constraint, or to strange lands which provide a haven from ethnic violence. Old hatreds and old memories are provoked; some to die in the glow of unification, some to inflame passions long muted by state control.

Similarly, within those western European states of greater apparent stability, past divisions surface to accentuate separatism, to fuel demands for greater independence, to reinforce the characteristics of nationality through historic language and culture. Divisions of nationality and of state administration become increasingly temporal, and hang in delicate balance. At the same time, and at the other extreme of organizational endeavor, pan-European groups seek to exploit cross-national cooperation; to create stronger trading, scientific, cultural and military power bases, the better to peddle their wares on a world stage. National pride brings financial supremacy and individual sovereignty into strange conflict with this multi-lingual, European federation club.

Insecurity and unfamiliarity seek solace in the known, the familiar, the friendly and the past. That British cities are being modeled to resemble Dickensian film sets is not surprising. Post-modernism was a way of picking up some threads from the richness of history, heritage and tradition that had been pushed aside, to be rediscovered almost anew by a fresh generation of architects. A breed of buildings emerged, with historical architectural elements that looked as if they had come out of a box of child's building blocks, a kind of multi-colored instant 'Lego", which some hoped might just as easily be dismantled. This apparent rootlessness of conviction and purpose, seemed to suggest that architecture had had the rational stuffing of modernism knocked out of it, and was wandering aimlessly looking for a fresh cause.

To an extent the preoccupation with constructivism and deconstruction can be seen as part of this search for an architectural language which would reconcile the scientific rationality of problem solving, with an aesthetic that would be individualistic and interpretational, able to resolve the issues of scale and context which pervade our cities, without resort to history. But these are in danger of becoming internal architectural languages out of touch with the society they are intended to serve. They portray an architecture of destruction, one that is as unfriendly and unfamiliar as that they seek to supplant: a comic-strip architecture of entertainment, to be viewed in a familiar, comfortable, well-lit and secure environment. Or is an architecture of deconstruction an environmental foretaste of the daily deconstruction of industry, employment and finance?

But technology remains one of the prime sources of inspiration for architects and designers, and the source of a perennial paradox. It is both the root for an aesthetic that will represent the current mood, and the facilitator of socially generated needs. The idea of the technological cottage, full of the most up to date electronic gadgets and equipment, self-sufficient and cheap to run, providing instant access to the world of work and pleasure, seemingly by a single remote control from a familiar armchair, is not longer new. The point is that both because of and despite the

advances of technology, it is user-friendly; because the technology would be inaccessible if it was not, and because, in a world of constant change, it provides an equally constant and familiar social anchor. After the ravages of wartime and the vandalism of the subsequent modern movement, a built environment which is user friendly, familiar and safe has become a form of social security.

But to those for whom state security had deadened the will, and almost snuffed the candle of innovation, it is a different story. For them, the built environment is a place to conserve memories of an individualistic and more dynamic past; a place to innovate anew, building upon those memories to erase the political vandalism of the intervening years. In both east and west, the past fifty years is seen as destructive of the individuality and uniqueness of the city, whether under the dead hand of totalitarianism, in both eastern and western guises, or under the equally dead but shiny hand of a market economy.

The city of today is not the place for a single architecture, a single attitude, a single politics or a single God; but the setting for a mixture of buildings from different periods for different purposes, each a reflection of its time and the ever-changing idiosyncrasies of the people who use it. We must seek architectures for our cities that do not offend; but that make significant landmarks where these are to be made, that sit unobtrusively in the background when appropriate, that fit the urban pattern and sustain its diverse, multi-cultural activities. This infers a city which sustains change and in so doing sustains itself – a city that is a permanent form of social security for its inhabitants.

Inasmuch as the successful home permits personalization and provides for the individuality of its occupants, neighborhoods and cities equally reflect familiarity of place and identity of location. The landmarks of the past provide for that familiarity and identity, more so than do many from the present. Yet a city must be dynamic, able to change without apparently changing, offering opportunity for enterprise without diminution of its familiarity and identity, encouraging that which identifies and develops uniqueness above that which is everyday.

New City State

This dynamism of change has brought cities into competition with each other, each outbidding the other for supremacy of one form or another; each making careful self-appraisal of its attributes and potentialities in order to attract a diminishing amount of money, and a diminishing market. Without an inherent identity and strength a city is seen to struggle, even to decline. And in a diminishing market an inability to compete – with jobs, with environment, with homes – means that migration to the more successful city becomes inevitable. A city on lines of communication, offering easy transportation to the next, facilitates interchangeability of jobs with security of home base, and has the ability to draw on a larger population for events of the increasing importance it needs to sustain its prestige. The dangers of this inter-city rivalry become obvious. The race is on; the fittest will prosper, the weak will decline.

Throughout Europe cities are competing: the state capitals of Germany with one another over the qualities of their parks, transportation, galleries, orchestras, education, and so on; the decentralized cities of France keen to outdo each other for national prestige. Cities are in competition for government and EU funds; for trade fairs, conferences, universities; national institutions, world and regional headquarters; national and world events. Each wants to attract more people, more trade, more money; and can only do so by offering something special, something unique. Identity, character,

sense of place, quality, are the watchwords. The rewards are great, the competition severe.

A reliable source of labor, good schools and other facilities are obvious assets, but in themselves they are no longer enough. A quality of environment can sustain a quality of life, and a city which invests in its environment is one which is more likely to succeed when other assets seem equal. European Union legislation is aimed at benefiting those cities which address this very point, thereby fueling the rivalry.

The city state of fourteenth century Italy and the New Towns of the Dukes of Zähringen are obvious historical parallels; one rivaled another for power and prestige; civic buildings and events brought individuality, identity and difference. The quality of planning and architecture plays a significant part, now as it did then, in the regeneration of the European city.

An Agenda

The emergence of the new City State is already establishing a fresh social, economic and political agenda. Much of its content is being derived from parts of Europe where the strength of regionalism and the purpose of the city were never entirely submerged by universality; and where the manner of physical intervention within the fabric of the city belongs to an older, and some would say unmodernized, professional order. Urban design has emerged as a multi-disciplinary something new, when in reality it is a turning back of the professional clock to times when the term did not exist, but the job was actually done better.

'I used to think there was a thing called urban design. I now think it is called architecture. We have to remember that there was no such subject as urban design in the days when we did it well. The

term did not exist. The more I think of what in recent years we have come to call urban design or what foreigners call urbanism, the more I think that this is architecture... We have to enlarge the concept of architecture and not try to slip in between it and planning something called urbanism.' (Esher, 1984)

The agenda for urban design, whoever in fact does it and however it may come to be described, infers a shift away from the merely visual and sculptural aspects of urban decision making, without of course losing sight of them, to embrace the social, economic and technical parameters upon which the new City State is being founded. Sustainability, interdependence, identity, clarity of purpose, and security are here proposed as keywords in any agenda for urban design that is intended to achieve a functioning order and a unique identity for the future city.

Interdependence

Interdependence infers the mixing of functions because each relies on the other's proximity for sustenance. The concept of proximity both enlarges and diminishes the notion of distance. The expanding proximities of communications are poles apart from the shrinking proximities of pedestrian orientation, where increasingly more facilities are demanded within a walking distance that, at 10 minutes or half a mile, has remained fairly constant since it was rediscovered at Radburn, New Jersey, when the motor car was in its ascendancy. (Stein, 1958) The blinkered expertise of institutional investment, which conditions the separation of shopping, industry and housing, is overdue for reform. One can begin to argue that future pensions might better be secured by investment in development that was naturally sustainable rather than artificially controlled.

Housing needs to be encouraged back into the city center, and served with essential needs rather than fashion accessories. Offices, service industries, light manufacturing and specialty production, need to be more closely grouped and grouped alongside housing, according to levels of access and pollution rather than rate-determined use classes. Public functions need to be decentralized along lines of public communication, to enrich and identify areas outside the center and spread the prosperity of the city, rather than concentrated into mono-functional ghettos controlled by time and crime. The worst excesses of the nineteenth century city which beget current planning, can now be controlled by qualitative and quantitative environmental measures, in order to permit a return to the perennial values of neighborliness, self-help, philanthropy, esteem and interdependence for which it stood.

Identity

In the new City State identity replaces conservation. Values are changing so that every aspect of life becomes concerned with conservation, which is as much, if not more, about the future than the past. Local civic groups might be concerned to encourage urban identity through a variety of civic projects, to promote civilization and culture, civility and citizenship. As urban vigilantes their concern would be to secure the city's visual identity, rather than be bothered about conformity to universally perceived notions of good taste that succeed only in making everywhere look like everywhere else. Without a role which defines and enhances difference and uniqueness they could have no place.

Conservation is all-pervasive. Conservation of the past as the unique root which identifies the present and the future goes almost without saying. Almost; because too often it is the uniqueness which is missed in the mission to conserve at all costs. Conservation of the future infers that it is imperative to conserve at all costs. But it is real costs that are at stake now: the cost of conserving energy for the future, the cost to the environment of the consumption of fossil fuels, of pollution and waste, the cost of generating power from natural energy, the cost of doing something that will be sustainable in the future. All of these demand an unblinkered view of conservation, and the ability to assimilate whatever is necessary to achieve them in conservation of a living organism.

Solar collectors, wind generators, heat sinks, trombe walls, atria and conservatories must become as much a part of the social and economic urban scene as the church spires, defensive walls and moats, town halls and market places, which we now seek to conserve, contributed to the urban scene in their day. Technical progress will generate devices and forms yet unknown. Conservation takes on a new meaning in the context of sustainability. Conservation of energy infers that the veil of historical preservation and look-alike caution be lifted to accommodate these new forms. It may be argued that they are acceptable away from historical precedent, in the same way that shiny retail and industrial boxes are acceptable out of town. But if, in so doing, peripheral growth is perpetuated, then the reasons for their existence will have been denied. Should we hide technical progress out of sight, while it powers a historical pastiche? Should we not reveal it as part of a living identity that is acceptable, perhaps even desirable, once it is seen to have a social and economic purpose?

Clarity of Purpose

It is, after all, only a clarity of purpose which can provide the will to achieve these, or any other goals. While national and local administrations pull in different directions, while people are at odds with their masters, little can be achieved except by a rule of law which

smacks of dictatorship, however benevolent this may appear to be. In a devolved democracy public participation becomes paramount, not by the election of representatives to lucrative talking-shops in another city or another country, not by the lip-service of public inquiries, or by the fending-off of public disquiet by palliative measures, but by a process of local democracy that makes clear the purpose of changes and arrives at decisions which clearly reflect local opinion about them. The accelerating pace of competition provides the spur to imaginative decisions and overcomes much divided opinion, but without a competition having a clarity of purpose to those who should benefit from winning, it will become a mere spectator event: a post match brawl, a television saga, a newspaper campaign.

The media provide the agora of today, the public meeting place, the forum for debate. The purpose of a city's open spaces are denied, the space between buildings open to offer to the highest bidder, the car. Gradually the car is being pushed back, to regain space within the city for the pedestrian. But to what purpose is this space other than exclusion of the car and, one believes, a reduction in the number of accidents? Pedestrianized space has become an area to fill again, almost embarrassingly because of its size, with coarse imitations of bygone paving, antique bollards and signposts, kiosks, franchised barrows and musical beggars – a scene from My Fair Lady! What is it: a parade ground for the latest fashion uniform, a conduit between car park, bus station and shopping mall, a last resort for the ostracized smoker, somewhere to drop off a salvationary coin or two?

The original open space pattern upon which the pedestrianized precinct has been implanted, had a distinct clarity of purpose. The major open space was a market place, for trade and periodic festivals, there may have been other open spaces associated with town hall or church, for public meetings or religious ceremonies; surrounding streets served trading purposes with an intensity that is paralleled today in the indoor shopping mall; residential squares served as neighborhood gardens and playgrounds. Ambiguity is the hallmark of most of these spaces today, the purpose of their delineations gone. Open spaces are proposed in many a new urban development, and apparently without any sense of the vagaries of weather, are universally portrayed for investors and planning authorities as posing grounds for beautiful people on sunny days.

Redefinition is needed. Inasmuch as the space within buildings is tightly controlled by management costs, and must increasingly be accountable for its energy efficiency and pollutants, so too must the space outside. The administration of our competitive City State will not take too kindly to the cost of its maintenance, unless it serves a purpose for the city upon which a value can be placed. Perhaps it is a heat sink pond, a space to secure regulatory sunlight on south facing solar collectors or trombe wall, a mass of trees to absorb carbon dioxide; perhaps it is a local market place or the venue for a latter day festival, a cultural and performance arena, a twenty-first century agora to take over from, or be taken over by, a now ineffectual media…

Security

Sadly, as inequalities are exposed by both stagnating economy and soaring inflation, as the poor get relatively poorer and the rich relatively richer, as the costly habits of eradicating a downtrodden existence bite, so crime appears to increase. Yet while it is on the increase the city continues to attract, continues to provide a haven of security for a sustained existence. The balance is a precarious one. And of the items on this agenda for urban design, security is perhaps the most urgent, but may remain as the most insoluble and intractable in democratic terms. The images of earlier City States are dominated by the forms and devices of security; defensive measures by which the city was secured from attack without, and individual holdings were secured from attack within.

Post-Script

Between seven and four hundred years ago the city states of northern Italy and the munificence of the Dukes of Zähringen, supplied the venues for the cultural tours and international conferences of today. Within their defensive walls are preserved an unsurpassed richness of art and architecture, a calmness and a self-sufficiency, a unique sense of place and purpose. Then, the idea of city generated a fervor about supremacy, attracted artists and craftsmen to embellish it, artisans to trade upon its prosperity serving time-honored values of supply and demand, others to camp outside its walls in hope of a secure home within, or to tend the surrounding land which fed the city.

Ernie Scoffham, B. Arch. Ph.D., FRSA, is Reader in Urban Architecture and Director of the Center for Urban Design at the University of Nottingham, Nottingham, UK.

Chapter Thirty-Three

Marketing Local Identity;
The Importance Of The Physical

Bill Erickson and Marion Roberts

It is now common to suggest that the traditional identity of local places is being eroded by the invasion of global corporations, retailing their products through a world-wide market, through time-space compression enabling distant places to seem familiar, through the dispersal of migrant communities and cultures across continents. It appears that everywhere, anywhere is becoming the same. Simultaneously in a fight for economic survival, cities are tussling to attract their share of multinational capital, for headquarters, soft drink plants or factories, emphasizing the unique qualities of their town or city. As they struggle to do so, places become products to be marketed and promoted, using glossy leaflets and videos.

Yet as ordinary places come to be sold in commodified form, extraordinary places provide areas of real experience. Theme parks, shopping malls and heritage centres are marketed to millions; to millions, these manufactured places are simply part of the everyday.

Our research started from these observations; that there are tensions between the local and the global, that there are shifting relations between the authentic experience and the mediated perception. While these shifts have been studied elsewhere, for example by David Harvey, as urban designers we are interested in their influence on the design and production of the built environment. In this paper we shall consider these divisions further and move on to describe some empirical work which we undertook on city marketing. Finally we shall end,

with some questions about the role of urban design in all of this.

Identity is an elusive concept. It can be defined as the qualities that make an individual, or place, capable of being specified or singled out, that make it unique and separate. Conversely identity can also refer to perfect sameness between individuals, to the state of being identical. No two cities can be described as identical and the notion of city identity is most usually explored in the former sense of the word, yet in doing so it remains useful to consider two tendencies, of increasing distinctiveness and toward uniformity. In this light identity can be explored as a range between these two extremes and as processes which tend toward one or the other.

As individuals we all form personal identities and an understanding of our location within social groupings and in space has long been recognized as fundamental in this process. Places (cities) and their identity are bound to experience and emotion; that is, we recognize similarities and differences between ourselves, other people and other places. Place identity is an essential part of self-identity. The places we share and their meanings form a "collective self-identity of the community". The identity of our built environment is thus both raw material and the product of social practice. This reflexive process produces "authentic" or "real" places where populations are bound over time to location through inter-subjective experience, meaning and action.

The apparent loss of this authentic place bound experience has been the cause of much alarm. It was well documented by Relph twenty years ago who lamented that this authentic relationship with place was being eroded by the forces of modern capital, rendered inauthentic. He described the main manifestations of this as; the production of synthetic or pseudo-places such as Disneyland, the standardization of buildings and products, formless and giant developments such as suburbia and skyscrapers and instant or non-permanent buildings. In this process the personal relationship with place is reduced or mediated due to forces such as: the mass communication of ideas, the role of centralizing bureaucracies and the globalizing power of "big business". In the two decades since Relph's book we have seen the rise of what Harvey describes as the Condition of Postmodernity. Our everyday experience is increasingly mediated, vicarious and shaped by mass consumerism. Further, as Jameson argues, under the intense pressure of the ubiquitous reproduction of the real as image we have lost the wish to make a "syntactic" connection between past, future and present. The distinction between the authentic and the manufactured is increasingly confused.

Are authentic places the product only of pre-industrial homogeneous societies and experienced today only by "residual" communities as some post-modern commentators suggest? Geographers have long rejected the simplistic notion of place with a clearly defined boundary and a simple fixed or singular identity. Individual districts maybe home to multiple populations each with a differing sense of place. Patrick Wright for example evokes the contrasting responses of the different groups who live in Stoke Newington in London, minority communities, Jews, Irish, Afro-Caribbean, white middle class gentrifiers together with the "residual" indigenous white working class.

Places are sources of strong sentiments and while their identities may be compound or complex they continue as the basis of ideology and collective action because territorial place-based identity, particularly when conflated with race, ethnic, religious and class differentiation, is one of the most pervasive bases for both progressive political mobilization and reactionary politics. Cities are increasingly complex and confusing places. However so that we may interact at a functional level we seek order in this confusion and attach meanings to the environment. We continue to attach and extract identities from the city. However as Harvey warns us, as traditional values are broken down so new mythologies of power can be established and our search for authenticity is open to exploitation. We have witnessed a similar imposition in the marketing of consumer products, which uses our desire to recreate our personal identities through the linking of artifacts (products) with emotion, desire and action. One might expect therefore that city identity and image to be exploited in the commodification and marketing of places.

Marketing has been seen as increasingly important by city managers in Britain, as elsewhere, most of whom now engage in some form of place promotion. The increased pressure on city managers to compete for investment and "market" their locality has led to a renewed interest in local difference. To examine the type of impact this may be having on City Identity we looked first at the manner in which cities "sell" themselves, that is attract mobile capital to their locality. There becomes apparent a tension between local interest and the needs of capital. Unlike places, goods and capital and are now extremely mobile, the spatial network in which global capital operates is more or less uniform, dictated by a system of proximities communications but is fragmented by pressures of local difference including loyalties of class, gender, race and special interest, which may include, incidentally an interest for place. Jameson characterizes this as a kind of "schizospace" a space looking out and looking in. This tension is evident in the marketing material we examined. For example Solihull, which is a metropolitan district in England includes in its material under the slogan of "a place to work" imagery of a motorway network and factory locations while under the slogan of "place to live" exhibits imagery of a group of historic locations.

Marketing places poses particular problems since they differ from the traditional concept of a consumer product in marketing theory; places are immobile, multi-faceted and non-priced. Marketing involves the construction and projection of particular images about a place. These are transmitted, via promotional material in an attempt to confirm expectations and to extend awareness of that location. This also involves the redefinition of the city as an "urban product". Such definitions can be difficult, but essentially they consists of the physical entity of the city together with a range of services which that city can offer. Most cities in the UK offer the basic physical requirements for modern industry or commerce given the mobility of goods and capital. It is locational advantages and transport services which provide competitive edge and become frequent features of promotional material. In our study, location and transport are the most common element of a promotional publication. Such added amenity frequently represents the major value of the urban product. Other obvious amenities include commercial and financial services, a skilled workforce, good housing and abundance of recreational activities and these are also frequently featured in the material.

Marketing material essentially seeks to allay any doubts regarding possible disbenefits, this tends to produce a marked uniformity in form and content. However in order to be successful the material must produce a memorable, and therefore unique, image. In their promotions cities tend to claim generic amenity plus special unique features. To be memorable and provide impact a strong sense of identity must emerge from promotional material. This may be attempted through the form of the material itself, some cities for example use very arresting graphics or provide a video, or alternatively seek to emphasize famous and unique features of the place.

We found several elements used frequently to emphasize difference. Civic buildings are common, especially town halls which act as a metaphor for community (and of the body funding the promotion), shopping centers and theaters. Unlike tourist brochures these documents tend not to catalogue historic and monumental building but do include them usually in association with other activities such as shopping, housing or recreation. Other "heritage" locations feature especially industrial ones such as canals but appear in the context of recreation. Interestingly cities with a strong historic reputation such as Bath or York play down the heritage theme and stress the existence of modern facilities and communications while places with a weak or negative image may stress what history they do have. Thus Solihull again, is presented as an historic rural village. Where a particular natural feature such as a river or port exists it too is emphasized. Few cities adopt a modern image, most preferring the rural or the traditional. A notable exception to this is the Glasgow's Alive promotion which concatenates modern and traditional images to suggest dynamic place.

While business people may be able to make informed decisions regarding the needs and location of their business this may also necessitate their contemplation of living in a new location. Here too basic amenities are projected in promotional material; shopping, educational and recreational facilities. However less tangible attributes are also important and these are more difficult to value and to project; quality of life, sense of belonging, sense of community. As people are selecting a new home for themselves, their families and their employees and not simply a business location the comparison of the evaluative image becomes less analytical and more imaginative. There is a need to project an identity for the city as well as an image which combines favorable attributes.

Marketing cities needs then to include identity. Pre-modern city identity was established through local materials and frequently associated the mode of production; the fishing village and the mining town but with the majority of people now working in the service sector these associations are no longer available. This shift is paralleled by an increasing importance in the value of "quality of life" issues as a locational factor for business and pressure to commodify local identity. In our study images concerned with lifestyle such as; shopping, leisure, education and housing facilities were nearly as common as those stressing business and locational advantage. Further those images in which features of local identity were apparent tended to be those associated with lifestyle. The marketing message appears to be "this is a good location for your business PLUS this is an enjoyable place to live" The projected image needs to engender the expectation of place-bound meaningful and positive experiences. However the marketing material may be directed at people who have no direct experience of the place involved and have only vague impressions of the city and its communities.

It is not surprising therefore to see a number of images appealing to stereotypes and especially those associated with leisure. Shopping high streets and market squares are common, mostly pedestrian, and featured in a general and familiar view. Rural imagery is ubiquitous and is even associated with metropolitan areas; flowers, gardens, heritage buildings and sport are all common as are those of the shopping high street or mall. Bath and York are not portrayed as historic centers but rather as places of the everyday. These images are not those of extraordinary events or scenes, rather they are of the social patterns of daily life which appeal to a desire for vitality and for place. Here too one can trace the impact of a schizophrenic attitude to locality, the desire to suggest that a particular experience is sated by

an appeal to stereotypical and familiar. Rather than appeal to group experiences which are the basis of authentic place formation these are directed at the individual in much the same manner as consumer advertising. They present the myth of the countryside as the simplest and immediate real experience- a return to a pre-industrial age with a direct relationship with production and with nature. They also appeal to consumption itself as the experience of the real.

One is lead to speculate about the nature of the experiences portrayed. Are they those of the authentic place- bound relationship between city and citizens? Was Relph wrong? Is authenticity safe, perhaps even nurtured by a renewed interest in locality? Alternatively we can see these images as the commodification of the everyday in the public realm. Do they represent a sanitized and packaged view of how the city should be if it is to appeal to the "movers and shakers" of business? Do they represent the appropriation of the authentic by capital in the name of prosperity?

Sharon Zukin argues that all sense of local authenticity will inevitably be appropriated by the larger forces of the market economy and that the urban designer's role lies in manipulating style and urban comfort. She posits a new model for the urban experience; that of Disneyland, one in which our expectations are formulated by marketing and our experiences mediated through a commercialized process, where the urban environment becomes a product for visual consumption. Here the syntactic relation to history is severed in the constant recycling of the familiar. However is this transformation inevitable, complete and irreversible. We hope not. We have shown how identities can be plural, relative and dynamic, rather than absolute and fixed. Surely it is our task to facilitate their rapid development in the face of mounting pressures upon them.

Spaces can and indeed are, appropriated by their resident populations at particular times. All cities have such examples; Housing estates where social groupings based on violence and youth culture, born of social inequality create "no go areas" in which the normal social values and conventions, such as the rule of law, are rejected. In many cities districts have been transformed by the rapid influx of and domination by ethnic, gay or other minority populations. Such groupings may result from particular attributes which at that location offers (amenities such as religious buildings, gay bars or specialist food stores) or economic necessities. Most cities have had a "red-light zone" or a "China Town" Indeed these identities are the product of difference, it is they which shatter the homogeneity of the urban product. And yet it is these local identities which are rare in city marketing, [which conforms to the market view].

In a hyper-mobile economy we are increasingly free to choose where we live. We move to places that suit our selves. One may think also of areas of gentrification; picturesque or historic locations where the built environment has acquired value as social capital. Here new populations unite to form powerful lobby groups to protect, reinforce and even manufacture the qualities they value in the environment but in so doing redefine their social grouping in terms of the place.

In these and other examples authentic place bound socio-spatial identities can be witnessed evolving. These are. not the authentic identities described by Relph where populations and places form one another in an even flow of space and time. These are populations which appropriate place or which create themselves out of place but which may then enter into a reflexive relation with it.
We believe that city managers can contribute to the nurturing of social-spatial identities but that such identities are unpredictable and shifting. The task is to allow populations to engage with their environment, to invigorate attachments to existing places and to foster new attachments rather than relying on existing stereotypical imagery and vacuous meanings. The very forces seen as acting against local identity, such as mass advertising, can be brought to its aid. In this instance one might think of the famous "I ❤ NY" campaign. Managers and designers can encourage in and invigorate new forms of place making. As researchers we see our next task as exploring those strategies already being adopted to this end. We have already made a study of one such example; the use of public art in urban redevelopment and, as we argue in another paper at this conference, this strategy may result in conflict, or failure but also in vivid successes.

Bill Erickson, B. Arch., M.A., M.Sc., School of Urban Development and Planning, Faculty of the Environment, University of Westminster, London, U.K.

Dr. Marion Roberts, B. Sc. (Hons.), Dipl. Arch., School of Urban Development and Planning, Faculty of the Environment, University of Westminster, London, U.K.

Ecology

Ökologie

Dietmar Hahlweg explaining the "Green in Erlangen" program of ecological improvements.

Chapter Thirty-Four

Ecological Principles For New Urban Areas

Dietmar Hahlweg

I would like to start by mentioning a sentence which is used more and more, "Think globally, act locally." In the 1970's our citizens in the U.S. and in Europe started to use this sentence because of information about developments around the globe. In the beginning of the 1970's we started to make ecology an important political issue. We heard that Mayor Casellati of Venice was selected in 1971 as one of the first politicians in Italy who was fighting for this issue.

Now since the conference in Rio, we use the term "sustainable development"; that means development that takes care of resources, not only to provide good living conditions in the community where we are planning and making decisions, but around the globe. And to contribute to this big task, since the conference in Rio, all the countries who took part in this conference decided to make sustainable development an important official goal. And they decided on Agenda 21, which says that they will try, in every community and every country, to act in the same way.

Now the main goals are to try to prevent damage to nature and to ecology, and to save resources as much as possible. That means -- and it was mentioned already by Mayor Ungern-Sternberg, who talked about the principles of new urban areas -- that one of the principles in our cities should be to plan the new city in a way that there is a possibility to use energy as rationally as possible, for instance, by district heating, and to save energy.

Another principle is to try to save as much water as possible. Use the water which comes as rain and not put it into the sewage, but try to let it seep back into the ground, and save this ground water.

Another principle is to reduce garbage and recycle as much as possible. And it is very important to also mention that we need to prevent unnecessary traffic. From all that we know, it costs a lot of energy, makes a lot of noise, and is not good for our clean air.

Now, talking about new developments, new urban areas, I think that it is important to stress the point that the key to most of these goals is reasonable density. We know that this is easy to say, but there are many countries, especially the United States where they have a very large percentage of low density, where most people want to have their own house. The ideal is my home is my castle and this castle should be on a large lot, and there should be no trespassers. This ideal creates density problems. So, I think we agree that reasonable density is the key to most of these ecological goals.

I would like to mention a few of the great advantages which were made possible by reasonable density. To save space is very important in the protection of natural land, which is lost by development in our cities and communities in all our countries almost every day. And this development will have to end, and if we do not stop this, then in more and more regions people will have to go by car or metro miles and miles in order to come to an area which is not changed by development. So, density saves space and natural landscape.

This is very important because if you save space, natural landscape, then you have easy access from the densely planned neighborhood to this free landscape. And this saves not only time to go there, you can go there by foot or by bicycle, and it is not necessary to use the car and go far away.

Now, density also makes possible district heating. It makes it possible to save energy by building townhouses, as we have in England and also in other countries. You save energy by densely planned neighborhoods. And there is no doubt that density makes it economically feasible to have an attractive public transportation system. It is impossible to have attractive transportation in a dispersed planning situation.

Density also makes it possible to have mixed use. To have shops which really have an economic base, because there are enough clients in order to make it possible to run a business, or a café or restaurant in this new development. And density also makes it possible to bring living, dwelling, and working together.

Now, I have enough experience and not only successes in mind when I talk about this topic. I know how very difficult it is to find the right density. Mr. Salzano said it is one of the main tasks of planners and politicians to find how densely such new developments can be planned. And there is no question that the quality of this planning has to be even better and more attractive, and therefore is more complicated and difficult than just planning a very nice suburban area.

So, I think that this is a very necessary, but also very interesting, task for us all, to plan new developments that make density possible, and to make these new developments aesthetic, and socially successful.

Higher density is necessary from the ecological point of view, but density also offers advantages for social and safety reasons.

So I think we should take a new approach to reasonable density for the sake of ecology, and for the sake of the people in our cities.

Dr. Dietmar Hahlweg is former Lord Mayor of Erlangen, Germany and Member of the IMCL Board.

Ökostadt 2000
Ein Siedlungsmodell

Rainer Mayerhofer, u.a.

Wenn sich die Städte wie bisher weiterentwickeln, dann werden dort nach glaubhaften Prognosen zwei Drittel der Weltbevölkerung unter zunehmend schlechter werdenden Umweltbedingungen zu leben haben, die wesentlichen vitalen Bedürfnissen nicht mehr gerecht werden. Die Richtung dieser Entwicklung, mit Verschwendung von Ressourcen und insbesondere von Energie, mit starker Belastung der Umwelt und Beeinträchtigung des Wohlbefindens der Menschen, ändert sich nur langsam. Erschwerend kommt hinzu, daß nur in kleinen Teilbereichen isolierte Verbesserungen unternommen, daß im wesentlichen nur eindimensionale Maßnahmen realisiert wurden (z.B.: Erhöhung des Mindestwarmeschutzes in den Bauordnungen, Errichtung entlegener kleiner Einfamilienhaussiedlungen mit Optimierung der Sonnenenergienutzung wie z.B. die "Solar Subdivisions" in New Mexico, Einführung des Katalysators) und zu wenige, bzw. zu wenig weitreichend vernetzte Lösungsansätze untersucht werden.

Nur ökologisch funktionierende Städte bieten die Chance, natürliche Landschaften im notwendigen Ausmaß zu erhalten, einen umweltverträglichen Energiehaushalt zu erreichen und der Umweltverschmutzung entgegenzuwirken.

Während alle einschlägigen Raumordnungsprogramme einen komplexen, die Ökologie weitgehend berücksichtigenden Zielkatalog aufweisen, werden nur bei wenigen vor der Realisierung stehenden Projekten erste Schritte zu einer Vernetzung getan.

(Zum Beispiel sind in dem primär als Wohnstadt geplanten Niedrigenergie-Stadtteil "Solar City" in Linz-Pichling, der von einer Straßenbahnlinie erschlossen werden soll, neben 6.000 - 8.000 Wohneinheiten auch Gewerbeflächen vorgesehen)

Erforderlich wäre ein grundsätzliches Umdenken in Richtung auf einen ganzheitlichen Ansatz und zwar auf allen Ebenen:

- der Überörtlichen Raumplanung (Regionalplanung),

- der Örtlichen Raumplanung (örtliche Entwicklungs-, Flachenwidmungs- und Bebauungsplanung) und

- der Objektplanung.

Zielvorstellungen

Mit dem Projekt "Okostadt 2000" wird eine solche Alternative zur derzeitigen Stadtentwicklung angeboten:

Anstelle einer weiteren Verdichtung der Ballungsräume - wo eine ökologische Stadtentwicklung infolge der vorhandenen festgefügten Strukturen kaum oder nur sehr langsam erfolgen kann - und insbesondere anstelle einer weiteren Zersiedelung im Umland der Großstädte werden neue, weitgehend eigenständige Siedlungseinheiten abseits der Verdichtungsgebiete angestrebt, die zur Gänze nach geänderten Prinzipien strukturiert werden sollen.

- Der Mensch und die Natur bilden den Maßstab fur die Entwicklung von Technik und Wirtschaft und nicht umgekehrt - die Lebensweise soll sich an der Sicherung hoher Lebensqualität für die Menschen durch die langfristige Erhaltung der natürlichen Lebensgrundlagen orientieren.

- Bei allen Aktivitäten sollen die Belastungen für die Gesundheit der Menschen und für die Umwelt durch die Anwendung von Verfahren minimiert werden, welche die Entstehung von Schadstoffen sowie die Ausbeutung der Vorräte der Erde (Rohstoffe und Energie) durch möglichst geschlossene Kreislaufe weitgehend vermeiden.

- Das wichtigste Ziel der Stadtplanung muß darin bestehen, Bedingungen zu schaffen, unter denen sich die Bewohner wohl fühlen. Eine wesentliche Voraussetzung dafür stellt die Beachtung der sozialen Auswirkungen bei allen technischen Lösungen dar. Die bauliche Struktur sollte die Entstehung einer Organisationsform der Gemeinschaft begünstigen, die ein friedliches Zusammenleben fördert und größtmögliche Sicherheit (Vermeidung von Unfällen, Schutz vor Gewalt) gewährleistet. Durch das Zusammenwirken zahlreicher Einzelmaßnahmen im Rahmen einer ökologischen Gesamtstruktur soll die Stadt als Lebensraum wieder an Attraktivität gewinnen.

- Die Funktionsmischung bildet die Grundlage für die räumliche Verteilung aller Lebensbereiche. Sie wird auf überörtlicher und örtlicher Ebene in Form der dezentralen Konzentration optimiert:
Bei allen Einrichtungen soll einerseits eine größtmögliche Dezentralisierung soweit sie wirtschaftlich sinnvoll ist - angestrebt werden, andererseits ist zur Optimierung von Weglängen und zur Nutzung von Synergieeffekten eine gewisse Konzentration erforderlich.

Die Ökostadt ist ein Modell fur eine flächensparende städtische Bauweise sowie eine umwelt- und sozialverträgliche Gestaltung technischer und wirtschaftlicher Einrichtungen.

Das Schwerpunkt - Achsen - Prinzip

Eine lineare Siedlungsentwicklung entlang einer Achse stellt die Alternative zum ungeordneten flächenhaften Wachstum der Ballungsräume dar. Das Schwerpunkt-Achsen-Prinzip ist nicht neu. Es ist beispielsweise in einem bereits 1972 vom Deutschen Bundestag formulierten "Zielsystem zur räumlichen Ordnung und Entwicklung der Verdichtungsräume in der Bundesrepublik Deutschland" enthalten. Konsequent umgesetzt wurde dieses Prinzip bei den Trabantenstädten Stockholms, die im Umkreis von max. 800 m um die Haltestellen der Schnellbahn mit einer Verdichtung der Bebauung in der Nahe der Haltestelle errichtet wurden.

Die Ökostadt als neue Siedlungseinheit bildet einen Schwerpunkt an einer Entwicklungsachse, um die optimale Anbindung an benachbarte Orte durch ein öffentliches Verkehrsmittel zu ermöglichen. Ein günstiger Standort wäre neben einer historisch gewachsenen Kleinstadt gegeben, deren Funktion als zentraler Ort durch ergänzende Einrichtungen in der neuen Siedlungseinheit aufgewertet würde. Eine ausreichende Entfernung vom nächsten Ballungsraum (rund 50 km), der für die Ökostadt als zentraler Ort höchster Ordnung dient, sorgt dafür, daß Pendlerbewegungen in Grenzen gehalten werden. Die Achse kann durch eine bestehende, gering belastete, Regionalbahnstrecke (die meist aber nicht optimal trassiert ist) oder durch eine in das bestehende Netz eingepaßte Neubaustrecke (als Stadtbahn für den Nahverkehr etwa nach dem Vorbild von Karlsruhe) erschlossen werden.

Wesentlich ist dabei die Abstimmung des Angebotes der an der Entwicklungsachse geiegenen Siedlungen aufeinander, sodaß benachbarte Siedlungen einander ergänzen. Der wichtigste Unterschied zu vielen neuen Siedlungen (meist "Schlafstädte") besteht aber in der Funktionsmischung innerhalb der Siedlungseinheiten, insbesondere durch die Anordnung ausreichender Arbeitsplätze zur Vermeidung von Pendlerbewegungen.

Bisherige Versuche zum Ausbau von Siedlungen nach dem Schwerpunkt-Achsen-Prinzip waren nur teilweise erfolgreich. Die Entwicklungsstrategie für die Region Basel sieht das Entstehen neuer Schwerpunkte entlang der bestehenden Bahnlinien durch die Ansiedlung neuer Arbeitsplätze und neuer Wohnungen vor. Auch in einigen Trabantenstädten Stockholms sind Arbeitsstätten vorhanden. Aber sowohl in Basel als auch in Stockholm ist es nicht gelungen zu erreichen, daß die Menschen weitgehend in ihrem Wohnort auch ihren Arbeitsplatz finden. Gründe dafür könnten sein, daß diese Siedlungen nahe an den Ballungsraumen liegen und daß insbesondere der motorisierte Individualverkehr wegen der nicht kostendeckenden Preise zu billig ist.

In einer Studie der Planungsgemeinschaft Ost (der österreichischen Bundesländer Burgenland, Niederösterreich und Wien) wurde ein Modell entwickelt, das in der großräumigen Entwicklung den Zielen der Ökostadt nahe kommt: durch "Urbanisierung der Land-Städte" soll der "Suburbanisierung des Um-Landes" (des Ballungsräumes Wien) entgegengearbeitet werden - die Neubautätigkeit bei Wohnungen, aber auch bei Arbeitsplätzen, soll auf geeignete, nicht zu nahe am Ballungsraum gelegene, regionale Zentren (Kleinstädte) konzentriert werden .

Das Schwerpunkt-Achsen-Prinzip bietet die besten Voraussetzungen für Verkehrslösungen im Umweltverbund: innerhalb der Siedlung Fußgänger und Radfahrer, in den Außenbeziehungen öffentlicher Verkehr.

Die Stadt der kurzen Wege als städtebauliches Prinzip

Die Siedlungseinheiten der Ökostadt sind von der Einwohnerzahl her so ausgelegt (ca. 5.000-10.000 Einwohner), daß sie einerseits die Anordnung wirtschaftlich tragfähiger Einrichtungen für alle wesentlichen Funktionen erlauben (Untergrenze), andererseits eine fußläufige Erreichbarkeit aller dieser Einrichtungen garantieren (Obergrenze).

Als wichtige Rahmenbedingung ist eine ausgewogene Bevölkerungsstruktur erforderlich - alle Altersgruppen und sozialen Schichten sollten vertreten sein. Damit wird die Entstehung eines sozialen Klimas der Verantwortung und Solidarität unterstützt.

(Diese Forderung läßt sich aus den negativen Erfahrungen ableiten, die bei der Besiedelung neuer Stadtteile mit einseitiger alters- und schichtspezifischer Bewohnerstruktur gemacht worden sind.)

Aus der Vorgabe, alle Wege innerhalb der Stadt in max. 15 Minuten zu Fuß zurücklegen zu können, ergibt sich ein Durchmesser des Siedlungsgebietes von etwa 1,0 bis 1,2 km;

Das Ziel der Flächeneinsparung führt zwangsläufig zu einer kompakten Stadt. In Verbindung mit den erforderlichen, kleinräumig zugeordneten städtischen Folgeeinrichtungen entstehen die erwünschten kurzen Wege. Dabei spielt ein ausgewogenes Verhältnis von Wohnungen und Arbeitsplätzen die Hauptrolle. Um dieses zu erreichen, wird die Entwicklung eines neuen Instrumentariums für eine untereinander koordinierte Vergabe von Wohnungen und Arbeitsplätzen erforderlich sein.

Arbeitsplätze entstehen einerseits bei den von den Bewohnern der Ökostadt benötigten Einrichtungen für die städtischen Funktionen, andererseits in Produktions-, Handels- und Dienstleistungsbetrieben unterschiedlicher Branchen, bei denen besonderer Wert auf ökologische Verträglichkeit der erzeugten Produkte und der angewendeten Produktionsverfahren gelegt wird.

Ansätze zu einer Methode für eine gezielte Ansiedlung von Einrichtungen zeigen sich etwa bei der Vorgabe eines Branchenmix für Einkaufszentren. Eine ähnliche Vorgangsweise müßte auf die verschiedenen Einrichtungen im gesamten Siedlungsbereich ausgedehnt werden.

Bei der räumlichen Verteilung der Einrichtungen aller städtischer Funktionen (die gleichzeitig alle Arbeitstätten der Ökostadt umfassen) werden die Prinzipien der dezentralen Konzentration angewendet. Ihre Lage orientiert sich an der Häufigkeit der Nutzung, an der Erreichbarkeit für die Benutzer und an der optimalen Belieferung mit Gütern.

Insbesondere sollen Einrichtungen mit Transportbedarf für große Warenmengen und/oder schwere Produkte an der Hauptachse - der Trasse eines Schienenverkehrsmittels - liegen (Handelsbetriebe

innerhalb der Siedlung, produzierendes Gewerbe am Stadtrand), um Belastungen durch den Güterverkehr zu minimieren. Bei allen anderen Einrichtungen steht der Personenverkehr als Standortkriterium im Vordergrund - die nur einmal in der Ökostadt erforderlichen Einrichtungen (Schule, Veranstaltungssaal usw.) bilden das Zentrum, um für alle Bewohner möglichst gleich gut erreichbar zu sein; die häufiger benötigten Einrichtungen (täglicher Bedarf) sind in Subzentren oder an einer Nebenachse zusammengefaßt. Auf der dezentralsten Ebene sind den Wohnbauten insbesondere Freizeit- und Erholungseinrichtungen (Spiel- und Sportplätze, Gemeinschaftseinrichtungen, kleinere Grünanlagen) flächig zugeordnet.

Infolge der geringen Ausdehnung der Ökostadt ist der Zugang zu den - natürlichen oder gestalteten - übergeordneten Grünräumen an der Bebauungsgrenze fußläufig gegeben.

Diese Siedlungsstruktur ermöglicht den Bewohnern eine hohe Mobilität, weil infolge der geringen Entfernungen zwischen Einrichtungen, die häufig aufgesucht werden müssen, viele kurze Wege miteinander gekoppelt werden können.

Mobilität

Der Begriff Mobilität wird häufig fälschlich als Synonym für Verkehrsleistung verwendet. In der modernen Verkehrsplanung hat sich dagegen die folgende Definition durchgesetzt:

Mobilität wird durch die Anzahl der Wege, die in einer bestimmten Zeit erledigt werden können, bzw. durch die Anzahl der nutzbaren Gelegenheiten beschrieben. Eine hohe Mobilität ist daher nicht durch die Zurücklegung langer Strecken gekennzeichnet, sondern durch die große Anzahl von erreichten Zielen in der gleichen Zeiteinheit.

Der Personenverkehr innerhalb der Ökostadt wird von Fußgängern dominiert, denen ein zusammenhängendes, dichtes Wegenetz zur Verfügung steht, das sichere und weitgehend ungestörte Fortbewegung ermöglicht. Da Fußgänger sehr umwegempfindlich sind, sollen wichtige Ziele (im Zentrum, in den Subzentren und an der Hauptachse) möglichst auf direktem Weg erreichbar sein. Die Verbindungen ins Zentrum sollen auch Wetterschutz bieten - schattenspendende Bäume sowie Regenschutz in Arkaden und an der Hauptachse in Form einer Passage.

Für den internen Verkehr werden nur wenige Fahrzeuge benötigt. Am häufigsten werden Fahrräder eingesetzt: als Privat- oder Mietrad, für Botendienste, als Transportrad usw.. Nur für einige spezielle Aufgaben sind Kraftfahrzeuge erforderlich: als Einsatzfahrzeug, für die Müllsammlung oder als Montagefahrzeug für Handwerker. Diese sollen auf niedrigen Energieverbrauch und geringe Emissionen optimiert und zur Erhöhung der Sicherheit nur für die erforderliche bzw. zugelassene Geschwindigkeit (Tempo 30) ausgelegt sein.

Die Hauptwege für den Fußgänger- und Radverkehr führen als Wander- und Radwanderwege ins Umland der Ökostadt weiter und sind somit auch ein Symbol für die angestrebte Verbundenheit der Stadt mit ihrer Region.

Die Verbindung von der Ökostadt nach außen wird durch ein öffentliches Schienenverkehrsmittel (Stadtbahn, Schnellbahn oder Bahnstrecke) hergestellt. Die im Stadtzentrum liegende Haltestelle ist für Fußgänger optimal zugänglich. Sie bietet auch zahlreiche Dienstleistungen im Rahmen einer Mobilitätszentrale an: Fahrplanauskünfte vom regionalen bis zum internationalen Verkehr, Disposition bedarfsorientierter Verkehrssysteme (Rufbus, Anruf-Sammeltaxi) in der Region, Fahrrad- und eventuell Autovermietung, Fahrradbotendienst, Mobilitätsberatungen für Privatpersonen und Betriebe ...

Beim Güterverkehr werden die meisten Innovationen notwendig sein. Ein großer Teil davon ist zwar in neuen Konzepten für die Citylogistik bereits enthalten, aber noch nicht umfassend umgesetzt. Die wesentlichste Rolle spielt dabei ein Güterverteilzentrum, dessen Hauptaufgaben logistische Dienste, Lagerhaltung und die Verteilung der mit der Bahn und (zu einem nur kleinen Teil) mit LKWs angelieferten Güter in der Ökostadt sind. Für die Belieferung der Handelsbetriebe und die Zustellung schwerer Waren (Möbel, Elektrogeräte, etc.) zu den Kunden müßten noch stadtverträgliche Kleintransporter (etwa Elektrofahrzeuge) entwickelt werden.

Energieversorgung, solare Niedrigenergiebauweise

Das bestimmende Element in der baulichen Struktur stellt die Orientierung der Gebäude zur Sonne dar, um eine höhere Wohnqualität und einen größtmöglichen Wärmegewinn durch passive Sonnenenergienutzung zu erzielen. Durch weitgehende Vermeidung von Energieverlusten, durch aktive Nutzung der Sonnenenergie, den Einsatz von Langzeitspeichern und Energiegewinnung aus Wind, Biomasse und Wasserkraft kann der Einsatz fossiler Energiequellen auf ein Minimum reduziert werden.

Solares Bauen, das zugleich umweltschonend und energiesparend ist, läßt sich primär im städtischen Raum verwirklichen, wo kompakte, großvolumige Bauformen mit geringem Grundverbrauch möglich sind.

Walking, bicycling, public transportation: Erlangen, Germany

Werner Schwenke

Chapter Thirty-Seven

Integrated Transportation Planning
Strasbourg, France

Roland Ries

Despite continuous improvements in the road network during the last 30 years, the increase in the number of individual cars and their share in the Strasbourg transport system has led to problems of congestion whose intensity and effects are strongly felt in the central part of the urban area and around the main thoroughfares leading to the center. This, in fact, is where:

- the appeal is the strongest

- the concentration of activities is the most dense

- the framework and characteristics of roads and highways inherited from the past are the least adapted to car traffic.

The effects of traffic congestion are numerous, not merely in respect of an efficient transportation system, but also in relation to the functioning of the city as a whole and the quality of environment offered in central housing areas:

- the traffic conditions for traveling by car have continued to deteriorate with journeys that are increasingly long and uncertain and innumerable parking problems. The excessive energy consumption of cars is also another factor to be considered.

- apart from the relative stagnation over the past 15 years in the means of public transport offered, the running of the Strasbourg bus network also appears to be a cause for concern on several accounts: the commercial pace is slow, regularity is difficult to ensure at certain hours and the running costs are increasing.

- as a result of the saturation on main trunk roads caused by motorized traffic (cars and buses together), access to the city center has also not improved in the last ten years. Such a situation is scarcely compatible with an objective of fostering economic and cultural progress in the urban Strasbourg center. Moreover, logistic functions and urban supplies to the city center have, in particular, been affected by the intense traffic, leading to problems of isolation.

- the quality of the environment has continued to deteriorate as a result of pollution largely generated by the increasing use of motorized means of transport. At a time when the quality of the environment is a top social priority, various kinds of ecological and social pollution in urban areas can be observed.

Urban development and the morphological characteristics of areas have been totally conditioned by using cars as a primary mode of transport. The public space taken up by cars has greatly contributed to limiting other urban applications by the local authorities and public road maintenance services. The traffic conditions for those on foot and handicapped persons have steadily declined due to cars parked on sidewalks and the difficulties in crossing roads with heavy congestion. The indispensable links between different urban functions, particularly housing and stores have also been rendered more difficult.

The Strasbourg Urban Area Project (1990) advocates, in the sector of urban transport, the implementation of a strategy determined by three fundamental objectives:

• to find a new balance among the different modes of traveling inside the urban area, by developing a system of public transport whose essential feature will be a tramway network in special lanes, towards which, the reorganized bus services will be directed. The additional use of different transport modes will also be encouraged by setting up inter-modal transfer junctions which are well organized and appealing.

• to complete the network of main road links in order to connect the major areas of the city (by remedying the existing structural drawbacks of an excessively radial network).

• to draw up a traffic/parking scheme in the main center of the urban area (and when required, in the central areas of the outskirts) which would facilitate:

    • the reduction in through traffic on the main thoroughfares to the city center to reserve them specifically for purposes of access and connections. Certain public areas saturated by traffic would be used for other purposes. Thus, a new organization of areas and roads with an excessive flow of traffic would help to redefine the center's identity (notably by laying out pedestrian precincts presenting a certain continuity, from the cathedral to the Station and the Centre Halles and also in the protected sector of "Petite-France").

    • the integration of all the modes of transportation including two-wheeled vehicles and pedestrians, by taking into account safety requirements and complementarity of the different modes and also certain demands pertaining to a reduction in pollution and improvement in the environment.

    • the construction of proper parking facilities adapted to the needs of residents (= long periods) and those using the center. Building new parking lots around the *epicenter* and redefining parking conditions to encourage people to park for short periods in the city center are also part of the policy.

Moreover, the global transport/environment approach taken in this respect also involve the following:

• promoting electric traction in the *epicenter* (tramway, electric vehicles) and taking effective measures to reduce the pollution in certain central neighborhoods.

• producing long term changes in the habits of those using the center.

The reorganization undertaken in the field of urban transportation is a result of voluntarist actions, forming an integral part of urban progress and better living conditions.

In particular, the new layout of the central zone of the city is proof of a strong and explicit determination:

- to strengthen the economic framework of the city center, by enhancing the appeal of the service sector zone in the *epicenter* and relieving the congestion of the central zone by providing a possibility of spatial extension (both towards the North-West in the Gare and Halles areas and towards the South in the "Etoile" sector.

- to promote actions which enhance the central urban fabric and improve living conditions in order to preserve as large a population as possible in central neighborhoods. This strategy of development entails the following:

  - encouraging diverse uses of public areas, cleared of car traffic

  - launching safeguard operations for protecting the architectural heritage.

  - launching rehabilitation programs for old houses

  - carrying out regular operations for improving public squares, urban reforestation

  - promoting various social and cultural activities, open air markets, etc. by designing new layouts for public squares, thus making them suitable for hosting such activities.

  - facilitating delivery of supplies to the city.

- to develop tourist economy by means of actions promoting urban tourism on a long term and an efficient organization of tourist transportation.

The objectives of the Urban Transportation Scheme of Strasbourg, thus integrated in a global plan of rehabilitating urban areas in decline and protecting the "urban organism", represents a major challenge for the improvement of the city and the environment.

The "tramway project" of the Strasbourg Urban Community is a generic term, which includes the actual tramway infrastructure (in its own lanes) and also a certain number of related operations which would gear down the anticipated effects of this project.

- the first phase of the tramway network construction (in specific lanes) operates between Hautepierre and Illkirch, via the city center. This first line which is 12.6 kms. long (7.8 miles) and has 23 stations at an average distance of 400 meters (437 yards), will be operational in September 1994 and will have 26 trams, each with a capacity of 230 passengers and a headway of four minutes during peak hours. Thanks to a low floor throughout the length of the tram, access on board will be easy, even for persons with limited mobility.

- The program of reorganizing the urban bus network - undertaken at the same time as the tramway construction - is also an integral part of the public transport strategy.

The actions, which are a concrete illustration of the development and modernization of the bus network shall be progressively implemented from 1993 to 1996, and consist in:

- laying out bus lanes with the flow or against the flow of the traffic, to increase the commercial pace of buses, and also in order that buses on outward and return journeys be found on the same avenue.

- improving access on board with the progressive introduction of buses with lowered floors and higher platforms.

- designating new bus stops by installing electronic panels and information facilities to improve the legibility of routes at bus stops, and in certain stations, providing the possibility of making easy connections with other transport networks.

- installing electronic traffic control devices at cross roads, adapted to buses having right of way.

- developing an integrated tariff system, applied to journeys made by tram and bus and if the case may be, for cars parked in parking lots on the outskirts.

All these actions aim to create a positive and attractive image of public transport and propose quality services for greater harmony between offer of services and consumer require-ments in the field of transport.

Setting up inter modal transfer junctions:

Transfer facilities between the different modes of transport and setting up a truly integrated multi-modal network are vital aspects of an efficient public transport system.

The setting up of several inter-modal transfer hubs, which is part of the Strasbourg Urban Community "tramway project", aims to integrate in the most efficient way, the different transport modes "tramway", "bus", "rail", "bicycle", "motor vehicle" and "walking" and optimize the synergy effects between the different networks.

Replanning Pedestrian Precincts:

Pedestrian precincts in the *epicenter* are a fundamental aspect of the "tramway project", for developing the shopping area and also as a means of reinforcing the residential and cultural role of the city center. The purpose of the operations undertaken in central areas (place Kléber, place de la Gare, place de Lattre, place d'Austerlitz...) is to improve the environment quality of central neighborhoods and also provide more urban space for city dwellers. These projects aim to find a solution to the steady deterioration in "urban decor", by emphasizing the physical characteristics of the city and fostering the notion of urban design.

- The place Kléber, which had until the beginning of 1992 a traffic of around 50,000 vehicles per day, was an important area to redesign. The new layout of this square and its adjacent streets (22 Novembre, Francs-Bourgeois, Grandes Arcades) should help to fulfill its role as a cultural and shopping area. This project, drawn up by the architect firm CLAPOT represents an investment of 36 million FF (financed by the local authorities and the Strasbourg urban Community).

- The construction of a vast pedestrian precinct in the heart of the *epicenter* of Strasbourg will make it possible to link pedestrian precincts built during the past two decades in tourist and shopping areas

Suzanne H. Crowhurst Lennard

Drawing of a newly pedestrianized Place Kléber, exhibited in the square while work progressed (1993).

("cathedral", "Petite France" and "Gutenberg") and will help in reducing through traffic from the two trunk roads North-South.

Laying out Cycle Lanes

Encouraging the use of cycles is another major aspect of the "tramway project", with the proposal of special cycle lanes and appropriate signs, thus making cycling in the city safe, convenient and continuous. The use of two-wheeled vehicles is exceptional in France, but represents almost 15% of traveling modes in Strasbourg.

A real network of cycle lanes is being designed in the main urban center so as to offer a certain continuity with the lanes previously built in the outskirts (almost 130 kms. - 80 miles) with the network (which is mainly radial).

Roland Ries, Deputy Mayor for Transportation Planning, Strasbourg, France.

193

Chapter Achtunddreißig (a)

Städtisches Leben und Verkehr

Helmut Holzapfel

Der Vortrag geht von der Vorstellung aus, daß nicht technische Innovation den Umgang mit dem Verkehr und der Stadt der Zukunft prägen wird, sondern daß eine Veränderung wesentlich auch von einem Wechsel in Lebensstil und -einstellung der Menschen ausgeht.

"Über Entfernung und Freiheit" könnte man das Thema auch nennen. Es handelt nämlich nicht vorrangig um Verkehrsprobleme, sondern wie sich Raumorganisation auf uns, die Menschen, auswirkt und was wir mit ihr zu tun haben. Ich werde zwei sehr raumwirksame Formen unserer Lebensorganisation darstellen - den "entfernungsintensiven Lebensstil" und etwas, das ich "erfahrungsintensiven oder urbanen Lebensstil" nenne. Das erstere gibt es und das zweite ist eine Vorstellung einer möglichen Zukunft - deshalb werde ich auch den Übergang zwischen diesen Lebensstilen schildern. Dies alles ist mit Fragen des städtischen Raumes und seiner Organisation eng verbunden.

1. Was ist eigentlich "Lebensstil"?

Unter einem Lebensstil verstehe ich die Gesamtheit von Verhaltensweisen von Menschen: Also wie Menschen ihr Geld ausgeben, wie sie ihre Zeit nutzen, wie sie ihre Orte wechseln, und insofern Gesamtheit, daß ich immer die Person, den Menschen dahinter in der Tat als Gesamtpersönlichkeit betrachte und ihn nicht in Einzeldaten zerstückele. Zeitbudgetstudien zum Beispiel - so nützlich oder weniger nützlich sie sein mögen - zeigen nur einen Ausfluß der Verhaltensweisen von Menschen. Also was sie in bestimmten Zeiten tun, ist ja nur eine Sache. Sie bewegen sich ja gleichzeitig an Orten, sie sind gleichzeitig Menschen, die Motive haben. Dieses alles meine ich mit Lebensstil.

Und wenn ich nun einen Lebensstil idealisiere und im weiteren beschreibe und ihn als typisch für die modernen westlichen Industriegesellschaften darstelle, so ist es natürlich so, daß dies in der Tat eine Idealisierung, eine Abstraktion von der Realität ist und niemand hier natürlich genau diesen Lebensstil so vollführt, wie ich ihn im weiteren schildere. Er kommt also so in der Realität nicht vor. Er wäre jedoch nicht typisch, wenn wir uns in Elementen dieses Lebensstils nicht wiedererkennen würden und wenn er in der Tat nicht typische und wesentliche Teile dessen bezeichnete, was wir heutzutage vollführen.

Ich nenne ihn den "entfernungsintensiven Lebensstil". Das heißt genauer, es ist ein Lebensstil, der durch folgende Elemente gekennzeichnet ist. Man fährt erstens immer weiter weg und hält dies zweitens meistens für intelligent. In kurioser Weise demonstrierte etwa die Deutsche Bundesbahn dies in einer Werbung, die so lautet: "Jetzt aber nichts wie weg und egal, wohin, und zurück, und das für 130,- DM." Dies soll laut Werbung auch noch "intelligent" sein. Das ist für mich eine neue Definition von "Intelligenz". Aber hieran wird deutlich, was ich meine mit entfernungsintesiverem Lebensstil. Es wird für gut gehalten offenbar von dem Werber und offenbar von seiner Kundschaft, weiter weg

Dinge zu machen, wobei es ziemlich egal ist, was dort stattfindet.

Die Fakten, die man jetzt einmal etwas weniger polemisch dem gegenüberstellen kann, beziehen sich auf die Verkehrsentwicklung der letzten 30 Jahre seit 1960. Kurz zusammengefaßt: Die Anzahl der Wege pro Tag und Einwohner blieb in der Bundesrepublik etwa gleich. Dies sind Durchschnittsdaten aus Befragungen und daher auch mit Fehlern behaftet, auf die ich aber hier nicht näher eingehe, denn dieser Tatbestand ist davon weniger betroffen. Gleichzeitig hat der Autoverkehr zugenommen. Dies kann man jetzt so interpretieren: Wir fahren eigentlich genau so oft weg, wir machen auch fast dasselbe, führen ähnliche Aktivitäten aus, nur wir tun dies alles immer weiter weg. Das heißt, die durchschnittlichen Entfernungen über den Tag haben zugenommen. Die gewonnene Geschwindigkeit mit dem Automobil ist praktisch nur in Reiseweite umgesetzt worden, nicht unbedingt in eine größere Vielfalt von Aktivitäten.

Wie hat das weiter ausgesehen? Entfernungsintensiver Lebensstil definiert sich eben nicht nur dadurch, daß wir fahren, sondern er definiert sich nun auch dadurch, daß andere längere Strecken zu uns hinfahren. Das gilt für Ziele des Tourismus oder dafür, daß die Produkte, die wir konsumieren, von immer weiter weg herkommen.

Entfernungsintensiver Lebensstil heißt natürlich gleichzeitig: Hohes Maß an Ähnlichkeit überall. Was in den letzten 30 Jahren passiert ist, interpretiere ich als Verlust von Erlebnissen. Der entfernungsintensive Lebensstil drückt sich darin aus, daß ich nur dann etwas erlebe, wenn ich ganz, ganz weit fahre, denn alles andere kenne ich schon, und es ist mit mir auch schon verschwunden. Nehmen wir etwa unsere Urlaubsfahrten: In den 60er Jahren sind ja viele von uns nach Griechenland gefahren und wer heute mal hinfährt und ein bißchen waches

Auge hat, der weiß, was sich verändert hat. Auf einer griechischen Insel konnte man noch Ende der 60er Jahre einen Markt finden, wo praktisch kein einziges Produkt aus der Bundesrepublik Deutschland vorrätig war. Das waren nur alles lokale Produkte, die aus dem einheimischen Land waren. Wenn man heute dort einen beliebigen Markt aufsucht, hat man zu 80% Produkte, die in Deutschland wahrscheinlich auch erhältlich sind, und etwa zu 30% Produkte, die in der Bundesrepublik gefertigt worden sind, so daß man hier ein hohes Maß an Ähnlichkeit hat. Die entfernungsintensive Gesellschaft beseitigt eben Unterschiede.

Kennzeichnend für diesen ganzen Prozeß ist die geringe Relevanz des Raumes, also daß wir auch Raumvernichtung betreiben. Dabei geschieht gleichzeitig etwas ganz anderes mit der Zeit, die immer wichtiger wird. Gleichzeitig wird aber der Raum immer unwichtiger Raum und Raumüberwindung, der Zwischenraum zwischen verschiedenen Destinationen interessiert uns überhaupt nicht mehr. Uns interessieren lediglich noch die Ziele. Das Einfamilienhaus mit Doppelgarage ist für mich ein weiteres Symbol des entfernungsintensiven Lebensstils. Das gehört sozusagen dazu und ist der Traum, der ja gleichzeitig mit dem Automobil das kennzeichnet, was die Menschen lange Zeit wirklich oder angeblich gewollt haben. Das frißt natürlich Raum. Und jeder, der einmal so entfernungsintensiv gelebt hat wie ich, und die Freude hatte, mit dem Flugzeug über Los Angeles hinwegzufliegen (und da runterzug-ucken und das Schachbrettmuster interessant findet, nach einer Viertelstunde guckt er wieder runter, und es ist immer noch dasselbe, und nach einer halben Stunde Flug ist darunter immer noch dasselbe), der weiß, zu welchen Siedlungsstrukturmustern das führt und zu welcher Ausbreitung in die Landschaft, und wie diese typische Lebensweise, wie diese Form dann sich sozusagen in den Raum ergießt, und er weiß, wie unwichtig dann Raum wird.

195

Das waren verschiedene Indizien des entfernungsinternen Lebensstils. Es waren eigentlich nur Beschreibungen, die ich mit einigen wertbehafteten Bemerkungen versehen habe. Dieser Lebensstil nun ist in der Tat etwas, wofür die Politiker meinen, wirklich zu planen. Und das sei etwas, so meinen sie, was die Menschen wollen in ihrer Mehrheit. Und es ist wohl ernst zu nehmen: Es gibt immer wieder Befragungen von Bausparkassen über etwa eben das Einfamilienhaus mit Doppelgarage. "Wollt Ihr das?" Und alle sagen "ja".

Als ich den europaeinheitlichen Supermarkt einmal als Verlust geschildert habe bei der EG-Kommission, hat der zuständige Kommissar für Verkehr gesagt: Nein, er sei derjenige, der das wolle, das sei die Gleichwertigkeit der Lebensbedingungen in Europa, daß man überall das gleiche einkaufen könne, das sei der Lebensstil, für den er als Politiker und Sozialdemokrat eigentlich arbeite. Und ich habe gesagt, "dafür würde ich nicht arbeiten". Und er sagte mir auch: Es gibt eben nur eins, diesen gleichen Supermarkt oder das, was ich eingefordert habe, nämlich ein Nachtfahrverbot für Lkw's in Europa. Er sagt, "dann kann ich das nicht realisieren, den gleichen Supermarkt, da brauchen wir wieder den regional-spezifischen." Und ich habe gesagt: "Mehr Regionalspezifität - nicht zurück ins Mittelalter, aber mehr Regionalspezifizität als heute würde ich als interessanter und erlebnisreicher empfinden."

Das Erlebnis selbst braucht mittlerweile Entfernung, weil, um noch etwas erleben zu können, ich weit weg fahren muß, weiter weg als früher, um noch Differenz zu sehen - eben dann z.B. bis hin nach Amerika, obwohl dort die Supermärkte auch noch eine frappierende Ähnlichkeit mit den hiesigen aufweisen.

Der entfernungsintensive Lebensstil ist nicht zuletzt durch eine starke Rolle staatlicher und bereits überstaatlicher Regelungen hochde-terminiert und überraschungsfrei. Das "über-raschungsfrei" habe ich bereits versucht, etwas zu definieren. Nun das "hochdeterminiert": Es ist etwas, was auf den ersten Blick vielleicht überrascht. Denn das "hochdeterminiert" bedeutet ja "unfrei", ich will also sagen, daß der entfernungsintensive Lebensstil gerade keine Freiheit schafft.

Einige Indizien: Wenn alles weiter weg ist, kann ich es nicht selbst erobern, ich benötige Hilfsmittel. Das ist eigentlich das, was viele Leute übersehen. Das geht beim Schulkind los. Die Schulen wurden seit den 60er Jahren immer weiter konzentriert, so daß in dünn besiedelten Regionen, ja oft sogar schon im Stadtumland, der Schulbus zur Regel wird. Damit wird praktisch das transportierte Kind generiert, während das Kind früher selbst noch Erfahrungen machte. Ich bin als Kind noch selbst zur Schule gelaufen, ich hatte während dieses Weges natürlich bestimmte Erlebnisse, Freunde, Bekannte, die ich besucht habe, ich weiß genau, welche Ereignisse während meines Schulweges aufgetreten sind, was für wichtige Erlebnisse ich gemacht habe. Das tritt natürlich heute alles nur stellvertretend noch im Schulbus auf. Auch Landschaft wird nur noch von außen gesehen. Und der entfernungs-intensive Lebensstil reproduziert sich bereits selbst, denn die Freunde, die ich während der Fahrt und auf der Schule gewinne und die ich aufsuchen muß, um sie dann zu treffen, wohnen natürlich nicht mehr in meinem eigenen Ort, sondern sie wohnen vielleicht ganz am anderen Ende des Einzugsbereichs der Schule, und ich werde dann meist von meiner Mutter (selten vom Vater) hingefahren, was gleichzeitig wieder einen hoch-determinierten Lebensstil schon als Kind bedeutet. Für mich, als ich Kind war, waren die Freunde die interessantesten, die ich nicht haben sollte, wo meine Eltern gesagt haben, "nein, mit dem nicht", die haben mich sehr interessiert, und die anderen waren eigentlich nicht so interessant. Die Wahl hat ein Kind heute nur noch sehr eingeschränkt, weil, wenn es dauernd gebracht wird, haben die Eltern natürlich sowohl über die Zeit als auch über die Freunde die vollständige Kontrolle, was in meinem Fall zumindest äußerst ärgerlich gewesen wäre.

Diese Determination, die bei den Kindern schon anfängt, die setzt sich natürlich fort. Wenn alles von weiter weg kommt, kann ich mich auch nicht mehr selbst versorgen, ich bin in hohem Maße abhängig: abhängig von Prüfinstanzen, von Leuten, die mir sagen, was in einem Produkt eigentlich drin ist. Wenn die Molkerei am Ort ist, weiß man noch ziemlich genau, was sich dort abspielt: Man kennt einen, der die Molkerei kennt, und weiß zum Beispiel, wenn der sagt, ach, das ist aber dreckig in unserer Molkerei und es ist gar nicht so in Ordnung, dann wird es bemerkt und diskutiert und abgestellt. So etwas hat es ja früher gegeben. Wenn der Quark in Deütschland zentral von der Firma "Südmilch" kommt, habe ich stattdessen Qualitätskriterien. Die Stiftung "Warentest" testet mit Geschmackstestern, Chemikern und Profiessern fünf verschiedene Quarksorten, und ich suche aus was angeblich sehr empfehlenswert ist. Das heißt, ich bin auf andere angewiesen, um zu entscheiden, was läuft überhaupt. Ja, das Risiko ist für mich auch nicht mehr selbst kontrollierbar. Es gibt ja die Definition der Risikogesellschaft von Beck, der sagt, daß eben auch die Risiken in dieser Gesellschaft gar nicht mehr abschätzbar seien und der Staat denzufolge die Risiken kontrollieren muß.

Ist das nun Freiheit oder nicht Freiheit?

Ich behaupte Zeit ist in der heutigen Industriegesellschaft in hohem Maße determiniert, und es ist für viele Leute ungeheuer schwer, selbst ihre Zeit zu organisieren. Unsere Zeit ist überhaupt das am meisten von anderen bestimmte Gut. Während wir den Raum gewinnen, haben wir die Autonomie über die Zeit verloren. Das ist eine ganz wichtige Tatsache.

Autonomie über Zeit hieße, daß ich selbst darüber verfügen könnte.

Schauen wir uns einmal bei einem Kind den Kalender an. Es gibt ja schon den Schülerkalender für Sechsjährige. Und dann betrachten wir mal den Wochenplan an, und gucken uns einmal an, wenn wir uns selbst an unsere eigene Jugend erinnern, ob wir auch so etwas gehabt haben. Meine Erinnerung würde mich sehr trügen, wenn ich so etwas gehabt hätte.

Das heißt also, hier ist praktisch bereits eine enorme Verplanung der kindlichen Zeit eingetreten. Dies hat natürlich auch Wirkung auf die Erwachsenen-Zeit. Denn wenn vor allem Frauen das Kind vom Schwimmtraining zum Pfadfindertreffen und dann wieder zum Kindergeburtstag fahren müssen, bleibt natürlich wenig für ihre eigene Freizeit. Da sind also schon sehr enge Parameter, die praktisch wieder einschränkende Wirkung haben.

Jetzt habe ich versucht, die entfernungsintensive Gesellschaft zu beschreiben, ich habe versucht, sie in einigen Bereichen bewußt negativ zu thematisieren, und zwar in einem ganz zentralen Punkt, nämlich in dem, was sie eigentlich bringen soll, dem Freiheitsgefühl und der Freiheit am Beispiel unserer Zeitorganisation. Ich habe gerade gesagt, sie ist in hohem Maße unfrei, und sie ist es durch etwas, was die Leute überhaupt nicht mögen, nämlich durch staatliche Intervention.

Der Staat sagt uns, wie schnell wir gehen müssen. Ich erkläre polemisch die sogenannte Richtlinie für Lichtsignalanlagen zur eigentlichen Verfassung der Bundesrepublik Deutschland. Ich erkläre, sie ist wichtiger als die Verfassung, weil mir in dieser Richtlinie vorgeschrieben wird, die kaum einer kennt (natürlich im Gegensatz dazu, daß wohl einige Menschen wissen, daß es eine Verfassung gibt), wie schnell ich über die Straße gehen muß. Wenn wir langsamer gehen, droht uns, vom

197

Auto überfahren zu werden. Ein üblicher Wert dafür ist z.B. 0,8 m pro Sekunde, nicht einmal sehr langsam. Die Lichtsignalanlage selbst schreibt natürlich auch vor, wann ich die Straße überqueren muß, sie schreibt mir auch vor, wo ich die Straße überqueren muß. Wenn wir also in der Nähe der Ampel statt direkt dort die Straße überqueren - der "zumutbare Umweg" beträgt 50 m rechts und 50 m links nach einschlägigen Gerichtsurteilen - wenn wir das zu nahe machen in diesem hochdeterminierten System, dann, wenn wir angefahren werden, sind wir selbst Schuld und müssen praktisch die Beule im Auto bezahlen, wenn uns ein Auto rammt, oder unsere Haftpflichtversicherung muß das tun, wenn wir haftpflichtversichert sind.

Außer den Lichtsignalanlagen, die es erst seit den 20er Jahren in Deutschland gibt, gibt es in dieser entfernungsintensiven Gesellschaft eine Vielzahl von Regelungen, die Ingenieure und Fachleute beschäftigen. Dies geht von den Ampeln bis zu Vorschriften über die Breite der Lkw's und Normen über die beleuchtung unserer Städte, die oft weit entfernt, etwa in Brüssel, in Büros ausgedacht werden.

2. Probleme des Übergangs

Jetzt kommt die Frage, ob die Menschen überhaupt etwas ändern wollen. Wenn man sagt, es gibt einen übergang von diesem Lebensstil auf einen anderen, könnte man einwenden: Die Menschen sind doch offenbar alle ganz glücklich mit diesem Lebensstil, man könnte sagen, dieser entfernungsintensive Lebensstil mit Haus mit Doppelgarage usw., wie ich es Ihnen geschildert habe, sei doch attraktiv. Und in der Tat, es spricht viel dafür. Auch die Leute in der Dritten Welt wollen, so heißt es, diesen Lebensstil.

Dazu eine kleine Geschichte: Mit einer Delegation aus China fuhr ich durch Nordrhein-Westfalen und zeigte dieser den Ruhr-Schnellweg B 1, auf dem die Fahrzeuge in einem gigantischen Stau standen, die Luft war schlecht. Ich sagte also: "Setzen Sie in China nicht so stark auf die Autos." Und der Übersetzer übersetzte das: "In China soll man nicht so viele Autos haben. Schauen Sie her, zu was das bei uns geführt hat." Die Chinesen sahen sich wechselseitig an, und der Übersetzer übersetzte mir die Rückfrage der Chinesen. "Wieso macht Ihr es denn, wenn es so blöd ist?"

Diese Geschichte zeigt, daß eine Erkenntnis, aus der wir keine Konsequenz ziehen, auch niemanden glauben läßt, daß man sie wirklich ernst meint. Die Chinesen wollen natürlich auch so fahren wie wir, und ohne ein überzeugendes Vorleben hier wird man Änderungen auch andernorts nicht vollziehen. Und das ist natürlich angsterregend, daß alle das machen wollen, was wir machen.

Wenn es also unter anderem das Auto ist, das diesen Lebensstil hochdeterminiert und unfrei macht, ist natürlich die Frage, ob die Menschen überhaupt frei sein wollen. Das ist natürlich ein wichtiger Punkt. Wenn Menschen sich in starke Abhängigkeiten begeben haben, wenn meine Analyse also richtig ist, dann wäre natürlich die Frage: Wollen die Menschen überhaupt frei sein, freier? Wollen sie etwa überhaupt freie Zeit zur Verfügung haben?

Wenn man Menschen neue Freiheiten gibt, besteht das Risiko, daß sie dann erst einmal mit diesen Freiheiten nicht glücklicher, sondern unglücklicher sind, daß sie ihre Befreiung aus der Abhängigkeit der entfernungsintensiven Gesellschaft, diesen übergang, vielleicht damit bezahlen müssen, daß sie anfangs gar nicht wissen, was sie denn tun sollen. Das muß natürlich nicht so sein. Auf einer autofreien Insel, wo ich mit Kindern war, habe ich festgestellt, daß Kinder dieses Problem überhaupt nicht haben. Das haben hauptsächlich Erwachsene. Kinder brauchen da etwa einen Tag, bis sie wirklich nach keiner Fernsehsendung mehr fragen und sich dann in der Tat selbst unterhalten. Da scheint es diese Fähigkeit noch zu geben.

Autonomie statt Auto, das scheint mir ein wichtiger Punkt zu sein. Wenn es denn so ist, daß der entfernungsintensive Lebensstil uns hoch determiniert, sind wir natürlich umso besser dran für die Chancen möglicher Alternativen, je mehr ein Drang nach Autonomie in den Menschen da ist, inwiefern sie noch in der Lage sind, sie selbst sein zu können und statt draußen irgendwo, in sich selber Motive und Antriebe noch finden.

3. Alternativen

Alternativen zum bestehenden Lebensstil dürfen natürlich nicht moralisch begründet werden. Das wäre der allergrößte Fehler. Moral stärkt immer das Bestehende. Das heißt, wenn man übergehen will auf einen neuen Lebensstil, wird man mit einer abstrakten Moral kontraproduktiv wirken. Man wird damit immer das Bestehende starken, indem man Schuldgefühle hervorruft und Kreativität schwächt.

Die Alternative, die ich stattdessen im Kopf habe, ist, wirklich Spaß und Lebensfreude wiederzufinden, was in dem räumlichen Aspekt in der Nähe und im Nahbereich dann natürlich auch heißt, Beziehungen zu entwickeln zur eigenen Stadt, zur Natur und zu anderen Menschen, und sich wieder an Lebendigkeit zu freuen, während man sich gegenwürtig-ja hauptsächlich an Technik und technischen Substituten von Lebendigkeit erfreut. Das würde dann auch heißen, daß man automatisch sozusagen als Nebenprodukt sich wieder um diese Lebendigkeit kümmert und daß so etwas wie ein etwas friedvolleres Verhältnis zur Natur dabei herauskommt.

Da bin ich schon bei dem neuen Lebensstil. Es muß sich dabei um einen Lebensstil handeln, der sich definiert nicht durch mehr Reglementierung, sondern durch einen Abbau von Reglementierung. Das heißt, wir müssen erkennen, die Nähe, unsere Stadt, unsere Region bietet uns die Möglichkeit, weniger reglementiert zu sein, weniger abhängig zu sein, weniger von technischen Schäden oder Risiken abhängig zu sein. Sie bietet uns mehr Optionen.

Reduktion der Durchlässigkeit des Raumes heißt auch mehr Urbanität und weniger Reglementierung. Es heißt, daß wir nicht mehr weit fahren müssen, weil man die Postämter (wie in Deutschland) mit Hinweis auf allgemeinen Autobesitz zentralisiert hat. Daß wir nicht nach Brüssel fahren müssen, um mit einer Delegation bei der EG zu demonstrieren, bloß weil wir ordentliche Äpfel haben wollen. Solche Dinge sind Bestandteil der entfernungsintensiven Gesellschaft. Da wir alle in Europa unsere Äpfel austauschen wollen und natürlich dann auch erwarten, daß die Größen alle gleich sind in den Geschäften bedeutet, daß wir noch zusätzlich einen Reglementierer in Brüssel haben müssen. Wir scheinen darauf angewiesen zu sein, jemanden zu haben in Brüssel, der entscheidet, wie unsere Äpfel aussehen. Das gehört zum entfernungsintensiven Lebensstil. Die Leute, die meinen, so etwas definieren zu müssen, meinen es gut mit uns. Man vermutet wohl in der EU-Bürokratie, daß wir selbst nicht ordentlich entscheiden könnten, was ein guter Äpfel sei, weil wir das eben nicht mehr wußten, insbesondere bei einem Äpfel, der weit herkomt. Aber sie meinen es zu gut mit uns. Sie verplanen uns. Und das hat mit der Entfernung und mit dem, wo die Dinge herkommen, und mit der Austauschbarkeit direkt etwas zu tun.

Das Gegenbild zum entfernungsintensiven Lebensstil heißt für mich erfahrungsintensiver, städtischer Lebensstil. Das wäre ein Lebensstil, der uns Neuigkeiten bringt, neue Erfahrungen, ohne das wir viel reisen müßten. Und solche Neuigkeiten müssen einem zuallererst einmal auffallen - vielen ist das so gegangen beim Fahrradtrend, der vor ca. 15 Jahren anfing, als sie zum ersten Mal in ihrer Stadt wieder mit dem Fahrrad fuhren und plötzlich merkten, auch da ist ja ein Weg, den habe ich noch nie gesehen, und da kann ich aber einen Baum sehen, den finde ich sehr schön, und da habe ich einen Platz, wo ich mich hinsetzen kann. Das sind zum ersten Mal neue Erfahrungen gewesen.

Das Problem ist, daß im Laufe der Entwertung des Raumes niemand auf diese Gegenden geguckt hat und wir im Laufe der Zeit dort alles zerstört haben. Gerade wenn wir den Stadtrand uns seine Entwicklung anschauen, in Westdeutschland, sehen wir das. In den neuen Bundesländern waren zumindest noch bis vor einem halben Jahr die Stadtränder Gegenden, wo man in der Tat aus der Stadt heraus mit dem Fahrrad direkt wandern und spazieren gehen konnte. Heute fangt dort bereits der bei uns übliche Speckgürtel von Supermarkten, Flachhallen und Stadttangenten an sich zu etablieren, über den man praktisch nicht hinwegkommt in die stadtnahen Erholungs-gebiete mit eigener Kraft. Dann gibt es auch wieder die Menschen, die dann das Fahrrad aufs Autodach schnallen, um erst einmal herauszufahren aus diesen häßlichen Zonen. Vielleicht sollte man wenigstens darauf achten, daß man dort noch autonom, also aus eigener Kraft, aus der Stadt herauskommt. In den alten Bundesländern in Deutschland mußten solche Wege erst geschaffen werden.

Zeiten müßten neu organisiert werden. Es müßte uns in der Tat gelingen, Möglichkeiten wieder zur eigenen Lebensgestaltung in der Nähe anzubieten, wobei ich bestimmte Dinge unheimlich schwierig reversibel sehe. Der übergang wird nicht einfach. Wir können bestimmte soziale Organisationsformen, wenn sie einmal weg sind aus der Welt, nicht mehr neu schaffen. Das ist also oft ein hilfloses

Projekt, etwa wenn es wegen der geringen Dichte in neuen Stadtteilen nicht genügend Kinder gibt, die autonom zusammen eine Gruppe bilden könnten, die einmal unabhängig übers Feld streift.

Aber auch das können wir auf den autofreien Inseln erfahren: Die Kinder lernen so viel autonomer andere Kinder kennen und entwickeln dabei auch Verfahren, wie sie wechselseitig mit anderen Kindern umgehen während dieser Urlaubszeit. Andere Kinder werden zum ersten Mal nicht von den Eltern mitgebracht und vorgestellt. Und dann bilden die Kinder sogar eigene Gruppen und streifen dort durch die Gegend. Und abends kommen sie irgendwie verdreckt zu Hause an und haben mehr gelernt, als wenn wir den ganzen Tag versucht hätten, denen nun durch einen soziologen Unterricht in Gruppendynamik zu geben. Das sind die Gegenbilder einer nicht entfernungsintensiven Gesellschaft.

Fuß und Rad sind die Verkehrsmittel dieser erfahrungsintensiven Gesellschaft, und sie findet vor allem in unseren Städten statt. Und es gehört dazu, daß wir auch etwas lernen, was wir bei der allgemeinen Zeitknappheit gar nicht genug betonen müssen, nämlich wieder lernen, Dinge zu betrachten. Wir alle sind dauernd von Fahrplänen und Zeiten geprägt und schauen immer auf die Uhr, auch ich nehme häufig nicht mehr wahr an vielen Stellen, was eigentlich wahrzunehmen sich lohnte. Das würde also auch mit einer Neu-organisation von Zeit zu tun haben. Wir sollten versuchen, wieder zu lernen, Dinge zu betrach-ten, so schwierig das vielleicht anfangs fällt.

Wie kann also der Übergang von Lebensstilen geschehen? Natürlich kann das nicht von oben organisiert werden! Man kann das als Politiker nicht anordnen und kann sagen: Die Zeit der entfernungsintensiven Gesellschaft ist vorbei!

Wir werden also eher so etwas wie eine Einladung an die Menschen aussprechen, die natürlich das Risiko hat, ausgeschlagen zu werden. Und wir werden versuchen müssen, staatliche Zwänge abzubauen, um exemplarische Experimente durchzuführen, um das zu fördern.

Eine staatliche Zwangsmaßnahme ist die Subventionierung des Automobils mit unseren Steuergeldern, also auch mit denen von Menschen, die gar kein Auto haben. Das Auto ist hochsubventioniert, die Autofabriken sind hochsubventioniert. Daimler Benz ist der Konzern in der Bundesrepublik Deutschland, der die allermeisten Forschungsgelder kassiert. Und es gibt eine EU-Studie, die wenig bekannt ist, die zeigt daß in allen europäischen Autofabriken die staatlichen Subventionen über den Gewinnen liegen, d.h. ohne die Subventionen würden diese Fabriken bereits seit Jahren Verluste machen. Eine Subventionsform liegt in der steuerlichen Absetzbarkeit, dem Steuervorteil von Betriebsfahrzeugen, von Jahreswagen. Das sind Subventionen, deren Beendigung natürlich Verschiebungen hervorrufen würde.

Die Subventionierung im Straßenbaubereich wird immer deutlicher, weil die Kosten dort enorm in die Höhe gehen. Und wer in der Vergangenheit einmal die Subventionen der öffentlichen Haushalte sich anguckt, der sieht, wie hoch subventioniert über Jahre hinweg der Straßensektor war. Man hat natürlich erst in Autobahnen investiert, ohne daß man ein entsprechendes Steueraufkommen hatte aus den Automobilen. Und erst in der Folge kam der Autotrend. Das ist in fast allen Ländern so gelaufen. Das heißt, wir haben staatlich schon eine Menge für das Auto getan, seinen Erfolg gestützt. Der Abbau der hohen Subventionierung des Autos muß also die erste Forderung sein.

Die zweite Forderung muß sein, Experimente zu ermöglichen oder zu fördern, wo Menschen wieder autofreie Erfahrungen in der Nähe machen können. Ich finde solche Erlebnisse wichtig, ich finde sie vor allem für die Kinder wichtig, die dadurch eine Möglichkeit haben, sich später vielleicht daran zu erinnern, um dann bei der Neuorganisation der Städte nach menschlichen Muster davon zu profitieren.

4. Schluß

Wenn unser Lebensstil sich ändert, dann kann man das nur zusammen mit den Menschen machen. Und noch so intelligente Steuerung durch ökonomische Maßnahmen kann nur ein Mittel sein. Wir müssen den Menschen also klar sagen, was wir wollen, welche Risiken sie eingehen und welche anderen Entwicklungen ein neuer Lebensstil bringt. Wenn sie die nicht wollen, sondern die Risiken des Bestehenden, dann können wir in der Tat wenig machen. Hier bin ich aber optimistischer als viele Ökologen, weil ich in der Tat Indizien sehe, daß der entfernungsintensive Lebensstil sich selbst entzaubert. Es kann gelingen, daß wir einen anderen Lebensstil finden, der den Menschen mehr Lebensqualität in ihren Städten bringt und von dem ganz als Nebenprodukt die Umwelt enorm profitiert. Es kann gut sein, daß wir dann eine Tendenz haben, daß das Auto wieder das wird, was es eigentlich ist: Ein Produkt, das in bestimmten Zeiten des 20. Jahrhunderts einmal ganz modern war, das man aber dann irgendwann zweckgerichtet nur noch in den Bereichen benutzt, wo seine Benutzung noch Sinn macht, und das ist eher selten.

Prof. Dr. Ing. Helmut Holzapfel ist Professor der Verkehrsplanung, Universität Kassel, und Ministerialdirigent, Ministerium für Wohnen, Städtebau und Verkehr, Sachsen-Anhalt.

Chapter Thirty-Eight (b)

Urban Lifestyle and Transportation Policy

Helmut Holzapfel

Let me start by telling you what I'm not going to talk about. I'm not going to say that the motor car is very bad, and that we have to abolish it immediately. I think a lot of people have repeated this and quite often it is understandable, if you see the damage motor cars do to our city. But it's not the right way to persuade people to a new policy, as Roland Ries from Strasbourg has done. And if you listened to him, you heard that it is the combination of a new quality of life with better transportation and a very beautiful city that leads people to a different policy. So the main thing is, I'm not talking about transport policy, I'm talking about lifestyles, how people want to live, and about new policies - how to build cities where you don't need motor cars anymore!

I'm starting with a short illustration as well. At our conference last year in Kassel, we made a walk through the city with a lot of Americans and I gave everybody participating in the conference a walking stick, just to show them that pedestrian transport can be very important. And on this walking stick there was a sign and it said "It's beautiful here", and this meant that we, being pedestrians, want a beautiful city! One of the main reasons that many people have a car (and that is very important) is that they want to run away from their ugly place where they live, but all they do is get to another ugly place because a lot of motor cars are around. So the main reason why we have so many motor cars is that we built bad cities.

So I will talk about two lifestyles. One lifestyle, is what I call the Distance Intensive lifestyle.

This means that people drive a lot. And I must explain how wrong city planning and building helps to create what I call the Distance Intensive lifestyle. And then I will talk about a second lifestyle, which I call the urban lifestyle. It's a lifestyle full of new experiences and it is not distance intensive.

Let's first talk about the Distance Intensive lifestyle. The distance intensive lifestyle is something very easy to understand because you can see it everywhere. It is a kind of ideal of our society where, on the big roadside ads you can read that today you must be in Marlboro country and tomorrow you must be in Egypt to smoke your Camel cigarette. So you are everywhere in the world, but you're not at home! All the time you're traveling, and traveling. You see in Germany, especially in Eastern Germany where no one speaks English because in the schools they have been taught Russian all the time, but if you look at the ads, everything is in English and the East Germans can't understand what is really in the advertisement. Nobody knows, nobody cares.

The worldwide global ads for Marlboro country are everywhere. So you have a high similarity of this distance intensive lifestyle. We travel a lot, we have to be everywhere. But not at home. Our German railway company had a big ad last year, "Get away from your place immediately, Deutschebahn." So they don't care where you go. The main thing is you get away from your place. And if you look at some of our cities, you understand very well why people do this.

But not only do we travel, our products travel as well. What was once produced in my region, now has to come from distant areas. Go to a shop in Freiburg and you will find butter from Ireland. And go to a British shop and you will find butter from Bavaria. What is the difference between butter from Bavaria that you would have to transport it to England? And what about Irish butter being transported at the same time in a big lorry to Germany and the lorry on it's way goes all through Europe. This destroys much of our environment.

There is a very well-known story in Germany about a yogurt produced in Stuttgart. This yogurt was produced by the Südmilch factory in Stuttgart and it's a strawberry yogurt. It's even exported to Britain. I saw it in Britain about two weeks ago. This yogurt jar, before it is produced, has already been transported 8,000 kilometers. How can this be? The strawberries in the yogurt come from Poland. The glass comes from about two hundred miles away, and then the label is printed somewhere in France because it's the cheapest printing. And all this then is put together, including the milk that is coming from a cow far away. And before it is ready for you, it's a global yogurt.

The experience of the distance intensive lifestyle is symbolized in city planning by two objects. One is the supermarket. The supermarket looks similar all around the world nowadays. Not only do the products look very similar, but the shop itself looks very similar. The supermarket stands as a symbol for this distance intensive lifestyle. It was supposed to symbolize freedom of choice, but if you really look into it, it's just the opposite.

And the second object that is typical for this global lifestyle is something that looks very square, simple, and has a garage beside it. It's the single family home. I think this is the one thing we have to talk about. If you want to change to an urban lifestyle we can't have the single family home with two garages beside it.

This creates a city that has a low density, a city that is not nice.

As I told you, in Kassel we are doing the pedestrian walk through the city. I'm having my student groups walk through the city. And we do these walks mainly in nice areas, but sometimes we do it in single family home areas. And you learn that no one is on the streets. And if you look into these houses no one is there. About 20-30% of the people are on holiday, because they're flying away from their nice house, they don't want to see it anymore, obviously. They want to see something else. It's so nice, they want to go away! And the rest of it, there's no one at home because people are at work to get the money for this very expensive house. And the area is just empty.

Sometimes you see children who are very lonely there because they cannot find friends. They are so far away that mothers and fathers have to bring them to the other children. So it's not nice for children as well, because in these areas children are in a poor position to find friends. I remember when I was young living in a European city, the best friends I had were those where my parents said, "Don't go to these people". And I found them on the streets of the city. Nowadays my children are completely controlled with whom they have contact, because a lot of their friends live in these single family home areas. And we have to bring them there by motor car. They can't go there on their own. It's a big improvement for German children now if they have bicycles, they can go there on their own. This gives them more autonomy and more freedom.

Distance intensive cities and distance intensive lifestyles determine the lives of people in ways they don't really perceive. One form of control is symbolized by my watch. Look at what this distance intensive lifestyle has meant to children. My children have calendars where every day in the week you say, "Well, you have to go to sports on Monday afternoon between

3:00 and 5:00, there is a trainer," and we have all this high degree of control of time all through the day. When I remember my own youth, I had no such calendar. I just walked out in the road, had some experience, played football when I liked to, found other places. My children have a football trainer in a special place because they can't play on the road because there are too many cars around they could destroy. And so they have to be driven around in the city with the car, to the school, and to the kindergarten and they don't experience it for themselves. A lot of my own experiences came on my way to school.

What would be a change in lifestyle, and what would be this different lifestyle? This different lifestyle would be more autonomous, more multi-functional spaces in the city, less control. A lot of the control in the city comes through the car, but much more control is exercised as well by buildings. Look at our schools in Germany, for instance, where children are. We have very large schools now because some very efficient person said one day, "Efficient schools must be large enough for 1,500 pupils, or 2,000 pupils." The school must look like a factory, then it's efficient, obviously, at that scale. This means distance intensity because you have to bus the children to this school.

Look at single family housing areas. What can you do if the single family house gets unpopular someday? What can you do with these areas? Knock them down, or do what? Our medieval cities could be reused. They could be used for living, they could be used for offices. And now sometimes offices are changed into dwellings, so you could use them in multi-functional ways. A single family housing area can't be reused for any other purpose.

What can be done by our planners? Look at the regions around your own city again. Try to find the products from this region. Make the city attractive to your own people. I was in Bremen about four weeks ago and they have a big problem with traffic there, and a big problem with new roads to be built. And when you ask those people what they do on the weekend they say, "Well, Bremen is ugly, there's a lot of traffic around and so we get into our cars and travel far away where it's nicer." And then they come to a region where everybody else is going and they find themselves in a huge car park where there are a lot of cars, and then they go back to Bremen. Other people are going to Bremen and having their holiday there. And if you look at Bremen's advertisements you find that they don't advertise their own region to their own persons in their own city. They don't tell the people in Bremen, "Well, make your holiday in and around Bremen, it's very nice." If you ask the tourist agencies they say, "Oh, we're sending our leaflets all around the world to tourists from Tokyo and everywhere." But if you ask, "Are you sending your leaflets to your own citizens?" No. Why not? Why not get persons interested in their own city again? Why not attract people to their own places again? Because they don't believe in what they've built! The architects and city planners in Bremen don't find their own place really attractive.

Regional consumption, regional holidays, a new lifestyle with less motorization. Can this be possible? I think it is possible, and it can be very attractive to the citizens in European cities. This leads to ideas such as in Bremen, where there are living quarters where you don't have any more motor cars, where people quite really say, "Well, we want to live here without a car." The first step would be to have good, dense, multi-functional living quarters, and the research done by transportation engineers in these living quarters shows that you have half the motorization of other areas. So it is quite automatic that if people are satisfied with their environment, they have fewer cars. And then the next idea may be that all those persons that don't own a motor car, like myself for instance, would tell you, "I don't want to support the motor car anymore."

So if you want to change transportation policy you have to offer a positive alternative, a lively and beautiful city where you don't need a motor car any more.

Prof. Dr. Ing. Helmut Holzapfel is Professor of Transportation Planning at the University of Kassel, and Director of Transportation in the Ministry for Housing, Urban Planning and Transportation for the State of Sachsen-Anhalt, Germany.

Venedig - Vorbild einer autofreien Stadt ?

Egon Grund

Venedig erscheint zunächst als ein unvergleichbarer Sonderfall. Im allgemeinen Bewußtsein ist es eine vom Tourismus geprägte "Museumsstadt". Dabei wird verkannt, daß in diesem einmaligen Gebilde eine normale Bevölkerung - vom Touristen kaum bemerkt - wohnt, lebt und arbeitet. Und der Tourismus ist, obwohl immer wieder vermutet, keineswegs die wesentliche wirtschaftliche Grundlage. Der Fremdenverkehr überlagert die Normalstrukturen. Industriearbeitsplätze befinden sich im Festlandbereich der Kommune. Die Hauptinsel (Centro Storico) hat ca. 80.000 Einwohner. Sie ist ein Oberzentrum mit den entsprechenden privaten und öffentlichen Verwaltungen, aber auch vielen Handwerks-betrieben und vor allem einer großen Zahl von Läden und Geschäften (50.000 Arbeitsplätze, ca.10% tourismusabhängig). Venedig ist - von kleineren Urlaubsorten abgesehen - weltweit die einzige autofreie Stadt.

Das Centro Storico ist jedoch mit dem Auto wie mit Bahn und Bus erreichbar. Doch sobald man beim Parkhaus, auf der Parkinsel oder am Busbahnhof angekommen ist, muß auf das öffentliche Verkehrsmittel umgestiegen, zu Fuß gegangen oder ein Taxiboot benutzt werden. Dabei wäre es denkbar, daß an Stelle eines Autos jeder Haushalt ein entsprechendes Motorboot besitzt. Das ist aber nicht der Fall. Nur ganz wenige sind Eigentümer eines privaten Motor-bootes. Es scheitert schon an den hohen Kosten. Wesentlich ist jedoch, daß man eine kommunale Abstellerlaubnis (= Parkplatz) braucht, um die Zulassung zu bekommen. Da der Wasserstraßen-raum begrenzt ist, gibt es nur sehr wenige Genehmigungen.

Da motorisierter Individualverkehr nahezu vollständig fehlt, hat der öffentliche Personennahverkehr herausragende Bedeutung. Die Haltestellen der Vaporetti - Bussen vergleichbare Wasserfahrzeuge mit größerem Fassungsvermögen - erschließen das Centro Storico flächendeckend, d.h. die Gehwegentfernungen zu den Haltestellen sind sehr kurz.

Der Canal Grande ist der Hauptverteiler und durch seine eigentümliche Form - ein umgekehrtes S - erschließt er die gesamte Hauptsiedlungsfläche. Das wird deutlich in der nebenstehenden Abbildung. Im übrigen dient das vielfach verzweigte Wasserstraßennetz dem Wirtschafts- und Sonderverkehr, also der Versorgung der Bevölkerung mit allen nur denkbaren Gütern und Dienstleistungen.

Stellen wir uns vor, eine "Normalstadt" von ca. 80.000 Einwohnern wäre in dieser Weise erschlossen:

Der gesamte motorisierte Individualverkehr endete an einem Punkt, d.h. das Prinzip des Kopfbahnhofes wäre angewendet. Innerhalb der Stadt gäbe es keinen privaten Autoverkehr.

Das Fahrstraßennetz stünde allein den öffentlichen Verkehrsmitteln einschließlich Taxis und dem Wirtschaftsverkehr zur Verfügung. Auch die Einwohner könnten, falls sie es unter diesen Umständen überhaupt für sinnvoll halten würden, ein Auto zu besitzen, dieses nur außerhalb der Stadt benutzen. Sie müßten - wie in Venedig - ihren Wagen im Parkhaus am Stadtrand oder weiter außerhalb abstellen.

Sind das utopische Vorstellungen? Wäre die Versorgung der Bevölkerung unter solchen Bedingungen überhaupt möglich? Wären die Arbeitsplätze in zumutbarer Weise erreichbar?

Ein derartiges Verkehrssystem hätte ganz bestimmte Auswirkungen auf die städtebauliche Struktur. In Venedig wird das besonders deutlich, es ist ein Musterbeispiel für eine "Stadt der kurzen Wege". Weil nicht ständig ein eigenes Fahrzeug gleichsam griffbereit vor der Haustür zur Verfügung steht, ist z.B. der Einkauf größerer Mengen unzweckmäßig. Große Kaufhäuser, Supermärkte und Einkaufszentren gibt es deshalb nicht. Stattdessen existiert eine Vielzahl von Einzelläden, die in die Wohnbebauung einbezogen sind und schnell zu Fuß erreicht werden können. Kindergärten und Schulen liegen dicht beieinander innerhalb der Wohngebiete. Es gibt keine großen Schulzentren. Auch die Einrichtungen der Universität sind über die Wohnbereiche verteilt. Ebenso sind Krankenhäuser, Ambulatorien und Altenheime in die Wohnbebauung integriert.

Das alles setzt selbstverständlich eine dichte Bauweise voraus. Dadurch stehen die Einwohner immer wieder vor der Wahl, entweder zu Fuß zu gehen, oder das öffentliche Verkehrsmittel zu benutzen. Vielfach ist der Fußweg günstiger. Die Folge ist, daß im Centro Storico 63,4% den Weg von der Wohnung zur Arbeits- oder Ausbildungsstelle zu Fuß zurücklegen, 35,5% den "Bus", d.h. einen Vaporetto nehmen und nur 1,1% dafür ein privates Fahrzeug benutzen.

Wie müßte eine "Normalstadt" beschaffen sein, um sich solchen venezianischen Verhältnissen wenigstens anzunähern?

Die Schwierigkeiten liegen beim Parkraum und beim öffentlichen Verkehr. Ohne durchgreifende Einschränkung der Parkraumansprüche sowohl im Kernbereich als auch an den Zufahrtstraßen ist ein Zurückdrängen des motorisierten Individual-verkehrs zugunsten des öffentlichen Verkehrs nicht zu erreichen. Solange die Ziele des Innen-stadtgebietes direkt angefahren werden können und Abstellplätze im Straßenraum und Park-häuser in zentraler Lage zur Verfügung stehen, bewirken sehr stark verbesserte ÖPNV-Systeme zwar Zuwächse bei den Fahrgastzahlen, aber der motorisierte Individualverkehr geht nicht zurück. Es entsteht dann mehr Verkehr, d.h. es wird mehr mit den öffentlichen Verkehrs-mitteln gefahren, aber insgesamt nicht weniger mit dem Auto. In Städten mit besonders attraktiven ÖPNV-Systemen ist kein einschneidender Rückgang des motorisierten Individualverkehrs (MIV) eingetreten. In Zürich und Freiburg sank die Verkehrsleistung des MIV um etwa ein bis zwei Prozent, in Karlsruhe stieg der Autoverkehr weiter an.

Anstelle der mannigfachen Parkmöglichkeiten in der Innenstadt müßte ein P+R-System geschaffen werden, bei dem die einzelnen Parkmöglichkeiten in der Mehrzahl wesentlich weiter vom Kernbereich entfernt lägen. Ein derartiges P+R-System funktioniert aber nur, wenn gleichzeitig der größte Teil der Innenstadt - d.h. ein sehr viel größerer Bereich als die engbegrenzte Fußgängerzone - nicht mehr für den motorisierten Individualverkehr zugänglich ist. Anderenfalls wird die Mehrzahl der Autofahrer immer wieder versuchen, doch noch eine Parklücke im Stadtinnern zu finden. Auch durch "intelligente" Parkleitsysteme ist dieser Suchverkehr nicht auszuschalten. Voraussetzung für die Funktionsfähigkeit eines solchen P+R-Systems mit außerhalb liegenden Auffangparkplätzen ist also, daß in der Innenstadt nur noch der "notwendige Verkehr" zugelassen wird.

Der Umfang vorhandener Fußgängerzonen ist im wesentlichen stets auf den zentralen Geschäftsbereich beschränkt. Indem die Attraktivität der Fußgänger-Geschäfts-Zone ständig gesteigert wurde, verminderte sich gleichlaufend die Qualität der anschließenden Gebiete. Würden die Bereiche, in denen der Fußgänger Vorrang hat, deutlich vergrößert, könnte die unausweichliche Entwertung, die bei Fußgängerzonen üblicher Größe in den umliegenden Wohngebieten eintritt, vermieden werden. Bei hinreichender Größe einer Zone mit stark eingeschränktem Individualverkehr wäre ein Ausgleich der Konzentration von Verkaufsflächen im Geschäftszentrum und der rückläufigen Entwicklung in den umliegenden Bereichen denkbar. Die übermäßige Anziehungskraft des Hauptgeschäftsgebietes würde dann gemindert und die Standortgunst gleichmäßiger verteilt.

Das anzustrebende Endziel stufenweise zu verwirklichen - wäre ein vom motorisierten Individualverkehr weitgehend befreiter Bereich, der etwa die Größenordnung der Hauptsiedlungsfläche von Venedig hätte. Um das zu verdeutlichen, zeigt die nebenstehende Abbildung einen Maßstabsvergleich mit vorhandenen Fußgängerzonen.

Bis zum venezianischen Extrem zu gehen hieße, auch den Bewohnern der Innenstadt das Benutzen ihres Autos innerhalb des Sperrbezirkes zu untersagen, falls es nicht zum "notwendigen Verkehr" gehört. Das ist politisch kaum durchsetzbar, obwohl oder gerade weil es die Innen-stadtbewohner selbst sind, die den größten Teil des Autoverkehrs dort verursachen.

Unter Umständen wird ein Wandel dadurch hervorgerufen, daß die Zustände in den Innen-städten immer unerträglicher werden. Dort sollten wenigstens die öffentlichen Stellplätze deutlich verringert und verhindert werden, daß neue hinzukommen.

Auch für ein Steigern des ÖPNV-Anteils ist Voraussetzung, daß der motorisierte Individualverkehr wirksam eingeschränkt wird. Gleichzeitig mit dem Einrichten größerer Fußgängergebiete müßte der öffentliche Verkehr drastisch verstärkt werden (Bedienungshäufigkeit und Beförderungsgeschwindigkeit). Der Kernbereich wäre durch Linien zu ergänzen, die mit Spezialfahrzeugen (Citybusse) betrieben werden.

Die Übertragbarkeit der geschilderten Prinzipien auf eine "Normalstadt" wurde anhand eines Fallbeispiels (Göttingen) untersucht.

Der für den MIV nicht allgemein zugängliche Bereich ist erheblich größer als die vorhandene Fußgängerzone. Dieser Verkehr wird auf Tangenten geleitet, die den Sperrbezirk umgeben. Die Zufahrten am Rande des Bezirks sind durch selbsttätig bewegliche Schranken oder Poller, die mit maschinenlesbaren Ausweiskarten bedient werden können, gesperrt. Halter von Kraftfahrzeugen, die zum "notwendigen Verkehr" zählen, bekommen derartige Dauerausweise. Die Bewohner des Bezirks erhalten ebenfalls - eventuell befristet - die entsprechende Erlaubnis. Nur an einem (im Norden), maximal an zwei Zugängen (Norden und Süden) wird Personal eingesetzt - nicht anders als bei bewachten Parkplätzen -, damit auswärtige Lieferanten, die keinen maschinenlesbaren Dauerausweis besitzen, passieren können. Auch die nicht oft, aber regelmäßig die Innenstadt anfahrenden gewerblichen Fahrzeuge bekämen die Erlaubnis.

Die P+R-Anlagen liegen bis auf eine größere Einrichtung im Bahnhofsbereich nicht am Rande der Sperrzone, sondern erheblich weiter außerhalb. Sie sind mit den Haltestellen von durchgehenden Buslinien verknüpft. Dabei handelt es sich um zusätzliche Linien, die nur mit einem Zwischenhalt von den Außenbezirken zum Stadtzentrum verkehren.

Außer den zusätzlichen und beschleunigten Linien werden innerhalb der Sperrzone zwei Citybus-Ringlinien installiert. Die eine führt vom Bahnhof aus durch die vorhandene Fußgängerzone, die andere folgt dem Verlauf des Innenstadtringes. Weil bei konsequenter Einschränkung des MIV dort eine Flächenreserve entsteht, finden sowohl die vorhandenen als auch die neuen Linien Platz. Damit kann der Innen-Stadtring, der bisher

vorwiegend dem MIV dient und den Kernbereich von der übrigen Innenstadt abschnürt, sinnvoll genutzt werden.

Dr.-Ing. Egon Grund, Stadtbaurat a.D.

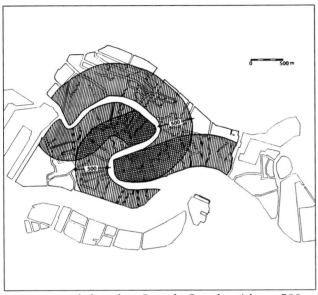

Area served by the Grand Canal with a 500m catchment area.

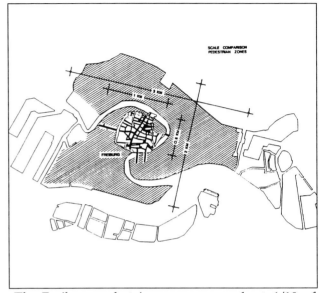

The Freiburg pedestrian area covers about 1/10 of Venice's main residential area.

Chapter Thirty-Nine (b)

Venice: A Model of a Car-free City?

Egon Grund

At first sight, Venice seems to be an incomparable special case. Most people think of Venice as the "City of Museums", dominated by tourism. Like any other city, however, this unique structure is inhabited by a normal population that lives and works here, though almost unnoticed by the tourist. Contrary to popular assumption, tourism is not even its economic basis. Tourism overlies the normal structures. Industrial enterprises are located in the community's mainland area. The main island (Centro Storico) has approximately 80,000 residents. There is a main centre with the usual private and public offices, but there are also many craft businesses and a particularly large number of shops and businesses (50,000 jobs, about 10 per cent of them dependent on tourism). Venice is - with the exception of some smaller holiday resorts - the only car-free city in the world.

BALANCED TRANSPORTATION SYSTEM

BALANCED TRANSPORTATION SYSTEM

The Centro Storico can be reached by car, rail, and bus. However, upon arrival at the multi-storey car park, on the parking island, or at the bus terminal, the traveler must change, to public means of transport, walk, or take a taxi-boat. One might expect households to own a motor boat instead of a car, yet this is not the case. Only few residents own a private motor boat. For one thing, there are the high costs. A second and even more important reason is that a parking licence issued by the community (parking space) is required for the registration of the boat. As there is only limited space on the waterways, only few licenses are issued.

As there is almost no motorised individual traffic in Venice, the local public transport system is of prime significance. The stops of the Vaporetti - vessels similar to busses but with a higher capacity - cover all of the Centro Storico, which means that walking distances to the nearest stop are always very short.

The Canal Grande is the trunk and because of its unusual shape - a reversed S -it serves the complete main residential area, as may be seen in the above figure.

Furthermore, the branched out network of waterways is also used for commercial and other special traffic, i.e., for supplying all kinds of goods and services to the population.

Imagine a "standard city" of about 80,000 inhabitants with the following traffic and transport system:

The entire private automobile traffic (motorised individual traffic) would end at one point, i.e., the principle of a dead-end station would be applied. There would be no private automobile traffic within the city. The streets would be used exclusively by public transport including taxis and commercial traffic.

If they regarded car ownership as at all useful, given the circumstances, residents could only drive outside the city limits. As in Venice, they would have to park their cars in the multi-storey car parks at the edge of the central area or even further away.

Is this a Utopia? Could the population still be supplied under these circumstances? Are trips to work and back still reasonably convenient?

Such a traffic system would have a certain impact on the urban structure. This impact can be seen clearly in Venice, which is a perfect example of a "City of Short Distances". For instance, shopping in bulk is impractical, as there is no private vehicle waiting for you in front of your house. Therefore, there are no department stores, supermarkets, or shopping centres. Instead, there is a variety of small shops, integrated into the residential area and always within walking distance. Kindergartens and schools are located side by side within the residential districts. There are no large school complexes. Even the university's facilities are spread out over the residential area. Likewise, hospitals, out-patient departments, and senior citizen's homes are integrated into the residential building area.

This, of course, requires a dense pattern of settlement. Thus residents are always faced with the choice between walking and using public transport. Often enough walking is more convenient. As a consequence, 63.4 per cent travel from their home to their workplace or school on foot, 35.5 per cent take the "bus", i.e., the Vaporetto and only 1.1 per cent use a private vehicle.

Which characteristics would such "standard city" need if it wanted to copy, or at least get closer, to the Venetian model?

Parking place and public transport usually pose the main problems. Without drastic restrictions on parking space in the core area as well as along access streets, no city will ever succeed in curbing motorised individual traffic in favour of public transport. As long as inner city destinations are still directly accessible by car and parking spaces are available in the streets and in centrally situated car parks, improved public transport systems may increase their passenger numbers, but private automobile traffic will not decrease. In fact, there will be more traffic, as there will be more public vehicles, while the car will not be used less. Those cities offering a particular attractive public transport system did not see a drastic decline in private automobile traffic. In Zurich and Freiburg, the motorised individual traffic performance went down by about one or two per cent, in Karlsruhe car traffic even continued to increase.

Instead of manifold parking facilities in the city centre, a park-and-ride system would have to be introduced, with the majority of its individual parking facilities being located much further away from the core area. However, such a P+R system can only operate successfully, if a major part of the city centre - a much larger area than the limited pedestrian areas - cannot be entered by private motor vehicles. Otherwise, the majority of drivers will keep trying to find a parking space in the city centre. Even "intelligent" parking management systems cannot eliminate this traffic caused by drivers searching for a parking space. Thus a precondition for the efficiency of such a P+R system with alternative parking provided at some points outside the central area is that only the "essential traffic" is granted permission to enter the city centre.

Existing pedestrian areas are commonly restricted to the central shopping area. The steady increase in the attractiveness of the pedestrian and shopping zone has correspondingly impaired the quality of adjacent areas.

If pedestrian zones were expanded considerably, the inevitable devaluation, which usually occurs in residential areas bordering on normal-sized pedestrian areas, could be avoided. if the area with strictly limited private traffic was large enough, the concentration of selling space in the city centre as well as the downward trend in adjacent areas might be compensated. The excessive appeal of the main shopping area would then be diminished and there would be a larger number of advantageous locations within this area.

The final aim - to be met step by step - is an area, that is largely freed from motorised individual traffic and about as large as Venice's main residential area. In order to illustrate this, the following figure shows a scale comparison with existing pedestrian areas.

Going to the Venetian extreme would involve prohibiting the inner city residents from using their cars within the restricted areas, unless they fall in the "essential traffic" category. Politically, this is hardly enforceable, although, or maybe just because, it is the city centre residents themselves who cause most of the car traffic in this area.

A change may be brought about by the fact that the situation in the city centres will become more and more unbearable. At least the number of public parking spaces in this area should be reduced considerably while the creation of new parking spaces should be prevented.

Neither will public transport play a more important role without restricting private car traffic. At the same time when larger pedestrian zones are established, public transport must be increased (service frequency and transport speed). New services for which special vehicles are employed (city buses) should be added in the central area.

The transferability of the above described principles to a "standard city" was investigated in a case study (Göttingen).

The area in which private car traffic is not generally permissible is considerably larger than the existing pedestrian zone. This traffic is directed onto a ring road surrounding the restricted area. The access points at the outside edge of this area are controlled by automatic barriers or posts which are operated with machine readable code cards. Keepers of vehicles considered "essential traffic" may obtain a permanent ID. Residents of this area are also given a permit, possibly for a limited period. Only at one access point (in the north) or at a maximum of two access points (north and south) staff is employed - similar to car parks with attendants - so that delivery vans from out-of-town may enter the city centre without a code card. Those commercial vehicles supplying inner city businesses regularly, yet not too frequently would also be given a permit.

With the exception of a major facility in the vicinity of the railroad station, P+R facilities are not located at the edge of the restricted area, but considerably further away. They are linked up to stops of direct bus service routes. These are additional shuttle service routes traveling from the outskirts to the city centre with only one more stop.

Besides the additional and rapid services, two citybus circle routes will be installed within the restricted area.

One of them runs from the station through the existing pedestrian zone, the other one runs along the inner ring road. Since a rigorous restriction on private automobile traffic will generate extra space, there will be sufficient space for existing and new public transport routes. As a result, the inner ring road, which

has up to now mainly been used by private vehicles and has cut off the core area from adjacent city centre areas, becomes available for a new, meaningful use.

Dr.Ing. Egon Grund is Stadtbaurat a.D. (Planning Director, retired) in Karlsruhe, Germany.

Chapter Forty

Towards a Pedestrian-Friendly Manhattan
Seen from a German Perspective

Rolf Monheim

From the perspective of a German visitor, Manhattan is an ideal place to create a pedestrian-friendly environment, both because of its potentials and because of its needs. He has the impression, however, that citizens as well as decision-makers and even many planners are not fully aware of this because their perception is misled by the physical dominance of the motorcar. They do not realize that the relative share of car users among all people traveling is extremely low, whereas the negative impacts, given the too high absolute numbers, are disastrous. Against that, most European cities during the last decade have changed their approach to transportation planning from car-orientation towards a more balanced development which is a condition to ensure their livability and sustainability. In this paper, some elements of these new strategies will be presented with a special reference to their meaning for a more pedestrian-friendly, and that means, a more livable Manhattan.

Perception of Problems

Transportation planning is the result of policy. This policy is determined by the main streams of opinion among citizens, and that means voters, on one hand, and by the perception of these opinions among politicians, administrators and the media, on the other hand (furthermore, there is a strong, but often hidden, influx of pressure groups like chamber of commerce or taxi drivers).

In Europe, and especially in Germany, several polls have shown a widespread criticism of car traffic among citizens which is highly underestimated, however, by decision makers and opinion leaders.

When citizens are asked what they consider (or: in their opinion is) the most important problem to be solved by those responsible for the city, in all cases traffic is mentioned by far most often.

In the case of interest conflict between the needs of cars with those of public transport, cycling and walking the so-called "green modes" - they do not see the solution in an improvement of road infrastructure but, in contrary, in a planning priority for the latter, notwithstanding disadvantages for car users. This is true for all urbanized areas in Germany as well as for the average in West- and, even more, in (former) East-Germany and in whole the European Community.

The personal opinion of decision makers in Germany is very close to the average citizen. A great bias, however, can be found in the perception of citizens' priorities by decision makers as well as, in the opposite way, in the perception of decision makers' priorities by citizens. In both cases, from outside the priorities are considered to be more car-oriented than they really are.

This bias of perception is well known to the citizens, as can be seen from answers to polls among citizens, whether they believe that politicians, journalists and administrators perceive the sentiments of citizens towards cars to be more hostile or more car-friendly than they really are. There is a very clear majority of those who are aware of the wrong perception among decision and opinion makers in favor of cars.

Some consider the knowledge of these priorities and perceptions to be without significance for planning because they see very often a contrast between declared opinions and real behavior. New trends, however, first have to be introduced into minds before they can become reality. In Germany (and even more in Switzerland and the Netherlands) meanwhile, it has been proved many times that the trend towards the car is not destiny but can be changed, with the result of an increasing use of public transport and cycling, and that the new trends prior to change transportation structures started at the level of opinions, discussions and studies.

The importance of walking, up to now is increased only within the large pedestrianized areas of city centers, whereas it is still not increasing for longer distances due to bad walking conditions and growing trip length. There is, however, an increasing number of studies on walking.

Objectives for a Sustainable Development

The limits of growth, as they have been shown by the Club of Rome, make necessary a change of direction in the trend of our development if we want the earth to survive. Traffic is only one of several fields of action. Others are energy and waste. The hierarchy of objectives for an environmentally more compatible and sustainable development is very similar. In all cases, first priority has to be given to a reduction strategy, that is: less energy consumption, less waste production and less traffic generation.

The energy crisis, which was caused by exploding oil prices, first had forced us to understand that economic growth is possible without increasing energy consumption but that, in the contrary, energy saving can become an important element of technical progress and economic growth. At the moment, we start to learn that lesson for our growing waste which cannot be handled anymore. The same has to be understood for our traffic, the increase of which for a much too long time has been seen as a sign of progress and an output in itself whereas, in the contrary, it is an input which ought to be minimized.

Notwithstanding all efforts to save traffic there always will be a need of mobility - just as energy is needed and waste produced. For this unavoidable - or socially accepted - mobility the green modes, e.g. walking, cycling and public transport, should be used as much as possible, in a similar way as environmentally more compatible energy sources and industrial materials have to be given priority. The change in the mode of transport requires a broad mixture of measures pulling the transportation of people and goods towards the green modes and pushing them away from the motorcar, the so-called stick and carrot strategies.

In those cases where it is impossible or unreasonable to use the green modes, the remaining car traffic has to be handled more safely, with less noise and less pollution that it is today. This often is made by techniques of traffic calming in a more narrow sense. The hazards from energy production and waste disposal have to be minimized in an analogous way.

The traffic calming philosophy results from a new understanding of mobility which was developed in a learning process. In the period of industrialization the increase of mobility had been considered as an important condition for economic growth. Afterwards, we were told that increasing mobility is inevitable in a growing economy and that the transport system had to be adjusted to the increasing demand.

An increasing awareness of the negative side effects of traffic on the environment and the livability of cities provoked doubts whether additional traffic really meant more prosperity. The first reactions were measures in the field of engineering (e.g. less fuel consumption and less poisonous fumes) and traffic management (e.g. speed control, lanes reserved to buses or high occupancy vehicles). Meanwhile there is an increasing understanding that more prosperity does not depend necessarily on more mobility. In the contrary, it can be said that traffic saving, in the same way as energy and waste saving, is an important condition for more prosperity based on a sustainable development.

Without this new understanding there is no chance to get the political support for a strategy towards traffic saving or, as John Roberts from London had called it, traffic degeneration. Small and densely populated nations like the Netherlands and Switzerland are ahead in this learning process and have demonstrated that it works (e.g. at Amsterdam, Delft, Basel and Zürich). The Zürich population is especially keen on saving money instead of wasting it for useless transportation expenditures (that is how you become and stay rich). In Germany, some cities have started this process, too (e.g. Erlangen, Freiburg, Munich). And it is again typical that these are the most prosperous ones! In the United States, Manhattan could become the ideal place to adopt such a new strategy if the decision making system would understand its enormous benefits for the quality of life, and

that means, for the success, if not survival, of the admired "Big Apple".

Traffic Saving for Manhattan

Traffic saving strategies are the most difficult ones and need the longest time to produce visible results. Manhattan already is an ideal place because of its density and mixture of functions. All possible efforts should be made to defend or to develop even further this mixture and to avoid the spreading out of mono-functional land uses. Especially affordable housing should be encouraged as much as possible. Pocket parks and well developed tree rows along traffic calmed streets can help to reduce the need to flee from urban pollution. Sufficient working facilities in the outer parts of New York can reduce the pressure of commuters on Manhattan.

Traffic saving is also possible by a better organization of peoples and goods transport. The enormous numbers of taxis, for instance, are necessary because public transport has, or is perceived to have, poor service and comfort. A similar example are mothers driving their children. And the distribution or collection of goods could be managed in a much more efficient way than it is today, with the benefit of a clearly reduced member, trip length and size of trucks.

Promotion of Walking

Walking is a very important part of the transportation system in Manhattan, both, as the only means for a trip and in combination with public transport (and with the car in those cases where parking is not possible immediately at the place of destination). But pedestrians have to overcome many impediments and risks, the reduction of which certainly would encourage more and longer trips on foot.

Safety is of especially high importance. Traffic safety mainly depends on the design of street crossings. It can be improved by "sidewalk caps" where, in the case of a parking lane, the sidewalk at an intersection is enlarged by the width of the parking lane. As a result the pedestrian who wants to cross the street has a better visual interaction with the approaching car driver and has to walk a shorter distance between the sidewalks of both sides of the street. Broad streets with a two-way traffic should have a pedestrians' island in the middle of the street where the pedestrians can stop until the traffic flow allows to cross the second half of the street.

In those cases where main roads are heavily used by pedestrians as well, the level of the sidewalk may continue across secondary side roads so that cars entering or leaving the side road across that sidewalk have to slow down and to acknowledge the priority of pedestrians (a good example for such a boulevard design can be found at Nuremberg - Königstraße.

Pedestrians should not be forced to use underpasses when crossing a street. There should always be the possibility for a safe crossing on ground level. The possibility to cross a street safely also depends very much on the speed and volume of car traffic. Their reduction, in addition, results in less noise and fumes, which makes it more pleasant - or less boring - to walk. Within the secondary network of urban streets, the speed of cars in most Germany cities is reduced area wide to 20 miles/hour. In shopping streets speed may be reduced even to 12 miles/hour or to pedestrians' speed by special traffic signs.

The width of the sidewalk should be broad enough to avoid congestion which, in some cases, can become an impediment for moving fast longer distances, especially at lunch time. Trees along the sidewalk are an important support for walking. The climatological effect of tall buildings on walking like shadow or wind should be considered as well.

Safety includes also that people are - and feel - safe from crime in an area. Even though transportation planning cannot solve social problems of a city, there are several possibilities to improve safety conditions, like cleanliness and good lighting. Furthermore, public uses on the ground floor attracting people all times of the day probably are the best means to give the feeling of safety whereas blank walls or derelict buildings are very disadvantageous.

Pedestrianization is the most effective measure to improve walking conditions. Originally, it was restricted to narrow shopping streets with high numbers of pedestrians. Meanwhile, in most German cities pedestrian precincts cover large parts of the retail core and include streets and places where important historical buildings, cultural, social or recreational functions can be found. In several cases, within the city core now networks of 3 - 6 miles are pedestrianized (see, for instance, Freiburg, Nuremberg or Munich).

Recently, the area-wide approach has led to the model of so-called "car free" or "pedestrian friendly" city centers which, in reality, are not car free, but allow only a limited access to cars. Residents and owners of private parking garages may enter the restricted area the whole day, emergency vehicles, public services and public buses as well. Visitors, on the other hand, are not allowed to enter the area.

The first application of such a system was made in Bologna, Italy. It became very famous and made possible a clear reduction in car traffic which, however still remains with a certain volume. Florence followed that model several years later with a very large area of restricted access.

In Germany, Lübeck was the first city to introduce this type of selected access. It started in 1989, in the beginning only as an attempt restricted to Saturday and Sunday (Lübeck has high numbers of tourists). Cars without a special permit, which is given by the city, are not allowed to enter the city core between 10:00 AM and 4:00 PM. If they have entered the area before that time they may continue their trip as long as they like. The access to public parking garages and large parking areas is free the whole day. It is planned to expand this regulation to all days of the week in 1995.

Aachen introduced the same regulation on Saturdays form 10:00 AM to 3:00 PM in 1991. It increased heavily the frequency of its public transport and offered special group fares. With the so-called "happy day ticket" a group of five persons can travel all day Saturday within the city boundaries as far and as often as they want at a price of only $3. The access to all but two parking garages is free the whole day on special access roads.

Erfurt was the third city to use that model in 1992. Some other cities like Bremen and Nuremberg have combined large pedestrian precincts with a system of traffic sectors: cars have to leave these sectors at the same side where they have entered it. There is no direct connection between sectors but only via the surrounding ring road.

The most utopian traffic-calming model has been developed in 1991 by the car factory BMW for its "home city" Munich. It is part of a traffic management scheme to reduce the pressure of car traffic step by step from the urban fringe towards the city center by giving less and less room to cars but more and more room to public transport, cycling and walking as one approaches the core area. Visitors who come by car and do not change to P+R in the urban fringe have to store it in automatic garages located along a ring road surrounding the city core. Within the core people walk or use small shuttle buses. Existing garages are changed to functions more adequate for a city center.

The fact that a car factory dares to develop such a model (while meanwhile is being transferred by BMW to smaller "model cities" like Dresden, Regensburg and Linz) shows deep changes in the political climate which increasingly puts under question the disastrous effects of heavy car traffic on quality of life. In Germany, we are still in the beginning of moving in a new direction. The first steps sometimes have caused heavy protest from car-oriented interest groups, but always have got a strong support from citizens, as many polls show. Area wide traffic-calming principles, in the long run, certainly will spread out in a similar way as pedestrian precincts did within the last three decades. New York has a great chance to become the fore-runner within the New World.

Rolf Monheim is a Professor in Applied Urban Geography at the University of Bayreuth, Germany.

Architektur mit hoher Qualität für öffentliche Verkehrsmittel

Jürgen Rauch

In meiner theoretischen wie auch in meiner praktischen Arbeit beschäftige ich mich mit Planungsaufgaben, welche mit architektonischen Mitteln eine Verbesserung für bauliche Anlagen des öffentlichen Verkehrs schaffen.

In fast allen Städten der Welt sind wir mit dem schnell wachsenden Problem, Menschen zu bewegen, konfrontiert, mit Verkehrsproblemen und den Erfordernissen der Mobilität. Von den relativ kleinen Städten mit 50.000 Einwohnern bis hin zu den großen Ballungszentren, in Europa beispielsweise London, Paris und Moskau, oder den kleineren Großstädten wie Berlin, Barcelona und den Städten des Ruhrgebietes, und außerhalb Europas, städtischen Ballungsräumen mit mehr als 15 Millionen Menschen, Tokio, Sao Paulo, Mexiko Stadt, gibt es eine große Zahl von Beispielen, die uns zeigen, daß ein großer Bedarf besteht, die derzeitige Situation zu verbessern.

Manche dieser Städte vergrößern sich mit Wachstumsraten, welche weit über dem Durchschnitt dessen liegen, was wir hier in Europa kennen. Ich möchte unter diesen Metropolen speziell die Großstädte in Südostasien nennen. In manchen davon (beispielsweise in der thailändischen Hauptstadt Bangkok) bringt die Dichte privater Kraftfahrzeuge alle Aktivitäten komplett zum Erliegen.

So sehen wir, daß der Individualverkehr keine hinreichende Problemlösung darstellt. Mittlerweile erkennen wir aber in den meisten Ländern Anstrengungen dahingehend, die wachsende Notwendigkeit zur Deckung des Verkehrsbedarfs ernstzunehmen und zu reagieren, hat doch der Zusammenbruch des Verkehrs auch schwere wirtschaftliche Auswirkungen: wir verschwenden eine Menge Zeit, Energie, und unsere Gesundheit. Darüberhinaus sehen wir uns einem starken Verfall unserer Lebensqualität gegenüber.

Ich denke, daß wir alle, in allen Ländern, in der wesentlichen Tatsache übereinstimmen, daß die Verringerung der Möglichkeiten der individuellen Mobilität durch die öffentliche Hand allein keine Lösung dieser immensen Problemstellung ist. Speziell an Orten, wo das private Kraftfahrzeug und das öffentliche Verkehrsmittel mit gleichen Wettbewerbsbedingungen nebeneinander existieren, sind Zwangsmaßnahmen gegenüber der Bevölkerung nutzlos: die persönliche Wahl des Verkehrsmittels für-- jeden einzelnen kann in die Richtung "weg vom privaten Kraftfahrzeug" nur durch, eine sichtbare Qualitätsverbesserung beim öffentlichen Verkehr beeinflußt werden.

Die Erhöhung der Kapazität schienengebundener Verkehrsmittel ist der einzig gangbare Weg, weniger "Motorlaufzeit" zu erhalten - natürlich ist dies auch ein Vorteil für unsere Umwelt und ein großer Impuls für die Volkswirtschaft der jeweiligen Länder.

Um die großen Städte in den Industrienationen wie auch in den sogenannten Schwellenländern am Funktionieren zu erhalten, ist es erforderlich, neue Verkehrssysteme zu errichten. In den Stadtzentren wird man neue Linien in eine zweite Ebene legen müssen, als aufgeständerte Bahn oder unter die Oberfläche. In kleineren Städten und in den Vorstädten der Metropolen wird man diese Verkehrsmittel an der Oberfläche errichten (Erlebniswert der Reise).

Wichtige Spezialaufgaben müssen auf effiziente Weise gelöst werden: Auch in einer technisch und infrastrukturell gut organisierten Metropole kann der öffentliche Verkehr allein den gesamten Verkehrsbedarf der Massen nicht lösen. Daher sollten und dürfen verschiedene Verkehrsmittel nicht in Konkurrenz leben. Wir brauchen die gesamte Kapazität aller Verkehrsträger, gut kombiniert je nach der Siedlungsstruktur der verschiedenen Zonen unserer Ballungsgebiete.

Da alle diese Vorhaben nur mit einem enormen Kostenaufwand verwirklicht werden können, ist es von großer Wichtigkeit, daß die Bewohner eines Ballungsgebietes wie auch die Tagesgäste einer Stadt das Massenverkehrsmittel mit seinen Einrichtungen gerne annehmen. Wir haben drei Wege, diesem Ziel näherzukommen:

- Der visuelle Eindruck der Haltestellen und der Fahrgastwägen muß zeigen, daß der Preis der Fahrt gerechtfertigt ist.

Welches sind die wichtigen Aspekte von Haltepunkten öffentlicher Verkehrsmittel in den Städten? Sie sind Haltepunkte von Bahnen, Orte, an denen man Informationen über die Fahrt erhalten kann, Orte, an denen die Wartezeit gut verbracht und gut genutzt werden sollte, wichtige Punkte in einem Netz von Linien, welches die Struktur und das Skelett einer Stadt oder eines Ballungsraumes

bilden, Orte, an denen Menschen zusammenkommen, Orte, die den Wert der Reise ausdrücken sollen, und die Imageträger einer Statt oder eines Stadtviertels.

- Die Umsteigeverbindungen zu anderen Verkehrsmitteln, sowie zwischen Auto oder Bus in weniger dicht bewohnten Gebieten mit Haltestellen oder Bahnsteigen von Stadtbahnen, U-Bahnen oder Zügen müssen so projektiert sein, daß die Wege leicht zu finden sind, daß sie sehr kurz oder in ihrem Verlaufe sehr interessant sind, und daß beim Umsteigen sehr wenig Zeitverlust entsteht.

Angenommen wir bewältigen die Aufgabe, alle erforderlichen Verkehrskapazitäten zu schaffen, müssen wir dabei dennoch eine Sache wesentlich verbessern: die Qualität der Schnittstellen und Verbindungswege zwischen den verschiedenen Verkehrsmitteln und die Übergänge zu den öffentlichen Räumen einer Stadt. Dabei sind die Gesichtspunkte der Funktion und auch der Architekturqualität der Bahnhöfe, der Haltestellen von Vorstadtbahnen und innerstädtischen Bahnen (U-Bahnen, Stadtbahnen) gemeint.

- Die Anmutungsqualität von Design und Innenausbau der Haltestellen und Bahnhöfe muß hoch sein. Dies kann man durch das Schaffen von Räumen mit sehr viel natürlichem, und dort wo es nicht möglich ist, einem hohen Maß an künstlichem Licht, mit heller Boden- und Wandverkleidung und schließlich mit einem Architektur-konzept und einer Raumanordnung erreichen, welche den Fahrgästen ermöglicht, schnell einen Überblick über die Station zu bekommen.

Der Gebrauch privater Kraftfahrzeuge ist in beinahe allen Gesellschaften ein Zeichen des Selbstbewußtseins der Menschen, das Auto wird bisweilen als wichtig erachtet, um in eine bestimmte soziale Schicht eingeordnet zu werden. Um diesen Irrtum zu korrigieren und die Menschen zum Benützen von Zügen, U-Bahnen oder Stadtbahnen in ihrer Funktion als äußerst effiziente und komfortable Transportmittel in der Stadt zu ermutigen, können wir aus Beispielen der Vergangenheit und der jetzigen Zeit lernen, und wir sollten diese Beispiele zu noch besseren Lösungen weiterentwickeln.

In der Geschichte der Bahnhofsgestaltung finden wir Ideen und Details, die wir auch in der heutigen Architektur für Verkehrsbauwerke verwenden können. Am Ende des vergangenen Jahrhunderts war die Bahn das wichtigste Transportmittel, in Europa wie auch in Nordamerika. Neben der Schiene gab es kein effizientes Transportmittel. Der Bahnhof war daher das Tor zur Stadt.

Die Faszination des Reisens wurde durch die Gestaltungsmittel der Bahnhöfe ausgedrückt; in den Bahnhöfen waren Einrichtungen, um die Wartezeit zu nutzen und um sich zu treffen. In den großen Bahnhöfen aus dieser Zeit gibt es Restaurants, manche davon mit elegantem, großartigen Interieur, wie das Beispiel des Restaurants "Le train bleu" im Pariser Gare de Lyon zeigt.

Die Bahnsteighallen wurden mit Eisenkonstruktionen überdacht. Die enorme Raumhöhe in diesen Bahnhöfen bereitet den ankommenden Fahrgästen einen adäquaten Empfang (Leipzig, Hauptbahnhof, Barcelona, Estació de França). Der Klassizismus war der Stil der Bahnhöfe, aber es gab auch einige Ausnahmen, welche mit utopischem Charakter errichtet oder geplant wurden.

Einige Stationsbauten in den Außenbezirken von London waren Teil eines Programmes für die "Corporate Identity" des Londoner U-Bahn-Systems. Es gibt kubische und zylindrische Bauten, jeweils an gut sichtbaren Stellen des Straßenraumes, die Orientierungspunkte und Erkennungszeichen sind, den endlosen Wohngebieten Identität verschaffen und den Fahrgästen behilflich sind, während der Fahrt mit dem Bus an der Oberfläche auf einfache Weise den Ort des Wechsels des Verkehrsmittels zu finden.

Kleine Läden für die Fahrgäste waren integrativer Teil des Interieurs der Schalterhallen. Auf den Bahnsteigen der U-Bahnen gabe es sogar Kioske (Hamburg, Klosterstern, errichtet 1929).

Die Moskauer U-Bahnhöfe wurden beinahe wie Paläste ausgestattet, und dies zu einer Zeit, als in den Ländern des Westens Bahnhöfe und Metrostationen ohne ornamentale Beigaben errichtet wurden. In der Metrostation Majakowskaja, erbaut 1938, erweckt eine indirekte künstliche Beleuchtung der Deckengewölbe den Eindruck, daß natürliches Licht den Raum erhelle.

Verbindung der Bahnhöfe mit dem öffentlichen Raum

Montreal besitzt ein großes System unterirdischer Verbindungen für Fußgänger zwischen den U-Bahnhöfen des Stadtzentrums, verbunden mit großen Innenräumen von Geschäftsbauten.

Das Design der U-Bahnhöfe ist sehr auf die Wirkung des Raumes ausgerichtet. Es gebraucht die Möglichkeiten von Brücken und Durchblicken. Stationen und Fußgängerwege sind zu einer Einheit mit großen Einkaufs- und Servicezentren zusammengeschlossen.

Eingangssituationen von Haltepunkten, vor allem Wege zu unterirdischen Räumen, erfordern die ganze Aufmerksamkeit des Planers. Es ist wichtig, den Fahrgast zur Bahn oder zur Oberfläche zu geleiten, mit interessanten Wegen, Raumsituationen, Plätzen und guter Beleuchtung.

In München wurden in den letzten Jahren im Hauptbahnhofsgebäude neue Ladeneinbauten fertiggestellt, in der Bahnsteighalle und in einem zweigeschoßigen Hallenbereich. Das Wechselspiel von Ziegel oder Beton mit Glas und Stahl bestimmt ihr Bild. Die Einbauten bilden einen kontrastierenden Dialog zur alten Bausubstanz.

Die Qualität der Beleuchtung und das Erfassen der räumlich-architektonischen Zusammenhänge einer Station

Die Untergrundbahnhöfe von Washington werden indirekt beleuchtet, sie bestehen aus geräumigen Hallen mit Punkten, von denen aus die Fahrgäste die Raumfolgen überblicken können, und mit gut sichtbaren Umsteige- und Verbindungswegen zu den Anschlußlinien .

Eine gewölbte Aluminiumdecke, mit welcher starke Lichtquellen in den Raum reflektiert werden, ist das Architekturprinzip der Münchner U-Bahnstation Fürstenried West. Die Bahnsteigkante wird mit besonders hoher Lichtintensität angestrahlt.

Der Münchner U-Bahnhof Dülferstraße ist ein Projekt, mit welchem wir betraut waren, in Zusammenarbeit mit dem Büro P. Lanz und der U-Bahnbehörde der Münchner Stadtverwaltung. Die Station wurde 1993 eröffnet, zur Zeit ist sie der Endbahnhof der Linie 2. Die Umsteigestation dieser U-Bahnlinie mit der S-Bahn zum Flughafen ist die vom selben Team entwickelte, momentan in Bau befindliche Station Feldmoching.

In der heutigen, aktuellen Gestaltung von Haltestellen des öffentlichen Verkehrs gibt es einige wichtige Aspekte für den Fahrgast: er muß schnell Informationen über Fahrplan und Umsteigeverbindungen erhalten, die Fahrt effizient fortsetzen können; die Haltestellenkonzeption muß den Übergang von und zu anderen Verkehrsmitteln so leicht wie möglich machen. Diese neuen Projekte kompensieren die Wartezeit mit der visuellen Qualität eines gut designten Bauwerks - sie sind eine mögliche Antwort auf die Bedürfnisse der Haltestation als Teil des öffentlichen Raumes und als Teil der täglichen Lebensumwelt.

Gebäude für das Umsteigen zwischen verschiedenen Verkehrsmitteln

Der Stockholmer Busterminal von Ralph Erskine verschmilzt mit einem Bürogebäude von 40.000 Quadratmetern Grundfläche, dem sogenannten "World Trade Center". Der Bau führt die räumlichen Erfahrungen des Reisens und der Arbeitswelt zusammen. Die Menschen sollen nicht auf miserable Weise auf Busse oder Züge in schäbigen oder zugigen Hallen warten. In diesem Gebäude kommen die Fahrgäste erst unmittelbar am Fahrzeug durch eine Glastüre aus dem angenehmen Innenraum. Der Busbahnhof verbindet Flughafenbus, Fernbussen, U-Bahnsystem und den nahegelegenen Hauptbahnhof.

Der North West Terminal in Chicago ist eine Kombination eines Bahnhofes für Einpendler mit einem Büro- und Geschäftskomplex an der Stelle eines früheren Fernbahnhofes, gleichzeitig ein Tor zum zentralen Geschäftsstraßenbereich der Innenstadt.

1994 eröffnete die Münchner Stadtverwaltung die neue Station Fröttmaning, mit Umsteigemöglichkeiten zu Bussen und einem großen Park-and-Ride-Parkhaus. Neue architektonische Formen sollen hier ausdrücken, daß der hohe Grad der Annehmlichkeit des Gebäudes der Weg ist, den öffentlichen Verkehr dem Bürger nahezubringen.

In Zürich gibt es gute Beispiele neuer Bahnhofsarchitektur. Die innerstädtische Station Stadelhofen symbolisiert die dynamische Bewegung des Zuges, unterhalb der Gleise befindet sich eine lange, teilweise natürlich beleuchtete Passage mit Läden, die den Weg des Fahrgastes zum Zug säumen. - Ein anderes erwähnenswertes Projekt ist das Ladengeschoß zwischen Bahnsteig und Oberfläche der Station Museumsstraße mit einem hellen Boden und qualitativ guter Beleuchtung.

Viele Architekturimpulse gehen von den Bahnhöfen der Alta Velocidad Espanola, der Hochgeschwindigkeitsbahn zwischen Madrid und Sevilla in Spanien aus. Der Bahnhof Atocha in Madrid von Rafael Moneo ist ein Endbahnhof dieser Linie. Die Fußgängerebene liegt unterhalb der Straßenebene, der Vorplatz ist eingetieft. Auf dem Wege zu den verschiedenen Ebenen gibt es variationsreiche Läden, Cafes und Restaurants, eine Verbindung zur Metro, einen Busbahnhof, der 8,5 Meter höher als die Metro gelegen ist. Die Parkebenen fassen über 800 Fahrzeuge. Die Bauaktivitäten erstreckten sich über zwei Abschnitte, einen Nahverkehrs- und einen Fernbahnhof, mit allen Funktionen und unter Berücksichtung der natürlichen Ökonomie der Bewegung. Der Architekt schuf hochwertig wirkende Räume, keine Durchgangsräume, durch die Einbeziehung des natürlichen Tageslichts.

In den Metrostationen von Barcelona kann man sehen, wie eine Bar das Ambiente eines Verkehrsbauwerkes verbessern kann.

Diese Beispiele zeitgenössischen Stationsdesigns zeigen architektonische Konzepte, die nicht nur die funktionalen Erfordernisse zur Bewältigung großer Fahrgastmengen erfüllen. Das Design der Stationen versucht, den Eindruck von räumlicher und architektonischer Qualität zu erzeugen, durch den kreativen Gebrauch von Material, von Lichtführung und Detail.

Visionen für die Zukunft

Bahnhofsdesign von hoher Qualität ist auch ein großer Vorteil für die Wirtschaft einer Stadt oder eines Stadtteils. Die kanadischen Städte Toronto und Montreal haben uns bereits die erfolgreiche Verbindung der Entwicklung von öffentlichen Verkehrsmitteln und Immobilienwerten beziehungsweise baulicher Entwicklung vorgeführt.

Unter den verschiedenen Zukunftprojekten gibt den interessanten Entwurf eines Park-and-Ride-Turmes, eine Diplomarbeit. Die Notwendigkeit, die Anzahl von Kraftfahrzeugen in einer Innenstadt drastisch zu senken, ergab die Idee, einen Turm für 10.000 Kraftfahrzeuge zu errichten, zusammen mit einer Zugverbindung in das Stadtzentrum. Die Brücke zwischen den beiden Teilen dieses Zwillingsgebäudes wird als Hotel genutzt. Dieser neue urbane Knotenpunkt kann auch zwischen mehreren Städten eines verstädterten Ballungraumes gebaut werden. Mannigfaltige Dienstleistungsangebote und Läden mit einer reichen Produktpalette können hier eingerichtet werden, Treffen und Geschäftermine können auf halbem Wege zwischen zwei Städten stattfinden.

Wir schlugen der Deutschen Bahn AG in einer Studie zur Verbesserung des Intercityhaltepunktes München-Pasing vor, zwischen das historische Bahnhofsgebäude und den

Bahnsteigbereich eine Halle zu bauen, mit Läden, Cafes und anderen Einrichtungen für den Fahrgast auf zwei Geschoßen. Die räumliche Idee ähnelt dem Typus der alten Ladenpassagen in den großen Städten Europas.

Noch in diesem Jahrzehnt soll die katalanische Metropole Barcelona an das Netz der TGV-Hochgeschwindigkeitszüge aus Richtung Paris-Lyon-Montpellier angeschlossen werden. Zwischen Barcelona und der letzten Station auf französischem Terretorium, Perpignan, wird der Bevölkerungsschwerpunkt Girona (ca. 200.000 Einwohner), ca. 100 Kilometer nördlich von Barcelona gelegen, einen Zwischenhalt des Schnellzuges bekommen.

In unserem Projektvorschlag, erarbeitet zusammen mit den lokalen Architekten Joaquim Bover u.a., gehen wir von einer effizienten Verknüpfung von Hochgeschwindigkeitszug, regionalen Zügen, Flugverkehr und Straßenverkehr aus, um den Hochgeschwindigkeitszug für möglichst viele Bewohner des sich in den vergangenen Jahren stark verstädternden Gebietes zugänglich zu machen.

Als Gebäudeform wurde ein in Grundriß und Höhenentwicklung geschwungener Körper entwickelt, der das Abbremsen eines sehr schnellen Verkehrsmittels ebenso wie das Beschleunigen dieses Zuges am anderen Ende der Bahnsteighalle symbolisiert. Eine große, weitgehend verglaste Halle empfängt den Fahrgast, darunter befinden sich Eingangshalle, Geschäfte und Cafes, sowie seitlich daran anschließend ein ebenfalls unter der Bahnsteig-halle liegender Busbahnhof und Parkflächen für den Individualverkehr.

In einer gut organsierten innerstädtischen U-Bahn- oder Stadtbahnstation können die Verbindungsebenen als Außenraum, aber auch als Galerien oder Passagen betrachtet werden.

Cafes oder Kneipen mit langer Öffnungszeit und die Möglichkeit, das Bahnsteiggeschoß zu überblicken, begünstigen die Akzeptanz der Bahnbenützung zu den städtischen Außenbezirken, auch in den späten Abendstunden. Kiosks und kleine Stehbars auf dem Bahnsteig, vielleicht auch ein Brunnen, verbessern die Atmosphäre einer Verkehrseinrichtung.

Das Bauen für den öffentlichen Verkehr in unseren Städten muß von hoher Qualität sein, um die Menschen zu ermutigen, Züge und Stadtbahnen as die effizientesten Transportmittel zu benützen.

Dr.-Ing. Jürgen Rauch ist Planer für Verkehrsbauwerke, München.

223

High Quality Architecture for Urban Public Transportation

Jurgen Rauch

In my theoretical studies as well as in my professional practice I work to improve built structures for public transport through architectural means.

In nearly all cities of the world we face the fast growing problem of moving people, of transport and the needs of mobility. Beginning with small cities with 50,000 inhabitants, up to the huge crowded areas, in Europe for example London, Paris and Moscow, or the smaller cities such as Berlin, Barcelona or the Rhein-Ruhr area, and outside Europe, cities of more than 15 million people, Tokyo, Sao Paulo, Mexico City - we have many examples of the big demand to improve the current situation. Some of these cities are expanding faster than the average rate we know here. I mention among these metropoles especially the cities in South East Asia. In some of them (one example is the Thai metropole of Bangkok) the density of individual cars leads to the complete stop of all activities.

It is clear that transport with individual cars is not a satisfactory solution to the problem. Meanwhile most countries are making efforts to resolve transportation problems because traffic congestion has also very heavy economical dimensions. We waste a lot of time, energy, and damage our health, and we face the fact of a heavy decrease of life quality.

I think we all agree that reducing mobility by public decree does not give the solution to this immense task. Especially where private cars and public transportation are in equal concurrency, trying to force people to give up the use of private cars is useless: people can only be influenced not to use the private car by a visible improvement of the quality of public transportation.

The increase of capacity of railway transportation is the only possible way to get less "time of running motors" - it is thus an advantage for our environment and an impressive "Plus" for the nations' economies. In order to maintain the well-functioning of big cities of highly industrialized countries as well as in countries which are industrializing at this time, it is necessary to continuously build new equipment for transportation. In the central districts of these cities new lines have to be located on a second level, that is elevated or underground. In smaller cities and in the outskirts of the metropoles, transportation will be located on the surface.

Important special tasks have to be resolved in an efficient way. Also in a technically and, regarding the infrastructure, well organized metropolis, public transportation alone can not be adequate to manage all the transportation needs of the masses. We need to use the common capacity of all transportation modes, well combined according to the settlement structure.

As these plans can only be realized by enormous costs, it is very important that the inhabitants of a city, as well as the guests arriving daily in a city, accept very well the mass transport facilities. Therefore we have three kinds of approach, each of them is very essential:

- The visual impression of the train stations and of the rolling stock has to express that the journey is worth the price.

Which are the important aspects of transport stations within cities? They are train stops, places to get information about the journey, places for spending the waiting time, important points in the transportation network which is the skeleton of an urban area, points where people meet, places which express the value of the journey, and the image of a city or a certain district within a city.

- The concept of intermodal links between individual cars or buses and the train stops of the light rail, metro or train system must be planned well, connections must be short and should be found very easily, longer corridors have to be designed in a very interesting way, they have to give the impression to the passenger that the loss of time was very small.

Supposing that we can furnish all capacities which are required, this is what we have to make better: the quality of the intermediate junction points between different transportation means among each other and with the public space of the city. This means the aspects of function and the architectural quality of railway stations, suburban and light rail train stops and metro stations.

- The quality of the design or interior design of the train stops has to be a high one. This can be achieved be creating spaces with a lot of natural or artificial light, with floor

and wall surfaces in bright colors, and last but not least, with an architectural concept which allows passengers to very quickly survey the station.

The use of private cars is, in nearly all societies, a sign of self-esteem, using a private car is sometimes considered to be important for a member of a certain social class. To correct this error and to encourage people to use trains, metro or light rail as the most efficient and comfortable means of moving through the city, we can learn from history and from good contemporary examples, in order to develop the basic ideas of these examples to even better solutions.

Beginning in the history of station design we can see details that we can use also today in architecture for transportation buildings. At the end of the last century the train was the most important means of transport, throughout Europe and North America. Apart from the railway there were no efficient means of transport. The station was the gate to the city. The fascination of traveling was expressed by the stations' design ideas; in the stations there were facilities for using the waiting time and for meeting each other. In the terminus stations of this era, there are restaurants, some of them with splendid interior, as the example of the "Le train bleu" restaurant in the Paris Gare de Lyon shows.

The roofs of the platform halls were built with iron constructions. The height of spaces in these stations is enormous, giving arriving passengers an adequate reception. (Leipzig, Hauptbahnhof, Barcelona, Estacio de Piranha). The classic language of architecture was the style of the stations, but there were also some exceptions which were built or planned with an eutopic character.

Several station buildings in the outskirts of London were part of a program for the "corporate identity" of the London Underground system. There are cubic or round buildings, in well visible points of the streets, which are landmarks, points of orientation and points of recognizing, helping the endless dwelling quarters to gain identity and helping passengers to easily find the point of change of the transport mode while traveling by bus.

Small shops for passengers were integral parts of the service hall interior. Kiosk facilities were even in the metro stations (Hamburg, Kloster-stern, built in 1929).

Moscow metro stations were built like real palaces; at a time when western countries built railway and metro stations without ornamental accessories. In the Mayakovskaya metro station, built in 1938, indirect artificial lighting in the ceiling domes give the impression of natural daylight.

Connection of Stations with Public Space

Montreal owns a big system of subterranean connections for pedestrians between the central city metro stations, connected with big inner spaces in office buildings. The design of the metro stations is a spatial design, using the possibilities of concrete, bridges, views. The stations and pedestrian subways are connected to huge shopping and service centres.

Station entrances require the planners' full attention, especially ways to subsurface spaces. It is important to lead passengers to the train or to the surface, accompanied by good light, and with interesting ways and places.

In Munich, shop insertions in the main station building were finished in the last years, in the platform hall, and in a second level. Concrete surfaces, glass and stainless steel are to be seen. The insertions form a contrast to the old substance of the building.

The Quality of Lighting and the Perception of the Architectural Space of a Station

Washington Metro stations are lit indirectly, and have huge halls with points from where passengers can overlook spaces and well visible connections to corresponding trains. The principle of a vaulted aluminum ceiling, where strong light sources are reflected into the space, guided the architecture of the Munich metro station Fürstenried West. Especially the edge of the platform is lit with high intensity.

The Munich Dülferstraße metro station is a project we were in charge of, in collaboration with the authorities of the Munich city administration. The station was opened in 1993, at this moment end of the line 2. The interchange station of this metro line with the airport train is Feldmoching metro station which is currently being completed.

In designing urban transport stations today there are several important aspects for the passenger: to be able to quickly gain information about train connections, to continue the journey efficiently, and to make the transition to another means of transport as easily as possible. These new metro projects will compensate the waiting time with the visual quality of a well designed building - giving a possible solution to the demands for the station as a part of public space and a part of the daily environment.

Buildings for Intermodal Connections

The Stockholm bus terminal by Ralph Erskine is integrated with the 40,000 square meter office block of the "World Trade Center", bringing together the experience of travel and work. People should not wait for buses or trains in shabby and draughty halls. Passengers and buses only meet right at the last moment. The bus station acts as link between airport buses, the metro system and the railway network at the nearby main station.

In 1994 Munich metro authorities opened the new Fröttmaning station with intermodal connection to urban and suburban buses, and with park-and-ride facilities. New architectural forms will also demonstrate that high convenience of building facilities is the way to introduce public transport into everyday life.

In Zurich there are good examples of new station architecture. The city center station Stadelhofen symbolizes the dynamic movement of the train, the lower level of the station is a long walkway under the rails, partly lit with natural light, with shops along the passenger's way to the train. Another good project is the level between the platform hall and the surface in the Zurich Museumsstraße station with a bright floor, and with shops for the passengers, with good quality light.

There are many architectural ideas in the stations of the high speed line between Madrid and Seville in Spain, the Alta Velocidad Española system. Madrid Altocha station designed by Rafael Moneo is one terminal of this line. The station square is of different levels, the traffic on the higher, the pedestrians on the lower level. On the way to the different levels there are various commercial activities. There is a connection to the metro, and a bus station 8.5 meters higher than the metro level. The building contains two parts, a commuter station, and a long distance station, connected with all functions by taking the natural economy of movements into consideration. The architect created worthy looking spaces, not only transition rooms, by including natural daylight.

These examples of contemporary station design explain architectural conceptions which not only satisfy the functional needs for huge passenger crowds, but also create sensations of spatial and architectural quality by creative use of material, lighting and detail.

In a well organized city centre metro station, connection levels can be seen as outside spaces as well as galleries. Cafes or pubs with long opening times and the possibility to overlook the platform hall favor the acceptance of suburban train transportation also in the late evening hours. Kiosks and stand-up lunch places on the platform, perhaps also a water fountain, can improve the atmosphere of the transport facilities.

Building for public mass transit should be of a high architectural quality in order to encourage people to use trains and tramways as the most efficient and comfortable means of transport.

Dr.-Ing. Jürgen Rauch is Planner for Buildings for Transport, Munich, Germany.

Stadtverträglicher Autoverkehr
- Struktur des LADIR-Verfahrens

Hans Jürgen Collin

1. Ausgangslage

Bei der praktischen Bearbeitung von städtischen Verkehrskonzepten wird nur zu selten von der Verfügbarkeit von Verkehrsflächen und der Verträglichkeit des Autoverkehrs ausgegangen.

Ein wesentlicher Grund dafür ist das Fehlen von entsprechenden Verfahren und Standards, mit deren Hilfe verträgliche Verkehrsmengen für Straßen und Flächen in Abhängigkeit von Grenzwertsetzungen berücksichtigt werden können.

Das entwickelte LADIR-Verfahren, basierend auf einer Forschungsarbeit im Auftrag der Bundesministerin für Raumordnung, Bauwesen und Städtebau, erlaubt die Ermittlung von Verträglichkeitsgrenzen für die Straßenbelastbarkeit durch den fahrenden Autoverkehr und ebenfalls die als verträglich anzusehende Gebietsbelastbarkeit durch abgestellte Autos.

Werden diese als Grenzwerte anzusehenden Belastungswerte mit den konkreten Verkehrsmengen verglichen, ist die Differenz als die Pkw-Verfügungsmasse anzusehen, die es z.B. durch das Maßnahmenspektrum der Verkehrsvermeidung, Verkehrsverlagerung oder Verkehrsberuhigung zu behandeln gilt.

2. Ziel des LADIR-Verfahrens

Die gegenwärtigen städtischen Verkehrssituationen erfordern einen akuten Handlungsbedarf in die Richtung, die Verkehrsbelastungen auf ein stadtverträgliches Niveau zu senken. In diesem Zusammenhang gilt es zu klären, was unter Stadtverträglichkeit zu verstehen ist. Im wesentlichen impliziert die Behandlung des Verträglichkeitsbegriffs drei Fragen:

- Welchen maximal möglichen Autoverkehr kann die Stadt bewältigen?

- Wieviel Autoverkehr ist zur Aufrechterhaltung der Funktionen der Stadt notwendig?

- Wieviel Autoverkehr ist zur Sicherung eines bestimmten Qualitätsstandards der städtebaulichen Umwelt verträglich?

Die Frage nach der Summe des maximal möglichen Autoverkehrs bezieht sich auf die technische Leistungsfähigkeit des Straßennetzes und der Flächenverfügbarkeit für den ruhenden Verkehr. In der Regel sind in den Städten diese Belastungsgrenzen erreicht oder überschritten. Die verfügbaren Flächen und finanziellen Rensourcen sind so knapp, daß mit Ausnahme von Einzelfällen keine Maßnahmen mehr ergriffen werden können, um die Leistungsfähigkeit der Anlagen des fließenden und ruhenden Autoverkehrs wesentlich zu erhöhen. Auf der

Wirkungsebene liegt hiermit ein Bereich vor, der bis zur völligen Unverträglichkeit reichen kann.

Die entscheidende Frage ist, ob das heutige Autoverkehrsaufkommen für die Funktionsfähigkeit der Stadt auch notwendig ist. In Fachkreisen wird weitgehend unterstellt, daß mit Mitteln der Organisation - vor allem der Umstieg vom Pkw auf Verkehrsmittel des Umweltverbundes - das städtische Verkehrsproblem zu lösen sei. Der notwendige Autoverkehr ergibt sich unter dieser Prämisse als Differenz zwischen dem heutigen Autoverkehr und dem durch andere Verkehrsmittel ersetzbaren Verkehr. Zusätzlich müssen hier auch die Strategien der Verkehrsvermeidung berücksichtigt werden.

Der so definierte Verkehr stellt die unterste Grenze der stadtverträglichen Belastbarkeit aus städtebaulicher und verkehrlicher Sicht dar und kann als verträglicher Belastbarkeitsbereich definiert werden.

Zwischen diesen Extremwerten rangiert eine zumutbare Verkehrsbelastung, die sich an Qualitätsstandards des städtischen Lebens orientiert, sich also nach den Ansprüchen der Stadtbewohner und Stadtnutzer auch außerhalb ihres Autos richtet und die Lebensfähigkeit der Stadt als tragende Größe beinhaltet.

Ziel des LADIR-Verfahrens ist es, die stadtverträgliche (zumutbare) Verkehrsbelastung durch den Autoverkehr für einen Planungsraum zu bestimmen. Hierbei kann der Planungsraum ein ausgewähltes Stadtgebiet oder eine Gesamtstadt umfassen. Grundsätzlich ist anzumerken, daß im Gegensatz zur maximal möglichen Verkehrsbelastung der Grenzwert für die stadtverträgliche Verkehrsbelastung - wie auch der notwendige Autoverkehr - innerhalb einer

Spannweite liegen kann. Der eigentliche Grenzwert ist abschatzbar in Abhängigkeit von den jeweiligen Bewertungskriterien im Kontext mit den städtebaulichen Situationen sowie den zu definierenden Ansprüchen an Verträglichkeiten bzw. Schutzbedürftigkeiten.

3. Struktur des LADIR-Verfahrens

In der städtischen Verkehrsplanung wird überwiegend von der aus den städtischen Nutzungen resultierenden - Nachfrage nach Verkehrsleistungen im fließenden und ruhenden Autoverkehr und selten von der Verfügbarkeit und Belastbarkeit von Verkehrsflächen ausgegangen. Die Struktur des LADIR-Verfahrens berücksichtigt diesen flächenbezogenen Ausgangsgedanken.

Bei der Ermittlung des als verträglich anzusehenden Autoverkehrs wird unterschieden nach Funktions- und Nutzungsansprüchen in unterschiedlichen städtebaulichen Situationen:

- Im Hauptverkehrsstraßennetz (HVS-Netz) werden in Abhängigkeit von fünf Kriterien 13 Hauptverkehrsstraßen-Typen vorgegeben und für diese die Verträglichkeit bezogen auf den fließenden Verkehr ermittelt.

- In Stadtgebieten wird in Abhängigkeit von drei Gebietstypen die Verträglichkeit durch den ruhenden Verkehr bestimmt.

- In Bereichen, die sich nicht eindeutig dem Hauptverkehrsstraßennetz oder einem Gebiet zuordnen lassen, müssen beide Prüfungen durchgeführt werden, um den maßgebenden Belastungsfaktor zu ermitteln.

PRIORITÄTEN IN DER VERKEHRSPLANUNG

Die Verträglichkeitsgrenzen werden durch drei Bereiche mit jeweils zwei Kriterien gekennzeichnet:

- Umwelt (Abgas, Lärm),

- Umfeld (Unfallgefährdung, Trennwirkung),

- Städtebau (Fläche, Stadtgestalt).

Allen Kriterien können Standards oder Grenzwerte für die verkehrliche Belastbarkeit und für die städtebauliche Verträglichkeit zugeordnet werden. Deren Einhaltung bzw. Überschreitung bestimmt das Maß der (Un)Verträglichkeit des Autoverkehrs.

Die zugehörigen Verträglichkeitsgrenzen für die Straßenbelastbarkeit beziehen sich im Detail sowohl auf städtebauliche Verträglichkeiten bezüglich Gehwegbreite, Straßenraumproportionen, Kfz-Höchstgeschwindigkeiten und Querungsansprüchen für nichtmotorisierte Verkehrsteilnehmer als auch auf verkehrliche Verträglichkeiten mit den Kriterien Lärm und sichere Fußgängerüberquerbarkeit.

Die Gebietsverträglichkeiten ergeben sich aus den Mindestbedingungen für Gehweg- und Fahrbahnbreiten und aus den städtebaulichen Verträglichkeiten bezogen auf Proportionen des Straßenraumes sowie den Vorgaben von maximalen Fahrbahnbreiten.

Das LADIR-Verfahren ist so offen konzipiert, daß die jeweiligen Zielvorstellungen über Stadtverträglichkeiten frei und nachvollziehbar Eingang finden können. Umfangreiche Datenerhebungen sind nicht erforderlich.

Die Belastbarksiten der zu Typen zusammengefaßten städtebaulichen Situationen lassen sich räumlich zusammenführen zu einer Aussage über die insgesamt noch stadtverträg-

liche Gesamtbelastbarkeit durch Autoverkehr für einen definierten Planungsraum.

Für die Bestimmung der stadtverträglichen Belastbarkeit werden Empfehlungen für die jeweiligen Verträglichkeitsgrenzen vorgeschlagen. Hierbei handelt es sich um Werte, die dem derzeitigen Kenntnisstand entsprechen, die von der Nutzung des Straßenraumes und Straßenumfeldes abhängen und normativen Charakter besitzen. Es sind somit keine scharfen, eindeutig bestimmbare Grenzwerte. Aus diesem Grund werden für die Gesamteinschätzung der Verträglichkeit drei Stufen bezogen auf die Zuordnung zu einem Anspruchsniveau unterschieden.

- Stufe 1: hohes Anspruchsniveau,

- Stufe 2: mittleres Anspruchenniveau,

- Stufe 3: niedriges Anspruchenniveau.

Mit Hilfe dieser Mehrstufigkeit wird erreicht, daß für jedes Kriterium spezifische Empfindlichkeiten angemessen berücksichtigt werden können.

Im Gegensatz zur Gebietsbelastbarkeit ist bei der Straßenbelastbarkeit eine überschreitung von Grenzwerten einzelner Kriterien möglich. So lassen sich im Hauptverkehrsstraßennetz - bezogen auf die Stadtverträglichkeit von Autoverkehr - für einzelne Abschnitte Unverträglichkeitsgrade bzw. Dringlichkeitsstufen für Maßnahmen zur Belastungsreduzierung ableiten, je nachdem, wieviele Grenzwerte über- bzw. unterschritten sind.

Dagegen folgt aus der Ermittlung der Anzahl im öffentlichen Straßenraum noch stadtverträglich abzustellender Autos (Gebietsbelastbarkeit) eher eine Gestaltungsaufgabe durch Erstellung eines Straßenentwurfs im Rahmen der Stadt- und Gebietsplanung.

4. Methodik des LADIR-Verfahrens

Die Bestimmung der Verträglichkeitsgrenzen stellt den ersten operationalisierten Schritt des LADIR-Verfahrens dar. Daran schließt sich als zweiter Schritt die eigentliche Berechnung der Belastbarkeit einer Straße oder eines Gebietes an. Die Ausführung dieser Berechnung für eine gesamte Stadt oder ausgewählter Stadtteile ermöglicht in einem dritten Schritt, die für den Planungsraum maximal verträgliche Anzahl von gleichzeitig im Straßennetz fahrenden bzw. im öffentlichen Straßenraum von Wohngebieten abzustellenden Autos zu bestimmen.

Entsprechend den unterschiedlichen Verkehrssituationen und städtebaulichen Anspruchsniveaus an Hauptverkehrsstraßen und in Stadtgebieten sind zwei verschiedene Berechnungspfade in das LADIR-Verfahren integriert

Pfad 1: Stadtverträgliche Straßenbelastbarkeit (HVS-Netz),

Pfad 2: Stadtverträgliche Gebietsbelastbarkeit

Die Straßenbelastbarkeit wird mit Hilfe verkehrlicher Belastbarkeiten und städtebaulicher Verträglichkeiten ermittelt. Die verkehrlichen Belastbarkeiten ergeben sich direkt aus dem Verkehrsablauf (Lärm, Unfallgefährdung). Die Grenzwerte können dementsprechend in verkehrsbezogenen Einheiten (Kfz/h) angegeben werden. Die städtebauliche Verträglichkeit ist demgegenüber nicht primär von der Anzahl fahrender Autos abhängig. So ist z.B. die Proportion des Straßenraums ein städtebaulich relevantes Merkmal. Die sich daraus ergebende verträgliche Fahrbahnbreite hat dabei nichts mit der möglicherweise (theoretisch) errechenbaren Kfz-Leistungsfähigkeit (von Fahrbahnquerschnitten) - ausgedrückt in Kfz/h - zu tun. Für eine Quantifizierung der städtebaulichen Verträglichkeit sind daher beschreibende Einheiten bzw. Dimensionen eingeführt worden.

Die Analyse der Grenzwertüberschreitungen liefert Hinweise, mit welchen Maßnahmen die Straße oder das Stadtgebiet verträglicher gestaltet werden kann. Nicht behandelt werden die Strategien und Maßnahmen, mit deren Hilfe die ermittelten Grenzbelastungen erreicht werden können.

Das LADIR-Verfahren zur Berechnung der stadtverträglichen Belastbarkeit durch Autoverkehr ist als offenes Verfahren konzipiert. Das heißt, die methodische Vorgehensweise ist vorgegeben, während die inhaltliche Ausgestaltung begrenzt wählbar ist. Damit besteht die Möglichkeit, die Grundlagen für die Bestimmung der Verträglichkeit anhand der jeweiligen umweltpolitischen Zielsetzungen in einer Kommune sowie aktueller Erkenntnisse festzulegen und auch zu modifizieren.

Da es sich bei dem LADIR-Verfahren um die Entwicklung eines Rechenverfahrens handelt, wird auch nicht auf Fragen eingegangen, die sich z.B. mit der gewünschten sozialen Funktion des Straßenraums oder mit der noch vertretbaren Art und Intensität der Straßenrandnutzung auseinandersetzen.

5. Ausblick

Um den vom Verkehr ausgehenden Unverträglichkeiten gezielt und wirksam begegnen zu können, ist die Implementierung und Umsetzung einer neuen Art von integrativer, ganzheitlicher Entwicklung von Verkehrskonzepten notwendig. Hierzu gehört auch eine neue Struktur der Verkehrsentwicklungsplanung.

Grundlegender Ansatz ist, daß nur auf der Basis von Grenzwerten für eine stadtverträgliche Verkehrsbelastbarkeit der Stellenwert des Autoverkehrs relativiert und genau definiert wird und nur darauf aufbauend geeignete Strategien und Konzepte in Richtung Verkehrsvermeidung entwickelt und die Verkehrsarten des Umweltverbundes (zu Fuß, Fahrrad, ÖPNV) gezielt gefördert werden können.

Insgesamt sollte sich eine um das LADIR-Verfahren erweiterte Verkehrsentwicklungs-planung aus fünf Bearbeitungsblöcken zusammensetzen:

I. Rahmenbedingungen und Situations-analyse,

II. Bestimmung der stadtverträglichen Belastbarkeiten,

III. Abschätzung von Veränderungs-notwendigkeiten: Ist/Sollvergleich und Dringlichkeitsreihung von Maßnahmen,

IV. Konzeptentwicklung und Wirkungs-abschätzung,

V. Durchführbarkeitsaspekte.

Speziell in den Blöcken II. und III. sind die aus dem LADIR-Verfahren resultierenden Ansätze und Rechenregeln anzuwenden.

Auf dieser Grundlage sind dann Informationen und Daten vorhanden, um z.B. die Substitutionspotentiale des Autoverkehrs zielgerecht ausschöpfen zu können oder auch Strategien und Maßnahmen zu entwickeln, die zu einer Umsetzung der ermittelten Grenzbelastungen beitragen können. Hiermit sind Fragen angesprochen, auf welche Fahrtzwecke, Nutzergruppen und Fahrtziele sich der städtebaulich noch verträgliche Autoverkehr aufteilen sollte.

Ganz sicher sind auch die Teilergebnisse aus diesen Bearbeitungsblöcken geeignet, um in der Diskussion mit der Bevölkerung und den Meinungsträgern, auch auf der Ebene der Beeinflussung des Verkehrsverhaltens und der Verkehrspolitik, zu wirkungsvolleren und einsichtigeren Vorstellungen und Vorgehens-weisen als bisher zu gelangen.

Notes:

1) Mitautoren sind: Peter Müller, Institut Wohnen und Umwelt und Wulf Rüthrich, Cooperative, beide Darmstadt

Prof. Dr. Ing. Hans Jürgen Collin ist im Vorsitz der Arbeitsgruppe Unabhängiger Stadt- und Verkehrsplaner, Braunschweig, Deutschland.

PART THREE

New Urban Neighborhoods:
Work in Progress

DRITTER TEIL
Neue Stadtteile für urbanes Leben:
zum derzeitigen Sachstand

Principles

Grundsätze

Chapter Forty-Three (a)

Ten Guidelines for the Planning and Development of a New Urban Neighborhood

Sven von Ungern-Sternberg

1. A neighborhood which is planned and constructed nowadays mirrors our modern society. Furthermore it has to reveal our vision of the world of tomorrow. It should particularly translate into built reality our idea of a liberal and democratic social order, of a pluralistic community and of the dignity of each individual.

Therefore, the planning of a new neighborhood should not be left exclusively to city planners and engineers - as indispensable as they are. This kind of a project has to be, from the very start, an interdisciplinary undertaking. It should be understood as a community task which includes already during the preliminary stages pedagogues, psychologists, ecologists, politicians concerned with cultural and educational problems as well as many other experts from various subdisciplines.

2. Our pluralistic social system requires variety. Therefore we have to avoid and combat any form of ghettoization and social segregation. Responsible urban design unites people. It brings them together instead of separating them. It breaks with the fatal "ideology of segregation" which was typical for urban planning of the past decades.

In practice this means that the project management for the entire new neighborhood has to remain under the coordination and responsibility of public authorities. It is their task to organize a variety of investors and building owners. In its methodical approach this is the denial of a dominant private developer or general contractor who plans, builds and markets the new neighborhood. This means also that a multitude of architects providing different design options, is necessary. One of the main tasks of project management is the organization and coordination of this multitude of mostly private building owners and architects who complement each other.

3. Urban development still fulfills the task of "social engineering". This means on one hand "mixed use" for working and living. Old and young, people with and without physical handicaps, locals and foreigners should, if possible, be brought together instead of being concentrated in special buildings. Otherwise they will be systematically separated and segregated from the community. This should be achieved by maintaining a certain share of barrier-free homes within the general housing. Community facilities should bring together different generations whenever this is possible, instead of separating them and fencing them off from one another. Low cost housing should include small parcels and should be mixed with privately financed housing. In order to exclude the existing risk of discrimination, the buildings and facilities of the low cost housing should not reveal any social classification.

4. Far-sighted urban development should not only consider the changing needs of modern society but also foresee possible future trends.

237

Thus the changing role of women requires new conceptions of the residential plans. The increasing number of "single households" and single parents, the "traditional" families which need to be strengthened, the older people who want to remain in their familiar environment, all of them expect different and individual answers. Therefore the floor plans should offer the possibility of diverse uses. Therefore a reasonable share of barrier-free homes and easy access to buildings for the handicapped are required. Therefore also public space planning has to take into account the needs of the handicapped.

In view of a plan which is especially adapted to the needs of women and families, new forms of experimental urban development need to be encouraged and realized within reasonable limits.

5. From the very beginning, security requires special attention on the part of the planners. That means that police experts, women representatives, children's offices have to be included at an early stage. Unfortunately we have to be prepared for the fact that the problematic area of public security is going to become even more explosive in the course of future decades and that it will be of utmost importance for the quality of life and the social cohesion of the various neighborhoods. As far as the general planning of city construction is concerned, relatively little money is needed in order to create positive conditions here as well. This concerns the arrangement of dwellings and house entrances, the coordination of public, semi-public and private rooms as well as topics such as visibility and social control.

As far as traffic policy is concerned, possible dark zones can be avoided by thinking ahead. Dark and uncontrollable subways belong to the past. The layout of paths in the green zones is as important as the layout of parking lots. Unfortunately the area of public security has been very much neglected in the past decades and needs to be redefined.

6. A good neighborhood of tomorrow has to adopt a farsighted traffic policy. Larger urban developments have to be based on public transportation in the cities, with the streetcar being the "backbone". New neighborhoods have to be planned according to the existing streetcar system as the main axis.

The bus has only a supplementary function as a transportation means. General construction planning has to concentrate its efforts from the very beginning on building a city for bike riders, these efforts being often neglected or even smiled at. Compared to the train and road systems, this is only a low cost factor but extremely effective in terms of a cost-profit analysis.

Developers should have the courage to experiment on a moderate scale with neighborhoods without cars or at least without parking lots. But it would be unrealistic to try to banish the car in our century. This would risk putting public space, streets and places at a serious disadvantage due to non-existent traffic.

The recovery of public space, streets and places as meeting points and centres of social life is of utmost importance in any urban and traffic planning for a new neighborhood. Being the expression of a "democratic urban planning", this public space has to be open and accessible to all citizens, regardless of their status or age. Thus, public space becomes a "structured invitation" to all citizens to meet, make contacts and communicate with each other. Therefore the specific layout and ambiance of public space play a key role in the formation and fostering of a sense of neighborhood, a sense of identity, and the creation of emotional bonds.

7. Urban development for tomorrow means also ecological consciousness in urban design. Therefore clear guidelines and tasks have to be set up at an early stage of the planning. This applies to the traffic policy which has to avoid unnecessary traffic from the start, offering eco-friendly alternatives combined with reasonable restrictions. This applies also to the energy policy which offers low energy systems for housing requirements, district heating systems as well as options for solar heating. This applies finally to resource programs (waste reducing and recycling systems, reduced surface sealing etc.).

8. In the context of decentralized conceptions of urban development policies, the necessary infrastructures have to be created in the neighborhoods, if possible at the same time that the occupants move in. This applies not only to the usual social and cultural facilities, but also to shopping facilities serving daily needs. By creating markets in the center, unwanted "plastic shopping malls" in the green areas can be avoided. In this way, shopping facilities are within walking distance and at the same time contacts between neighbors are encouraged. From the socio-political standpoint this is a positive factor which reduces also avoidable motorvehicle traffic.

Large shopping centres in the neighborhoods themselves are also unwanted. On the contrary, preference is given to different smaller commercial and service facilities, the so-called "mixed use concept".

According to the principle "small is beautiful" smaller, easily comprehensible units are to be created in all areas of life, which encourage the formation of a sense of neighborhood, of emotional bonds and personal identification. Personal identification with the new district and the direct neighborhood is an essential factor which is often overlooked by the planning technocrats. However, in order to grow together, people need the attachment to their neighborhood and the feeling that they are at home.

9. Urban development has to focus on the future. Therefore it has to be receptive to future developments, changing social conditions of the coming decades, which are unknown to us today, which we often foresee but sometimes cannot even recognize in their outlines. If our present decisions are irreversible, problems and difficulties are going to await us in the future, due to changing conditions and needs. Therefore, foresighted planning has to offer mobility and freedom for the future, flexibility in the use of homes, mobility within the existing housing space, "robustness" of the definite planning, multiple possibilities of subsequent densification, reserve space - all these factors serve the object of open planning.

10. Finally, we should not forget that the planning and building of homes is not only done for the citizen but also with the citizen. Possibilities of citizen participation at an early preliminary stage of planning as well as in competitions should be pursued. But special attention should be paid also to the participation of occupants who exert their influence even after moving in. This may occur either during subsequent stages of the general construction planning or with respect to the concrete layout of the housing environment which has not yet been entirely planned. The result will be a stronger identification of the citizen in his own neighborhood and possibly also a quite individual and personalized structure of the immediate neighborhood. The complete layout of the house entrance area could, for example, be postponed to a date after the occupants actually moved in, in order to offer them the opportunity to participate in this project.

As to the larger neighborhoods, planning and realization have to take place stage by stage.

This way, the experience gained during preceding stages and steps can be integrated in the following stage. The fact that human society undergoes constant changes and developments, has to be reflected in the planning. This is the only way to reach the goal of urban planning, which is to take up social changes and to anticipate them lookingahead. And this is the only way to get as close as possible to fulfilling the ambitious claim of building neighborhoods for the citizens which meet their actual and future needs, and to make good cities.

Dr. Sven von Ungern-Sternberg is Erster Bürgermeister (Deputy Mayor) for the City of Freiburg, and Program Co-Chair for the 17th IMCL Conference.

Kapitel Dreiundvierzig (b)

Zehn Leitlinien für die Planung und Entwicklung eines neuen Stadtteils

Sven von Ungern-Sternberg

1. Ein in unserer heutigen Zeit geplanter und gebauter Stadtteil ist ein Spiegelbild unserer heutigen Gesellschaft. Er muß zudem unsere Visionen einer anzustrebenden künftigen Welt von morgen erkennen lassen. Insbesondere soll er unser Bild von einer freiheitlichen demokratischen Grundordnung, von einem pluralistischen Gemeinwesen und von der Würde eines jeden einzelnen Menschen in die gebaute Wirklichkeit umsetzen.

Daher darf die Planung eines Stadtteiles nicht ausschließlich Stadtplanern und Ingenieuren so unverzichtbar diese auch sind - anvertraut werden. Ein derartiges Vorhaben muß bereits im methodischen Ansatz ein interdisziplinäres Unterfangen sein. Es muß als Gemeinschaftsaufgabe begriffen werden, die bereits im Vorfeld Sozialwissenschaftlicher, Pädagogen, Psychologen, Kulturpolitiker, Ökologen und viele andere Fachleute aus unterschiedlichsten Teildisziplinen einbezieht.

2. Unsere pluralistische Gesellschaftsordnung setzt Vielfalt voraus. Daher müssen Monostrukturen, jedwede Formen von Gettoisierung und sozialer Segregation verhindert und bekämpft werden. Verantwortliche Stadtplanung verbindet. Sie führt zusammen und trennt nicht. Sie nimmt Abschied von der fatalen "Entmischungs-Ideologie" des Städtebaus vergangener Jahrzehnte.

In der praktischen Umsetzung bedeutet dies, daß das Projektmanagement für den gesamten neuen Stadtteil in der koordinierenden Verantwortung der öffentlichen Hand bleiben muß. Es ist deren Aufgabe, eine Vielfalt von Investoren und Bauherren zu organisieren. Dies ist im methodischen Ansatz eine Absage an einen dominierenden privaten Entwickler oder Generalunternehmer, der großflächig und rationell-nivellierend den neuen Stadtteil plant, baut und vermarktet. Dies bedeutet auch eine anzustrebende Vielzahl von Architekten mit individuellen gestalterischen Möglichkeiten. Eine der Hauptaufgaben des öffentlichen Projektmanagement ist die Organisation und Zusammensetzung dieser sich ergänzenden, zumeist privaten Vielfalt von Bauherrschaft und Architektenschaft.

3. Stadtplanung hat unverändert die Aufgabe des "social engineering". Dies ist zum einen "mixed use" zwischen Arbeiten und Wohnen. Alt und jung, Behinderte und Nichtbehinderte, Einheimische und Ausländer sollen zudem möglichst zusammengeführt und nicht in Sonderbauten konzentriert werden. Ansonsten werden sie tendenziell von der Gemeinschaft ab- und ausgegrenzt. Diesem Ziel dient ein durchgehender bestimmter Anteil von barrierefreien Wohnungen im allgemeinen Wohnungsbau. Gemeinschaftseinrichtungen sollen, wo immer möglich, generationsübergreifend zusammenführen und nicht einander trennend voneinander "abschotten". Der "soziale Wohnungsbau" soll möglichst kleinparzelliert sein und mit freifinanziertem Wohnungsbau gemischt werden. Die Form von Gebäuden und Siedlungskörpern soll im sozialen Wohnungsbau so gestaltet werden, daß soziale Zuordnung nicht ablesbar ist und die damit verbundene Gefahr von Diskriminierung unterbleibt.

4. Weitsichtige Stadtplanung muß auf geänderte Nutzungsanforderungen unserer Zeit und bereits erkennbare Tendenzen für morgen eingehen. So bedingt die veränderte Rolle der Frau in der heutigen Zeit neue Grundrißkonzeptionen für die Wohnung. Die zahlenmäßig dominierenden "Single-Haushalte", die steigende Zahl von Alleinerziehenden mit Kindern, die weiterhin zu stärkenden "traditionellen" Familien, die älteren Menschen, die in ihrer vertrauten Wohnumgebung bleiben möchten, alle erwarten unterschiedliche und individuelle Antworten. Daher Grundrisse mit möglichst viel Offenheit für unterschiedliche Nutzungen. Daher einen angemessenen Anteil

barrierefreier Wohnungen und behindertengerechten Zugänglichkeit zu Gebäuden. Daher auch behindertengerechte Ausgestaltung des öffentlichen Raumes.

Für frauen- und familiengerechte Konzeptionen müssen in überschaubarem Rahmen neue Wege des experimentellen Städtebaus gefördert und verwirklicht werden.

5. Dem Thema der inneren Sicherheit ist von Anfang an bei der Planung ein verstärktes Augenmerk zuzuwenden. Hierbei sind Experten der Polizei, Frauenbeauftragte, Kinderbüros frühzeitig mit einzubeziehen. Wir müssen uns leider darauf einstellen, daß das Thema der Öffentlichen Sicherheit in künftigen Jahrzehnten an Brisanz zunimmt und große Bedeutung für die Lebensqualität und das Miteinander in den einzelnen Stadtteilen erhält. Mit relativ wenig Geld können auch im Bereich der Bauleitplanung des Städtebaus positive Rahmen gesetzt werden. Dies gilt für die Anordnung der Wohnungen und Hauseingänge bis hin zur Abstimmung der öffentlichen, halböffentlichen und privaten Räume sowie den Belangen der Einsehbarkeit und sozialen Kontrolle. In der Verkehrspolitik können vorausschauend Dunkelräume vermieden werden. Nicht einsehbare Unterführungen gehören der Vergangenheit an. Die Wegeführung der Grünplanung ist genauso wichtig wie die Anordnung der Parkierung. Die Bedeutung der Bauleitplanung und des Städtebaus für den Bereich der öffentlichen Sicherheit ist viele Jahrzehnte leider sehr vernachlässigt worden und bedarf einer grundliegenden Neubewertung.

6. Ein guter Stadtteil für morgen muß von vorneherein die Gesichtspunkte einer weitsichtigen Verkehrspolitik berücksichtigen. Städtebauliche Fehlentscheidungen können im Nachhinein kaum noch durch verkehrspolitische Maßnahmen korrigiert werden.

Ab einer bestimmten Größenordnung muß in Städten der öffentliche Personennahverkehr mit der Straßenbahn als Rückgrat die entscheidende Grundlage der Stadtentwicklung sein. An der Straßenbahn als Hauptachse oder "Korsettstange" müssen sich die neuen Wohnquartiere ausrichten.

Das Transportmittel Bus hat lediglich ergänzende Funktion. Die Bauleitplanung hat von Anfang an das häufig unterschätzte oder gar belächelte Ziel einer fahrradgerechten Stadt zu berücksichtigen - im Aufwand gegenüber Bahn und Straße nur ein geringer Kostenfaktor - aber ungeheuer effektiv im Sinne einer Kostennutzungsanalyse.

In überschaubaren Dimensionen sollen mutig Experimente von autofreien oder zumindest stellplatzfreien Nachbarschaften angegangen werden. Es darf aber nicht realitätsfern das Auto aus der Existenz unserer Jahrzehnte einfach hinweggedacht oder hinweg gewünscht werden. Ansonsten besteht die Gefahr, daß der öffentliche Raum, Straßen und Plätze durch den ruhenden Verkehr nachhaltig geschädigt wird.

Den öffentlichen Raum, Straßen und Plätze verstärkt für den Menschen wieder als Erlebnis- und Begegnungsbereich zurückzugewinnen, kommt eine zentrale Bedeutung für jede Stadt- und Verkehrsplanung eines neuen Stadtteils zu. Als Ausdruck einer "demokratischen Stadtplanung" muß dieser öffentliche Raum für alle Bürger, unabhängig von Status und Alter, zugänglich und offen sein. Danach ist der öffentliche Raum eine "gestaltete Einladung" an die gesamte Bürgerschaft zum Kontakten, zum Aufeinanderzugehen, zum Gespräch und zur Begegnung. Die konkrete Ausgestaltung und Austrahlung des öffentlichen Raumes spielt daher eine Schlüsselrolle für das Entstehen und die Pflege von Nachbarschaften, Identifikation und emotionaler Bindung.

7. Stadtentwicklung für morgen ist zugleich ökologisch verantwortliche Stadtplanung. Vom Ansatz her müssen daher entsprechende klare Vorgaben und Rahmen die Stadtplanung leiten. Dies gilt für die Verkehrspolitik, indem vermeidbarer Verkehr von vorneherein verhindert wird und umweltfreundliche Alternativen in Kombination mit maßvollen Restriktionen als Angebote vorhanden sind. Dies gilt für die Energiepolitik durch Niedrigenergiegebote im Wohnungsbau, Fernwärmeverbund, Optionen für Solarnutzung. Dies gilt für ressourcenschonende Versorgung (z.B. Nutzung von Regenwasser) als auch für die Entsorgung (Mülleinsparungs- und Verwertungskonzepte, geringere Oberflächenversiegelung etc.).

8. Im Rahmen von dezentralen Konzeptionen der Stadtentwicklungspolitik müssen in den Stadtteilen die notwendigen Infrakstrukturen entstehen, möglichst zeitgleich mit dem Einzug der Bewohner. Dies gilt nicht nur für die üblichen sozialen und kulturellen Einrichtungen, sondern zugleich für die Versorgung des täglichen Gebrauchs im Bereich des Handels. Märkte- und Zentrenkonzepte können helfen, unerwünschte "Plastikstädte" auf der grünen Wiese abzuwehren. So wird eine füßläufige Versorgung gesichert, nachbarschaftlicher Kontakt gefördert. Dies ist sozialpolitisch erwünscht, es verringert unter verkehrspolitischen Vorzeichen aber auch vermeidbaren Kfz-Verkehr.

Unerwünscht sind auch große Shopping Center in den Stadtteilen selbst. Erwünscht sind vielmehr kleinparzelliertere unterschiedliche Handels- und Dienstleitungsangebote von "mixed-use Konzepten".

Nach dem Grundsatz "small is beautifull" sind in allen Lebensbereichen möglichst überschaubare, kleinräumige Einheiten zu entwickeln, die erste Nachbarschaften, persönliche Beziehungen und emotionale Bindungen fördern. Diese emotionalen Bindungen und gefühlsmäßigen Identifikation mit dem neuen Stadtteil und der unmittelbaren Nachbarschaft sind entscheidende Gesichtspunkte, die von Technokraten der Planung häufig übersehen werden. Für das Zusammenwachsen der Menschen sind die Bindungen zum Stadtteil und das Entstehen von Nachbarschafts- und Heimatgefühlen aber unerläßlich.

9. Stadtentwicklung muß auf die Zukunft ausgerichtet sein. Sie muß daher offen sein für künftige Entwicklungen, für geänderte gesellschaftliche Verhältnisse der nächsten Jahrzehnte, die wir heute nicht wissen, häufig erahnen, bisweilen in ihren Ansätzen aber noch nicht einmal erkennen können. Je irreversibler unsere Festlegungen in der heutigen Zeit sind, desto größere Schwierigkeiten und Probleme entstehen künftig bei veränderten Rahmenbedingungen und Bedürfnissen. Daher muß eine vorausschauende Planung Beweglichkeits- und Freiheitsgrade für künftige Zeiten einbauen: Flexibilität in der Nutzung von Wohnungen, Mobilität innerhalb des vorhandenen Wohnungsbestandes, "Robustheit" der festgelegten Planungen, vielfältige Nutzungsmöglichkeiten der vorhandenen öffentlichen Einrichtungen, Möglichkeiten der Nachverdichtung, Reserveflächen - all dies trägt dieser offenen Planungsrechnung.

10. Schließlich muß stets bedacht werden, daß nicht nur für den Bürger, sondern auch mit dem Bürger geplant und gebaut wird. Möglichkeiten der Bürgerbeteiligung in einem frühen Vorfeld von Planungen und bei Wettbewerben sind anzustreben. Besonderen Wert bei neuen Stadtteilen ist aber auch nach dem Einzug der ersten Bewohner auf eine Bewohnerbeteiligung zu legen, die auch nach Wohnungsbezug noch Gestaltungs- und Einwirkungsmöglichkeiten geben. Dies mag bei weiteren Abschnitten der Bauleitplanung sein oder in der konkreten Gestaltung des noch nicht restlos verplanten Wohnumfeldes. Dies führt zu einer stärkeren Identifikation des Bürgers in der eigenen Nachbarschaft und kann zudem zu der unverwechselbaren individuellen und persönlichen Ausformung des engsten Nachbarschaftsbereiches führen. So kann z.B. die gesamte Ausgestaltung des Hauseingangs-bereiches bewußt auf einen Zeitpunkt nach einem Bezug durch die Bewohner verlegt werden, um diese dann bewußt an diesem Vorhaben zu beteiligen.

Bei größeren Stadtteilen muß Planung und Umsetzung abschnittweise angegangen werden. So kann im Rahmen einer "lernenden Bauleitplanung" jeweils die Erfahrung vorangegangener Abschnitte und Stufen bei dem nächsten Schritt mit eingebracht werden. So wie die Gesellschaft allgemein sich in einer stetigen Fortentwicklung und Veränderung befindet, muß dies auch in den jeweiligen Planungsinhalten ihren Niederschlag finden. Nur so kann das Ziel der Stadtplanung, die gesellschaftlichen Veränderungen aufzugreifen und im Blick auf morgen zu antizipieren, erreicht werden. Und nur so kann der hohe Anspruch, einen Stadtteil für den Bürger, für seine tatsächlichen und seine künftigen Bedürfnisse Nachbarschaften zu bauen und Städtebau zu betreiben in einer möglichst großen Annäherung erreicht werden.

Dr. Sven von Ungern-Sternberg ist Erster Bürgermeister der Stadt Freiburg im Breisgau.

Zehn Thesen zur "Vorstadt"

Hans Stimmann

1. Das Leitbild ist nicht mehr die (Groß-) Siedlung, sondern die Vorstadt mit ca. 5 000 Wohnungen. Jede neue Vorstadt wird als städtebauliche Einheit ein neuer Teil der vorhandenen großstädtischen Struktur Berlins. Es geht nicht um den idealen Gesamtplan großmaßstäblicher Stadterweiterung, sondern um die Einfügung überschaubarer, planerisch, wirtschaftlich und zeitlich begrenzter Vorstadtprojekte.

2. Die Gebiete zeichnen sich durch eine differenzierte soziale sowie durch einen hohen Grad an Funktionsmischung aus. 20 % der Geschoßflächen sollen für Arbeitsplätze ausgewiesen werden. Die Wohnungen entstehen innerhalb unterschiedlicher Förderprogramme und Baustrukturen: Ein Drittel sozialer Wohnungsbau, ein Drittel frei vereinbarte Förderung und ein Drittel private Finanzierung/Eigentum. 80% der Wohnungen werden im Geschoßwohnungsbau und max. 20% der Wohnungen in individuellen Haustypen mit eigenem Grundstück errichtet.

3. Die neuen Vorstädte sollen eine eigene Identität bekommen, die einen Bezug zu den historischen Spuren und vorhandenen Nutzungen herstellt. Die ursprüngliche Parzellierung oder Bebauung sowie die Topographie gehen in den städtebaulichen Entwurf ein.

4. Um den komplexen Anspruch des Städtischen zu erfüllen, ist eine Dichte von 1,2 GFZ als unterste Grenze Voraussetzung. Dichte ist eine Bedingung für eine positive Energiebilanz, einen wirtschaftlichen Betrieb des Öffentlichen Nahverkehrs, für die Möglichkeit zum Verzicht auf das Auto, für eine wohnungsnahe Konsumentenversorgung und damit insgesamt für eine stadtökologisch positive Bilanz.

5. Die Vorstädte werden nach einem eher traditionellen städtebaulichen Muster entworfen. Hauptelemente sind Straßen und Plätze als Grundgerüst für Identität und Orientierung. Die Straßen folgen mit ihrer Einteilung in Fahrbahn, Bordstein, Bürgerstein, Baum/Hecke/Vorgarten, Haus konventionellen Mustern. Das Grundgerüst öffentlicher Straßen verhält sich neutral gegenüber den abschließend definierten Nutzungen der Baufelder.

6. Die Schulen und Kindertagesstätten sind öffentliche Bauaufgaben. Sie besetzen ganz bewußt städtebaulich wichtige Orte, wie Plätze oder Blockecken.

7. Unterschiedbare Häuser unterschiedlicher Größe bieten die Chance zur architektonischen Differenzierung und zur Identifikation der Bewohner mit ihrem Haus. Die Häuser werden jedoch nicht in künstlichen Hauseinheiten kleinteiliger Parzellen, sondern in wirtschaftlich sinnvollen Größenordnungen gebaut. Die Häuser haben eine maximale Höhe von vier Geschossen plus ausgebauten Dachgeschossen.

8. Das Bild der neuen Vorstädte ist im öffentlichen Bereich durch intensive Baumpflanzungen, Parkanlagen, Spielplätze

und Sportflächen geprägt. Die Gestaltung und Bepflanzung erfolgt nach Kriterien städtischer Gartenarchitektur, die aktuelle ökologische Forderungen (z. B. Regenwasserversickerung) einbezieht.

9. Der bauordnungsrechtlich geforderte Stellplatznachweis (0,5/pro Wohnung) soll grundsätzlich nicht im Blockinnenbereich, sondern im Straßenraum nachgewiesen werden. Beiderseitige Senkrechtaufstellungen, die den Straßenraum ästhetisch in einen Parkplatz verwandeln, sollen vermieden werden.

10. Die Projektsteuerung und die Realisierung erfolgt zu großen Teilen außerhalb der Verwaltung durch treuhänderische Entwicklungsträger oder über städtebauliche Verträge mit privaten Gesellschaften. Die Verwaltung übernimmt das Management.

Ergebnisse und Kritik: Berlin

Zwischenbilanz Frühjahr 1994

Die Umsetzung dieses Leitbildes und dieser Strategie in städtebauliche Konzepte erfolgte bisher in Karow-Nord, Buch, Buchholz-West, Altglienicke, bei den Rudower Feldern, den Staakener Feldern und in der Eisenacher Straße und begrenzt auch für die innerstädtischen Projekte "Eldenaer Straße", "Rummelsburger Bucht". Einen Sonderfall von der Größe und Nutzungsstruktur bildet die "Wissenschaftsstadt Johannisthal-Adlershof" und die "Wasserstadt Spandau".

Wenn man die bisherigen Erfahrungen des kurzen Planugsprozesses kritisch resümiert, läßt sich folgende Zwischenbilanz ziehen: Beginnen wir mit dem positiven, d. h. mit dem städtebaulichen Leitbild, das sich mit seinen klar definierten und gestalteten öffentlichen Räumen, mit seinen baumbestandenen Straßen, Plätzen und sorgfältig gestalteten Parkanlagen wohltuend von den indifferenten Siedlungsräumen früherer Zeiten unterscheidet. Der damit verbundene Gewinn ruhiger halböffentlicher Blockinnenräume sichert eine lange vergessene Qualität traditioneller Blockbebauung. Ob mit diesen Formen "Siedlungen im historischen Kleid" entstehen, ist abhängig von der Nutzungsstruktur der Vorstädte. Zentrales Element für den Erfolg der neuen Vorstädte ist die funktionale und soziale Mischung. Ob die soziale Mischung gelingt, ist wesentlich eine Folge der konsequenten Anwendung unterschiedlicher Förderwege. Die geplante Drittelung (ein Drittel erster Förderungsweg, ein Drittel vereinbarte Förderung, ein Drittel freifinanziert) ist bei den bisherigen Projekten ein Erfolg, insbesondere wenn man bedenkt, daß ein Teil der Mieter der vereinbarten Förderung - wegen der mit den Jahren ansteigenden Mieten - potentiell Eigentümer werden. Die nach 1995 knapper werdenden Wohnungsbauförderungsmittel werden zwangsläufig den Eigentumsanteil weiter erhöhen. Ob die immer noch in relativ großen Hauseinheiten (halbe Blöcke) gebauten Wohnungen wirklich eigentumsfähig sind, d. h. vor allem in der Konkurrenz zu den Einfamilienhausgebieten im ländlichen bzw. kleinstädtischen Umfeld Berlins bestehen können, wird die Zukunft zeigen. Die Parzellierung derart großer Gebiete trüge schließlich dazu bei, das Wachstum in kleineren Abschitten zu ermöglichen und damit auch wieder mehr Flexibilität bei der Gestaltung der Blöcke zu bekommen.

Ein weiteres zentrales Element der neuen Vorstädte ist die traditionelle Mischung von Wohnen und Arbeiten. Bei der Realisierung der Projekte ist jedoch die Forderung der Durchmischung von Wohngebieten mit Gewerbe- und Dienstleistungsstandorten durch die Entwicklungsträger nur bedingt steuerbar. Der Dienstleistungs- und Gewerbeanteil ist und bleibt marktabhängig. Wann und unter welchen Umständen diese teilweise extrem

verfallen. Das ist sicherlich die schlechteste Lösung, wenn man das Areal nicht als Vorratsfläche für später ansieht. Zwischennutzungen sind nur insoweit angezeigt, als sie das geplante Gesamtprojekt nicht hemmen.

Bleibt ein Teil der Gebäude stehen, so wird die städtebauliche Planung nicht leichter, sondern schwerer. Ein städtebaulicher Wettbewerb kann weiterhelfen. Wenn alle Beteiligten sich dem Ganzen verpflichtet fühlen, sollte sich ein Interessenausgleich erreichen lassen. Neue Formen der Beteiligung am Planungsprozess sind gefragt. Wo Stadtplaner, Architekten, interessierte Bürgergruppen, mögliche Investoren und Vertreter der Stadt in einem konstruktiven Dialog zusammengeführt werden, lässt sich ein tragfähiger Konsens leichter finden. Auch das bürgerschaftliche Leben im Quartier kann so bereichert werden.

Städtische Vitalität lebt von der Nutzungsvielfalt

Die Grösse der ehemaligen Militärflächen lässt ihre Gliederung zu. Sie erlaubt ein verträgliches Nebeneinander von unterschiedlichen Nutzungen. Insbesondere gibt die Konversion auch dem Wohnen in innenstadtnahen Bereichen wieder Raum. So kann der Abwanderung ins Umland entgegengewirkt werden. Schon um die Jahrhundertwende konnten die deutschen Großstädte ihre Bevölkerung nicht aus sich selbst heraus halten. Aber damals gab es eine gewaltige Zuwanderung, welche die Städte anschwellen liess. Heute geht die Bevölkerung kontinuierlich zurück, in der Stadt Stuttgart in den letzten beiden Jahren jeweils um mehr als 7.000 Einwohner. Dabei sind es gerade jüngere Personen mit mittlerem Einkommen, die abwandern. Sie suchen die eigenen vier Wände, können sie aber innerhalb der Großstadt nicht bezahlen und weichen deshalb aufs Umland, auch auf den zweiten Ring um

die Großstadt, aus. Dieser Bevölkerungsgruppe preiswertes Wohneigentum zu ermöglichen, ist stadt-politisch sinnvoll.

Die Planung von Städten ist immer ein Wagnis. Die "Stadt auf Probe" gibt es nicht - trotz allem experimentellem Städtebau. Im Labor kann man die Stadt nicht testen. Und Gebäude leben meist länger als die Ideen, die zu ihrer Errichtung geführt haben. Stadtplanung muss daher für künftige Entwicklungen offen sein. Sie muss versuchen, auch spätere Nutzer ins Auge zu fassen. Bei autofreien Quartieren z.B. ist zu bedenken, dass ihnen ewiges Leben schwerlich beschieden sein dürfte. Schon die Söhne und Töchter der ersten Generation können ein anderes Verhältnis zum Kraftfahrzeug haben. Eine gute Planung muss daher flexibel sein und Antworten für später bereit halten. Freiflächen können dem Wandel der Zeit entsprechend auch wieder umfunktioniert werden. Künftige Stellplätze lassen sich so - auch in zumutbarer Entfernung - einplanen. Umgekehrt können überzählige Stellplätze auch wieder zurückgebaut werden.

Raum für eigene Gestaltung sollte den Nutzern so weit wie möglich gegeben sein; und sei es nur, dass diese ihren eigenen Baum setzen können und die Aussengestaltung nicht einfach übergestülpt erhalten. Individualität soll sich entfalten. Auch im scheinbar Überflüssigen steckt ein Sinn.

Ohne Bebauungsplan geht es in der Regel nicht

Eine städtebauliche Planung ist schon deshalb erforderlich, weil ohne verbindliche Neuplanung nach deutschem Recht eine zivile Nutzung nur bei kleineren ehemaligen Militäranlagen innerhalb bebauter ortsteile zulässig ist. Die in der Praxis wichtigste Gruppe bilden jedoch die grösseren Gesamtanlagen, bestehend aus Kasernen,

Kasernenhof, Sport- und Exerzierflächen, Garagen und Werkstätten. Sie sind entweder dem Aussenbereich zuzurechnen (auch als "Aussenbereich im Innenbereich") oder als faktisches "Sondergebiet Militär" zu qualifizieren. Letzteres ist durch die militärische Zweckbestimmung geprägt. Diese fällt mit dem Ende der militärischen Nutzung nicht automatisch weg, sondem bleibt (nach § 34 Abs. 1 oder Abs. 2 BauGB) weiterhin Maßstab für die städtebaurechtliche Zulässigkeit. Gleichgültig, ob nun ein Aussenbereich oder ein militärisch geprägter Innenbereich vorliegt, eine zivile bauliche oder sonstige Neunutzung ist jedenfalls erst dann zulässig, wenn die kommunale Bauleitplanung in dem vom Baugesetzbuch vorgesehenen Verfahren einen neuen Nutzungsmaßstab geschaffen hat. Bewertungsmässig sind solche Grundstücke vorerst in aller Regel nur Bauerwartungsland .

Neue Instrumente im Städtebaurecht stehen zur Verfügung

Die Umwandlung ehemaliger Militärflächen ist eine Aufgabe der Gemeinden und muss von diesen politisch gesteuert werden. Dabei können Modelle einer Public-Private-Partnership weiterhelfen. Die deutsche Gesetzgebung hat hierfür im Baugesetzbuch wie auch im Massnahmengesetz zum Baugesetzbuch Instrumente geschaffen, die auf einen Interessenausgleich zwischen Gemeinde und Massnahmenträger abzielen. Dem städtebaulichen Vertrag (§ 6 MassnahmenG) und dem Vorhaben- und Erschliessungsplan (§ 7 MassnahmenG) ist das Ziel gemeinsam, den Erwerber oder Investor an den Wertsteiger-ungen der Grundstücke zu beteiligen. Diese privaten Partner der Gemeinde treten finanziell in Vorleistung. Sie kaufen Grundstücke und machen sie durch Erschliessung und Neu-ordnung in Abstimmung mit der Gemeinde baureif. Der auf diese Weise steigende Bodenwert kommt ihnen durch Veräusserung oder Vermietung zugute, soweit sie nicht nach

Massgabe abzuschliessender öffentlich-rechtlicher Ver-träge die Planungs- und Erschliessungskosten (so beim Vorhaben- und Erschliessungsplan) oder auch sonstige Aufwendungen bis hin zu den Kosten für Gemeindebedarfseinrichtungen (so beim städtebaulichen Vertrag) zu tragen haben.

Der Vorhaben- und Erschliessungsplan gründet sich auf die Initiative eines Investors. Die Planung ist auf ihn zugeschnitten. Fällt er aus, wandeln sich die Vorteile des Verfahrens, Flexibilität und Beschleunigung, ins Gegenteil. Für Developer kommt das Instrument nicht in Frage. Dasselbe gilt für grössere Areale, für deren Bebauung es mehrerer Investoren bedarf.

Besonders geeignet: Die städte-bauliche Entwicklungsmassnahme

Bei größeren Konversionsflächen ist namentlich an dieses Instrument (§§ 165 - 171 BauGB) zu denken. Weil sie den Grunderwerb der Gemeinden vorsieht und für diesen Zweck ein erleichtertes Enteignungsrecht bereit hält, muss sie vom "Wohl der Allgemeinheit" her geboten sein. Bei der Entwicklungsmassnahme fliesst der durch die Neuordnung bewirkte Wertzu-wachs der Gemeinde zu. Auf diese Weise sollen die Kosten gedeckt werden, die nach den Zielen und Zwecken der Entwicklung erforder-lich sind. Hierzu zählen auch Aufwendungen für Gemeindebedarfseinricht-ungen, nicht aber für sonstige Baumassnahmen.

Auch im Rahmen einer Entwicklungs-massnahme ist eine Public-Private-Partnership möglich. Die Gemeinde kann nämlich für die Entwicklung der Konversionsflächen zum Bauland einen Entwicklungsträger einschalten. Dieser wird nach dem Baugesetzbuch nur treuhänderisch für die Gemeinde tätig. Wenn er Grundstücke erwirbt, baureif macht und anschliessend veräussert, so handelt er zwar im eigenen Namen, aber stets auf Rechnung der

Gemeinde; er partizipiert daher nicht an den Wertsteigerungen der Grundstücke. Ausserhalb von förmlichen Entwicklungsmassnahmen nach dem Baugesetzbuch, lässt sich ein derartiges Treuhandmodell auch vertraglich mit der Gemeinde vereinbaren. Entscheidend ist dabei, dass kommunale Planungshoheit und wirtschaftliches Risiko zusammengeführt werden.

Die Entwicklungsmassnahme, die schon kraft Gesetzes auf Beschleunigung angelegt ist, wird durch den Entwicklungsträger noch weiter erleichtert. Dieser entlastet die Gemeinde auf vielfältiger Weise, durch ein professionelles Projektmanagement ebenso wie durch das Besorgen der Finanzierung. Zugleich kann die Entwicklungsmassnahme ausserhalb des Kommunalhaushalts abgewickelt werden.

Planung und Finanzierung hängen voneinander ab

Beides muss Hand in Hand gehen. Die Konversion militärischer Flächen ist ein vielschichtiger und langwieriger Prozess, der nicht stecken bleiben darf. Die erheblichen Kosten für Grunderwerb, Abbruch von Gebäuden, Altlastensanierung, Erschliessung und Schaffung von Gemeinbedarfseinrichtungen müssen daher von Anfang an bedacht werden.

Bevor die Finanzierung der Gesamtmassnahme sich nicht darstellen lässt, sollte die Gemeinde auch keine Konversionsflächen erwerben. Gerade dieser Grunderwerb ist aber bei der städtebaulichen Entwicklungsmassnahme, dem wichtigsten Instrument bei der Konversion, vom Gesetzgeber vorgesehen. Er bringt für die Gemeinde eine Reihe von Vorteilen: Die Gemeinde erhält nicht nur den durch die Neuordnung bewirkten Wertzuwachs und gewinnt so eine Finanzierungsquelle; sie kann in den Verträgen über die Weiterveräusserung

der neugeordneten Grundstücke auch ihre kommunalen Zielsetzungen für Wohnungsbau und Betriebsansiedlungen durchsetzen.

Wichtigste Finanzierungsquelle ist der Wertzuwachs der Grundstücke

Dieser hängt vor allem ab vom Inhalt der städtebaulichen Neuordnung und der Art der neuen Nutzung. So lassen sich die neugeordneten Grundstücke für Wohnzwecke meist teurer verkaufen als für gewerbliche Zwecke; Flächen für Eigentumswohnungen haben einen höheren Verkaufswert als solche für den sozialen Wohnungsbau. In den innenstadtnahen Bereichen der Großstädte kann die Bodenwertsteigerung zwischen Erwerb vor und Verkauf nach der Neuordnung, trotz der nicht geringen Einstandspreise, bis zu 800.- DM/m2 betragen.

Mit der Neuordnung von Konversionsflächen verfolgt eine Stadt zumeist mehrere kommunalpolitische Zwecke. Die Schaffung einer guten kommunalen Infrastruktur, auch mit einem Wirkungsgrad über die konkrete Konversionsfläche hinaus, kann ein Ziel sein, die Ansiedlung von Gewerbe ein anderes.

Viele Gemeinden wollen über die Konversion ihre Bürger mit preisgünstigen Mietwohnungen versorgen oder jüngeren Familien zum Wohneigentum verhelfen. Sie geben hierzu die ehemaligen Militärflächen nach deren Neuordnung zu einem geringeren Verkaufspreis ab (wobei auch ein geringerer Verkehrswert gegeben ist). Die praktische Erfahrung lehrt, dass sich eine Konversionsmassnahme finanziell nicht aus sich selbst heraus trägt. Sie ist vielmehr auf ein Finanzengagement der Gemeinde ebenso angewiesen wie auf die Unterstützung durch staatliche Förderprogramme. Die deutschen Bundesländer geben solche Unterstützungen in unterschiedlichem Maß. Die Bundesrepublik

Deutschland gewährt abgestufte Preisnachlässe beim Verkauf von Konversionsflächen. Sie beteiligt sich ferner an den Kosten der Altlastensanierung.

Weil mit einem Konversionsprojekt erhebliche Kosten verbunden sind und weil diese Kosten und ihre Deckung ganz wesentlich vom Inhalt der Neuplanung abhängen, kommt der Vorbereitungsphase besonderes Gewicht zu. Wird eine Entwicklungsmassnahme in Betracht gezogen, so sollte die Gemeinde möglichst frühzeitig (nach § 165 Abs. 4 des BauGB) Voruntersuchungen beschliessen und dies ortsüblich bekannt machen. Ab diesem Zeitpunkt stehen die entwicklungsbedingten Bodenwerterhöhungen des Grundstücks, wenn es später zu einer Entwicklungsmassnahme kommt, der Gemeinde zu. Beim Erwerb der Konversionsflächen durch Kauf oder Enteignung ist dies zu beachten.

Ein Beispiel aus der Praxis

Planung und Finanzierung einer Konversionsfläche stehen in einem wechselseitigen Verhältnis; sie bilden einen symbiotischen Verbund. Der Prozess der städtebaulichen Planung muss vorbereitet und begleitet werden durch Untersuchungen zu den Kosten und deren Finanzierung. In der Praxis haben sich als Einstieg ins Verfahren Machbarkeitsstudien bewährt, die mit alternativen städtebaulichen Szenarien arbeiten. Sie sollten sowohl mit einer Zeitplanung als auch mit einer Kosten- und Finanzierungsplanung verbunden sein. So lassen sie den Liquiditätsbedarf der einzelnen Jahre erkennen und geben Antwort auf die Frage, ob insgesamt ein Defizit oder ein Überschuss entsteht. Einnahmen und Ausgaben sollten zugleich für den gesamten mehrjährigen Konversionszeitraum indexiert werden, um der Preisentwicklung Rechnung zu tragen. In mehreren optimierungsschritten kann ein städtebauliches Leitbild entworfen und solange fortentwickelt werden, bis eine

sachgerechte planerische Konzeption mit tragfähiger Finanzierung gefunden worden ist.

Die optimierung kann sowohl über eine Reduzierung von Verkehrs- und Gemeindebedarfseinrichtungen als auch über eine planerische Neuverteilung der Nutzungsflächen gefunden werden. Nach dieser Methode ist die Landesentwicklungsgesellschaft Baden-Württemberg bei der Konversion der ehemaligen Vauban-Kaserne in Freiburg vorgegangen. Dieses Kasernenareal haben die französischen Streikräfte nach dem Zweiten Weltkrieg bis zum Jahre 1992 in Anspruch genommen und nach dem grossen Festungsbaumeister des französischen Sonnenkönigs, Sébastien le Prestre de Vauban, benannt, der Freiburg während der französischen Herrschaft (1679-1697) zur Festung ausgebaut hat.

Auf einer 34 ha grossen Teilfläche des noch innenstadtnahen Areals führt die Stadt Freiburg eine Entwicklungsmassnahme nach dem Baugesetz durch. Die Planung sieht überwiegend Wohnungen, daneben auch Gewerbe vor. In der Vorbereitungsphase sind von der Landesentwicklungsgesellschaft als Entwicklungsträger im Rahmen des optimierungsprozesses über 30 Nutzungsvarianten erarbeitet und mit einer entsprechenden Kosten- und Finanzierungsübersicht unterlegt worden. Schliesslich konnte ein tragfähiges städtebauliches Leitbild gefunden werden. Die Gesamtkosten belaufen sich auf 177 Mio. DM. Das Land Baden-Württemberg und die Stadt Freiburg teilen sich das im Saldo der Einnahmen und Ausgaben übrig bleibende Defizit von 10 Mio. DM je zur Hälfte. Das Verfahren hat Modellcharakter. Sein Ergebnis war im Sommer 1994 Grundlage für einen städtebaulichen Ideenwettbewerb.

Die Konversion militärischer Flächen hat die Kommunen überrascht. Sie war nicht vorherzusehen. Nunmehr stellt sie eine herausragende Aufgabe dar, die über die Jahrtausendwende hinausragt. So vielschichtig und schwierig diese Aufgabe auch erscheint, sie eröffnet doch enorme und unerwartete Chancen. Freilich verlangt sie einen langen Atem. Aber auch Rom ist nicht an einem Tag erbaut worden.

Dr. Walter Kilian ist Geschäftsführer der LEG Landesentwicklungsgesellschaft Baden-Württemberg mbH, Stuttgart, Deutschland.

Chapter Forty-Five (b)

New Uses of Former Military Areas

Walter Kilian

The end of the East-West conflict has lent new weight to the word "conversion." Used until now primarily in the academic areas of chemistry, physics, medicine, and religion, this term today particularly designates the transformation of military facilities and potentials for civilian purposes. Here, conversion stands for a complex procedure which covers the integration of former army members and civilian assistant workers into a new working life, as well as the transformation of ordnance factories or places of military research.

The communities in Germany are especially affected by the conversion of military property--of airports, troop training areas, barracks installations, and housing areas. For our country, through whose center the Iron Curtain passed for decades, was a preferred location for military installations.

The magnitude of military areas becoming available is tremendous.

This is especially true for the new German states in the area of the former German Democratic Republic. While in the West of Germany, that is, in the old German states, the military property becoming available consists of approximately 0.1% of the land area, the portion in the East is 23 times that. The absolute numbers are also correspondingly different. If it can be assumed that the conversion areas in the West make up approximately 25,000 hectares, the quantity in the new German states amounts to over 250,000 hectares; in the German state of Brandenburg alone, over 100,000 hectares exist. The installations formerly used by the Soviet Army are also sometimes especially large. The location of Wünsdorf near Berlin-the former seat of the German military leadership in World War II, and, until August 1994, the seat of the Supreme Command of the West Group of Russian troops-contains an area of 590 hectares, to which a troop training area of a further approximately 6,000 hectares is connected.

The challenge of the conversion of military areas, for this reason, has a greater dimension in the East of Germany. This applies to the financial expenditure as well as to the planning of urban development. In many places in the new German states, the housing area structure of a community is affected in its basic make-up. And the conversion must be managed by municipalities whose administrations are newly established or in reconstruction.

In the West, the forces were not only a burden, but also an economic factor whose discontinuation is frequently regretted especially in the smaller communities. The loss of workplaces and purchasing power has an effect, namely on the economically weaker regions. In Rheinland-Pfalz, which is, of the western German states, especially affected by the troop withdrawal, the detrimental effects are particularly concentrated in the rural areas. The conversion must set momentum for a new upswing in such areas.

New chances are being revealed in the conurbation.

Not all conversion areas are found--such as airports and troop training areas-outside of the populated areas. A considerable portion, up to 40%-deals with barracks installations within or immediately on the edge of the developed areas. Here, a new scope arises for the city planning especially in the big cities. For, in the city centers, available land for potential development has been fully exhausted in the last two decades.

Germany is, especially in its conurbation, a very densely populated country. The utilizing of still undeveloped regions for apartments, commerce, or a municipal infrastructure is not easily possible; it runs against ecological, legal, and political limits. The barracks installations which have become available are frequently found, on the other hand, in good inner city or near inner city locations. The origin of a portion of them is during the time of the emperors.

Some of these old barracks were already converted into civilian housing when the German Army was limited to 100,000 men after World War I. The majority of these barracks, however, came into being in the 1930's. While they were still more or less dissociated from the housing areas at the time of their foundation, they have, in the meantime, been pulled in by the ever-expanding city. Almost all have a connection to local public transportation at their disposal, and not seldom via subway or streetcar.

The size of these city-related areas varies greatly. Some installations, especially older barracks, are only 1-2 hectares. But areas of 50-100 hectares are no rarity, especially if adjacent housing installations, developed predominantly in the 1950's for the allied forces of the Americans, British, French, or Canadians, are added on. These "housing areas" frequently have the character of a separate suburb. Their becoming available relieves--noticeable in some locations--the German apartment market, even if the adaptation of the apartments to German conditions and norms is not inexpensive. Although this utilization is possible even without urban development planning, it should nevertheless be recommended. The loosely developed areas are in many ways suitable for a later filling with various construction and housing forms. Since a drastic redesigning is not required, though, the "housing areas" should remain outside of the following consideration.

The reorganization of the conversion areas is to be coordinated locally and beyond.

It does, in fact, protect the environment and makes short transportation routes possible. But it is simultaneously more difficult and more expensive than the original entire planning and development. First, the question exists of the new utilization, correct and appropriate to need. In the old German states, the goal of quickly creating a balance for lost economic power as well as living areas, especially of the economical sort, stands manifold in the foreground. In many eastern German communities, the areas becoming available clearly exceed the areas needed for housing development. In the East, as in the West of Germany, the conversion requires effort in order to attain economic feasibility and financability. Precise considerations of need are therefore just as indispensable as a new thinking through of the city development and the setting of temporal priorities.

Planning considerations cannot simply stop at the community borders. The embedding of the conversion in the beyond-local planning, especially in the regional planning, is legally required. Sometimes there exists no option other than intercommunity cooperation. Not far from the gates of Freiburg is the former Bremgarten Germany Army airport with a total area of 582 hectares. The installation finds itself on the boundary of four communities, each with less than 10,000 residents. These communities, along with 11 others, amongst them the city of Freiburg and the county of Breisgau-Hochschwarzwald, have joined together in an administration union to erect an industrial park whose realization will reach, in sections, far into the next millennium. The size of the industrial park has, at the same time, effects on the regional planning, in regards to the quantity and spatial distribution of commercial workplaces. Even the area utilization planning is being adapted; this ensues mutually through agreement (§ 204 Paragraph 1 Sentence 4 BauGB [Bau Gesetzbuch--building code]).

The area utilization planning as preliminary zoning for the entire community area must not, by the way, be temporally modified before the compulsory zoning by way of development planning in all conversion cases. The Baugesetzbuch (building code) (in § 8 Paragraph 3--

"parallel procedures") as well as the statute for specific provision to the building code (in § 1 Paragraph 2) permit giving priority to the development planning. This way, an immediate housing need can, particularly, be covered. The well-ordered entire urban development may not, of course, be impaired.

Inner city or near inner city conversion areas must nearly always be drastically reconstructed. Their expansion, more often than not, leaves a multitude of uses for apartments, jobs, culture, recreation, and social purposes. It also offers room for shopping centers. These also belong, in appropriate size and particularly in connection with offices, doctors' practices, and gastronomy, in the city. The inner cities need the retail trade; the retail trade, though, does not need the inner city. The generally smaller "filets" directly bordering the inner city, which can also be found in the small and medium-sized cities, require special planning care. The utilization mixture must here be fine, with great consideration of the cityscape.

The conflict of goals between demolition and preservation affects the economic feasibility.

Demolition is frequently demanded for structural installations on conversion areas. For buildings of purely military function, this demand must also be redeemed. Management buildings and workshops can also be used for civilian purposes. This is how, in the conversion area of Wünsdorf, all buildings should remain standing according to the present planning status. In addition, there are structural installations which hold a high rank as an expression of construction history and should therefore be preserved.

In all these cases, economic considerations are to be weighed up with contemporaneous claims to utilization. Here, the economic feasibility of the entirety cannot be disregarded. This also holds true for the consideration of the protection of monuments. Because if the reorganization cannot let itself be economically presented and therefore ceases, the conversion area will lie fallow and will threaten to become dilapidated. It is certainly the worst solution, if one does not see the area as a reserve for the future. Intermediate uses are appropriate only as long as they do not hinder the entire planned project.

Should a portion of the buildings remain standing, the urban development planning will not become easier; it will become more difficult. An urban development competition can further help. If all participants feel obligated to the entirety, a balance of interests should be attained. New forms of participation in the planning process will be in demand. When city planners, architects, interested citizen groups, possible investors, and city representatives can be led together into a constructive dialogue, a solid consensus will be easier to find. Even the citizens' life in the district can be enriched this way.

Urban vitality lives on the multitude of uses.

The size of the former military areas allows for their subdivision. It permits a peaceable neighboring of differing uses. In particular, the conversion even gives room for living space in the near inner city areas again. This can work against the migration to the surrounding countryside. Already at around the turn of the century, the German big cities could not maintain their populations. But then there was a monumental immigration which allowed the cities to swell. Today, the populations continually diminish--more than 7000 residents each year in the last two years in the city of Stuttgart. These are generally younger people with middle incomes who emigrate. They are looking for their own four walls, can't afford it within the big city, and therefore go to the surrounding countryside, even to the second ring of the big city. To make economical owned property possible to this population group would make good political sense.

City planning is always a venture. The "city on test" does not exist--despite all experimental urban planning. One cannot test a city in a laboratory. And buildings more often than not live longer than the ideas which led to their erection. City planning must therefore be open to future developments. It must attempt to contain even future users in its vision. In auto-free districts, for example, it must be considered that eternal life may hardly be granted. The sons and daughters of the first generation could already have a different relationship to automobiles. A good planning must therefore be flexible and keep answers prepared for the future. Free areas can also be reallocated corresponding to the changing times. Future parking places are to be planned--even in reasonable distance. On the other hand, abundant parking places can also be built back.

Room for individual structuring should be given to the users as much as possible; even if only to be able to plant their own trees so as not to simply force them to preserve the outside structure. Individuality should blossom. Even the apparent superfluous makes some sense.

As a rule, it does not work without a development plan.

Not lastly, an urban development plan is therefore necessary, because without a binding new plan in accordance with German law, civilian use is allowed only in smaller former military installations within built-up local sectors. The most important group in practical terms is made up, however, of the larger entire installations, consisting of barracks, barracks lot, sport and drill areas, garages, and workshops. They belong either to the outer area (also as "outer area of the inner area") or are qualified as actual "special military areas." The latter are characterized by the military purpose provision. This does not disappear immediately with the end of the military utilization; rather, it remains (according to § 34 Paragraph 1 or Paragraph 2 of the building code) as a standard of legal urban development permissibility. It does not matter whether an outer area or a military characterized inner area is in question; a civilian construction or other new utilization is only permissible if the communal zoning has created a new utilization measure by the procedure prescribed in the building code. Such properties are generally, for the time being and according to assessment, only future construction land.

New instruments in urban development law are available.

The transformation of former military areas is a task of the municipalities and must be politically controlled by them. Models of a public-private-partnership can further help with this. The German legislation has created instruments in the building code as well as in special provisions to the building code which target a balance of interests between the municipality and the party responsible for the measure. The mutual goal of the urban development contract (§ 6 of the special provision law) and the project and development plan (§ 7 of the special provision law) is to let acquirers or investors participate in the increase in value of the properties. These private partners of the municipality step in financially in advance. They buy the properties and prepare them for construction through development and reorganization in accordance with the municipality. The property value, which rises in this manner, is of benefit to the private partners through disposal or leasing, as long as they need not bear the planning and development costs (as in the project and development plan) in accordance with public legal contracts to be concluded, or even other expenditures up to the costs for essential equipment of the municipality (as in the urban development contract).

The project and development plan is based on the initiative of an investor. The planning is tailored to him. Should he drop out, the advantages of the procedure, flexibility and speed, become the opposite. For developers, the instrument is not an issue. The same applies for larger areas, for which construction requires several investors.

Especially suitable: The development measure for urban planning.

With larger conversion areas, this instrument, namely, is to be thought of (§§ 165 171 building code). Because it provides for the property acquisition by the municipalities and holds an alleviated eminent domain at its disposal for this purpose, it must be required by the "well-being of the general public." With the development measure, the value increase created by the reorganization is of benefit to the municipality. In this manner, the costs required for the goals and purposes of the development should also be covered. Expenditures for essential equipment of the municipality are part of these costs, but not for other construction measures.

A public-private-partnership is also possible within the realm of a development measure. The municipality can, namely, activate a development company for the development of the conversion area to construction land. It will become active for the municipality only as a trustee in accordance with the building code. If it acquires properties, prepares them for construction, and finally disposes of them, it is acting, in fact, on its own behalf, but always on account of the municipality, it does not participate, therefore, in the increase in value of properties. Aside from formal development measures in accordance with the building code, this kind of a trustee model can also be contractually agreed with the municipality. The deciding factor is that the communal planning sovereignty and the economic risk are brought together.

The development measure, which is built for speed on a legal basis, is further facilitated by the development company. It relieves the municipality in multiple ways, through professional project management just as through the procurement of the financing. At the same time, the development measure can be carried out outside of the communal household.

Planning and financing depend on each other.

Both must go hand in hand. The conversion of military areas is a complex and lengthy process which cannot get stuck. The considerable costs for property acquisition, demolition of buildings, contaminated site clean-up, development, and creation of essential equipment of the municipality must therefore be considered from the very beginning.

Until the financing of the entire measure materializes, the municipality should acquire no conversion areas. This very property acquisition is provided by the legislation, though, in the development measure for urban planning, which is the most important instrument during the conversion. It brings a series of advantages to the municipality: The municipality receives not only the value increase caused by the reorganization and therewith wins a source of financing; it can also carry through its communal goal-settings for apartment construction and places of business in contracts over the further disposal of the reorganized properties.

The most important source of financing is the value increase of the properties.

This depends, above all, on the content of the urban reorganization and the type of the new utilization. The reorganized properties can, more often than not, be sold more expensively for housing purposes than for commercial purposes; areas for owner-occupied apartments have a higher sale value than those for social apartment construction. In the near inner city areas of the big cities, the property value increase between acquisition before and sale after the reorganization, despite the rather expensive cost price, can consist of up to DM 800.00/m2.

With the reorganization of conversion areas, a city will pursue, for the most part, several communal-political purposes. The creation of a good communal infrastructure, even with an effectiveness above and beyond the concrete conversion areas, can be a goal; the establishing of commerce another. Many municipalities want to supply their citizens with economical apartments through the conversion or to help younger families with housing ownership. For this, they give up the former military areas at a lower sale price (whereby a lower market value is also given). Practical experience teaches that a conversion measure does not carry itself financially. It is, rather, dependent on a finance engagement of the municipality as well as on the support of state support programs. The German states give such support to a varying degree. The Federal Republic of Germany grants graduated discounts in the sale of conversion areas. It participates, in addition, in the costs of contaminated site clean-up.

Northeast, which is characterized by dense, built-out inner cities.

The third obstacle to inner city industrial development includes a myriad of governmental regulations and land use policies which, taken together, promote an anti-business climate which makes investment within traditional mill towns an unattractive alternative to suburbia. Some of these regulations and policies include:

- **Occupational Safety and Health Administration (OSHA) Regulations**

    OSHA requirements mandate that mills be free of asbestos, which is more the exception than the rule in most buildings. In addition, the majority of freight elevators within inner city industrial facilities are outdated and cannot meet the needs of modern production or safety requirements.

- **Environmental Protection Agency and Superfund Sites**

    The vast majority of manufacturing facilities have hazardous wastes or chemicals which can be found in or around the structure. In most states, these sites are not eligible for loans on buildings for sale until they are "clean". However, the costs of environmental clean-up are so high that owners will often leave the site as is, leaving many mills abandoned for years.

- **The Americans With Disabilities Act (ADA)**

    The ADA enforces accessibility requirements for persons with disabilities. For mill buildings, extensive ramping, as well as the installation of modern elevators are often too costly for manufacturers.

- **Housing and Urban Development (HUD) Flood Plan Regulations**

    Many mills are located in areas which have been designated either 50-or 100-year flood plains by HUD. With such a designation, financial lenders are reluctant to provide funds for facilities which are for sale or seeking to expand.

- **The National Register for Historic Places**

    The National Register was established to preserve the nation's industrial heritage through the protection of historic industrial structures. However, the Register can unwittingly contribute to the decay of these buildings. Efforts to modernize can be halted on the grounds that physical or structural changes might serve to denigrate these buildings' historic character. This conflict becomes particularly acute when federal dollars are requested for structural improvements and the mill is listed on the National Register. However, unless a mill is "moth-balled", a vacant structure will eventually decay, leaving it of little use for future generations to enjoy or utilize.

- **Non-Conforming Uses in Local Zoning Regulations**

    Non-conforming uses are those uses which are inconsistent with the uses prescribed by zoning regulations. In recent times, planners have come to recognize that these non-conforming uses might remain indefinitely. In an effort to phase them out, administrative procedures prohibit changes in use or expansion efforts. In addition, even if a mill is not a non-conforming use, those sites which are surrounded by residential neighborhoods may result in "nuisance" cases brought by land owners to combat manufacturing activities which may endanger the health or safety of residents.

Though these regulations were designed to protect the structural integrity of the mills, as well as the safety of those living around them, the end result is that revitalization of these potentially useful facilities is being deterred.

These factors taken together -- limitation of the mills for modern production practices, lack of availability of developable industrial land and stringent environmental regulations -- contribute to an overall image problem for inner city industrial development. Yet there are several examples of old factories in mill communities which have proven to be, not only attractive, but as functional as suburban manufacturing facilities. One, however, can dispute the fact that given the choice between old industrial sites and new suburban settings, for quality of life and cost savings, greenfield development is an attractive alternative.

Greener Pastures for Industry - An Exodus to the Suburbs

Where the inner city is constricted in terms of the limitations of structure, infrastructure, space and governmental support, suburbia offers tasteful single-story facilities, acreage, state-of-the-art infrastructure. Thus, the greenfield industrial park has become the place where Americans want to work. Indeed, new industrial centers are springing up across the United States, complete with their own regional shopping centers and recreational amenities. These low density, well planned, typically "clean" manufacturing facilities are welcome in many communities for their addition to the tax

base and creation of new jobs. This trend has been stimulated in part, by subsidies from state government.

A recent review of grants to Massachusetts cities and towns shows suburban communities receive a majority of state funds earmarked for industrial expansion. This favoritism can be found in the allocation of federal highway funds and environmental protection funds for upgraded sewage disposal, all of which often favor suburban areas.

Yet, the very factors which have drawn industry to the suburbs -- quality of life, open space and affluent neighborhoods -- have had negative effects both on the community itself and on the center cities which have been left behind.

Negative Impacts of Greenfield Development

Anyone who has visited Boston's Route 128, North Carolina's Golden Triangle or the Silicon Valley in California will marvel at these symbols of modern industry. Rather than billowing smokestacks and images of pollution, the image of the machine in the garden is evoked. Yet, this draw to the suburbs has come with immense social and economic costs to both the old and new sites of industrial development.

Many suburban communities, prior to both residential and economic development, enjoyed a rich tradition of agricultural production. Despite the fact that many working farms have not been as profitable, as perhaps an industrial site might be, there are an abundance of viable working farms. These farms can serve to maintain this history of agriculture as well as to provide a regional source for agricultural products. In addition, this open land contributes to a sense of escape from the pressures of urban life. The recent trend toward decentralization of cities has resulted in a seemingly endless spread of development.

This spread of development, particularly business and industrial, has drawn a relatively affluent population, looking to purchase homes close to their new places of work. In effect, this parallel exodus of jobs and people from the city has left behind those who cannot afford the high-priced, single-family detached homes of the suburbs. The alternative for many poor, minority or single-parent households is to commute long distances for the jobs which have been displaced from the city. This is dramatic-ally exemplified in the Silicon Valley as the lower paid production workers in the semi-conductor industry have been pushed to the edges of the Valley and endured up to three hours of commuting per day.

A second negative consequence of greenfield development has been the proliferation of increased suburban sprawl in light of low density zoning restrictions. It is not uncommon to find lot coverage below 20 percent, meaning that 80 percent of a greenfield site is not developable for industrial space. Thus, there is the never-ending search for new land and new space. This sprawl has lead to the creation of so-called "Edge Cities" which are characterized by suburban to suburban connections rather than suburban to center city connections.

A final draw back to suburban industrial development has been favoritism of "clean" industries over "heavy" industry such as steel, chemical or other manufacturers which may be perceived as "dirty" by the host community. Clearly, the company which enjoys a strong reputation as a corporate leader and who employs well-educated white collar workers will be courted by developers of suburban industrial parks. The underlying concern within all of these consequences of greenfield development is the issue of equity both for

manufacturers and for the people who work there.

Strategies Toward Balanced Development

From the previous sections, it is clear that changes in our political, social and economic fabric are creating changes that few of us expected. No government at any level has espoused a policy of industrial decay in our urban centers. No community leader has advocated the destruction of active farm land for industrial or commercial uses. And similarly, few private industrialists have accurately predicted the influence of new production techniques, social legislative enactments or world wide competition on the location of the American manufacturing firm. Yet, we have a full scale exodus from urban areas. We have the continued loss of farm hands. And our manufacturers are constantly looking to locate in new areas where efficient production, low cost labor and inexpensive transportation opportunities exist.

Inevitably, the result of all this activity is the unintentional dispersion of manufacturing to both suburban and rural areas. Ultimately, this dispersion will have serious effects for both the greenfield communities and the industrial centers which have been left behind. The destruction of agricultural land, open space, recreational areas and residential communities will be paralleled by a decline in positive economic growth, full employment and quality of life for traditional manufacturing cities. The search for newer, greener sites will result in the deterioration of the center city - and eventually change the face of the American landscape.

Through the employment of regional strategies, balanced approaches to greenfield and brownfield development can reverse the trend toward suburban sprawl. Following are a list of some practical strategies which planners and community leaders may utilize to encourage sound industrial and economic growth.

Development of Regional Strategies

As industrial development is far from insular and is dependent on regional resources for labor, material and markets, regional strategies provide a mechanism to better plan for industry.

Comprehensive Environmental Clean-up

One of the strongest deterrents to re-using older industrial buildings or sites in inner cities is the environmental clean-up procedure. This is not only an expensive task but is also very time consuming. Furthermore, the burden of the clean-up lies entirely with the current owner of the property. Often times these owners do not have the money necessary for the clean-up and are unable to either refinance or sell their property. Their only option is to abandon it.

The reuse and clean-up of these sites are of importance to the community in which they are located. Reuse and clean-up are also important to the bank or financial institution that holds the paper as well as the owner who would like to sell or reinvest. Due to these factors, there is need for a joint effort on the part of the state, the community, the bank and the owner to see that the process is carried out in a timely and efficient manner.

It is crucial that policies and land use regulations be established to encourage companies to clean-up hazardous sites on the premises. As long as manufacturers know they can simply abandon a contaminated site, older manufacturing facilities will remain unavailable for potential new investment and modernization.

Reparcelizing of Urban Industrial Land

Most industrial parcels in either center cities or mill communities are too small to accommodate new manufacturing or expansion of existing manufacturing. Furthermore, the current allowable floor to area ratio is around 20 percent - 30 percent in most communities as compared to 80 percent when the original lots were divided or the mills built. Industrial buildings are now one or two stories high as compared to the four-story mill complexes. Therefore, industry today needs more land for the same size of building than it did in yesteryears. This is practically impossible to get in inner cities.

Reparcelization powers enable the communities to consolidate small lots to form a bigger workable parcel. Reparcelization also allows a community to acquire, by eminent domain, parcels of land that are crucial to the area's revitalization plans. In Springfield, Massachusetts, for example, the city through a selective demolition program hopes to make older properties that are structurally and environmentally sound, but do not have room to expand or adequate parking, economically viable once again. Reparcelization can thus serve to maximize allowable density on urban land.

Investment Credits for Inner City Development

Industry should be provided with positive incentives to invest in urban areas rather than simply move to the suburbs to construct new facilities. Municipalities can offer a number of investment credits. Urban enterprise zones have been used successfully in parts of

Connecticut and in Philadelphia as vehicles to stimulate recovery in designated areas. Normally, an enterprise zone is a targeted economic opportunity area where a variety of inducements and financial incentives are in place. These could take the form of tax abatement for five or ten years, accelerated depreciation, grants and programs for venture capital, gap financing or loans for equipment and other capital expenditures.

Streamlining of the Permitting Process

Under current procedures, it is not uncommon for manufacturers or developers to wait up to two years for permits to either expand existing facilities or develop new ones. The quagmire of environmental and procedural requirements has only served to promote an anti-business climate within many urban areas across the country. In the time that it takes to simply wait for a permit, a new facility can be constructed in a green field site.

Where Do We Go From Here?

It is clear that the methods used to determine new industrial sites across the nation cannot continue as they are. The unintended consequences are leading to decay, neglect and lost opportunities. They are contributing to crime, an erosion of the work ethic and the creation of a permanent class of underemployed citizens. At the same time, our farmlands are threatened, our open spaces are carved up and our landscapes are becoming eroded.

It is recognized that efficient production, competitive pricing, high quality results and profitability are critical cornerstones to our economic base. Somehow we must maximize our existing resources in the center city.

If buildings are outmoded, they must be demolished such that the land can be used. If they can be revitalized, then public/private partnerships should be formed to take on the task. If the land is hazardous, it must be environmentally cleansed at the expense of the owners and the host community alike. If our infrastructures need to be upgraded then the community must live up to its responsibilities. In short, it is crucial that a pro-active brownfield strategy be developed that involves the private sector, the banks, governments at all levels and our academic and research centers.

Zenia Kotval Ph.D., AICP, Assistant Professor, Michigan State University, East Lansing, MI, USA.

New Urban Neighborhoods: Case Studies

Neue Stadtteile für urbanes Leben: Beispiele

Freiburg-Rieselfeld

Freiburg-Rieselfeld

Sven von Ungern-Sternberg

1. Vorgeschichte

Hätte man mich vor 15 Jahren gefragt, ob noch im Laufe der 90iger Jahre richtige neue Stadtteile in Freiburg geplant und verwirklicht werden würden, hätte ich die klare Antwort gegeben, nein, es sei nicht vorstellbar. Der Schwerpunkt der Stadtentwicklung liege in diesem Jahrzehnt in der Stadterneuerung und der inneren Verdichtung. Umbau gehe vor Neubau. Lediglich überschaubare Arrondierungen vorhandener Wohnbaugebiete seien erwünscht.

Heute gehen wir - wie in den 60iger Jahren - mit großem Engagement daran, auf dem Rieselfeld für 12.000 Bürger und auf dem Vauban-Gelände für 5.000 Bürger neue Stadtteile zu entwickeln. Die Gründe hierfür liegen auf der Hand. Wie allgemein in Deutschland hat auch in Freiburg, vor allem seit der zweiten Hälfte der 80iger Jahre, der Druck auf den Wohnungsmarkt stark zugenommen. Atypisch zu fast allen anderen deutschen Städten nimmt zudem in Freiburg seit Jahrzehnten die Bevölkerung durch Zuwanderung ständig zu. Entscheidend aber ist der stetig wachsende zusätzliche durchschnittliche Flächenverbrauch pro Einwohner. Dieser Vorgang ist vor allem durch gesellschaftliche Veränderungen hervorgerufen. Der dramatische Anstieg der "singles" in Einzelhaushalten ist in Freiburg als Universitätsstadt besonders hoch. Zugleich haben wir einen erheblichen Rückgang bisher untervermieteter Räume, bedingt durch den allgemeinen Wohlstand, aber auch durch den stark ausgebauten Mieterschutz. So wird von der Mehrheit unserer Bürger eine erheblich größere Fläche an Wohnraum "konsumiert". Dies führt dazu, daß der sozial schwächere Teil unserer Bevölkerung durch diese Verknappung am Wohnungsmarkt in zunehmend echte Situationen der Wohnungsnot gerät. Dieser Fehlbedarf, vor allen Dingen an preiswerten Wohnungen, zwingt die Politiker zum Handeln über die vorgesehenen Maßnahmen der inneren Verdichtung und Arrondierung hinaus, also zu dem Bau ganzer neuer Stadtteile.

Unter diesen Gesichtspunkten war es für Freiburg ein Glücksfall, daß das städtische Rieselfeld seit 1980 "ausgedient" hatte. Zu diesem Zeitpunkt wurde unser städtisches Kanalnetz an ein regionales Klärsystem angeschlossen. In einer langwierigen und sehr kontrovers geführten kommunalpolitischen Diskussion wurde in Freiburg der Zielkonflikt zwischen Ökologie (Landschaftsschutz für dieses Gebiet) und Sozialpflichtigkeit (Wohnversorgung) in einem Kompromiß gelöst. Anfang des Jahres 1991 entschied der Freiburger Gemeinderat, ein Viertel des Rieselfeldes, knapp 80 ha, als Bauland für einen neuen Stadtteil auszuweisen.

2. Städtebaulicher Ideen-Wettbewerb

Auf dieser Grundlage wurde im Sommer 1991 ein städtebaulicher und landschaftsplanerischer Ideenwettbewerb ausgelobt. Hierbei war kennzeichnend, daß das Wettbewerbsgebiet nicht nur das Gebiet des neuen Stadtteils selbst, sondern weit darüber hinaus ein über 1000 ha

Drittens gibt es eine Menge von Einzelpunkten, die der Gemeinderat sehr gerne angewandt sehen möchte, etwa frauenfreundlichere Grundrisse, die aber nicht in einer stringenten Form zwingende Voraussetzung für den Abschluß eines Kaufvertrages sind. Diese sollen in den individuellen Vertragsverhandlungen des Projektmanagements mit einem künftigen Investor als Empfehlung eingebracht werden, in der Hoffnung, daß nicht alle, aber doch ein großer Teil davon auch praktisch verwirklicht wird.

5. Inhalte der wesentlichen politischen Vorgaben

Ein in unserer heutigen Zeit geplanter und gebauter Stadtteil soll ein Spiegelbild der Gesellschaft sein. Er muß aber auch unsere Visionen einer anzustrebenden künftigen Welt von morgen erkennen lassen. Hierbei soll er unser Bild von unserer freiheitlichen demokratischen Grundordnung, von unserem pluralistischen Gemeinwesen und der Würde eines jeden einzelnen Menschen in die gebaute Wirklichkeit umsetzen. Dieses bedeutet konkret, daß Vielfalt organisiert werden muß, daß in dem neuen Stadtteil eine soziale Balance hergestellt wird und die konkreten sozialen Bedürfnisse berücksichtigt werden.

Der neue Stadtteil soll von der fatalen Entmischungsideologie im Städtebau Abschied nehmen. Die verschiedenen Bereiche Arbeiten und Wohnen müssen zusammengeführt werden. Die unterschiedlichen Gruppen unserer Bevölkerung sollen möglichst nicht getrennt, sondern zusammengeführt werden. Die heutigen Erkenntnisse der Verkehrspolitik und Ökologie müssen bei der Planung berücksichtigt werden. Die Gesichtspunkte der inneren Sicherheit müssen frühzeitig einbezogen werden. Die Planung muß offen für künftige gesellschaftliche Änderungen sein. Ein neuer Stadtteil soll nicht nur für den Bürger, sondern auch möglichst mit dem Bürger entwickelt werden.

All diese hehren Ziele müssen in einem gebündelten Gesamtmanagement möglichst aufeinander abgestimmt und optimiert werden.

6. Organisation der Vielfalt

Um Vielfalt zu organisieren, darf die Entwicklung eines Stadtteils nicht in die Hände eines einzigen oder einiger weniger externer Projektträger gegeben werden. Vielmehr muß das in der städtischen Hand befindliche Projektmanagement durch Planung und Marketing eine Vielfalt von einzelnen Bauträgern und künftigen Eigentümern organisieren.

So muß von der Planung her der städtebauliche Entwurf Kleingliedrigkeit und Aufteilbarkeit in Parzellen zulassen. Aufgabe des Managements ist es, möglichst viele Partner als Investoren zu finden. Dies ist für die Verwaltung sicherlich schwieriger, als mit einigen wenigen großen Partnern umzugehen, die dann jeweils möglichst viele Wohneinheiten bauen. Aber eine Vielzahl von Investoren als handelnde Personen mit jeweils unterschiedlichen Architekten, mit unterschiedlichen Finanzierungsmodellen und mit unterschiedlichen Nutzervorstellungen gewährleisten die anzustrebende Vielfalt am besten.

Dies bedeutet nicht, daß bei besonderer Konstellation ein Partner, der ein größeres Kontingent von Wohnungen bauen möchte, abgewiesen werden muß. So haben wir in der Zusatzversorgungskasse der deutschen Bauwirtschaft (ZVK) einen hervorragenden Partner mit einer hohen Zahl von Wohnungen, ca. 500 für das gesamte Wohngebiet.

Freiburg-Rieselfeld

Sven von Ungern-Sternberg

1. Vorgeschichte

Hätte man mich vor 15 Jahren gefragt, ob noch im Laufe der 90iger Jahre richtige neue Stadtteile in Freiburg geplant und verwirklicht werden würden, hätte ich die klare Antwort gegeben, nein, es sei nicht vorstellbar. Der Schwerpunkt der Stadtentwicklung liege in diesem Jahrzehnt in der Stadterneuerung und der inneren Verdichtung. Umbau gehe vor Neubau. Lediglich überschaubare Arrondierungen vorhandener Wohnbaugebiete seien erwünscht.

Heute gehen wir - wie in den 60iger Jahren - mit großem Engagement daran, auf dem Rieselfeld für 12.000 Bürger und auf dem Vauban-Gelände für 5.000 Bürger neue Stadtteile zu entwickeln. Die Gründe hierfür liegen auf der Hand. Wie allgemein in Deutschland hat auch in Freiburg, vor allem seit der zweiten Hälfte der 80iger Jahre, der Druck auf den Wohnungsmarkt stark zugenommen. Atypisch zu fast allen anderen deutschen Städten nimmt zudem in Freiburg seit Jahrzehnten die Bevölkerung durch Zuwanderung ständig zu. Entscheidend aber ist der stetig wachsende zusätzliche durchschnittliche Flächenverbrauch pro Einwohner. Dieser Vorgang ist vor allem durch gesellschaftliche Veränderungen hervorgerufen. Der dramatische Anstieg der "singles" in Einzelhaushalten ist in Freiburg als Universitätsstadt besonders hoch. Zugleich haben wir einen erheblichen Rückgang bisher untervermieteter Räume, bedingt durch den allgemeinen Wohlstand, aber auch durch den stark ausgebauten Mieterschutz. So wird von der Mehrheit unserer Bürger eine erheblich größere Fläche an Wohnraum "konsumiert". Dies führt dazu, daß der sozial schwächere Teil unserer Bevölkerung durch diese Verknappung am Wohnungsmarkt in zunehmend echte Situationen der Wohnungsnot gerät. Dieser Fehlbedarf, vor allen Dingen an preiswerten Wohnungen, zwingt die Politiker zum Handeln über die vorgesehenen Maßnahmen der inneren Verdichtung und Arrondierung hinaus, also zu dem Bau ganzer neuer Stadtteile.

Unter diesen Gesichtspunkten war es für Freiburg ein Glücksfall, daß das städtische Rieselfeld seit 1980 "ausgedient" hatte. Zu diesem Zeitpunkt wurde unser städtisches Kanalnetz an ein regionales Klärsystem angeschlossen. In einer langwierigen und sehr kontrovers geführten kommunalpolitischen Diskussion wurde in Freiburg der Zielkonflikt zwischen Ökologie (Landschaftsschutz für dieses Gebiet) und Sozialpflichtigkeit (Wohnversorgung) in einem Kompromiß gelöst. Anfang des Jahres 1991 entschied der Freiburger Gemeinderat, ein Viertel des Rieselfeldes, knapp 80 ha, als Bauland für einen neuen Stadtteil auszuweisen.

2. Städtebaulicher Ideen-Wettbewerb

Auf dieser Grundlage wurde im Sommer 1991 ein städtebaulicher und landschaftsplanerischer Ideenwettbewerb ausgelobt. Hierbei war kennzeichnend, daß das Wettbewerbsgebiet nicht nur das Gebiet des neuen Stadtteils selbst, sondern weit darüber hinaus ein über 1000 ha großes Gebiet umfaßte. Wichtig erschien die großräumige Einbindung des neuen Stadtteils in die vorhandene Nachbarschaft, seien es die landschaftlich geschützten Flächen im Westen, sei es ein benachbartes Gewerbegebiet im Süden, sei es vor allen Dingen der angrenzende Stadtteil Weingarten im Osten. Weingarten ist ein Stadtteil, der nach den Planungsideologien der 60iger Jahre gebaut worden ist. Große Wohnmaschinen und Monostrukturen sind kennzeichnend. Erhebliche soziale Brennpunkte belasten das Quartier und mittelbar die gesamte Stadt.

Es sollten städtebauliche Konzepte für den neuen Stadtteil mit seinen Naht- und Übergangszonen zum Naturschutzgebiet sowie zu der bestehenden Bebauung, gefunden werden. Die Wettbewerbsergebnisse wurden die Grundlage für die weitere Flächennutzungsplanung und den Landschaftsplan, für die konkreten Bebauungspläne und die dazugehörigen Grünordnungspläne.

Den ersten Preis erhielt eine Architektengemeinschaft aus vier Büros unserer Region. Diese wurde mit der weiteren Bearbeitung bis hin zu den Bebauungs- und Grünordnungsplänen beauftragt. Der preisgekrönte Entwurf gruppiert um die mitten durch das Gebiet geführte Stadtbahn, eine dichte sonnenorientierte Blockrandbebauung, die sich zu den Stadträndern hin auflöst. Der "besondere Pfiff" dieses Entwurfes ist, daß dem Schutz der Landschaft insoweit Rechnung getragen wird, als sich der Stadtteil aus seinem Zentrum heraus mit einer großzügigen Grünanlage nach Norden öffnet.

Ein orthogonales Straßennetz gliedert überschaubar den neuen Stadtteil, dessen Mittelachse die Stadtbahnlinie bildet. Entlang dieser Ost-West-Strasse sind die wichtigen zentralen Infrastruktureinrichtungen geplant. Die Bebauung geht von einem 5-geschossigen Wohnbogen, der zugleich auch Lärm-

schutzriegel gegen eine angrenzende Autostraße bildet, über zu einer klassischen Blockstruktur, die wir auch bei den hoch eingeschätzten Freiburger Stadtteilen der Gründerzeit kennen, bis hin zu zwei- bis viergeschoßigen Reihenhäusern. Der prämierte Entwurf bindet außerdem naturräumliche Elemente wie die Bachläufe sehr gut in die städtebauliche Situation ein. Darüber hinaus hat dieser Wettbewerb auch einen Energiesonderpreis erhalten.

3. Methodischer Ansatz des Projektmanagements

Ganz entscheidend für die weitere Entwicklung des Stadtteils ist der methodische Ansatz im Management. Bewußt wurde die weitere Entwicklung nicht an einen Projektmanager außerhalb der städtischen Verwaltung weitergegeben. Vielmehr wurde innerhalb der hoheitlichen Verwaltung, unmittelbar dem Baudezernenten unterstellt, ein städtisches Projektmanagement gebildet, das in neuen Formen und Zuständigkeiten ämter- und dezernatsübergreifend die administrativen Ressourcen bündelt.

In dieses Projektmanagement eingebunden ist eine Zusammenarbeit mit der Kommunalentwicklung Baden-Württemberg GmbH, deren "Know-how" in vielen Bereichen, etwa der Treuhandabwicklung, wir uns zu eigen machen. In diese Projektgruppe sind nicht nur die verschiedenen Ämter des Baudezernats, also Planungsamt, Tiefbauamt, Hochbauamt, Vermessungsamt, sondern auch die Finanzverwaltung sowie Fachämter der Kultur, Sozial und Umweltdezernate eingebunden. Des weiteren werden in einer sehr engen Zusammenarbeit mit dem Planungsamt die Preisträger mit der weiteren Bearbeitung des städtebaulichen Entwurfes betraut und sind in die Entwicklung der Bebauungs- und Grünordnungsplanung einbezogen.

Für die politische Rückkopplung ist wichtig, daß eine eigene gemeinderätliche "Arbeitsgruppe Rieselfeld" geschaffen worden ist. Diese tagt kontinuierlich und ist ständig an den wichtigen Weichenstellungen beteiligt und überwacht den Vollzug der politischen Vorgaben. Hier werden die Entscheidungen im Bauausschuß und im Gemeinderat vorbereitet und im Vorfeld früh abgestimmt. Zugleich ist auch die bürgerschaftliche Beteiligung mit dem Projektmanagement einerseits und der gemeinderätlichen Arbeitsgruppe Rieselfeld andererseits verbunden.

Das gesamte Rieselfeld steht in vollem Eigentum der Stadt Freiburg. So ist die Stadt über den Verkauf von Grund und Boden an die einzelnen Investoren in der Lage, die notwendigen öffentlichen Infrastruktur-maßnahmen in Höhe von ungefähr 280 Mio. DM zu erbringen, ohne den "normalen Haushalt" des Kämmerers zu belasten. Daher ist die Entwicklung des Rieselfeldes ein finanzielles In-sich-Geschäft, das vom städtischen Haushalt abgekoppelt ist und als Treuhandfinanzierung durchgeführt wird. Die wichtigen politischen Vorgaben werden von den gemeinderätlichen Gremien beschlossen. Die Veräußerung von Grund und Boden geschieht im gemeinderätlichen Finanz-ausschoß. Die gesamte Vermarktung wird jedoch im Projektmanagement vorbereitet.

Es ist ein Glücksfall, daß bei der derzeit schwierigen Situation kommunaler Haushalte die gesamte Entwicklung des neuen Stadtteils hierdurch finanziell abgesichert und langfristig kalkulierbar ist, d.h. unabhängig von den jeweiligen mühseligen Prozeduren der städtischen Haushaltberatungen geworden ist.

Die Entscheidung, ein eigenes Projekt-management gemeinsam mit der Kommunalentwicklung Baden-Württemberg GmbH aus Stuttgart einzurichten und die Gesamtverantwortung für das Projekt bis hin zur Vermarktung und Finanzabwicklung in hoheitlicher Hand der Bauverwaltung zu halten, hat sich heute bereits als richtig herausgestellt.

4. Umsetzung der politischen Vorgaben und Ziele

Wir kennen die Wirklichkeit der in den zurückliegenden Jahrzehnten neu gebauten Stadtteile in Deutschland und anderswo. Heute haben wir die Chance, aus den Fehlern und Erfahrungen zu lernen und eine an den erkennbaren Bedürfnissen der Bevölkerung ausgerichtete Konzeption für neue Stadtteile zu entwickeln. Hierzu ist Vorbedingung, daß Leitlinien mit klaren städtebaulichen und gesellschaftlichen Zielen frühzeitig diskutiert und dann vom Gemeinderat politisch verbindlich festgelegt werden. Insofern haben wir zunächst über Workshops, Seminare und Diskussionen in den verschiedenen gemeinderätlichen Gremien diese Ziele eingehend definiert und dann vom Freiburger Gemeinderat als Vorgaben beschlossen.

Bei diesen Zielen gibt es drei Ebenen: Zum einen die Vorgaben, die als hoheitliche Festsetzungen im öffentlichen Recht gegenüber jedermann verbindlich in der Bauleitplanung ausgewiesen werden. Zum zweiten gibt es eine Reihe von Zielen, die wir über hoheitliches Recht in der Bauleitplanung gar nicht verbindlich beschließen und umsetzen können, die aber aber als politische Vorgaben für uns sehr wichtig sind. Diese können wir über privatrechtliche Verträge verbindlich machen. Dies gilt z.B. für die Durchsetzung ökologischer Ziele. So darf nur an Investoren Grund und Boden verkauft werden, die sich verpflichten, den Beschluß des Freiburger Gemeinderats für Niedrigenergie auch anzuwenden.

Drittens gibt es eine Menge von Einzelpunkten, die der Gemeinderat sehr gerne angewandt sehen möchte, etwa frauenfreundlichere Grundrisse, die aber nicht in einer stringenten Form zwingende Voraussetzung für den Abschluß eines Kaufvertrages sind. Diese sollen in den individuellen Vertragsverhandlungen des Projektmanagements mit einem künftigen Investor als Empfehlung eingebracht werden, in der Hoffnung, daß nicht alle, aber doch ein großer Teil davon auch praktisch verwirklicht wird.

5. Inhalte der wesentlichen politischen Vorgaben

Ein in unserer heutigen Zeit geplanter und gebauter Stadtteil soll ein Spiegelbild der Gesellschaft sein. Er muß aber auch unsere Visionen einer anzustrebenden künftigen Welt von morgen erkennen lassen. Hierbei soll er unser Bild von unserer freiheitlichen demokratischen Grundordnung, von unserem pluralistischen Gemeinwesen und der Würde eines jeden einzelnen Menschen in die gebaute Wirklichkeit umsetzen. Dieses bedeutet konkret, daß Vielfalt organisiert werden muß, daß in dem neuen Stadtteil eine soziale Balance hergestellt wird und die konkreten sozialen Bedürfnisse berücksichtigt werden.

Der neue Stadtteil soll von der fatalen Entmischungsideologie im Städtebau Abschied nehmen. Die verschiedenen Bereiche Arbeiten und Wohnen müssen zusammengeführt werden. Die unterschiedlichen Gruppen unserer Bevölkerung sollen möglichst nicht getrennt, sondern zusammengeführt werden. Die heutigen Erkenntnisse der Verkehrspolitik und Ökologie müssen bei der Planung berücksichtigt werden. Die Gesichtspunkte der inneren Sicherheit müssen frühzeitig einbezogen werden. Die Planung muß offen für künftige gesellschaftliche Änderungen sein. Ein neuer Stadtteil soll nicht nur für den Bürger, sondern auch möglichst mit dem Bürger entwickelt werden.

All diese hehren Ziele müssen in einem gebündelten Gesamtmanagement möglichst aufeinander abgestimmt und optimiert werden.

6. Organisation der Vielfalt

Um Vielfalt zu organisieren, darf die Entwicklung eines Stadtteils nicht in die Hände eines einzigen oder einiger weniger externer Projektträger gegeben werden. Vielmehr muß das in der städtischen Hand befindliche Projektmanagement durch Planung und Marketing eine Vielfalt von einzelnen Bauträgern und künftigen Eigentümern organisieren.

So muß von der Planung her der städtebauliche Entwurf Kleingliedrigkeit und Aufteilbarkeit in Parzellen zulassen. Aufgabe des Managements ist es, möglichst viele Partner als Investoren zu finden. Dies ist für die Verwaltung sicherlich schwieriger, als mit einigen wenigen großen Partnern umzugehen, die dann jeweils möglichst viele Wohneinheiten bauen. Aber eine Vielzahl von Investoren als handelnde Personen mit jeweils unterschiedlichen Architekten, mit unterschiedlichen Finanzierungsmodellen und mit unterschiedlichen Nutzervorstellungen gewährleisten die anzustrebende Vielfalt am besten.

Dies bedeutet nicht, daß bei besonderer Konstellation ein Partner, der ein größeres Kontingent von Wohnungen bauen möchte, abgewiesen werden muß. So haben wir in der Zusatzversorgungskasse der deutschen Bauwirtschaft (ZVK) einen hervorragenden Partner mit einer hohen Zahl von Wohnungen, ca. 500 für das gesamte Wohngebiet.

Dieser Partner akzeptierte die Vorgaben der Stadt, sein Kontingent über mehrere Bauabschnitte zu verteilen und auch in den einzelnen Bauabschnitten kleinparzelliert, mehrere voneinander getrennte Standorte zu bebauen. Darüber hinaus lobt er Realisierungswettbewerbe aus und beschäftigt mehrere Architekten. Insofern ist auch bei größeren Partnern durch den methodischen Ansatz die Vielfalt organisierbar.

Für die Sozialstruktur des neuen Stadtteils ist die Vielfalt von hervorragender Bedeutung. Vielfalt bedeutet, daß dieser Stadtteil für alle Bürger da ist. Dies meint eine soziale Ausbalancierung zwischen finanzschwachen und finanzkräftigen Mitbürgern sowie zwischen Mietwohnungsbau und Eigentumsbildung. Dies heißt ein Miteinander von Älteren und Jüngeren, von Behinderten und Nichtbehinderten, von Einheimischen und Ausländern in weitgehender "Durchmischung". Daher wollen wir nicht, daß ältere Mitbürger oder Behinderte in großen Gemeinschaftsbauten konzentriert und damit bis zu einem gewissen Maße gettoisiert werden. Wir wollen vielmehr prozentuale Anteile von barrierefreien Wohnungen ganz allgemein im Wohnungsbau. Rahmenbedingungen sollen dazu dienen, daß Verbleiben von älteren Mitbürgern in ihrer vertrauten Umgebung zu erleichtern, wenn beispielsweise die Kinder ausgezogen sind.

Pluralismus heißt Abkehr von der Entmischungsideologie vergangener Jahrzehnte. Wohnen und Arbeiten muß wieder so weit als möglich zusammengeführt werden. Im Rahmen einer dezentralen Stadtentwicklungspolitik müssen wichtige Funktionen des täglichen Lebens möglichst fußläufig in der eigenen Nachbarschaft vorhanden sein. Dies alles kann nicht durch Städteplanung letztlich erzwungen werden. Aber es müssen Voraussetzungen und Rahmenbedingungen geschaffen werden, die all dies erleichtern und nicht erschweren. Aufgabe des Projektmanagements für den neuen Stadtteil ist es, diese politischen Vorgaben in hoheitlicher Hand zu strukturieren und praktisch umzusetzen. Die soziale Wirklichkeit soll möglichst mit der stadträumlichen gestaltenden Wirklichkeit übereinstimmen. Städteplanung ist unverzichtbar nach wie vor "social engineering".

7. Ausreichende Dichte schafft Urbanität

Wir bauen einen neuen Stadtteil und keine Siedlung. Neue Stadtteile sind mehr als Wohnungen und Siedlungen. Sie weisen eine urbane Gestalt und die erforderlichen Infrastrukturen auf. Dies kann nur dann geschaffen und gehalten werden, wenn eine ausreichende städtebauliche Dichte und damit eine angemessen große Mantelbevölkerung auf engem Raum vorhanden ist. Die Schlüsselfrage für die Entwicklung neuer Stadtteile ist daher eine ausreichende Dichte. Grund und Boden muß ohnehin angesichts der Knappheit unserer Ressourcen intensiver genutzt werden.

Für die verkehrspolitische Konzeption, diesen Stadtteil an die Straßenbahn anzubinden, ist ebenfalls eine ausreichende Dichte notwendig. Dies gilt gleichfalls für die Ansiedelung und ökonomische Bestandsfähigkeit von Einrichtungen im Handel und von Dienstleistungen. Bei uns in Freiburg ist daher als politische Vorgabe eine Mindestdichte von durchschnittlich 1,0 GFZ für den gesamten Stadtteil entwickelt worden. An der Hauptachse des neuen Stadtteils entlang der Stadtbahn gibt es sogar Bereiche, deren Dichte gegen 2,0 GFZ und darüber geht.

Dichte bedeutet natürlich nicht, daß Stadtteile aus hohen Wohntürmen und großen "Wohnmaschinen" bestehen müssen. Ausreichende Dichte kann auch in kleinparzellierten städtebaulichen Gliederungen erreicht werden. Daher gibt es eine Höhenbegrenzung des neuen Stadtteiles (nicht über 5 Geschosse). Daher gibt es die eingangs schon behandelte Vorgabe, auch größere Einheiten in kleinere überschaubare Nachbarschaften aufzulockern.

8. Verkehrspolitische Vorgaben

Eine wichtige Aufgabe war es, von vornherein die Grundsätze unserer Freiburger Verkehrspolitik auch in die Planung des neuen Stadtteils einzubringen. Eine Stadt, die den ÖPNV mit Vorrang versieht, muß daher für neue Stadtteile die Straßenbahn als Rückgrat und als "Korsettstange" planen. So ist auch beim neuen Stadtteil Rieselfeld die Stadtbahn die zentral angeordnete Hauptachse. Sie wird bereits im September 1997 fertiggestellt sein, d. h. möglichstzeitnah mit dem Einzug der ersten Einwohner des ersten Bauabschnittes. So können die neuen Bewohner des Stadtteils von Anfang an ihre Fahrgewohnheiten auf das Angebot der Stadtbahn ausrichten.

Neben dem Vorrang für den ÖPNV bestimmt eine eindeutige Fahrradpolitik den gesamten Stadtteil. Von Anfang an soll die Planung des neuen Stadtteils fußgänger- und fahrradfreundlich sein. Selbstverständlich werden alle Wohngebiete als Tempo30-Zonen ausgewiesen. Ausreichend viele Abstellplätze für Fahrräder werden von vornherein eingeplant und sollen nicht mühsam nachgerüstet werden.

Allerdings wird kein flächendeckender "autofreier Stadtteil" konzipiert. Dies hieße, die Realität unserer Gesellschaft zu verkennen und könnte dazu führen, daß die Qualität des öffentlichen Raums entscheidend gefährdet würde. Die gegenwärtigen Probleme in vielen Stadtteilen mit dem ruhenden Verkehr müssen uns zu denken geben. Daher haben wir im allgemeinen für die Wohnungen im Rieselfeld Stellplätze in Form von größenmäßig überschaubaren Tiefgaragen wohnungsnah vorgesehen.

Ziel der Freiburger Verkehrspolitik ist ohnehin nicht die Utopie, das Auto aus unserer Realität zu verdrängen. Vielmehr ist unser Ziel, interessante und praktische Alternativen auf dem Gebiete des ÖPNV und der Fahrradpolitik als Angebote zu entwickeln, damit der Kfz-Halter möglichst sparsam und ökonomisch sein Auto benutzt. Daher hat in den vergangenen 15 Jahren in Freiburg die Zahl der Autofahrten absolut einen Rückgang erfahren, obwohl die Zahl der vorhandenen Kfz sich in diesem Zeitraum um ca. 50% erhöht hat.

Wenn somit auch im allgemeinen Verkehrskonzept des neuen Stadtteils Rieselfelds direkt im Hausbereich befindliche Tiefgaragen allgemein vorgesehen sind, so ist dennoch in einzelnen Bauabschnitten ein Experiment für "autofreie Nachbarschaften" vorgesehen. Dies wird eng mit der selbstverwalteten Bürgerbeteiligung auf einer freiwilligen Basis abgestimmt und entwickelt.

9. Innere Sicherheit

Das Thema der inneren Sicherheit ist von Anfang an bei der Planung miteinbezogen worden. Spezielle Sicherheitshearings mit der Polizei, Familienorganisationen, städtischen Frauenbeauftragten, dem Kinderbüro und anderen Experten haben dazu geführt, daß auch hier frühzeitig Zielvorgaben für Bauleitplanung und Grundstücksverträge entwickelt werden konnten. Wir haben umfangreiche Kataloge zusammengestellt, die sowohl für die Wohnung, für das Haus, für das Wohnumfeld, aber auch für die städtebauliche Planung des Quartiers insgesamt den Aspekt der öffentlichen Sicherheit im künftigen Stadtteil berücksichtigen und auch Leitlinien für Investoren sein können. Leider sieht es so aus, daß das Thema der öffentlichen Sicherheit in künftigen Jahrzehnten an Brisanz zunehmen und eine noch größere Bedeutung für die Lebensqualität und das Miteinander in den einzelnen Stadtteilen erhalten wird. Ein Blick in das Ausland läßt nur erahnen, was auf diesem Sektor auf unsere Städte in Deutschland zukommen kann. Aber wir können, wenn wir vorausdenkend bei der Planung die Sicherheitsbelange berücksichtigen, mit wenig Geld in vielen Bereichen bessere Rahmenbedingungen für die öffentliche Sicherheit schaffen.

Dies gilt für die Anordnung der Wohnungen und Hauseingänge, für die Abstimmung der öffentlichen, halböffentlichen und privaten Räume, für die Einsehbarkeit des Straßenraumes und die soziale Kontrolle in der gesamten Nachbarschaft. Nicht einsehbare Unterführungen müssen der Vergangenheit angehören. Die Wegeführung der Grünplanung ist genauso wichtig wie die Anordnung der Parkierung. Die Bedeutung der Bauleitplanung und des Städtebaus für den Bereich der öffentlichen Sicherheit ist viele Jahre leider sehr vernachlässigt worden und bedarf einer grundlegenden Neubewertung. Gerade im Rieselfeld haben wir versucht, hier eine Korrektur einzuleiten.

10. Nutzerfreundliche Vorgaben für die Praxis

Ein neuer Stadtteil muß auch im Detail den geänderten Bedürfnissen und Entwicklungen der Gesellschaft Rechnung tragen. Natürlich wollen wir einen frauen- und kinderfreundlichen Stadtteil schaffen. Deshalb haben wir die Bauträger in vielen Gesprächen davon zu überzeugen versucht, daß geänderte Grundrisse der Rolle der Frau und der Situation der Kinder besser gerecht werden. Der traditionelle Grundriß (ein großes Familien-Fernsehzimmer, eine kleine Küche, kleinere Kinderzimmer, ein spezielles Schlafzimmer für die Eltern) entspricht eben nicht mehr den konkreten Bedürfnissen vieler Mitbürgerinnen und Mitbürgern unserer Zeit. Von daher haben wir Diskussionen angestoßen, die uns zu verbesserten Grundrissen führen. Dies kann in einer Aufwertung des Küchenbereiches, in der Gleichwertigkeit möglichst vieler Räume und damit auch in der Offenheit für unterschiedliche Nutzungen bestehen. Sowohl traditionelle Familien mit Kindern, als auch Alleinerziehende mit Kindern, "Singels" und Wohngemeinschaften müssen sich in diesen Grundrissen wiederfinden.

Deshalb geben wir auch grünes Licht für experimentellen Wohnungsbau, wie etwa bei einem Projekt "Stadt und Frau", das diese Gesichtspunkte besonders berücksichtigen möchte.

Den konkreten Bedürfnissen von älteren oder behinderten Menschen wird durch einen prozentualen Anteil barrierefreier Wohnungen, zumeist in den Erdgeschossen, im allgemeinen Wohngemenge Rechnung getragen. Hinzu treten zusätzliche Überlegungen für barrierefreie Zugänge zum Hauseingang. Von vornherein muß auch der öffentliche Raum in seiner Ausgestaltung die Gesichtspunkte der Behinderten, z.B. bei Straßenübergängen, miteinbeziehen. So sollen z. B. alle Straßenübergänge rollstuhlgerecht durch Absenkungen ausgebildet werden. Bei Ampelanlagen sollen akustische Signale für Blinde mit einem minimalen Mehraufwand von vornherein berücksichtigt werden.

Vor allem wird aber auch die Kinderfreundlichkeit des neuen Stadtteils durch das Angebot an Freiräumen und an Spielmöglichkeiten ein entscheidender Qualitätsmaßstab des Rieselfeldes sein. Daher ist es wichtig, Fachkundige zu diesem Bereich, das Kinderbüro oder den Familienverband, von Anfang an mit Rahmenbedingungen und Wünschen sich in die Planung einbringen zu lassen.

All diese Überlegungen, nutzerfreundliche Vorgaben für die Praxis einzubringen, sollen dazu beitragen, daß über die reine Funktion hinaus bereits von Beginn an eine höhere Identifikation, eine höhere emotionale Bindung und eine größere Verwurzelung der neuen Bürger mit dem eigenen Stadtteil und Wohnumfeld entsteht.

11. Zeitgleicher Ausbau der Infrastruktur

Wenn wir keine Siedlung wollen, sondern einen Stadtteil, so treten über das Angebot von Wohnungen umfassende Einrichtungen der Infrastruktur hinzu. Der neue Stadtteil muß im schulischen Bereich natürlich von Anfang an die notwendigen Angebote haben. So steht die Grundschule bereits mit dem Einzug der Bewohner des ersten Bauabschnittes ab Herbst 1996 zur Verfügung. Im Herbst 1997 nimmt in dem neuen Stadtteil das Kepler-Gymnasium, ein traditionelles Freiburger Gymnasium, das in den Westen verlegt wird, seinen Betrieb auf.

Damit wird ein schulisches Angebot entwickelt, das auch weit über den eigenen Stadtteil hinaus für die gesamte Stadt Freiburg wirkt. Für die Kinder sollen ein Kinderhaus und mehrere flexible Kinderbetreuungseinrichtungen nach neuen pädagogischen Gesichtspunkten geschaffen und damit Angebote im Vorschulbereich unter einem Dach verwirklicht werden.

Darüber hinaus ist besonders wichtig, daß es auch im Einkaufsbereich Angebote im Stadtteil selbst gibt. Die Politik der Stadt Freiburg ist im Rahmen des Märktekonzeptes darauf ausgerichtet, große Einkaufszentren vor den Toren der Stadt abzuwehren. Diese gefährden nicht nur die Innenstadt, sondern auch die einzelnen Stadtteile in ihren Ortskernen. Aber auch im Stadtteil selbst gilt eher der Grundsatz "small is beautiful". Dies bedeutet, daß wir ein

großes Shopping-Center im Stadtteil abgelehnt haben. Wir versuchen vielmehr, Angebote von Handel und Dienstleistungen gegliedert und in überschaubaren Größen zu organisieren. Natürlich wird dies sich vor allem im Bereich der Mittelachse, entlang der Stadtbahn, konzentrieren.

Im Projektmanagement wird bei der Vermarktung Investoren, die bereit sind, derartige kommerzielle Nutzungen vorzusehen, eine Priorität eingeräumt. Mir selbst schwebt vor, soweit als möglich das "shop-house" zu verwirklichen. Dieses shop-house entspricht ideal der Forderung nach Vielfalt und Durchmischung, enthält es doch unter einem Dach in den verschiedenen Geschossen Arbeiten und Wohnen zugleich.

Gemeinschaftseinrichtungen, die Kommunikation und nachbarschaftliche Bindungen entstehen lassen, werden auch durch die Kirchen geschaffen. Unser neuer Stadtteil wird neben konfessionellen Gemeinschaftseinrichtungen auch wieder den Neubau von Kirchen haben. Diese Bauten sollen in einem ökomenischen Geist von katholischer und evangelischer Kirche auf einem gemeinsamen Areal in der Mitte des Stadtteils geplant und verwirklicht werden. Die eigene Unabhängigkeit wird gewahrt, aber in einem gemeinsamen Wettbewerb und in gegenseitiger Abstimmung wird die Planung angegangen. Da die Kirchen erst in einigen Jahren auch aus finanziellen Gründen bauen können, wird es eine Pionierzeit geben. Hier haben wir den glücklichen Umstand, daß Ladenflächen, die jetzt im Zuge der Neubauten an der Stadtbahnachse errichtet werden sollen, aber wegen fehlender Mantelbevölkerung ökonomisch zunächst auf unsicheren Füßen stehen, für einige Jahre von den Kirchen angemietet werden. Von hier aus kann dann Seelsorge und Sozialarbeit bereits frühzeitig mit dem Einzug der ersten Bewohner geschehen. Später werden dann nach dem Bau der kirchlichen Einrichtungen diese Läden nicht mehr gebraucht und stehen der angestrebten kommerziellen Nutzung zur Verfügung. Dies ist eine interessante Abfolge, bei der sich die unterschiedlichen Interessenslagen gut ergänzen. Auch dies wird durch das städtische Projektmanagement organisiert.

Arbeiten und Wohnen wird nicht nur mit einer Durchmischung von Läden und Wohnen entlang der Stadtbahnachse und hier und dort in den Wohnquartieren erreicht, sondern es tritt ein eigenes kleines Gewerbemischgebiet im 2. Bauabschnitt des neuen Stadtteils ergänzend hinzu. Arbeiten und Wohnen sollen, als Erkenntnis aus dem Überwinden der Entmischungsideologie, wieder näher zusammenrücken. Hier wollen wir neben Dienstleistung und Handwerkern mit örtlichem Bezug auch generell interessante Arbeitsplätze in den Bereichen Umwelttechnologien, neue Medien usw. anbieten.

12. Ökologische Zielsetzung insbesondere im Energiebereich

Freiburg ist eine Stadt, die sich dem Umweltschutz verpflichtet fühlt. Daher müssen auch neue Stadtteile unter ökologischen Gesichtspunkten geplant und ausgeführt werden. So sind z. B. die energiepolitischen Vorgaben von großer Bedeutung. Bereits beim Wettbewerb war vorgesehen, daß in der Auslobung die Ausrichtung der Häuser so geschehen soll, daß Solarenergie möglichst gut genutzt werden kann. Hierfür hat der 1. Preisträger einen Sonderpreis für Energie bekommen. Dies ist entsprechend in die Bauleitplanung eingeflossen.

Noch größere Bedeutung im Rahmen der Energiepolitik haben Maßnahmen des Energiesparens. Daher beschloß der Gemeinderat, städtische Grundstücke nur dann an Investoren abzugeben, wenn sie zumindest in Wohnbereichen mit einer Energiekennzahl von 65 kWh/qm und Jahr errichtet werden. Dies wird konsequent für den gesamten Stadtteil angewandt, so daß hier wohl erstmals in der Bundesrepublik flächendeckend ein ganzer Stadtteil diese Niedrigenergiewerte erfüllt, die weit über das geltende deutsche Recht hinausgehen. In den Verhandlungen mit den Investoren wird im Bereich der Empfehlung weiterhin darauf eingewirkt, daß Gesichtspunkte der passiven Solarenergienutzung berücksichtigt werden.

Darüber hinaus werden unter ökologischen Vorzeichen spezielle Konzepte, z.B. bei der Regenwasserentsorgung (spezielle Versickerungsbereiche, Wurzelraumbehandlungsanlage im westlichen Rieselfeld), im Verkehrsbereich oder etwa für die Minimierung der Bodenversiegelung umgesetzt.

13. Bürgerschaftliche Beteiligung

Von Anfang an war uns wichtig, daß bei der Planung dieses neuen Stadtteils die Bürgerschaft miteinbezogen wird.

Dies galt bereits für die Vorbereitung zum städtebaulichen Wettbewerb, als es um den Text der Auslobung mit den grundlegenden Zielen ging. Dies galt später für die Festlegung der politischen Ziele durch den Freiburger Gemeinderat. Hier konnten die verschiedenen Arbeitskreise der Bürgerbeteiligung ihre Wünsche und Forderungen vorher formulieren und den Fraktionen und dem Gemeinderat vortragen, so daß sie zwangsläufig in deren Beratung einflossen. Und so hat auch der Gemeinderat in einer Reihe von Punkten bürgerschaftlich erhobene Forderungen als verbindliche Vorgaben mitübernehmen können.

In der ersten Phase der Bürgerbeteiligung wurde diese zwar nicht von der Stadt direkt, aber von der Kommunalentwicklung Baden-Württemberg im Rahmen des Projektmanagement organisiert und geleitet. In einer zweiten Phase stellte sich die bürgerschaftliche Beteiligung völlig auf ein selbstverwaltetes Modell um. Verschiedene Arbeitskreise organisieren sich selbst zu den unterschiedlichen Themen und erhalten lediglich materielle Unterstützung für ihre Arbeit durch die Stadt und selbstverständlich umfassende Informationen. Diese Arbeitskreise stehen in einem ständigen Kontakt mit der Projektgruppe und haben auch eine Rückkopplung mit der gemeinderätlichen Arbeitsgruppe Rieselfeld. So wird z.B. die Planung und der Bau von 8 Reihenhäuser im 2. Bauabschnitt gemeinsam mit dem Arbeitskreis "Gemeinsam Bauen und Wohnen" betrieben.

Geplant ist nach dem Einzug der ersten Bewohner im Rieselfeld, die bürgerschaftliche Beteiligung in eine dritte Phase überzuleiten, die dann die Form einer konkreten Bewohnerbeteiligung erhält. Gemeinsam mit der Evang. Fachhochschule Freiburg läuft von Sommer 1996 an ein Projekt "Quartiersarbeit im neuen Stadtteil Rieselfeld". Dieses Projekt soll mit dazu beitragen, daß mit Einzug der ersten Bewohner ein Gemeinwesen entsteht, das sich selbst trägt und auch neu Hinzuziehende integrieren kann. Ich verspreche mir von diesem Projekt eine große Ausstrahlung. Es hat eine wichtige Signalfunktion für das Leben auf einer "Baustelle" mit seinen besonderen Rahmenbedingungen.

14. Stand der Vermarktung

Entgegen der allgemeinen Situation auf dem Wohnungsmarkt in den Jahren 1995/96/97 ist die Vermarktung der ersten Bauabschnitte sehr zügig vorangegangen. Trotz mancherlei Befürchtungen haben die unterschiedlichen Auflagen und Rahmenbedingungen die Investoren nicht davon abgeschreckt, sich für ein Engagement für einen neuen Stadtteil mit den dargestellten Zielen als dauerhafter und stabiler Anlage einzusetzen. Die ersten Wohnungen sind im September 1996 bezogen worden. Die ersten beiden Bauabschnitte mit einem Volumen von knapp 2.200 Wohnungen waren bis zum Jahre 1996 mit über 80% vermarktet.

Neben den üblichen Wohnprojekten liegt der Schwerpunkt der städtischen Zielsetzungen in den weiteren Bauabschnitten in Modellprojekten für kosten- und flächensparendes Bauen unter besonderer Berücksichtigung passiver und aktiver energetischer Belange. Ein weiterer Schwerpunkt liegt in der Eigentumsbildung für Familien.

Stadtteilfeste und Begegnungsmöglichkeiten in der Einzugsphase haben den neuen Stadtteil Rieselfeld als künftigen Wohnort mit hoher Qualität noch stärker in das Bewußtsein der Öffentlichkeit gerückt. Die Akquisitions- und Werbepolitik für den neuen Stadtteil war maßgeblich dafür, daß auch insbesondere überregionale Nachfrage entstanden ist.

Insbesondere ist es gelungen, bei der Vermarktung die Pluspunkte für die Niedrigenergiebauweise überzeugend durchzusetzen. Allerdings sind in allen Phasen der Vermarktungs- und Planungsgespräche viel Mühen und Zeit aufzuwenden für Überzeugungsarbeit, um die Ziele und Empfehlungen des Gemeinderates sicherzustellen. Von entscheidender Bedeutung waren aber die konsequenten Bindungen im Kaufvertrag und die Tatsache, daß die Gebäude mit derartigen ökologischen Vorgaben eine bessere Bausubstanz und damit eine direkte Wertsteigerung für eine spätere Vermarktung erhalten haben.

15. Offenheit der Planung für eine ungewisse Zukunft

Eine wirklich vorausschauende und qualitativ gute Planung muß offen genug sein, um genügend Flexibilität für künftige, noch nicht vorhersehbare neue gesellschaftliche Situationen und konkrete Bedürfnisse zu haben. Die gesellschaftlichen Bedürfnisse sind nicht ein für alle Mal definiert, sondern ändern sich zum Teil in dramatischer Weise in kürzester Zeit.

Hier denke man nur an die Veränderung in der Situation der Familien und der Haushalts-strukturen oder an das veränderte Freizeitverhalten, das eine ganz andere Dimension unserer Lebenswirklichkeit eingenommen hat. Auch sei an die Entwicklung der Mobilität mit dem Phänomen Auto innerhalb weniger Generationen verwiesen, grundlegende Veränderungen in der Wirklichkeit unserer Städte, auf die sie in Jahrhundert entstandenen Strukturen überhaupt nicht eingerichtet sind.

Eine gute Planung muß jeweils aus der konkreten und gesellschaftlichen Situation heraus vorausschauende Antworten finden. Daher muß jede gute Stadtplanung in ihren Ansätzen offen sein, Bewegungsspielräume und Freiräume besitzen, um auf neue Nutzungsanforderungen und Bedürfnisse reagieren zu können.

Neben den funktionalen Notwendigkeiten spielt eine wichtige Rolle, daß emotionale Bindungen und gefühlsmäßige Verwurzel-ungen der Bevölkerung zum neuen Stadtteil entstehen. Natürlich müssen zunächst die konkreten Bedürfnisse an Wohnungen, Haus und Nachbarschaft "funktionieren". Aber darüber hinaus müssen Voraussetzungen geschaffen werden, die diese emotionalen Bindungen erleichtern. Dieses geschieht z. B.

durch den Ansatz "small is beautiful", bei dem überschaubare Gliederungen und Strukturen geschaffen werden, in dem sich der Einzelne wiederfinden kann. Es muß eine Vielfalt des Stadtteiles entwickelt werden, in dem Unterschiedlichkeiten und Individualitäten in Wohnung, Haus und Nachbarschaft ermöglicht werden. Auch eine gute Bürgerbeteiligung kann derartige emotionale Bindungen verstärken, weil der Einzelne an dem Entstehen der gebauten Wirklichkeit beteiligt gewesen ist.

Eine große Bedeutung kommt hierbei dem öffentlichen Raum zu. Er muß die Möglichkeit zu sozialen Kontakten, zu Begegnungen, zum Verweilen und zu Bindungen ermöglichen. All diese Komponenten müssen zusammenspielen. Nur so werden Menschen im neuen Stadtteil wohnen, die sich auch wirklich als Bürger dieses Stadtteils fühlen, sich mit ihm identifizieren und die notwendigen und erforderlichen sozialen Bezüge und Anker auswerfen, damit ein derartiger Stadtteil ausbalanciert und stabil gestaltet werden kann.

Wir haben ein großes Bündel von hochfliegenden Zielen. Wir sind uns bewußt, daß wir natürlich nur teilweise diese selbstgesetzten Vorgaben erreichen. Es ist aber ungeheuer spannend, in der heutigen Zeit aus den Erkenntnissen und Erfahrungen vorhandener Trabantenstädte zu lernen und einen neuen Versuch zu machen, neue städtische Wohnformen und dauerhafte Urbanität zu entwickeln. Wir werden manche Fehler, die in der Vergangenheit gemacht worden sind, hoffentlich vermeiden können. Wir wissen aber auch, daß manches, für das wir uns heute engagiert einsetzen, später anders gesehen und bewertet werden wird. Natürlich wissen wir, daß wir bereits heute sehenden Auges unter Sachzwängen und finanziellem Druck manche Kompromiße schließen müssen. Aber ich hoffe sehr, daß unsere Stadtteile, die wir jetzt bauen, ein wenig besser im Urteil der Geschichte dastehen als die Stadtteile der 60iger und 70iger Jahre aus heutiger Sicht. Es bleibt zu wünschen, daß unser Freiburger Rieselfeld einen brauchbaren Beitrag liefert.

Dr. Sven von Ungern-Sternberg ist Erster Bürgermeister der Stadt Freiburg, und Vorsitzender des Program Komittees.

Im Herbst 1997 erscheint die erste, umfassende und kritische Gesamtdarstellung des Projekts als Buch:

Stadterweiterung Freiburg Rieselfeld
Hrsg.v. Prof. Klaus Humpert
Mit Beiträgen von: Sven v.Ungern-Sternberg, Projectgemeinschaft Rieselfeld, Stadtplanungsamt Freiburg u.a. Ca.180 Seiten, viele Abbildungen und Zeichnungen in Farbe. Verlag avedition, Stuttgart.

Chapter Forty-Seven (b)

Freiburg-Rieselfeld

Sven von Ungern-Sternberg

1. Background

If anyone had asked me 15 years ago, if completely new urban districts in Freiburg would be planned and realized in the course of the 90s, I would have given a clear answer, no, inconceivable. The main focus of urban development during this decade lies in urban redevelopment and increasing the density of existing urban districts. Structural alteration has priority over erecting new buildings. Desired is only the calculated rounding off of existing residential areas.

Today - as in the 60s - we are forging ahead with great commitment in developing the new urban district of Rieselfeld for 12,000 and the Vauban site for 5,000 citizens. The reasons for this are perfectly obvious. As felt generally throughout the Federal Republic, Freiburg has also been experiencing strongly increasing pressure on the housing market, especially since the second half of the 80s. In contrast to almost every other German city an influx over the last few decades has led to an ever-increasing population in Freiburg. Decisive, however,

is the continuously growing additional average living floor space per inhabitant. This process is, above all, a result of social changes. As a university town, the dramatic increase in the number of singles in single-resident households in Freiburg is especially high. At the same time we have been experiencing a considerable decrease in the number of rooms being sublet, caused by the general affluence of today and the enhancement of tenants' rights. This has meant our citizens "consuming" a much great area of floor space. This scarcity on the housing market has been leading to the socially weaker members of our community finding themselves increasingly in the real situation of a housing crisis. This deficiency, especially of cheap apartments, is forcing politicians to take steps above and beyond the envisaged measures of increasing the density of existing housing and the rounding off of residential areas; namely, building completely new urban districts.

From these points of view it was a piece of luck for Freiburg that the municipal sewage farm (Rieselfeld) had finished serving its purpose by 1980. This is when our municipal sewage system was connected up to a regional sewage treatment system. In a lengthy and very controversial local political discussion the target conflict in Freiburg between ecology (landscape protection for this area) and social duty (providing housing) was solved with a compromise. At the beginning of 1991 the Freiburg Local Council decided to allocate one quarter of the Rieselfeld area, just under 80 hectares, as building land for a new urban district. The majority of the Rieselfeld area was initially placed under landscape protection and has now even been declared by order as of January 1996 as a nature conservation area.

2. Town Planning Concept Competition

On this basis in the summer of 1991 a prize was offered in a town planning and landscape planning concept competition. Significant here was that the competition not only encompassed the area of the new urban district itself, but far beyond this over an area covering over 1,000 hectares. It seemed important to consider the integration of the new urban district into a larger area, encompassing the existing neighborhood: the protected landscape areas in the West, the neighboring industrial estate in the South, above all, the adjacent urban district of Weingarten. Weingarten is an urban district built in accordance with the planning ideologies of the 60s, typified by huge housing units and mono-structures. This district suffers serious social problems, indirectly affecting the entire city.

Looked for were town planning concepts for the new urban district with its interface zones to the nature conservation areas, as well as the existing built-up areas, especially Weingarten. The competition results are the basis for the updating of the land development plan and the landscape plan in progress, concrete development plans and the relevant green space regulation plans.

The first prize was awarded to an architects' practice comprising four offices within our region which has also been commissioned to further develop their entry to include development plans and green space regulation plans. This first prize clusters densely arranged sun-oriented blocks, bordering a municipal streetcar line running through the center of the area, and which thins out at the edges of the urban district limits. That "extra something" in this draft is that the protection of the landscape is taken into account in that the urban district opens up from its center to the North as far as the Dietenbach plain. This competition solved the decisive question of linking up this new area with the existing urban districts and creating a distinctive urban quality, at the same time providing free green spaces and extensive protection of the conservation worthy Western Rieselfeld.

An orthogonal road network divides the new urban district into small areas, the municipal streetcar network forming the central axis. The important central infrastructure facilities are planned along the East-West line. Building starts with a curved five story housing block, which also acts as a noise barrier to the western ring road, followed by a classical block structure, reminiscent of the highly valued Freiburg urban district areas of the early city development era and includes two to four story town houses. The entry awarded first prize also integrates natural areas as well as small stream courses into the urban development situation. Moreover, this entry was also awarded a special prize for energy conservation.

3. Systematic Approach to Project Management

Absolutely decisive for the further development of this urban district is the systematic approach in project management. It was decided quite purposely not to pass on the further development to a project manager outside the municipal administration. On the contrary, a municipal project management team was established as a section within the Freiburg Building Administration Office, directly responsible to the "Erster Bürgermeister" channeling the administrative resources into new interdepartmental and interdivisional constellations and competencies.

This project management includes cooperation between the Kommunalentwicklung Baden-Württemberg GmbH, whose know-how we have adopted in many areas, such as trust company management. This project group not only involves many offices of the Construction Division and the Town Planning Department, Civil Engineering Department, Building Construction Department, Surveyor's Office, but also the Fiscal Administration Department as well as the Cultural Affairs, Social Services and the Environment Divisions. Furthermore, in very close cooperation with the Planning Office, the prize winners will be entrusted with the further development of the urban development plan and are contributing to the development of the building plans and green space regulation plans.

With respect to political feedback, it is important that an independent local political "Rieselfeld working group" has been established. This meets regularly and is always involved in making important decisions and monitors the implementation of political guidelines. The decisions are prepared by the Building Committee and the Local Council and agreed upon in advance. At the same time townspeople are making contributions to the project management team, on the one hand, and the Rieselfeld local council working group, on the other.

The entire Rieselfeld area is owned by the City of Freiburg. This means that, by selling land to the individual investors, the City is able to come up with approximately 280 million DM

without having to debit the treasurer's "normal budget". Hence, the development of Rieselfeld is a financially self-contained enterprise, independent of the Local Council budget and trust company financing. The important political guidelines are decided on by the local council committees. The sale of land is the responsibility of the finance committee. Marketing, on the other hand lies completely in the hands of the project management team.

In all it is a piece of luck that in light of the difficult situations of municipal budgets the financing for the entire development of the new urban area is assured and safe cost estimates can be made for the long term, i.e., independent of the respective arduous procedures of the Local Council budget discussions.

The decision to set up a municipal project management team in cooperation with the Kommunalentwicklung Baden-Württemberg GmbH from Stuttgart and the overall responsibility for the project, including marketing and finance management, under the Local Authority sovereignty of the Building Administration Department has proved to have been correct right up to the present day.

4. Implementation of Political Guidelines and Objectives

We know the reality of the newly erected urban districts in Germany and elsewhere in decades gone by. Today we have the chance to learn from the mistakes and experience gained and to develop the recognizable needs of a resident-oriented concept for a new urban area. In this context, it is prerequisite that the guidelines with clearly defined town planning and social objectives are discussed at an early stage and then laid down politically in a binding form by the local council. To this extent, starting with workshops, seminars and discussions in the various local council committees, we defined these objectives exhaustively. These were then agreed upon as binding guidelines by the Freiburg Local Council.

These objectives cover three levels: first, the guidelines, which are legitimized as municipal stipulations in public law binding for everyone involved in the construction outline planning. Second, there are a number of objectives which we cannot make binding or implement as a municipal stipulation in the construction outline planning which are, however, very important for us as political guidelines. We can make these binding by contracts drawn up according to civil law. This is the case for achieving ecological objectives, for example. This means that land may only be sold to investors who commit themselves to abiding by the decision made by the Freiburg Local Council on low-energy building construction.

Third, there are numerous individual points which the Local Council would very much like to see implemented: more women-oriented ground plans, which should, however, not be an absolutely compulsory requirement for concluding a purchase agreement. These are envisaged as recommendations in the individual contract negotiations of project management with a future investor, in the hope that not all but at least a greater part will be realized in practice.

5. Subject Matter of the Important Political Guidelines

An urban district planned and built in our current age should be a reflection of our society. However, it must also mirror our visions of a future world of tomorrow worth aspiring to. In doing so it should convert our concept of our liberal democratic basic fundamental order, our pluralistic community structure and the dignity of every individual

person into the reality built. In concrete terms this means that multiplicity must be organized in such a way that in a new urban district a new social balance is established and the concrete social needs are taken into account. The new urban district should say goodbye to the fatal segregation ideology in town planning. The various areas of working and living must be brought closer together. The different groups of our population should not be kept separate, but be integrated as greatly as proves feasible. Today's knowledge of traffic policy and ecology must be taken into account in the planing. Public security considerations must be taken into account at an early stage. Planning must be flexible to meet future social structural changes. A new urban district should not only be for the local residents, but, where possible, also be developed with their involvement.

All of these noble objectives must be coordinated and optimized as effectively as possible in a channeled overall management plan. It goes without saying that there will be many conflicts in these objectives. It is a foregone conclusion that not all of the objectives will be achieved, but that one can only partially realize some of them and that many compromises will have to be accepted.

6. Organizing Multiplicity

To organize multiplicity the development of an urban district cannot be entrusted to the hands of a single or only a few project management contractors. Rather, the public project management scheme must organize a multiplicity of individual building contractors and future owners by appropriate planning and marketing.

This means the urban district development plan must make provision for small units and division into lots. The management team has the task of finding as many partners as investors as possible. This is certainly more difficult from an administrative point of view than cooperating with a few large partners who should each build as many housing units as possible. However, it is the multiplicity of investors, each with their own different architects, with different financing models and different user concepts which will best ensure the multiplicity being striven for. This does not mean that given a special constellation a partner who would like to build a larger contingent of apartments will necessarily be rejected. On the contrary, we have found an excellent partner in the Zusatzversorgungs-kasse der Bauwirtschaft (Building Trade Supplementary Benefit Insurance Scheme), constructing a large number of apartments; namely, about 500.

In negotiations this partner, who also played a kind of "icebreaker" role in the early planning phase, has stated its willingness to distribute its contingent over several of the building phases and also within these phases to build on small lots in several widely-separated sites. Furthermore, it offered prizes in a project realization competition and employs several architects. This means that even in the case of larger partners it is possible to organize the systematic approach of multiplicity.

As far as the social structure of the new urban district is concerned, multiplicity is of eminent importance. Multiplicity means that this urban district is there for all citizens. This means a social balance between low-income and high-income fellow citizens as well as between building tenant and owner-occupied property. This means a thorough mixture of the living and working alongside one another of young and old, disabled and non-disabled, locals and foreigners. Hence, we do not want older citizens or the disabled concentrated in large communal buildings, leading, to some extent, to a ghettoization. Rather, we want a certain percentage allocation of unspecified apartment

occupancy in home building. Prevailing structural conditions should serve to facilitate older citizens remaining in their familiar surroundings, when the children have moved out, for example.

Pluralism means departure from the segregation ideology of the last few decades. Living and working must be integrated as much as is feasible. Within the framework of a decentralized urban development policy important facilities for everyday life must be available within the local neighborhood, wherever possible, within walking distance. In the final instance, this cannot all be imposed by urban planning. However, conditions must be created which promote all this and do not make it more difficult. One of the tasks of the project management team for a new urban district is to structure these guidelines at a Local Authority sovereignty level and to implement them in practice. Social reality should tally with the reality of urban development. In my opinion, urban planning is still indispensable social engineering.

7. Adequate Density Creates Urbanism

We are building a new urban district and not a settlement. New urban districts are more than just apartments and settlements. They have an urban structure and the necessary infrastructure. This can only be created and maintained when there is an adequate town planning density and, hence, an appropriately large local residential population over a small area. The key question for the development of a new urban district is thus adequate density. Considering the scarcity of our resources, land must in any case by used more intensively.

The traffic policy plan to link up this urban district to the streetcar network also requires adequate density. This is also true for the settlement and economic viability of trades and services. For us in Freiburg, therefore, a political guideline figure of an average minimum density of 1.0 GFZ (= Floor Area Ratio) has been selected for the entire urban district. On the main axis of the new urban district along the streetcar line there are even some areas with a density of 2.0 GFZ and above.

This, of course, does not mean that urban districts must comprise high towers and huge housing blocks. Adequate density can also be achieved in small-lot town planning developments. For this reason there is a height limit in the new urban district (not to exceed five stories). Hence, as in the guideline already mentioned, larger units are to be broken up into smaller more manageable neighborhoods.

8. Traffic Policy Guidelines

One important task from the outset was to also integrate the basic principles of our Freiburg traffic policy into the planning of the new urban district. A city which gives priority to a PTN (Public Transportation Network) must thus plan the streetcar network as the backbone and "stays" of the new urban district. The new urban district will develop along it as a main axis. Characteristically, the streetcar line runs directly through the center of the new urban district. It will be completed in September 1997, that is as soon as possible after the first residents have moved into the housing of the first building phase. In this way the new residents can adapt their commuting habits to the streetcar right from the onset.

Alongside the priority for the PTN, a clear cycle traffic policy is to be applied to the entire urban district. Right from the onset, the planning of this new urban district should meet the needs of pedestrians and cyclists. It goes without saying that all streets in the residential areas will have 30 km/hour speed limit. An adequate number of cycle parking spaces have already

been accounted for in the planning stage, much easier than adding these at some future date.

On the other hand, a car-free urban district is not envisaged. This would mean not recognizing the reality of our society and could lead to the quality of public spaces being decisively endangered. The current problems in many urban districts with parked vehicles must make us reflect on our policies. For this reason we have generally decided to provide apartments in Rieselfeld with parking spaces in adjacent, small, clearly laid out underground car parks.

The aim of the Frieburg traffic policy is in any case not the utopia of ousting the car from our reality, but, in pursuing policies of alternatives, creating conditions where the use of cars can be kept to a minimum. Nevertheless, within a clearly outlined framework, experimental "car-free neighborhoods" are to be planned. This is to be agreed upon and developed in close cooperation with a self-governed citizens' group on a voluntary basis.

9. Public Security

From the onset the topic of public security has been an integral factor in the planning. Special security hearings with the police, City Officer for Women's Affairs and the Children's Office led to the early development of the objective guidelines of construction outline planning and building plot contracts. There are comprehensive lists not only for apartments, houses, living environment, but also for the urban development plan as a whole which give consideration to the aspect of public security in the future new urban district. Unfortunately, it would appear that in the decades to come the topic of public security will become an increasingly important and explosive issue with regard to the quality of life and living together in the individual urban districts. However, if one thinks ahead during the planning phase of security measures, it will be possible with a small investment to create favorable conditions in many areas.

This applies to the arrangement of apartments and front doors, the coordination of public, semi-public and private rooms, the clear layout of the street system and social control throughout the entire neighborhood. Subway labyrinths belong to the past. Public footpaths in the green spaces are just as important as the arrangement of parking spaces. For many years the significance of construction outline planning and town planning with regard to public safety has unfortunately been very much neglected and requires a fundamental reappraisal. It is with Rieselfeld that we have attempted to begin correcting this state of affairs.

10. User-Friendly Guidelines for Implementation

A new urban district must also take the details of the changing needs and developments of society into account. It can be taken for granted that we wish to create an urban district which meets the needs of women and children. For this reason, in a series of discussions with the building contractors we have attempted to convince them to improve ground plans to do better justice to the role of women and the situation of the children. The traditional ground plan (a large family/TV room, a small kitchen, small children's rooms, a special bedroom for the parents) no longer corresponds to the concrete needs of many citizens of our time. This means that we have sparked off discussions which will lead us on to improved ground plans. This can be giving greater importance to the kitchen area, similar size for the majority of the rooms, enabling much more flexibility in their use. Both traditional families with children as well as one-parent families with children, singles and

communes should have the feeling that their needs have been met.

Thus, we have also given our OK for experimental building projects such as "City and Woman", which wishes to give special attention to these aspects. The concrete needs of older or disabled persons is taken into account by a certain percentage of obstacle-free apartments, mainly on the ground floor, dispersed throughout the whole district. In addition, consideration is being given to obstacle-free access to the front door. From the start, public areas must be designed bearing the needs of the disabled in mind, e.g., street crossings. It is thus planned that all street crossings should have curb ramps. For a minimum extra cost traffic lights should be equipped from the start with acoustic signals for the blind.

Above all, however, the needs of children, met by the provision of free spaces and playing facilities, will contribute decisively to the quality of the new urban district of Rieselfeld. From the start it is therefore important to incorporate the recommendations and wishes of experts in this area, the Children's Office or the Family Association in the planning phase.

All these considerations to include user-friendly guidelines for the implementation phase are intended to make a contribution towards going further than mere functionality and from the start promote a feeling of great identification, greater emotional commitment and greater deep rootedness with their urban neighborhood and surroundings on the part of the new citizens.

11. Simultaneous Consolidation of the Infrastructure

If we do not want a settlement but an urban district, then the provision of housing must be supplemented with comprehensive infrastructure facilities and services. The new urban district must, of course, provide schools for the first residents. Thus an elementary school has been completed during the first building phase as the first residents move in at the end of 1996. In the autumn of 1997 Kepler Gymnasium, a traditional Freiburg grammar school, to be moved form the North of the City to the West, is to open its doors.

The schools being built will also take on children from other areas of the City of Freiburg. A Kinderhaus (day care center for young children) and several flexible children's care centers are to be built, taking new pedagogical insights into account, and hence make provisions for preschool children under a single roof.

Furthermore, it is especially important to provide shopping facilities in the urban district itself. The policy of the City of Freiburg is to remain within the framework of the market concept of keeping large shopping centers outside the city gates. This would not only endanger the city center but also the centers of the individual city districts. This said, the appropriate slogan in Rieselfeld is rather "small is beautiful". This means that we rejected a large shopping center in the urban district itself. Rather, in as much as is financially feasible, we will attempt to integrate viable trades and services commensurate with the size of the community. These will, or course, tend to be concentrated along the central axis parallel to the streetcar line.

With regard to marketing project management will give priority to those who are prepared to contemplate such commercial applications. For my own part, I can envisage a large contingent of "shop houses". This shop house fulfills the demand for multiplicity and variety ideally, with the mixture of trades and living accommodation in the different stories under one roof.

The Church also contributes to establishing community centers, communication and neighborhood commitment. Along with denominational community centers, our new urban district will see the erection of new churches. In line with the ecumenical trends within the Protestant and Catholic church these buildings are to be built on common grounds in the middle of the urban district. Each will retain its independence, but the planning will be a joint venture with mutual agreement. Since, for financial reasons, the churches will not be able to begin construction for a number of years, there will be a pioneer period. Here we are fortunate enough that the shopping areas which are to be built as the streetcar line axis is being constructed but which, due to the lack of local residents, is initially financially unviable for investors to develop, will be let to the church for a few years. This means that pastoral and social work can be conducted from here by the time the first residents take up occupation. At a later date, after the churches have been built, these buildings will no longer be required and will become available for commercial ventures. This is an interesting sequence, which complements the various interests well. This project will also be conducted under municipal project management.

Working and living is not only achieved by a mixture of shops and apartments along the streetcar axis and erecting housing units here and there, but a small multifarious industrial estate will supplement this during the second building phase of the new urban district. In light of the insight gained from overcoming the ideology of segregation, working and living should once again come closer together. In addition to services and craftsmen with a local interest, it is our intention to provide jobs of general interest in the fields of environmental technology, new media, etc.

12. Ecological Objectives with a Special Emphasis on Energy Considerations

Freiburg has been adorning itself for many years with a reputation as a city for environmental protection. Independent of whether this is completely applicable, this new urban district should, of course, become an environmentally conscious urban district. The energy policy guidelines are thus of great significance. Even as early as the competition it was envisaged that a prize could be offered for entries which took the alignment of the houses into account such that solar energy should be optimally exploited. The winner of the first prize received a special prize for energy considerations. Correspondingly, this has been integrated into construction outline planning.

Of even greater importance in the energy policy guidelines are energy saving measures. For this reason the local council agreed to sell plots only when the investors, at least in the housing sections, could build with an energy quotient of 65 kWh/m^2 and year. This is being applied to the entire urban district, so that for the first time ever in the Federal Republic a complete urban district will fulfill these low-energy standards over the entire area, considerably below the levels stipulated in the Thermal Preservation Order and current legislation. In the negotiations with investors, recommendations will be given to induce them to take aspects of the use of passive solar energy into account.

Moreover, in the interest of ecological considerations special concepts such as rain water disposal (special seepage areas, biological rainwater conservation system in western Rieselfeld), in the traffic sector or minimizing ground surface sealing are to be implemented.

13. Citizen Participation

From the start we considered it important that the citizens of Freiburg be involved in the planning of this new urban district.

This has already been the case in the preparation of the town planning competition when it came to formulating the fundamental objectives in the text for the public promise of reward. This was true later for the stipulation of the political objectives by the Freiburg Local Council. Here the various citizen working groups could formulate and present their wishes and demands to the factions and local council so that they inevitably had some influence in their consultations. In this way the local council has been able to adopt a number of citizens' proposals as binding guidelines.

During the first phase of citizen participation, this was not organized and directed by the City Council itself, but by the Kommunalentwicklung Baden-Württemberg GmbH within the scope of the project management plan. In a second phase citizen participation was conducted entirely on a self-organized basis. Different working groups have been organizing themselves to deal with different topics, merely receiving material support for their work and, of course, comprehensive information from the City. These working groups are in constant contact with the project group and also have feedback to the Rieselfeld Local Council Working Group. One result of this is, for example, the joint planning and building of eight town houses in the second building phase with the working group "Gemeinsam Bauen und Wohnen" (Build and Live Together).

After the first occupants have moved into Rieselfeld it is planned to lead citizen participation on into the third phase, which will then take on a concrete form. In cooperation with the Kontaktstelle für praxisorientierte Forschung e. V at the Freiburg Protestant College of Social Studies a project will begin in the summer of 1996 entitled "Community work in the new urban district of Rieselfeld". This project is intended to contribute to the emergence of a community as the first occupants move in, which is also capable of integrating those who move into the district at a later date. I have high hopes of this project having far-reaching effects. It has a special signal function for life on a "building site" with its special conditions.

14. Openness in Planning for an Uncertain Future

Truly forward-looking and qualitatively good planning must be open enough to possess sufficient flexibility for future, as yet unknown new social situations and concrete needs. Social needs cannot be defined for all time, but change dramatically in certain areas in a very short period of time. Here we need only think of the changes in the situation of the family and structure of households. We need only think of the phenomenon of leisure time, which has taken on a completely different dimension in our lives today. And we need only think of the development in mobility with the phenomenon of the car which our cities were not originally designed for at all.

Good planning must find answers to the concrete forward-looking social situations. This means that good town planning must always be open in its approach, possess room for movement and modification, to be able to react to new user requirements and needs.

In addition to the functional necessities an important role is played by the emotional commitment and a feeling of deep-rootedness of the population which emerges in a new urban district. Naturally, to start with the concrete needs for apartments, house and neighborhood must "function". Going beyond this, conditions must be created to enhance these emotional commitments. This takes place, for example, with the starting point "small is beautiful", a clearly laid out structure which each individual can identify himself with. There must be a multiplicity within the urban district, in which the differences and individuality in apartments, house and neighborhood is made possible. Good citizen participation can also enhance such emotional commitments as the individual is involved in the emergence of the constructed reality.

Great significance is attached to public space and buildings. There must be opportunities for making social contacts, meeting people, places to linger. All these components must interact. It is only in this way that people living in a new urban district will really feel they are residents of this district, identify themselves with it and make the necessary and required social contacts so that such a district can take on a balanced and stable form.

As you can see we have a large package of high-flying objectives. I am convinced that a number of practical beginnings are here to realize these objectives so that it does not stop at being a purely academic discussion and the chances for implementation missed.

We are aware, of course, that we can only achieve a certain percentage of all this. It is incredibly exciting in today's age to learn from the knowledge and experience of already existing satellite towns and to make a new attempt. We will hopefully avoid making some mistakes made in the past. However, we also know that much of what we see today will be considered in a different light at a later date. Already today, under the pressure of financial considerations, we are forced to make certain compromises. However, I hope that the urban districts we are now building will later be judged more favorable in our history than the urban districts of the 60s and 70s are looked upon today.

Dr. Sven von Ungern-Sternberg is Erster Bürgermeister of Freiburg im Breisgau, Germany, and Co-Chair, Program Committee.

Kapitel Achtundvierzig

Ein neuer Lübecker Stadtteil

Volker Zahn and Christopher Guhr

Rahmenbedingungen

Die Hansestadt Lübeck ist Oberzentrum einer Wirtschaftsregion, deren Einzugsbereich seit Herstellung der Deutschen Einheit wieder das traditionelle Mecklenburger Umland mit einbezieht (218.000 EW Stadt Lübeck, ca. 450.000 EW Einzugsbereich Region).

Die Hansestadt ist Standort mehrerer Hochschulen, u. a. einer Medizinischen Universität und einer dazu stadträumlich gelegenen Fachhochschule (Bauwesen, Angewandte Naturwissenschaften, Elektrotechnik, Maschinenbau, Wirtschaftsingenieurwesen, Akademie für Hörgeräte-Akustiker). Diese bilden positive Ansätze für zukünftige Entwicklungen.

Der Ausbau des Hochschulstandortes verbindet gleichermaßen kommunale und landes-politische Zielsetzungen. Mit der Neuordnung des Hochschulareals soll ein neuer Lübecker Stadtteil entwickelt werden, in dem innovative Forschungs- und Studienmöglichkeiten an der Nahtstelle zwischen Medizin, Naturwissen-schaften, Technik und Wohnen angesiedelt werden sollen.

Diese in Schleswig-Holstein einmalige funktionale und räumliche Konstellation auf einem ausbaufähigem Standort soll über die Region Lübeck hinaus wirken. Stadt und Land gehen davon aus, daß mit der Entwicklung des Hochschulstadtteils auch bundesweite Nach-fragepotentiale aktiviert werden.

Der Hochschulstadtteil ist das umfangreichste Projekt für die langfristige lübecker Stadtentwicklung.

Seit den 70er Jahren wurde in Lübeck kein neuer Stadtteil mehr gebaut. Der Hochschulstadtteil leitet somit nach den umfangreichen Stadterweiterungen der Gründerzeit, der 20er und 30er Jahre und den Nachkriegsjahrzehnten die 4. Phase der Stadterweiterung ein. Auch im Land Schleswig-Holstein wird dieses Großprojekt auf absehbare Zeit seinesgleichen suchen. Für den Hochschul-stadtteil sind die Impulse durch das Land und die Hansestadt gesetzt. Diese gilt es jetzt zu konkretisieren und zügig umzusetzen.

Leitidee

Der städtebauliche Rahmenplan bildet die konzeptionelle Grundlage für die Entwicklung des Hochschulstadtteils.

Der neue Stadtteil hat eine Gesamtgröße von 230 ha und umfaßt damit etwa die zweifache Größe der Lübecker Altstadt. Gegenwärtig werden davon 60 ha durch Kliniken und Hochschuleinrichtungen genutzt. Für eine Neubebauung stehen 80 ha zur Verfügung. Die verbleibenden 90 ha sind als Landschafts- und Grünflächen von jeglicher Bebauung freizuhalten.

Die Potentiale für eine Neubebauung umfassen ca. 700.000 m2 Bruttogeschossfläche. Etwa ein

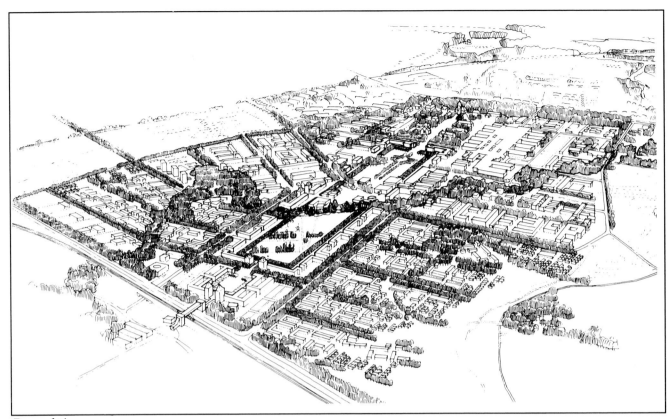

Perspektive

Drittel davon entfallen jeweils auf die Entwicklung von **Wohngebieten** (2.500 WE), eines **Wissenschafts- und Technologieparks** und die **Erweiterung der Hochschulen**.

Die Leitidee für den Hochschulstadtteil ist ein, den bebauten Raum stark prägender "Campus". Dieser **Stadtpark** bildet die Stadtteilmitte und setzt die axiale Symmetrie der heute unter Denkmalschutz stehenden, ältesten Krankenhausanlage bis an die Bahnlinie fort.

Die Längsseiten des Parks werden durch baulich klar gefäßte Randstrukturen begrenzt. Hier sollen die zentralen **Stadtteileinrichtungen** angesiedelt werden. Im weiteren sind um den Park alle anderen Nutzungen angeordnet: nach Norden und Süden die Wohngebiete, nach Westen zur B 207 die

Technologiebereiche, nach Osten die Erweiterungen der MUL/FHL.

Die engräumliche Nachbarschaft von Wohnen, Arbeiten, Lehre, Forschung, Freizeit und medizinischer Versorgung bietet günstige Voraussetzungen für einen "**Stadtteil der kurzen Wege**".

Ein weiterer Grüngürtel mit einer Folge von Teichen und Regenwasserrückhaltebecken durchzieht den Stadtteil diagonal. Er verbindet somit den breiten Uferstreifen am Landgraben im Süden mit ausgedehnten Kleingärten im Norden des Stadtteils.

Die "**Adressenbildung**" und Erschließung für den neuen Stadtteil erfolgt ausschließlich von Westen über die B 207 neu. Ausnahmen davon bilden die Universitätskliniken, deren Adresse weiterhin die Ratzeburger Allee bildet.

Die Hansestadt Lübeck ist Eigentümerin der Liegenschaften. Die Vergabe der Grundstücke erfolgt mit weitgehenden, **umweltorientierten Bindungen** zum Wasser- und Bodenschutz, zur Energieversorgung und zur ökologischen Bauweise.

Das **Verkehrskonzept** hat modellhaften Charakter und stellt die Belange des Umweltverbundes in den Vordergrund. Es minimiert die motorisierten Verkehrsbeziehungen und reduziert die Stellplatzforderungen der Landesbauordnung maßgeblich. Der Mönkhofer Weg sowie eine, von der B 207 in den Stadtteil abzweigende Hauptstraße sind für den ÖPNV (Schiene) reserviert. Der Rahmenplan hält eine Option für einen Haltepunkt der Deutschen Bahn AG an der Strecke Lübeck-Ratzeburg offen.

Die **Realisierung** des Gesamtprojektes wird mehr als ein Jahrzehnt benötigen. Der Hochschulstadtteil erhält somit eine langfristige Perspektive für die lübecker Stadtentwicklung. Durch räumliche Verknüpfung der Kliniken, Hochschulen, Wohngebiete und Technologie-bereiche liegt eine planerische Konzeption vor, die der Entwicklung Für künftige Aufgaben breiten Raum läßt.

Grünordnung und Landschaftsplanung

Eine landschafts- und sozialverträgliche Grünordnung ist Prämisse für den Hochschulstadtteil. Gleichwertig ist dabei die Begründung der Wohnquartiere, der Technologieflächen, der Klinikbereiche und der Hochschulen zu betrachten.

Dem Rahmenplan liegen folgende landschafts- und grünplanerischen Ziele zugrunde:

- Schutz der Landgraben-Niederung als ökologisches Verbundsystem von Ost nach West (Landschaftsschutzgebiete Ringstedtenhof und Wakenitz).

- Ausbildung eines offenen Vorflutsystems.

- Entwicklung von Naturerlebnisflächen,

Der Stadtpark (120 x 800 m), ca. 10 ha, ist die grüne Mitte des Stadtteils und bildet die Voraussetzung für eine kommunikative Erholungsnutzung. Er soll mit Bäumen an den Rändern und dazwischen liegenden Rasen/Wiesen bei Einbeziehung der vorhandenen Knicks extensiv gestaltet werden.

Der den Stadtteil diagonal durchquerende Graben bildet eine gestalterische Zäsur mit Wasser und hohen Uferstauden. Die feinere Oberflächentextur des Stadtparks wird von der rauheren Natur des Grabens durchschnitten.

Die Blockbebauung und das abgestufte Verkehrssystem geben ein Gestaltungspotential vor, daß sowohl in der Gebäude- als auch in der Freiraumplanung Möglichkeiten schafft, eine kleinteiligere, an den jeweiligen Bedürfnissen der Bewohner orientierten Gestaltung vorzusehen. Je nach Zielvorstellung kann eine Durchdringung oder auch Trennung von öffentlichem, halböffentlichem und privatem Raum erfolgen.

Wohngebiete

Der Hochschulstadtteil umfaßt ein Wohnungskontingent von ca. 2.500 WE und zusätzlich 600 Wohnungen für Studenten und Personal. Damit ist der Hochschulstadtteil der bedeutendste Wohnungsbaustandort auf absehbare Zeit für Lübeck. Er bietet die Perspektive für eine langfristige Bedarfsdeckung für den öffentlich-geförderten und freifinanzierten Wohnungsbau. Der Hochschulstadtteil muß daher nach den Zielsetzungen für eine langfristige Stadtentwicklung unabhängig von kurzfristigen Bedarfsschwankungen entwickelt werden.

Die Wohnbebauung ist verkehrlich und infrastrukturell mit den angrenzenden bestehenden Wohngebieten und Freiräumen verknüpft. Sie ist flächensparend konzipiert und läßt sich in eigenständigen Bauabschnitten entwickeln.

Zugrundegelegt ist ein Schlüssel von ca. 75% für den Geschoßwohnungsbau und 25% für Eigenheime (Stadthäuser, Reihen- und Einfamilienhäuser). Das planerische Konzept bietet angesichts schrumpfender Haushaltsgrößen sowie sich wandelnder Wohnbedürfnisse Spielräume für eine bedarfsgerechte Modifizierung, für neue Wohnformen und Eigeninitiativen.

Die im Rahmenplan konzipierte orthogonale Rasterung mit Blockstrukturen für den Geschoßwohnungsbau sowie mit Gebäudetypen für den Eigenheimbau bilden das städtebauliche Grundkonzept.

Die Einhaltung des Programms von ca. 2.500 WE erfordert auch aus ökologischen Gründen überwiegend eine dichte, geschlossene Blockstruktur und die Anlage von Parkhäusern bzw. Tiefgaragen.

Durch die dichte Blockbebauung in Kombination mit einer zentralen Wärmeversorgung (BHKW, Fernwärme) werden die klimarelevanten Emissionen gegenüber allen anderen städtebaulichen Strukturen ganz erheblich gesenkt (bis zu 40% weniger Emissionen gegenüber Reihenhäusern).

Für die Konkretisierung der Wohnbebauung soll ein Gestaltungsrahmenplan aufgestellt werden. Dieser soll als Orientierung für den weiteren Entwurfsprozeß dienen, damit die einzelnen Bauabschnitte, Teilbebauungen, und Architekturen sich zu einer interessanten städtebaulichen Ordnung verbinden und eine eigene Gestaltqualität dieses Stadtteiles ergeben (Gebäudebreiten, horizontale und vertikale Gliederung, Dachformen, Materialwahl, Farbgebung, etc.).

Der Rahmenplan enthält Entwicklungsmöglichkeiten für drei voneinander unabhängige Wohngebiete. Die Quartiere "Nördlich Stadtpark" und "Südlich Stadtpark" sind zur Stadtteilmitte orientiert und haben zusammen eine Größe von 12 ha. Hier sind ausschließlich Blockstrukturen in Geschoßbauweise für 1.800 Wohnungen vorgesehen (drei bis vier Geschosse plus Staffel).

Das Quartier "Wohnen am Landgraben" ist zur freien Landschaft orientiert und hat eine Größe von 13 ha. Hier sind ausschließlich offene Eigenheimstrukturen mit Stadt-, Reihen und Einfamilienhäusern für 450 Hauseinheiten vorgesehen (zwei bis drei Geschosse plus Dach).

Stadtteilmitte und zentrale Einrichtungen

Der große Stadtpark bildet die geographische Mitte des Hochschulstadtteils. Diese "Grüne Lunge" wird an der nördlichen und südlichen Längsseite jeweils durch eine markante Randbebauung gefaßt. Hier sollen die Grundversorgungseinrichtungen für den Stadtteil angesiedelt werden. Die grüne Mitte und die städtische Randbebauung bilden somit auch die gesellschaftliche Mitte des Stadtteils.

Die Parkrandbebauungen werden jeweils durch doppelzeilige Baustrukturen mit Überdachten Innenhöfen ausgebildet. So ist ein hohes Maß an Flexibilität für unterschiedlichste Nutzungen und für sich ändernde Ansprüche gegeben. Eine breite Palette von Stadtteileinrichtungen (Handel, Gastronomie, Hotel, Jugendeinricht-ungen, Schule, Kindergarten, Kirche, etc.), Büros und Dienstleistungen, Arbeitsplätzen, Forschungseinrichtungen der Hochschulen und der Technologiebereiche soll sich in der Stadtteilmitte mit der Nutzung "Wohnen zum Park" überlagern. Diese dichte Mischung der Funktionen soll die wünschenswerte Urbanität fördern.

Erweiterung medizinische Universität und Fachhochschule

Der Rahmenplan Hochschulstadtteil sieht umfangreiche Erweiterungsmöglichkeiten der Medizinische Universität vor (Bestand 160.000 m2 BGF, zusätzliches Potential 190.000 m2 BGF).

Das Wissenschaftsprofil der Medizinischen Universität soll durch neue Studienangebote technischer Fachrichtungen differenziert und erweitert werden (Biomedizintechnik, Mikrosystemtechnik, Informatik). Zunächst sind 450 Studienplätze in diesen nicht- medizinischen Disziplinen vorgesehen, langfristig sollen diese Fachrichtungen weiter ausgebaut werden.

Der Rahmenplan sieht ebenfalls umfangreiche Erweiterungen der Fachhochschule vor (Bestand 35.000 m2 BGF; zusätzliches Potential 70.000 m2 BGF).

Zur Milderung der extremen räumlichen Überlastung an der FHL sollen in einer ersten Ausbaustufe 560 flächenbezogene Studienplätze, in einer zweiten Stufe weitere 850 Studienplätze geschaffen werden. In diesem Zusammenhang werden zusätzliche Laborgebäude, Hörsäle und Forschungsbauten erforderlich.

Der Aushau des Hochschulstandortes Lübeck stellt eine der bedeutendsten Zukunftsinvestitionen im Land Schleswig-Holstein dar. Nach derzeitiger Finanzplanung des Landes sind für vordringliche Baumaßnahmen der MUL und der FHL insgesamt ca. 800 Millionen DM vorgesehen.

Dazu gehören:

- Hörsalzentrum/Audi max, auch für öffentlich-kulturelle und gesellschaftliche Stadtteilaktivitäten.

- Erweiterung der Zentralen Hochschulbibliothek, Verdoppelung des vorhandenen Bauvolumens.

- Lehr- und Forschungseinrichtungen für Medizintechnik- und Informatik.

- Erweiterung Mensa, Verdoppelung des vorhandenen Bauvolumens.

Wissenschafts- und Technologiepark (WTP)

Die Entwicklung des WTP soll zu einer Stärkung des Wirtschafts- und Wissenschaftsstandortes Lübeck führen. Schwerpunkt ist die Förderung der endogenen regionalen Wirtschaftsstruktur.

Angestrebt werden Neugründungen und Ansiedlungen innovativer und marktfähiger

Unternehmen. Durch den Ausbau der Hochschulen, durch die Förderung von Technologietransfer und durch das Angebot an Serviceleistungen sollen günstige Rahmenbedingungen für diese Gründungen geschaffen werden. Dabei wendet sich der WTP an Interessenten, welche primär kenntnisintensiv und nicht vorrangig produktionsorientiert sein sollen. Gefragt sind also Betriebe, die neue Produkte entwickeln wollen.

Dabei bietet die räumliche Bindung an den Hochschulstadtteil einen wechselseitigen Nährboden von WTP, regionaler Wirtschaft und Hochschulen für technologische Initiativen und Entwicklungsprojekte. Es liegt auf der Hand, daß die Besetzung interdisziplinärer Technologiefelder eine Koordinierung von Hochschulen und privater Wirtschaft voraussetzt. Durch die Vernetzung von Wohnen, Forschung, Lehre, Medizin, Naturwissenschaft und Technikentwicklung kann für den WTP ein geistig-materiell förderndes Umfeld entstehen.

Um die EU-weiten Erfahrungen bei der Entwicklung vergleichbarer Technologiekonzepte zu nutzen, wurde bei der Europäischen Kommission ein entsprechender Antrag gestellt. Das "Sprintgutachten" wurde im Dezember 1994 genehmigt und wird von der EU mitfinanziert. Die Gutachter aus Frankreich, Niederlande, England und des Fraunhofer-lnstituts werden ein Zwischenergebnis bis Sommer 1995 vorlegen. Wesentlich wird dabei sein, die Chancen für den Standort Lübeck herauszuarbeiten, sowie den mittel- und langfristigen Flächenbedarf einzuschätzen.

Das rahmenplanerische Konzept plaziert den WTP räumlich an den Westrand des Hochschulstadtteils mit vier Bauabschnitten. Er erhält somit eine optimale Anbindung und repräsentative Adresse am "Stadtteileingang"

mit Anbindung an das städtische Verkehrsnetz und an die geplante Ostseeautobahn A 20.

Über die Entwicklungsmöglichkeiten des WTP hinaus ist ein weiterer Impuls zur Wirtschaftsentfaltung der Stadt gegeben. An den Rändern zum Stadtpark konzentrieren sich die Funktionen Wohnen und Arbeiten. Diese räumliche Mischung bietet günstige Voraussetzungen für verkabelte Arbeitsbereiche.

Die Entwicklung von zukunftsweisenden Arbeitsmöglichkeiten könnte für Schleswig-Holstein Modellcharakter erhalten (Modell "Arbeiten und Wohnen").

Verkehrskonzept

Für den Hochschulstadtteil wurde ein stadtverträgliches Verkehrskonzept entwickelt, in welchem die Flächen für den RV so gering wie möglich gehalten und die Belange des Umweltverbundes gestärkt werden. Der Stadtteil der "kurzen Wege" bietet dafür günstige Voraussetzungen durch seine engräumliche Mischung von Wohnen, Arbeiten, Lehre, Forschung, Versorgungs- und öffentlichen Einrichtungen, Kliniken und Erholungsflächen.

Gegenüber dem nach der Landesbauordnung für den Stadtteil ermittelten Bedarf von ca. 10.000 Stellplätzen für Autos ergibt die qualifizierte Nachfrage einen Bedarf von ca. 6.000 Plätzen (Doppel- und zeitlich verschobene Nutzung). Lediglich dieser reduzierte Ansatz soll bei der Bedarfsdeckung zugrundegelegt werden.

Voraussetzung für die Entwicklung des Stadtteils ist der Bau der verlängerten Berliner Straße/B 207 neu in einem ersten Bauabschnitt bis Stadtteileingang. Damit ist eine Anbindung an das Hauptstraßennetz der Hansestadt und im späteren an die A 20 gegeben.

Ver- und Entsorgung

Die Schmutzwasserentsorgung sowie die Versorgung mit Wasser, Gas und Elektrizität sind problemlos.

Die Regenwasserableitung ist konfliktreich zu beurteilen. Um negative Auswirkungen infolge Flächenversiegelung auf den Niemarker Landgraben und die Wakenitz zu vermeiden, soll die Regenwasserentsorgung durch die Ausbildung eines offenen Vorflutsystems mit einer Folge von Regenrückhaltebecken gewährleistet werden.

Naturhaushalt und Ökologie

Mit der Realisierung des Hochschulstadtteils sind erhebliche Eingriffe in den Naturhaushalt unvermeidbar:

- Überbauung/intensive Nutzung reichstrukturierter Wiesen/Weiden (Feuchtbiotop im Sinne des § 15 a Landesnaturschutzgesetz).

- Eingriffe in Quellbereiche, Reduzierung des natürlichen Landschaftspotentials.

- Der Versiegelungsgrad (Ableitung von Regenwasser) führt zu negativen Auswirkungen auf die benachbarten Gewässer.

- Erhebliche Eingriffe in die hydrologischen Verhältnisse.

Zur Verminderung der negativen Auswirkungen auf Boden und Wasser sowie zur Sicherstellung umweltorientierter Zielsetzungen werden folgende Maßnahmen angestrebt:

- Ausreichende Dimensionierung der Rückhalteteiche.

- Verwendung von versickerungsfähigen, wasserspeichernden Belegen auf Flächen für Erschließungsanlagen.

- Zwischen Straße und Bebauung werden Vorgärten mit der Funktion durchgängiger Grünzonen und Straßenbegleitenden Baumpflanzungen angelegt.

- Begrünung von Gebäudefassaden als durchgehendes Thema.

- Verbleib des Bodens am Baugelände (Wälle, Erdhügel etc.).

- Energiebewußte Bauplanung (konstruktiv-bauphysikalische Aspekte).

- Wärmeenergieversorgung durch zentrale Anlagen (BHKW).

- Gebäude für Solarnutzung und Photovoltaik optimieren.

- Dezentrale Kompostierung, Müll- und Wertstofftrennung.

- Getrennte Wassersysteme für Trink- und Brauchwasser.

- Regenwasser für Brauchwassernutzung ermöglichen (2. Wasserkreislauf).

Zum Ausgleich der genannten Konflikte werden folgende, weitergehende Grundsätze für die Stadtteilentwicklung angestrebt:

- Alle Wohngebäude erhalten Solardächer, der Hochschulstadtteil wird als "Solarstadt" mit bundesweitem

Modellcharakter entwickelt. Auch die Technologiebereiche sollen Solardächer in Kombination mit Gründächern erhalten.

- Ein Teilbereich des Stadtteils wird als "Autofreies Stadtquartier" entwickelt. Die Nutzungsmischung im Stadtteil bietet dafür günstige Ansätze (Unterstützung durch das Modell "Stattauto").

- Der hohe Versiegelungsgrad durch Tiefgaragen in den Blockinnenbereichen soll durch den Bau "dezentraler Parkhäuser" verringert werden.

- Im Stadtteil soll eine "Naturerlebnisfläche" entwickelt werden.

Entwicklungsgesellschaft Hochschulstadtteil

Der Hochschulstadtteil muß als umfassendes Gesamtprojekt betrachtet werden. Die Größenordnung und Komplexität dieses für die Lübecker Stadtentwicklung außerordentlich bedeutsamen Projektes bedeutet einen "Quantensprung" gegenüber den vergleichsweise sehr viel kleineren Baumaßnahmen der vergangenen Jahrzehnte. Nur bei Sicherstellung eines Übergreifenden Managements mit Kompetenzen, welche über die Strukturen der Stadtverwaltung hinausreichen, mit Erfahrungen von vergleichbaren Großprojekten und mit Profi-Marketing ist zu gewährleisten, daß unkoordinierte Einzelmaßnahmen nicht zu einer städtebaulichen "Torso-Bildung" führen.

Die Entwicklungsgesellschaft muß die Interessen der Stadt Lübeck hinsichtlich der Realisierung als Gesamtkonzept wahren. Das bedeutet, daß die unter privatwirtschaftlicher Sicht einzuordnenden "unrentierlichen Kosten" (für Gemeinbedarfseinrichtungen/Schule/ Kindergarten, Kleingartenersatz, zentraler

Stadtpark/ Grünflächen, Ausgleichsmaßnahmen nach dem Naturschutzrecht etc.) von den renditebringenden Nutzungen (Wohnungsbau, Technologie- und Entwicklungsbereiche) ausgeglichen und nicht zu einseitigen Lasten des städtischen Haushaltes führen dürfen.

Planungsdaten "Hochschulstadtteil"

- Der neue Stadtteil hat eine Gesamtgröße von 230 ha. Gegenwärtig sind davon 60 ha durch Kliniken und Hochschuleinrichtungen genutzt. Für zusätzliche bauliche Aktivitäten stehen 80 ha zur Verfügung. 90 ha sind als Landschafts- und Grünflächen von Bebauung freigehalten.

- Der gegenwärtige Baubestand umfaßt 200.000 m2 BGF, die Potentiale für die Neubebauung betragen 700.000 m2 BGF.

- Mit der Entwicklung des Hochschulstadtteils sind neben städtebaulichen Zielsetzungen gleichrangig Ziele und modellhafte Maßnahmen für den Umweltschutz, für ein stadtverträgliches Verkehrskonzept Umweltverbund/ Parkraumbewirtschaftung), für Ausgleich und Ersatz unvermeidbarer Eingriffe in den Naturhaushalt, für ökologisches Bauen, zur Energieversorgung, zur Abfallentsorgung sowie zum Wasser- und Bodenschutz verankert.

  Die Wohngebiete sollen generell für die Nutzung von Solarenergie ("Solarstadt") und der Wissenschafts- und Technologiepark mit Solardächern in Kombination mit Gründächern als Modellprojekt entwickelt werden.

- Die Hansestadt Lübeck ist im Besitz der Liegenschaften. Sie hat es in der Hand, die Vergabe von Grundstücken mit derartigen Bindungen zu versehen.

- Der Ausbau der Medizinischen Universität umfaßt eine Erweiterung des Zentralklinikums, den Bau weiterer Fachkliniken, Forschungsstätten, Einrichtungen der Krankenversorgung und Rehabilitation sowie die Ausweitung des Studienangebotes durch nicht-medizinische Disziplinen (Klinikbetten: Bestand 1.100/Ziel 1.400; Studienplätze: Bestand 1.300/Ziel 1.800).

  Das mittel- und langfristige Entwicklungspotential und Bauvolumen für die MUL wird auf 140.000 bis 190.000 m2 BGF ausgelegt. Das entspricht einer Verdoppelung des vorhandenen Baubestandes (derzeit ca. 160.000 m2 BGF).

- Der Ausbau der Fachhochschule umfaßt die Erweiterung bestehender sowie den Bau zusätzlicher Laborgebäude, Hörsäle und einer zentralen Verwaltung. In einem ersten Bauabschnitt ist die Erweiterung um 560, in einem zweiten um zusätzliche 850 flächenbezogene Studienplätze vorgesehen (Studienplätze: Bestand 3.000/Ziel 4.500).

  Das mittel- bis langfristige Entwicklungspotential/Bauvolumen für die FHL und die gemeinsamen Einrichtungen mit der MUL wird auf 70.000 m2 BGF ausgelegt. Das entspricht dem zweifachen des vorhandenen Baubestandes (derzeit ca. 35.000 m2 BGF).

- Das Programm wird durch gemeinsame Einrichtungen der MUL und der FHL ergänzt, wie Auditorium Maximum, zentrale Hochschulbibliothek, Erweiterung Mensa, Lehranstalten für Medizintechnik und Informatik.

- Der Hochschulstadtteil soll ein umfangreiches Wohnungsbauprogramm aufnehmen. Das Kontingent liegt bei 2.500 Wohnungen, zusätzlich 600 Studenten- und Personalwohnungen (Bestand WE ca. 700/Ziel ca. 4.000).

- Zugeordnet sind Infrastruktureinrichtungen für die Stadtteilversorgung. Dazu gehören eine Grundschule, Kindertagesstätten, wohnungs- und arbeitsplatznahe Einzelhandels-, Dienstleistungs- und Freizeiteinrichtungen, Kirche, Hotel, etc.. Das Entwicklungspotential wird auf 35.000 m2 BGF ausgelegt.

- Die Ansiedlung gewerblich-technologischer Entwicklungs- und Forschungseinrichtungen soll die vorhandene Standortgunst durch räumliche und funktionale Kooperation mit den Hochschulen und dem Laserzentrum nutzen. Angestrebt wird die Konzeption eines Wissenschafts- und Technologieparks.

  Das mittel- bis langfristige Entwicklungspotential/Bauvolumen für den WTP wird auf 190.000 bis 220.000 m2 BGF ausgelegt. Dafür wird eine Fläche von ca. 18 ha Größe bereitgestellt.

- Im Stadtteil werden zukünftig mehr als 7.000 Menschen wohnen, 8.000 Menschen einen Arbeitsplatz (Bestand ca. 4000)haben sowie 6.500 Studierende eine Berufsausbildung erhalten. Insgesamt werden hier etwa 20.000 Menschen in räumlichen und sozialen Kontakt treten.

Senator Dr. Volker Zahn Dipl. -Ing., Baudezernent der Hansestadt Lübeck, Deutschland.

Christoph Guhr Dipl. -Ing., Stadtplanungsamt der Hansestadt Lübeck, Deutschland.

Chapter Forty-Nine

Carpi and Imola

Edoardo Salzano

Two Different Cities, Two Different Objects...

Carpi and Imola are two cities, both in the Regione Emilia-Romagna, one at the North, the other at the South of Bologna.

They have approximately the same size: about 60 thousand inhabitants. They are both very active and rich cities. I am consultant to the City Government of Carpi for the Master plan, and consultant to the City Government of Imola for a new settlement, Quartiere della Giuliana.

I shall illustrate some aspects of both works, because, even at different scales and with different goals (a master plan on one hand, and on the other hand a project for a small settlement of 500 dwellings) there is - I think - a development of the same idea.

...And One Idea: The "System of Qualities"

The modern city consists of houses, linked by roads, covered by cars. It is built up as a continuous conglomerate of concrete and asphalt: behind the houses and roads lie some open spaces - free for children and garbage, often for the one and the other together.

I think that we must reverse this way of living in the city. We must project it as a **continuous network** where pedestrian paths and bicycle-paths link all the sites of social, physical and environmental quality. That means the spaces and the buildings that people use as members of a community: churches and schools, community buildings and sport grounds, theaters and museums, libraries and markets, hospitals and cemeteries, parks and public gardens, clubs and - finally - open spaces dedicated to meetings and to being together, to conversing and to discussion. And it means also the spaces and buildings where nature and history have imprinted the sign of beauty or rarity or memory: riversides and woods, historical centers and castles, panoramic views and archeological zones, geological and natural monuments and cultural goods.

Carpi: The Master Plan

An aerial view of Carpi shows that it is a compact city. The master plan shows what we call "confini della cittá", the boundaries of the city. The choice we made was to indicate that the city had encountered its limits, and that the shape of Carpi is now concluded. So we established a kind of greenbelt, a continuous belt of open spaces reserved for parks and soft sport- and play- grounds, for woods to be established, for protected agriculture and so on.

What we call the "System of qualities" are the public spaces and the public buildings, the most important environmental and artistic values (such as the historical center, the archeological zones, the riversides, the ancient buildings and so on). And you can see a continuous network of pedestrian paths and cycle paths, obtained or in the plans of urban renewal, or by reducing the space for cars in some of the actual roads.

The "System of qualities" tries to bind together urban and country spaces: the spots within the city, normally assigned to daily needs and opportunities, and those outside the city, normally the goal of week end promenades.

Imola: The Project of the New Settlement La Giuliana

Quartiere della Giuliana is a new settlement of more than 500 dwellings. The owners of the area and promoters of the realization are the Municipality and the Azienda Multiservizi Intercomunale (about 50% of the area), and three private and cooperative promoters. About 30% of residential buildings will be social housing.

The neighborhood della Giuliana is located between the center of Imola and the area called Pedagna, where during the 1970s and 1980s was developed a settlement of about 5.000 inhabitants. One of the aims of the improvement plan was to connect the two existing neighborhoods of Pedagna and Cappuccini. The great difficulty to create a real connection is due to the fact that several buildings, lots, open areas, roads are poorly located at the facing edges of the two quarters. Moreover the local municipality has decided to construct a high-speed road North-South and an important school, creating two consistent barrier between the Quartiere della Giuliana and the center of the city.

A New Model of Suburb

Imola's suburbs present some negative aspects such as: a great number of linear blocks and point blocks, out of scale with their surround-

ing; streets with car ports on both sides; one family houses with gardens, separated from the public spaces by walls, fences or hedges; too wide asphalt areas used for parking.

The principal aims of the improvement plan is to carry out a different model of urban suburb.

The new layout tries to combine the rules of the urban design of the European cities of the nineteenth century ("rue corridor", tree-lined promenades, residential courts, squares with built-up facades) with some typical element of the "forma urbis" (townscape) of the local historical center such as the central "plaza" or streets with "portici".

The original dimension and function of those elements are maintained. It would be a great mistake to project too wide open spaces, streets with a great number of vehicular lanes, squares used like crossing or traffic circles.

The Topic Lines

A *main road*, arriving from the South and connecting the neighborhood with the settlement Pedagna, forms the central axis of a "T", in which the two lateral branches reach the surrounding roads, that lead to the city center.

A *"piazza"* is the center of the neighborhood, where the most important public facilities, the church, and shops are located.

A sequence of *public open spaces* (gardens, playgrounds, covered market place, etc.) is connected through narrow green paths, opening the view towards the wooded hills at the West. All the private open spaces of the residential courts face on the sequence of green spaces.

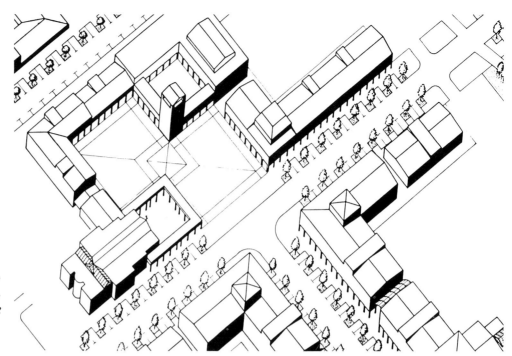

Imola (Bologna, Italy). Quartiere della Giuliana. Axonometric view of the center.

A *wooded park* surrounds the hill where the central co-generation facility is located. In the large safety zone placed North-East of the settlement will be located the high speed road.

The Courts

Buildings are organized around courts. Each court will be realized by a consortium of promoters (two of them by the Municipality). They are actually preparing the architectural projects, according to the rules established by the layout. These rules establish that:

- the house can have from two to four floors, the higher one facing the main road and the "piazza";

- front elevations of buildings facing the main road must be aligned at the edge of the road and have a continuous "portico" at ground floor, according to a regional tradition;

- all residential houses must have brick walls, respecting a regional tradition and having a better maintenance;

Open spaces of courts must be organized as gardens. Not more than 30% of the surface of each courtyard can be paved. The private car ports can be realized only under the ground floor of the buildings.

Buildings of central courts can have part of the floors used for non residential uses, such as public and private offices, shops, commercial and craft activities, restaurants, etc.

The "Piazza"

Quartiere della Giuliana is the first settlement in Imola where is located a central square with built-up facades. The layout of the "piazza" is obtained by the intersection of two squares overlapped at one corner, defining one area as the religious space (the project proposes on one side the location of a church), the other the civil space (a civic center faces on it).

Vehicular roads don't cross the square. Public facilities, shops and flats face on it, in the same way as on the "piazza" of historical centers in small neighborhoods and villages.

The ratio between the height of buildings and the width of the square aims to create a sense of intimacy. The mix of functions and the characters of buildings is intended to exert the "sense of identity".

Main Street

The central street has a wide section, but only the two central lanes are dedicated to vehicular circulation. On both sides are located parks, tree-lines, cycling lanes and wide sidewalks. Near the piazza sidewalks become "portici". Some little shops and stores face on them.

The tower of the civic center is located with respect to the axis with the central street, as a visual attraction.

The highest density of buildings corresponds to the richness of functions. Nevertheless buildings never have more than 3 or 4 floors.

Also this physical and functional concentration reproduces the character of ancient towns. In this way both functionality and a good townscape of the neighborhood can be obtained.

The Green Areas

The new settlement has many kinds of green areas.

Around the neighborhood a great safety zone, partially wooded, protects dwellings from noise and pollution.

The safety zone becomes a real park near the hill of the co-generation heating and power-plant. The park is connected with the residential courts through cycling lanes and paths. From the top of the hill it's possible to look across the whole neighborhood.

Inside the settlement green areas are organized in a series of gardens, joined to each other by green paths. All gardens can be reached from the residential courts without crossing vehicular roads. Traffic calming is provided every time the cycling lanes, that connect the green areas of the settlement, cross vehicular roads.

The project of gardens favour social aspects and are intended to allow the inhabitants to enjoy a sure and quiet leisure. Wider or more natural gardens are situated not so far from the new neighborhood.

Conclusion

I'm not sure that the ideas that we had projecting the master plan of Carpi and the new settlement of Imola will became reality. The quality of both the administrations is very good, quite exceptional for my country. But between the designs and the reality there is always a gap. We hope it will not be too large.

Edoardo Salzano is Dean of the School of Urban Planning at the University of Venice, Italy.

Chapter Fifty

Antwerp Revives its Urban Neighborhoods

Bob Cools

Introduction

In another paper I attempted to demonstrate that a real Urban Revival is needed if we are to preserve the urban civilisation!

- We should all be aware, moreover, that this must be a priority, certainly at European level today and at world level tomorrow .

- We also came to see that cities, like human beings, are founded on a subtle balancing act.

- All over Europe we encountered the phenomena of the depopulation of cities, inner city degeneration and impoverishment and a growing area of tension between the urban fabric and the working of the urban mechanism.

- Everywhere we look, we find a weakening of the urban basis or mainstay.

- So city administrators should try to find one another and look for common solutions. This was how Europe came to have two urban networks, Eurocités and Club des Eurométropoles.

I am well aware that it is risky to try and offer solutions. It gives the impression of always wanting to be right. It is perhaps safer to raise questions and pose problems.

I will now tell you how, starting in 1971, we in Antwerp tried to put "our" theories into practice with varying degrees of success.

I. Antwerp

Antwerp is Flanders' largest and most prominent city, but also its most convivial. It is located in the north west of Europe on the River Scheldt, 50 miles from the North Sea. It is part of the Kingdom of Belgium and is only 35 miles away from Brussels, the European administrative capital.

Today Antwerp is Europe's second largest seaport and the world centre of the diamond trade.

Furthermore, Antwerp is a commercial and transport centre, but also a centre for the chemical and photographic industries. The electronic industry also has a presence there.

Antwerp was and still is a city of art and culture. In fact, Antwerp was Cultural Capital of Europe in 1993.

The seaport of Antwerp has its origins in Gallo-Roman times and by the 13th century was already an international port. By the 16th century, it was a world seaport and metropolis of the West. In the 17th century, Antwerp became a city of baroque art with Rubens, Van Dyck, Jordaens, Teniers and other artists.

However, in the 18th century Antwerp was lost from international view and with the French Revolution it became a "French" city and remained so for more than twenty years. Then the 19th century brought a revival, a real comeback, with the independence of the Belgian Provinces following the Napoleonic wars. We then had to contend with two world wars, but eventually a tremendous period of growth and prosperity followed in the sixties.

All these chapters left their mark on the urban fabric.

1983 brought a major administrative "reshuffle". The city was amalgamated by law with the seven surrounding municipalities with the result that the new city numbers almost 500,000 inhabitants. However, this does not mean that the ideal solution was found. City and region are still looking for the right structures, for the Antwerp region has more than 1.5 million inhabitants.

Be this as it may, the city of Antwerp today accounts for 11% of the G.N.P., 20% of Belgium's foreign trade and 16% of the jobs in Flanders. Moreover, we estimate that while one Fleming in ten lives in Antwerp, almost two in ten working Flemings earn a living there.

Furthermore, Antwerp is a city which attracts a good deal of tourism, particularly from the Netherlands, but also Germany, France, Great Britain and a whole series of other countries.

Antwerp undoubtedly constitutes a part of Europe's cultural identity. Consciously or unconsciously, the city's great past lives on in all of us. The fact that Antwerp was a "Weltwirtschaft" (world economy) or a "Welt für sich" (world unto itself) in the 16th century, to use the words of Fernand Braudel and Immanuel Wallerstein, has of course had a strong influence on us, and indeed still has.

Consequently, our urban heritage dates not so much any more just from the Middle Ages, but mainly from the Renaissance. Seen in this way, our heritage is of dual origin, Gothic and Renaissance. Many of our stepped gables are reconstructions of earlier wooden facades in a later sand and brickstone architecture. This was all incorporated and opened up in a more spacious 19th-century arrangement. The late-Gothic cathedral gives the whole a majestic air. So we owe everything to the River Scheldt, "L' Escaut, ce signe clair vers la mer" (The River Scheldt, this clear sign towards the sea). It is hardly surprising either that the port economy has a prevailing presence and is our number-one concern. This of course affects events in the city.

Today, however, we know that the international economy feels increasingly at home in an impressive metropolitan environment with a reputation for culture, rather than in industrial zones.

II. The turning of the tide or ... of the urban clearance policy

The fifties ushered in the first misrepresentations of the "misunderstood" functionalism. That meant urban renewal by means of slum clearance, by eradicating the lay-out of the city and erecting concrete blocks, not only on the outskirts but also in the 19th-century neighbourhoods and even in the very heart of the historic centre. People only reacted when there were plans afoot to erect three blocks of dwellings between our unique renaissance town hall and the mediaeval Butchers' Hall, after first removing the old fabric with its characteristic stepped gables. For the rest, the whole inner city would soon be turned over to the mono-office culture.

All this of course went hand in hand with the usual phenomena, namely motorization and suburbanization, followed by turning the cities into motorways and the financial erosion of the city.

Moreover, the Belgian system of personal taxation that supplements the municipalities works very much to the disadvantage of our cities .

The non-existence of a proper urban planning commission for city and region has of course meant that people have gone on carving up the open areas. This is what you might call the infernal circle, or the threat from the outside and from within. Since 1982 almost 50,000 citizens have abandoned Antwerp for the green belt, while 25,000 immigrants from north Africa have settled in the city.

1) The regional physical plan, a consciousness raising process

Environmental planning finally arrived in Belgium in 1962 and that meant voting for a law on environmental and physical planning and urban development .

The authorities now wanted to move fast. Consequently the provincial planning phase was skipped so that work could commence at the regional planning stage .

I was asked to help draw up the regional plan for Sint-Niklaas. This mainly entailed looking for opportunities for the port and industry to expand physically, since space on the right bank of the river had been exhausted.

At a later date, in 1976 to be precise, I was made "the person responsible" for drawing up the regional plan for Antwerp. This involved real pioneering work. Moreover, it is true to say that to this very day the regional plan is still the only working document we have when making decisions about land use. However, it is clear that we have now reached the stage where it needs to be revised and should be put to the test on an environmental master plan for the whole of the Flemish region.

At any rate, it is as a result of these activities that I became aware of the very weak position of the city vis-a-vis the metropolitan area. Consequently, I launched (among other things) the "City on the River" planning concept. This was based on the principle that while it is the city's location on the river that typifies Antwerp, sadly, both city and port are growing away from the river. Our objective here was clearly to encourage those living in the city to stay so as to restore some balance between living and working. At that time e.g. 50,000 people were employed in the old inner city of Antwerp, while only 25,000 lived there.

In 1970, as the first ever alderman for environmental planning and urban development of the city of Antwerp, I was given the political opportunity to show that I could convert theories into practice. This required a rapid approach, partly so as to convince others and partly by way of demonstration for the surrounding area.

2) The first "commando assignments"

First and foremost there was the challenge of the area around the Butchers' Hall, to which I have already referred. It is an area which illustrates pretty well everything that was ever expressed on the subject of how to tackle cities in the postwar period. The area is located in the heart of old Antwerp, in the triangle formed by the cathedral, town hall and Butchers' Hall.

There had been a V bomb attack and after World War II this was the pretext for reorganising out of existence everything that was left, including the original street lay-out. A succession of projects were presented.

- Project number one: three blocks of dwellings.

- Project number two: building with patios.

- Project number three: hotel with quality catering facilities.

- Project number four: garden city project in the public housing sector.

I tried to give the final project the form it has today.

In so doing, we allowed ourselves to be guided by the following considerations:

a/ to preserve the original lay-out of the streets;

b/ to save and renovate what still remained of the old buildings in the area and to protect it as a monument where necessary;

c/ to give the area a residential purpose, preferably in the public sector, with a few essential shops;

d/ to apply the planning rule of "harmony with the surroundings";
e/ to build in brick, even using old bricks wherever possible, vertical architecture, pitched roofs;

f/ to create open spaces in such a way that there can be oases of peace in the centre of the city;

g/ to create a traffic-free zone. Only about 234 homes on a total area of approximately 1.5 ha.

I called it "a donor heart for old Antwerp" with all the risks that that entails. I think I can safely say that that heart still beats today. I do hear a number of remarks about "kitsch" from the avant-gardist architecture set, but my response is: "when I came along practically everything had already been demolished. "Hyper-architecture" would not have been right here". However I take responsibility for the project as it is today and I still believe that it was my first successful "commando assignment". I should add that we were able to realise the whole project because the land was owned by the city and we were able to erect it with a housing corporation which also belonged to the city. Consequently, we were not obliged to pay the market price for the land, otherwise I think we would have had great difficulty in getting started.

- I quickly launched another "commando assignment" with a view to capturing another bridgehead. This, too, is symptomatic of the turning of the tide. It was the sixties and in a neighbourhood near the Butchers' Hall the city council was intending to demolish the old barracks (known as the "Prekerskazerne") and to replace it with public housing. I tried to approach the project from a different standpoint, but was only partly successful in this. After the barracks had been demolished, we planted the whole area with vegetation. Only one block of dwellings remained, surrounded by greenery. The rest of the new dwellings were erected according to the existing street design but round the new park, in vertical architecture with pitched roofs. The old existing buildings were completely integrated into the whole. The result was a considerable improvement for the old Sint-Andries area.

- Another project involved rehabilitating the area in the immediate vicinity of the old Sint-Andries Church.

- Next we tackled the historical Veemarkt (Cattle Market) and the surrounding area, which includes St. Paul's Church. This linked up with a project in the area around the church itself in the Zwartzustersstraat (Black Sisters' Street).

Together these "commando assignments" signified a thousand new or renovated dwellings spread over the old inner city, in the vicinity of the river. We hoped they would serve to benefit the surrounding area in a variety of ways. In a number of cases we were totally successful. In other places we were not. The main reasons for this were, as I came to realise, that it is not enough to romantically advocate a mix of functions in the old city, because often the new residents in the renovated areas of the city are inconvenienced by office workers during the day and in the evenings and at night by those out enjoying recreation. So increasingly we have to seal off the renovated districts because of this type of nuisance; a factor which should not be underestimated when endeavouring to bring city dwellers practically up to the walls of the town hall.

The technique we applied was always the same. We put together a brochure outlining the proposed rehabilitation, distributed them among those citizens and users concerned, organised information evenings and evenings for public comment, processed what came in by way of contributions and comment during the course of new public meetings and produced a written procedure. The execution of the project would follow.

During execution, action was taken with regard to:

- the public domain, particularly with the creation of pedestrian zones;

- the housing stock, mainly the provision of public housing by one of our housing corporations;

- the monuments and historic buildings which were listed and protected by Royal Decree;

- improving the fabric by creating open spaces and planting green areas.

3) Urban neighbourhood approach

We drew up a master plan for the whole inner city. It was even ratified by Royal Decree on March 25th 1980. It was no easy task, for here we actually had to turn the tide and break away from a number of situations and procedures which had developed.

The aim of the master plan was of course to restore the balance in that area on several fronts. So as to be able to do this, we had to issue vertical regulations for land use. For example, in certain parts of the area in question, the regulations specified that there could be a shop at street level, but that the premises above were for residential use only. Shop owners were also offered financial incentives for living above the shop. In this way, mixed areas of offices and dwellings began to develop. In other words, living in the area became more or less an obligatory part of urban planning. Urban planning regulations were introduced simultaneously with this first series of specifications for the use of buildings. A regulation about harmonisation was promulgated, i.e. no more high-rise buildings in our city and any further development had to fit in with the existing buildings. This explains why you will only see three skyscrapers in the city centre, "sins", one might say, of the fifties and sixties.

At this point we took a look at all the listed buildings in the inner city and we established that only about forty buildings, mostly large monuments, were protected by Royal Decree. The smaller-scale architecture, the highly-typical stepped gables, the attendant architecture with the lovely cityscape effects, were not protected and, what was worse, in many cases they were labeled as slums and so doomed to disappear or to be dismantled and reconstructed in an open-air museum. I found this appalling. Consequently, a campaign was launched and more than 1,000 buildings and parts of buildings were given the protection of a Royal Decree. So I would even go so far as to say that today the essence of Antwerp's heritage is safeguarded for the future. Yet we must remain on our guard. It came to light very recently that a protection by Royal Decree offers no absolute guarantee; indeed, our very own city council has just razed a stepped gable to the ground in the most brutal manner.

Efforts were also made to tackle the traffic situation. I worked on the premise that eventually traffic would be partially or totally banned from the whole inner city area. Today 20% of it is closed to traffic. The major axis - the Meir-Leysstraat proved the biggest obstacle to achieving this and, in fact, we did not succeed in turning it into a pedestrian zone until 1992, when the prospect of Antwerp Cultural Capital of Europe was on the horizon.

So I believe that the master plan for the inner city is one of the most important documents I have succeeded in putting together during my political career.

We went on to prepare two more, namely one for the south of Antwerp and one for Stuivenberg, a typical 19th-century neighbourhood which manifests the socio-xenophobic problems I have already referred to on several occasions. These plans were not executed to the same degree, the reason being that in 1983 the city underwent the institutional shock of amalgamation.

The old city of Antwerp with its 200,000 inhabitants was now merged with the periphery and its almost 300,000. I became burgomaster of this new city. Our immediate concerns were now of a financial, rather than directly urban development, nature. As I have explained repeatedly, the financial problems stem partly from the lack of solidarity between city and region. In other words, we see time and time again that urban problems arise at a higher level than the purely urban.

In conclusion we can say that considerable impetus was given from the bridgeheads to recapture old Antwerp's urban fabric, at least in the old inner city. A great deal of work remains to be done with regard to the 19th-century neighbourhoods.

III. The consequences of the amalgamation between the City of Antwerp and the suburbs in terms of environmental and urban planning

One might ask whether a municipal boundary really has such a great influence on environmental planning; well, it has an enormous influence. After all, surrounding municipalities often steer counter to the city and they have just one ambition: to suck the city dry. If you remove that boundary and look at the area in its entirety, then of course you have a totally different picture and you sense the kinship more than the resistance. So the whole unit also becomes much more balanced. Prior to amalgamation, the city of Antwerp covered an area of 13,000 ha (including 10,000 ha of port zone). Now, after the amalgamation, the city covers 20,373 ha. This fact and the 300,000 additional inhabitants (300,000 from the suburbs + 200,000 from the city of Antwerp) make all the difference. The traffic situation can be seen in a wider context; there is scope for polycentrism; the need to strive for a balance between living and working in all neighbourhoods is not so great as it used to be. We have a chance to save large areas from development and to apply the planning regulations contained in the master plan for the inner city to the former suburbs as well. In this way the scale and volume of the whole of the new city can be safeguarded.

So the time had come to draw up a global master plan for the new city. The technique and the procedure we applied were more or less those applied previously to the old part of the city. It took a long time, seven years, but it was eventually approved by the council in 1990. The master plan had to serve a dual purpose. On the one hand, it had to provide the new city with a strategic plan and an urban vision, and, on the other hand, it had to issue guidelines for an immediate and specific approach in the urban areas and neighbourhoods.

But the plan's overriding objective was very clearly to call a stop to the phenomenon of suburbanization that had taken hold all around the city and to define the contours of the city more clearly.

Two important features are: clamping down on (automobile) traffic and developing an efficient public transport network. On a tactical level this means that an all out effort is to be made to improve both the quality and quantity of the available housing, with the emphasis of course still on public housing and urban renewal. The "bridgeheads" which were taken during the "commando assignment" now became "rehabilitation areas" recognised by the government. Some fifteen of them were earmarked. They are areas which one might call enlarged bridgeheads, yet which do not encompass a whole neighbourhood or urban area. The problem is, however, that while the city did its job and considerably improved the public domain there, the higher authorities defaulted on their financial contribution. Much goodwill had been fostered and expectations raised, only to be dashed because of the default on the part of the higher authorities.

The global master plan proposes new concentration points for regional functions, it proposes an additional urban backbone, a so-called east-west axis, it draws attention to the belt of 19th-century neighbourhoods and it proposes to plant a ringroad wood in the suburbs.

The suburbs should acquire a character of their own which will reject the name "banlieu" or "outskirts". The various urban areas should gain recognition by building gatehouses which would become the visible sign of polycentrism.

We believe that the Global Master Plan needs to be looked at again, as part of the master plan for Flanders which the higher authorities have promised. An opportunity at last to foster a more harmonious unity between city and region.

Bob Cools is the Honorary Mayor of Antwerp, and President of the Municipal Centre for Health Care and Social Welfare.

(Umweltprojekte, Fachforen, Exkursionen, Kinderbetreuung).

Die vom Seniorenbüro ausgehenden Aktivitäten sollen in das Bürgerinformationssystem eingebracht werden. Zugleich können die älteren Menschen von den Informationen und Beratungsmöglichkeiten dieses Angebots zur Unterstützung ihres Lebensalltags profitieren.

Ebenso wie bei der Agentur für Jugendarbeit hat das Seniorenbüro daneben die Funktion, für die inhaltliche wie organisatorische Verzahnung mit der offenen Altenarbeit Sorge zu tragen, die im Stadtteilzentrum und in den Verfügungsflächen im Wohnnahbereich vorgesehen ist.

Bürgerpartizipation und -engagement

Gerade in der heutigen Zeit ist es besonders wichtig, daß die Menschen Kommunikations- und Begegnungsmöglichkeiten außerhalb ihrer Privatsphäre verfügbar haben, aktiv an den Belangen ihres Gemeinwesens teilhaben können sowie Gelegenheiten und Anregungen für gesellschaftliches Engagement erhalten. Das soziale und kulturelle Stadtteilzentrum bietet hierfür ausgezeichnete Voraussetzungen:

- Es werden Räume geschaffen für Ausstellungen, Musik- und Theateraufführungen, Bürger- und Vereinsversammlungen, öffentliche und private Feste;

- es dient als Anlaufpunkt für Selbsthilfegruppen sowie als Lernort für Bildungsangebote und Qualifizierungsmaßnahmen verschiedener Träger;

- es wird ein Planzellenverfahren als Instrument der Information, Gestaltung und Selbstorganisation für die Bürger geschaffen, um sie in kommunale Handlungsprozesse einzubeziehen und

ihre unterschiedlichen Kompetenzen (Daseins-wissen) zur Entfaltung zu bringen;

- für das Stadtteilzentrum selbst wird ein Programmbeirat unter Beteiligung der Bürgerinnen und Bürger, der Initiativen und Vereine gebildet;

- über die Einrichtung und der hierin Aktiven wird ein gemeinsames Konzept zur Förderung von ehrenamtlichem sozialen und ökologischen Engagement, von Beratung und Fortbildung für Ehrenamtliche entwickelt.

4. Organisationsstruktur

Das themen- und fachbereichsübergreifende Handlungskonzept für die soziale und kulturelle Stadtteilarbeit muß sich dementsprechend auch in den organisatorischen Strukturen des Angebotssystems widerspiegeln.

Für das Stadtteilzentrum wird eine ressortübergreifende Trägerschaft angestrebt, für die ein adäquates Organisationsmodell allerdings noch zu entwickeln ist. Die erforderlichen Fachkräfte aus dem Kultur-, Jugend-, Sozial- und Umweltbereich sollen in einem interdisziplinären Team zusammenarbeiten. Hieraus hervorgehen soll auch eine Koordinationsstelle für die Angebote und Aktivitäten in den Verfügungsflächen im Wohnnahbereich sowie für die zukünftige Stadtteilrunde - einem regelmäßigen Diskussions- und Kooperationsforum, durch das die Zusammenarbeit der verschiedenen sozialen Organisationen und Vereine im Stadtteil organisiert wird.

Mit dem Bau des Stadtteilzentrums soll 1997 begonnen werden; der Betriebsbeginn ist für das Jahr 2000 geplant. Unter dem Aspekt, daß die soziale Infrastrukur mit dem Baufortschritt erfolgen soll und die Bürger bereits frühzeitig in die Planungs- und Umsetzungsphase einbezogen werden sollen, ist vorgesehen, Anfang 1997 einen Stadtteilladen vor Ort einzurichten. Der Stadtteilladen hat insbesondere die Aufgabe, die Bürger zu informieren und zu beraten, Initiativen zu unterstützen, Nutzungsinteressen an den Verfügungsflächen zu koordinieren sowie die Mitwirkung an der Ausgestaltung des Stadtteilzentrums zu fördern und zu organisieren.

Der Stadtteilladen soll außerdem eng mit dem Anwaltsplaner zusammenarbeiten, der ab 1996 seine Tätigkeit aufnimmt, und der insbesondere die Aufgabe hat, die Interessenartikulierung der Bürger zu fördern, zu bündeln und gegenüber der Stadt zu vertreten. Die Aktivitäten des Stadtteilladens sollen von der fachbereichsübergreifenden Arbeitsgruppe mit getragen und begleitet werden. Die Anregungen und Wünsche von seiten der Bürger werden wiederum in die laufende Planungsarbeit für den Stadtteil einbezogen

Dr. Werner Heye, Referat für Stadtentwicklung, Stadt Hannover, Deutschland.

Chapter Fifty-Two

Plans for a University Urban Village near Aberdeen, Scotland

John Thompson

The City of Aberdeen in the Grampian region of Scotland is a thriving "North Sea Oil" city with a requirement in the regional structure plan to provide approximately 3,300 new homes in the area. Six miles southwest of the city centre on the southern bank of the River Dee, Blairs College Estate, formerly a Catholic seminary, offers an exceptional opportunity to provide the new homes through the creation of an urban village.

At an early stage, developer John Muir spotted the potential for an urban village at Blairs and, working with the Estate's Trustees, the Roman Catholic Church, invited John Thompson to organize and facilitate a Blairs Estate Community Planning Weekend, to test the feasibility of the idea. In accordance with Urban Village principles of participation at local level this five-day interdisciplinary community consultation event allows all interested parties - landowners, residents, local businesses, the wider community, the public sector and consultants and so on - to get together (not normally easy to achieve) during two days of workshops and planning for real sessions to address the issues involved and come up with often radical ideas and recommendations.

Blairs Estate comprises the College buildings, which include the main school with potential for conversion to a variety of uses, a beautiful chapel which continues to serve the local community, a museum, a theatre, a library and a variety of outbuildings which could be converted into workshops. Coupled with the 1100 acres of land and scattered steddings, the estate offers a wide range of social and commercial opportunities that could ultimately provide employment for up to 50% of the residents.

The Planning Weekend began with a public launch attended by local people, dignitaries, neighboring landowners and other key players. The event was given a high profile by the Aberdeen Press and Journal stimulating a good turn-out for the two days of public workshops and Planning for Real sessions. The workshops covered such topics as housing, economic development and establishing a new community, ecology and environment. For those unfamiliar with the Estate, guided tours were available so that an appreciation of its potential could be made. Planning for Real sessions looked at the design of the village, the constraints and opportunities of using the existing buildings, getting about the village and integrating the infrastructure with existing and proposed transportation systems.

Immediately following the public sessions the Weekend Team of architects, urban designers, ecologists, and planners analyzed and evaluated all the information and ideas and within two days, gave a slide show presentation of the outcome to a large local audience in the main hall of the College. Within a further few days the results of the Weekend were available in a report which formed the basis of a planning application for the redevelopment of the Estate as an urban village.

A decision on the provision of new housing in the Aberdeen area has still to be finally approved and in the Autumn of 1995 John Muir invited John Thompson & Partners, to hold a design charrette at Blairs to explore the possibilities of incorporating a university campus into the proposed urban village. The Robert Gordon University in Aberdeen has outgrown its present buildings, with faculties scattered throughout the city, and is looking for a site that will provide a residential campus for students and house the Science and Technology faculties.

The design charrette mirrored Planning Weekend process with a short, intensive period of work; this time the consultation process included representatives of the University, the client, architects, urban designers, planners and environmentalists. The resulting scheme demonstrates how these faculties could be integrated into the village together with a proposed Science and Technology Park and has received the public backing of the University.

The Estate offers the University an opportunity to relocate to a campus that has enough space for growth and to be an integral part of an established community. The sharing of infrastructure and a wide range of facilities including shops, library, banks, playing fields and sports hall, would add to their viability and both village and university would benefit from direct links to the proposed science and technology park.

The integration of the three components for the proposed urban village creates a significantly enhanced economic future, strengthening the urban village. A mix of uses gives the best long-term guarantee of sustainability for a new community. The economic impact that comes from this integration in turn creates a major post-oil economic growth role in the local area, with economic spin-off for the region as a whole.

John Thompson, RIBA, John Thompson & Partners, London.

319

Former Military Sites: Case Studies

Ehemalige Militärflächen: Beispiele

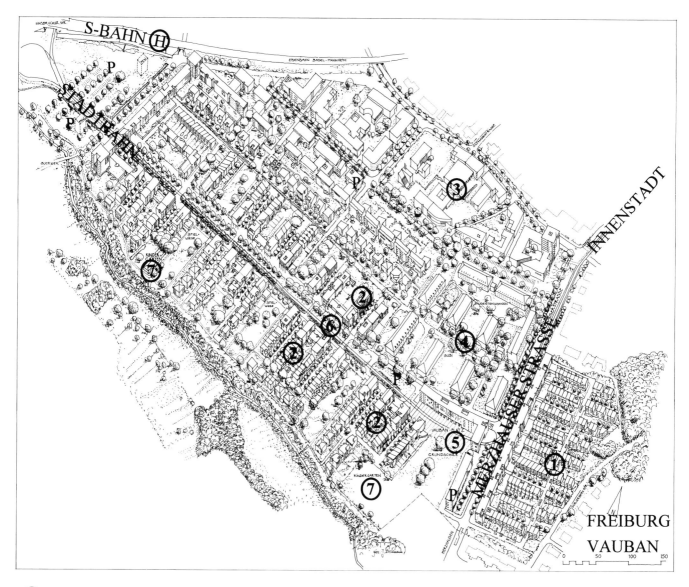

1. Solarsiedlung
2. Stellplatzfreie Quartiere
3. Gewerbe
4. Studentisches Wohnen + Selbsthilfeprojekt
5. Stadtteilzentrum mit Grundschule
6. Quartiermitte mit Wochenmarkt
7. Kindergarten
P Standort Parkierungsanlage

Kapitel Dreiundfünfzig

Von der Kaserne zur Gartenstadt Vauban

Sven von Ungern-Sternberg and Volker Jescheck

1. Situation

Die ehemalige Vauban-Kaserne liegt 2,5 km vom Stadtzentrum Freiburgs entfernt am südlichen Stadtrand. Das Gebiet liegt landschaftlich reizvoll am Fuße des Schwarzwaldes. Hier beginnt die Toskana Deutschlands, wie eine überregionale Tageszeitung dieses Landstrich einmal bezeichnete: Wohnen, wohin andere in Urlaub fahren.

Die Mannschaftsgebäude stammen größtenteils aus den 30er Jahren. Ein Sammelsurium häßlicher Blechhallen kam später hinzu. Die Qualität des künftigen Wohngebietes wird durch den Baumbestand bestimmt: Wohnen im Park, nicht auf dem Parkplatz.

Das Gelände wurde 1992 von den Forces Francaises en Allemagne (FFA) geräumt. 1993 beschloß der Gemeinderat, die ehemalige Kaserne zu kaufen. Die erschlossenen Baugrundstücke werden reprivatisiert. Die Erlöse finanzieren die Infrastruktur, ohne den kommunalen Haushalt zu belasten.

2. Gartenstadt Vauban

Grundlage für den Bebauungsplan ist der städtebauliche Entwurf einer Stuttgarter Arbeitsgemeinschaft aus Architekten, Landschaftsarchitekten und Verkehrsplanern. Die Gruppe (Kohlhoff und Kohlhoff, Luz und Partner, Billinger) war 1994 als Sieger aus einem Architektenwettbewerb hervorgegangen.

Der Entwurf knüpft an die Vorbilder der Gartenstadtbewegung an: Geringe Höhenentwicklung der Gebäude, viele kleine Parzellen, bescheidene, von Vorgärten gesäumte Erschließungsstraßen. Auf dem 38 ha großen Gelände werden einmal 5.000 Menschen wohnen und 1.000 arbeiten. Die bauliche Dichte ist wesentlich höher, als in den historischen Gartenstadtsiedlungen. Aber die Einwohnerdichte dürfte sich nicht sehr unterscheiden, weil heute ein vielfaches der damaligen individuellen Wohnfläche beansprucht wird. Ebenezer Howard und andere Protagonisten sahen in der Gartenstadt die Alternative zur Metropole: Soviel Land wie möglich, so viel Stadt wie nötig. Das Vauban-Quartier bietet Arbeitsplätze, Büroflächen, ein Stadtteilzentrum, Grundschule und Kindergärten. Auf kleinen Grundstücken von etwa 160 m2 bis 300 m2 soll es breiten Bevölkerungsschichten möglich sein, ein Eigenheim zu bauen oder zu erwerben.

Howards Idee autarker Gartenstädte blieb Utopie. Als Siedlungsform aber gilt die Gartenstadt auch heute noch vielen Menschen als erstrebenswert. Das Vauban-Quartier wird ein kleiner Stadtteil mit komplexen Beziehungen zur Gesamtstadt sein.

3. Umweltfreundliche Verkehrskultur

Die Stadt Freiburg stärkt seit Jahrzehnten erfolgreich umweltfreundlichen Stadtverkehr: Fußgänger, Radfahrer, Stadtbahn, Busse und ein attraktives Tarifkonzept.

Angesichts der stadtnahen Lage ist die heutige Busverbindung, die im Zuge der Besiedlung des Vauban-Quartiers ausgebaut wird, gut. Für den Bau einer Stadtbahn, die noch kürzere Fahrzeiten und mehr Komfort bietet, sind die Flächen freigehalten. Eine S-Bahn-Haltestelle ist zusätzlich geplant. Die Nordseite der Hauptallee ist allein Fußgängern und Radfahrern vorbehalten.

Im Vauban-Quartier wird zusätzlich eine altbewährte Idee aufgegriffen: Wohnbereiche ohne Autos, Parken an den Siedlungsrändern. Dafür hat sich der Begriff "Stellplatzfreie Quartiere" etabliert. Gegen größere Parkierungsanlagen bestehen wegen der Anonymität, der gestalterischen Mängel und der schwierigeren Rechtsverhältnisse Vorbehalte. Schlechte Beispiele der Großsiedlungen aus den 60er und 70er Jahren haben maßgeblich zu dieser Einschätzung beigetragen. Im Vauban-Gelände sollen die Gemeinschaftsgaragen überwiegend als kompakte automatische Garagenanlagen gebaut werden. Die Autos werden dort ähnlich wie in einer Einzelgarage abgestellt und durch industrielle, computergesteuerte Regaltechnik auf freie Plätze transportiert. Angsträume werden vermieden. Die Bodenversiegelung wird gegenüber ebenerdiger Parkierung und Tiefgaragen erheblich reduziert.

Private Transporte, Anlieferung, Müllabfuhr und andere Dienste können auf schmalen Straßen problemlos abgewickelt werden. Die Stellplätze liegen 50 - 300 m von den Wohnungen entfernt. In den Wohnstraßen gibt es keine öffentlichen Parkplätze. Besucher können nur gebührenpflichtig parken, entweder in den Garagenanlagen oder auf der Hauptallee. Der öffentliche Raum dient dem sozialen Leben. Nach dem Mischungsprinzip sind in den Wohnstraßen alle Nutzer gleichberechtigt und haben aufeinander Rücksicht zu nehmen. Die stellplatzfreien Quartiere erlauben noch weitergehende Ziele: Wohnen für Menschen ohne eigenes Auto. Für diesen Fall werden Flächen reserviert, um Stellplätze später nachrüsten zu können.

Dadurch, daß alle Häuser mit Fahrzeugen erreichbar sind, ist prinzipiell auch konventionelles Parken auf dem eigenen Grundstück möglich, falls sich das Konzept der stellplatzfreien Quartiere nicht bewährt. Der öffentliche Raum hat sich in allen Epochen den wandelnden gesellschaftlichen Bedürfnissen anpassen müssen. Flexibilität ist deshalb eine Grundforderung an Stadtsysteme.

4. Stadtökologie

Das Flächenwachstum der Städte und Dörfer wird vielfach als Zersiedlung angeprangert. Der Verzicht auf neue Siedlungsflächen hat sich aber als nicht sozialverträglich herausgestellt: Horrend gestiegene Mieten und Bodenpreise auf der einen Seite, zunehmender Protest gegen die Nachverdichtung der bestehenden Stadtteile auf der anderen Seite sind die Folge.

Für das Vauban-Quartier kann glücklicherweise eine bereits besiedelte Fläche umgenutzt werden, so daß schon vom Ansatz eine günstige Öko-Bilanz gezogen werden kann. Neue Wege beschreitet die Stadt Freiburg mit der Regenwasserableitung. Wegen der ungünstigen Bodenqualität und der dichten Bauweise kann auf dem Baugrundstück nicht versickert werden. Die Fachingenieure haben deshalb ein System aus Rinnen und Gräben ersonnen, in denen das

Wasser gesammelt wird und durch den Einbau von Rigolen (Kiespackungen) über die belebte Bodenschicht einwandfrei ins Grundwasser gelangt.

5. Niedrigenergiebauweise und Solarsiedlung

Der Energieverbrauch und Schadstoffausstoß werden durch Nahwärmeversorgung, Niedrigenergiebauweise und Solaranlagen begrenzt. Wohngebäude haben im gesamten Vauban-Gelände die Energiekennzahl von 65 kW/qm und Jahr einzuhalten. Nach dem Rieselfeld wird auch der zweite neue Freiburger Stadtteil mit deutlich besserem Energiestandard gebaut, als es der Gesetzgeber verlangt.

Doch selbst dieser Standard soll in Teilbereichen überboten werden: Die Stadt Freiburg verhandelt mit einem Investor, der auf dem ehemaligen Kasernensportplatz östlich der Merzhauser Straße eine Solarsiedlung bauen will. Den Verkehrslärm soll ein langes, gut gegliedertes "Sonnenschiff" abhalten. Im Erdgeschoß sind Läden, in den beiden folgenden Geschossen Gewerberäume und Wohnungen geplant. Darüber sollen südorientierte Maisonette-Wohnungen quer zur Längsachse des Sonnenschiffs aufgesetzt werden. Auf der ruhigen Seite sind zwei- und dreigeschossige Reihenhäuser vorgesehen. Die Solarsiedlung wird im Passivhausstandard gebaut. Der Heizenergiebedarf wird bei 15 KW/qm und Jahr liegen. Aktive Solarelemente machen aus den Passivhäusern Plusenergiehäuser. Über das Jahr gerechnet sollen die Häuser mehr Energie erzeugen als sie verbrauchen. Dieser hervorragende Energiestandard würde auf 20% der Wohnfläche des Vauban-Geländes realisiert werden.

Auch zahlreiche private Bauherren haben signalisiert, Passivhäuser bauen zu wollen. Die dafür optimale Nord-Süd-Orientierung ist auf über 50% der Grundstücksflächen gegeben. Die reine Lehre ausschließlicher Nord-Süd-Orientierung halten wir aber nicht für vertretbar. Die planerisch erwünschte Öffnung des Quartiers nach Süden zur Landschaft erfordert auch Ost-West orientierte Häuser. Damit wird zugleich klimatischen Belangen Rechnung getragen und ein abwechslungsreiches Stadtbild erzeugt.

6. Partizipation durch das Forum Vauban e.V.

Partizipation begleitet die Stadtplanung seit den späten 60er Jahren als politische Forderung. Ursprünglich war sie Betroffenenbeteiligung, meist in Sanierungsgebieten.

Bei der Planung neuer Stadtteile gibt es noch keine Betroffenen. Deshalb hat die Stadt Freiburg selbst die Partizipation künftiger Bewohner sowie fachlich oder bürgerschaftlich interessierter Menschen ins Leben gerufen. Das Forum Vauban e.V. hat sich als Träger der Partizipation angeboten und seit anderthalb Jahren effektiv und professionell gearbeitet. Mit fachlicher Kompetenz und politischem Geschick hat das Forum Vauban e.V. vor allem auf die Themen Verkehr, Energie, Entwässerung und Quartiersmitte Einfluß genommen. Die Chancen, die im städtebaulichen Entwurf angelegt sind, wurden nach unserer Einschätzung durch die Partizipation weiter entfaltet. Grenzen der Einflußnahme sind aber dort, wo übergeordnete Interessen tangiert werden oder Einzelaspekte derart überzogen werden sollen, daß andere Belange ins Hintertreffen geraten.

Künftig wird das Forum Vauban eine maßgebliche Rolle bei der Organisation von Baugruppen und Bauherrengemeinschaften spielen. Das Ziel einer kleinparzellierten Grundstücksvergabe ist auch Grundsatz der Stadtverwaltung. Gemeinsames Ziel von Stadt und Forum ist es, die kleinen Kräfte im Vauban-Quartier zu stärken. Demokratie und Pluralismus sollen sich in Vielfalt und Kleinteiligkeit der Formen ausdrücken. Deshalb muß das stadtplanerische Konzept für die Zukunft offen und flexibel bleiben.

7. UN-Konferenz Habitat II

Das Projekt Vauban wurde vom Deutschen Nationalkomitee Habitat II für die gleichnamige UN-Konferenz, die Anfang Juni 1996 in Istanbul stattfand, ausgewählt. Unter der Leitidee "Nachhaltige Siedlungen in einer zur Verstädterung strebenden Welt" gilt Vauban als Modell für best practises. Der methodische Ansatz der lernenden Planung, das planerische Gesamtkonzept und der kooperative Planungsprozeß mit dem Forum Vauban e.V. haben dieses erfreuliche Echo hervorgerufen.

Mit den harten Realitäten der riesigen Metropolen in der dritten Welt wollen wir uns redlicherweise nicht messen. Die Fragestellung, ob Autos in automatischen Parkregalen oder in Tiefgaragen abgestellt werden sollen, mag angesichts hygienischer Mängel in zahlreichen Millionenstädten unwesentlich erscheinen. Habitat II sollte uns glückliche Bewohner des reichen Nordens zur Bescheidenheit mahnen. Bauliche Dichte, Mischung von Wohnen und Arbeiten, hohe städtische Freiraumqualitäten, lokale soziale Netze, Priorität des öffentlichen Nahverkehrs, sparsamer Umgang mit Wasser und fossiler Energie sowie Nutzung der Wind- und Sonnenkraft sind wesentliche Elemente nachhaltiger Stadtentwicklung.

Dr. Sven von Ungern-Sternberg ist Erster Bürgermeister der Stadt Freiburg, und Vorsitzender des Program Komittees.

Volker Jeschek Dipl. Ing. ist Architekt in dem Stadtplanungsamt, Freiburg, Deutschland.

Freiburg, Vauban-Gelände
Verkehrs- und Parkierungskonzept, Stand August 1995

Hans Billinger

Günstige Lage des Vauban-Geländes in der Stadt Freiburg - hohe städtebauliche Dichte ist anzustreben

Das Vauban-Gelände

- liegt nur 3 km von der Innenstadt entfernt, also in günstiger Fahrrad Entfernung,

- hat guten Anschluß über eine Buslinie,

- verfügt über die Aussicht, beim öffentlichen Verkehr durch Stadtbahn und S-Bahn in vorzügliche Erschließungsqualität aufzurücken,

- bietet nahebei hohe Freiflächen- und Erholungsqualitäten,

- weist eine Vielzahl von städtischer Infrastruktur in der Umgebung auf und

- läßt innerhalb von Fußgänger- und Fahrrad-Entfernung viele Arbeitsplätze finden.

Bei diesen Rahmenbedingungen empfiehlt es sich, möglichst hohe Städtebauliche Dichte anzustreben, aus ökonomischen und ökologischen Erwägungen. Wohnungen hier

- verursachen, im Unterschied zu Baugebieten weiter draußen, geringere

städtebauliche und verkehrstechnische Erschließungskosten,

- bringen eine höhere Auslastung der bestehenden und geplanten Verbindungen des öffentlichen Verkehrs,

- bieten bessere Chancen einer Verkehrsmittelwahl der Bewohner zugunsten der Verkehrsmittel des Umweltverbundes und

- mindern ganz allgemein den Energieverbrauch für den motorisierten Verkehr, also der Summe von Autoverkehr und öffentlichen Verkehr.

Hervorragende Wohnqualität bei hoher städtebaulicher Dichte läßt sich nur erreichen, wenn es gelingt, die Belästigungen und den Flächenverbrauch für den Autoverkehr zu minimieren.

Lösungsansätze Verkehr

Im Sinne dieser Grundgedanken sind als verkehrsplanerische Ansätze zu nennen:

- Der stadtplanerischen Pflege der Fußgänger- und Radverbindungen inner-halb des Wohngebietes und im Anschluß an das Umland gebührt hoher Rang.

- Dazu gehört ergänzend die nahe Ansiedlung - also in Fußgängerentfernung und in Radentfernung - von Einzelhandel, Dienstleistungen und Arbeitsplätzen.

- Die Buserschließung und die spätere Stadtbahn sind im Schwerpunkt des Wohngebietes geplant.

- Verkehrssicherheit: weite Bewegungsräume für Kinder, Behinderte und Alte sollen bei der Abwägung hohes Gewicht gewinnen können, gegenüber der Bequemlichkeit der Autonutzung.

- Schutz der Wohnungen vor Lärm und Abgasen des Autoverkehrs: außerdem sollen große autoverkehrsarme Pufferzonen in Abwägung stehen mit der nahen Autoverfügbarkeit.

- Die Erregbarkeit des Wohngebietes mit Pkw soll mengenmäßig nicht begrenzt sein. Das heißt für das Parkierungskonzept, daß es für den Wohnbereich keine Verknappung des Parkstandsangebotes geben soll.

- Kfz-Fahrten der Notdienste und des Serviceverkehrs sowie Ver- und Entsorgungsfahrten mit Lkw sind zu gewährleisten.

Mehr Wahlfreiheit für die Wohnungsqualität

Ein neues Angebot an Wohngebietstypen: autoverkehrsarm, Parken nur am Rand

Die Praxis der Anwendung der Landesbauordnung definiert die Grenze der "zumutbaren" Entfernung von der Wohnung zum Stellplatz bei 300 m. Nach der herkömmlicher Auffassung der Bauträger und Vermerkter von Wohnungen erwarten Bauherren und Mieter eines Wohngebietes die Autostellplätze jedoch näher an den Wohnungen. Gehentfernungen

von 100 m oder 200 m werden - dieser Auffassung zufolge - als nicht mehr akzeptabel angesehen. Dementsprechend sind in der Vergangenheit auch immer nur relativ eng begrenzte autoverkehrsfreie Wohnquartiere gebaut worden und alle Wohnungen bleiben im nahen oder mittleren Einwirkungsbereich von Lärm und Abgasen des Autoverkehrs.

An der herkömmlichen Auffassung sind jedoch Zweifel angebracht: Zu erwarten ist, daß es ein nennenswertes Potential an Bauherren und Mietern gibt, die einem weiten Autoreifen Bewegungsraum ihrer Kinder und einem großen Abstand ihrer Wohnungen zu Lärm und Abgasen des Autoverkehrs den Vorrang geben, vor nahe angeordneten Autostellplätzen.

Zum Potential dieser Nachfrage zählen:

a) diejenigen Haushalte, die bewußt ohne (eigenes) Auto leben wollen. In einer Stadt der Größe von Freiburg haben 35 bis 40% der Haushalte kein Auto, das sind rund 40 000 Bürgerinnen und Bürger. Ein Teil davon hat sich ganz bewußt gegen ein eigenes Auto entschieden. Das Modellgebiet Bremen-Hollerland belegt dies. Dort finden sich 230 Haushalte zusammen, die sich verpflichten, kein eigenes Auto besitzen zu wollen. Dies an einem Standort der deutlich ungünstigere Lagebedingungen für ein Leben ohne Auto als das Vauban-Gelände bietet.

b) Haushalte, die über ein Auto verfügen wollen, die Stellplatz-Entfernung aber bewußt nachrangiger sehen, als es der konventionellen Auffassung entspricht.

Wie oben ausgeführt, gibt es allerdings auf dem Wohnungsmarkt keine Wohngebietstypen, die im Sinne dieser Gruppen weniger auto-orientiert angelegt sind. Für die Gruppe b) gibt es also keine Chance, durch das Abstellen ihres Autos weiter entfernt von der Wohnung in einem autoverkehrsarmen Wohngebiet leben zu können und, noch gravierender, die Gruppe a) kann derzeit aus ihrem persönlichen Autoverzicht überhaupt keinen Gewinn für ihre Wohn- und Umweltqualitäten ziehen.

In einer Repräsentativerhebung hat das Institut für angewandte Sozialwissenschaft (INFAS) Januar/Februar 1995 in Berlin 1 093 ausgewählte Personen unter anderem zum Thema autofreies/autoarmes Wohnen befragt. Die Ergebnisse zu Interesse, Akzeptanz und Voraussetzungen sind zusammengefaßt im Anhang aufgenommen. Danach kann - wenn die Einatzbedingungen des Autos in einem Wohnquartier mit Konsequenz neu definiert sind - mit einem hohen Interesse an dem neuen autoverkehrsarmen Wohngebietstyp gerechnet werden. Gleichermaßen berichtet das Forum Vauban e. V. vor Ort aus Freiburg.

Ein autoarmes Wohnquartier hat ökologische und ökonomische Vorteile nicht nur für die Bewohner, sondern für die ganze Stadt

Der Verzicht seiner Bürger auf ein eigenes Auto und die Akzeptanz einer größeren Entfernung zwischen der Wohnung und dem Autostell-platz betreffen nicht nur persönliche Belange der Bauherren und Mieter, sondern sie nützen auch der Stadt insgesamt in erheblichem Umfang:

- Bürger ohne eigenes Auto haben eine Mobilitätskultur mit dem Ergebnis:

    - weniger Verkehrsgefährdungen geht auf die Mitbewohner aus,
    - Energieverbrauch, Verkehrslärm und Schadgasemission sind geringer,
    - die Stadt spart an Baukosten und Unterhaltskosten für Fahrbahnen,
    - die öffentlichen Verkehrsmittel erfahren eine höhere Auslastung,

- die Bürger haben eine stärkere Ortsbindung; Versorgungs-, Kultur und Freizeitangebote im Stadtgebiet werden mehr benutzt.

- Bürger, die es (wegen der damit verbundenen persönlichen Vorteile) vorziehen, ihr Auto von ihrer Wohnung 200 m oder 300 m entfernt zu parken, benutzen ihr Auto überlegter und weniger häufig. Ihre Mobilitätskultur (und die damit verbundenen Vorteile für ihre Mitbürger) nähert sich denen der Bürger ohne eigenes Auto.

"Lernende Planung" als Weg für die Erprobung

So liegt es auch im Interesse der gesamten Stadt Freiburg, die Möglichkeiten eines neuen Verkehrs- und Parkierungskonzeptes auszuloten und es drängt sich die Idee auf, mit dem Schaffen einer größeren Wahlfreiheit im Wohnungsbau praktisch zu erkunden, wieviele Bürger an einem Stadtquartier interessiert sind, das sich einen Schritt weiter vom Auto befreit als üblich.

Der Bebauungsplan bietet also Wahlfreiheit für die Wohnungsqualität:

Bereich A: Östlich der Merzhauser Straße gibt es die herkömmliche Zuordnung der Autostellplätze zu den Wohnungen, in Tiefgaragen und in Parkdecks an der Merzhauser Straße gelegen (rund 1 100 Ew, 20%).

Bereich B: Im westlichen Teil gibt es 4 Quartiere mit den Autostellplätzen für etwa ein Viertel deren Wohnungen in/am Haus und für etwa drei Viertel der Wohnungen mit den Autostellplätzen am Rand des Wohngebietes mit herkömmlichen Stellplatz-Entfernungen zwischen 30 m und 200 m (rund 2 400 Ew., 50%).

Bereich C: Außerdem weist der westliche Teil 3 Quartiere aus, mit moderat höheren als den herkömmlichen Stellplatz-Entfernungen, nämlich mit 150 m bis 350 m. Sie sind im Süden am Dorfbach gelegen, im Grünen, ruhig und weit von den Autoabgasen. Die Bus-Stadtbahn-Haltestelle im Boulevard liegt höchstens 200 m entfernt (rund 1500 Ew., 30 %).

Alternative für die Bereiche B und C: Die städtebauliche Struktur der Gebiete B und C vermag es daneben aber auch, statt der Parkierung am Rand der Quartiere, die Autos direkt im/am Haus parken zu lassen. Dann entstehen allerdings als Nachteile:

- die Wohn-Nutzfläche wird kleiner,

- die Wohnanger müssen die Zufahrten zu den Garagen aufnehmen, sie fallen dann als hochwertige, wohnungsnahe Bewegungsräume der Kinder aus und verlieren an Qualität als Aufenthaltsraum für die Erwachsenen und weiterhin,

- die Anlieger des Boulevards haben die 8fache bis 20fache Autoverkehrsmenge (je nach Betriebsfall der Ziffern 7 und 8) zu ertragen. Die Wohnungen werden sich wegen des Lärms vom Boulevard mehr abschirmen. Die soziale Kontrolle und die persönliche Sicherheit sinken.

Empfohlen wird, die im Vauban-Gelände gegebene einmalige Chance zu nutzen, verbesserte Wahlfreiheit für die Wohnqualität zu erproben. Dazu sollte, wenn im westlichen Teil gebaut wird, als erstes ein Quartier nach dem System des Parkens am Rande des Quartiers verwirklicht werden. Es kann im Bereich B oder C liegen.

Mit einer solchen ersten Baustufe kann der Markt getestet werden. Sollten sich schlechte Erfahrungen ergeben, dann kann im weiteren die obengenannte Alternative greifen, in allen oder in einem Teil der Quartiere das Parken im/am Haus zu wählen. Erfüllt sich dagegen die Erwartung der Planer und es findet die hohe Wohnqualität vielseitigen Anklang, die durch das Parken am Rand der Quartiere erreicht wird, dann sind die Weichen gestellt, für alle westlichen Quartiere den Vorschlag des Parkens am Rand zu verwirklichen.

Der Bebauungsplan eröffnet also nicht nur Wahlfreiheit für die Bewohner zwischen unterschiedlichen Wohnqualitäten, sondern er erlaubt es auch, aus einer ersten Baustufe des westlichen Teiles Erfahrungen für das weitere Vorgehen auszuwerten. Er birgt also auch Wahlfreiheit für die Entscheidungsträger. Die Planung wird deshalb als "lernende Planung" bezeichnet.

Für den westlichen Teil ist ein Baufortschritt vor der Merzhauser Straße ausgehend nach Westen angebracht und dementsprechend ist als erste Baustufe - im Sinne der lernenden Planung - das an Schule und Zentrumsbereich unmittelbar anschließende Wohnquartier als autoverkehrsarmes Quartier vorgeschlagen. Die Verkehrserschließung des Boulevards beeinträchtigt dieses südöstliche Quartier des westlichen Teiles nicht.

Erst bei den weiteren Baustufen wirkt sich ein erhöhter Kfz-Verkehr auf dem Boulevard belästigend auf die Wohnquartiere aus. Erst dann ist es für den Entwurf der Bebauung entlang des Boulevards entwurfsbestimmend, ob die Quartiere konventionell erschlossen werden, der Boulevard also mit dem ungünstigsten Fall der Kfz-Erschließung belastet ist oder, durch eine Entscheidung für autoverkehrsarme benachbarte Quartiere, der Boulevard nur geringen Kfz-Verkehr zu tragen haben wird.

Hans Billinger, Verkehrsplaner, Planungsbüro Billinger, Stuttgart, Deutschland.

Chapter Fifty-Five

Converting a Military Facility to an Urban Townscape

Andreas Feldtkeller

The breakdown of the eastern communist regimes has opened a door all over the world for a transfer to civil use of large areas previously used for military purposes. This offers a unique opportunity, not only because, for the first time in history, war is disappearing from cityscape, but also because this sudden military withdrawal has created a spatial vacuum that may be filled by a new urban vision.

During the last century Tübingen's defensive town wall became obsolete. Its place was taken by the closed military area with its own walls, with barracks, drill courts, and sheds for modern weapons.

When the historic town walls were pulled down a process of enormous urban expansion began. In our time, the abandonment of the military areas within the modern city may be the beginning of a development of similar importance.

In 1991 and 1992 the French army, garrisoned in Tübingen since World War II, abandoned an area of approximately 400 acres. Immediately after the withdrawal was announced, the local authorities claimed the area.

It is important to recognize that restructuring a former military area is completely different from developing agricultural land. The area is not fertile soil but waste land. Military land has no economic value. It is not owned by private individuals, but by the state. In many cases the state is not interested in the future use of the area.

Originally the grounds were expropriated for military use without compensation. The present owner—the state—however, wishes to make as much profit as possible by selling the ground. It is difficult to know what is the correct price of the ground and buildings, because the area has not participated in urban development and the concomitant increase of real estate value.

The area is accessible, with streets in place, and there are water mains, electricity, street lighting, sewer systems, etc., but to a lesser extend than would be required for urban development.

There may be a great deal of ground contamination, and this requires a complicated examination process. Not until that process has been finished can one estimate the time and cost involved in making the ground usable for construction.

At the same time, there is the political and economic expectation that one can immediately make use of the area and its buildings. In summary, there is a strange mixture of possibilities, expectations and perils.

Periphery or Center

Military areas created fifty or one hundred years ago on land that was, at that time, on the edge of a settlement, are today surrounded by residential and industrial areas.

In Tübingen these areas form a ribbon-like zone within the southern outskirts of the town. Parallel to that ribbon is Bundesstrasse 27, a highway that, during the next two decades is planned to be transformed into a tunnel. The military area and the highway together form an embarrassing barrier between neighborhoods.

Together with strips of unused land on both sides of the highway, the former military areas are approximately 600 acres. Since that whole area is surrounded by already built areas it has significance for Tübingen's planning policies.

Planning Aims and Principles

Former military areas situated within the built area of a city provide the opportunity to correct deficiencies in the adjacent neighborhoods. The city council of Tübingen has, therefore, decided to use the conversion area to develop new urban qualities for the whole of the southern parts of the city.

In 1990 the German planning legislation made it possible to declare a larger area of the town suitable for reconstruction as "Städtebaulicher Entwicklungsbereiche". That means, the local authorities have to acquire all parts of the area, and to sell the newly constituted lots, after development, to a broad range of interested people. When the city purchases the land the city must not pay more than the estimated value of the land if there was no further development. With the money earned from selling the land the city is able to pay for a large part of the necessary social, cultural and technical infrastructure. Furthermore, the city council can decide on the aims of development without respect to the wishes of any private landowner.

The main idea for the redevelopment of Tübingen's Südstadt (former military area) is to create a new urban core in the middle of the existing built areas. Consequently, we are planning a district consisting of quarters with an urban scale and mixed use. Living and working, daily life and leisure activities will be again brought nearer to each other. This will give the Südstadt an innovative quality: the Südstadt will get a new backbone that, we hope, will be very attractive.

The Meaning of Mixed Use

Since World War II planners have been accustomed to think in terms of separate areas for residential use, industrial districts, shopping areas, sports centers, etc.. Today we acknowledge that by isolating the different activities of our lives we destroy the urban complexity of the city. Social segregation in various forms is the result. The city loses its validity as a framework for social life.

If we intend to make cities again more livable in the future we have to find ways of bringing the various activities together again in a new way. Plans are urgently needed that allow investors to install small and medium sized businesses and trades in districts that are, at the same time, used for residential purposes. Blocks of such a mixed use will very easily house different groups of inhabitants that, otherwise, would be segregated in special areas for the rich, the poor or different ethnic groups.

However, the idea of mixing activities and groups is alien to today's society. Therefore, we shall succeed with that idea only if we pursue

Tübingen -- the 400 acre former French military base (foreground) close to the historic city (background left).

our vision with great determination, and if we use every opportunity to realize it.

The Planning Process

Now in Tübingen, after three years of planning, we are prepared to enter the necessary negotiations with people willing to build houses, workshops, stores and apartments.

We began the planning process by defining the planning aims, and by holding a competition for architects and urban designers. The competition was won by five students at Stuttgart University. Based on this result we worked out an urban design plan, a framework with principles, showing the relationship between built structures and streets, squares and urban green areas.

The urban design plan has been the object of broad discussion, not only in the city council, but equally in hearings open to an interested public, at round tables dedicated to special topics, and in smaller circles concerned with special projects (such as, for instance, the installation of a special cooperative car sharing rental system.)

At the same time, we have been concerned with negotiations for the acquisition of the military land, and with the investigation of the land contamination. These questions are not yet fully answered.

First Realizations

If you take over former military land for civilian purposes it is almost impossible to keep the land and buildings unoccupied until you have finished planning and made other preparations. Therefore, in Tübingen we decided to put to use immediately as many of the buildings as possible, without alterations and modernization; and also without the final clarification of the financial conditions for assuming ownership at a later date.

There were 460 residential units available, many in poor condition. They have been divided up between the Federal Republic, the State and the City. Without any delay we accepted people in emergency situations into the 230 apartments under our responsibility. We pay rent to the Federal Republic, which still owns the buildings. For necessary repairs to 120 apartments it will be necessary to spend 70,000 DM per flat.

The people who are living in the former military apartments today are our partners in discussions concerning our plans to construct more buildings on the site.

In addition, there are former workshops and sheds that we have given away for temporary industrial use. Other sheds of poorer quality have been demolished.

In five former barracks, accommodations for students were created by the university. There are already 550 students living in the Hindenburg area today. When the area is complete there will be 450 more students in new buildings.

Second Step: Infrastructure

Still, without owning the land, we started to build up the first parts of the infrastructure. The technical work of the local authority started with a system of district heating, that, later will extend to all other parts of the development. We started to build a new sewer system, new water and electricity networks. At the same time the city began establishing social and cultural activities in the existing buildings.

These included five kindergartens (three privately supported), a house for kids, a primary school, rooms for therapeutic work with young people, a house for the Volkshochschule (adult education) a house with the office of the Stadtsanierungsamt (city planning) and rooms for meetings of all types The next efforts will be to restore two gymnasiums (one in cooperation with two dance and sports clubs).

All these projects are accompanied by a continual reevaluation of the usefulness of remodeling garrison buildings. By repairing existing buildings we are able fairly quickly to make space available at a low cost. As Jane Jacobs already emphasized, it is important in an urban area to have some substandard buildings that can guarantee the survival of low income businesses. Reusing existing buildings provides the opportunity for self-help and cooperative enterprises. This is a way to save money. The problem is that the owner, the Federal Republic, until now has been unwilling to sell the property at a low enough price. Our argument continues to be that, if the price is not low enough, the city could order the demolition of these buildings.

Pollution

A few words about the problem of pollution. The removal of contaminants must be solved before development can take place. In our country, the owner of former military installations, the State, is prepared only to remove contaminants that cause immediate dangers, for instance, polluted subsoil. It is up to the local authority interested in developing the area to prove that there is an immediate danger.

Planning Procedure

Negotiations with investors cannot start until one can finalize the transfer of ownership. Our idea is not to give the future lots to building companies, but to give the land to persons willing to build for their own use—apartments, houses, workshops, small industrial plants, offices, ateliers, and shops.

We want to create small lots, on which one can build shop/houses and townhouses, next to one another, with three to five stories. And we intend to sell the lots at a fixed price.

In order to realize this idea it will be necessary to organize a service to form cooperatives of groups of small investors. That service ought not to be combined with brokerage activities. In the bills of sale it will be specified that the city has the right to repurchase the land at a defined price, if it is later offered for sale.

Planning for Reduced Car Traffic

Negotiations with investors will be made on the basis of the preliminary building regulations approved by the city council. The final building regulations are to be approved at a time when two thirds of the land is sold.

When we negotiate the sale of land we will also discuss with the buyer possibilities for reducing car traffic. We propose that people take their car only as far as the next bus stop, or that they renounce a car of their own. There will be the possibility for those who do not own a car to rent a car by the hour during the day, at modest rates. The idea is to have large parts of the urban area with reduced car traffic. People -- children as well as the elderly -- should consider the street primarily as their living space, rather than as a vehicular thoroughfare.

City as a Workshop

During the last fifty years productive work has abandoned the urban scene. Bringing productive work back into the city is an essential part of reconstructing the urban quality of an area. Mixed land use means, therefore, finding productive trades that are likely to work in a district with a mixed use character.

In a mixed use quarter there is less sensitivity to noise than in purely residential areas. Children can profit from that, in that they may again be allowed to play in the streets.

The presence of work in an urban area affords new opportunities for youth. Tübingen already has its trade schools in the southern part of the town quite near to the conversion area. Together with the urban development, the city intends to encourage a close cooperation between secondary and trade schools, and the growing trades in the area.

Andreas Feldtkeller is Stadtbaudirektor (Planning Director) for the City of Tübingen, Germany.

Conversion of Previous Military Sites:
Examples in Kassel

Folkert Lüken-Isberner

I work for a company, which is engaged in research, planning and development for the Federal State of Hessen, which lies in the centre of Germany. The company- is owned by the State and works under contract for various ministries, as well as for regional and local authorities. Very soon after it became known that the national and NATO forces intended giving up their military sites, our company initiated its own research for the State - in order to give the politicians a basis for negotiating. Regarding the extent to which Hessen is affected, the state lies further down the scale in comparison with other Federal states, - nevertheless a special program for conversion was already introduced in 1992; this program promoted among other things planning and consulting, which for the most part have been delivered by the State's own development company, for example, through ongoing "Conversion Guidelines". The support from this subsidy program is directed mainly at the relatively weaker areas (central and northern Hessen). I would like to tell you about one such "Conversion case".

Given the financial state of the majority of local authorities, politicians and town planners cannot buy land up speculatively, rather they are forced to consider development strategies, which contain rather less maneuver for public use and are subject more to the interests of private investors. Consequently urban development - our theme - is restricted in its realization and multi-purpose character.

I now come to my prototype: It concerns a town with a population of 200,000 called Kassel. This is the main town of the northern part of the State of Hessen, lying halfway between Hannover and Frankfurt and is internationally known for the world's largest art exhibition "Documenta".

The town of Kassel was up until the recently begun reduction of forces an important military base. In addition the town has been an important centre for arms manufacture since the beginning of the industrialization (and still is). Parts of the military production have been nevertheless already converted into manufacturing for civilian purposes.

Since the fall of the internal German border, the Kassel military base is no longer of strategic importance; so that valuable tracts of land have become available for urban development. Three inner city garrisons are completely empty, one other is partly evacuated.

The town has a tradition in redeveloping military sites and complexes.

In the course of the last centuries, many old inner city military bases have been relocated to the town boundary due to site requirements and have made way for other mainly public uses. Such a migration to the town boundaries is best compared with that of the industrial estates. This phenomenon can be seen of course in many towns, just as the dismantling of fortifications resulting in providing new land and thoroughfares for the public sector demonstrate the most significant conversion measures at the beginning of modern times: the well known Kassel Friedrichplatz was in its time the largest late barock town square in Europe and thanks its origins to such developments.

After the two World Wars it was natural for the local authority to take over permanently many of the military establishments during the phase of demilitarization, so long as they weren't repossessed for temporary military uses, for example, by the allied forces after the second World War.

At that time the less damaged garrisons in Kassel were mainly converted into flats, administration buildings, schools and social institutions, training grounds converted to sport and playing fields; spontaneous walkways (marching routes) united previously isolated areas again for the first time with neighbourhood areas.

In one example, considering it in today's context, a particularly valuable temporary civilian development was built; old military administration buildings, workshops and living quarters were converted to a clinic, two law courts, two schools and sport halls. Even if in those early years of the fifties, redevelopment was not by far completed, that is to say, this complex was built in conditions of land shortage, this concentration of facilities had a very strong durable impact on the neighbouring newly built residential areas, which had very little social structure of their own. Through the repossession of the two garrisons by the military a few years later, the community infrastructure was again removed from the expanding urban area without any replacement. An urban development became an enclosure again, for which recently planning was proposed without an opportunity for a

community component. At the moment ,this very location is next in line for conversion; it lies adjacent to the newly built Intercity-Express Railway Station in the west side of town, and one would be to-day happy, to have there a similar requirement for this area.

The earliest conversion program of the post war era is already almost history.

Before the current wave of available military complexes came to the town, already in the eighties the conversion of a previous garrison on the outskirts of the town into a small urban area had begun. This remote area (outside of the main transport system) was after 1945 never again used for military purposes, rather it became rather desolate. After the Federal Government handed over this location for a symbolic 1 DM, a comprehensive development plan was started, without any pressure of time for completion, and was turned into a residential area with high living, working and environmental qualities. A planned extension will improve the already existing community services and public utilities.

The new potential for conversion.

What was achieved in this conversion, with a lot of investment in a period of high demand for housing and with a scarcity of suitable land, is not easily transferable to the recent new additional sites with favourable development potential, since the possible demand for further housing doesn't match the large areas of land. In addition, there is competition between the different locations with the simultaneous release of land or possibly a concentration of "higher value uses" at the already mentioned more attractive location sited directly beside intercity express station (ICE), which has been significant for the town's development.

While one can count here on a certain self dynamic for development and consequently this location is clearly anchored in the political awareness, a location on the town boundary is worthy of attention, in order to examine its development potential for an urban area. Just this location shall be presented in more detail, since it probably characterizes a typical urban development, which is common to most areas and is part of planning and political discussion.

It concerns a garrison built in the beginning of our century, with moderate site benefits.

My previous characterized garrisons exist from the time of the large armaments program of the Nazi period, that means, they were stamped out of the earth in one piece and consist mainly of one building style. The garrison on the southern town boundary on the other hand was gradually built, with the first section in 1912. Later extensions resulted in a trebling in size: accordingly the architecture and surroundings illustrate quite different styles - in accordance with the period and function - and gives the appearance of an urban development of quality. All important public utilities are represented in this "town within a town" (which has much in common with many garrisons of this size - 20 hectares). In this multipurpose development lies the challenge for a concept for subsequent use within the context of an urban area with exceptional profile. This is often least recognized by the supporters of the quick sale (just as here, where already irreversible decisions have been made before the expiry of the procedure for planning, which omits a consideration for the benefits of residential development. We must as town planners and consultants present these areas, which are still to be developed and of course finally to be sold, as areas with unmistakable architectural and urban qualities.

Using the principle of clear identity we developed a planning model, which promotes durability and an emphasis on multi-purpose uses: industry, offices, housing, sport and leisure centres. This model is not sensational, rather undisputed, classical. And quick sales aspirations are also considered, since the site lends itself to such development. The often promoted argument using the nearby urban motorway for industrial use only is not valid due to the size of the site. Naturally the planned industrial use will be situated in that noisy part of the complex. But through a belt of industrial buildings, a new sound absorbing town boundary will be created, which will permit the remaining development, among others housing.

The model advocates such residential development, which can satisfy the high demand from lower income groups. For which it requires planning and development concepts, which are cost-saving (including a high proportion of self help) and suitable forms of capital and financing bodies. Through the already existing residential areas and a good city centre infrastructure within walking distance, the new development is of a manageable size and the danger of a stigma for the new inhabitants does not occur. Through the high quality facilities of the surrounding environment a minimal change in the transport system is required, as the local tram system connects the site with the entire transport system of the town. The significant reduction in soil closure allows the creation of adjacent green spaces and climatical surfaces.

The implementation of the plan has begun.

A process orientated master plan, which shall develop the joint economical and development aims parallel and be carried over into the first stages of implementation, has already had its first setbacks: the department for the promotion of industry has taken a sector for relatively inferior new development (extensive land use, few qualified jobs, large car park) without adequate discussion with the town planners. This first development is so massive, that the urban area concept threatens to become an absurdity as such.

I wish to mention a rather particular problem for implementation, which has its roots in the technical infrastructure, but brings with it greater consequences: the whole underground supply system namely is not compatible with the town utilities system, as we know it with "civil planning"; so that the technical development of this new adjoining land can only be organized through special complicated legislative contracts or through expensive relocation of access points. The military, as sole owner, didn't need to follow civilian standards. Also this problem may exist in many similar cases and can make any development, which is based on surface utilities, become quickly unrealistic.

Dr. Folkert Lüken-Isberner, Hessische Landesentwicklungs- und Treuhandgesellschaft, (HLT), Company for Research, Development and Planning, Ltd., Wiesbaden/Kassel, Germany.

Kapitel Sechsundfünfzig (b)

Konversion ehemaliger Militärflächen: Kassel

Folkert Lüken-Isberner

Angesichts der kommunalen Finanzschwäche können Kommunalpolitiker und Stadtentwickler in der Überzahl nicht in die Bodenbevorratung gehen, sondern sind stark auf Planungsinstrumentarien angewiesen, die relativ wenig Steuerungsmöglichkeiten im kommunalen Interesse beinhalten und somit sich oft zu stark Einzelinteressen von Investoren unterordnen. Einer städtischen Quartiersentwicklung aber - unser Thema - sind in ihrer Prozeßhaftigkeit und urbanen Nutzungsvielfalt damit enge Grenzen gesetzt.

Ich komme zu meinem Beispiel.

Es handelt sich um eine 200.000 Einwohner-Stadt mit Namen Kassel. Sie ist die Metropole des nördlichen Teils des Landes Hessen, liegt auf halber Strecke zwischen Hannover und Frankfurt und ist international am ehesten durch die "Documenta", der weltgrößten Kunstschau, bekannt.

Die Stadt Kassel war bis zum Beginn der jüngst begonnenen Reduzierung der Streitkräfte ein wichtiger Militärstandort. Zudem war die Stadt seit Beginn der Industrialisierung auch wichtiger Standort der Rüstungsproduktion (und ist dies noch immer). Teile der wehrtechnischen Produktion wurden allerdings bereits konvertiert in zivile Produktionssektoren.

Seit dem Fall der innerdeutschen Grenze ist der Militärstandort Kassel, da strategisch nicht mehr interessant, zur Bedeutungslosigkeit geschrumpft, so daß an mehreren Orten der Stadt zugleich z. T. wertvolle Flächen für die Stadtentwicklung verfügbar werden. Drei innerstädtisch gelegene Kasernen sind vollständig freigezogen, eine wird teilweise frei.

Die Stadt hat eine Tradition in der Umwandlung von militärischen Flächen und Anlagen

Im Laufe der Jahrhunderte sind längst viele ehemalige innerstädtisch gelegene Militäreinrichtungen im Zuge modernerer Standortanforderungen in die städtische Peripherie abgewandert und haben Raum für andere meist öffentliche Nutzungen eröffnet. Eine solche Randwanderung war der der Industriestandorte am ehesten vergleichbar. Dieses Phänomen gilt selbstverständlich vielenorts, wie auch die Schleifung der Festungsanlagen mit dem Ergebnis der Gewinnung neuer öffentlicher Freiflächen oder Straßen ja die bedeutsamsten Konversionsmaßnahmen zu Beginn der Neuzeit darstellen: Der bekannte Kasseler Friedrichsplatz als seinerzeit größter spätbarocker Stadtplatz Europas hat z. B. so seine Entstehung zu verdanken.

Nach den Weltkriegen war es für die Kommune sozusagen "natürlich", viele Einrichtungen des Militärs sich in der Phase der Demilitarisierung anzueignen auf Zeit, sofern sie nicht durch militärische Interimsnutzung weiterbeansprucht wurden, z. B. seitens der Alliierten nach dem II. Weltkrieg. Damals wurden die wenig zerstörten Kasernen in Kassel in größerem Umfang zu Wohnungen, Verwaltungen, Schulen und Sozialeinrichtungen, Exerzierplätze zu Sport- und Spielflächen umgewandelt; spontane Wegeführungen (Trampelpfade) verbanden die

vordem isolierten Areale mit den benachbarten Stadtteilen wieder oder neu.

In einem Fall entstand eine aus heutiger Sicht besonders "hochwertige" zivile Interimsnutzung: vormals militärische Verwaltungs-, Wirtschafts- und Unterkunftsgebäude nahmen eine Klinik, zwei Gerichte, zwei Schulen sowie Sporteinrichtungen auf. Wenn in diesen frühen 50er Jahren auch der Wiederaufbau lange noch nicht beendet war, also dieses Nutzungsgeflecht unter Bedingungen der räumlichen Defizite entstand, so gingen von der Agglomeration dieser Einrichtung doch sehr starke quartiersbildende Wirkungen aus auf einen im Umfeld neu entstehenden Wohnbezirk, der kaum über eigene Sozialinfrastruktur verfügte. Schon durch die Wiederinbesitznahme der zwei Kasernen durch das Militär nach wenigen Jahren wurde die quartiersbildende Infrastruktur dem wachsenden Stadtteil weitgehend ersatzlos wieder entzogen. Aus einem Stadtteil-Baustein wurde wieder ein eingezäuntes Areal, auf dem Flächennutzungsplan entstand neuerlich eine Fläche ohne die Möglichkeit einer kommunalen Entwicklungsaussage.

Derzeit steht genau dieser Standort erneut zur Konversion an; er ist in unmittelbarer Nähe zu dem um den Inter-City-Express-Bahnhof neu entstandenen Westzentrum der Stadt gelegen, und man wäre heute froh, dort ein qualitativ ähnliches Nachfrageprofil zu haben.

Das jüngste Konversionsprojekt der Nachkriegszeit ist fast schon Geschichte

Bevor die derzeitige Welle der Freiwerdung militärischer Liegenschaften auf die Stadt zukam, wurde bereits in den 80er Jahren mit der Umwandlung einer ehemaligen Kaserne im Außenbereich zu einem neuen kleinen Quartier begonnen. Dieses verkehrlich abseits gelegene Gebiet mit ursprünglich geringer städtischer Standortqualität war nach 1945 nicht wieder militärisch genutzt worden, stattdessen zu einem desolaten Wohnstandort verkommen.

Nachdem der Bund der Stadt die Liegenschaft symbolisch für 1 DM überließ (!), konnte eine umfassende städtebauliche Planung ohne zeitlichen Druck erfolgen und wurde unter Einsatz regulärer Sanierungsmittel ein Wohnungsquartier entwickelt mit hohen Wohn-, Arbeits- und Umfeldqualitäten. Eine geplante Erweiterungsmaßnahme wird die schon vorhandenen Gemeinbedarfs- und Versorgungseinrichtungen demnächst tragfähig machen.

Die neuen Konversionspotentiale

Was in diesem gerade erwähnten, bereits realisierten Konversionsfall mit hohem Mitteleinsatz in Zeiten hoher Wohnungsnachfrage und knapper Bodenverfügbarkeit gelang, ist nicht ohne weiteres übertragbar auf die heutigen neu hinzugekommenen, deutlich größeren Standortpotentiale mit höherer Standortgunst, denn das Nachfragepotential nach Wohn- u. a. Nutzungen entspricht nicht dem groß dimensionierten Flächenzugang. Zudem gibt es eine Konkurrenz der verschiedenen gleichzeitig freigewordenen Standorte untereinander bzw. möglicherweise eine Konzentration "höherwertiger" Nutzungen an dem schon erwähnten attraktiveren Standort mit Lage in unmittelbarer Nähe des für die Stadtentwicklung bedeutsam gewordenen Haltepunktes des schnellen Schienenfern-verkehrs (ICE). Während hier mit einer gewissen Eigendynamik der Entwicklung zu rechnen ist und von daher dieser Standort im politischen Bewußtsein deutlich verankert ist, ist einem peripherer gelegenen Standort besondere Aufmerksamkeit zu schenken, um ihn auf seine Entwicklungsfähigkeit zum Quartier zu überprüfen. Genau dieser Standort

soll hier etwas genauer präsentiert werden, da er vermutlich einen städtebaulichen Typus charakterisiert, der an vielen Orten anzutreffen ist und dort Gegenstand planerischer und stadtpolitischer Erörterung ist.

Es handelt sich um eine Kaserne aus den 10er Jahren mit mittlerer Lagegunst

Die bisher von mir charakterisierten Kasernen stammen aus der Zeit der großen militärischen Aufrüstungsprogramme der NS-Zeit, d. h. sind in einem Stock aus dem Boden gestampft worden und verfügen weitgehend nur über Typenbauten. Unsere Kaserne am südlichen Stadtrand ist dagegen sukzessive entstanden, mit ihrem ersten Abschnitt 1912. Spätere Erweiterungen ließen die Anlage auf das Dreifache wachsen; entsprechend bildet sich heute die Bauten- und Freiraumstruktur - je nach Entstehungszeit und Funktion - ausgesprochen differenziert ab und erscheint als städtebaulich-visuelle Qualität. Alle wichtigen Funktionen von Stadt kommen sichtbar vor in dieser "Stadt in der Stadt" (was sie wiederum mit vielen Kasernen dieser Größenordnung - 20 ha - gemein hat). In dieser städtebaulich-funktionalen Vielfalt liegt das eigentlich Herausfordernde für ein Nachnutzungskonzept i. S. eines Quartiers mit ausgeprägtem Profil. Dies wird von den Akteuren des schnellen Vermarktens oft zuwenig erkannt (so auch hier, wo bereits irreversible Entscheidungen vor Ablauf eines städtebaulichen Zielfindungsverfahrens gefällt wurden, die ein Denken in Quartiersqualitäten vermissen lassen). - Uns als Stadtplaner und Berater der Stadt muß es darum gehen, die zu entwickelnden und selbstverständlich letztlich zu vermarktenden Flächen zuvor als Orte mit unverwechselbaren stadtfunktionalen und städtebaulichen Qualitäten darzustellen.

Aus dem Befund der Unverwechselbarkeit entwickelten wir ein Planungsleitbild, welches auf Nachhaltigkeit und starke Nutzungs-mischung setzt: Gewerbe, Büros, Wohnen, Sport- und Freizeitanlagen. Dieses Leitbild ist nicht sensationell, eher ein unstrittiges, klassisches. Und angesichts schneller Vermarktungsambitionen war und ist dafür zu werben, denn der Standort gibt diese Entwicklung her. Die oft angeführte nahe Stadtautobahn als Argument für eine reine Gewerbenutzung sticht bei der Größe des Areals nicht. Selbstverständlich wird in diesem gestörten Flächenteil die vorgesehene gewerbliche Nutzung liegen. Aber durch eine bandartige bauliche Ausprägung der Gewerbe-bauten entsteht eine neue schallabsorbierende "Stadtkante", die die übrigen Nutzungen, u. a. Wohnen, verträglich werden lassen.

Das Leitbild plädiert für solche Wohn-nutzungen, die die hohe Nachfrage aus unteren Einkommensschichten befriedigen kann. Dazu bedarf es planerischer und baulicher Konzepte, die kostensparend sind (dabei hohe Selbsthilfe-Anteile bergen) sowie angepaßter Finanzier-ungs- und Trägerschaftsformen. Durch das Vorhanden-sein gewachsener Wohnungs-quartiere sowie ein infrastrukturell voll ausgestattetes Stadtteilzentrum in fußläufiger Nähe gerät die neue Wohnnutzung in tragfähige Größenordnungen bzw. ist die Gefahr einer Stigmatisierung für die neuen Bewohner nicht gegeben. Durch die hohen Ausstattungsqualitäten des Umfeldes ist eine verkehrsminimierende Umsetzung möglich, zudem bindet eine Straßenbahn den Standort an das Verkehrssystem der Gesamtstadt an. Die deutliche Verringerung der hochgradigen Versiegelung läßt wohnnahe Grünflächen und klimaaktive Oberflächen entstehen.

Die Umsetzung der Planung hat begonnen

Eine prozeßorientierte Masterplanung, die die stadtwirtschaftlichen und städtebaulichen Teilziele idealerweise parallel entwickeln und in erste Umsetzungsschritte überführen soll, hat bereits erste Blessuren hinnehmen müssen: so hat das Ressort Wirtschaftsförderung ohne genügend Absprache mit den Städtebauern eine Teilfläche für relativ "minderwertige", Neunutzung okkupiert (hoher Flächenver-brauch, wenig qualifizierte Arbeitsplätze, großer Parkplatz). Diese erste Ansiedlung ist so massiv, daß das Quartierskonzept als Ganzes ad absurdum geführt zu werden droht.

Ein ganz besonderes Umsetzungsproblem möchte ich erwähnen, welches seine Ursache in der technischen Infrastruktur hat, aber Folgen von hoher Tragweite mit sich bringt: Das gesamte unterirdische Versorgungssystem nämlich ist von seiner Lage her nicht am Fahrerschließungssystem orientiert, wie wir es vom "zivilen Städtebau" her kennen; so daß ist die technische Erschließung der neu zuge-schnittenen Grundstücke nur über rechtlich komplizierte Sonderverträge bzw. über (teure) Neuverlegung der Trassen zu regeln ist. Das Militär als Allein-Eigentümer hatte sich an keinen zivilen Normen zu orientieren. Auch dieses Problem dürfte in vielen vergleichbaren Fällen existieren und kann eine städtebauliche Planung, die sich lediglich am Oberirdischen orientiert, schnell unrealistisch werden lassen.

Folkert Lüken-Isberner ist in der Hessische Landes-entwicklungs- und Treuhandgesellschaft, Gesell-schaft für Forschung, Planung, Entwicklung, Kassel, Deutschland.

Chapter Fifty-Seven (a)

Lee Barracks in Mainz-Gonsenheim

Herbert Fessenmayr

The tract of land of approximately 30 ha in size in the Mainz suburb of Gonsenheim had been used as a barracks since the 1930s.

It is located between Canisiusstrasse and Erzbergerstrasse, and very close to the center of the suburb. Thus almost all services and utilities are available in the vicinity. Two local public transport routes serve the area just a short distance away.

Originally located outside of the city, the barracks are now surrounded by built-up areas. To the south, west and east, residential areas adjoin. To the north is the Erzbergerstrasse which is heavily used as a motorway feeder road. Weserstrasse on the western boundary of the site also has a heavy traffic load.

Buildings occupy only a small part of the barracks grounds. Of striking appearance is the row of large administrative and accommodation buildings following Canisiusstrasse in an elegant curve. They were erected as three-storied u-shaped blocks in 1939/40 and determine the street's appearance.

A striking feature in the axis of the entrance building is the site of the former parade ground which has since been kept free of buildings and preserved as an area of lawn.

These striking elements of the site were a determining feature of the design prepared for the urban planning structural concept produced by the firm Trojan, Trojan and Neu in Darmstadt:

- the layout of the former parade ground as a green space of approximately 2.5 ha in size as the center of the new district;

- retention of the former accommodation and administrative buildings along Canisiusstrasse as buildings shaping the cityscape.

In addition to the large central park, the urban planning design offers further public or semi-public open spaces and areas. The transition zone from the residential buildings to the technical college links these two utilizations together by arranging joint utilizations and recreation areas in the public space.

Internal access differentiates between access roads, residential roads and housing paths. The latter allow one to expect a high utilization value as recreation and play areas, especially for children, in front of house entrances. A network of footpaths provides access to the inside areas of the blocks.

On the south-eastern side of the park, a public playground is planned which at this point will be readily accessible via the footpath and cycle track network, and provides a linking point to the neighboring residential district (the former American housing area).

The development plan structure permits the implementation of various dwelling types and a small-size parceling-out of the areas. In this way, the desired diversity in architecture and ownership forms can be achieved.

The four-story "top buildings" can be implemented first and foremost as apartment housing. Here in the internal area of the blocks private and also communal open space utilization are possible. The tent-like structure with three-storied construction permits house-types with a maisonette-like arrangement of the apartments or also row housing with private open space utilization.

Public transport access to the area is provided by a bus route crossing the site in a west-east direction, with a catchment area covering the technical college (main source of passengers) and parts of the two residential districts west and east. In addition to this, the southern part of the plan area is connected at a short walking distance with the tram stop in Elbestrasse offering good links with the city's public transport network.

The vehicle access points for the districts east and west of the park are not linked together. In the central section of the site, the pathways provided for pedestrians and cyclists in a north-south direction are not crossed by motor traffic. Access to the residential districts is provided in an east-west direction by footpaths. These footpaths link the new residential area with the housing area "An der Sandflora", adjoining to the east, via a children's playground.

The social structure of the future residents is not yet known at the present state of planning. However, by means of planning law guidelines in the development plan on the one hand (fixing of locations for dwellings suitable for support through public funds and stipulating their proportion in the total number of dwell-

ings) and by means of contractual provisions when disposing of building plots to the future building owners/investors it is intended to exercise influence on the age and social structure so that a heterogeneous "healthy population mix" can be achieved, avoiding any formation of ghettos. Thus a total of 10% of the dwelling units to be created are to be implemented as publicly financed apartments which will be distributed around the individual districts in the planning area. In addition to this, each investor is to be contractually required to provide two dwelling units suitable for the mobility impaired within the scope of each project. Together with the condominium apartments planned anyway, and the student hostel already in existence at the Canisiusstrasse location, it will thus be possible to achieve a balanced social structure in the plan area as a whole.

Participation of the public in the replanning of the former barracks site has been on a broad basis up to now. Already in the course of the first structural discussions and then following that in the phase of outline urban planning, public meetings were held in the suburb of Gonsenheim, thus offering the opportunity for information and discussions on the concepts presented. Great use was made of this possibility by the public. All interested sections of the population were addressed here. There was no special participation of future residents or investors at this stage of planning.

In the course of the building development plan proceedings, the advance involvement of the public stipulated under the Building Code (BauGB) in accordance with § 3 para 1. The building development plan draft, which had been revised in the meantime, will be presented in published form in June/July 1995. As the plan will have reached its final form after this stage in procedure, the first step in marketing construction land can then follow, i.e. the future building owners can announce their interest in the acquisition of construction plots from the development agency, the municipal property management company GVG.

Positive design rules, such as in the form of design bylaws, have not been stipulated. The urban planning basic structures are to be seen from the response made by the draft author to the existing garrison buildings along Canisius-strasse, which are to be retained, and are laid down definitively in the development plan (the areas of land to be built on, building heights, access).

The architectural quality of the individual buildings is to be safeguarded within the context of the selling off of the plots of land to building sponsors, i.e. the development agency GVG will only dispose of plots of land when the builder has previously agreed the architectural design of the project concerned with the city planning office. In this "presentation procedure", the draft plan author of the outline urban plan will have the right to have a say in the decisions.

The planning area is located in the direct vicinity of the main shopping area in Gonsenheim, "Breite Strasse" which is also intended to take on the main supply of goods and services for everyday requirements. The residents of the planning area will thus participate in the everyday life of the suburb of Mainz-Gonsenheim.

In addition to the centrally located green open space, which will take on play and local recreation functions for all age groups, the public playground located at the eastern boundary of the plan area offers the possibility of integrating the residential area "Am Müllerwäldchen" (former US housing area) located outside into the open space system of "G 124". In addition to this, all the play and local recreation functions are integrated into an inter-connected network of footpaths and cycle tracks. The external prerequisites for the

creation of communication and so a community are thus present.

Starting out from the availability of public and private supply facilities located in the direct vicinity and easily accessible by foot along Breite Strasse, there is to be primarily residential utilization within the plan area. The provision of an independent supply center within the plan area itself would fail on account of the lack in sufficient number of an adequate population, i.e. in order to exist, individual shops and supply facilities would be dependent on motorized customers from outside of the plan area. The "economy access" stipulated for the plan area would not, however, be able to cope with this additional traffic, the possibility to accommodate shop utilizations and other uses less sensitive to noise, such as catering establishments, in the western and north-western boundary zone, where motorized traffic can reach the properties directly from outside and not affect the residential areas within the planning area. Utilizations of a public nature in the plan area are just the sports hall already located in the northwest and the technical college proposed for the whole northern part of the plan area.

As already explained, all kinds of denser dwelling can be implemented in the urban planning structures stipulated in the development plan, with the exception of detached dwelling houses.

The building structures proposed within the context of the restructuring of the barracks site are initially a response to the situation found present in the rear section of the already existing garrison building. From an ecological standpoint, the resultant north-south alignment of the rows of buildings and the accompanying mainly west-east alignment of the dwellings do not, it is true, offer the most optimal prerequisites for passive utilization of solar energy, but this is compensated for by the urban planning advantages.

However, within the context of the implementation, there is quite certainly a possibility for installing equipment for utilizing solar energy, especially in the roof area.

When this new district is being implemented, the rain water occurring in the area is to be allowed to seep away and not be led into the public sewer network. The underground is very good for seepage purposes; what would also be meaningful would be to collect the rain water and use it.

Herbert Fessenmayr is the Acting Director of Planning for the City of Mainz, Germany.

Kapitel Siebenundfünfzig (b)

Umnutzung der Lee Barracks, Mainz

Herbert Fessenmayr

Das Gelände von ca. 30 ha Größe im Mainzer Stadtteil Gonsenheim war seit den 30er Jahren als Kaserne genutzt.

Es befindet sich zwischen der Canisiusstraße und der Erzbergerstraße und sehr nahe am Zentrum des Stadtteils. Somit ist in der Umgebung die Versorgung größtenteils sichergestellt. Zwei Linien des ÖPNV tangieren das Gelände in geringen Abständen.

Ursprünglich außerhalb der Stadt gelegen, ist die Kaserne mittlerweile von Bebauung umgeben. Nach Süden, Westen und Osten schließen sich Wohngebiete an. Im Norden befindet sich die Erzbergerstraße, die als Autobahnzubringer stark befahren ist. Auch die Weserstraße an der Westgrenze des Geländes hat eine hohe Verkehrsbelastung.

Das Kasernengelände ist nur zu einem geringen Teil bebaut. Auffallend ist die Reihe der großen Verwaltungs- und Unterkunftsgebäude, die in elegantem Schwung der Canisiusstraße folgen. Sie wurden in den Jahren 1939/1940 als u-förmige Blocks in dreigeschossiger Bauweise errichtet und prägen das Bild der Straße.

Auffallend ist in der Achse des Eingangsgebäudes die Anlage des ehemaligen Exerzierfeldes, das seither von Bebauung freigehalten und als Rasenfläche erhalten wurde.

Diese markanten Elemente des Geländes waren entwurfsbestimmend in der Erarbeitung des städtebaulichen Strukturkonzeptes, durch das Büro Trojan, Trojan und Neu in Darmstadt:

- die Gestaltung des ehemaligen Exerzierfeldes zu einer Grünanlage mit ca. 2,5 ha Größe als Mitte des neuen Quartiers;

- der Erhalt der ehemaligen Unterkunfts- und Verwaltungsbauten entlang der Canisiusstraße als stadtbildprägende Gebäude;

Der städtebauliche Entwurf bietet neben dem großen zentralen Park weitere öffentliche oder halböffentliche Frei- und Platzflächen. Die Übergangszone von der Wohnbebauung zur

Fachhochschule verknüpft diese beiden Nutzungen durch die Anordnung gemeinschaftlicher Nutzungen und Aufenthaltsflächen im öffentlichen Raum.

Die innere Erschließung differenziert Erschließungsstraßen, Anliegerstraßen und Wohnwege. Letztere lassen einen hohen Nutzungswert als Aufenthalts- und Spielflächen, besonders für Kinder, vor den Hauseingängen erwarten. Ein Fußwegenetz erschließt die Blockinnenbereiche.

An der Südostseite des Parks ist ein Kinderspielplatz geplant, der an dieser Stelle gut über das Fuß- und Radwegenetz erreichbar ist und einen Verknüpfungspunkt zum benachbarten Wohnquartier (ehem. Housing Area der Amerikaner) darstellt.

Die Bebauungsstruktur ermöglichen die Realisierung unterschiedlicher Wohnungstypen und eine kleinteilige Parzellierung der Flächen. Damit ist auch die gewünschte Vielfalt in der Architektur und in den Eigentumsformen realisierbar.

Die viergeschossigen "Kopfbauten" sind in erster Linie als Geschoßwohnungsbau realisierbar. Hier sind im Blockinnenbereich private und auch gemeinschaftliche Freiflächennutzungen möglich. Die zeilenartige Struktur mit dreigeschossiger Bebauung ermöglicht Stadthaustypen mit maisonette-artiger Anordnung der Wohnungen oder auch Reihenhäuser mit privater Freiflächennutzung.

Die ÖPNV-Erschließung des Gebietes erfolgt durch eine in West-Ost-Richtung das Gebiet querende Buslinie deren Einzugsbereich die Fachhochschule (Hauptfahrgastaufkommen) und Teile der beiden Wohnquartiere West und Ost abdeckt. Darüber hinaus ist vor allem der südliche Teilbereich des Plangebietes über die in fußläufiger Erreichbarkeit liegende Straßen-

bahnhaltestelle in der Elbestraße gut in das ÖPNV-Netz der Stadt eingebunden.

Die Kraftfahrzeugerschließung für die Quartiere östlich und westlich des Parks ist nicht miteinander verbunden. Im Zentralen Bereich des Gebietes wird die Wegeführung für Fußgänger und Radfahrer in Nord-Süd-Richtung nicht von motorisiertem Verkehr gekreuzt. Die Wohnquartiere sind in Ost-West-Richtung durch Fußwege erschlossen. Diese Fußwege verknüpfen das neue Wohngebiet über einen Kinderspielplatz mit dem östlich angrenzenden Wohngebiet "An der Sandflora".

Die Sozialstruktur der zukünftigen Bewohner ist zum derzeitigen Planungsstand noch nicht bekannt. Durch planungsrechtliche Vorgaben im Bebauungsplan einerseits (Festsetzung von Standorten für förderfähige Wohnungen und deren Anteil an der Gesamtzahl der Wohnungen) und durch vertägliche Festlegungen bei der Veräußerung von Wohnungsbaugrundstücken an die zukünftigen Bauherren / Investoren, soll jedoch Einfluß auf die Alters- und Sozialstruktur genommen werden, so daß eine heterogene, "gesunde Bevölkerungsmischung" erreicht und eine Ghettoisierung vermieden werden kann. So sollen insgesamt 10 % der zu schaffenden Wohneinheiten als Sozialwohnungen realisiert werden, die räumlich auf die einzelnen Quartiere im Plangebiet verteilt sind. Darüber hinaus soll jedem Investor vertraglich aufgegeben werden, im Rahmen seines Vorhabens 2 behindertengerechte Wohneinheiten zu erstellen. Zusammen mit den ohnehin vorgesehenen Eigentumswohnungen und dem am Standort Canisiusstraße bereits vorhandenen Studentenwohnheim, wird im Plangebiet insgesamt somit eine ausgewogene Sozialstruktur erreicht werden können.

Die Beteiligung der Bürger an der Umplanung des ehemaligen Kasernenareals hat bis zum heutigen Tag breiten Raum eingenommen. Bereits im Zuge erster struktureller

Überlegungen und daran anschließend in der Phase der städtebaulichen Rahmenplanung wurden Bürgerversammlungen im Stadtteil Gonsenheim durchgeführt und somit Gelegenheit zur Information und zur Diskussion der vorgelegten Konzepte gegeben. Seitens der Bürger wurde von dieser Möglichkeit reger Gebrauch gemacht. Angesprochen wurden in diesem Zusammenhang alle interessierten Bürger; eine spezielle Beteiligung zukünftiger Bewohner bzw. Investoren gab es zu dieser Planungsphase nicht.

Im Verlauf des eigentlichen Bebauungsplanverfahrens wurde dann noch die vom Baugesetzbuch (BauGB) vorgeschriebene vorgezogene Bürgerbeteiligung im Sinne des § 3 Abs. I durchgeführt. Der zwischenzeitlich überarbeitete Bebauungsplanentwurf wird im Juni / Juli 1995 dann in die öffentliche Auslegung gebracht werden. Da der Plan nach diesem Verfahrensschritt im Prinzip seine endgültige Form erreicht haben wird, kann sich dann der erste Schritt der Baulandvermarktung anschließen, d. h. dann können die zukünftigen Bauherren ihr Interesse am Erwerb von Baugrundstücken bei der Entwicklungsträgerin, der städtischen Grundstücksverwaltungsgesellschaft GVG, anmelden.

Positive Gestaltungsvorschriften, etwa in Form von Gestaltungssatzungen, werden nicht vorgegeben. Die städtebaulichen Grundstrukturen ergeben sich aus der vom Entwurfsverfasser gegebenen Antwort auf die vorhandenen und zu erhaltenen Garnisonsgebäude entlang der Canisiusstraße und sind im Bebauungsplan festgeschrieben (die bebaubaren Grundstücksflächen. Gebäudehöhen, Erschließung).

Die architektonische Qualität der einzelen Gebäude soll im Rahmen der Grundstücksveräußerung an die Bauherren sichergestellt werden, d. h., die Entwicklungsträgerin GVG wird Baugrundstücke erst dann veräußern, wenn der Bauträger die architektonische

Gestaltung der entsprechenden Vorhaben zuvor mit dem Stadtplanungsamt abgestimmt hat. In diesem "Moderationsverfahren" erhält der Entwurfsverfasser des städtebaulichen Rahmenplanes Mitspracherecht.

Das Plangebiet liegt in unmittelbarer Nachbarschaft der Gonsenheimer Hauptgeschäftslage "Breite Straße", die auch die Hauptversorgung mit Gütern und Dienstleistungen des täglichen Bedarfes übernehmen soll. Die Bewohner des Plangebietes werden daher am täglichen Leben des Stadtteils Mainz-Gonsenheim teilnehmen.

Als städtebauliche Mittel im Plangebiet selbst fungiert die zentral gelegene öffentliche Grünanlage, die als Stadtteilpark auch den Einwohnern des gesamten Stadtteils Mainz-Gonsenheim offenstehen wird und insofern auch wichtige Kommunikationsaufgaben für alle Bevölkerungsgruppen ausfüllen wird.

Auf der Ebene des Plangebietes sind hier zum einen die o. a. öffentlichen Grünanlagen als auch die auf Quartiersebene vorgesehenen privaten Spielstraßen zu nennen, die das Quartier Ost und West jeweils in Nord-SüdRichtung durchziehen und als Begegnungs- und Spielfläche dienen sollen. Insbesondere das Spielen im Beobachtungsfeld der elterlichen Wohnung kann hier im Mittelpunkt stehen. Kleinkinderspielplätze sind in den Blockinnenhofen der Geschoßwohnbauten integriert.

Neben der zentralgelegenen Grünfläche, die Spiel- und Naherholungsfunktionen für alle Altersstufen aufnehmen wird, bietet der am östlichen Plangebietsrand liegende öffentliche Spielplatz die Möglichkeit, daß außerhalb gelegene Wohngebiet "Am Müllerwäldchen" (ehemalige Housing-Area) in das Freiflächensystem des "G 124" zu intregrieren. Darüber hinaus sind alle Spiel- und Naherholungsfunktionen in ein durchgängiges Fuß- und Wegenetz integriert. Die äußeren Voraussetzungen für das Entstehen von Kommunikation und somit Gemeinschaft, sind somit gegeben.

Ausgehend von der in unmittelbarer Nachbarschaft und in guter fußläufiger Erreichbarkeit gelegenen öffentlichen und privaten Versorgungseinrichtungen entlang der breiten Straße, soll im Plangebiet primär Wohnnutzung realisiert werden. Der Aufbau eines eigenständigen Versorgungszentrums im Plangebiet selbst wird an der nicht in ausreichendem Umfang vorhandenen Mantelbevölkerung scheitern, d. h., einzelne Läden und Versorgungseinrichtungen wären, um existieren zu können, auf motorisierte Kundschaft von außerhalb des Plangebietes angewiesen. Die im Plangebiet vorgehaltene "Sparerschließung" würde diese zusätzlichen Verkehrsaufkommen jedoch nicht verkraften, die Wohnqualität würde darunter leiden. Es besteht deshalb lediglich die Möglichkeit, in der westlichen und nordwestlichen Randlage, wo der motorisierte Verkehr direkt von außen auf die Grundstücke gelangen kann und die Wohnquartiere im Inneren des Plangebietes nicht beeinträchtigen kann, Ladennutzungen und andere lärmunempfindlichere Nutzungen, wie z. B. Betriebe des Beherbergungsgewerbes, unterzubringen. An Nutzungen mit öffentlichem Charakter befinden sich im Plangebiet lediglich die im Nordwesten bereits vorhandene Sporthalle und die im gesamten nördlichen Plangebiet vorgesehene Fachhochschule.

Wie oben bereits ausgeführt, lassen die im Bebauungsplan vorgehaltenen städtebaulichen Strukturen, mit Ausnahme des freistehenden Wohnhauses, alle Arten des verdichteten Wohnens zu.

Die im Rahmen der Umstrukturierung des Kasernengeländes vorgeschlagenen Baustrukturen antworten zunächst auf die vorgefundene Situation im rückwärtigen Bereich der bereits vorhandenen Garnisonsgebäude. Die so

entstandenen Nord-Süd-Ausrichtung der Gebäudezeilen und die damit einhergehende überwiegend West-Ost-Ausrichtung der Wohnungen bietet zwar unter ökologischen Gesichtspunkten nicht die optimalsten Voraussetzungen zur passiven Nutzung von Solarenergie, was jedoch durch die städtebaulichen Vorteile kompensiert wird.

Im Rahmen der Realisierung besteht jedoch durchaus die Möglichkeit, insbesondere im Dachbereich Einrichtungen zur Nutzung der Solarenergie einzubauen.

Bei der Realisierung dieses neuen Quartiers soll das anfallende Niederschlagswasser im Gebiet versickert und nicht der öffentlichen Kanalisation zugeführt werden. Der Untergrund ist sehr gut versickerungsfähig; sinnvoll wird auch das Sammeln des Niederschlagswassers und der Gebrauch als Grauwasser sein.

Herbert Fessenmayr, Leitender Baudirektor, Stadtplanungsamt, Stadt Mainz, Deutschland.

Herbert Hoover Siedlung, Heilbronn

Andrea Nussbaum, u.a.

1. Idee "kaufen statt mieten"

Die Stadtsiedlung Heilbronn GmbH ist das erste Unternehmen in der Bundesrepublik, welches ehemals militärisch genutzte Wohnungen als Eigentumswohnungen auf den Markt gebracht hat. Bereits Ende 1992 hat die Stadtsiedlung eine ehemals amerikanische Wohnsiedlung in der John F. Kennedy Straße angemietet und an Heilbronner Wohnungssuchende weitervermietet. Dadurch entspannte sich der Wohnungsmarkt insbesondere bei der Nachfrage nach größeren Familienwohnungen. Schneller als erwartet, wurde auch die zweite große Siedlung in der Herbert-Hoover-Straße frei. Bei dieser Wohnanlage bot sich die Möglichkeit, Eigentum für Familien zu schaffen, die sich eine Neubauwohnung in dieser Größenordnung nicht leisten können.

2. Standort

Bei der Wohnsiedlung Herbert-Hoover-Straße handelt es sich nicht um eine Anlage im "üblichen Kasernenstil". Die 13 Gebäude mit insgesamt 288 Wohnungen sind "campusartig" angelegt, in unmittelbarer Nachbarschaft eines bevorzugten Wohngebietes unterhalb der Weinberge und des Heilbronner Waldes.

3. Sozialstruktur

Die Gebäude werden vorwiegend von jungen Familien mit Kindern bewohnt. Die Altersgruppe der 30- bis 35- jährigen ist prozentual am höchsten vertreten (siehe Statistik). Auch verschiedene Generationen finden wieder zueinander; es kommt öfter vor, daß Eltern und Kinder sich eine Wohnung im selben Gebäude bzw. im benachbarten Gebäude kaufen.

4. Beteiligung der Öffentlichkeit

Der Gedanke, die Wohnungen nicht zu vermieten, sondern zu verkaufen, war recht kühn. Allen Beteiligten war bewußt, daß bis zu diesem Ziel ein schwieriger und risikoreicher Weg zu begehen war. Daß die Sache einen guten Abschluß fand, lag hauptsächlich daran, daß von Anfang an offene Gespräche zwischen den Verhandlungspartnern (Bundesvermögensamt, Oberfinanzdirektion, Bundesfinanzministerium, Stadt Heilbronn und Stadtsiedlung Heilbronn GmbH) geführt wurden. Auch die örtliche Presse wurde durch eine offensive Informationspolitik in die Verhandlungen eingebunden.

5. Identität und Raumwirkung

Auf unterschiedliche Weise hat man versucht, von dem "Kasernenstil" wegzukommen und die Attraktivität der Wohnsiedlung zu steigern.

Beispiele:

- Unterschiedliche Farbgestaltung der Häuser.

- Balkonanbau (die Wohnung wurde um einen "Raum im Freien" erweitert).

- Aufwendige Gestaltung der Freiräume (z.B. unterschiedliche Grünflächen, verschiedene Kinderspielplätze...).

6. Öffentliche städtische Plätze, Gemeinschaftssinn

In der Wohnanlage gibt es keinen Durchgangsverkehr. Die Straße sowie alle Wege und Plätze bieten sich als Kommunikationsflächen an. Die Spielplätze auf den einzelnen Hausgrundstücken fördern durch Sitzbänke, Pergolen, Grillplätze den Gemeinschaftssinn; sie sind insbesondere Treffpunkt junger Mütter. Städtische Plätze sind ein vorhandener Abenteuerspielplatz sowie das Jugendhaus.

7. Kinder und Jugendliche

Die großzügige Gestaltung der Grünflächen sowie die 14 Spielplätze laden zum gemeinsamen Spiel geradezu ein.

8. Grundstücke, Nutzung

Die Stadtsiedlung Heilbronn GmbH hat das Gesamtgrundstück mit einer Größe von ca. 948.050 m2 vom Bund erworben. Es wurde in 13 Hausgrundstücke mit großzügig gestalteten Außenanlagen sowie öffentliche Grünflächen, Parkierungsanlage und Spielplätze aufgeteilt.

In der Wohnanlage gibt es neben den 13 Hausgrundstücken ein großes Einkaufszentrum zur Deckung des täglichen Bedarfs, einen Kindergarten, eine Grundschule, eine Sporthalle (die gleichzeitig als Veranstaltungshalle genutzt wird). ein Jugendhaus, eine Kirche sowie ein Schnellrestaurant.

9. Wohnmöglichkeiten

Die Wohnanlage besteht aus 13 Gebäuden mit insgesamt 288 Eigentumswohnungen. Dabei handelt es sich um sehr geräumige 3-Zimmerwohnungen mit ca. 100 qm und 4-Zimmerwohnungen mit ca. 126 qm Wohnfläche.

Vor Verkaufsbeginn führte die Stadtsiedlung eine Art "Marktforschung" durch. In der örtlichen Presse wurden Anzeigen mit Wohnflächen, kurzer Baubeschreibung und Kaufpreisen geschaltet. Zusätzlich wurde ein Besichtigungswochenende veranstaltet, bei dem sich über 400 Interessenten von der Qualität der Wohnungen überzeugen konnten.

Von insgesamt 600 schriftlichen Anfragen konnte die Stadtsiedlung 210 feste Reservierungen vermerken. Die Vermarktungschancen der Wohnungen waren hervorragend.

Durch die günstigen Verkaufspreise (durchschnittlich DM 245.000,00 für eine modernisierte 3- Zimmerwohnung bzw. DM 285.000,00 für eine 4- Zimmerwohnung), und dem zusätzlichen Angebot einer sehr günstigen Finanzierung über unsere Hausbank, konnte Eigentum für breite Schichten geschaffen werden. Die Wohnungen wurden fast ausschließlich an Selbstnutzer verkauft.

Mit den umfangreichen Modernisierungs- und Instandsetzungsarbeiten wurde im Januar 1994 begonnen und Ende April 1995 waren planmäßig alle Gebäude an die künftigen Eigentümer übergeben. Die Hauptaktivitäten erstreckten sich auf die Instandsetzung der Wohnräume, den Anbau von Balkonen, die Außengestaltung sowie auf die Gartengestaltung.

10. Ökologische Prinzipien, Verkehr

Die bereits vorhandenen großzügigen Grünflächen wurden erhalten und der Baumbestand
weiter erhöht.

Die notwendige Stellplatzanlage wird durch
Baumpflanzungen begrünt und als Ober-
flächenbelag wurden Rasengittersteine aus
recyceltem Kunststoff bzw. eine wasser-
gebundene Decke zum Einsatz gebracht.

Auf eine weitere Nachverdichtung wurde
verzichtet. Die Beheizung der Gebäude erfolgt
umweltfreundlich über eine Fernheizung.

In der Wohnanlage gibt es keinen Durchgangsverkehr. Es handelt sich um eine reine
Wohnstraße, durchsetzt von Fußgänger-
überwegen und Verbindungswegen zu den
einzelnen Gebäuden bzw. öffentlichen
Einrichtungen.

Beim Bezug des ersten renovierten Gebäudes
wurden bereits zwei Stadtbuslinien
eingerichtet.

*Andrea Nussbaum, Stadtplanungsamt, Stadt
Heilbronn, Deutschland.*

Former Industrial Areas: Case Studies

Ehemalige industriellen Anlagen: Beispiele

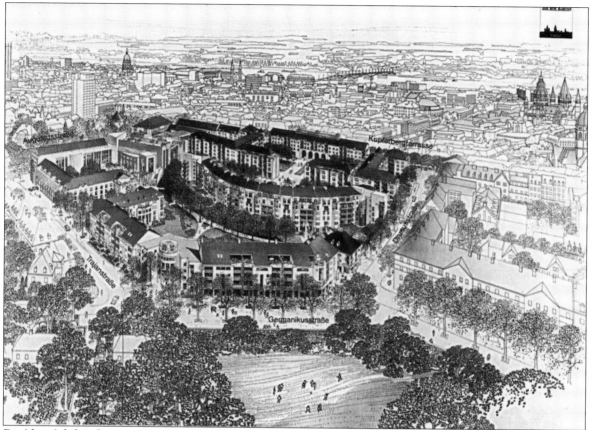

Residential development on Kästrich, Mainz

Residential Development on Kästrich, Mainz

Herbert Fessenmayr

On a topographical elevation overlooking the old quarter of Mainz, the Romans erected a castellum for their legions over 2,000 years ago. In the subsequent period, this plateau was incorporated into the military installations of the fortress of Mainz. With the industrialization following the dismantling of the fortifications in the last century, commercial establishments were located there with several breweries. After the companies were moved elsewhere for economic and urban planning reasons, the obvious thing to do was to put the area with its enormously favorable location - direct link with the city center, connection with green belt and relative proximity to the main railway station - to an adequate use.

By means of an urban planning competition, a solution was found in 1983 doing justice to the challenge presented. With the change in utilization of the city district of Kästrich, the old crown of the city of Mainz was exchanged for a new one. Behind this symbolic interpretation is to be found one of the largest linked urban renewal schemes in former West Germany. Over the past ten years, an industrially used site of almost 4 ha in a central location in the inner city with a wonderful view was reconstructed as a prestigious residential area. The entire residential development was constructed by the company Deutsche Bau- und Siedlungs-Gesellschaft, Frankfurt.

Four hundred, fifty-one dwellings of various sizes for over 1,000 residents, an apartment house, a city hotel with bathing and recreational facilities open to the public, doctors' and lawyers' offices, restaurants and shops for everyday requirements were constructed, together with parking space for 770 cars in underground garages. The total costs amounted to some DM 250 million.

In order to achieve as optimum an intermix of residents as possible, there is a wide range of accommodation to choose from, from a two-room apartment through a town house with tenant's garden to a spacious five-room maisonette apartment with roof terrace. The real estate cannot be purchased for private ownership and without exception is for tenancy on a rent basis.

One sociological objective was to break out of the anonymity of conventional multi-story accommodation and to promote the achievement of independence by the residential units following the model of the single-family house. Individually styled house entrance zones, and the communicatory and at the same time dividing design of the public, semi-public and private sectors contribute just as much to this as taking account of a sensible vision screening.

Well-founded and constantly updated analyses of requirements, close collaboration by all parties involved, well-directed public relations work and implementation in manageable sections led to a residential community growing together with the neighborhood. What has also brought about this acceptance of a new city district by the public are neighborhood festivals, the inviting design of a fountain courtyard in the manner of those to be found in Mediterranean countries, the arched hall as a popular meeting point with its incomparable view over the old part of Mainz, the public access to the excavated Roman gateway at the center of the site and the urbanly eventful quality of the outdoor areas offering possibilities for all ages to sojourn a while in their playgrounds, arcades, niches and terraces.

Great importance was attached to the sensitive adaptation and activation of links with neighboring buildings. Traditional elements from the surroundings were taken up and interpreted, habitual pedestrian links were maintained. A public lift rising five stories links the city center of Mainz with the new city district, a facility of advantage for pedestrians and the mobility-impaired. An integrated and differentiated network of cycle tracks and footpaths, the direct link with local public transport, the banning of cars from the inner residential area by accommodating them in underground garages, thus not allowing parked cars to spoil the surroundings, lead to a solution for traffic access in keeping with our times.

Noise abatement requirements and heat insulation measures were optimized to a high degree, leading to an increase in living comfort, as well as to a reduction in consequential costs. Attention was also paid to constructing buildings using environmentally friendly materials and environmentally sustainable methods. Thus, for example, a rubble recycling plant on the site utilized for the most the demolition material consisting of natural rough stone and brick material, reusing it as aggregate or backfilling material. In this way, it was possible not only to avoid transporting rubble away, but also deliveries by truck cause wear and tear to the roads and a nuisance for the neighbors.

What has been created has proved its worth and led astonishingly quickly to an independent local district awareness among the residents. The utilization, planning and implementation of the development may be described as exemplary urban renovation in which the constraints of a construction site with cultural heritage (Roman castellum baroque casemates, industrial installations) had to be overcome. The State of Rhineland-Palatinate and the City of Mainz have already awarded the building development prizes for the architecture and sponsorship.

Herbert Fessenmayr is the Chief Building Director for the City of Mainz, Germany.

Kapitel Neunundfünfzig (a)

Wohnanlage auf dem Kästrich, Mainz

Herbert Fessenmayr

Auf der topographischen Erhöhung über der Mainzer Altstadt errichteten die Römer vor mehr als 2.000 Jahren ein Kastell für ihre Legionen. In der folgenden Zeit wurde dieses Hochplateau in die militärischen Anlagen der Mainzer Festung eingebunden. Mit der Industrialisierung nach der Entfestigung im vergangenen Jahrhundert vollzog sich dort eine Gewerbeansiedlung von mehreren Brauereien. Nachdem aus wirtschaftlichen und städtebaulichen Gründen die Firmen verlegt worden waren, bot es sich an, dieses Areal mit seiner enormen Lagegunst - direkte Anbindung an das Stadtzentrum, Verknüpfung mit dem

Grüngürtel und mittelbare Lage zum Hauptbahnhof - einer adäquaten Nutzung zuzuführen.

Über einen städtebaulichen Planungswettbewerb fand man 1983 eine Lösung, die der gestellten Herausforderung gerecht wurde. Mit der veränderten Nutzung des Stadtquartiers auf dem Kästrich wurde die alte Stadtkrone von Mainz gegen eine neue ausgewechselt. Hinter dieser symbolhaften Deutung verbirgt sich eine der größten zusammenhängenden Stadtsanierungsmaßnahmen der alten Bundesländer in Deutschland. Hier wurde in den vergangenen 10 Jahren ein industriell genutztes Areal von fast 4 ha in zentrale und aussichtsbegünstigter Lage der Innenstadt zu einem wertvollen Wohngebiet umgebaut. Die gesamte Wohnanlage wurde von der Deutschen Bau- und Siedlungs-Gesellschaft, Frankfurt, errichtet.

Für mehr als 1.000 Bewohner entstanden 451 Wohnungen unterschiedlicher Größe, ein Appartementhaus, ein Stadthotel mit öffentlich zugänglichen Bade- und Freizeitanlagen, Praxen, Restaurants und Läden für den täglichen Bedarf sowie 770 Kfz-Stellplätze in Tiefgaragen. Die Gesamtkosten betrugen rund 250 Mio. DM.

Um eine möglichst optimale Durchmischung der Bevölkerung zu erreichen, ist das Wohnungsangebot breit gefächert und reicht vom 2-Zimmer-Appartement über das Stadthaus mit Mietergarten bis hin zur großzügigen 5-Zimmer-Maisonettewohnung mit Dachterrasse. Die Liegenschaften können nicht im Privateigentum erworben werden und sind ausnahmslos auf Mietbasis zu bewohnen.

Ein soziologisches Ziel war, die Anonymität des überlieferten Geschoßwohnungsbaues aufzubrechen und die Verselbständigung der Wohneinheiten nach dem Vorbild des Einfamilienhauses zu fördern. Individuell

gehaltene Hauseingangszonen und die vermittelnde und zugleich trennende Gestaltung der öffentlichen, halböffentlichen und privaten Bereiche tragen ebenso dazu bei wie die Berücksichtigung eines sinnvoll Sichtschutzes.

Fundierte und fortschreibende Bedarfsanalysen, eine enge Zusammenarbeit aller Beteiligten, eine gezielt Öffentlichkeitsarbeit und die Realisierung in überschaubaren Abschnitten führten zu einer in sich wachsenden Wohngemeinschaft mit der Nachbarschaft. Zu dieser Akzeptanz eines neuen Stadtquartiers auch durch die Öffentlichkeit gehören Stadtteilfeste, die einladende Gestaltung eines Brunnenhofes als Aufenthaltsort nach dem Muster südlicher Länder, die Bogenhalle als beliebter Treff mit ihrem unvergleichlichen Blick über die Mainzer Altstadt, der öffentliche Zugang zu dem freigelegten Römertor inmitten der Anlage und die stadträumlich erlebnisreiche Qualität der Außenbereiche, die mit ihren Spielplätzen, Arkaden, Nischen und Terrassen Aufenthaltsmöglichkeiten für alle Altersklassen bieten.

Großer Wert wurde auf die einfügsame und aktivierende Verknüpfung mit der Nachbarschaftsbebauung gelegt. Überlieferte Gestaltungselemente aus der Umgebung wurden interpretierend aufgegriffen, über-kommene Wegbeziehungen weitergeführt. Ein öffentlicher Aufzug über 5 Etagen verbindet fußgängerfreundlich und behindertengerecht die Mainzer Innenstadt mit dem neuen Stadtquartier. Ein integriertes und differenziertes Netz von Fahrrad- und Fußwegen, die direkte Anbindung an den öffentlichen Nahverkehr, die Verbannung des Autos aus dem inneren Wohnfeld durch Unterbringung in Tiefgaragen ohne Stellplatzverschandelung der Umgebung führen zu einer zeitgemäßen Lösung der Verkehrserschließung.

Schalltechnische Anforderungen und wärmedämmende Maßnahmen wurden in einem

hohen Maße optimiert und führten zu einer
teigerung des Wohnkomforts sowie zu einer
Reduzierung der Folgekosten. Ebenso wurde
darauf geachtet, daß die Gebäude mit
umweltfreundlichen Werkstoffen und umwelt-
schonenden Methoden entstanden. So
verwertete z.B. eine Trümmeraufbereitungs-
anlage vor Ort das weitgehend aus Natur-
bruchstein und Ziegelmaterial bestehende
Abbruchgut, das als Zuschlagsstoff oder
Auffüllmaterial wieder verwendet wurde.
Dadurch konnten nicht nur Abfuhren sondern
auch Zulieferungen mit ihrer Straßen-
beanspruchung und Belästigung der Anlieger
vermieden werden.

Das Realisierte hat sich bewährt und führte
erstaunlich schnell zu einem eigenständigen
Quartiersbewußtsein der Bewohnerschaft.
Nutzung, Planung und Abwicklung der
Bebauung können als vorbildliche Stadtern-
euerung bezeichnet werden, bei der die
Zwänge eines Bauplatzes mit kulturellem Erbe
(Römerkastell, barocke Kasematten, Industrie-
anlagen) zu überwinden waren. Das
Bundesland Rheinland-Pfalz und die Stadt
Mainz haben das Bauvorhaben bereits mit
Architektur- und Bauherrenpreisen
ausgezeichnet.

*Herbert Fessenmayr, Leitender Baudirektor, Stadt-
planungsamt, Stadt Mainz, Deutschland.*

Chapter Sixty

The Search for Neighbourhood in Ultimo-Pyrmont, Sydney

Peter Webber

Introduction

Notions of neighbourhood as cozy communities in parkland settings, with community facilities, school and shops all within a quarter-mile radius, pervaded the ideas of early 20th Century planning theorists from at least Clarence Perry and Clarence Stein onwards: "... the common denominator for the arrangement of space is the family ... a mother knows that her child will have no traffic streets to cross on his way to school, ... the housewife may have an easy walk to the shopping centre ... and the man of the house may find convenient transportation to and from work ..." wrote the authors of one of the standard planning texts of the 1950's. In most cities of the western world, this vision of the utopian suburban neighbourhood faded almost before it could be realized, with the increased personal mobility offered by the motor vehicle, the new communication media, and gender roles which began to conform less and less to the stereotyping of this quaint mid-century prose.

In the inner urban areas of the major metropolitan cities where demolition and "urban renewal" were advocated to improve social conditions, this conventional wisdom about neighbourhood was seen to have little relevance. Social theorists, contemporaries of Perry and Stein, observed that with the development from the village and the small town, "when the neighbourhood has broken up into smaller and more isolated units which are separated according to their diverse interests, we can call a community a city." Only a decade later Lewis Mumford wrote that it was the emphasis on "critical choices, the purposive associations, and the rational ends of the secondary group which is one of the main functions of the city. The city is in fact the physical form of the highest and most complex types of associative life."

It is a sad commentary on the collective ability of 19th and 20th century city builders that in the vast urban agglomerations which comprise our cities, only rarely - and sometimes it seems accidentally, - does the physical form provide opportunities for joyful expression of that life. All too commonly the inner urban environment is socially dysfunctional at best. Small exceptional areas of Manhattan and other North American cities analyzed and celebrated by authors such as Jane Jacobs for their positive qualities are a reminder that the task may be challenging, but not impossible.

Pyrmont-Ultimo - Physical Context and Management Framework

A testing contemporary challenge in Sydney is the ambitious proposal to transform a somewhat desolate inner urban area into a vital part of the city. The Ultimo-Pyrmont peninsula adjoins the central city and shares with it the waterfront of Darling Harbour. It has spectacular views of city skyline and many sites enjoy superb harbour views and access. From the middle of the 19th century it served as the workhorse for the city. Some of its major activities have been quarrying sandstone for building, iron foundry, flour milling, sugar refining, building materials manufacture, dairy products processing and distribution, fish marketing, ship building and woolstorage. It has accommodated the major power generation plant and the city waste incinerator. Its population at the turn of the century numbered of the order of 30,000 and there is strong evidence that the tough working-class environment inspired a strong sense of community loyalty, - which perhaps exhibited the essential characteristics of a traditional "neighbourhood". As industry declined and waterfront activities closed, population dropped to 5,000 in 1974 and to only 1,800 in 1978. Schools closed, community support facilities declined and housing decayed, or was demolished. Today the finger wharves on the eastern foreshore are little used and the privately-owned industrial waterfront sites are mostly vacant. Ultimo-Pyrmont presents opportunities both for creating a model environment for an inner-urban community, and for profit-driven private speculation.

In New South Wales planning powers ultimately reside in the State Government rather than the City, and in 1989 the State established a task force to develop proposals for the future of Ultimo-Pyrmont. The "City-West Strategy" was published in 1990. A statutory Regional Environment Plan was approved by the Minister for Planning and gazetted in October 1992. Master Plans have been prepared to provide a framework for physical development of major sites. A statutory State Government authority - City West Develop-ment Corporation, - has been established to manage government-owned land, promote infrastructure and encourage private investment. The stated objectives of planning strategies are to develop new communities with emphasis on balanced environmental management, conservation of the built heritage, co-ordinated public transport, and a mix of residential and commercial development. Ambitious early plans projected population numbers growing to 20,000 with employment opportunities

increasing from the present 14,000 to 40,000 - although such projections are subject to constant revision.

All three levels of Australian government have involvement in the process. The State Government has initiated innovative planning proposals and sought to ensure that financial returns on State-owned properties would be maximized through its Development Corporation. It has permitted high levels of development potential on privately-owned land, through floor-space index and other controls included in planning instruments, - although all development is strongly constrained by environmental criteria in the same instruments.

The Australian Government has endorsed the project and through its national "Building Better Cities" program has provided funding for a new light rail link, as well as for some subsidized housing for low income earners, and for open space and community facilities.

The City Council has day-to-day responsibility for planning, development control of all land other than that owned by the State or excluded for master-planning purposes, but ultimately is answerable to the State Minster for Planning in the event of disputes. It is also responsible for community planning and support services.

Formal Planning Policies

The principles set out in the statutory Regional Plan begin with a commitment to enhancing the status of the city "as a financial, commercial, residential and tourist city of world standing". The twenty four "principles" which follow give by far the strongest emphasis to developing and controlling the physical form of the environment: economic and formal considerations have priority. An Urban Development Plan, - essentially an advisory code consequential to the requirements of the Statutory Plan, - is a 72-page document almost exclusively concerned with the built form, infrastructure, environmental criteria and physical amenities. It deals for the most part very sensitively with these issues but it is not its role to develop a social agenda. Similarly a series of Master Plans, primarily for the vacant or disused sites, address almost exclusively the physical form of future development. Throughout these documents diagrams, plans and descriptions give clear direction as to building heights and alignments, conservation of heritage items, location of public parks and squares, access for pedestrians and vehicles, and the types of land use and activities to be encouraged or permitted.

By contrast the social objectives - whilst not entirely neglected, - are articulated only in the most abstract terms. The Regional Plan calls for "a wide range of housing and employment opportunities, and educational, recreation and cultural activities", "a high quality mixed living and working environment", "a socially diverse residential population representative of all income groups", "different kinds of housing, including affordable housing, to ensure that low to moderate income households may continue to be able to live in City West", and "the needs for social facilities and services to be accommodated". The Urban Development Plan by definition addresses only those social concerns which are consequential to the built form, such as sunlight access, privacy, ecological issues, and access for disabled people.

The Master Plans are similarly preoccupied with formal issues and were presented complete with block models and drawings, illustrating idealized concepts for inner-city living. The "Vision Statement" in the Plan for the critical area of land largely owned by the CSR company, is no more explicit, using terms such as "a mixed-use working and living environment containing a high level of urban activities ..." An accompanying sketch of this latter-

day Land of Cockaygne depicts citizens in smart dress embracing as they gaze at sparkling water and blue skies, with tables in the foreground laden with seafood and other delicacies. "Housing mix", "social diversity", "opportunities for commercial activity and employment compatible with a high quality residential environment", are concepts variously invoked in the section setting out Land Use objectives, as well as "... community facilities ... consistent with the needs of the resident population and workforce". The Master Plan for the contiguous area of Pyrmont Point is equally bland; although nominating specific square metres of permissible business use on each defined building site, it is silent as to the nature of the social structure in the residential accommodation areas.

In the Master Plan for Pyrmont Bay the large Government-owned site on the waterfront facing to the city, and adjacent to the residential areas of Pyrmont, has been specifically allocated for a casino. This is a vast development in advanced stages of planning, and in addition to gaming facilities will include two large theatres, a major hotel, a high-rise residential apartment block, a retail arcade, food hall, and parking for 2,500 cars. The social, environmental and economic impacts will inevitably be substantial. The building form and management of traffic and infrastructure have been closely monitored and controlled, but beyond endorsement for the employment-generating capacity of the development, there is little evidence of policies addressing the social implications of such a large intervention into this part of Pyrmont.

Another important component of the range of planning policies is the Public Domain Strategy. This comprehensively describes the various parks and public places, existing or proposed, - and the network of paths proposed to link them. It includes provisions for "structured and unstructured recreational activities" from children's play areas to cycling tracks, - but does not demonstrate any correlation between facilities and projected population characteristics, although it does provide as an appendix a sample survey of preference of existing residents and workers.

The absence of specific social planning policies is intriguing, given that adoption of physical planning criteria, - particularly those relating to building height and density - had in fact gone a long way towards determining the population profile. Characteristics such as low proportion of young children, predominance of adults in the 20-49 years age bracket, low proportion of home ownership, low average household size, and high level of transience are all typical of inner urban high density areas of the type proposed.

Early Development Initiatives

Within the framework of the planning policy documents there are various large development projects already completed, under construction, or in advanced planning stages. An elevated freeway and connecting bridge - which had been planned long before the present proposals for Ultimo-Pyrmont -, is now close to completion. It will remove much surface traffic from the streets, but has a very serious adverse impact on a wide swathe of properties close to its route. A new light rail system will follow the route of an existing goods rail line; it is in advanced stages of planning and promises to provide good public transport to the city.

A series of large residential blocks have been approved. These are private developments which exploit to the maximum the potential building bulk permitted by planning codes. In many areas development to a height of 28 metres (approx. 10 storeys) is allowed, subject to satisfaction of environment criteria. A number of proposals have been refused by the City Council for failing to provide a satisfactory level of private or public amenity, but numer-

ous buildings have achieved consents, and these given rise to considerable concern. Almost invariably they have been built to the maximum permissible height and are comprised of mainly one and two-bedroom apartments. Whilst indoor and rooftop recreation facilities are provided in some cases, they are unsuited to families with children, have minimal contact with the spaces around, and engender the social isolation and remoteness from the community which is characteristic of buildings of this form. Several are built unduly close to the new expressway and other front narrow streets which afford inadequate levels of amenity in terms of sunlight access, both to the residential accommodation and to the public street.

In parallel with these private investment initiatives, government has a commitment to funding up to 700 residential units for low income earners, 600 of which are euphemistically termed "affordable housing". The first 20 are now completed with a further 68 under construction. The majority of these will be low-rise, developed in small increments and located and designed sensitively in a way which by comparison with the privately funded projects should enhance opportunities for residents to integrate with the community.

The casino complex, - likely to be in operation from 1997, - will bring large numbers of people to Pyrmont. It has been estimated that there will be a daily total of about 5000 employees working in three daily shifts, and several thousand hotel and apartment residents, and casino visitors. Some employees no doubt will live nearby, but the casino will lure an overwhelmingly transient population, - local interstate, and international, - who will have only the most ephemeral links to the Ultimo-Pyrmont community. Some residents and commercial interests welcome the development, but many view it as a gross intrusion which will be incompatible with the development of the community. The building design provides for some degree of physical integration by means of such devices as pedestrian through-links, awarding to street frontages, low-scale podium-type buildings fronting streets, and attractive foreshore landscaping, but the nature of the operation inevitably predisposes it to being perceived and largely operating as an introverted "fortress".

The outcome of developments to date has been an estimated increase in residential population to over 6,000 people and employment workforce of close to 16,000. Extrapolation of growth estimates suggest that it is realistic to anticipate that there will be over 17,000 residents and 49,000 employees in Ultimo-Pyrmont by the third decade of the 21st century.

Social Planning Initiatives

The set of circumstances, - historical, economic and political, which have given rise to these early years of planning in Ultimo-Pyrmont are not uncharacteristic of the inner-city environment of other large metropolises, - a partly derelict environment, a small surviving working-class population undergoing gentrification, substantial reliance on profit-driven private-sector investment, and an unwritten assumption, - driven by economic and physical determinist rationale that employment opportunities and physical regeneration will resolve social dilemmas. The conspicuous absence of convincing social planning policies in the key planning documents, and the isolationist nature of initial private developments would suggest that the likelihood of the emergence of a cohesive community ethos is minimal. Fortunately a series of initiatives developing in parallel with formally promulgated policy gives hope that this would be an unduly pessimistic assessment, and does not take into account the vitality which has been infused into the debate by the existing community, the commitment of the City Council to improving the quality of the social and physical environment, and the more recent actions by State Government authorities to convert vague "principles" into specific policies.

The elected City Council representing the community has been very active in consulting and working with community groups. The State Government authorities are increasingly following this model. Two residents' Precinct Committees, - for Pyrmont to the north and Ultimo to the south, were established by Council and have had a very significant input into planning decisions at local level. They have been influential in shaping the form of new parks and playgrounds, street closures and landscaping, community centres and recreation facilities; they are consulted in relation to all development proposals in their areas. Some very attractive environments are beginning to emerge in existing residential streets previously degraded by through-traffic and uncontrolled parking. A separate group representing primarily business interests is also active in bringing an important commercial perspective into discussion, although this is not always consistent with the position of residents. Representative community committees have been established to ensure that residents' views are taken into account when major developments are proposed or studies undertaken: these include groups which advise on management of construction traffic, the development of a new park at Pyrmont Point, development of traffic, parking and transport policies, and a current open space study. The Council has adopted a detailed strategy to levy and manage contributions from development proposals for the purpose of providing public amenities and services.

The State Government Department of Planning and its City West Development Corporation, - recently amalgamated within the one Department, - have during the last year prepared a series of social planning documents which should fill much of the previous policy vacuum. They variously address recreation needs, quality-of-life issues, ecologically sustainable development, economic strategy, human infrastructure strategy, and affordable housing implementation and management. A comprehensive "human services strategy" has been formulated.

As resident population grows it is likely to have an increasingly powerful voice in shaping of policy. The very large residential and commercial areas in Pyrmont which are as yet largely undeveloped and in early planning stages will in future be subject to the closest scrutiny, with the real prospect that a human dimension will be integrated into the early formal concepts. These areas are potentially extremely attractive residential environments with varied topography, enchanting views and easy access to city and harbour. A concern must be not whether this will be a satisfactory place to live and work, but whether it will become an exclusive elite environment which may return high profits to owners and developers but remain aloof from the nearby community.

Conclusion: Questions Rather than Answers

Ultimo-Pyrmont will be redeveloped as a busy urban area. It may yet well develop some of the idiosyncratic qualities which make for a vibrant and memorable environment,-the qualities which characterize a Greenwich Village, a Chelsea, a left Bank. It can never be a "neighbourhood" in the suburban sense of the term, but can it develop the rich fabric of over-lapping interests visualized by Mumford, and at the same time, develop the mutually supportive networks which characterize a caring society? Can it become a balanced, - rather than exclusively gentrified community - which satisfies the social needs not only of the affluent and upwardly mobile, but also the elderly, the incapacitated, the lonely and the very young? Can the somewhat belated initiatives now in place make up for the apparent vacuum in initial planning policy documents?

Is it unrealistic to expect that it should have been possible to pre-plan significant details of the social agenda rather than to rely upon only the broadest and vaguest of positions? Is it inevitable that critical elements of the urban form must first be established before these questions can be addressed? Since a study of historical precedent reveals that it is often those environments which have robust aesthetic and physical qualities which survive over centuries to provide satisfying urban ambiance, - a Place des Vosges in the Marais or the terraces of Paddington in Sydney, - is it indeed legitimate to determine the physical environment in advance of the knowledge of any details of the social agenda, with confidence that infinitely adaptable human beings will create a vital social life within a pre-ordained physical habitat?

A close monitoring of the experience of Ultimo-Pyrmont over the next three decades should provide some fascinating answers.

Peter Webber is Professor of Architecture at the University of Sydney, Australia.

Kapitel Einundsechzig

Marktredwitz, Innenstadt-Süd

Max Wittmann

Standort

Das Projekt, "Innenstadt Süd" grenzt unmittelbar südlich an die historische Altstadt. Das gesamte zur Neuordnung anstehende Areal umfaßt eine Größe von ca. 6 ha. Auf einer Fläche von ca. 3,8 ha befanden sich bis Ende des Jahres 1985 bzw. bis Ende 1993 produzierende Gewerbebetriebe. Durch den Freistaat Bayern und die Gesellschaft zur Altlastenbeseitigung Bayern, München, erfolgt in modellhafter Form eine Altlastensanierung des gesamten Areals. Diese Arbeiten werden Ende 1995 bzw. im östlichen Bereich des Plangebietes Ende 1996 abgeschlossen.

Sozialstruktur

Die Zahl der Bewohner innerhalb des Projektes "Innenstadt Süd" hat aufgrund der vorwiegend ehemals gewerblich genutzten Grundstücke nur untergeordnete Bedeutung; insgesamt wohnen in dem Gebiet derzeit ca. 50 Einwohner. Aufgrund der städtebaulichen Planungen sollen zur Stärkung der Bevölkerung in der Altstadt ca. 150 neue Wohneinheiten für ca. 350 Personen geschaffen werden. Angestrebt wird eine Mischung von öffentlich gefördertem und frei finanziertem Wohnungsraum im Verhältnis von 40 zu 60 v.H.

Beteiligung der Öffentlichkeit

Die durchgeführten Voruntersuchungen im Rahmen der Stadtsanierung und Stadtenwicklung, die Gutachten zur Einzelhandels-entwicklung und zum innerstädtischen Verkehr, das Ergebnis des städtebaulichen Ideenwettbewerbes und die Bauleitplanung wurden in öffentlichen Bürgergesprächen und Seminaren, Fachgesprächen mit den verschiedensten Interessengruppen der Stadt und den einzelnen Grundstückseigentümern und künftigen Nutzern in umfangreichen Gesprächen vorgestellt und erörtert. Es wurde außerdem eine eigene Arbeitsgruppe "Innenstadt Süd" mit Vertretern der politischen Parteien, den verschiedenen Fachverbänden (u.a. Einzelhandel) und der Verwaltung eingerichtet, die sich sehr eingehend mit der Planung und Gestaltung des Projektes und dessen Auswirkung auf die gesamte Stadt befaßt hat.

Identität und Raumwirkung

Bereits vor Auslobung des städtebaulichen Ideenwettbewerbes wurden im Rahmen der Bestandsanalyse insbesondere Kriterien zu Identität, Raumkanten und Maßstab aufgestellt. In dem städtebaulichen Ideenwettbewerb und in der Bebauungsplanung wurden diese grundsätzlichen Aussagen konkretisiert.

Öffentliche städtische Plätze

Die städtebauliche Struktur entwickelte sich aus der starken Anlehnung an die topografische Situation. Ergänzt durch die grünordnerische Konzeption werden die Freiflächen entsprechend ihrer spezifischen Funktion gestaltet und in das gesamte Stadtgefüge integriert.

Im Kernbereich des neuen Bauquartiers entsteht ein städtischer Platz, der sich in Form und Dimension an den Marktplatz anlehnt, jedoch entsprechend seiner Funktion als Quartiersplatz innerhalb der Wohnbebauung eine besondere gestalterische Ausprägung erhält. Dieser sogenannte Anger wird als multifunktionaler Kommunikationsbereich ausgebildet und durch die Baumstellung in strengen Reihen gefaßt. So entsteht ein "architektonischer" grüner Platz als Kontrast zu den südlich angrenzenden naturnahen Grünflächen. Die öffentliche Grünfläche entlang der Kösseine verbindet die bereits vorhandenen Freiflächen zu einem durchgehenden städtischen Grünzug mit Anschluß an die freie Landschaft. Ein angestauter Teich mit einer zugeordneten baulichen Nutzung bildet einen attraktiven Anziehungspunkt innerhalb dieser neuen Freiflächengestaltung.

Gemeinschaftssinn

Wesentlicher Wert bei der Planung und Gestaltung des Projektes wurde auf die Integration und Stärkung der gewachsenen Altstadt gelegt. Auf der Grundlage dieser Zielsetzungen werden derzeit die Realisierungsplanungen ausgearbeitet.

Kinder und Jugendliche

Die entsprechend gestalteten und ausgerichteten Straßen, Plätze und Grünflächen bilden ein funktional und gestalterisch gestuftes Freiflächensystem, angefangen vom städtischen Markt als Stadtzentrum, über den streng formal begrünten Anger, bis hin zur naturnahen Bachaue der Kösseine. Die Folge dieser unterschiedlich gestalteten Räume erhöht die Lebensqualität für die Bewohner und insbesondere für die Kinder und jugendlichen Menschen.

Ältere und Behinderte

Aufgrund der Lage und räumlichen Zuordnung zur Altstadt und öffentlichen Einrichtungen ist bei der Wohnbebauung vorrangig auch an die Realisierung von Wohnungen für ältere und behinderte Menschen gedacht. Trotz der zentralen Lage und vorgesehenen Dichte der Bebauung ist durch die Freiraumgestaltung und Baukörperstellung eine hohe Wohnqualität gerade auch für ältere Menschen zu erwarten.

Grundstücke

Die Größe der künftigen Grundstücksflächen wird im wesentlichen bestimmt durch die städtebauliche Anordnung der Gebäude und Umgriff der Freiflächen. Für den 1. Bauabschnitt - westlicher Teil des Plangebietes - wurde derzeit ein Investitions- und Entwicklerwettbewerb öffentlich ausgeschrieben. Wesentliche Grundlage für die Entscheidung bei der Auswahl der Investoren wird der Anspruch an die bauliche Gestaltung sein.

Gemischte Nutzung

Das Gebiet "Innenstadt Süd" liegt im unmittelbaren Übergangsbereich zwischen Altstadt - Einkaufsschwerpunkt für die Region mit einem Einzugsbereich von ca. 80.000 Einwohnern - und südlich angrenzenden Wohnbereichen. Durch eine entsprechende Nutzungsmischung von Läden, Dienstleistung, öffentliche Einrichtungen und Wohnen soll ein lebendiger Stadtbereich entwickelt werden, der die Altstadt sinnvoll ergänzt und bereichert und nicht in Konkurrenz zu ihr tritt. So ist u. a. die Außenstelle eines Geologischen Landesamtes - ein geowissenschaftliches Analytik- und Forschungszentrum - und die Errichtung eines Einzelhandelsmagneten zur Stärkung der überörtlichen Handelsfunktion.

Wohnmöglichkeiten

In dem Plangebiet sind im nördlichen Bereich - zur Altstadt orientiert - Wohnungen und Appartements in dem 2. bzw. 3. Obergeschoß vorgesehen. Im südlichen Bereich des Plangebietes sind Wohnungen im sozialen und freifinanzierten Wohnungsbau in unterschiedlichen Größen vorgesehen.

Ökologische Prinzipien

Im Hinblick auf Stadtklima, Boden und Wasserhaushalt sind verschiedene Maßnahmen innerhalb des Plangebietes vorgesehen. Die bislang durch strenge Böschungen gefaßte und kanalisierte Kösseine erhält durch Abflachen des nördlichen Uferbereiches und Bepflanzung standortgerechter Auengehölze ein natürliches Ufer mit Überschwemmungsbereich. Im Bereich der Wohnbebauung wird das Dachwasser gesammelt und möglichst über offene Gräben weitergeleitet. Großkronige Alleebäume in den Straßenräumen und auf dem Angerbereich sowie entlang der Kösseine tragen dazu bei, Staub zu filtern und das Stadtklima zu verbessern. Außerdem ist Dachbegrünung auf den Zwischenbauten der Büro- und Geschäftsgebäude zur Reduzierung der sich aufheizenden Flächen vorgesehen.

Ferner wird für das gesamte Gebiet ein Energieversorgungskonzept für eine zukunftsweisende möglichst primär energiesparende und schadstoffarme Wärme- und Stromversorgung für das gesamte Areal und die angrenzenden bereits bestehenden Bebauungen in der Innenstadt erstellt. Zu untersuchen sind insbesondere Varianten mit konventioneller getrennter Wärme- und Stromerzeugung sowie Möglichkeiten der Wärmekraftkoppelung mit Blockkraftheizwerken.

Verkehrsplanung

Die verkehrliche Erschließung und Anbindung des Projektes "Innenstadt Süd" wurde auf der Grundlage einer umfassenden Verkehrsanalyse für die gesamte Innenstadt erstellt. Im Sinne eines möglichst störungsfreien Verkehrsflusses der Hauptverkehrsstraßen wurden die Zufahrtsmöglichkeiten auf wenige geeignete Stellen konzentriert. Hauptaugenmerk wurde insbesondere auf ein zusammenhängendes Fuß- und Radwegenetz gelegt. Weiteren Schwerpunkt bildet die Schaffung von unterirdischen Parksystemen sowohl für die öffentlichen als auch für die privaten Stellplätze der einzelnen Nutzungen auf dem Gelände.

Max Wittmann, Geschäftsführer, STEWOG, Stadtentwicklungs- und Wohnungsbau GmbH, Stadt Marktredwitz

Housing Areas: Case Studies

Wohnanlagen: Beispiele

Elevation fragment of new housing estate in Janów West, Lódz, Poland.

Chapter Sixty-Two

Ecological Principles for Mass Housing

Renata Mikielewicz

Various land development structures are our every day surroundings. They influence the way of our life even if we do not take conscious notice of it.

Mass housing is a typical and prevalent fabric of land development in most contemporary polish cities. It influences the way of life of hundreds of people in extreme ways. Large parts of our cities developed as amorphous and nondifferential patterns, very unique and unrecognizable ones.

Frank Lloyd Wright once wrote: *"Urban happiness of the properly citified citizen consists in crowding in confusion - lured by the hypnotic warmth, pressure and approbation of the crowd? The screech and mechanical uproar of the big city turns the citified head, fills citified ears - as the song of birds, wind in the trees, animal cries, or as the voices and songs of his loved ones once filled his heart. He is sidewalk happy."* Talking about restructuring mass housing is also thinking about the return to such values which in a city are missed. In mass housing structures. we can say, they are doubly missed. We have not created a good city form. We have not created a good natural surrounding. Flats and open space that do not satisfy the peoples' needs, have in the end, the effect of a gray, depressive world influencing in invisible ways the minds of the people living there.

Mass housing as an urban form, developed from modernist thinking and spread through all the country, overgrew forms of both the settlement and the buildings, losing the connection with the natural environment and peoples' needs to identity themselves with the surroundings they live in. People who live in mass housing districts feel alienated from environmental values even if the urban form was primarily thought of as one which should improve living conditions, giving to the inhabitants more free, well illuminated and ventilated space than the 19th century city.

If we aim to create a better environmental form of housing estates, it is necessary to analyze the types of these structures in their historical evolution.

Mass housing estates, or whole districts, appeared in the townscape of the city of Lódz generally after 1945. Before the second world war such kinds of land development have existed in the form of social and cooperative housing as small complexes in different parts of the city. But we could not describe these complexes as mass housing in the same way we describe post-war structures. From the period of 1918-1939, there are two outstanding housing estates in Lódz, which together with the Warsaw WMS cooperative estates (district Zoliborz) constituted the avant-garde branch of Polish architecture of this time. Both estates comprise three-, or four-storied buildings of stair-well and balcony-access type, built closed, elongated courtyards in one case, and situated at right angles to streets in the other one. "Most postwar housing construction can be regarded as social housing, but the products mostly lack the freshness of ideas of the pioneer period. They rarely step beyond the technological routine of their construction."

Mass housing in Lódz after 1945 was situated outside the central core of the city. The historical structure of the 19th century core, except one estate of high-rise buildings (so called "Manhattan"), was left almost intact. Such a situation was caused by the small degree of wartime devastation.

The structures can be grouped in three stages: social-realistic, functionalist traditionally constructed and large panel prefabricated. The panel systems are introduced in the 1960s (small and medium size). Only social realism estates were planned with the use of "traditional aesthetic" - using the patterns of traditional street, arcades, squares etc.. In Lódz the built complexes (Old Market Sq. Estate) were not so oversized as other social-realism housing examples (Warsaw, Berlin etc.). In only a few cases, new housing districts kept the traces and the constrains of the existing urban structure. Single one-family houses on fenced lots remained in the middle of the ten-storied building structures. Through all that time the houses were destined to future demolition and their standard and comfort lagged behind what we could expect from residential housing. But these "implants" have every chance to be a good starting point in the restructuring process.

The housing complexes of the 1960s were built mostly of four-storied buildings. The flats are small, built in an "economical way". The standard regulation change came first in the late 1970s. But even the latest regulations allow rooms with some substandard solutions, concerning the comfort of space (for example, minimal width of rooms - 2,4 m). Higher building standards came into use later. The lack of social and commercial services have increased with time. Also the urban design and architectural solutions have become more and more impersonal. Some earlier estates (1960s) also have green areas with fully grown trees - existing trees were preserved in design - where greenery gave more individual character to the prefabricated housing units.

The 1980s brought change in the way the urban structure was formed. Now we can see also changes in architectural forms. But in all these projects and realizations, something is missing and this is, for sure, "the town feeling".

In the late 1980s, we can notice a stronger tendency to abandon the prefabricated mass housing in favor of row-, or one-family houses. This process was characteristic not only for the best-situated group of people. It is also very peculiar that some layouts of the urban plans for row-housing (also the quality of the inner space of these buildings) copy the structure and feeling of prefabricated mass housing areas.

Flats in mass housing were always the main aspiration of a great number of people. For those who moved in the first generation from the country into the town it was also a symbol of better social status. (Lódz is one of extreme examples of such migration process.) So we cannot expect the complete devaluation of that kind of space within a short period of time.

There were attempts to improve the quality of postwar mass housing already in the early 1980s but the activities stopped at analyses of possibilities and needs of inhabitants and first designs. These plans were made without ecological approach to the problems.

The scale of the restructuring needs shows the number of flats. Mass housing in Lódz comprise 88% of the total number of flats. And this process still continued (in 1990 about 87% of built flats - in Lódz - were built in large-panel prefabrication.

In the new economical social and political reality an urgent need to restructure the mass housing districts is recognizable. But this need is related more to inhabitants and users of that space than to local authorities. Changing the urban fabric of such areas, which were built without necessary social and commercial infrastructure is going on spontaneously and without any planning, not providing a better environment. The current processes concentrate mostly on an increase in the number of shops and other services, but not public utilities. It is all the more important to look for such solutions which integrate the structures with the older city core. Transforming processes need a plan and an environmental approach to restructuring methods. And then even if we used in design ecological technologies (as solar collectors, green roofs etc.) we do not have a real ecological design.

Any design must be multifaceted because single-purpose solutions to problems tend to create other problems. The same principle applies to redesign and restructuring solutions. To be valid one needs the integration of all design objectives as for example, composition values, social needs, improvement of natural habitats, climate and water etc.. Ecology in urban design presumes that in particular.

As already remarked, the need to restructure the mass housing districts is urgent. Especially in the new reality after 1989 we need solutions which can help to soften, or even prevent, undesirable social incidents and destruction of buildings.

The latest master plan for the city of Lódz only partly takes into consideration the problem of restructuring mass housing areas. Only the outskirts of housing districts are preserved and foreseen as recreational areas, and as such foreseen to be integrated in the whole ecosystem of the town. Mass housing estates themselves are described as territories for adaptation processes.

Existing opportunities are often unrecognized. A real potential exists for beneficial change. In the analyses for the redesign restructure plan, it is necessary to rediscover through the insights

that ecology provides, the nature of the mass housing units.

The restructuring plan should first of all contain connections with the whole city structure, and then focus on details. Looking from an ecological point of view we also say that *"the new concept of urbanization asks for building continuity, which implies that each building should not be a finite object, but an element of the continuum that requires a dialogue with the other elements to complete its own image"*. (The Machu Picchu Charter, 1978)

Buildings and urban infrastructure giving a frame-work of life directly determine living conditions for all living organisms. They also influence and change irreversibly the development of specific climatic conditions, alteration of soil and water habitat. They affect energy flow and matter cycle among natural elements of the urban ecosystem. This leads to a rise of the self-degrading system and in nature unbalanced, self-degrading ecosystems can exist only for a short period of time. The natural processes contribute to the physical form of the city, which in turn is altered by it. A wide basis of import (in ecological meaning) is used by a town sometimes in whole region-scale. In our design we cannot forget also the matter cycle chain. Even if we talk here only about parts of the town we should not forget that a city is an ecosystem as a whole.

The creation of well integrated, multifunctional areas was also one of the postulates of the Machu Picchu Charter. This document, presented and signed in 1978 during the XIIIth World Congress of UIA in Mexico, based on the 1933 Athens Charter, considers in contrast to it *"that human communication is a predominant factor in determining the very existence of the city. Consequently city planning and housing must recognize this fact (...) the quality of life and its integration with the natural environment ought to be a fundamental goal in the formulation of living spaces"* (The Machu Picchu Charter, 1978).

373

Redesign solutions relate to mass housing structures, which are mostly suburban, outside districts of the town, should take into consideration the essential task to create multifunctional corridors (for example, climate, natural, recreational) which join the town with open areas. Redesign should also promote the reconstruction of natural cycle, which means enhancing natural vegetation structure and sanitation of soil-water relations in order to improve health and climatic conditions in the micro- scale of individual, differently used areas. In the case of the city of Lódz, it is necessary to search for solutions enabling spatial links with external urban areas, preserving the river valleys transverse arrangements. The cheapest way to improve the quality of urban form of such districts seems to be the development, extension and restructuring of their green areas. As generally known, the role of greenery is not only restricted to climatic action, it exerts also an influence on the psychical and emotional sphere of man.

In the hope that the practical application of theory is relevant and useful to the urban designer, talking about ecology principles could enlarge his way of seeing the problems of redesigning and restructuring mass housing areas. We have to learn to understand, especially as architects and urban planners, that aesthetic priorities are secondary to the insights of ecological determinism. It looks necessary to develop an integrated concept for urban redesign of such areas based on ecological principles and conservation values. Ecology as the foundation for a philosophy of restructuring mass housing seems the only way to real improvement in a long term view.

Finally, all designers involved in the changing process - architects, landscape architects and town planners - are confronted with the question of methodology.

- How to reconcile even the basic needs of energy, environment and natural resource conservation with the traditional thinking about urban plans ?

- How to deal with the alienation of the urban society from environmental values ?

- How to use in redesign the understanding of the natural process that contributed to the physical form of land development and which in turn was altered by the total urban form of built environment?

Every redesign project must find the right, unique solutions.

Answers to these questions will determine whether the process of redesigning and restructuring mass housing areas will be a success and a real, used chance to make large parts of our cities livable again.

Zusammenfassung

Restrukturisierung vom verdichteten Wohnbau: Die Möglichkeiten und Vorteile von Beutzung ökologischer Prinzipien im städtebaulichen Wiederentwerfen

Verdichtete Wohnbaustrukturen beeinflussen das Leben Hunderten von Leuten. Das ist die typischste und verbreiteste Bebaungsart in den meisten heutigen polnischen Städten. Diese städtebauliche Form, die ihre Wurzeln in der modernistischen Theorie hat, prägt die Formen von Gebäuden und Siedlungstypen und hat den Zusammenhang zwischen der Naturumwelt und dem Bedurfnis von Leuten sich mit der Umgebung, wo sie leben, zu identifizieren, völlig verloren.

In der neuen ökonomischen, sozialen und politischen Realität besteht ein dringendes Bedürfnis, die Massenwohnstrukturen zu revitalisieren. Die Strukturänderungen solcher Gebiete, die ohne nötige Sozial- und Dienstleistungen gebaut waren, unterliegen einem spontanem und nicht durchplanten Prozess, der nicht zu einer wirklichen Verbesserung der Menschenumwelt dient.

Der Transformationsprozess braucht einen Raum- und Entwicklungsplan. Die Revitalisierungsmethode braucht ökologische Grundlagen. In diesem Referat versucht man die Wichtigkeit des Verstehens und Benutzens ökologischer Grundlinien in den Restrukturierungs- und Revitalisierungs- prozessen in den verdichteten Wohnbau- gebieten zu zeigen, und bemüht sich, die Methode und die Instumente zu finden und zu beschreiben, die durch ökologische Denkweise einem Planer alle Determinanten des Entwurfs vereinigen helfen. Die Möglichkeiten solcher Handlungen sind auf Beispielen für die Stadt Lódz in Polen gezeigt.

Renata Mikielewicz, M.A. Dip. Arch., Institute of Architecture and Urban Design, Technical University of Lódz, Poland.

Kapitel Dreiundsechzig

Städtebauliche Qualitäten im Wohnungsbau
Neubrandenburg Lindenberg-Süd

Stefan Resch

Der 1952 von der damaligen DDR-Regierung gefaßte Beschluß, Neubrandenburg zur Bezirksstadt zu erklären, war der bisher wohl stärkste Entwicklungsimpuls für die Stadt nach ihrer Gründung. Es erfolgte ohne rasante Entwicklung von etwa 20 000 Einwohner auf fast 90 000 Einwohner 1989. Nach dem Wiederaufbau der Innenstadt wurden rings um die Stadt neue Wohngebiete angelegt, in denen heute jeweils zwischen 10 000 und 25 000 Einwohner überwiegend in Plattenbauten leben. Bei aller Kritik an den Plattenbauten und den damit verbundenen Problemen der Monostruktur hat die Stadt jedoch dadurch einen sehr hohen Anschlußgrad an die Systeme der technischen Versorgung, insbesondere bei Abwasser und Fernwärme.

Parallel zum Wohnungsbau wurden große Betriebe des Bauwesens, der Nahrungsgüterproduktion, der Pharmazie, des Maschinenbaus u.a. angesiedelt; einen breiten Raum nahmen Verwaltungsfunktionen ein. Der für Deutschland typische Mittelstand existierte zu DDR-Zeiten in Neubrandenburg nicht, woraus sich heute einige Probleme ableiten. Mit der politischen Wende 1989/90 wurde die wirtschaftliche Basis der Stadt fast völlig zerstört und etwa 4 000 Wohnungsuchende wurden als "Altlast" übernommen. Diese Situation muß man kennen, um die Entscheidungen, die 1990 und kurz danach getroffen wurden, verstehen und einordnen zu können.

Ausgebend von der Tatsache, daß 1990 etwa 3/4 aller Haushalte in Neubauwohnungen (Baujahr ab 1970) wohnte, die nach dem Prinzip der Großplatte errichtet wurden, und daß rund 90 % des Wohnungsbestandes sich im Eigentum zweier Wohnungsunternehmen befand, ist die hohe Nachfrage nach Eigenheimen, insbesondere nach freistehenden Einfamilienhäusern zu erklären. Darüber hinaus besteht eine deutliche Nachfrage nach preisgünstigen Miet- oder Sozialwohnungen. Demgegenüber ist die Nachfrage nach Eigentumswohnungen noch vergleichsweise gering.

Auch wenn sich die Bevölkerung Neubrandenburgs zwischen 1989 und 1994 auf rund 82 000 Einwohner reduzierte (negatives Wanderungssaldo, Geburtenrückgang), besteht dennoch ein deutliches Wohnraumdefizit. Nach vorliegenden Einschätzungen, die insgesamt noch als zu niedrig eingestuft werden sollten, ist bis zum Jahr 2000 ein Zuwachs von 4 000 Wohnungen erforderlich, um das Wohnraumdefizit abzubauen. Vor allem bezieht sich die Wohnungsnachfrage auf zwei bis Dreiraumwohnungen, insbesondere für "Singlehaushalte" und Alleinerziehende. Dieser relativ hohe Anteil an den Wohnungssuchenden resultiert u.a. aus dem Anstieg von Ehescheidungen sowie aus dem vermehrten Auszug von erwachsenen Kindern aus dem jeweiligen Elternhaushalt. Darüber hinaus besteht jedoch auch ein Wohnungsfehlbedarf bei großen Wohnungen für Familien mit Kleinkindern.

Ein weiterer Grund für den Nachholbedarf in der Wohnraumversorgung resultiert aus dem personenbezogenen Wohnflächenbedarf. Während durchschnittlich die Wohnfläche pro Person in den alten Bundesländern Deutschland bei etwa 37 qm liegt, beträgt sie in den neuen Bundesländern rund 27 qm, in Neubrandenburg muß der Bewohner im Durchschnitt mit 22 qm Wohnfläche auskommen.

Der bis zur Jahrtausendwände durch den Neubau von mindestens 4 000 Wohnungen zu deckende Wohnungsbedarf soll - so ist es vorläufig geplant - in Form von Miet- und Eigentumswohnungen zu etwa 60 % sowie in Form von Familieneigenheimen zu etwa 40 % erfolgen. Neben Wohnungsbaumaßnahmen im Zusammenhang mit einer gebietsverträglichen Nachverdichtung in bestehenden Wohngebieten konzentriert sich der Wohnungsneubau in Neubrandenburg z. Z. auf vier größere Standorte mit je 800 bis 1000 Wohnungen:

- Lindenberg-Süd
- Brodaer Höhe
- Am Brodaer Holz
- An der Schlehenhecke

Zwei kleinere Standorte mit jeweils 100 bis 120 Einfamilien- oder Doppelhäusern sind bereits bebaut.

In Anbetracht der zuvor geschilderten Situation auf dem Neubrandenburger Wohnungsmarkt wurde in der Stadt Neubrandenburg frühzeitig damit begonnen, geeignetes Wohnbauland auszuweisen und zügig geltendes Baurecht zu schaffen. Eines der ersten nach der Wende von der Stadt ausgewiesenen Neubaugebiete war das Wohn- und Gewerbegebiet Lindenbergsüd, das mit seinen über 800 wohneinheiten und rund 2 000 neuen Arbeitsplätzen als eines der größten zusammenhängenden Neubauprojekte in den neuen Bundesländern galt.

Gleichzeitig mit der Teilkompensation der bestehenden Wohnraumnachfrage in Neubrandenburg wird auf dem Lindenberg-Süd das Ziel verfolgt, Arbeitsstätten in verträglicher Form den Wohnstandorten zuzuordnen. Aus der Beschlußvorlage der Ratsversammlung der Stadt Neubrandenburg vom 29.11.1990 heißt es hierzu:

"Das Gebiet ist als allgemeines Wohngebiet entsprechend der Baunutzungsverordnung einzustufen. Von den als ausnahmsweise zulässigen Funktionen sollen auch als Möglichkeit zugelassen werden:

- sonstige nichtstörenden Gewerbebetriebe,
- Anlagen für die Verwaltung,
- Betriebe des Beherbergungsgewerbes,
- Tankstelle an der Bundesstraße.

Das für den Lindenberg-Süd geplante Zentrum soll in erster Linie gebietsversorgenden Charakter haben. Geplant sind eine Einkaufspassage mit kleinen Geschäften und Gaststätten, kulturellen Zwecken dienende Einrichtungen sowie Einrichtungen der örtlichen Versorgung."

Das etwa 53 ha große neue Wohn- und Gewerbegebiet Lindenberg-Süd liegt im Süden der Stadt etwa 4 km vom Stadtzentrum entfernt, direkt an der nach Neustrelitz verlaufenden bundesstraße 96. Das Gebiet wird sowohl im Süden als auch im Westen durch das sogenannte "Nemerower Holz", ein zum Naherholungsgebiet entwickelter Wald, begrenzt. Nördlich hiervon, also in Richtung Stadtzentrum, erstreckt sich heute ein Gewerbegebiet. Östlich wird das Planungsgebiet durch die 4spurige Bundesstraße 96 begrenzt, woran sich eines der grössten in der Entstehung befindlichen Gewerbegebiete Neubrandenburgs anschließt.

Das neue Wohn- und Gewerbegebiet Lindenberg-Süd wird über eine Hauptsammelstrasse im wesentlichen parallel zur Bundesstraße erschlossen. Von dieser Hauptsammelstraße ausgehend werden über ja einen Sammelstraßenring der nördliche und südliche Teil des Wohngebietes angebunden. Die innergebietliche Erschließung erfolgt über verkehrsberuhigte Anliegerstraßen bzw. über Mischverkehrsflächen.

Der Bereich zwischen der Haupterschließungsstraße und der Bundesstraße wird als eingeschränktes Gewerbegebiet oder als Mischgebiet ausgewiesen und soll als Pufferzone gegenüber dem Wohnungsbau dienen.

Für die Gestaltung des Wohngebietes wurden von vornherein einige Prämissen vorgegeben:

- Die Forderung nach unterschiedlichen Wohnformen einerseits und die sensible Lage des Standortes im Landschaftsraum andererseits waren Ausgangspunkt des Gedankens, von Ost nach West für 3- bis 4geschossige Bebauung über 2geschossige Reihenhäuser bis zum freistehenden Eigenheim Vorgaben zu machen.

- Die quartiersweise Vergabe an Bauträger hatte zum Ziel, innerhalb eines Quartiers einheitliche Gestaltungsmerkmale zu erreichen, während von einem Quartier zum nächsten gestalterische Spannungsfelder gewünscht waren. Damit meinen wir, eine erste Antwort auf die Monotonie der Plattenbauten anderer Wohngebiete gefunden zu haben. Es braucht nicht verheimlicht zu werden, daß dieser Gedanke einem in den 80er Jahren gebauten Wohngebiet im Dänischen Odense abgeschaut wurde.

- Die Durchgrünung des Wohngebietes im öffentlichen und privaten Raum als Reaktion auf die ohnehin starke Durch-

grünung der Stadt Neubrandenburg und der Standortsituation im speziellen.

Das Vorhaben "Lindenberg-Süd" wurde als Forschungsvorhaben des "Experimentellen Wohnungs- und Städtebaus" (EXWOST) beantragt und bestätigt. Mit der Projektforschung wurde die Firme "Schwerin Consult" beauftragt. Mit der Aufnahme in das Forschungsprogramm waren zwei grundsätzliche Ziele verbunden. Zum einen sollte das bereits in der Erschließung befindliche Wohn- und Gewerbegebiet um weitere, über die im Bebauungsplan ausgewiesenen Städtebau qualitäten hinausgehende städtebauliche und umweltorientierte Qualitäten ergänzt und weiterentwickelt werden.

Tragende Funktionen bei der Realisierung dieses Projektziels kamen den beiden Projektbereichen "Verfahrensmanagment" und "Öffentlichkeitsarbeit" zu.

Zum anderen war das erklärte Ziel dieses Modellvorhabens die Förderung von Akzeptanz und Motivation von möglichst allen am Planungs- und Bauprozeß beteiligten Akteuren zum ökologischen orientierten Planen und Bauen. Dabei wurde neben Aspekten des kosten- und flächensparenden sowie des umweltgerechten Bauens und Wohnens auch besonders der Schaffung einen bewohner- und nutzerfreundlichen Wohnumfeldes große Bedeutung beigemessen. In diesem Zusammenhang wurde darüber hinaus angestrebt, ein modellhaftes Konzept für eine an ökologischen Kriterien orientierte Bestandspflege zu entwickeln, das eine frühzeitige Beteiligung der potentiellen Nutzer (Haus- und Wohnungseigentümer) vorsieht.

Mit Hilfe einzelner Projektbausteine sollte im Rahmen der Projektforschung insbesondere untersucht werden, ob auf ein im Planungsverfahren bereits weit fortgeschrittenes Wohnungsbauvorhaben noch Einfluß genommen werden kann, weitergehende als die im Bebauungsplanentwurf ausgewiesenen Qualitätsstandards zu verankern. Motivations- und akzeptansfördernde Aktivitäten sollten vor allem für die Bau- und Nutzungsphase im Hinblick auf ökologisch orientiertes Bauen und Wohnen im Vordergrund stehen, die es zu bewerten und zu begutachten galt.

Die Projektbegleitung durch "Schwerin Consult" bildete die Klammer zwischen den routinemäßigen Planungsarbeiten der Stadt und der Neubrandenburger Wohnungsgesellschaft als Erschließungsträger. Um die forschungsbezogenen Bausteine zu integrieren, wurde eine projektbegleitende Arbeitsgruppe gebildet, die sich folgenden Themen zuwandte:

- Möglichkeiten der Einflußnahme auf den in der Überarbeitung befindlichen Bebauungsplan (Genehmigungsphase), um zusätzliche städtebauliche Qualitäten zu verankern.

- Bau- und siedlungsökologische sowie gestaltungsbezogene Fragestellungen, die konkreten Bezug zu den Ausführungs- und Hochbauplanungen im Projektgebiet hatten.

- Fragen der Planung, Steuerung und Ausgestaltung von Aktivitäten im Rahmen der Öffentlichkeitsarbeit.

- Beratungen bei Umsetzungsstrategien von Ergebnissen in die Planungs- und Ausführungsarbeiten bei den kommunalen Planungsträgern, aber auch bei der kommunalen Wohnungsgesellschaft.

Die projektbegleitende Arbeitsgruppe tagte 13 mal und wurde durch häufige Abstimmungsrunden ergänzt. Den Höhepunkt bildeten drei durchgeführte Planungswerkstätten. Im Ergebnis der Tätigkeit konnten:

- Regelquerschnitte von Straßen zugunsten von Straßenbegleitenden Grundflächen reduziert werden,

- ehemals zwei Zentrumsbereiche zu einem städtebaulich zusammenhängenden Zentrum ohne Störung durch Autoverkehr zusammengelegt werden,

- der Grünflächenanteil im gesamten Gebiet weiter erhöht werden,

- der Versiegelungsgrad verringert werden, - die Verwendung von versickerungsfreundlichen Belägen und Materialien durchgesetzt werden.

Die Schaffung einen Beratungsbüros für umweltgerechtes Bauen wurde mit dem Ziel verfolgt, speziell sie Bauträger und Bauherren, die auf dem Lindenberg-Süd bauen wollen, möglichst umfassend, verständlich und pragmatisch über das Thema des umweltgerechten Bauens und Wohnens zu informieren und zu beraten. Es wurden umfangreiche Recherchen mit dem Ergebnis durchgeführt, daß Materialien zum ökologischen Bauen für Bauträger und Bauherren zusammengetragen und anwendungsorientiert aufbereitet wurden. Neben der Bearbeitung spezieller Themen aus dem Bereich des ökologischen Bauens, deren Ergebnis in Form von Informationsblättern ausgelegt und verteilt wurden, lag ein weiterer Arbeitsschwerpunkt in der Erstellung einer sogenannten "ökologischen Baufibel", die zu den einzelnen Themen des ökologischen Bauens Grundlageninformationen, anwendungsorientierte und verfahrenstechnische Hinweise bietet sowie auch mögliche Bezugsquellen ökologischer Baustoffe und Materialien benennt.

Die zu besprechenden Themen reichten in dem Beratungsbüro von Einzelaspekten des umweltgerechten Bauens, wie z.B. Anlage zur Regenwassernutzung oder Brauchwassererwärmung, energiesparende Wärmedämmung mit umweltfreundlichen Materialien usw. bis hin zu komplexen umweltfreundlichen Alternativen unter Wirtschaftlichkeitsaspekten im Zusammenhang mit ganzen Baube-schreibungen. Die Beratungsangebote wurden nicht nur von interessierten Bauherren des Wohngebietes Lindenberg-Süd wahr-genommen, sondern auch von Bauinteres-sierten aus der Stadt und der Region Neubrandenburg.

Was wurde erreicht?

Das mit dem Bebauungsplan erarbeitete Grünkonzept stellt hohe Ansprüche und wurde nur im Detail noch verändert. Auch wenn heute noch nicht allzuviel zu sehen ist, wird die Realisierung des Grünkonzeptes einen wesentlichen Wertanteil an der Qualität dieses Wohngebietes haben. Die Grundlagen dazu wurden mit der Standortwahl an sich, der Vernetzung öffentlicher und privater Freiflächen sowie dem entstehenden Fuß- und Radwegenetz geschaffen.

Eingebettet in diese günstige Ausgangs-situation haben im Ergebnis der Beratung eine Reihe von Bauherren den Sinn ökologischen Bauens erkannt. Die ersten Sonnenkollektoren in der Stadt Neubrandenburg befinden sich auf dem Lindenberg-Süd, mehrere Bauherren wählten Poroton, Fibuton oder den in Neubrandenburg hergestellten Kalksandstein als Baustoff, obwohl ihr ursprüngliches Projekt andere Baustoffe vorsah.

Wer erwartet hat, daß ich hier das Muster-beispiel ökologischen Bauens vorstelle, den habe ich sicher enttäuscht. Mir ging es viel mehr darum, Ihnen darzustellen, daß auch dort, wo sich das Nord-Süd-Gefälle und das Ost-West-Gefälle treffen (ich beziehe dies hier auf Deutschland), Menschen zu Recht anspruch auf Lebensqualität haben und daß es engagierte Kollegen gibt, die sich dieser Aufgabe stellen.

Vielleicht war es gerade die Zeit unmittelbar nach der Wende 1989/90, die es relativ leicht machte, neu gegebenen Handlungsspielraum selbst auszufüllen.

Stefan Resch, Dipl. Ing., Amtsleiter, Stadt-planungsamt, Stadt neubrandenburg, Deutschland.

Waterfront Areas: Case Studies

Waterfront-Bereiche: Beispiele

Kapitel Vierundsechzig

Düsseldorf ist an den Rhein zurückgekehrt

Kurt Schmidt

Düsseldorf, die Landeshauptstadt des Bundeslandes Nordrhein-Westfalen, hat heute 565 000 Einwohner innerhalb der Stadtgrenzen. In einem Radius von 50 km um die Stadt leben jedoch ca. 9 Millionen Menschen. Düsseldorf liegt geografisch am Rhein, war jedoch durch eine Hauptverkehrsstraße mit täglich bis zu 55 000 Fahrzeugen vom Rhein getrennt und ist heute an den Rhein zurückgekehrt.

Doch zuerst ein geschichtlicher Rückblick

1815 wurde Düsseldorf preußisch und Hauptstadt eines Regierungsbezirks, ab 1824 Versammlungsort der neugegründeten Provinzialstände. 1839 wurde eine erste feste Verbindung zum linken Rheinufer, eine Schiffbrücke errichtet. Düsseldorf entwickelte sich im Rahmen der Industrialisierung zur Verwaltungsstadt, Ausstellungsstadt, Kunststadt und zum Schreibtisch des Ruhrgebietes.

1888 beschloß die Stadtverordnetenversammlung den Bau eines Handels- und Industriehafens im Rheinknie der Lausward südlich der Altstadt und nördlich der 1870 eröffneten Eisenbahnstrecke über den Rhein nach Neuss. Der Sicherheitshafen nördlich der Altstadt wurde aufgegeben, er mußte der festen Straßenbrücke nach Oberkassel weichen.

1898 folgte der Beschluß, die Rheinufer mit der rechtsrheinischen Hochwassermauer und dem linksrheinischen Vorland neu auszubauen. Ein Beschluß, durch den die Stadt Düsseldorf ein neues Gesicht zum Rhein erhielt. Lassen Sie mich aus einem Gutachten des Hamburger Ingenieurs Andreas Meyer zitieren, in dem Herr Meyer auf die städtebaulichen Chancen hinweist, die sich aus dem geplanten Projekt ergeben:

"Eine breite, hoch angelegte, zweckmäßig geführte und gut gepflegte Uferstraße erschließt der Stadt die von der Bevölkerung lange entbehrte Zugänglichkeit und Benutzbarkeit ihrer schönen Lage am Rheinstrom. Von dieser Lage ist eigentlich nichts mehr übrig geblieben, der Aufenthalt an dem vernachlässigten Ufer ist unerquicklich. Düsseldorf hat seine Front seit langen Jahren in ausgesprochener Weise vom Rhein abgewendet, und dies wird von allen Seiten als ein großer Mangel der sonst so schönen Stadt empfunden und gerügt."

1902 war die neue Promenade hergestellt, die neben ihrer Funktion als Hochwasserschutz einen repräsentativen Boulevard und eine Autostraße auf der oberen Terrasse, und auf der unteren Terrasse, dem "Unteren Werft", eine Industrieverladehafennutzung aufnahm. Dieses Nebeneinander von Promenade, Autoverkehr und Industrienutzung war Ausdruck einer Epoche, in der der industrielle Aufschwung einen hohen gesellschaftlichen Stellenwert hatte. Gleichzeitig wurde diese Uferbefestigung nach Norden weitergeführt. Es wurde dort durch Aufschüttung der Golzheimer Insel ein 45 ha großes hochwasserfreies Gelände geschaffen, auf dem im Jahre 1902 die große Industrie-, Gewerbe- und Kunstausstellung stattfand, und auf dem sich heute der Rheinpark und der Ehrenhofbereich befinden.

Die 1902 geschaffene Promenade vor der Altstadt wurde im Laufe der letzten Jahrzehnte immer mehr vom Autoverkehr aufgefressen und für die Fußgänger entwertet. Täglich benutzten die als Bundesstraße 1 ausgewiesene Rheinuferstraße bis zu 55.000 Kraftfahrzeuge.

1946 wurde Düsseldorf von der britischen Militärregierung als Landeshauptstadt bestimmt. Nach provisorischen Unterbring-ungen im Operhaus und im Theatersaal der Firma Henkel fand das neue Parlament seinen Sitz im ehemaligen Ständehaus der preußischen Rheinprovinz.

1973 entsprach das Ständehaus nicht mehr den Anforderungen des Parlaments des größten deutschen Bundeslandes. Eine Erweiterung an Ort und Stelle in den vorhandenen Park hinein scheiterte an den Bürgereinsprüchen. Die Mitglieder des Parlaments reagierten empfind-lich und drohten, den Landtag in eine andere Stadt zu verlegen.

Seitens der Stadt reagierten wir sofort und übergaben dem Landtagspräsidenten bereits Ende April 78 alternative Überlegungen zu einem "Landtag am Rhein". Inzwischen hatten wir im Hafenbereich eine Entwicklung einge-leitet, auf die ich noch zurückkommen werde.

Wir konnten den Landtag von der Richtigkeit dieses Standorts überzeugen. 1979 fand für diesen Bereich ein erneuter Wettbewerb statt. Der erste Preis fiel am 22. Februar 1980 auf das Büro Eller, Meier, Walter.

Die grüne Achse vom Rhein zum Rhein

Das Leben einer Stadt fließt genausowenig kontinuierlich wie es unsere eigenen Leben tun. Äußere Einflüsse bringen Brüche und Einschnitte, andere Ereignisse sind von uns gewollt, Teilnahme an Olympiaden oder Bundesgartenschauen sind Anlässe, Jubiläen fordern zu besonderen Aktivitäten heraus. Für uns Planer bedeutet das immer Bündelung der Kräfte auf ein Ziel und auf einen zeitlichen Horizont.

1988 wurde Düsseldorf 700 Jahre alt. Bei einem Besuch der Bundesgartenschau in Stuttgart im Mai 1977 reifte der Plan, daß sich die Stadt Düsseldorf am Vorabend des Jubiläums, also 1987 für eine Bundesgartenschau bewerben solle. Am 30. Juni 77 erfolgte bereits ein entsprechender Ratsbeschluß.

Zur Gestaltung der Gartenschau schrieben wir einen europaweiten Wettbewerb aus, der sich bewußt nicht auf das Gelände südlich des Volksgartens beschränken sollte, sondern das Gebiet vom Fleher Wäldchen am Rhein über die Universität und deren Botanischen Garten, über das Gartenschaugelände, über Oberbilk und den Hauptbahnhof, über die Innenstadt und die Altstadt umfassen sollte, dort den Rhein wieder erreichend: "Grüne Achse vom Rhein zum Rhein" war das Thema.

Von dem langgehegten Wunsch, diese grüne Achse um eine tiefgelegte Rheinuferstraße am Rhein zu ergänzen, konnten wir Planer damals nur träumen.

Die Tieflegung der Rheinuferstraße

Ich hatte bereits erwähnt, daß es nicht leicht war, den Landtag für einen Standort am Rhein südlich der Kniebrücke zu überzeugen. Das für das Landtagsgebäude vorgesehene Grundstück war durch die als Hochstraße geführte B 1 in Verlängerung der Rheinuferstraße vom Stadt-gebiet getrennt. Dem Land wurde zugesagt, diese Hochstraße durch eine tiefgelegte Straße zu ersetzen, wenn die erste U-Bahnstrecke in der Innenstadt abgeschlossen und eine Finanzierung in Aussicht sei.

Anfang 1986 zeichnete sich eine Finanzierungsmöglichkeit ab, da der damalig zuständige Landesminister Christoph Zöpel zweckgebundene Straßenbaumittel weniger in Neubauten und mehr in Maßnahmen zur Verbesserung der Lebensqualität in den Städten lenkte. In Gesprächen mit der Landesregierung wurde deutlich, daß eine Tieflegung der Straße sich nicht auf den Landtagsbereich beschränken könne, sondern mindestens den Rheinuferbereich der Karlstadt und Altstadt mit einbeziehen müsse.

Alle Beteiligten waren sich darüber einig, daß eine solche Maßnahme mit ihrem hohen Kostenvolumen (eine halbe Milliarde DM wurde damals als Obergrenze gesehen) nur verantwortbar ist, wenn sie tief in die angrenzenden Stadtgebiete hinein eine Verbesserung der Lebensqualität bewirkt. Zwei Planergruppen, bestehend aus Stadtplanern, Architekten, Landschaftsplanern und Verkehrsplanern wurden aufgefordert, in einer ersten Ideenphase alle Chancen dazu auszuloten. Anfang 1987 lagen die Ergebnisse beider Gruppen vor.

Zur Beurteilung und weiteren Begleitung der Arbeiten wurde eine Lenkungsgruppe gebildet, bestehend aus den Vertretern des Rates, der Landesregierung, des Regierungspräsidenten, der Verwaltung und vier externen Fachberatern. In einer ersten Beurteilung hat die Lenkungsgruppe im März 87 die Arbeiten kritisch betrachtet und vorläufige Empfehlungen ausgesprochen. Vorläufig deshalb, weil bisher keine Kostenschätzungen vorlagen und die einzelnen Vorschläge noch weitergehend untersucht werden sollten.

Im Juni 87 trat die Lenkungsgruppe erneut zusammen, um nunmehr eine Zielrichtung und einen Zeithorizont für die weiteren Arbeiten vorzugeben. Am 15.7.1987 erfolgte der Grundsatzbeschluß im Rat. Im Dezember 89 war das erforderliche Planfeststellungsverfahren abgeschlossen. Am 14.12.89 erfolgte

der Baubeschluß im Rat, und am 20.12.89 wurden die ersten Aufträge an die Baufirmen erteilt. In einer ungeheuren Kraftanstrengung und unter persönlichem Einsatz aller Beteiligten waren alle Hürden genommen, alle Widersprüche ausgeräumt, war die Durchführung nicht mehr aufhaltbar.

Parallel zur Bauphase des Tunnels wurde die Planung zur Gestaltung der Oberfläche durch die in der ersten Phase getrennt arbeitenden und nunmehr zusammengeführten Planergruppen weitergeführt.

Eine nicht veränderte Rahmenbedingung war dabei die denkmalgeschützte Hochwassermauer. Lediglich im Bereich des Burgplatzes am alten Schloßturm konnte sich der Landeskonservator eine Veränderung vorstellen, wenn hier durch einen Wettbewerb eine städtebaulich hervorragende Lösung gefunden würde. Auf Wunsch des Planungsausschusses wurde dieser Wettbewerb auf den Bereich zwischen den beiden Brücken ausgedehnt. Die Gruppe um Herrn Prof. Fritschi erhielt den ersten Preis.

Ein besonders schwieriges Problem zeigte sich bei der wünschenswerten Einbeziehung von Künstlern bei der Gestaltung der Oberfläche. Die Finanzlage der Stadt hatte sich nach Vereinigung beider deutscher Staaten erheblich verschlechtert. Den zu einem Wettbewerb aufgeforderten Künstlern konnte nicht zugesichert werden, daß überhaupt Geld zur Verwirklichung ihrer Ideen vorhanden sein würde. Die Ergebnisse waren entweder nicht befriedigend oder nicht in die vorhandene Planung integrierfähig. Einigkeit bestand und besteht nur darin, daß dort kein Platz für "Abstellkunst" ist.

Um auf den durch die Tieflegung neu gewonnenen Flächen auch für Kinder Angebote zu machen, haben wir durch Schulwettbewerbe die Kinder in die Planung einbezogen. Wir wollten wegkommen von herkömmlichen Spielplatzausstattungen. Ich hoffe, daß sich hier noch einiges entwickelt. Ich sehe das, was jetzt gebaut ist, als Grundausstattung, die Überlagerungen aushält.

Die Entwicklung am alten Hafen

Parallel zu der geschilderten Entwicklung muß ein zweites Vorhaben gesehen werden, das eng mit dem Projekt der Tieflegung der Rheinuferstraße verknüpft ist: Die Bebauung südlich des Rathauses im Bereich des alten Hafens, der 1810 zugeschüttet wurde.

Diesen Planungsbereich kennzeichnet eine lange Reihe von nichtausgeführten Planungen. 1911 und 1925 wurden Wettbewerbe für Rathausneu- und Erweiterungsbauten durchgeführt, ohne zu einer Realisierung zu führen. In den fünfziger Jahren wurde die Idee eines Rathausneubaus wieder aufgenommen. Der erste Preisträger sah ein 46-geschossiges Hochhaus vor. Der Entwurf wurde durch einen Bebauungsplan abgesichert.

Anfang der 70er Jahre wurde diese, den Maßstab der Altstadt sprengenden Planung aufgegeben und erneut ein Wettbewerb mit dem Ziel einer der Altstadt angepaßten Bebauung mit einer Nutzungsmischung von Wohnen, Läden und nicht störenden Gewerbe ausgeschrieben. Das Ergebnis, das eine von der verkehrsreichen Rheinuferstraße und damit vom Rhein abgewendete Blockbebauung vorsah, wurde ebenfalls durch einen Bebauungsplan gesichert, der 1984 rechtskräftig wurde.

Bei Beginn der Bauarbeiten 1985 wurde überraschenderweise festgestellt, daß vom Bereich des alten Hafens und der Zitadelle mehr erhalten war, als vermutet wurde.

Als sich 1986 die Chance eröffnete, die Rheinuferstraße tief zu legen und vor dem Baugebiet anstelle der verkehrsreichen Straße eine Promenade zu errichten, hatten sich die Rahmenbedingungen grundlegend verändert.

Es folgten hitzige Debatten, fachliche Diskussionen. Sollen die historischen Teile liegen bleiben? Sind sie sichtbar zu machen? Oder können sie der späteren Aufschüttung des Ufers entsprechend angehoben werden? Ich selbst war damals für eine didaktische Lösung, bei der historische Bezüge sinnlich aber nicht lagegenau wieder sichtbar gemacht werden. Die Entscheidung fiel zugunsten der reinen Lehre der Denkmalpflege.

Ein neuer Wettbewerb wurde durchgeführt. Das Ergebnis ist verwirklicht. Hier wurde exemplarisch und überdeutlich dargestellt, welchen Chancen die Tieflegung der Verkehrsstraße für Düsseldorf bedeutet. Die Stadt öffnet sich wieder zum Rhein!

Der Hafenbereich

Von 1896 an wurde der Handels- und Industriehafen schrittweise bis zu einer Größe von 212 ha ausgebaut. Seine Funktionen sind heute:

- Das Kraftwerk Lausward, von dem aus zugleich die Fernwärmeversorgung für die Innenstadt erfolgt,

- der Handelshafen mit den Umschlagmöglichkeiten Schiene/Straße/Wasser,

- der Industriehafen mit den Weizenmühlen und Futterbetrieben,

- der Sporthafen.

1973 wurde dem Rat der Stadt Düsseldorf ein Gutachten vorgelegt, daß für die 212 ha große Hafenfläche zwei Alternativen vorsah:

Alternative I: Schrumpfung um 53 ha;

Alternative II: Schrumpfung um 99 ha.

In seinem Beschluß vom 18.7.74 blieb der Rat der Stadt Düsseldorf noch unterhalb der Alternative I und beschloß eine Schrumpfung um nur 33 ha.

Nach der Erörterung dieses Ratsbeschlusses in den Fachausschüssen des Rates, in der Verwaltung, mit der Hafenwirtschaft und der IHK, wurde am 8. Juli 76 dieser Beschluß auf eine Fläche von nunmehr noch 19 ha zurückgenommen. Gründe waren "inzwischen veränderte Umstände":

Die finanzwirtschaftliche Situation der Stadt,

- die veränderte Nachfragesituation nach Wohnungen und Büroflächen,

- exakte Kostenuntersuchungen verschiedener städtischer Dienststellen.

1978 wurde der Bau des Fernmeldeturms durch das Büro Harald Deilmann geplant. Wir hatten diesen Standort im Hinblick auf den Ausblick von der geplanten Aussichtsplattform und dem geplanten Restaurant ausgewählt. Unter diesen neuen Bedingungen hatten wir diesen Bereich dem Landtag zum Bau des neuen Landtagsgebäudes angeboten. Die Landzunge am Zollhafen wurde öffentliche Grünfläche, südlich des Fernmeldeturms boten wir das Grundstück dem WDR an. Aus einem Wettbewerb ging das Büro Parade als Sieger hervor.

Damit war die vom Rat freigegebene erste Phase mit 10 ha schneller bebaut als erwartet. Eine Freigabe der 2. Phase beiderseits der Kaistraße mit 9 ha sollte eigentlich erst nach 2010 erfolgen. Aber die Ereignisse überholten die Beschlüsse. Am 26.1.89 faßte der Rat einen

neuen Beschluß für die Phase 2 mit folgender Zielrichtung:

Die bauliche und visuelle Gestalt sollte geprägt sein

- durch Erinnerungen an den alten Hafen (Liegenlassen von Schienen im Pflaster, Erhalt von Kränen usw.)

- durch Erhalt und Umnutzung von Gebäuden

- durch kontrastreiche Neubauten

- durch Einbeziehung des Yachthafens

- durch raffiniert organisierte scheinbare Umordnung.

Die Nutzung sollte vorrangig bestimmt sein

- durch Medieneinrichtungen mit den ergänzenden Betrieben und weiterhin
- durch kleine Büroeinheiten, besonders für kreative Berufe

- durch kulturelle Einrichtungen (private Trägerschaft)

- durch Gastronomie

- durch spezifischen Einzelhandel

- durch Kunsthandwerk

- durch Atelier und/oder Wohnen

- durch Freiflächen, die zeitlich begrenzte Nutzungen zulassen.

Wie geht es weiter?

1990 wurde das gesamte Hafengelände von der Stadt an die Stadtwerke verkauft. Gemeinsam mit den Stadtwerken haben wir 1992 einen

Rahmenplan für die weitere Entwicklung des Hafens erarbeitet. Er zeigt die mittelfristigen Perspektiven auf. Danach können wir über die Landzunge der Speditionsstraße planerisch verfügen.

Aber langfristig haben wir natürlich schon Bilder in uns. Ein Sporthafenbereich durch eine Schleuse auf gleichen Wasserstand gehalten. Eine umgewandelte Fläche, auf der sich Wohnen, Arbeit und Freizeit ergänzen. Eine weiterentwickelte Uferpartie rund um den Bogen und in Hamm weiterlaufend. Aber diese Träume geben wir an unsere Enkel weiter.

Ausblick

Als Planer müssen wir Träume haben. Aber wir dürfen es nicht dabei belassen. Wir müssen alle Energie und Kreativität dazu verwenden, diese Träume in eine Verwirklichung umzusetzen.

Jede Stadt hat eine eigene Melodie, die gilt es zu erkennen. In Düsseldorf ist diese Melodie bestimmt von den großzügigen Alleen der Königsallee, der Heinrich-Heine-Allee, der Immermannstraße und der Luegallee.

In Oberkassel wird der alte Güterbahnhof umgewandelt. Aus einem Wettbewerb ging eine Idee hervor, bei der das für Düsseldorf typische Motiv der Allee aufgegriffen und in Fortsetzung der Luegallee weitergeführt wird.

Bei der Neuordnung im nördlichen Derendorf auf dem Landesgrundstück nördlich der Tannenstraße und auf dem aufgegebenen Gelände der Firma Rheinmetall tritt diese Melodie der prägenden Allee wieder auf. Der dort geplante Grünzug wird Teil eines größeren Grünzuges sein, der vom Nordpark ausgehend über den Nordfriedhof, das neue beplante Gelände und den Derendorfer Güterbahnhof, den Malkastenpark erreichen

wird. In einer großen Form wird er Derendorf und Golzheim umgreifen, ähnlich wie es der klassizistische Grünzug des Hofgartens mit der Königsallee, dem Kaiserteich und Spee'schen Graben um die Altstadt und Karlstadt tut.

Nördlich des Hauptbahnhofes wird die Post ihre umfangreichen Flächen aufgeben. Hier befinden wir uns noch der Zielfindungsphase. Im Herbst werden wir den Vorschlag zu einem Rahmenplan als Grundlage für einen städtebaulichen Ideenwettbewerb vorlegen.

Die Stadt Düsseldorf hat in ihren engen kommunalen Grenzen wenig Platz zur Ausdehnung. Der Schwerpunkt der Planung wird in den nächsten Jahren weiter in der Innenentwicklung liegen. Ich habe versucht, aufzuzeigen, welche Entwicklungen es da noch gibt.

Düsseldorf ist an den Rhein zurückgekehrt. Die täglichen 55.000 Kraftfahrzeuge sind unter der Erde verschwunden.

An einem Wochenende im Juni dieses Jahres haben die Bürger der Stadt und der Region die Allee in Besitz genommen. Der Landtag, die Staatskanzlei, das Rathaus und der Westdeutsche Rundfunk hatten ihre Türen geöffnet. Auf der anderen Rheinseite standen die Drachen am bewölkten Himmel über der Rheinwiese. Den Abschluß krönte ein Feuerwerk mit gleißenden Wasser-, oder richtiger, Feuerfällen von den beiden Brücken. - Düsseldorf war an den Rhein zurückgekehrt.

50 Jahre nach der Entscheidung, Düsseldorf zur Hauptstadt von Nordrhein-Westfalen zu machen, wird der Stadtumbau am Ufer des Rheinstroms in überzeugender Weise sichtbar.

Dipl. -Ing. Kurt Schmidt, Leiter des Stadtplanungsamtes Düsseldorf, Deutschland.

Chapter Sixty-Five

A Comprehensive Land Use Plan For San Francisco's Waterfront

Eva Liebermann

History

Between 1850 and 1870 the city grew from 25,000 to 150,000 inhabitants. Commerce and manufacturing of textiles, shoes, machinery and food products, located mainly along the waterfront, flourished. The State Legislature in 1863 created a Board of State Harbor Commissioners, entrusting it with the permanent control of harbor installations in the city. In 1890 construction began on the Great Seawall (completed in 1914) which extended from China Basin to the foot of Taylor Street. Even after the transcontinental railroad reached Oakland in 1869 bulky goods from the East coast and Europe continued to travel around Cape Horn for another 30 years. For over 100 years San Francisco remained the largest port on the Pacific coast.

The earthquake of 1906 and the subsequent fire obliterated Downtown, Chinatown and parts of the waterfront, but the city was rebuilt in record time constructing 20,000 buildings in three years. Between 1912 and 1930 many of the finger piers along the waterfront were built in order to satisfy the need for more docking facilities. During the thirties waterborne commerce declined. Because of the construction of the Oakland Bay Bridge and the Golden Gate Bridge ferry service to the 1896 completed Ferry Building was also drastically reduced. At their peak, ferry boats had carried 50 million passengers per year, about 100,000 per day. World War II represented a new height of maritime activities with the embarkation of troops, transportation of goods, ship building and repair happening all along the waterfront. For a few months at the end of the war San Francisco was the largest port in the United States.

The waterfront continued to prosper between 1950 and 1960 due to busy passenger traffic (4000 ships per year). But then the demand for Port facilities as offered in San Francisco steadily declined. Airline travel took over. Break bulk operations gave way to containerized cargo. While San Francisco's response to this change was slow, Oakland aggressively pursued federal grants to convert its mudflats to modern container terminals. Foreign competition in shipbuilding and ship repair dealt another blow to maritime activity at the Port. Although San Francisco eventually did invest in container facilities at Pier 94, Oakland was able to capture 92% of the San Francisco Bay Area Market share.

The Challenge

Today, San Francisco, the once thriving port, is at an important point of decision: how much land and facilities to allocate for maritime-industrial use: cargo shipping, ship repair, fishing, ferries, cruise ships, recreational boating, and how, on the other hand, to use outdated breakbulk piers, shipbuilding and repair docks, maritime support facilities, decaying wharfs and the balance of land on the seven and a half mile waterfront that has not yet been converted to non-maritime commercial, residential and open space uses.

Introduction to the Port

Nearly the entire seven mile long Bay waterfront of the city of San Francisco is publicly owned. This stems from the fact that most of this land was former tideland, filled by the State of California to provide docks and wharfs to facilitate commerce. This land is impressed with a "public trust" on behalf of all the people of California. The Port became the trustee of this land in 1968. As a condition of the transfer the State required the City to create a Port Commission with the authority to use, operate and manage the port.

The Port receives no financial support from the City's General Budget and relies solely on revenues from the property under its stewardship to fulfill its mandate which is to promote maritime commerce, navigation, fisheries and public access and protect natural resources. Its facilities are old and maintenance costs have outpaced revenues. Revenue generating opportunities are severely limited because of land use regulations imposed on the Port.

San Francisco has one of the most regulated waterfronts in the world. In addition to local zoning and Master Plan policies which apply to all city property, port lands are further regulated by (1) State laws, and (2) the Bay Conservation and Development Commission (BCDC). This is a State Agency set up in 1969 with the specific purpose of preserving San Francisco Bay and regulating development on its shores.

Under (1) public trust laws, Port property can never be sold or used for private purposes. This has been interpreted to mean that housing and non-maritime office is not allowed anywhere on Port property. Permitted uses are limited to maritime commerce, navigation, fisheries, and public recreation. BCDC (2) is even stricter, permitting only water-dependent uses and discouraging any further filling of the Bay.

These regulatory limitations combined with citizens' resistance to certain land use developments on port land (e.g. hotels, sailing center, new cruise terminal) have prevented new activities on the waterfront.

Thus the Port is attempting to balance the often competing interests of its maritime and commercial tenants with its public trust responsibilities to the people of the State of California, and its responsibilities to the people of San Francisco whose waterfront it oversees.

Planning Initiative

In November 1990, San Francisco voters adopted an initiative which required preparation of a comprehensive waterfront land use plan for Port properties with maximum feasible public input. It should be noted here that San Franciscans are especially adroit in using "the public process." They honed their political skills in their fight and eventual victory at stopping federally sponsored freeways. A public referendum on any issue can be called through the petition of only 10% of the people that voted in the previous election. San Franciscans freely make use of voter initiatives for planning issues.

The citizen initiative coincided with the 1989 earthquake which focused San Francisco's attention on the waterfront, particularly in the Ferry Building area. The double-decker freeway which had encircled the downtown area and thereby cut it off from the waterfront and the Ferry Building, was damaged to such an extent that it had to be torn down. Local authorities recognized this opening up of the waterfront as a positive outcome of an otherwise devastating event and a great opportunity to reconnect the City with its waterfront. They persuaded CALTRANS, the responsible state agency, not to rebuild the 35-years-old freeway but to seek alternative traffic solutions. The removal of the freeway will also allow the City to build a grand civic open space in its place, adjacent to the waterfront. The space is presently being designed.

Planning Process

The Waterfront Plan was prepared under the direction of the Waterfront Plan Advisory Board, a 27-member citizens body, appointed specifically for this process by the Mayor, City Council and Port Commission. The Advisory Board was carefully selected to represent a diversity of interests on the waterfront including maritime industry, labor unions, and neighborhood and citywide representatives. During three years, planning staff and the Advisory Board met twice a month in public meetings to craft the land use plan.

The planning effort was divided into three phases. In Phase I locations and sizes of land parcels were identified for: cargo-shipping and other water-dependent uses such as fishing, ship repair, cruise ships, recreational boating ferries, marinas and historic ships, based on industry-specific analysis of existing needs and growth-potential. These maritime-industrial and water-dependent uses were considered to have first priority in the allocation of land.

In Phase 11, the remaining port property not used by or reserved for maritime use was considered for other desirable non-maritime uses such as public access, open space, mixed use commercial development, public facilities (e.g. museums) and housing. In Phase 11 the first two phases were integrated into the comprehensive land use plan and evaluated with respect to their overall compatibility and environmental impacts.

The preparation of the Waterfront Land Use Plan has been guided by six goals:

1. To reunite the City with its waterfront

2. To reserve enough land for maritime uses

3. To revitalize the waterfront to create jobs, revenues, public amenities and benefits to the Port, City and State.

4. To provide a variety of activities for all San Franciscans and visitors to enjoy.

5. To facilitate appreciation and enjoyment of the Bay, by providing parks, plazas, walkways and open spaces at the water's edge.
6. To respect the historic character of the waterfront while creating new opportunities.

7. To achieve exemplary design quality in new developments.

Comprehensive Land Use Plan

The Port jurisdiction extends from Fisherman's Wharf in the north to India Basin to the south. The Plan envisions the creation of five sub-areas, each with its own inherent conditions, character, and development objectives.

1. **Fisherman's Wharf**: Fishing and Tourist/ Visitor Area

Fisherman's Wharf extends from Aquatic Park to Pier 39 and which sports the fishing harbor, fish handling facilities and a lively tourist area with shops, restaurants and hotels. The objective is to enhance it as a fishing and visitors center. This will be achieved by rebuilding the Hyde Street Pier for the fishing fleet and adding 88 berths as well as by modernizing Pier 45 according to stringent Federal Standards and by adding a Fisheries Research center. The existing ship museum, ferries and excursion boats will be retained in an improved arrangement. A new open space will be created in the very center of the area for get-togethers, festivals, outdoor markets by moving parking to an underground garage.

2. **Northeast Waterfront**: Recreational boating, public use, commercial uses and gateway area:

This area extends from Pier 35 to Pier 7. The objective is to protect the existing cargo operations. However, if these are going to be consolidated with the other maritime operations in the southern waterfront, the area is to be opened up for recreational maritime operations complemented with public uses and commercial services. New development should be designed to protect and enhance the historic maritime character of this part of the waterfront. The area is also seen as the gateway to Chinatown and North Beach.

3. **Ferry Building Area**: Transit, civic, visitor, commercial area:

The Ferry Building area stretches from Pier 5 to Folsom Street. It is dominated by the historic Ferry Building and Agriculture Building situated where Market Street meets the Embarcadero Roadway which encircles the entire waterfront. The objective for this area calls for the preservation and restoration of the historic buildings and their use as major transit, civic use, visitor and conference center and a gateway to the city. Ferries, hydrofoils, water taxis, excursion boats and historic ships would be complemented with uses such as public market, visitor center, conference facilities and shops.

4. **South Beach/China Basin Area**: Maritime, entertainment, housing area

The waterfront between Pier 22-1/2 and Mariposa Street is referred to as South Beach/China Basin. The objective here is to continue the existing maritime activities. These together with the yacht harbor at Pier 40 will retain a maritime presence. The existing land uses in this area also include sizable residential development on island parcels.

New uses proposed in the plan are family amusement, nighttime entertainment and more housing on inland lots.

5. **Southern Waterfront**: Industrial Maritime area

The area between Mariposa Street and India Basin is called the southern waterfront. The Port's Land Use Plan targets this area as the center of the industrial maritime operations. Much of the area is undeveloped and the two existing container terminals have operated well below capacity for years. Although cargo shipping in the Bay Area is projected to increase fourfold by 2020, there are many variables that will determine where that business will take place.

The objective for this area is to aggressively pursue cargo shipping but allow interim (10-20 years) uses to generate revenue from these parcels.

Eva Lieberman is Senior Planner for the Planning Department of the City and County of San Francisco, California.

Chapter Sixty-Six

Seaway Transportation in the Istanbul Metropolitan Area

Tülay Kilinçaslan

Introduction

The old city of Istanbul is situated on the European shore of the Bosphorus, a strait linking the Black Sea with the Sea of Marmara. The scenery on both sides of the strait is varied and beautiful. Several villages line each shore with numerous fine residences on the European side; the city of Istanbul lies at the southern end of the strait. Guarding the entrance to the Marmara, the city of Istanbul strategically occupies a triangular promontory and is washed on the north by the Golden Horn (Haliç), a narrow inlet which forms an excellent harbour. A broad valley, through which there once flowed a small stream, the Lycus, divides the promontory from the west to the southeast into two masses of elevated ground a long ridge overlooking the Golden Horn and an isolated hill in the southwest. The ridge consists of six eminences, so that, altogether, there are seven hills.

The Golden Horn, spanned by the Atatürk and Galata Bridges, divides old Istanbul. Facing Istanbul on the Asiatic side are Üsküdar (ancient Chrysopolis) and Kadiköy (ancient Chalcedon). Greater Istanbul embraces not only Üsküdar and Kadiköy but an almost uninterrupted, though narrow, ribbon of settlements on both sides of the Bosphorus and, for a considerable distance, on both the European and Asiatic shores of the Sea of Marmara. The inhabited areas of the city proper stretch from old Istanbul to Küçükçekmece, about 33 kilometers to the southwest and, on the opposite shore, from Üsküdar to Pendik, a distance of about 30 kilometers.

Istanbul has always been a cosmopolitan city. The population of Istanbul has been increasing steadily since 1930. The census figures of 1945 showed 860,558 persons within the city limits; that of 1960 showed 1,465,535. In 1990 the total population was 10 million. The city structure and urban transportation system are closely related. The expansion of the city in certain directions caused the improvements of transport services to these areas. Today, transportation in the city is served by several public transport modes: buses, minibus jitneys, light rail transport, and a limited number of ferries and low-capacity sea buses connecting the old city with the villages of the Bosphorus and the Asiatic coast of Marmara Sea and the Golden Horn. A subway system is currently under construction.

Waterside Settlements

Istanbul, by taking advantages of her location, has utilized the unique opportunity provided by seaway transportation. The use of rowboats, the first public transport vehicles, to carry passengers and freight increased rapidly during the 19th century. During the 19th century upper-class bureaucrats and members of minority populations started to live along the Bosphorus. Waterside residences on the Bosphorus, as well as on Golden Horn, were accessible by rowboats. The number of rowboats tied to piers in Istanbul increased from 3996 in 1802 to 19,000 in 1844. With sizes varying from two to twelve oars, these row-boats were operated on a shuttle system basis. Boats became an indispensible part of the city life.

Development of the settlements on the shores of Bosphorus accelerated the demand for seaway transportation. Both a Russian and an English ferry-boat started to operate on the Bosphorus in 1837. In 1844 the first Ottoman seaway transport company was founded and began to operate daily ferry services along the coastline of the Marmara. In 1851, another private company, the Sirket-i Hayriye, was founded but its operations were limited to the Bosphorus.

In 1905 paddle-wheel steamers were replaced with screw-driven boats and the daily number of passengers on the Bosphorus increased to 49,000 in 1912. Another maritime transportation company started carrying 22,300 passengers per day along the coast of the Golden Horn. Settlements along the shores of Istanbul expanded as the number of boats increased. The quiet, peaceful atmosphere of the daily boat trips always attracted people. The fact that intra-city transportation was carried out by boat lines encouraged the expansion of Istanbul along the coasts.

Istanbul Transport System

By the end of the 1920's, Istanbul had developed in strips that were parallel to the sea coast and the railroad tracks, due to the fact that intracity transportation had been left to large scale rail and sea transportation firms. During those years, horse-drawn trams and railroads were first introduced to the urban transportation system.

The first motor car entered Istanbul around the year 1908. An increase in the number of motor cars in Istanbul occurred after the First World War. In 1927 53,600 passengers were carried per day by motor cars and horse carriages. During the years 1926 and 1927 another development concerning public transportation occurred: the beginning of bus services. Although limited, the increase in the use of automobiles and buses created new demands for the construction of roads outside, as well as within the city. Several wide boulevards opened. The rise in the number of motor vehicles caused a resultant increase in the number of car-ferries.

Istanbul retained its characteristics of being a sea-shore city up until the end of the 1960's. After this decade, however, the city began to spread out into all directions. Historical relationship of the Istanbul resident with its seas disappeared. It became increasing difficult for city residents to reach the shore and the sea began to lose its effectiveness as a means of transportation.

In 1973 the first Bosporus Bridge and beltways were officially opened to use. The opening of the bridge caused alterations in the land use pattern and changed the transportation mode between Asia and Europe. In spite of this change the maritime lines retained its attractiveness and carried 325,100 passengers per day in 1975.

By 1970 small enterprises had become dominant in the public transportation system. It has been estimated that minibus jitneys and other small entrepreneurial transport means were carrying an average of 695,000 passengers per day. A total of 9.3% of commuters preferred the use of private vehicles; 57.4% utilized the vehicles of small enterprisers, while 33.3% used public vehicles.

Motorboat *dolmushes* (jitneys) also appeared as an additional type of small entrepreneurial service in maritime transportation. In 1970, 43 motorboats with passenger capacities varying between 40 and 150 were in operation, and these have been estimated to have transported 30,000 passengers per day. The city-operated maritime lines were carrying 325,100 passengers per day.

The city center began to spread towards the north and the density increased along the Bosphorus shores. It began to lose its residential characteristics. The beauty deriving from the combination of unique architecture of the elegant residences with green areas began to deteriorate.

In 1975 a total of 1,193,000 persons were employed in the city of Istanbul. 998,000 (84%) worked on the European side while 195,000 (16%) worked on the Asian side. Same year the percentages of the total population on both sides of the Strait were 72% and 28% respectively. These percentages show that travel demand between Asia and Europe was continuing. This demand was shared by a variety of transportation vehicles, but mainly by buses.

With the opening of the second Bosphorus Bridge and its connecting beltways the formerly unified central city area began moving towards the east, the west, the north-west, and the north-east to form a multi-poled metropolitan area. The pressure from the steadily increasing population along the shores of the Bosphorus escalated density on the European side.

The land use patterns and macroforms which are related to the transportation systems not only resulted in the dissolution of the relationship with the shore, but also resulted in a web of settlements within a metropolis covering an area having a diameter of 75 kilometers for which it has become extremely difficult to provide transportation services.

Currently small capacity transportation services, such as taxis and minibus jitneys, hold a larger share in total transportation modes than large capacity buses. The share of rail transportation which has been providing service to the city for many long years totals 6.8%, while sea transportation's share of the total does not exceed 8.4%.

Maritime Transportation in the Metropolitan Areas

Various sizes and types of vessels are used to provide maritime transportation in world-wide metropolitan areas. Technological advances have also brought about a steady stream of changes in maritime conveyances and new types of vessels have been developed for use in inter-city transportation. Besides the traditional slow-sailing, local sized vessels, hovercraft, hydrofoil, and catamaran type high-speed vessels are being used in many metropolitan areas.

The urban life styles of both Hong Kong and Venice include a close relationship with the sea and sea vessels are used for a multitude of purposes in both cities. Venice and Hong Kong provide traditional boat tours for its tourists, as does Istanbul, especially during the summer months. The boat trips down the Bosphorus afford a stunning view of the city center surrounded by numerous historical buildings.

Organization methods used are very important in terms of reduction of loading times. One example of an effective maritime transportation system is that of Hong Kong which has piers and loading systems that are conducive to fast arrival and departure. Double deck boats and piers permit fast loading. The city of Vancouver has used new technologies with sea buses to reduce boarding time. Small jitney boats in Vancouver, Canada and passenger boats on the Thames in London provide service with only one captain and one sailor.

As the twenty-first century brings the commuter increased stress, greater significance is being given to urban transportation systems which are at once both more comfortable and safer. The need for the development of public transportation, rather than individual transportation systems is also becoming more obvious. Seaway transportation causes less pollution, saves energy. Another positive feature of this kind of transportation is that it is a quite relaxing service. When taking all these factors into consideration, many agree that sea transportation should be given more significance.

Development Of Maritime Transportation in the Istanbul Metropolitan Area

Istanbul is situated along an extended body of water but, currently, only a small portion of the sea shore has been reserved for recreational and entertainment purposes. The fact that only 7% of all transportation in the Istanbul metropolitan area consists of maritime transportation is ample proof that the concept of water, especially so the characteristic of being a seaside city has become abstracted from the every day life of the city.

According to a research conducted in 1993, fifty percent of all sea trips taken in the Istanbul metropolitan area are for work purposes. In addition to the high rate of work related transportation there was also an increased number of trips for entertainment, shopping, and educational purposes. A quarter of the passengers using these lines are traveling for educational purposes and this kind of travel is of course clustered among certain periods of the year. In spite of its unique suitability for

this kind of purpose the total number of instances of sea travel for entertainment purposes has never exceeded 13%.

Passengers who prefer seaway transportation are spread over a very wide area in the city. There is no maritime service allowing passengers to travel between outlying points in the city. The number of passengers who must travel from one outer area into the central city only to transfer in order to reach another outer point should not be underestimated.

Very comfortable sea buses provide rapid service connecting the eastern and western shores of the Marmara Sea. In spite of the fact that passengers prefer these kinds of vessels they have not been designed to carry a large number of passengers. Sea buses are primarily utilized by upper income level individuals.

Conclusion

The shore is a source providing a variety of utilization possibilities, both in terms of its land and its sea uses. It is both natural and inevitable that seaside cities like Istanbul should have development patterns that stretch along its sea shores. The shore is an important source with the potential of being used as a recreational area. In addition to the importance of the shore as a settlement area, the potential that the shore carries for providing public transportation must also be taken into consideration.

Realistic solutions can be brought to the fore if the inter-city transportation plan is developed according to research based on the fundamental characteristics of the various services arising out of a transportation system and if the proposed solutions are based on hard facts.

In the search for solutions to transportation problems various experiences have proved that more benefits would be derived from low-cost applications before making endeavors which require high cost investments. Various countries have developed systems in which high passenger capacity vehicles transport passengers within a boundary surrounding the city center. These vehicles provide services within and to the points of high passenger demand. Small capacity modes of transportation are used to transfer passengers from this boundary to outlying districts. In Istanbul the efficient use of large capacity vessels in maritime lines could be utilized to meet the high demands of passengers to travel to the city center.

One of the current aims in the development of mass transportation systems is to minimize the negative influences to the environment caused by transportation vehicles. The use of sea vessels as mass transportation becomes even more attractive to seaside cities when their non-polluting, and energy saving features combined with their relaxing characteristics are taken into consideration.

The number of pier closures is constantly increasing even though efforts should be underway to develop the types of piers and vessels. In metropolitan area boat terminals are not only points that provide transfer opportunities. They should also be considered as settings which have a strong influence over social and cultural effects. The lives of city residents could attain new dimensions if these characteristics of terminal are taken into consideration. A network of maritime lines that are spread along the entire coast will lead to the development of a life style which includes the interconnection of the land and the sea.

Once a city which lived in unison with the sea, Istanbul is again waiting to be reunited with its waters. The health and the beauty of the city could return if an efficiently operated seaway transportation were operationalized, and the traffic problems of the city could be considerably lightened with a sea transportation system. With a maritime transportation system that is in operation during the day and night the water upon which the city was born and those same waters that gave the city its history for generations may be returned to Istanbul.

Tülay Kilinçaslan, Ph.D., Arch. Eng. teaches in the Faculty of Architecture, Department of Urban and Regional Planning at Istanbul Technical University, Turkey.

Revitalisierung von Hafen- und Ufer-Bereichen in Hamburg

Dirk Schubert

Durch Werften- Stahlkrise und Containeris-ierung des Güterumschlags sind nicht nur zehntausende von Arbeitsplätzen verloren gegangen, sondern auch große Brachflächen im Hafen entstanden, wie z.B. bei den Umschlags- und Lagerflächen für Erz und Kohle sowie bei den Mineralölbetrieben. Diese Industriebrachen bestehen zum großen Teil aus kontaminierten Böden, die vor einer neuen Nutzung gereinigt werden müssen. Der tiefgreifende strukturelle Wandel, dem viele Hafenstädte seit Ende der sechziger Jahre unterliegen, wird vor allem in zwei Richtungen thematisiert: Einmal als Problem des Niedergangs und der wirtschaft-lichen, technologischen und räumlichen Re-Strukturierungen von Häfen und Hafen-regionen und zum anderen als Planungs-aufgabe, die häufig brachgefallenen Uferbereiche, die "Waterfront" wieder zu reaktivieren und neuen Nutzungen und Verwertungen zuzuführen.

Auch in Hamburg ging mit der Abnahme der ökonomischen Bedeutung des Hafens bald eine Zunahme der öffentlichen Aufmerksamkeit über den weiteren Umgang mit den hafen-nahen Flächen einher. Mit dem Zusammen-wirken öffentlicher und privater Investitionen (Private-Public-Partnership) und neuer Plan-ungen der Behörden sollte die Re-Integration der Häfen und Uferzonen in das städtische Gefüge betrieben werden. In Hamburg ist es vor allem der Streifen entlang des nördlichen Elbufers mit Blick über die Elbe auf das gegenüberliegende südliche Elbufer - das Hamburger Hafenpanorama schlechthin - an dem sich diese Bemühungen zunächst festmachten. Anfang der achtziger Jahre gab es

hier heterogene, teilweise suboptimale Nutz-ungen und eine Mischung von Bauten aus der Zeit von der Mitte des letzten Jahrhunderts bis in die Nachkriegszeit. Diese Kulisse prägte die Hamburger "Visitenkarte" für mit dem Schiff ankommende Besucher.

In anderen Städten begonnene, oder bereits abgeschlossene Projekte der "Waterfront Revitalization" ließen auch Hamburg Mitte der achtziger Jahre initiativ werden. Bei allen diesen Vorhaben anderer Hafenstädte sollte die jeweils ökonomisch abnehmende Bedeutung der Häfen durch neue Planungen für die Uferrandzonen kompensiert werden. Es sollten neue Nutzungen gefunden werden und erlebbare Identifikationsmerkmale und Anzie-hungspunkte für Bewohner, Besucher und Touristen, aber auch anspruchsvolle Arbeits-plätze geschaffen werden. Da Hamburg aufgrund seiner damaligen geopolitischen Randlage im westeuropäischen Wirtschafts-raum bei der zunehmenden interkommunalen und internationalen Konkurrenz um Firmenansiedlungen weiter ins Hintertreffen zu geraten drohte, wurden an den Umbau der Uferzonen große Erwartungen der Aufwertung mit positiven Folgen für die Stadt geknüpft.

Daher sollten Investoren diese "Filetstücke" für Neuansiedlungen schmackhaft gemacht werden. Bausenator Wagner formulierte die Aufgabenstellung wie folgt: "In vielen euro-päischen und außereuropäischen Hafenstädten - Partner Hamburgs im Welthandel - gibt es seit einigen Jahren in den innenstadtnahen Hafengebieten erhebliche wirtschaftliche und bauliche Veränderungen. Besonders in den reizvollen Übergangszonen zwischen City und Hafen entstehen ganz neue, interessante und lebendige Stadtviertel. Die nicht mehr benötigten Hafenflächen werden dort für die Entwicklung von Gewerbe-, Dienstleistungs- und Industriebereichen ebenso genutzt wie für Wohnstandorte. Kopenhagen, Rotterdam, London und New York, um nur wenige Beispiele zu nennen, haben diesen Weg bereits erfolgreich beschritten". Die Diskus-sionen um die Revitalisierung von Hafen- und Uferzonen beziehen sich in Hamburg auf sehr unter-schiedlich geprägte Strukturen:

- Flächen im Bereich des Hafengebietes, die brachgefallen sind und/oder suboptimal genutzt sind. Sie könnten im Rahmen eines Flächenrecyclings neuen gewerblichen Nutzungen zugeführt werden. Auch Wohnnutzungen sind in Teilbereichen denkbar. Zur Umsetzung derartiger Wohn-gebietsplanungen müssen diese Flächen allerdings aus dem Hafengebiet (und der Zuständigkeit des Amtes für Strom- und Hafenbau) herausgeschnitten werden, da im Bereich des Hafens keine Wohnungen liegen dürfen.

- Flächen für Hafenerweiterungen, die im Rahmen des Hafenplanes festgelegt sind. Hier ist vor allem Altenwerder zu nennen, ein ehemaliges Fischerdorf, das bereits vor Jahren geräumt wurde, und einem geplanten Containerterminal weichen sollte. Das Planfeststellungsverfahren läuft noch, nach Abschluß soll sofort mit den Bauarbeiten begonnen werden.

- Flächen im Bereich des Harburger Binnenhafens. Für den ehemals unabhängig und in Konkurrenz zu Hamburg von Preußen betriebenen kleineren Schleusen-hafen und die Speichergebäude, Lager-häuser und Silos sind Ideenwettbewerbe durchgeführt worden und Umnutzungs-konzepte entwickelt worden.

- Flächen am südlichen Elbufer, den früheren Standorten der Werften. Diese inzwischen freigeräumten Flächen liegen genau gegenüber dem Stadtzentrum, bilden also den Blickfang vom nördlichen auf das südliche Elbufer. Hier gibt es Pläne für ein neues Logistik- und Bürozentrum, die aber wegen der problematischen Verkehrs-erschließung (Elbtunnel, oder Fähre) noch nicht realisiert worden sind.

- Flächen am nördlichen Elbufer, östlich des Fischmarktes. Dieser Bereich umfaßt die "Hafenstraße", die Landungsbrücken, Neu-bauten von Gruner und Jahr an den Vorsetzen, die Fleetachse, die Speicherstadt und die Kehrwiederspitze.

- Flächen in Hammerbrook, einem von Kanälen durchgezogenen vormals gewerb-lichindustrielle genutztem Gebiet, nördlich der Elbe, daß nun als Erweiterungsgebiet der Hamburger City mit Bürohäusern ("City-Süd") bebaut worden ist.

Die Aufgaben der Revitalisierung und Neuordnung stellen sich für diese Flächen von der Lagegunst, der Verkehrsanbindung, dem Gebäudebestand, den Altlasten und den Planungsmöglichkeiten her sehr unter-schiedlich dar. Es gibt daher keine allgemein-gültigen Patentrezepte der Revitalisierung von Hafen- und Uferzonen, sondern es ist wichtig die lokalen Besonderheiten präzise zu analysieren, Potentiale vor Ort und Konfliktlinien zu erkunden und die Bewohner und Gewerbetreibenden in die Diskussionen um eine Neuordnung dieser Bereiche einzubeziehen.

Das nördliche Elbufer und die "Perlenkette"

Die folgende Skizze von Projekten und Planungen bezieht sich stadträumlich nur auf das nördliche Elbufer und den Bereich zwischen Neumühlen und dem Fischmarkt. Für die Vorhaben am nördlichen Elbufer wurde von der Bauverwaltung der pfiffige Begriff der "Perlenkette" gefunden. Dieses Konzept ging davon aus, daß für diesen Bereich keine flächendeckende Strategie möglich sei, sondern daß punktuelle spektakuläre Vorhaben mittel- bis langfristig auch positive Anstoßeffekte und eine Aufwertung dieser Hafenrandzonen bewirken könnten. Oberbaudirektor Egbert Kossak organisierte 1985 das 2. Hamburger Bauforum, um in einer internationalen Architektenrunde Ideen für Bauten am Nordufer der Elbe entwickeln zu lassen. Das Ergebnis des Bauforums war ein Stadtbild- betontes Potpourri verschiedenster Architektur-ansätze. Einer der Teilnehmer bewertete das Bauforum als "Animations- Spektakel mit einem Architektur-Buquet aus Stilblüten". Mit der "Erfindung" der "Perlenkette" für das nördliche Elbufer war durch Bauforen, Wettbewerbe und die Berichterstattung in den Medien das Thema "Hamburg zurück an die Elbe" weit über Hamburg hinaus diskutiert worden. Einer breiten Hamburger öffentlichkeit wurden hier die scheinbar ausschließlich positiven Möglichkeiten der Attraktivitätssteigerung des Hafenrandes präsentiert.

Räumlich bezogen sich die Vorschläge des Bauforums auf den westlichen Bereich des nördlichen Elbufers zwischen Neumühlen und dem Fischmarkt. Dieser Bereich ist durch einen ca. 18-23 Meter hohen Geesthang und einen flachen Uferstreifen geprägt. Schon in der Zeit des Nationalsozialismus gab es Planungen für diesen Bereich und mit dem einzigen Hochhaus, daß Hitler hier zulassen wollte - "da Hamburg so etwas Amerikanisches hätte" - sollte das "Gesicht Hamburgs der Elbe zugewandt werden". Kritiker bemängelten daher durchaus zu Recht formale Ähnlich- keiten zwischen den Entwürfen von Gutschow aus der Zeit des "3. Reiches" und einigen Ideen des Bauforums, besonders ein spanischer Entwurf hatte sich mit Monumentalität auf der ganzen Länge des Planungsgebietes "hervorgetan". Aber die Vorstellungen zu

Hamburgs "Elb-Gesichtern" haben sich auch gewandelt. Oberbaudirektor Kossak argument- ierte: "An Gutschows Konzept war nicht die Idee an sich - die Stadt an die Elbe zu bringen, der Hafenstadt Hamburg eine Orientierung zur Elbe und zum Hafen zu geben - falsch. Die Funktionen und der städtebauliche Mabstab, in denen Gutschow seine Ideen verwirklichen wollte, waren falsch". Wie wichtig eine repräsentative "Elbfassade" für Hamburg ist, ist durchaus umstritten. Der Blick von der Elbe auf die Stadt hat für die meisten Besucher, die mit der Bahn, dem Auto oder Flugzeug kommen, an Bedeutung verloren. Sie bietet sich noch den Passagieren der von See kommenden Schiffe und kommt eigentlich nur noch den Teilnehmern einer Hafenrundfahrt zu Gute.

Den Veranstaltern des Bauforums ging es aber nicht nur um eine Revitalisierung in der schmalen Zone des nördlichen Elbufers, es sollte ein "integriertes Programm" für die Hafenrandentwicklung und für die innere Stadt mit den benachbarten Bereichen St. Pauli- Süd, Altona, Ottensen bis Hammerbrook entwickelt werden" mit dem vier Ziele intendiert waren:

- die City brauche Erweiterungsraum, besonders zwischen Zollkanal und Norderelbe, also in Richtung Speicherstadt;

- die Erlebbarkeit des Hafens solle in den Vordergrund gestellt werden und als gemeinsames Ziel von Städtebau und Hafenentwicklungspolitik sei das Südufer der Elbe zwischen Finkenwerder und Elbbrücken funktional und baulich zu aktivieren, also auch Sichtbezüge herzustellen;

- die Reeperbahn und St. Pauli, die "Sailorstown" sei als Arbeitsstätte und Wohnort, als Touristenattraktion und Ort der Kultur und des Vergnügens zu revitalisieren;

- am Nordufer der Elbe seien Standorte in "atmosphärischer Situation" für Medien und Hafenwirtschaftsbetriebe zu schaffen.

1987 wurden "Leitlinien zur Entwicklung des nördlichen Elbufers" vorgestellt. Es ging um eine städtebauliche Konzeption, die davon ausging, Arbeiten und Wohnen, Einkaufen und Freizeiteinrichtungen, Kultur- und Tourismus am Hafenrand mit einander zu verbinden, und zwar durch "behutsames Einfügen" in die vorhandene Struktur von Gebäuden und Freiflächen. Skizzieren am Beispiel der Planungen und Bauten am nördlichen Elbufer - im Westen der "Perlenkette beginnend - die Probleme und Chancen der Revitalisierung.

Das klobige Gebäude, das ehemalige Union-Kühlhaus in Neumühlen - ein Wahrzeichen der Hafentopographie - bildet das westliche Ende der Perlenkette. Nach einem "zufälligem" Brand wurde das Gebäude abgerissen und auf den Grundmauern - in Form und Maßen am alten Kühlhaus orientiert - wieder aufgebaut und zu einem Augustinum-Luxusseniorenheim.

An dem Beispiel der östlich angrenzend - auf der Elbe liegenden - Container-Wohnschiffe lassen sich Widersprüche zwischen architektonisch- planerischen Ambitionen sowie wohnungs- und sozialpolitischen Notwendigkeiten und Notlösungen besonders gut illustrieren. Auf den Wohnschiffen in Neumühlen - direkt neben dem Augustinum - werden Flüchtlinge zwangsweise bis zu einer Dauer von maximal drei Monaten "erst"-untergebracht, bevor sie dann in andere Gemeinschaftsunterkünfte verlegt werden. Derzeit leben ca. 2.200 Flüchtlinge aus 47 verschiedenen Ländern, davon 1.400 bosnische Kriegsflüchtlinge, auf den Wohnschiffen in Mehrbettkabinen oder Schlafsählen. Die Schiffe sind abgelegen von jeglichen Versorgungseinrichtungen und Dienstleistungen. Die Kosten für die Erstunterbringungen auf den drei Wohnschiffe beliefen sich 1995 auf 31,65

Mio. DM., für die schlechteste Unterbringungsform wird das meiste Geld ausgegeben und fast könnte man meinen, daß damit eine abschreckende Wirkung erzielt werden solle. Möglichkeiten hier etwa eine multikulturelle Begegnungsstätte vorzusehen und ein positives Zeichen der deutschen und Hamburger Integrationswilligkeit von Flüchtlingen und Asylbewerbern zu setzen, sind nicht verfolgt worden.

Auf der nördlichen Straßenseite befindet sich das zweigeschossige unter Denkmalschutz stehende - und mustergültig renovierte - Gebäude der Lawaetz-Stiftung, dessen Nutzern nun bald der Elbblick verstellt sein wird. Denn die Flächen gegenüber der Lawaetz-Stiftung und die Freiflächen vor den Wohnschiffen sollen nun mit vier 8-geschossigen Gebäuden bebaut werden, für die östlicher gelegenen Grundstücke gibt es allerdings noch keine Investoren. Vorwiegend sind Büronutzungen vorgesehen, der Wohnungsanteil ist noch umstritten, derzeit aber mit nur 15% vorgesehen. Die Wohnschiffe und die Bewohner sind nicht in die Planung einbezogen, sondern es wird davon ausgegangen, daß sie bald überflüssig werden.

Der östlich weiter anschließende Bereich besteht aus den Kaispeichern D, F, und G, die in den zwanziger Jahren gebaut wurden und weiter östlich aus meist zweigeschossigen Gebäuden, die von der Fischmarkt-Altona GmbH zur Fischverarbeitung genutzt werden. Für die Fischmarkt-GmbH arbeiten ca. 2.000 Beschäftigte, die Firma ist zu 100% im Besitz der Stadt. Der Fisch wird allerdings mit LKWs angefahren und abtransportiert, die Wasserseite ist zur Anlandung von Fisch bedeutungslos. Die Stadt möchte die Betriebe auslagern, um die Plätze an finanzkräftige Investoren zu verkaufen. Aber die Pachtverträge laufen noch bis 2008.

Vor den Gebäuden der Fischmarkt-Altona GmbH wurde fahrtschiffe und die England-

401

fähre wurde ein neuer architektonisch spektakulär gestalteter Terminal gebaut, seine wichtige Funktion als Ort des Abschieds und kaum erfüllt, da der Sichtkontakt vom Ufer zu den Schiffen völlig unterbunden ist. Das Gebäude wurde von den Londoner Architekten Alsop & Lyall und der Architekten-gemeinschaft "Medi-um" entworfen. Die Verlagerung von den Landungsbrücken zu dem neuen Terminal erfolgte, da die Betreiber eine schnellere Abfertigung und einen eigenen Terminal wünschten und die Schiffe in diesem Bereich der Elbe besser manövrieren können. Die Büros im Gebäude werden vorwiegend von nicht-hafenbezogenen Firmen genutzt.

Für den Bereich des östlich angrenzenden Holzhafens hat es einen vom Investor (Büll & Liedtke) ausgeschriebenen Wettbewerb gegeben, den der Holländer Kees Christianse gewonnen hat. "Wuchtige Blöcke aus Backstein, Glas und Stein", so das Hamburger Abendblatt sollen entstehen und Kritiker haben moniert, daß es sich bei dem Projekt eher um Klötze als um Perlen handeln würde. Baubeginn für den Investor soll Ende 1995 sein. In dem Projekt war ursprünglich eine Mischnutzung vorgesehen, aber ob auch Wohnungen gebaut werden, ist sehr fraglich.

Drei gründerzeitliche Großbauten, die Hafenmühle, der Speicher und die Mälzerei prägen in östlicher Richtung den Bereich vor dem Fischmarkt. Diese Gebäudestrukturen bleiben erhalten, während im Inneren ein vollständiger Umbau stattfindet. Der Speicher wird von Green-Peace genutzt werden, die hier ihre Einrichtungen in Hamburg konzentrieren wollen. Die Mühle, das ehemalige Stadtlagerhaus wird entkernt und ca. 80 Wohnungen sollen hier entstehen. Das gegenüberliegende Gebäude, eine Mälzerei, wird ebenfalls total entkernt und soll vorwiegend mit Büros und Designer- und Möbelgeschäften belegt werden.

Weiter in östlicher Richtung befindet sich die alte Fischauktionshalle, die in den siebziger Jahren ihre Funktion verlor, 1982 modernisiert wurde und zu einem (selten genutzten) Veranstaltungszentrum umfunktioniert worden ist. Am Fischmarkt sind neue Sozialwohnungen entstanden, die den historischen Markt wieder einfassen. Der Fischmarkt ist aber seit langem kein Fischmarkt mehr, sondern eher ein Trödelmarkt und findet nur noch sonntags statt.

Insgesamt weist der Bereich zwischen Augustinum und Fischmarkt eine sehr heterogen Struktur auf, Nutzungen sind fragmentiert und die Wohnbevölkerung weist große soziale Unterschiede auf. Derzeit sind im Gebiet noch ca. 2/3 des Gewerbes hafenbezogen. Aber das hafentypische Milieu und Gewerbe wird immer stärker durch kapitalkräftigere Nutzungen verdrängt. Die einmalige Chance bei der Neuplanung einen Uferweg entlang des ganzen Bereiches vorzusehen, wurde vertan. Die relativ hohen Büroflächenanteile bei den Neubauten und die damit verbundene neue Arbeitsbevölkerung werden Konflikte zwischen "Altbewohnern" und den "neuen" eher steigern. Die Attraktivität des Gebietes für Hamburger und Touristen mit dem hier (westlich) anschließenden Elbwanderweg führt teilweise (vor allen an Wochenenden und Feiertagen) zu erheblichen Verkehrsbelastungen und Staus.

Die Zukunft der Vergangenheit

An den Umstrukturierungsbemühungen am nördlichen Elbufer werden unterschiedliche Konfliktlinien deutlich. In den hafennahen Stadtteilen und Uferbereichen wohnten früher in der Regel eher einkommensschwächere Bevölkerungsgruppen, die entweder im Hafen gearbeitet haben, oder nach dem Rückzug der Hafennutzungen hier mietpreisgünstige Wohnungen gefunden haben. Das Interesse der international agierenden Developer zielt dagegen in der Regel auf den Bau von

Büroeinheiten und Wohnungen für das obere Bevölkerungsdrittel ab. Die städtebaulichen und sozialen Konsequenzen der bisher realisierten Projekte der Perlenkette sind also ambivalent. Auf der einen Seite ist es gelungen neue Entwicklungsimpulse in diesen Bereich zu ziehen, aber mit Aufwertung und Umnutzung gehen Konflikte um Verdrängung und Gentrification einher. Das Bemühen Hamburgs in der wirtschaftlich problematischen Phase Mitte der achtziger Jahre internationale Investoren um (fast) jeden Preis nach Hamburg zu ziehen, erweist sich im Nachhinein als übereilte Strategie, mit der Chancen auf eine behutsamere und sozialverträglichere Revitalisierung unter Berücksichtigung endogener Potentiale vertan wurden.

Viele Städte sind nun aber in letzter Zeit unsicher geworden im Umgang mit den "Filetstücken" am Hafen. Welche Nutzungen, welche Träger und welche Investoren werden sich nicht nur kurzfristig, sondern langfristig als sozial- umweltverträglich und sinnvoll erweisen? Es handelt sich in vielen Städten immerhin um die letzten großen Flächenreserven, die z.B. für Entwicklungsmöglichkeiten und Wohnbauflächen zur Verfügung stehen, die als Flächenrecycling in einen neuen Verwertungskreislauf eingebracht werden können und sich zudem bestens vermarkten lassen. Die Möglichkeit der Neugestaltung der städtischen Hafen- und Uferbereiche ist nach einer Phase der Verwahrlosung und Unkenntlichmachung eine einmalige Chance, wobei schwierige Planungsprobleme gelöst werden müssen und neue Planungskulturen eingeübt werden können. Dabei handelt es sich aber nicht nur eine architektonische Gestaltungsfrage, es geht vielmehr um komplexe planerische, organisatorische, politische, trägerschaftliche, ökonomische, ökologische, juristische und finanzielle Fragen.

Bei der Realisierung von Projekten am nördlichen Elbufer in Hamburg kommt erschwerend und verteuernd hinzu, daß Flutschutzmaßnahmen vorzusehen sind,

Altlasten zu berücksichtigen sind und Gründungskosten meist höher liegen als bei anderen Vorhaben. Bei der derzeitigen Haushaltslage Hamburgs ist die Versuchung naheliegend, Grundstücke aus dem kommunalen Bestand möglichst teuer an private Investoren zu veräußern und die eingenommenen Mittel zur Haushaltssanierung zu verwenden. Damit werden allerdings wichtige Steuerungsmöglichkeiten in diesem Bereich vertan und Chancen, die Revitalisierung der Hafen- und Uferzonen zu einem nachhaltigen und sozialverträglichen Stadtumbau zu nutzen. Mit dem inkrementalistischen Planungsansatz der "Perlenkette" sind zudem räumliche wohnungs- und stadtteilbezogene Effekte von einzelnen Projekten kaum steuerbar. Es ist daher besonders wichtig, bei diesen zentrumsnah gelegenen Flächen die Vorhaben auf Sozialverträglichkeit und nachhaltige Effekte für die zukünftige Stadt(teil)entwicklung hin sorgfältig zu prüfen und nicht nur auf vage "trickle down" Effekte zu hoffen. Bei der Umplanung der Uferzonen bestehen einmalige Chancen diese für die lokale Bevölkerung, aber auch für die Gesamtstadt und Besucher von auswärts mit dem Ziel der Revitalisierung zu nutzen, die nicht vertan werden sollten.

Dirk Schubert, Pd.Dr., Arbeitsbereich Städtebau III, Objektbezogene Stadtplanung, Technische Universität Hamburg-Harburg, Hamburg, Deutschland.

PART FOUR
Recommendations

VIERTER TEIL
Empfehlungen

The Freiburg Statement on New Urban Neighborhoods

Conclusions based on presentations and discussions of IMCL Board Members and invited speakers at the 17th International Conference on Making Cities Livable, Freiburg, September 5-9, 1995.

The overriding purpose of a new urban neighborhood is the care and culture of human beings.

The new urban neighborhood must provide an optimal physical and human landscape for its inhabitants to live together. Its architecture and design must encourage social life, social learning and sociability, and encourage a sense of community among all who live there, including children and the elderly, women and men, well-to-do and less well-off, native and foreign born.

It is important to learn from the traditional wisdom of city making, and to avoid the deplorable errors of modern developments at the periphery of the world's cities.

On the basis of the work of the conference, seven interrelated principles are proposed . To be effective, these principles must be implemented together.

1.   Plan for a heterogeneous social composition. Pay special attention to children and the elderly. Interweave a variety of scattered, small scale, low income housing with diverse forms of market rate housing.

2.   Develop the neighborhood around a central, traffic free urban space, designed to facilitate good social life, public events, community markets and festivals. To facilitate the multifunctional character of this central public space, include architectural and design characteristics that have guaranteed the success of traditional urban public places: visual enclosure, human scale, mixed use shop/houses, a dramatic and lovable architectural center-piece, focal points, seating, paving and nature.

3. Include housing, work opportunities, and shopping, civic, cultural and health facilities in a continuous fine textured, high density, low rise urban fabric, concentrated around the central urban space.

4. Involve active and continuous participation of all segments of the population in the planning and design, including future homeowners and business people, investors and near-by local residents; as well as architectural students, children and young people as surrogate representatives. Develop a dynamic, participatory, incremental design process to avoid the authoritarianism of a grid plan.

5. The architectural identity of a new urban neighborhood must be rooted in the collective memory of the region, reflecting through design guidelines those architectural and spatial characteristics most highly valued by the local community.

6. **Emphasize pedestrian, bicycle and public transportation networks to link residential, workplace, schools, and shops to the central urban place, and to the city of which it is a part. Strongly discourage automobile use.**

7. **Socially responsible development principles are also ecologically responsible: minimizing commuting distances, emphasizing pedestrian movement, conserving energy use, facilitating district heating through high density, employing passive solar urban design principles to regulate the external environment, and passive solar architecture principles to regulate the internal environments.**

Kapitel Achtundsechzig (b)

Die Freibürger Erklärung über Neue Stadtteile

Schlussfolgerungen aus Vorträgen und Diskussionen der IMCL-Vorstandsmitglieder und eingeladener Redner der 17. Internationalen Konferenz zum Thema Making Cities Livable Freiburg, Deutschland, 5.-9. September 1995

Der höchste Zweck eines neuen Stadtteils besteht darin, der Pflege und optimalen Entwicklung der in ihm lebenden Menschen zu dienen.

Der neue Stadtteil muss für das Zusammenleben seiner Bewohner eine optimale physische und menschliche Landschaft bieten. Architektur und Gestaltung müssen soziales Leben, soziales Lernen, sowie gesellliges Zusammensein fördern; sie sollten die Gemeinschaftsfähigkeit aller, die dort leben, fördern, von Kindern und alten Menschen, Frauen und Männern. Wohlhabenden und weniger Wohlhabenden, Einheimischen und Fremden.

Es ist wichtig, von der traditionellen Weisheit des Städtebaus zu lernen, statt die Irrtümer der modernen Entwicklungen an den Rändern der Städte unserer Welt zu wiederholen.

Auf der Grundlage der Konferenzarbeit werden sieben zusammenhängende Prinzipien vorgeschlagen. Um wirksam zu sein, müssen diese Prinzipien auch gemeinsam umgesetzt werden.

1. Pläne für eine gemischte soziale Zusammensetzung. Berücksichtige insbesondere Kinder und ältere Menschen. Verknüpfe eine Vielfalt von preisgünstigen, über das ganze Gebiet verstreute Wohnungen mit kleinem Grundriss, mit verschiedenen Wohnungsformen, die zu marktüblichen Preisen angeboten werden.

2. Lege den Stadtteil um einen zentralen, verkehrsfreien städtischen Raum an, der dafür vorgesehen ist, ein gutes soziales Leben, öffentliche Veranstaltungen, Gemeindemärkte und Feste leicht zu ermöglichen. Um den multifunktionalen Charakter dieses zentralen, öffentlichen Raumes zu fördern, nutze die Eigenschaften, die den Erfolg traditioneller öffentlicher Räume sichergestellt haben: sichtliche Geschlossenheit, menschlicher Massstab, gemischte Nutzung "shop/houses" für Wohnen und Gewerbe, ein dramatisches und beliebtes Gebäude, mehrere Treff- und Brennpunkte, Sitzgelegenheiten, schöne Pflasterung und nicht zuletzt Natur.

3. Beziehe Wohn-, Arbeitsstätten und Einkaufsmöglichkeiten, aber auch öffentliche Einrichtungen, Einrichtungen für Kultur und Gesundheitswesen in ein kontinuierliches, feinstrukturiertes Stadtgewebe mit hohe Dichte ein, das sich um den zentralen städtischen Platz konzentriert.

4. Berücksichtige bei Planung und Gestaltung die aktive und dauernde Teilnahme aller Bevölkerungsgruppen einschliesslich

künftiger Hauseigentümer und Geschäfts-
leute, Investoren und angrenzender
Bewohner; schliesse dabei auch
stellvertretend für die künftigen Bewohner
Kinder, Jugendliche und Studenten der
Architektur mit ein. Entwickle einen
dynamischen Entwurfsprozess, in dem alle
teilnehmen können, um nicht einen
autoritären Rasterplan zu erliegen.

5. Die architektonische Identität eines neuen
Stadtteils muss im kollektiven Gedächtnis der
Region verankert sein und mittels
gestalterischer Leitlinien eben diese
architektonische und räumliche Wesens-
merkmale reflektieren, die von der örtlichen
Bevölkerung geschätzt werden.

6. Lege besonderen Wert auf Vekehrsnetze für
Fussgänger, Radfahrer und öffentlichen
Verkehr, um Wohngebiete, Arbeitsstätten,
Schulen und Geschäfte mit dem zentralen
städtischen Platz und der Stadt zu verbinden,
zu der der Stadtteil gehört. PKW-Benutzung
ist mit allen zu Gebote stehenden Mitteln zu
entmutigen.

7. Sozial verantwortliche Entwicklung ist auch
ökologisch verantwortliche Entwicklung:
Verringerung des Pendlerverkehrs, Förderung
des Fussgängerverkehrs, sparsamer Umgang
mit Energie, Ermöglichung von Fernheitzung
durch hohe Dichte, Verwendung von
passiven, solaren, städtischen Gestaltungs-
prinzipien für Plätze und Strassen und
passiven, solaren Architekturprinzipien für
die Gestaltung der Innenräume.

Contributors / Mitarbeiter

Dr. Klaus Andrä, *Architect and author, Berlin, GERMANY.* **Dr. Klaus Andrä**, *freier Architekt, Berlin, DEUTSCHLAND.*

Hans Billinger, *Verkehrsplaner, Planungsbüro Billinger, Stuttgart, DEUTSCHLAND.*

Prof. Dr. Klaus Brake, *Forschungsinstitut Region und Umwelt, Carl von Ossietzky Universität, Oldenburg, DEUTSCHLAND.*

Dr. Ing. Peter Breitling, *Architekt und Universitäts-Professor Emeritus, Institut für Städtebau, Graz, ÖSTERREICH. Member of the IMCL Board.*

Dipl. Ing. Klaus Brendle, *Architekt, Lübeck, DEUTSCHLAND.*

Dr. Rolf Böhme, *Lord Mayor of Freiburg im Breisgau, GERMANY.*

Antonio Casellati, *former Lord Mayor of Venice, ITALY.*

Prof. Dr. Ing. Hans Jürgen Collin, *Mitglied des Vorsitzes der Arbeitsgruppe Unabhängiger Stadt- und Verkehrsplaner, Braunschweig, DEUTSCH-LAND.*

Bob Cools, *Honorary Mayor of Antwerp; President of the Municipal Centre for Health Care and Social Welfare, Antwerp, BELGIUM.*

Bill Erickson, B.Arch., MA, *School of Urban Development and Planning, Faculty of the Environment, University of Westminster, London, ENGLAND, UK.*

Andreas Feldtkeller, *Planning Director for the City of Tübingen, Tübingen, GERMANY. Member of the IMCL Board.* **Andreas Feldtkeller**, *Leiter des Stadtsanierungsamtes der Stadt Tübingen, Tübingen, DEUTSCHLAND.*

Herbert Fessenmayr, *Chief Building Director for the City of Mainz, Mainz, GERMANY.* **Herbert Fessenmayr**, *Leitender Baudirektor, Stadt-planungsamt der Stadt Mainz, Mainz, DEUTSCHLAND.*

Prof. Dr. Phil. Arno Gruen, *Psychoanalyst and author, Zurich, SWITZERLAND.*

Dr. Ing. Egon Grund, *Planning Director, retired, Karlsruhe, GERMANY.*

Christoph Guhr, Dipl. -Ing., *Stadtplanungsamt der Hansestadt Lübeck, Lübeck, DEUTSCHLAND.*

Dr. Dietmar Hahlweg, *former Lord Mayor of Erlangen, GERMANY. Member of the IMCL Board.*

Dr. Werner Heye, *Referat für Stadtentwicklung der Stadt Hannover, Hannover, DEUTSCHLAND.*

Prof. Dr. Ing. Helmut Holzapfel, *Professor of Transportation Planning, University of Kassel; Director of Transportation, Ministry for Housing, Urban Planning and Transportation for the State of Sachsen-Anhalt, GERMANY.* **Prof. Dr. Ing. Helmut Holzapfel**, *Professor der Verkehrsplanung, Universität Kassel; Ministerialdirigent, Ministerium für Wohnen, Städtebau und Verkehr, Sachsen-Anhalt, DEUTSCHLAND.*

Dr. Walter Kilian, *Executive Director, LEG Baden-Württemberg Regional Development Corporation Stuttgart, GERMANY.* **Dr. Walter Kilian** *ist Geschäftsführer der Landesentwicklungsgesell-schaft Baden-Württemberg mbH, Stuttgart, DEUTSCHLAND.*

Tülay Kilinçaslan, Ph.D., Arch. *Eng., Faculty of Architecture, Department of Urban and Regional Planning at Istanbul Technical University, TURKEY.*

Zenia Kotval Ph.D., AICP, *Assistant Professor, Michigan State University, East Lansing, Michigan, USA.*

Henry L. Lennard, Ph.D., *Chairman of the Advisory Board of the IMCL Council, Carmel, California, USA. Formerly Professor of Sociology in Psychiatry, University of California Medical School, San Francisco, California, USA.*

Dr. Ing. Hans Stimmann, *Planning Commissioner, City of Berlin, Berlin, GERMANY.* **Dr. Hans Stimmann**, *Senatsbaudirektor der Stadt Berlin, Berlin, DEUTSCHLAND.*

John Thompson, RIBA, *John Thompson and Partners, London, ENGLAND, UK.*

Dr. Sven von Ungern-Sternberg, *Deputy Mayor, City of Freiburg im Breisgau, GERMANY. Co-Chair, Program Committee for the 17th IMCL Conference, Freiburg im Breisgau.* **Dr. Sven von Ungern-Sternberg**, *Erster Bürgermeister der Stadt Freiburg im Breisgau, DEUTSCHLAND. Vorsitzender des Programm-Kommitees der 17. IMCL Konferenz, Freiburg im Breisgau, DEUTSCHLAND.*

Peter Webber, *Professor of Architecture, University of Sydney, Sydney, AUSTRALIA.*

Max Wittmann, *Geschäftsführer, STEWOG, Stadtentwicklungs- und Wohnungsbau GmbH, Marktredwitz, DEUTSCHLAND.*

Senator Dr. Volker Zahn, Dipl. -Ing., *Baudezernent der hansestadt Lübeck, Lübeck, DEUTSCHLAND.*

Acknowledgements

The editors of this book wish to acknowledge their thanks to the City of Freiburg, for support of the 19th International Making Cities Livable Conference in making available the facilities of the City, including the Historisches Rathaus, the Gerichtslaube, and the Historisches Kaufhaus.

Special thanks are also extended to members of the IMCL Board who advised on the organization of the Freiburg program, especially AltOberbürgermeister Dietmar Hahlweg, (Erlangen, Germany); Prof. Edoardo Salzano, (Venice, Italy); Prof. Derek Drummond (Montreal, Canada); and Gianni Longo (New York, USA).

We would also like to express our indebtedness to the following people who have supported the work of the IMCL Conferences over the years: Prof. Peter Breitling (Graz, Austria); Mayor Antonio Casellati (Venice, Italy); Mayor Bob Cools (Antwerp, Belgium); Prof.

Jaques Kaswan (Berkeley, CA, USA); Prof. Rolf Monheim (Bayreuth, Germany); Mayor Joseph P. Riley, Jr. (Charleston, SC, USA); Philip Sapir (Washington DC); Prof. Hartmut Topp (Kaiserslautern, Germany); Wolf von Eckardt (Jaffrey, NH, USA); and William H. Whyte (New York, USA).

The Making Cities Livable movement owes a great deal to the work and vision expressed by the following pioneers of city livability: Jane Jacobs; Alexander Mitscherlich; Lewis Mumford; H.R.H. The Prince of Wales; Bernard Rudofsky; Wolf von Eckardt; and William H. Whyte.

Special thanks also to the many staff members who helped to prepare the manuscript in California, and especially to Chris Krüger.

Biographical Notes

Sven R. von Ungern-Sternberg *studierte in Freiburg im Breisgau und Edinburgh Rechts- und Wirtschaftswissenschaften (Dipl.-Volkswirt) und promovierte über Internationales Recht zum Dr.-Jur. Er engagierte sich frühzeitig in der praktischen Kommunalpolitik, wurde 1971 in den Freiburger Stadtrat gewählt und war bereits 1973 Vorsitzender der CDU-Fraktion. 1978 wurde er Baubürger-meister und ist seit 1983 in dieser Funktion Erster Bürgermeister von Freiburg. Damit ist er nahezu 20 Jahre für die Planungs-, Bau- und Verkehrspolitik dieser Stadt verantwortlich. Darüberhinaus engagierte er sich seit Jahrzehnten aktiv in der Regionalpolitik.*

Seit 1994 its er im Beirat der IMCL-Konferenzen und "Co-Chairman" des Programm-Komittees.

Suzanne H. Crowhurst Lennard *received a B.Arch.(Hons.) from the Department of Architecture, Bristol University; RWA Dipl. from the Royal West of England Academy of Architecture, Bristol, U.K.; and Ph.D.(Arch.) in Human Aspects of Architecture and Urban Design from the University of California, Berkeley. She has taught architecture at the University of California, Berkeley; Oxford Polytechnic in Oxford, England; and at other universities in the U.S. and Europe; and consults for cities on urban space design.*

Her work has received awards from the National Endowment for the Arts; the Graham Foundation for Fine Arts; and the Royal Institute of British Architects.

Dr. Crowhurst Lennard is Director of the International Making Cities Livable Council; Organizer of the International Making Cities Livable Conferences; and Editor of the Making Cities Livable Newsletter. She is author of **Explorations in the Meaning of Architecture;** *co-author of* **Public Life in Urban Places;** *and* **Livable Cities Observed** *(with H.L. Lennard).*

Henry L. Lennard *was educated at the Wasa Gymnasium, Vienna, and received a Ph.D. from Columbia University, New York. He taught and directed research programs at Columbia University, and at the University of California in San Francisco, where he was Professor of Sociology in Psychiatry and Director of the Family Study Station. Dr. Lennard has received awards from The National Science Foundation; The National Institute of Mental Health; and the Commonwealth, William T. Grant, and Johnson Foundations.*

Among his books are: **Patterns in Human Interaction; Mystification and Drug Misuse; Ethics in Health Care; The Psychiatric Hospital;** *and* **Livable Cities Observed** *(with S.C. Lennard). His articles have appeared in* **Science, The Smithsonian, The American Psychologist, Archives of General Psychiatry,** *and many other professional journals.*

Dr. Lennard is currently working on a book on **The Good City for Children and Youth.**